C# 7 and .NET Core: Modern Cross-Platform Development

Second Edition

Create powerful cross-platform applications using C# 7, .NET Core, and Visual Studio 2017 or Visual Studio Code

Mark J. Price

BIRMINGHAM - MUMBAI

C# 7 and .NET Core: Modern Cross-Platform Development

Second Edition

First published: March 2016

Second edition: March 2017

Production reference: 1210317

Published by Packt Publishing Ltd.
Livery Place
35 Livery Street
Birmingham
B3 2PB, UK.
ISBN 978-1-78712-955-9

www.packtpub.com

Credits

Author

Mark J. Price

Reviewer

Fabio Claudio Ferracchiati

Commissioning Editor

Aaron Lazar

Acquisition Editor

Nitin Dasan

Content Development Editor

Siddhi Chavan

Technical Editors

Sunith Shetty

Abhishek Sharma

Copy Editor

Zainab Bootwala

Project Coordinator

Izzat Contractor

Proofreader

Safis Editing

Indexer

Francy Puthiry

Graphics

Abhinash Sahu

Production Coordinator

Nilesh Mohite

About the Author

Mark J. Price is a Microsoft Certified Trainer (MCT) and Microsoft Specialist: Programming in C# and Architecting Microsoft Azure Solutions, with more than 20 years of educational and programming experience.

Microsoft
CERTIFIED
Trainer

Microsoft
Specialist
Programming in C#

Microsoft
Specialist
Architecting Microsoft Azure Solutions

Since 1993, Mark has passed more than 80 Microsoft programming exams and specializes in preparing others to pass them too. His students range from professionals with decades of experience to 16 year old apprentices with none. He successfully guides all of them by combining educational skills with real-world experience in consulting and developing systems for enterprises worldwide.

Between 2001 and 2003, Mark was employed full-time to write official courseware for Microsoft in Redmond, USA. His team wrote the first training courses for C# while it was still an early alpha version. While with Microsoft, he taught "train-the-trainer" classes to get other MCTs up-to-speed on C# and .NET.

Currently, Mark creates and delivers training courses for Episerver's Digital Experience Cloud, the best .NET CMS for Digital Marketing and E-commerce.

In 2010, Mark studied for a Postgraduate Certificate in Education (PGCE). He taught GCSE and A-Level mathematics in two London secondary schools. He holds a Computer Science BSc. Hons. Degree from the University of Bristol, UK.

Thank you to my parents, Pamela and Ian, for raising me to be polite, hardworking, and curious about the world. Thank you to my sisters, Emily and Juliet, for loving me despite being their awkward older brother. Thank you to my friends and colleagues who inspire me technically and creatively. Lastly, thanks to all the students I have taught over the years for motivating me to be the best teacher that I can be.

About the Reviewer

Fabio Claudio Ferracchiati is a senior consultant and a senior analyst/developer using Microsoft technologies. He works for React Consulting (`www.reactconsulting.it`). He is a Microsoft Certified Solution Developer for .NET, a Microsoft Certified Application Developer for .NET, a Microsoft Certified Professional, and a prolific author and technical reviewer. Over the past ten years, he's written articles for Italian and international magazines and co-authored more than ten books on a variety of computer topics.

www.PacktPub.com

For support files and downloads related to your book, please visit www.PacktPub.com.

Did you know that Packt offers eBook versions of every book published, with PDF and ePub files available? You can upgrade to the eBook version at www.PacktPub.com and as a print book customer, you are entitled to a discount on the eBook copy. Get in touch with us at service@packtpub.com for more details.

At www.PacktPub.com, you can also read a collection of free technical articles, sign up for a range of free newsletters and receive exclusive discounts and offers on Packt books and eBooks.

https://www.packtpub.com/mapt

Get the most in-demand software skills with Mapt. Mapt gives you full access to all Packt books and video courses, as well as industry-leading tools to help you plan your personal development and advance your career.

Why subscribe?

- Fully searchable across every book published by Packt
- Copy and paste, print, and bookmark content
- On demand and accessible via a web browser

Customer Feedback

Thanks for purchasing this Packt book. At Packt, quality is at the heart of our editorial process. To help us improve, please leave us an honest review on this book's Amazon page at `https://www.amazon.com/dp/1787129551`.

If you'd like to join our team of regular reviewers, you can e-mail us at `customerreviews@packtpub.com`. We award our regular reviewers with free eBooks and videos in exchange for their valuable feedback. Help us be relentless in improving our products!

Table of Contents

Preface

There are C# books that are thousands of pages long that aim to be comprehensive references to the C# programming language and the .NET Framework.

This book is different. It is concise and aims to be a fast-paced read that is packed with hands-on walkthroughs. I wrote this book to be the best step-by-step guide to modern cross-platform C# proven practices using .NET Core.

I will point out the cool corners and gotchas of C# so you can impress colleagues and employers and get productive fast. Rather than slowing down and boring some readers by explaining every little thing, I will assume that if a term I use is new to you, then you will know how to Google it.

At the end of each chapter is a section titled *Practice and explore*, in which you will complete hands-on practical exercises and explore topics deeper on your own with a little nudge in the right direction from me.

You can download solutions for the exercises from the following GitHub repository. I will provide instructions on how to do this using Visual Studio 2017 and Visual Studio Code at the end of `Chapter 1`, Hello, C#! Welcome, .NET Core!

`https://github.com/markjprice/cs7dotnetcore.`

What this book covers

`Chapter 1`, *Hello, C#! Welcome, .NET Core!*, is about setting up your development environment and using various tools to create the simplest application possible with C#. You will learn how to write and compile code using Visual Studio 2017 on Windows, or Visual Studio Code on macOS, Linux, or Windows. You will learn about the different .NET technologies: .NET Framework, .NET Core, .NET Standard, and .NET Native.

`Chapter 2`, *Speaking C#*, is about the C# language---the grammar and vocabulary that you will use every day to write the source code for your applications. In particular, you will learn how to declare and work with variables of different types.

`Chapter 3`, *Controlling Flow, Converting Types, and Handling Exceptions*, is about writing code that makes decisions, repeats a block of statements, converts between types, and handles errors. You will also learn the best places to look for help.

`Chapter 4`, *Using .NET Standard Types*, is about commonly used .NET Core types that are part of .NET Standard and how they are related to C#. You will learn about the .NET Standard class library assemblies and the NuGet packages of types that allow your applications to connect existing components to perform common practical tasks, such as manipulating text, storing items in collections, and implementing internationalization.

`Chapter 5`, *Debugging, Monitoring, and Testing*, is about debugging tools, monitoring, diagnosing problems, and testing your code to remove bugs and ensuring high performance, stability, and reliability.

`Chapter 6`, *Building Your Own Types with Object-Oriented Programming*, is about all the different categories of members that a type can have, including fields to store data and methods to perform actions. You will use OOP concepts, such as aggregation and encapsulation. You will learn about the C# 7 language features such as tuple syntax support and out variables.

`Chapter 7`, *Implementing Interfaces and Inheriting Classes*, is about deriving new types from existing ones using object-oriented programming (OOP). You will learn how to define operators and C# 7 local functions, delegates and events, how to implement interfaces about base and derived classes, how to override a type member, how to use polymorphism, how to create extension methods, and how to cast between classes in an inheritance hierarchy.

`Chapter 8`, *Working with Databases Using Entity Framework Core*, is about reading and writing to databases, such as Microsoft SQL Server and SQLite, using the object-relational mapping technology known as the Entity Framework Core.

`Chapter 9`, *Querying and Manipulating Data with LINQ*, is about Language INtegrated Query (LINQ)---language extensions that add the ability to work with sequences of items and filter, sort, and project them into different outputs.

`Chapter 10`, *Working with Files, Streams, and Serialization*, is about managing the filesystem, reading and writing to files and streams, text encoding, and serialization.

`Chapter 11`, *Protecting Your Data*, is about protecting your data from being viewed by malicious users using encryption and from being manipulated or corrupted using hashing and signing.

`Chapter 12`, *Improving Performance and Scalability with Multitasking*, is about allowing multiple actions to occur at the same time to improve performance, scalability, and user productivity.

`Chapter 13`, *Building Universal Windows Platform Apps Using XAML*, is about learning the basics of XAML that can be used to define the user interface for a graphical app for the Universal Windows Platform (UWP). This app can then run on Windows 10, Windows 10 Mobile, Xbox One, and even HoloLens.

`Chapter 14`, *Building Web Applications Using ASP.NET Core MVC*, is about learning the basics of building web applications with a modern HTTP architecture on the server side using ASP.NET Core MVC. You will learn about the startup configuration, authentication, routes, models, views, and controllers that make up ASP.NET Core MVC.

`Chapter 15`, *Building Mobile Apps Using Xamarin.Forms and ASP.NET Core Web API*, is about learning the basics of how to take C# mobile by building a cross-platform mobile app for iOS and Android that calls a service built on ASP.NET Core Web API. The client-side mobile app will be created with Visual Studio for Mac and the server-side Web API service will be created with Visual Studio Code, both running on macOS.

`Chapter 16`, *Packaging and Deploying Your Code Cross-Platform*, is about publishing your apps and libraries, creating and distributing NuGet packages, and deploying your code cross-platform and to the cloud.

`Appendix`, *Answers to the Test Your Knowledge Questions*, has the answers to the test questions at the end of each chapter.

What you need for this book

You can develop and deploy C# on many platforms, including Windows, macOS, and many varieties of Linux. For the best programming experience, and to reach the most platforms, I recommend that you learn the basics of all members of the Visual Studio family: Visual Studio 2017, Visual Studio Code, and Visual Studio for Mac.

My recommendation for the operating system and development tool combinations is as follows:

- Windows 10 for Visual Studio 2017
- macOS for Visual Studio for Mac
- macOS for Visual Studio Code

The best version of Windows to use is Microsoft Windows 10 because you will need this version to create Universal Windows Platform apps in `Chapter 13`, *Building Universal Windows Platform Apps Using XAML*. Earlier versions of Windows, such as 7 or 8.1 will work for all other chapters.

Who this book is for

If you have heard that C# is a popular general-purpose cross-platform programming language used to create everything, ranging from business applications, web sites, and services, to games for mobile devices, Xbox One, and the Windows 10 desktop to tablet and phone platforms, then this book is for you.

If you have heard that .NET Core is Microsoft's bet on a cross-platform .NET future, optimized for server-side web development in the cloud, and client-side mobile development with Xamarin, combined with a cross-platform development tool in Visual Studio Code, then this book is for you.

Conventions

In this book, you will find a number of text styles that distinguish between different kinds of information. Here are some examples of these styles and an explanation of their meaning.

Code words in text, database table names, folder names, filenames, file extensions, pathnames, dummy URLs, user input, and Twitter handles are shown as follows: "`Controllers`, `Models`, and `Views` folders contain ASP.NET Core classes and `.cshtml` files for execution on the server."

A block of code is set as follows:

```
// storing items at index positions
names[0] = "Kate";
names[1] = "Jack";
names[2] = "Rebecca";
names[3] = "Tom";
```

When we wish to draw your attention to a particular part of a code block, the relevant lines or items are set in bold:

```
// storing items at index positions
names[0] = "Kate";
names[1] = "Jack";
names[2] = "Rebecca";
names[3] = "Tom";
```

Any command-line input or output is written as follows:

```
dotnet new console
```

New terms and important words are shown in bold. Words that you see on the screen, for example, in menus or dialog boxes, appear in the text like this: "Clicking the **Next** button moves you to the next screen."

Warnings or important notes appear in a box like this.

Good Practice

Recommendations for how to program like an expert appear like this.

Reader feedback

Feedback from our readers is always welcome. Let us know what you think about this book—what you liked or disliked. Reader feedback is important for us as it helps us develop titles that you will really get the most out of.

To send us general feedback, simply e-mail `feedback@packtpub.com`, and mention the book's title in the subject of your message.

If there is a topic that you have expertise in and you are interested in either writing or contributing to a book, see our author guide at `www.packtpub.com/authors`.

Customer support

Now that you are the proud owner of a Packt book, we have a number of things to help you to get the most from your purchase.

Downloading the example code

You can download the example code files for this book from your account at `http://www.packtpub.com`. If you purchased this book elsewhere, you can visit

`http://www.packtpub.com/support`and register to have the files e-mailed directly to you.

You can download the code files by following these steps:

1. Log in or register to our website using your e-mail address and password.
2. Hover the mouse pointer on the SUPPORT tab at the top.
3. Click on Code Downloads & Errata.
4. Enter the name of the book in the Search box.
5. Select the book for which you're looking to download the code files.
6. Choose from the drop-down menu where you purchased this book from.
7. Click on Code Download.

Once the file is downloaded, please make sure that you unzip or extract the folder using the latest version of:

- WinRAR / 7-Zip for Windows
- Zipeg / iZip / UnRarX for Mac
- 7-Zip / PeaZip for Linux

The code bundle for the book is also hosted on GitHub at `https://github.com/PacktPublishing/CSharp-7-And-NET-Core-Modern-CrossPlatform-Development-Second-Edition`. We also have other code bundles from our rich catalog of books and videos available at `https://github.com/PacktPublishing/`. Check them out!

Downloading the color images of this book

We also provide you with a PDF file that has color images of the screenshots/diagrams used in this book. The color images will help you better understand the changes in the output. You can download this file from `https://www.packtpub.com/sites/default/files/downloads/CSharp7andDotNETCoreModernCrossPlatformDevelopmentSecondEdition_ColorImages.pdf`

Errata

Although we have taken every care to ensure the accuracy of our content, mistakes do happen. If you find a mistake in one of our books—maybe a mistake in the text or the code—we would be grateful if you could report this to us. By doing so, you can save other readers from frustration and help us improve subsequent versions of this book. If you find any errata, please report them by visiting `http://www.packtpub.com/submit-errata`, selecting your book, clicking on the Errata Submission Form link, and entering the details of your errata. Once your errata are verified, your submission will be accepted and the errata will be uploaded to our website or added to any list of existing errata under the Errata section of that title.

To view the previously submitted errata, go to `https://www.packtpub.com/books/content/support`and enter the name of the book in the search field. The required information will appear under the Errata section.

Piracy

Piracy of copyrighted material on the Internet is an ongoing problem across all media. At Packt, we take the protection of our copyright and licenses very seriously. If you come across any illegal copies of our works in any form on the Internet, please provide us with the location address or website name immediately so that we can pursue a remedy.

Please contact us at `copyright@packtpub.com` with a link to the suspected pirated material.

We appreciate your help in protecting our authors and our ability to bring you valuable content.

Questions

If you have a problem with any aspect of this book, you can contact us at `questions@packtpub.com`, and we will do our best to address the problem.

1
Hello, C#! Welcome, .NET Core!

This chapter is about setting up your development environment; understanding the similarities and differences between .NET Core, .NET Framework, .NET Standard, and .NET Native; and using various tools to create the simplest application possible with C# 7 and .NET Core.

Most people learn complex topics by imitation and repetition rather than reading a detailed explanation of theory. So, I will not explain every keyword and step. The idea is to get you to write some code, build an application, and see it run. You don't need to know the details of how it all works yet.

In the words of Samuel Johnson, author of the English dictionary of 1755, I have likely committed "a few wild blunders, and risible absurdities, from which no work of such multiplicity is free. "I take sole responsibility for these and hope you appreciate the challenge of my attempt to "lash the wind" by writing this book about .NET Core and its command-line tooling during its rocky birth during 2016 and 2017.

This chapter covers the following topics:

- Choosing your development environment
- Installing Microsoft Visual Studio 2017 for Windows
- Installing Microsoft Visual Studio Code for Windows, macOS, or Linux
- Understanding .NET
- Writing and compiling code using the .NET Core CLI tool
- Writing and compiling code using Microsoft Visual Studio 2017
- Writing and compiling code using Microsoft Visual Studio Code
- Managing source code with GitHub

Choosing your development environment

Before you start programming, you will need to choose an **Interactive Development Environment** (**IDE**) that includes a code editor for C#.

The most mature and full-featured IDE to choose is **Microsoft Visual Studio 2017**, but it only runs on the Windows operating system.

The most modern and lightweight IDE to choose, and the only one from Microsoft that is cross-platform, is **Microsoft Visual Studio Code**, and it will run on all common operating systems, including Windows, macOS, and many varieties of Linux, such as Red Hat Enterprise Linux (RHEL) and Ubuntu.

To help you decide if Visual Studio Code is right for you, I recommend that you watch the following video, Beginner's Guide to VS Code: Up and Running in Ten Minutes: `https://channel9.msdn.com/Blogs/raw-tech/Beginners-Guide-to-VS-Code`

To create apps for iOS (iPhone and iPad), tvOS, macOS, and watchOS, you must have OS X or macOS, and Xcode. Although you can use Visual Studio 2017 with its Xamarin extensions to *write* a cross-platform mobile app, you still need OS X or macOS, and Xcode to *compile* it. So, in `Chapter 15`, *Building Mobile Apps Using Xamarin.Forms and ASP.NET Core Web API*, I will show you how to use **Visual Studio for Mac** running on macOS to create a Xamarin cross-platform mobile app for iOS and Android that calls a web service hosted on ASP.NET Core.

The following table shows which IDE and operating systems can or must be used for each of the chapters in this book:

Chapters	**IDE**	**Operating systems**
1 to 12, 14, 16	Visual Studio 2017	Windows 7 SP1 or later
	Visual Studio Code	Windows, macOS, or Linux
13	Visual Studio 2017	Windows 10
15	Visual Studio for Mac	macOS

Good Practice
If you have the option, then I recommend you try all the coding exercises with both Visual Studio 2017 on Windows, and Visual Studio Code on macOS, Linux, or Windows. It will be good for you to get experience with C# 7 and .NET Core on a variety of operating systems and development tools.

To write the second edition of this book, I used the following listed software, as you can see in the following screenshot:

- Visual Studio Code version 1.10.2 and Visual Studio for Mac Preview 4, on macOS Sierra version 10.12.3
- Visual Studio 2017 on Windows 10 (in a virtual machine)
- Visual Studio Code on Red Hat Enterprise Linux (in a virtual machine)

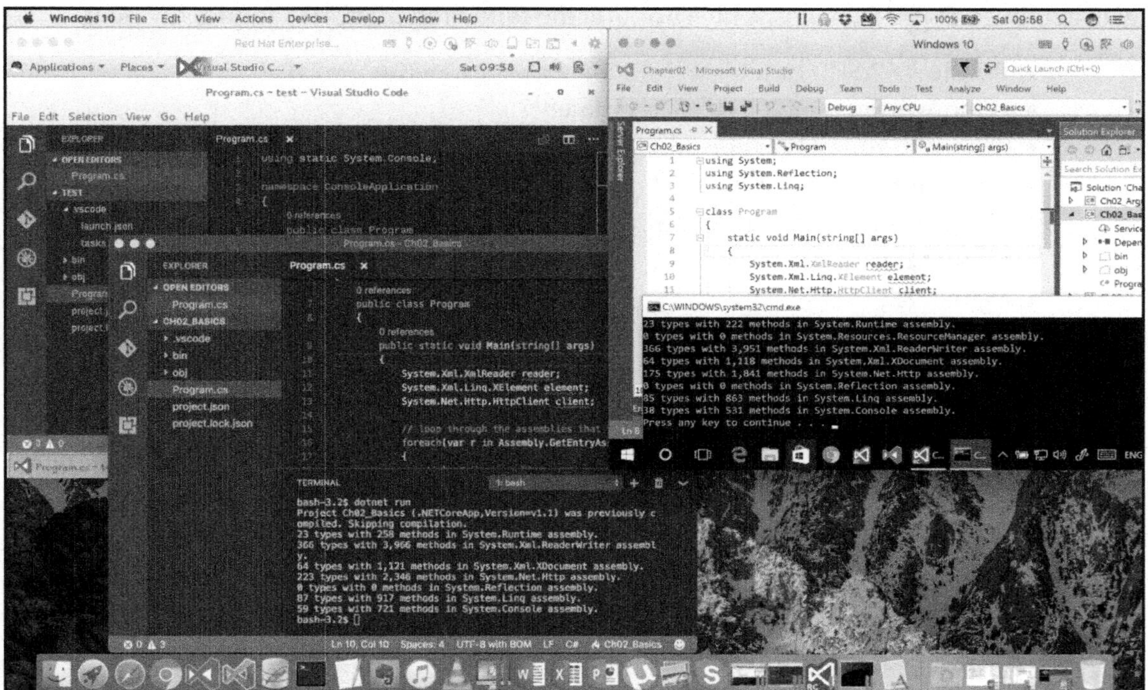

Using alternative C# IDEs

There are alternative IDEs for C#, for example, **MonoDevelop** and **JetBrains Rider**. You can install either of these two IDEs with the help of the following URLs:

- For MonoDevelop IDE, visit `http://www.monodevelop.com/`
- For JetBrains Rider, visit `https://www.jetbrains.com/rider/`

Cloud9 is a web browser-based IDE, so it's even more cross-platform than the others. It is growing in popularity. Here is the link: `https://c9.io/web/sign-up/free`.

Deploying cross-platform

Your choice of IDE and operating system for development does not limit where your code gets deployed. .NET Core currently supports the following platforms for deployment:

- Windows 7 SP1, or later
- Windows Server 2008 R2 SP1, or later
- OS X El Capitan (version 10.11) and macOS Sierra (version 10.12)
- Red Hat Enterprise Linux 7.2
- Ubuntu 14.04 LTS, 16.04 LTS
- Linux Mint 17
- Debian 8.2
- CentOS 7.1
- Oracle Linux 7.1
- Docker

Docker and Linux OSes are popular server host platforms because they are relatively lightweight and more cost-effectively scalable when compared to operating system platforms that are more for end users, such as Windows and macOS.

In the next section, you will install Microsoft Visual Studio 2017 for Windows. If you prefer to use Microsoft Visual Studio Code, jump ahead to the section titled, *Installing Microsoft Visual Studio Code for Windows, macOS, or Linux*.

Installing Microsoft Visual Studio 2017 for Windows

You can use Windows 7 SP1 or later to complete most of the chapters in this book, but you will have a better experience if you use Windows 10.

Since October 2014, Microsoft has made a professional-quality edition of Visual Studio available to everyone for free. It is called the **Community Edition**.

Microsoft has combined all its free developer offerings in a program called **Visual Studio Dev Essentials**. This includes the Community Edition, the free level of Visual Studio Team Services, Azure credits for test and development, and free training from Pluralsight, Wintellect, and Xamarin.

Download and install **Microsoft Visual Studio 2017** from the following link:
`https://www.visualstudio.com/downloads/`

Choosing workloads

On the **Workloads** tab, choose the following, as partially shown in the following screenshot:

- **Universal Windows Platform development**
- **.NET desktop development**
- **ASP.NET and web development**
- **Azure development**
- **Mobile development with .NET**
- **.NET Core cross-platform development**

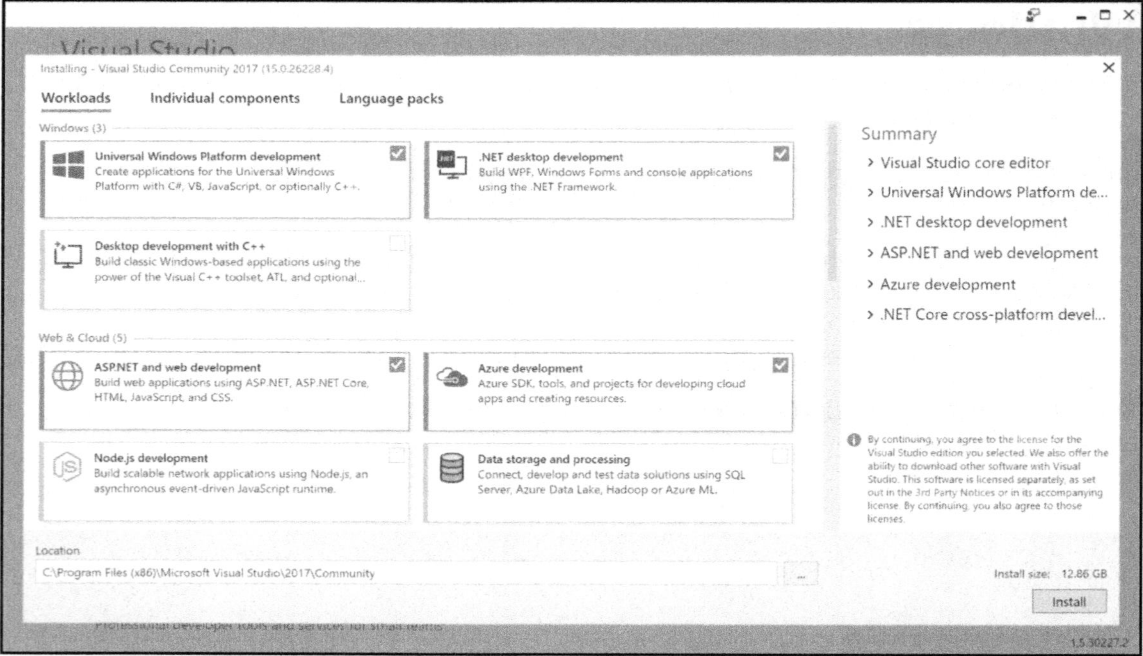

Choosing additional components

On the **Individual components** tab, choose the following additional components, as shown in the following screenshot:

- **Class Designer**
- **PowerShell tools**
- **Git for Windows**
- **GitHub extension for Visual Studio**

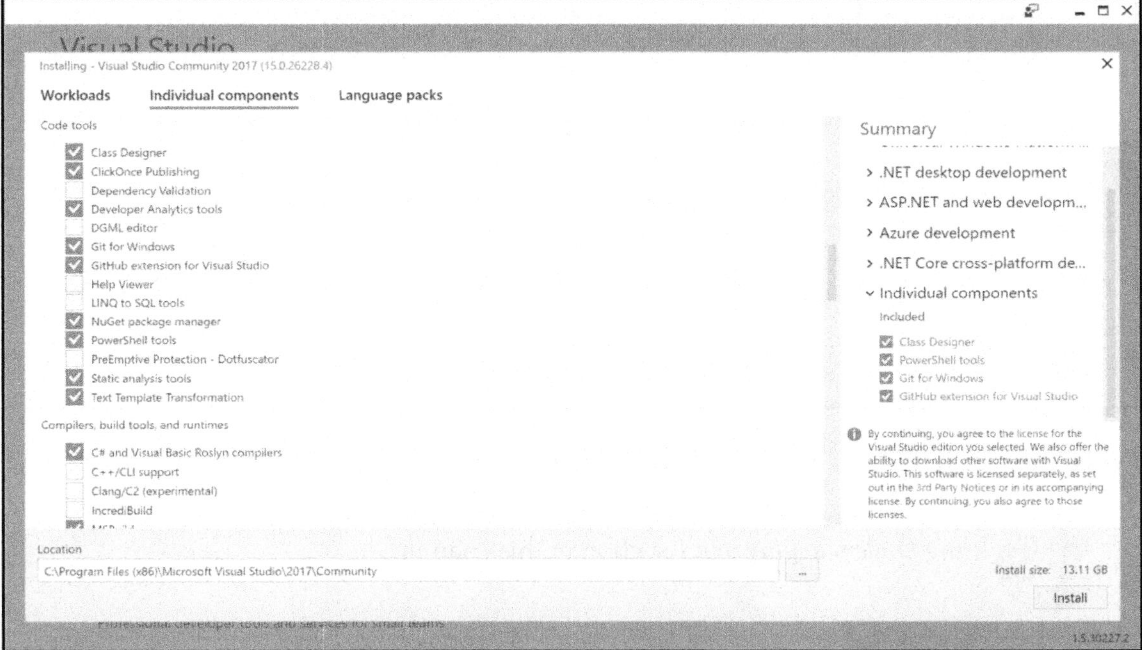

Click **Install**, and wait for the installer to acquire the selected software, and install it, as shown in the following screenshot:

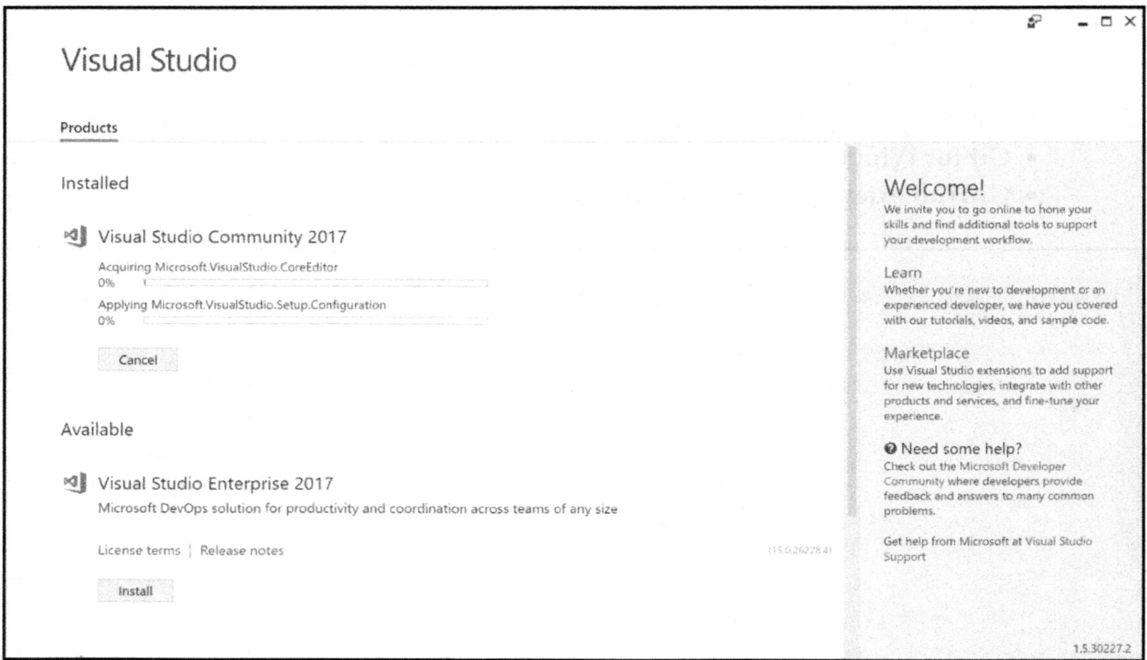

When the installation is complete, click **Launch**.

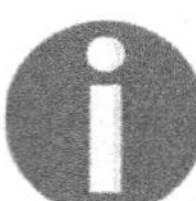

While you wait for Visual Studio 2017 to install, you can jump ahead to the *Understanding .NET* section in this chapter.

Signing in to Visual Studio 2017

The first time that you run Visual Studio 2017, you will be prompted to sign in. If you have a Microsoft account, for example, a Hotmail, MSN, Live, or Outlook e-mail address, you can use that account. If you don't, then register for a new one at the following link: `https://signup.live.com/`.

Choosing your settings

When starting Visual Studio 2017 for the first time, you will be prompted to configure your environment. For **Development Settings**, choose **Visual C#**. For color theme, I chose **Blue**, but you can choose whatever suits you, as shown in the following screenshot:

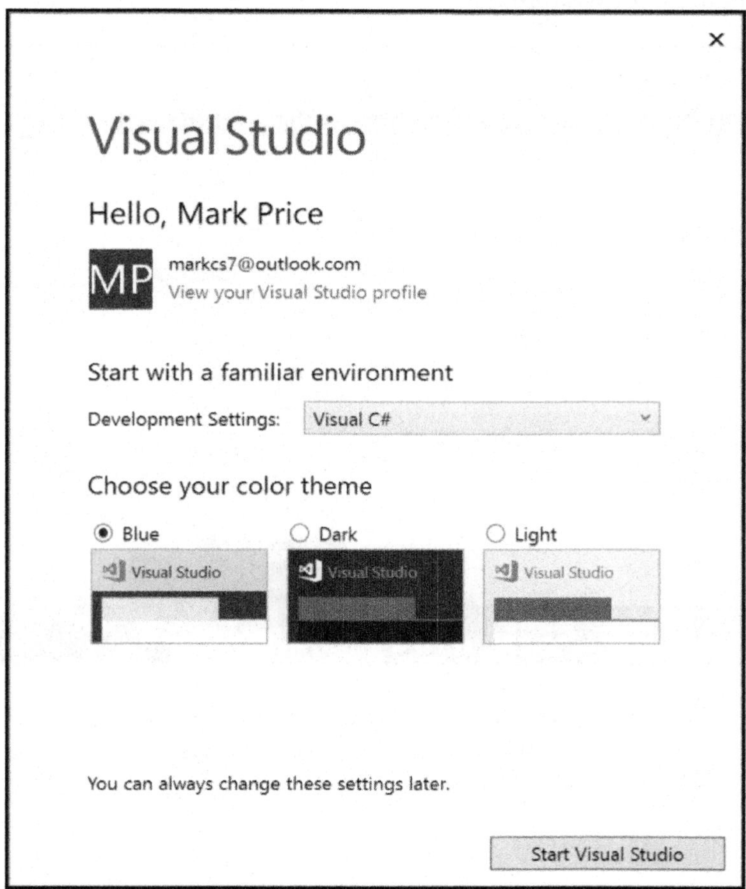

Reviewing Visual Studio's user interface

You will see the Microsoft Visual Studio user interface with the **Start Page** open in the central area. Like most Windows desktop applications, Visual Studio has a menu bar, a toolbar for common commands, and a status bar at the bottom. On the right is the **Solution Explorer** that will list your open projects:

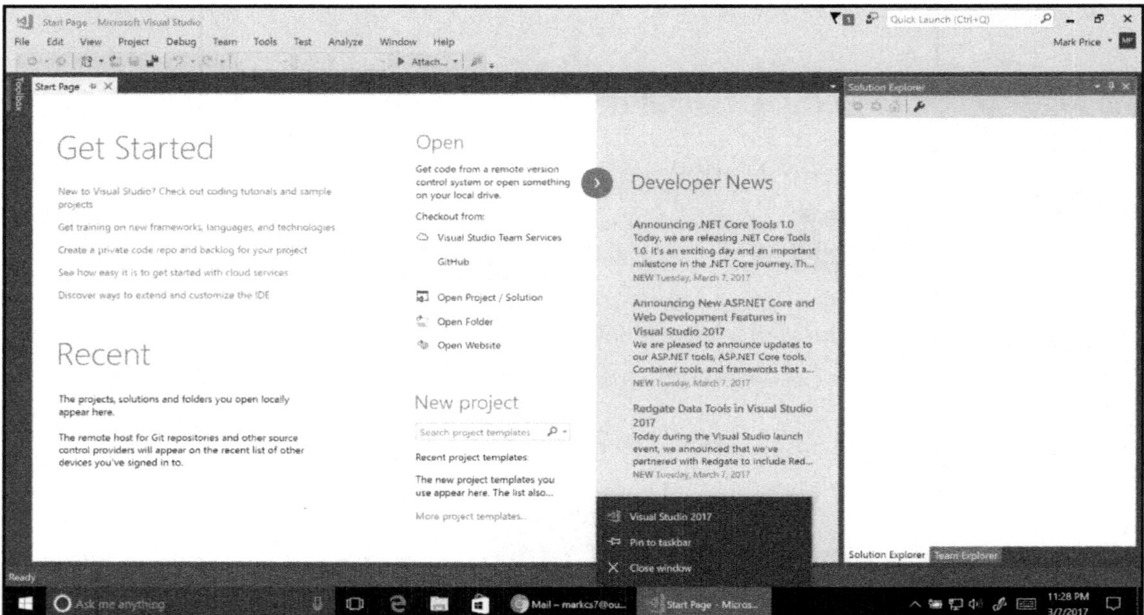

To have quick access to Visual Studio in the future, right-click on its entry in the Windows taskbar and select **Pin to taskbar**.

Installing Microsoft Visual Studio Code for Windows, macOS, or Linux

Between June 2015 and March 2017, Microsoft released a new version of **Visual Studio Code** every month (except for December 2016 because even Microsoft employees deserve a break for Christmas). Visual Studio Code has rapidly improved, and has surprised Microsoft with its popularity. Even if you plan to use Visual Studio 2017 as your primary development tool, I recommend that you learn how to use Visual Studio Code and the .NET Core command-line tool as well.

You can download Visual Studio Code from `https://code.visualstudio.com/`.

Installing Microsoft Visual Studio Code for macOS

In this book, I will show examples and screenshots of Visual Studio Code by using the version for macOS. The steps for doing the same with Visual Studio Code for Windows and variants of Linux is very similar, so I will not repeat the instructions for every platform.

After downloading Visual Studio Code for macOS, drag and drop it to your `Applications` folder, as shown in the following screenshot:

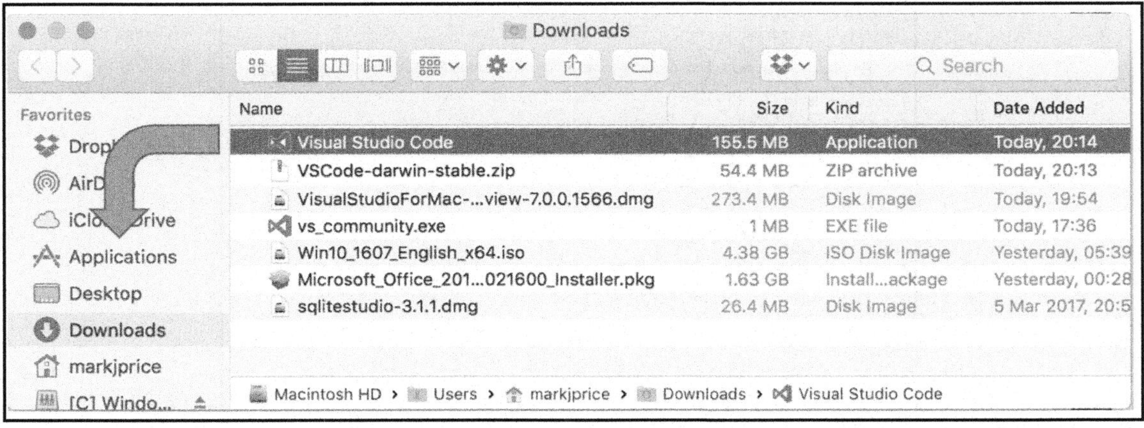

Installing .NET Core for macOS

You will now need to install the .NET Core SDK for macOS. The full instructions, including a video to watch, are described at the following link, and I have included the basic steps in this book for your convenience: `https://www.microsoft.com/net/core#macos`.

Installing Homebrew

The first step is to install Homebrew (if you don't already have it).

Start macOS's **Terminal** app and enter the following command at the prompt:

```
/usr/bin/ruby -e "$(curl -fsSL
https://raw.githubusercontent.com/Homebrew/install/master/install)"
```

Terminal will prompt you to press RETURN to continue, and then prompt for your password, as shown in the following screenshot:

```
markjprice — ruby -e #!/System/Library/Frameworks/Ruby.framework/Versions...
Last login: Tue Mar  7 17:18:54 on console
Marks-MBP-13:~ markjprice$ /usr/bin/ruby -e "$(curl -fsSL https://raw.githubuser
content.com/Homebrew/install/master/install)"
==> This script will install:
/usr/local/bin/brew
/usr/local/share/doc/homebrew
/usr/local/share/man/man1/brew.1
/usr/local/share/zsh/site-functions/_brew
/usr/local/etc/bash_completion.d/brew
/usr/local/Homebrew
==> The following existing directories will be made group writable:
/usr/local/bin
/usr/local/share
/usr/local/share/man
/usr/local/share/man/man8
==> The following existing directories will have their owner set to markjprice:
/usr/local/bin
/usr/local/share
/usr/local/share/man
/usr/local/share/man/man8
==> The following existing directories will have their group set to admin:
/usr/local/bin
/usr/local/share
/usr/local/share/man
/usr/local/share/man/man8
==> The following new directories will be created:
/usr/local/Cellar
/usr/local/Homebrew
/usr/local/Frameworks
/usr/local/etc
/usr/local/include
/usr/local/lib
/usr/local/opt
/usr/local/sbin
/usr/local/share/zsh
/usr/local/share/zsh/site-functions
/usr/local/var

Press RETURN to continue or any other key to abort
```

Installing OpenSSL

The second step is to use Homebrew to install OpenSSL, which is required by .NET Core.

At the prompt, enter the following commands:

```
brew update
brew install openssl
mkdir -p /usr/local/lib
ln -s /usr/local/opt/openssl/lib/libcrypto.1.0.0.dylib  /usr/local/lib/
ln -s /usr/local/opt/openssl/lib/libssl.1.0.0.dylib /usr/local/lib/
```

Terminal will output messages as shown in the following screenshot:

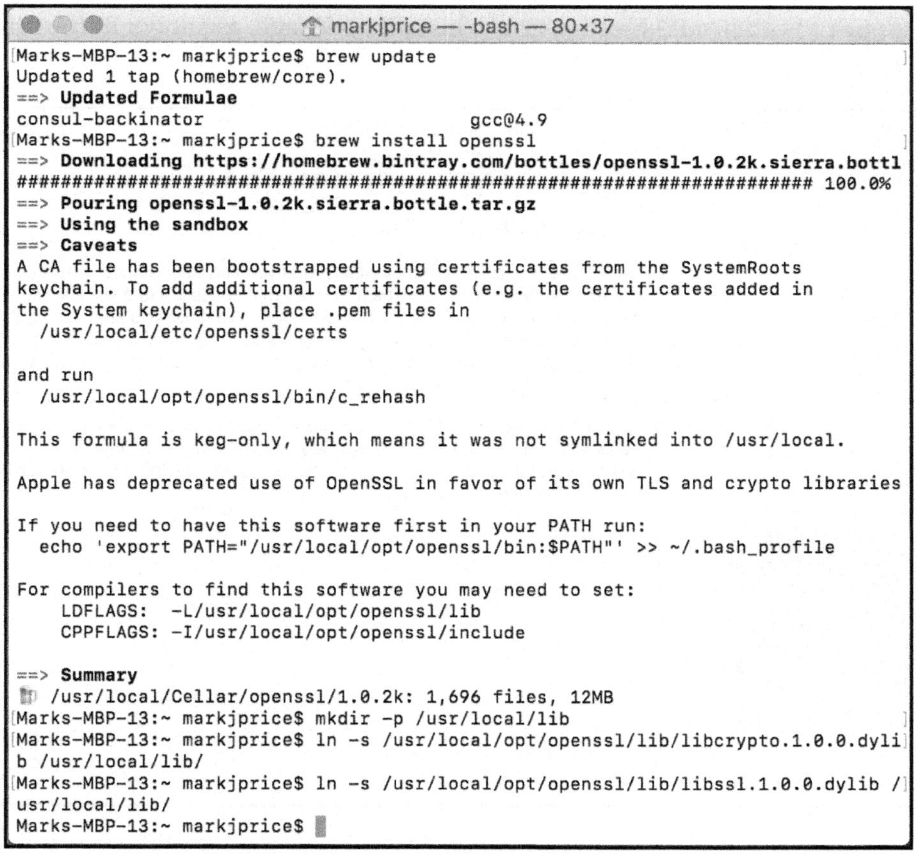

```
markjprice — -bash — 80×37
Marks-MBP-13:~ markjprice$ brew update
Updated 1 tap (homebrew/core).
==> Updated Formulae
consul-backinator                          gcc@4.9
Marks-MBP-13:~ markjprice$ brew install openssl
==> Downloading https://homebrew.bintray.com/bottles/openssl-1.0.2k.sierra.bottl
######################################################################## 100.0%
==> Pouring openssl-1.0.2k.sierra.bottle.tar.gz
==> Using the sandbox
==> Caveats
A CA file has been bootstrapped using certificates from the SystemRoots
keychain. To add additional certificates (e.g. the certificates added in
the System keychain), place .pem files in
  /usr/local/etc/openssl/certs

and run
  /usr/local/opt/openssl/bin/c_rehash

This formula is keg-only, which means it was not symlinked into /usr/local.

Apple has deprecated use of OpenSSL in favor of its own TLS and crypto libraries

If you need to have this software first in your PATH run:
  echo 'export PATH="/usr/local/opt/openssl/bin:$PATH"' >> ~/.bash_profile

For compilers to find this software you may need to set:
    LDFLAGS:  -L/usr/local/opt/openssl/lib
    CPPFLAGS: -I/usr/local/opt/openssl/include

==> Summary
   /usr/local/Cellar/openssl/1.0.2k: 1,696 files, 12MB
Marks-MBP-13:~ markjprice$ mkdir -p /usr/local/lib
Marks-MBP-13:~ markjprice$ ln -s /usr/local/opt/openssl/lib/libcrypto.1.0.0.dyli
b /usr/local/lib/
Marks-MBP-13:~ markjprice$ ln -s /usr/local/opt/openssl/lib/libssl.1.0.0.dylib /
usr/local/lib/
Marks-MBP-13:~ markjprice$
```

Installing .NET Core SDK

The third step is to download the **.NET Core SDK** installer for macOS (x64) from the following link: `https://www.microsoft.com/net/download/core`.

The .NET Core SDK installer package installs .NET Core version 1.1.1 and the .NET Core Command Line Interface (CLI) tool version 1.0.1. Yes, the version numbers are confusing! A single CLI tool with its own version number is used for multiple versions of .NET Core runtime. .NET Core 1.1.1 is the **Current** branch and gets new features and bug fixes. .NET Core 1.0.4 is the **Long Term Support (LTS)** branch and only gets bug fixes. Both were released on March 7, 2017 with Visual Studio 2017.

Run the `dotnet-1.1.1-sdk-osx-x64.pkg` installer package, as shown in the following screenshot:

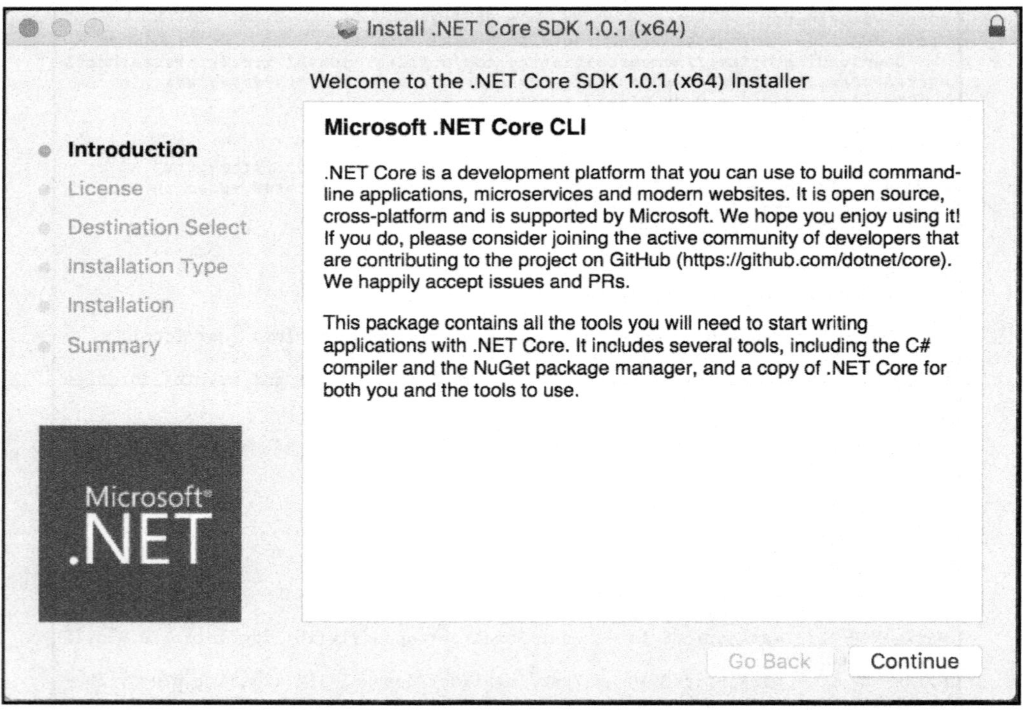

Click **Continue**, accept the license agreement, click **Install**, and then, as shown in the next screenshot, click **Close**:

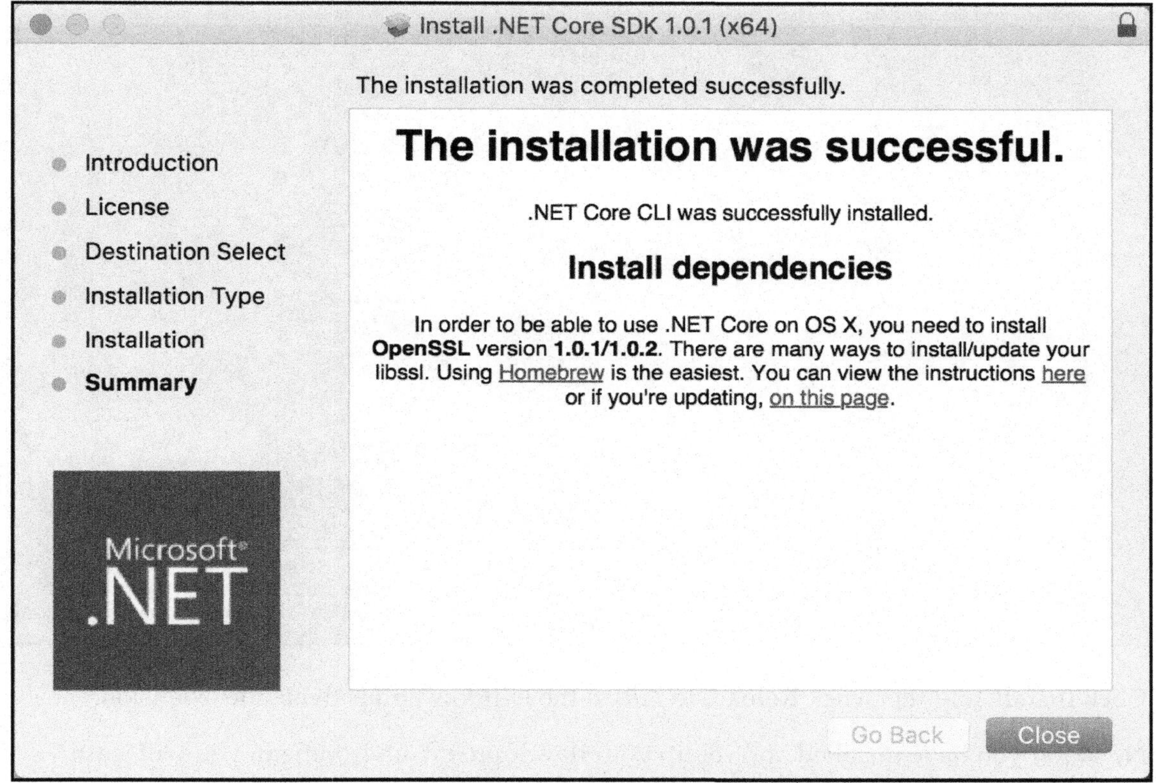

Installing the Visual Studio Code extension for C#

This extension is not necessary but it provides IntelliSense as you type, so it's very handy to install.

Launch **Visual Studio Code** and click the **Extensions** icon, or choose **View** | **Extensions**, or press *Cmd* + *Shift* + *X*.

C# is the most popular extension so you should see it at the top of the list, as shown in the following screenshot:

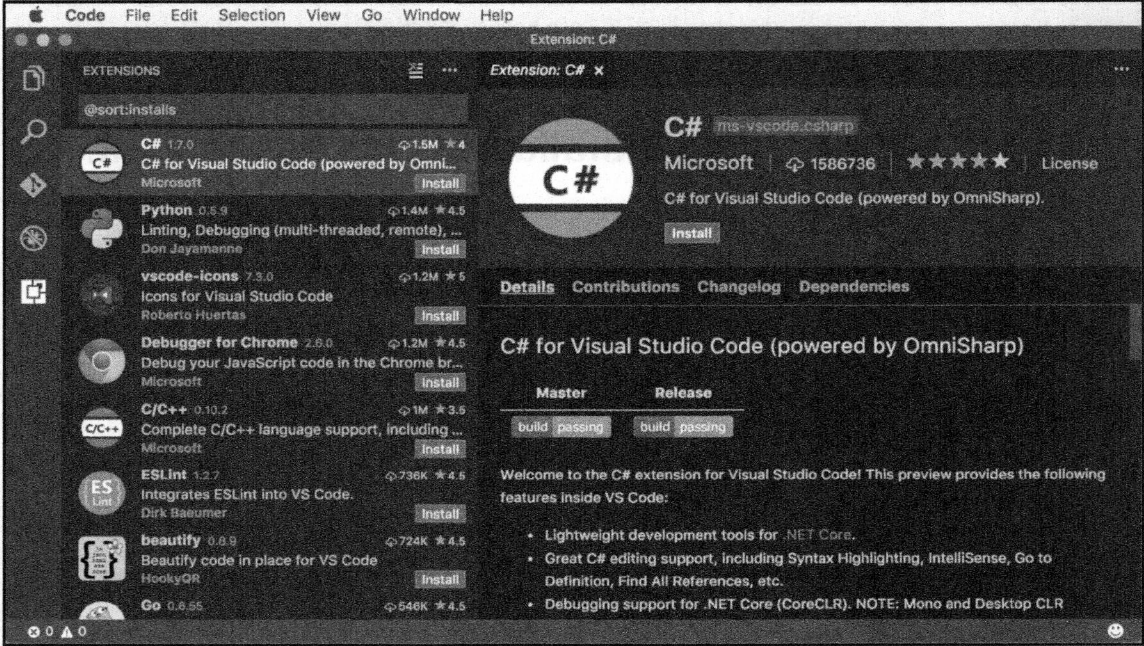

Click **Install**, and then click **Reload**, to reload the window and activate the extension.

Now that you have installed and set up your development environment, you will learn some background about .NET before diving in to writing code.

Understanding .NET

.NET Framework, .NET Core, .NET Standard, and .NET Native are related and overlapping platforms for developers to build applications and services upon.

Understanding .NET Framework

Microsoft's .NET Framework is a development platform that includes a **Common Language Runtime** (**CLR**) that manages the execution of code, and provides a rich library of classes to build applications.

Microsoft designed .NET Framework to have the possibility of being cross-platform, but Microsoft put their implementation effort into making it work best with Windows.

Practically speaking, .NET Framework is Windows-only, and a legacy platform.

Understanding the Mono and Xamarin projects

Third parties developed a .NET implementation named the Mono project that you can read more about here: `http://www.mono-project.com/`.

Mono is cross-platform, but it fell well behind the official implementation of .NET Framework. It has found a niche as the foundation of the **Xamarin** mobile platform.

Microsoft purchased Xamarin in 2016 and now gives away what used to be an expensive Xamarin extension for free with Visual Studio 2017. Microsoft renamed the **Xamarin Studio** development tool to **Visual Studio for Mac** and has given it the ability to create ASP.NET Core Web API services. Xamarin is targeted at mobile development and building cloud services to support mobile apps.

You will use Visual Studio for Mac in `Chapter 15`, *Building Mobile Apps Using Xamarin.Forms and ASP.NET Core Web API* to create a mobile app for iOS and Android that calls an ASP.NET Core Web API service.

Understanding .NET Core

Today, we live in a truly cross-platform world. Modern mobile and cloud development has made Windows a much less important operating system. So, Microsoft has been working on an effort to decouple .NET from its close ties with Windows.

While rewriting .NET to be truly cross-platform, Microsoft has taken the opportunity to refactor .NET to remove major parts that are no longer considered **core**.

This new product is branded as **.NET Core**, which includes a cross-platform implementation of the CLR known as **CoreCLR**, and a streamlined library of classes known as **CoreFX**.

Scott Hunter, Microsoft Partner Director Program Manager for .NET, says, "Forty percent of our .NET Core customers are brand-new developers to the platform, which is what we want with .NET Core. We want to bring new people in."

The following table shows when important versions of .NET Core were released, and Microsoft's schedule for the next major release:

Version	**Released**
.NET Core RC1	November 2015
.NET Core 1.0	June 2016
.NET Core 1.1	November 2016
.NET Core 1.0.4 (LTS) and .NET Core (Current) 1.1.1	March 2017
.NET Core 2.0	Scheduled for release in Q3 2017

Good Practice
If you need to work with .NET Core 1.0 and 1.1, then I recommend that you read the announcement for .NET Core 1.1, although the information at the following URL is useful for all .NET Core developers:
`https://blogs.msdn.microsoft.com/dotnet/2016/11/16/announcing-net-core-1-1/`

Streamlining .NET

.NET Core is much smaller than the current version of .NET Framework because a lot has been removed.

For example, **Windows Forms** and **Windows Presentation Foundation** (**WPF**) can be used to build **graphical user interface** (**GUI**) applications, but they are tightly bound to Windows, so they have been removed from .NET Core. The latest technology used to build Windows apps is the **Universal Windows Platform** (**UWP**), and UWP is built on a custom version of .NET Core. You will learn about it in `Chapter 13`, *Building Universal Windows Platform Apps Using XAML*.

ASP.NET Web Forms and **Windows Communication Foundation** (**WCF**) are old web application and service technologies that fewer developers choose to use for new development projects today, so they have also been removed from .NET Core. Instead, developers prefer to use ASP.NET MVC and ASP.NET Web API. These two technologies have been refactored and combined into a new product that runs on .NET Core named **ASP.NET Core**. You will learn about **ASP.NET Core MVC** in `Chapter 14`, *Building Web Applications Using ASP.NET Core MVC*, and **ASP.NET Core Web API** in `Chapter 15`, *Building Mobile Apps Using Xamarin.Forms and ASP.NET Core Web API*.

The **Entity Framework** (**EF**) 6.x is an object-relational mapping technology to work with data stored in relational databases such as Oracle and Microsoft SQL Server. It has gained baggage over the years, so the cross-platform version has been slimmed down and named **Entity Framework Core**. You will learn about it in `Chapter 8`, *Working with Databases Using Entity Framework Core*.

Some common but old data types in .NET Framework have been removed from .NET Core, such as `HashTable` and `ArrayList` in `System.Collections`, but can be added back using a separate class library or NuGet package. Some data types in .NET that are included with both .NET Framework and .NET Core have been simplified by removing some members. For example, in .NET Framework, the `File` class has both a `Close` and `Dispose` method, and either can be used to release the file resources. In .NET Core, there is only the `Dispose` method. This reduces the memory footprint of the assembly and simplifies the API you must learn.

As well as removing large pieces from .NET Framework to make .NET Core, Microsoft has componentized .NET Core into NuGet packages: small chunks of functionality that can be deployed independently.

.NET Framework 4.6 is about 200 MB and must be deployed as a single unit. .NET Core 1.0 is about 11 MB. Eventually, .NET Core and all its NuGet packages may grow to hundreds of megabytes. Microsoft's primary goal is not to make .NET Core smaller than .NET Framework. The goal is to componentize .NET Core to support modern technologies and to have fewer dependencies so that deployment requires only those packages that your application needs.

Understanding .NET Standard

The situation with .NET today is that there are three forked .NET platforms, all controlled by Microsoft:

- .NET Framework
- Xamarin
- .NET Core

Each have different strengths and weaknesses because they are designed for different scenarios. This has led to the problem that a developer must learn three platforms, each with annoying quirks and limitations.

So, Microsoft is working on defining .NET Standard 2.0: a set of APIs that all .NET platforms must implement. At the time that I write this, in March 2017, there is .NET Standard 1.6, but only .NET Core supports it; .NET Framework and Xamarin do not.

.NET Standard 2.0 will be implemented by .NET Framework, .NET Core, and Xamarin. For .NET Core, this will add many of the missing APIs that developers need to port old code written for .NET Framework to the cross-platform .NET Core. However, Microsoft warns that some APIs will be "implemented", but throw an exception to indicate to a developer that they should not actually be used! You will learn how to handle this in `Chapter 2`, *Speaking C#*.

.NET Standard 2.0 is the near future of .NET, and it will make it much easier for developers to share code between any flavor of .NET, but we are not there yet. Microsoft says .NET Standard 2.0, and .NET Core 2.0, are scheduled for release in Q3 2017. That could mean July 1, 2017, but based on previous experience, I think late September 2017 is more realistic.

The following diagram summarizes how the three variants of .NET (sometimes known as app models) will share the common .NET Standard 2.0 and infrastructure:

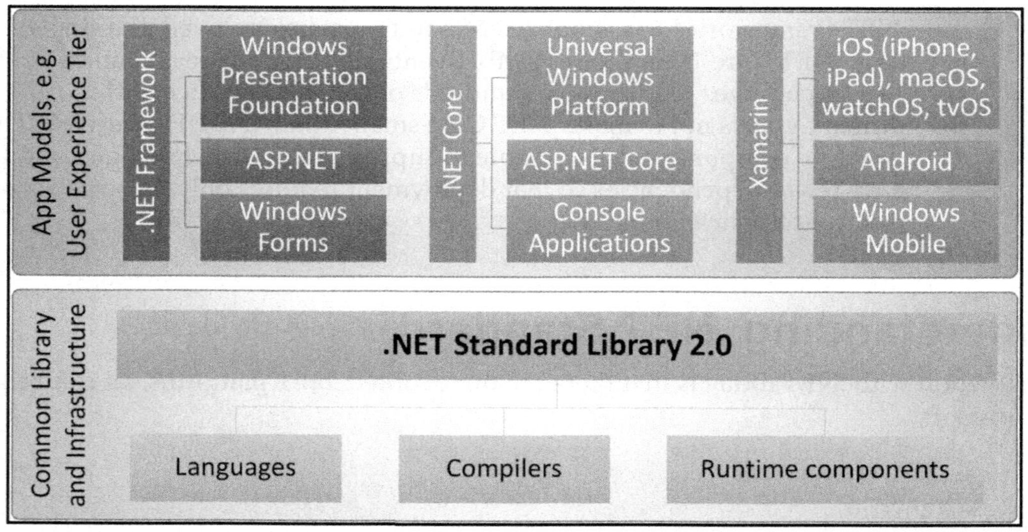

.NET used in this book

The first edition of this book focused on .NET Core, but used .NET Framework when important or useful features had not been implemented in .NET Core. Visual Studio 2015 was used for most examples, with Visual Studio Code shown only briefly.

The second edition has been purged of all .NET Framework code examples. It has been rewritten so that all code is pure .NET Core and can be written with either Visual Studio 2017 or Visual Studio Code on any supported operating system.

The only exceptions are in `Chapter 13`, *Building Universal Windows Platform Apps Using XAML*, that uses .NET Core for UWP and requires Visual Studio 2017 running on Windows 10, and in `Chapter 15`, *Building Mobile Apps Using Xamarin.Forms and ASP.NET Core Web API*, when we will write a Xamarin mobile app with Visual Studio for Mac.

Understanding .NET Native

Another .NET initiative is .NET Native. This compiles C# code to native CPU instructions **ahead-of-time** (**AoT**) rather than using the CLR to compile intermediate language (IL) code **just-in-time** (**JIT**) to native code later.

.NET Native improves execution speed and reduces the memory footprint for applications. It supports the following:

- UWP apps for Windows 10, Windows 10 Mobile, Xbox One, HoloLens, and **Internet of Things** (**IoT**) devices such as Raspberry Pi
- Server-side web development with ASP.NET Core
- Console applications for use on the command line

Comparing .NET technologies

The following table summarizes and compares .NET technologies:

<table>
<tr><th>Technology</th><th>Feature set</th><th>Compiles to</th><th>Host OSes</th></tr>
<tr><td>.NET Framework</td><td>Mature and extensive</td><td rowspan="3">IL executed by a runtime</td><td>Windows only</td></tr>
<tr><td>Xamarin</td><td>Mature and limited to mobile features</td><td>iOS, Android, Windows Mobile</td></tr>
<tr><td>.NET Core</td><td>New and somewhat limited (until .NET Core 2.0)</td><td rowspan="2">Windows, Linux, macOS, Docker</td></tr>
<tr><td>.NET Native</td><td>New and somewhat limited</td><td>Native code</td></tr>
</table>

Writing and compiling code using the .NET Core CLI tool

When you install Visual Studio 2017, or the .NET Core SDK, a **Command Line Interface (CLI)** tool named `dotnet` is installed as well as the .NET Core runtime.

`dotnet` has the following commands that all work on the project in the current folder:

- `dotnet new console`: creates a new console application project
- `dotnet new classlib`: creates a new assembly library project
- `dotnet new web`: creates a new empty ASP.NET Core project
- `dotnet new mvc`: creates a new ASP.NET Core MVC project
- `dotnet new webapi`: creates a new ASP.NET Core Web API project
- `dotnet restore`: downloads dependencies for the project
- `dotnet build`: compiles the project
- `dotnet test`: runs unit tests on the project
- `dotnet run`: runs the project
- `dotnet migrate`: migrates a .NET Core project created with the preview CLI tools to the current CLI tool MS Build format
- `dotnet pack`: creates a NuGet package for the project

- `dotnet publish`: compiles and publishes the project, either with dependencies or as a self-contained application

You will learn how to build, package, publish, and deploy your .NET Core applications and assemblies in `Chapter 16`, *Packaging and Deploying Your Code Cross-Platform*.

Before we use CLI tools such as `dotnet`, we need to write some code!

Writing code using a simple text editor

If you are using Windows, start **Notepad**.

If you are using macOS, launch **TextEdit**. From the **TextEdit** menu, choose **Preferences**, clear the **Smart quotes** check box, and then close the dialog. From the **Format** menu, choose **Make Plain Text**.

Or run your favorite plain text editor.

Enter the following code:

```
class MyApp { static void Main() {
System.Console.WriteLine("Hello, C#!"); } }
```

C# is case sensitive, meaning that you must type uppercase and lowercase characters exactly as shown in the preceding code. C# is not whitespace sensitive, meaning that it does not care if you use tabs, spaces, and carriage-returns to layout your code however you like.

You can type the code all in one line or spread it out over multiple lines and indent your lines. For example, the following code would also compile and have the same output:

```
class
      MyApp       {
 static                    void
Main          (){System.      Console.
    WriteLine(       "Hello, C#!");         }       }
```

Of course, it's best to write your code in a way that other programmers, and yourself months or years later, can clearly read!

If you are using Windows Notepad

In Notepad, from the **File** menu, choose **Save As...**.

In the dialog box, change to drive `C:` (or any drive which you want to use to save your projects), click on the **New folder** button, and name the folder `Code`. Open the `Code` folder, and click the **New folder** button, and name the folder `Chapter01`. Open the `Chapter01` folder, and click the **New folder** button, and name the folder `Ch01_HelloCS`. Open the `Ch01_HelloCS` folder.

In the **Save as type** field, select **All Files** from the drop-down list to avoid appending the `.txt` file extension, and enter the file name as `MyApp.cs`, as shown in the following screenshot:

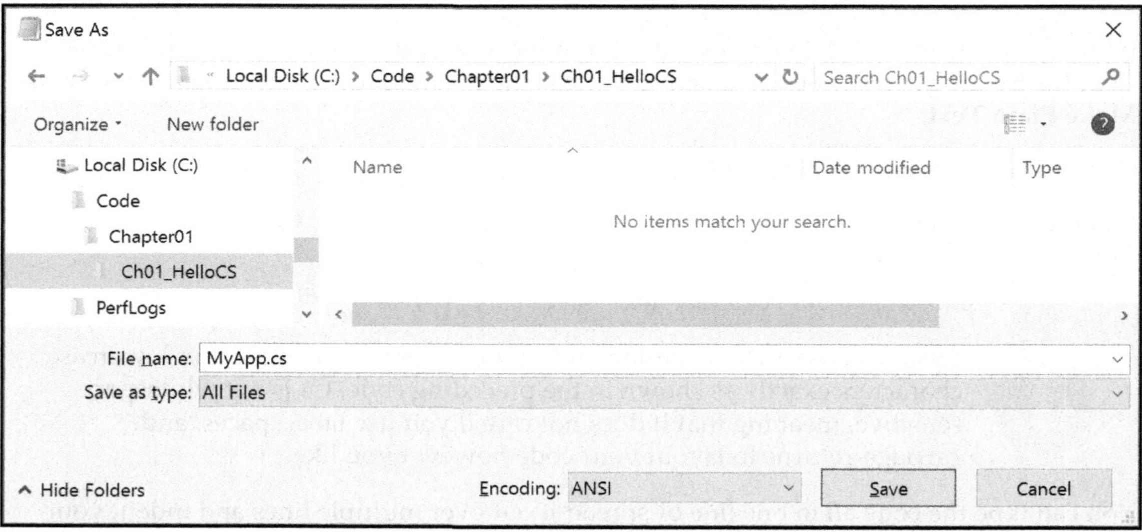

Your code in Notepad should look something like the following screenshot:

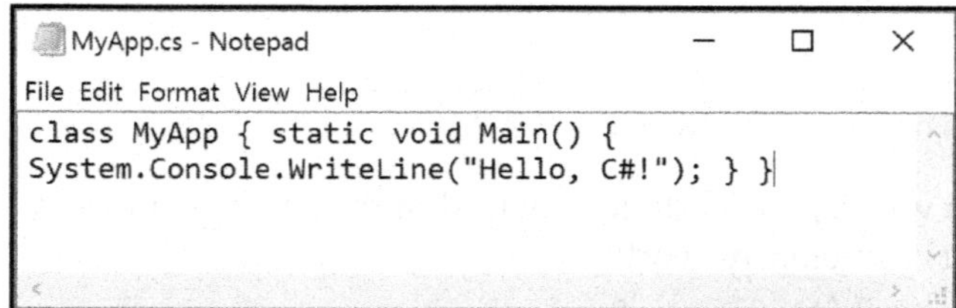

If you are using macOS TextEdit

In **TextEdit**, from the **File** menu, choose **Save...**, or press *Cmd* + *S*.

In the dialog box, change to your **user** folder (mine is named **markjprice**) or any directory in which you want to use to save your projects, click on the **New Folder** button, and name the folder `Code`. Open the `Code` folder, and click the **New Folder** button, and name the folder `Chapter01`. Open the `Chapter01` folder, and click the **New Folder** button, and name the folder `Ch01_HelloCS`. Open the `Ch01_HelloCS` folder.

In the **Plain Text Encoding** field, select **Unicode (UTF-8)** from the drop-down list, uncheck the box for **If no extension is provided, use ".txt"** to avoid appending the `.txt` file extension, enter the filename as `MyApp.cs`, and click on **Save**, as shown in the following screenshot:

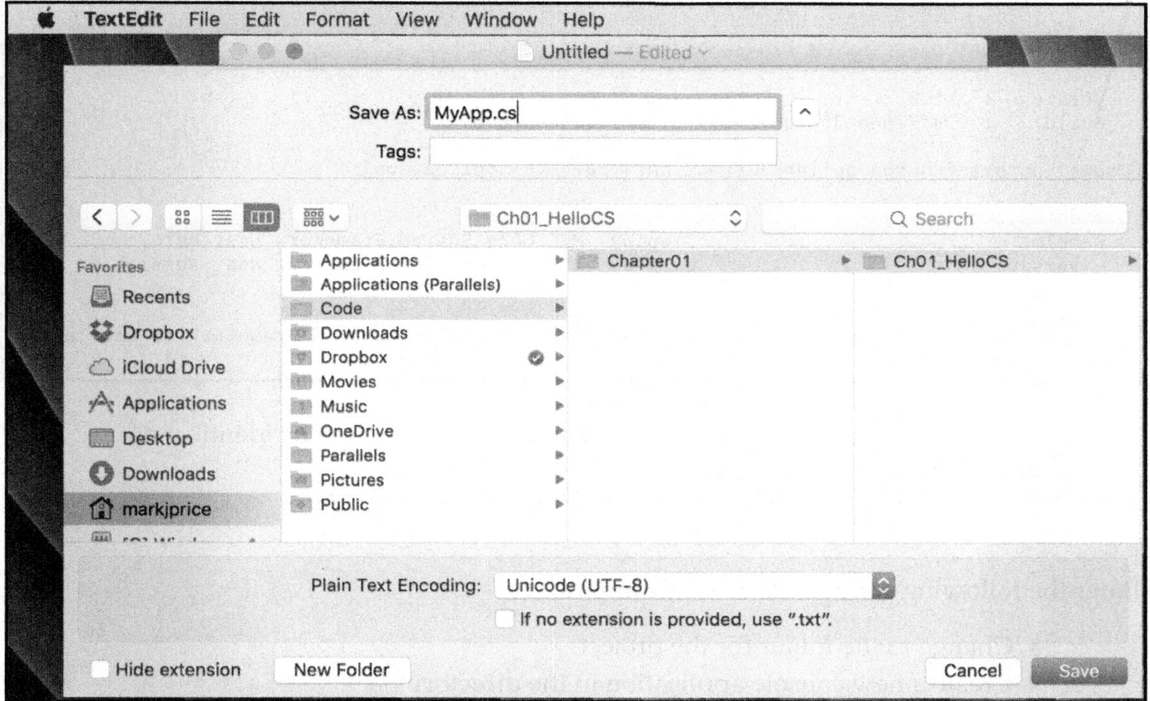

Compiling code using the .NET Core CLI tool

If you are using Windows, start **Command Prompt**.

If you are using macOS, launch **Terminal**.

At the prompt, enter the following command:

```
dotnet
```

You should see the following output describing the `dotnet` CLI tool:

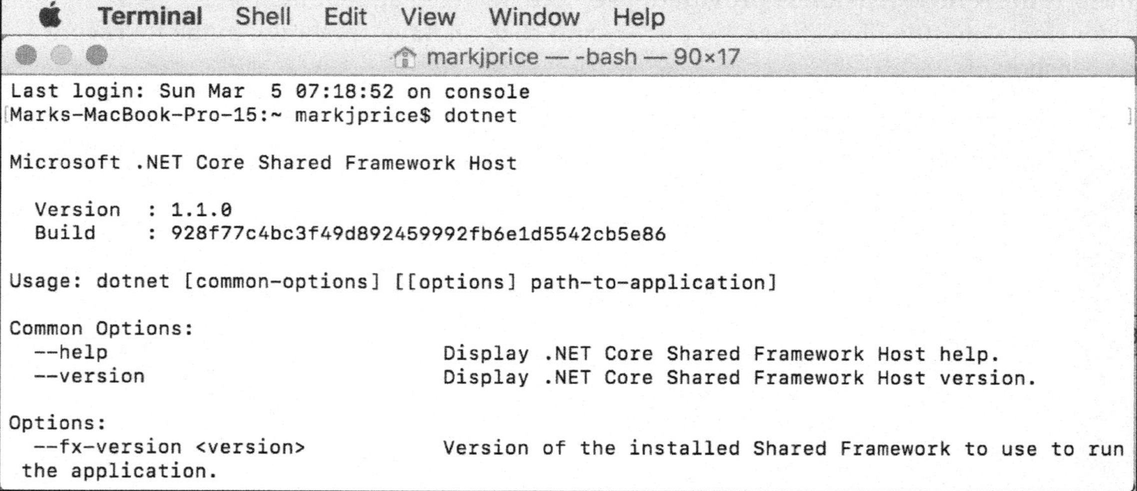

The output from the `dotnet` command-line tool will be identical on Windows, macOS, and Linux.

Enter the following commands at the prompt to:

- Change to the folder for the project
- Create a new console application in the directory
- List the files that the `dotnet` command-line tool created

If you are using Windows, in **Command Prompt**, enter:

```
cd C:\Code\Chapter01\Ch01_HelloCS
dotnet new console
dir
```

If you are using macOS, in **Terminal**, enter:

```
cd Code/Chapter01/Ch01_HelloCS
dotnet new console
ls
```

The first time that you execute a `dotnet new` command, your **local package cache** must be populated. This should only take a few moments.

You should see that the `dotnet` tool has created two new files for you:

- `Program.cs`: source code for a simple console application
- `Ch01_HelloCS.csproj`: a project file that lists dependencies and project-related configuration

For this example, we must delete the file named `Program.cs` since we have already created our own class called `Program` in the file named `MyApp.cs`.

If you are using Windows, in **Command Prompt**:

```
del Program.cs
```

If you are using macOS, in **Terminal**:

```
rm Program.cs
```

In all future examples, we will use the `Program.cs` file generated by the tool rather than manually create our own.

Restoring packages and running the application

At the prompt, enter the following commands:

```
dotnet restore
dotnet run
```

After a few seconds, all the packages needed by our code will be downloaded, the source code will be compiled, and your application will run, as shown in the following output on macOS:

```
Terminal  Shell  Edit  View  Window  Help
Ch01_HelloCS — -bash — 113×21
Marks-MBP-13:Ch01_HelloCS markjprice$ dotnet new console
Content generation time: 59.9867 ms
The template "Console Application" created successfully.
Marks-MBP-13:Ch01_HelloCS markjprice$ ls
Ch01_HelloCS.csproj      MyApp.cs                Program.cs
Marks-MBP-13:Ch01_HelloCS markjprice$ rm Program.cs
Marks-MBP-13:Ch01_HelloCS markjprice$ dotnet restore
  Restoring packages for /Users/markjprice/Code/Chapter01/Ch01_HelloCS/Ch01_HelloCS.csproj...
  Generating MSBuild file /Users/markjprice/Code/Chapter01/Ch01_HelloCS/obj/Ch01_HelloCS.csproj.nuget.g.props.
  Generating MSBuild file /Users/markjprice/Code/Chapter01/Ch01_HelloCS/obj/Ch01_HelloCS.csproj.nuget.g.targets.
  Writing lock file to disk. Path: /Users/markjprice/Code/Chapter01/Ch01_HelloCS/obj/project.assets.json
  Restore completed in 955.37 ms for /Users/markjprice/Code/Chapter01/Ch01_HelloCS/Ch01_HelloCS.csproj.

  NuGet Config files used:
      /Users/markjprice/.nuget/NuGet/NuGet.Config

  Feeds used:
      https://api.nuget.org/v3/index.json
Marks-MBP-13:Ch01_HelloCS markjprice$ dotnet run
Hello, C#!
Marks-MBP-13:Ch01_HelloCS markjprice$
```

Your source code, the file `MyApp.cs`, has been compiled into an assembly named `Ch01_HelloCS.dll` in the subfolder `bin/Debug/netcoreapp1.1`. For now, this assembly can only be executed by the `dotnet run` command. In `Chapter 16`, *Packaging and Deploying Your Code Cross-Platform*, you will learn how to package and publish assemblies for use on any operating system that supports .NET Core.

Fixing compiler errors

If the compiler displays errors, read them carefully, and fix them in your text editor. Save your changes and try again.

At the prompt, you can press the up and down arrows on your keyboard to cycle through previous commands you have entered.

A typical error might be using the wrong case, a missing semicolon at the end of a line, or a mismatched pair of curly braces. For example, if you mistyped a lowercase `m` for the `Main` method, you would see the following error message:

```
error CS5001: Program does not contain a static 'Main' method
suitable for an entry point
```

Understanding Intermediate Language

The C# compiler (named **Roslyn**) used by the `dotnet` CLI tool converts your C# source code into **intermediate language (IL)** code and stores the IL in an **assembly** (a DLL or EXE file).

IL code statements are like assembly language instructions, but they are executed by .NET Core's virtual machine, known as the **CoreCLR**.

At runtime, the CoreCLR loads the IL code from the assembly, JIT (just-in-time) compiles it into native CPU instructions, and then it is executed by the CPU on your machine.

The benefit of this two-step compilation process is that Microsoft can create CLRs for Linux and macOS as well as for Windows. The same IL code runs everywhere because of the second compilation process that generates code for the native operating system and CPU instruction set.

Regardless of which language the source is written in, for example, C# or F#, all .NET applications use IL code for their instructions stored in an assembly. Microsoft and others provide disassembler tools that can open an assembly and reveal this IL code.

Actually, not all .NET applications use IL code! Some use .NET Native's compiler to generate native code instead of IL code, improving performance and reducing memory footprint, but at the cost of portability.

Writing and compiling code using Microsoft Visual Studio 2017

We will now recreate a similar application using Visual Studio 2017. If you have chosen to use Visual Studio Code, I still recommend that you review these instructions and screenshots because Visual Studio Code has similar, although not as extensive, features.

I have been training students to use Visual Studio for over a decade, and I am always surprised at how many programmers fail to use the tool to their advantage.

Over the next few pages, I will walk you through typing a line of code. It may seem redundant, but you will benefit from seeing what help and information Visual Studio provides as you enter your code. If you want to become a fast and accurate coder, letting Visual Studio write most of your code for you is a huge benefit!

Writing code using Microsoft Visual Studio 2017

Start Visual Studio 2017.

Navigate to **File** | **New** | **Project...** or press *Ctrl* + *Shift* + *N*.

From the **Installed** | **Templates** list on the left, expand **Visual C#**, and choose **.NET Core**. In the list at the center, choose **Console App (.NET Core)**. Enter the name `Ch01_WelcomeDotNetCore`, set the location to `C:\Code`, enter `Chapter01` as the solution name, and click on **OK** or press *Enter*, as shown in the following screenshot:

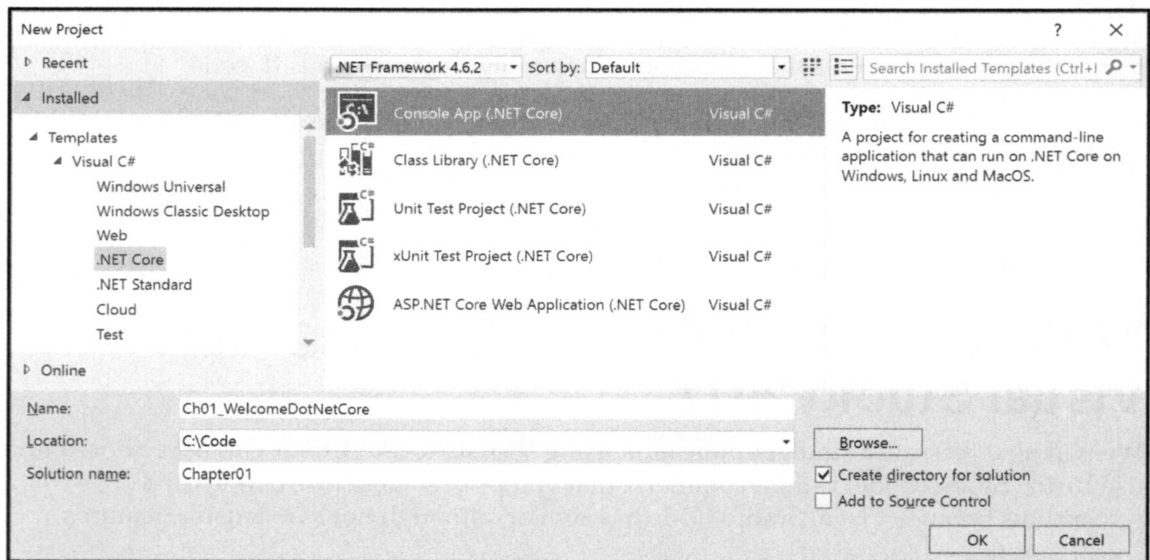

Ignore the target set to .NET Framework 4.6.2. That drop-down list box does not affect .NET Core projects!

Coding with Visual Studio's editor

In the code editor, delete the statement on line **9** that says, `Console.WriteLine("Hello World!");`

Inside the `Main` method, type the letters `sy`, as shown in the following screenshot, and note the IntelliSense menu that appears:

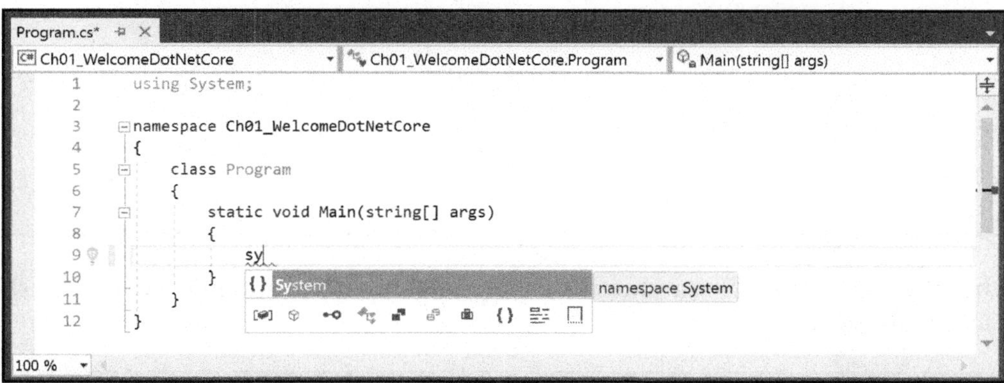

IntelliSense shows a filtered list of **keywords**, **namespaces**, and **types** that contain the letters `sy` and highlights the one that starts with `sy`, which happens to be the namespace that we want—`System`.

Type a dot (also known as decimal point or full stop).

IntelliSense automatically completes the word `System` for you, enters the dot, and displays a list of types, such as `AggregateException` and `Action`, in the `System` namespace, as shown in the following screenshot:

Type the letters `con`, IntelliSense shows a list of matching types and namespaces, as shown in the following screenshot:

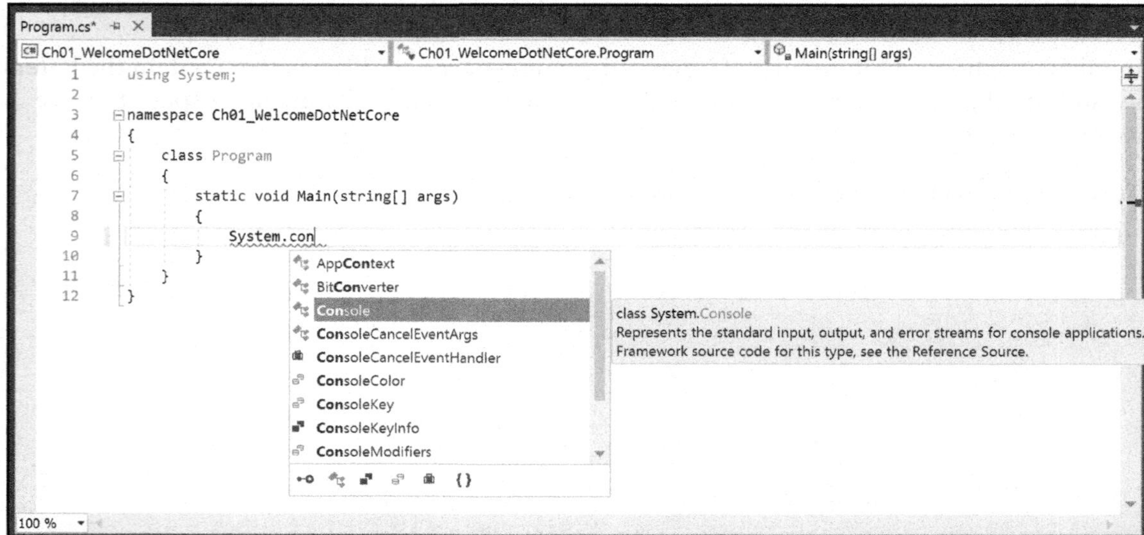

If the one you want is not selected, you can press the up and down arrows on your keyboard to highlight it. For now, **Console** is already selected, so just type a dot.

IntelliSense shows a list of the **members** of the `Console` class, as shown in the following screenshot:

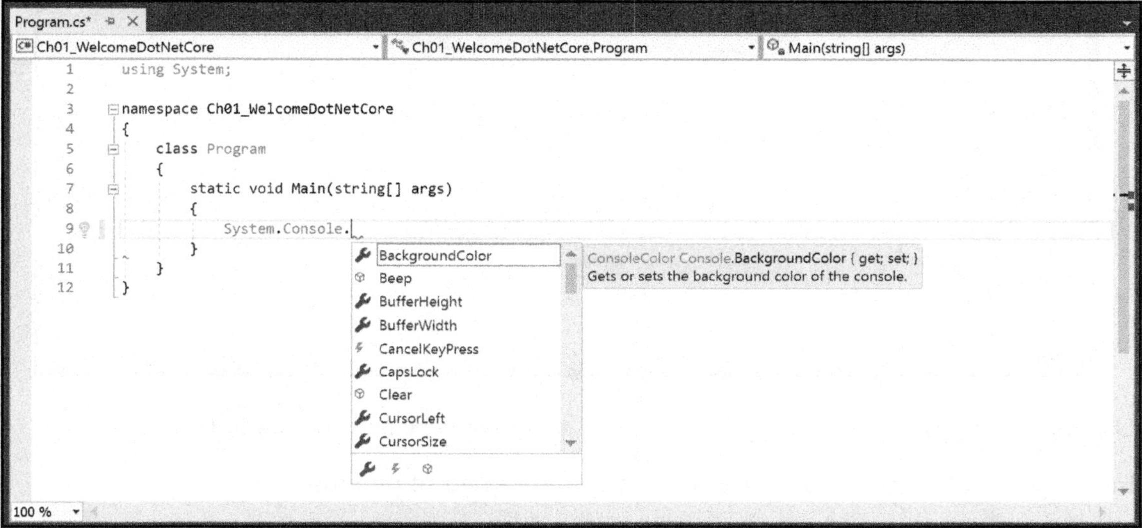

Members include **properties** (attributes of an object, such as `BackgroundColor`), **methods** (actions the object can perform, such as `Beep`), **events**, and other related things.

Type the letters `wr`. IntelliSense shows two matching members containing these letters, as shown in the following screenshot:

```
Program.cs*
Ch01_WelcomeDotNetCore    Ch01_WelcomeDotNetCore.Program    Main(string[] args)
using System;

namespace Ch01_WelcomeDotNetCore
{
    class Program
    {
        static void Main(string[] args)
        {
            System.Console.wr
        }                    Write
    }                        WriteLine
}
100 %
```

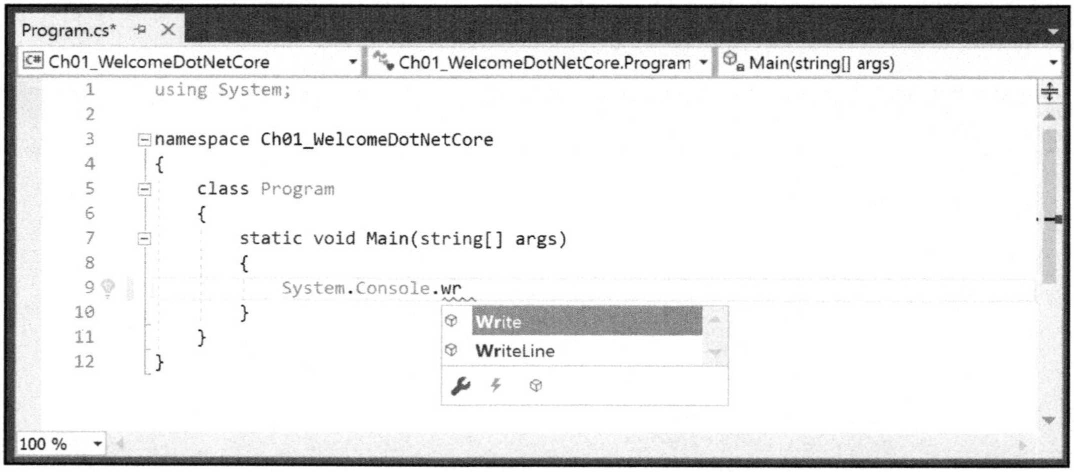

Use the down arrow to highlight `WriteLine` and then type an open parenthesis `(`.

IntelliSense autocompletes `WriteLine` and enters a pair of parentheses.

You will also see a tooltip telling you that the `WriteLine` method has 18 variations, as shown in the following screenshot:

```
Program.cs*
Ch01_WelcomeDotNetCore    Ch01_WelcomeDotNetCore.Program    Main(string[] args)
using System;

namespace Ch01_WelcomeDotNetCore
{
    class Program
    {
        static void Main(string[] args)
        {
            System.Console.WriteLine()
        }   ▲ 1 of 18 ▼ void Console.WriteLine()
    }       Writes the current line terminator to the standard output stream.
}
100 %
```

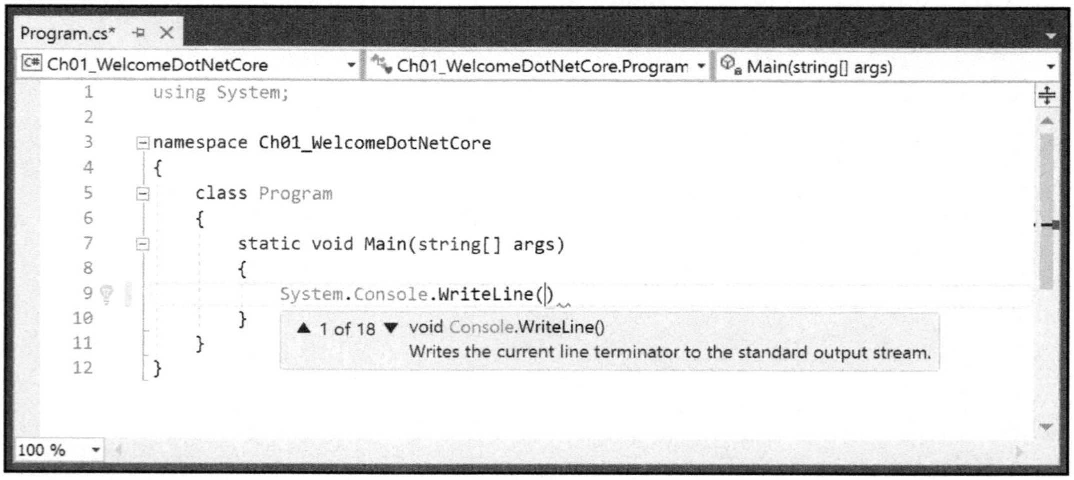

Type a double quote ("). IntelliSense enters a pair of double quotes for you and leaves the keyboard cursor in between them.

Type the text `Welcome, .NET Core!`, as shown in the following screenshot:

```
Program.cs*
Ch01_WelcomeDotNetCore    Ch01_WelcomeDotNetCore.Program    Main(string[] args)
using System;

namespace Ch01_WelcomeDotNetCore
{
    class Program
    {
        static void Main(string[] args)
        {
            System.Console.WriteLine("Welcome, .NET Core!")
        }
    }
}
100 %
```

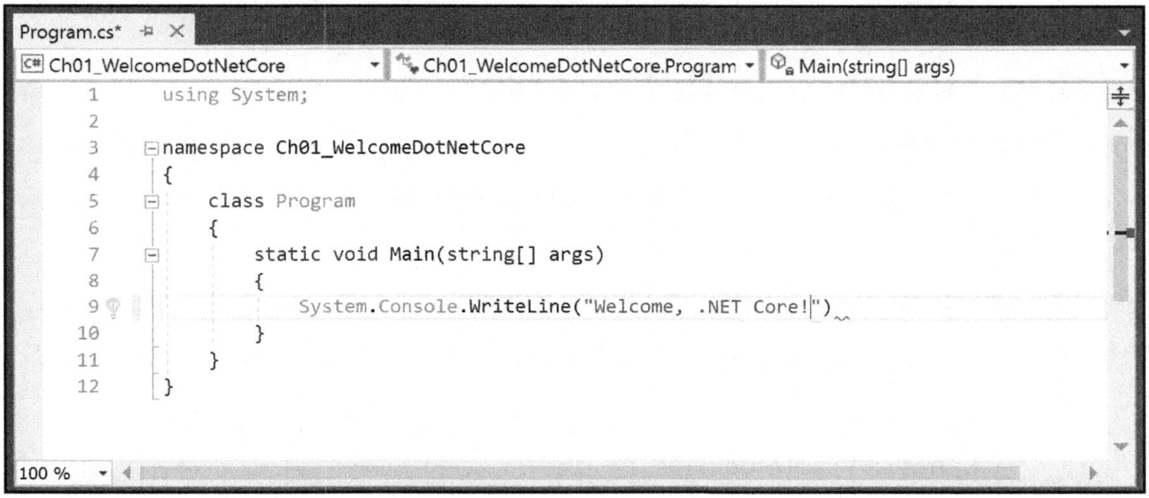

The red squiggle at the end of the line indicates an error because every C# statement must end in a semicolon. Move the cursor to the end of the line and type a semicolon to fix the error.

Compiling code using Visual Studio 2017

From the **Debug** menu, choose **Start Without Debugging** or press *Ctrl + F5*.

Visual Studio's status bar tells us that **Build started...**, then **Build succeeded**, and then your console application runs in a command prompt window, as shown in the following screenshot:

```
C:\Windows\system32\cmd.exe
Welcome, .NET Core!
Press any key to continue . . .
```

To save space in this book and to make the output clearer, I will usually not include screenshots of output from console applications as I did in the previous screenshot. Instead, I will show the output like this:

```
Welcome, .NET Core!
```

Fixing mistakes with the error list

Let's make two deliberate errors:

- Change the `M` of the `Main` method to the lowercase letter `m`.
- Delete the `e` at the end of the method name, `WriteLine`.

From the **Debug** menu, choose **Start Without Debugging** or press *Ctrl* + *F5*.

After a few seconds, the status bar tells us that **Build failed** and an error message appears, as shown in the following screenshot:

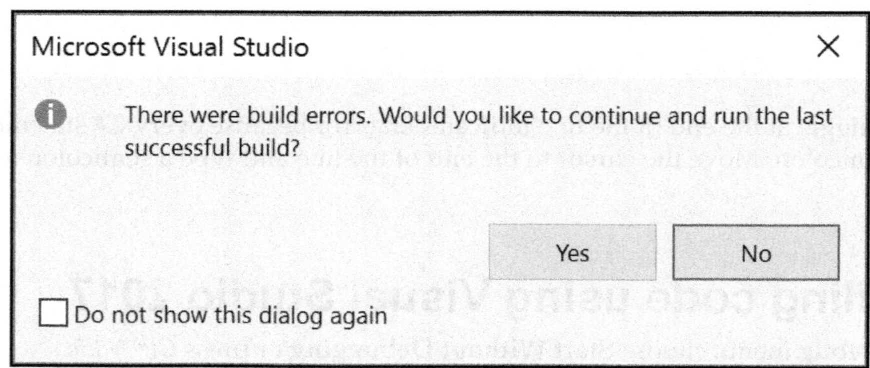

Click **No**.

The **Error List** becomes active, as shown in the following screenshot. You can also view the **Error List** by pressing *Ctrl* + *W*, *E*:

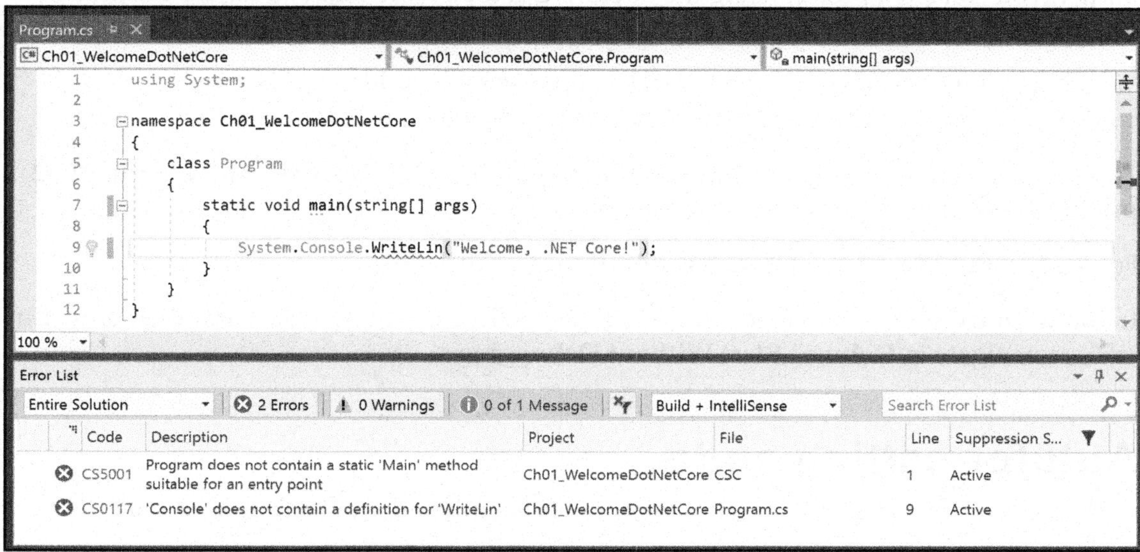

The list can be filtered to show **Errors**, **Warnings**, and **Messages** by clicking on the toggle buttons in the toolbar at the top of the **Error List**.

If an error shows a file and a line number, for example **File**: **Program.cs** and **Line**: **9**, then you can double-click on the error to jump to that line causing the problem.

If it's a more general error, such as the missing `Main` method, the compiler can't tell you a useful line number. You might want a method named `main` as well as a method named `Main` (remember that C# is case sensitive, so you're allowed to do that). However, Visual Studio can also analyze your code and provide messages with suggestions for improvements, such as telling you that method names should begin with an uppercase character.

As shown in the preceding screenshot, fix the two errors, and rerun the application to ensure that it works before you continue. Note that the **Error List** updates to show no errors.

Adding existing projects to Visual Studio 2017

Earlier, you created a project using the `dotnet` CLI tool. Now that you have a solution in Visual Studio 2017, you might want to add the earlier project to the solution.

Navigate to **File** | **Add** | **Existing Project...**, browse to the folder `C:\Code\Chapter01\Ch01_HelloCS`, and select the file `Ch01_HelloCS.csproj`.

To be able to run this project, in the **Solution Explorer**, right-click **Solution 'Chapter01' (2 projects)**, and choose **Properties** or press *Alt* + *Enter*.

For the **Startup Project**, click **Current selection**, and click **OK**.

In **Solution Explorer**, click on any file inside the `Ch01_HelloCS` project, and then press *Ctrl* + *F5*, or navigate to **Debug** | **Start Without Debugging**.

Autoformatting code

Code is easier to read and understand if it is consistently indented and spaced out.

If your code can compile, then Visual Studio 2017 can automatically format it, nicely spaced and indented for you.

In **Solution Explorer**, double-click the file named `MyApp.cs`, as shown in the following screenshot:

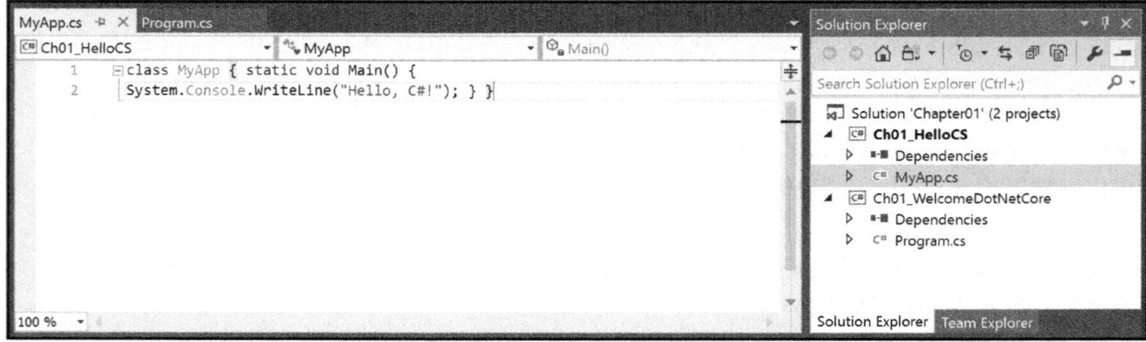

Navigate to **Build** | **Build Ch01_HelloCS**, or press *Shift* + *F6* and wait for your code to build, and then navigate to **Edit** | **Advanced** | **Format Document**, or press *Ctrl* + *E, D*. Your code will be autoformatted, as shown in the following screenshot:

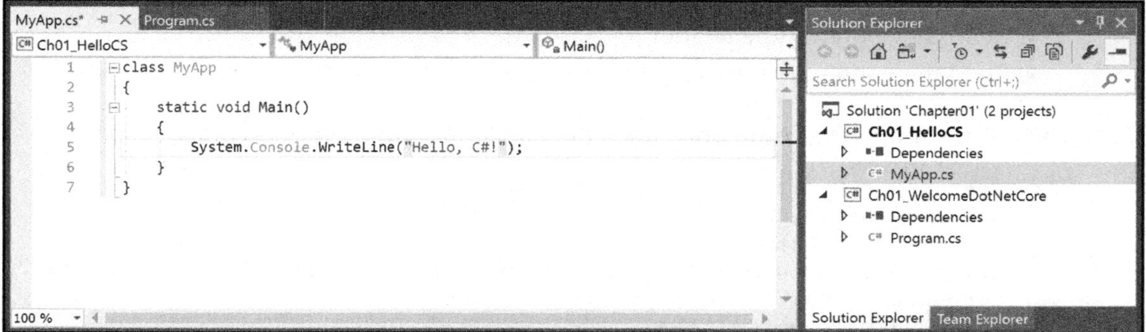

In Visual Studio Code, either right-click and choose **Format Document**, or press *Alt* + *Shift* + *F*.

Experimenting with C# Interactive

Although Visual Studio has always had an **Immediate** window with limited **read-eval-print loop** (**REPL**) support, Visual Studio 2017 includes an enhanced window with full IntelliSense and color syntax code named **C# Interactive**.

In Visual Studio 2017, from the **View** menu, choose **Other Windows**, and then **C# Interactive**.

We will write some interactive code to download the **About** page from Microsoft's public website.

This is just an example. You don't need to understand the code yet!

At the **C# Interactive** prompt, we will enter commands to do the following:

- Reference the `System.Net.Http` assembly
- Import the `System.Net.Http` namespace

- Declare and instantiate an HTTP client variable
- Set the client's base address to Microsoft's website
- Asynchronously wait for a response to a GET request for the **About** page
- Read the status code returned by the web server
- Read the content type header
- Read the contents of the HTML page as a string

Type each of the following commands after the > prompt and then press *Enter*:

```
> #r "System.Net.Http"
> using System.Net.Http;
> var client = new HttpClient();
> client.BaseAddress = new Uri("http://www.microsoft.com/");
> var response = await client.GetAsync("about");
> response.StatusCode
OK
> response.Content.Headers.GetValues("Content-Type")
string[1] { "text/html" }
> await response.Content.ReadAsStringAsync()
"<!DOCTYPE html ><html
xmlns:mscom="http://schemas.microsoft.com/CMSvNext"
xmlns:md="http://schemas.microsoft.com/mscom-data" lang="en"
xmlns="http://www.w3.org/1999/xhtml"><head><meta http-equiv="X-UA-
Compatible" content="IE=edge" /><meta charset="utf-8" /><meta
name="viewport" content="width=device-width, initial-scale=1.0"
/><link rel="shortcut icon"
href="//www.microsoft.com/favicon.ico?v2" /><script
type="text/javascript"
src="http://ajax.aspnetcdn.com/ajax/jQuery/jquery-
1.7.2.min.js">\r\n // Third party scripts and code linked to
or referenced from this website are licensed to you by the parties
that own such code, not by Microsoft. See ASP.NET Ajax CDN Terms of
Use - http://www.asp.net/ajaxlibrary/CDN.ashx.\r\n
</script><script type="text/javascript"
language="javascript">/*<![CDATA[*/if($(document).bind("mobileinit
",function(){$.mobile.autoInitializePage=!1}),navigator.userAgent.ma
tch(/IEMobile\\/10\\.0/)){var
msViewportStyle=document.createElement("style ...
```

The following screenshot shows what Visual Studio 2017 should look like after you've entered the above commands into the **C# Interactive** window:

```
C# Interactive
Microsoft (R) Roslyn C# Compiler version 2.0.0.61104
Loading context from 'CSharpInteractive.rsp'.
Type "#help" for more information.
> #r "System.Net.Http"
> using System.Net.Http;
> var client = new HttpClient();
> client.BaseAddress = new Uri("http://www.microsoft.com/");
> var response = await client.GetAsync("about");
> response.StatusCode
OK
> response.Content.Headers.GetValues("Content-Type")
string[1] { "text/html" }
> await response.Content.ReadAsStringAsync()
"<!DOCTYPE html ><html xmlns:mscom=\"http://schemas.microsoft
>
100 %
C# Interactive   Error List
```

Roslyn is the name of the C# compiler. Roslyn version 1.0 was for C# 6. Roslyn version 2.0 is for C# 7.

Other useful windows

Visual Studio 2017 has lots of other useful windows, including the following:

- The **Solution Explorer** window for managing projects and files
- The **Team Explorer** window for source code management tools
- The **Server Explorer** window for managing database connections and resources to manage in Microsoft Azure

If you can't see a window you need, go to the **View** menu to make it reappear or learn its keyboard shortcut, some of which are shown in the following screenshot:

View | Project | Build | Debug | Team | Tools

Code	F7
Solution Explorer	Ctrl+W, S
Team Explorer	Ctrl+`, Ctrl+M
Server Explorer	Ctrl+W, L
SQL Server Object Explorer	Ctrl+`, Ctrl+S
Call Hierarchy	Ctrl+W, K
Class View	Ctrl+W, C
Code Definition Window	Ctrl+W, D
Object Browser	Ctrl+W, J
Error List	Ctrl+W, E
Output	Ctrl+W, O

If your keyboard shortcuts are different from the ones in the preceding screenshot, it is because you picked a different set when you installed Visual Studio. You can reset your keyboard shortcuts to match the ones used in this book by clicking on the **Tools** menu, then clicking on **Import and Export Settings...**, choosing **Reset all settings**, and then choosing to reset to the **Visual C#** settings collection.

Writing and compiling code using Microsoft Visual Studio Code

The instructions and screenshots in this section are for macOS, but the same actions will work with Visual Studio Code on either Windows or Linux. The main differences will be native command-line actions such as deleting a file: both the command and the path are likely to be different. The `dotnet` CLI tool will be identical on all platforms.

Writing code using Visual Studio Code

Start Visual Studio Code.

Navigate to **File** | **Open...**, or press *Cmd* + *O*.

In the dialog box, open the `Code` folder, select the `Chapter01` folder, click the **New Folder** button, enter the name `Ch01_WelcomeDotNetCore`, and click **Create**, as shown in the following screenshot:

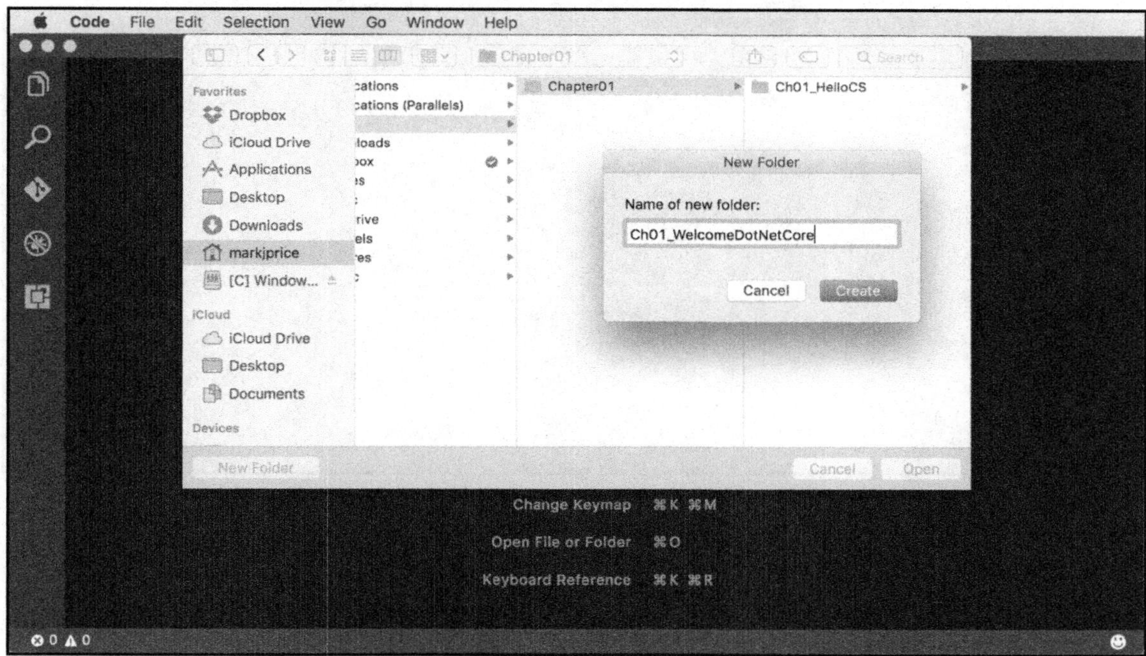

Select the **Ch01_WelcomeDotNetCore** folder, and click **Open** or press *Enter*.

In Visual Studio Code, navigate to **View** | **Integrated Terminal**, or press *Ctrl* + `.

At the **Terminal** prompt, enter the following command:

```
dotnet new console
```

You will see that the `dotnet` command-line tool creates a new console application project for you in the current folder, and the **Explorer** window shows the two files created, as shown in the following screenshot:

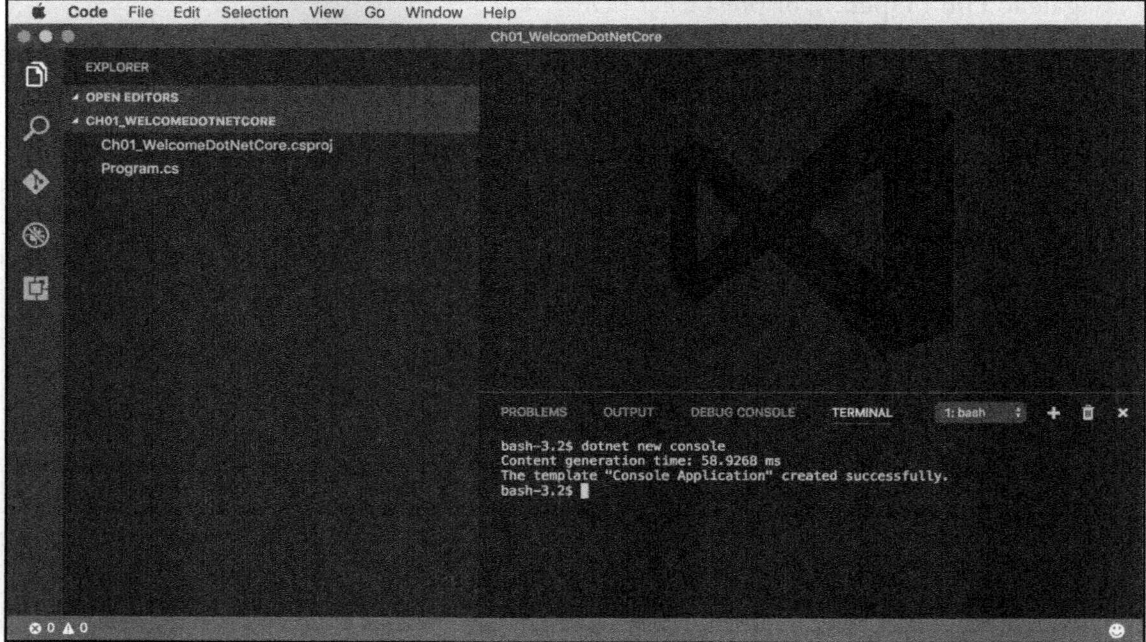

In the **Explorer** window, click on the file named `Program.cs` to open it in the editor window.

The first time that you do this, C# dependencies will be updated for your platform. This will take a few moments.

When you see the warnings about required assets and unresolved dependencies, click **Restore** and **Yes**, as shown in the following screenshot:

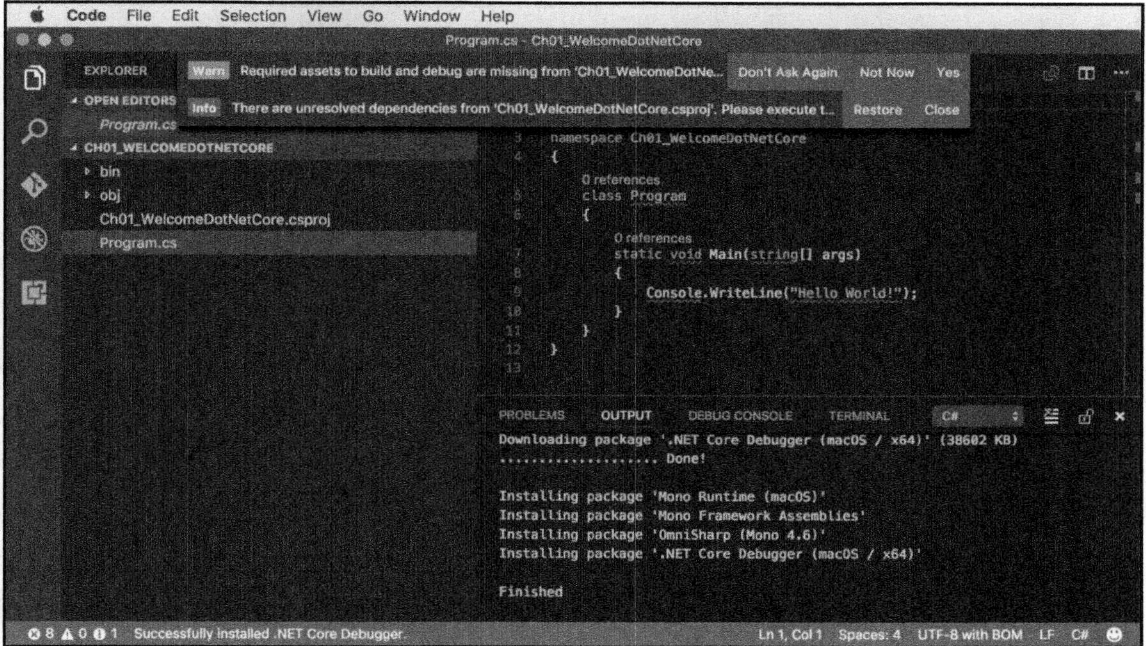

Modify the text that is being written to the console to say, `Welcome, .NET Core!`

On the **File** menu, choose **Auto Save**. This toggle will save the annoyance of remembering to save before rebuilding your application each time!

Compiling code using Visual Studio Code

Navigate to **View** | **Integrated Terminal** or press *Ctrl* + ` and enter the following command:

```
dotnet run
```

The output in the **Terminal** will show the result of running your application, as shown in the following screenshot:

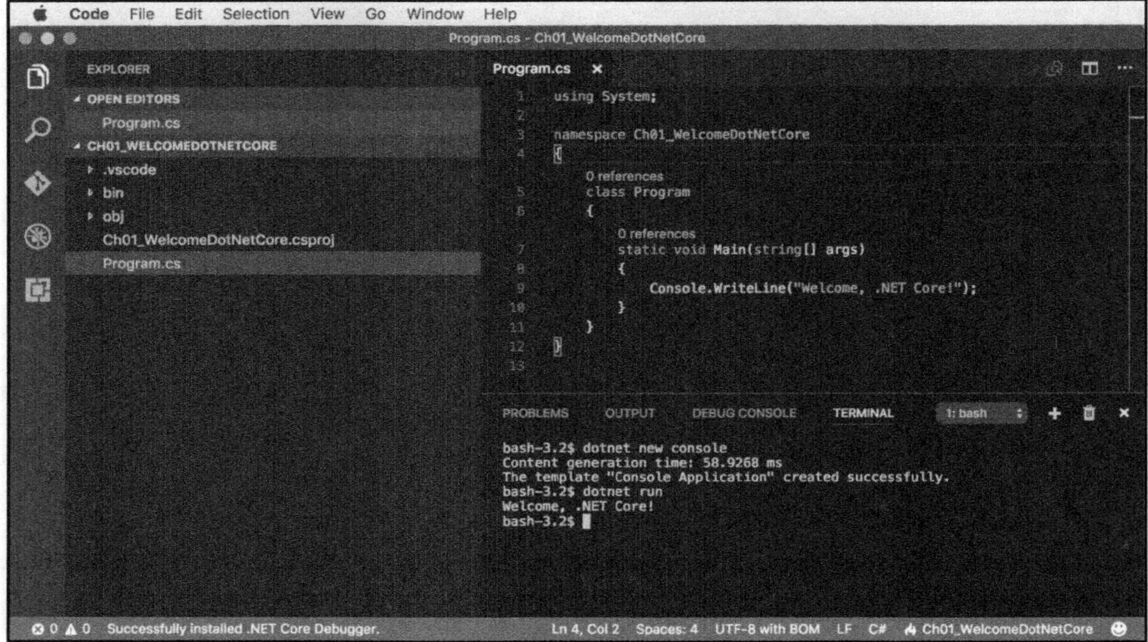

You now know how to create and build simple .NET Core applications for Windows and macOS (and Linux is just as easy).

You will be able to complete almost all the chapters in this book using either Visual Studio 2017 on Windows or using Visual Studio Code on macOS, Windows, or Linux.

Managing source code with GitHub

Git is a commonly used source code management system. GitHub is a company, website, and desktop application that makes it easier to manage Git.

I used GitHub to store solutions to all the practical exercises at the end of each chapter at the following URL:

`https://github.com/markjprice/cs7dotnetcore.`

Using Git with Visual Studio 2017

Visual Studio 2017 has built-in support for using Git with GitHub as well as Microsoft's own source code management system named **Visual Studio Team Services**.

Using the Team Explorer window

In Visual Studio 2017, navigate to **View** | **Team Explorer** to see the **Team Explorer** window:

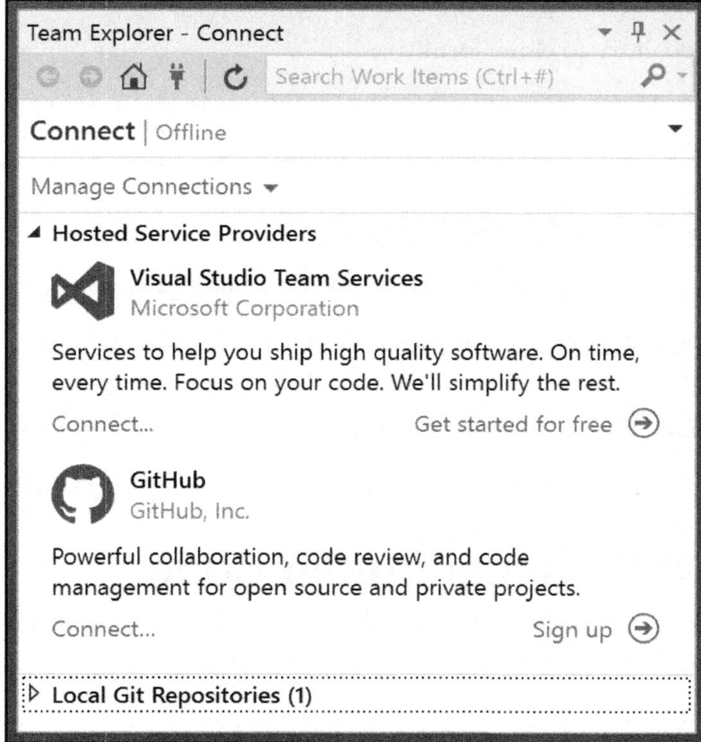

Although it is a good idea to sign up with an online source code management system provider, you can clone a GitHub repository without signing up for an account.

Cloning a GitHub repository

In the **Team Explorer** window, expand **Local Git Repositories**, click on the **Clone** menu, and then enter the following URL of a Git repository to clone it: `https://github.com/markjprice/cs7dotnetcore.git`.

Enter a path for the cloned Git repository:

```
C:\Code\Repos\cs7dotnetcore
```

Click on the **Clone** button.

Wait for the Git repository to clone locally.

You will now have a local copy of the complete solutions to all the hands-on practice exercises for this book.

Managing a GitHub repository

Double-click on the `cs7dotnetcore` repo to open a detail view.

You can click on the options in the **Project** section to view **Pull Requests** and **Issues** and other aspects of a repository.

You can double-click on an entry in the **Solutions** section to open it in the **Solution Explorer**.

Using Git with Visual Studio Code

Visual Studio Code has support for Git, but it will use your OS's Git installation, so you must install Git 2.0 or later first before you get these features. You can install Git from here: `https://git-scm.com/download`.

If you like to use a graphical user interface, you can download GitHub Desktop here: `https://desktop.github.com`.

Configuring Git at the command line

Launch **Terminal**, and enter the following command to check your configuration:

```
git config --list
```

The output should include your username and e-mail address, because these will be used with every commit that you make:

```
...other congfiguration...
user.name=Mark J. Price
user.email=markjprice@gmail.com
```

If your user name and e-mail has not been set, to set your user name and email, enter the following commands, using your own name and e-mail, not mine:

```
git config --global user.name "Mark J. Price"
git config --global user.email markjprice@gmail.com
```

You can check an individual configuration setting like this:

```
git config user.name
```

Managing Git with Visual Studio Code

Launch **Visual Studio Code**.

Navigate to **View** | **Integrated Terminal** or press *Ctrl* + ` and enter the following commands:

```
cd Code
mkdir Repos
cd Repos
git clone https://github.com/markjprice/cs7dotnetcore.git
```

It will take a minute to clone all the solutions for all the chapters to your local drive, as shown in the following screenshot:

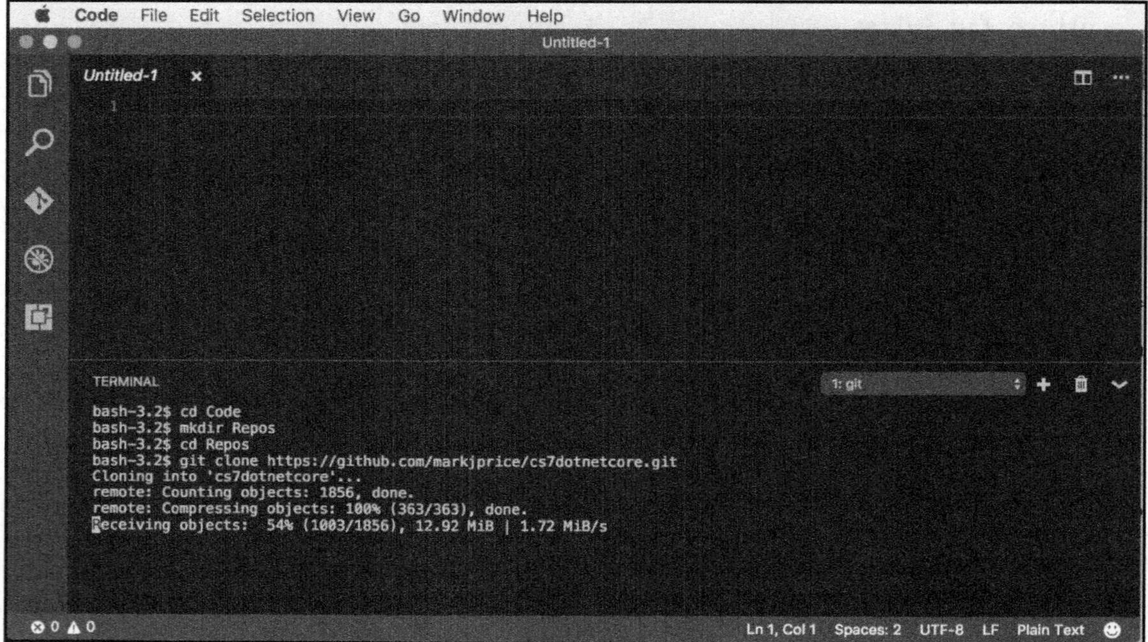

It is best to open one project folder at a time because the `cs7dotnetcore` repository does not include any dependencies, so you will need to restore them using the `dotnet restore` command, or wait for Visual Studio Code to prompt you after opening a folder.

For more information about source code version control with Visual Studio Code, visit: `https://code.visualstudio.com/Docs/editor/versioncontrol`.

Practicing and exploring

Test your knowledge and understanding by answering some questions, get some hands-on practice, and explore with deeper research into the topics covered in this chapter.

Exercise 1.1 – test your knowledge

Answer the following questions:

1. Why can a programmer use different languages, for example C# and F#, to write applications that run on .NET Core?
2. What do you type at the prompt to build and execute C# source code?
3. What is the Visual C# developer settings keyboard shortcut to save, compile, and run an application without attaching the debugger?
4. What is the Visual Studio Code keyboard shortcut to view the Integrated Terminal?
5. Is Visual Studio 2017 better than Visual Studio Code?
6. Is .NET Core better than .NET Framework?
7. How is .NET Native different from .NET Core?
8. What is .NET Standard and why is it important?
9. What is the difference between Git and GitHub?
10. What is the name of the entry-point method of a .NET console application and how should it be declared?

Exercise 1.2 – practice coding anywhere

You do not need Visual Studio 2017 or Visual Studio Code to practice writing C#.

Go to one of the following websites and start coding:

- .NET Fiddle: `https://dotnetfiddle.net/`
- Cloud9: `https://c9.io/web/sign-up/free`

Exercise 1.3 – explore topics

Use the following links to read more details about the topics covered in this chapter:

- **Welcome to .NET Core**: `http://dotnet.github.io`
- **.NET Core Command Line Interface (CLI) tool**: `https://github.com/dotnet/cli`
- **.NET Core runtime, CoreCLR**: `https://github.com/dotnet/coreclr/`
- **.NET Core Roadmap**: `https://blogs.msdn.microsoft.com/dotnet/2016/07/15/net-core-roadmap/`
- **.NET Standard FAQ**: `https://github.com/dotnet/standard/blob/master/docs/faq.md`
- **Visual Studio Documentation**: `https://docs.microsoft.com/en-us/visualstudio/`
- **Visual Studio Blog**: `https://blogs.msdn.microsoft.com/visualstudio/`
- **Git and Team Services**: `https://www.visualstudio.com/en-us/docs/git/overview`
- **The easiest way to connect to your GitHub repositories in Visual Studio**: `https://visualstudio.github.com/`

Summary

In this chapter, we set up the development environment, used Windows' Command Prompt and macOS's Terminal to compile and run a console application, used Visual Studio 2017 and Visual Studio Code to create the same application, and discussed the differences between .NET Framework, .NET Core, .NET Standard, and .NET Native.

In the next chapter, you will learn to speak C#.

2
Speaking C#

This chapter is about the C# language—the grammar and vocabulary that you will use every day to write the source code for your applications.

Programming languages have many similarities to human languages, except that in programming languages, we can make up our own words, just like Dr. Seuss!

In a book written by Dr. Seuss in 1950, *If I Ran the Zoo* states that:

> *"And then, just to show them, I'll sail to Ka-Troo And Bring Back an It-Kutch a Preep and a Proo A Nerkle, a Nerd and a Seersucker, too!"*

To learn to speak C#, you will need to create some simple applications. To avoid overloading you with too much information too soon, the first few chapters of this book will use the simplest type of application: a console application.

This chapter covers the following topics:

- Understanding C# basics
- Declaring variables
- Building console applications
- Operating on variables

Understanding C# basics

Let's start with looking at the basics of the grammar and vocabulary of C#. In this chapter, you will create multiple console applications, each showing a feature of the C# language.

To manage these projects with Visual Studio 2017, we will put them all in a single solution. Visual Studio 2017 can only have one solution open at any one time, but each solution can group together multiple projects. A project can build a console application, a Windows desktop application, a web application, and dozens of others.

To manage these projects with Visual Studio Code, which does not support solutions, we will manually create a container folder named `Chapter02`. If you would like to use Visual Studio Code, skip to the section titled *Using Visual Studio Code on macOS, Linux, or Windows*.

Using Visual Studio 2017

Start Microsoft Visual Studio 2017. In Visual Studio, press *Ctrl* + *Shift* + *N* or choose the **File** | **New** | **Project...** menu.

In the **New Project** dialog, in the **Installed** | **Templates** list, expand **Other Project Types** and select **Visual Studio Solutions**. In the list at the center, select **Blank Solution**, type the name `Chapter02`, change the location to `C:\Code`, and then click on **OK**, as shown in the following screenshot:

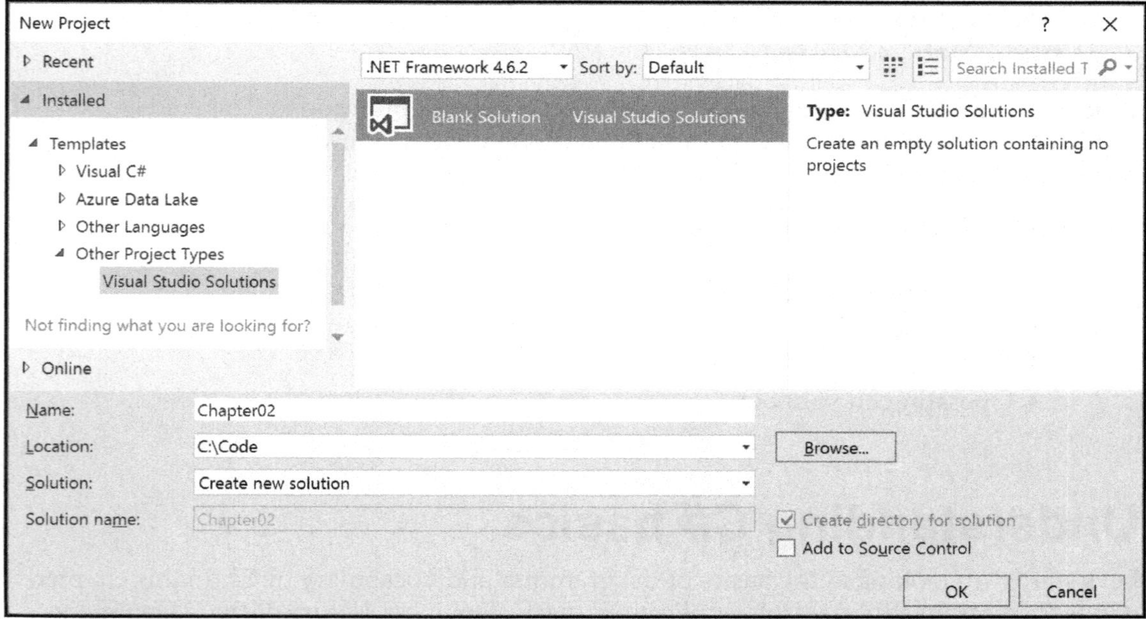

If you were to run **File Explorer**, you would see that Visual Studio has created a folder named `Chapter02` with a Visual Studio solution named `Chapter02` inside it, as shown in the following screenshot:

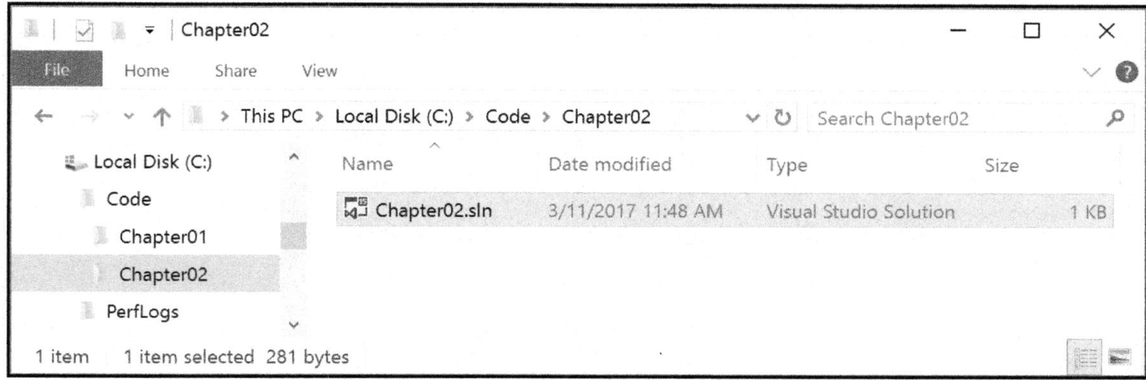

In Visual Studio, navigate to **File** | **Add** | **New Project...**, as shown in the following screenshot. This will add a new project to the blank solution:

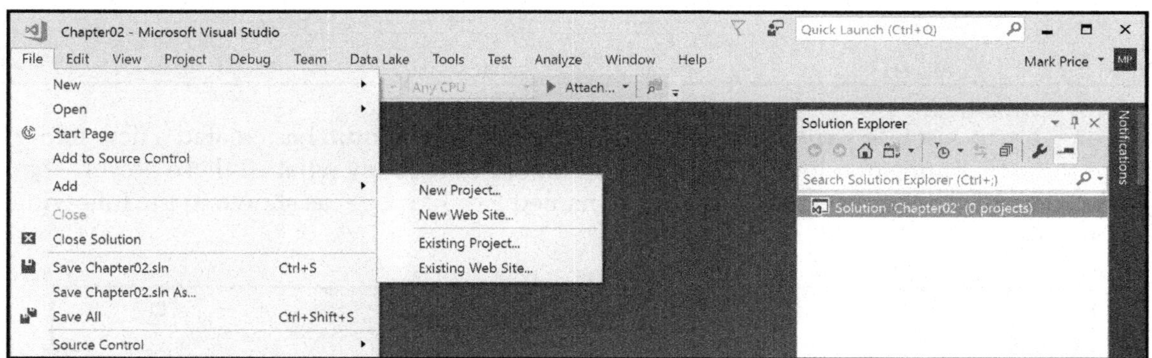

In the **Add New Project** dialog, in the **Installed | Templates** list, expand Visual C#, and select .NET Core. In the list at the center, select **Console App (.NET Core)**, type the name `Ch02_Basics`, ensure that **.NET Framework 4.6.2** (or later) is selected at the top, and then click on **OK**, as shown in the following screenshot:

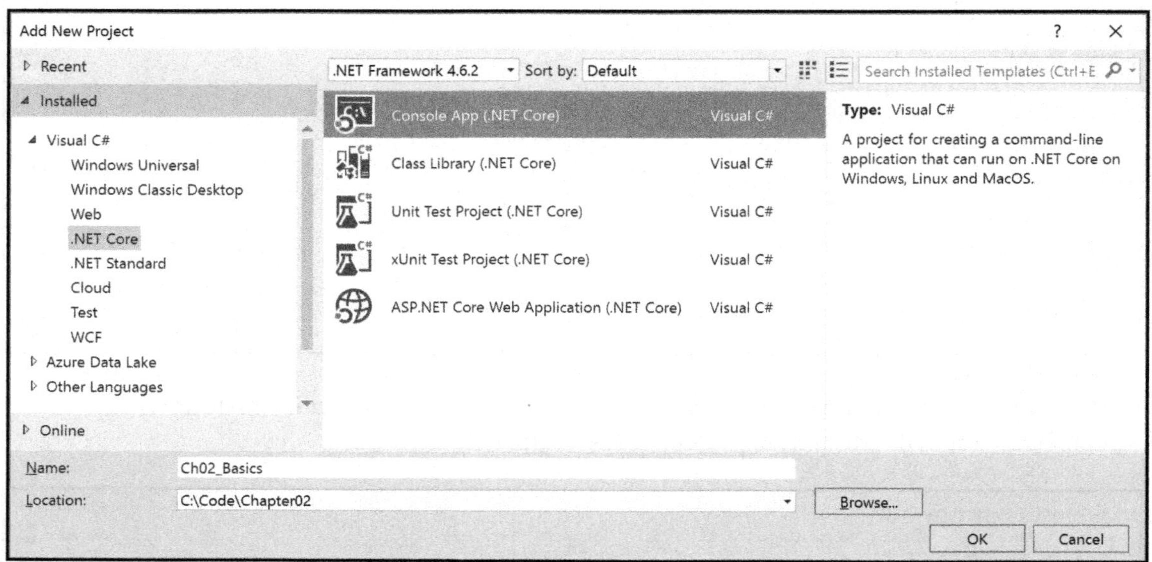

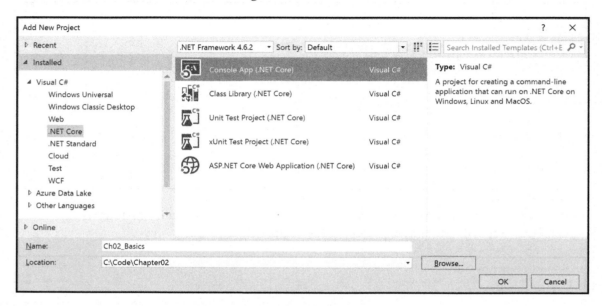

If you were to run **File Explorer**, you would see that Visual Studio has created a new folder with some files and subfolders inside it. You don't need to know what all these do yet. The code you will write will be stored in the file named `Program.cs`, as shown in the following screenshot:

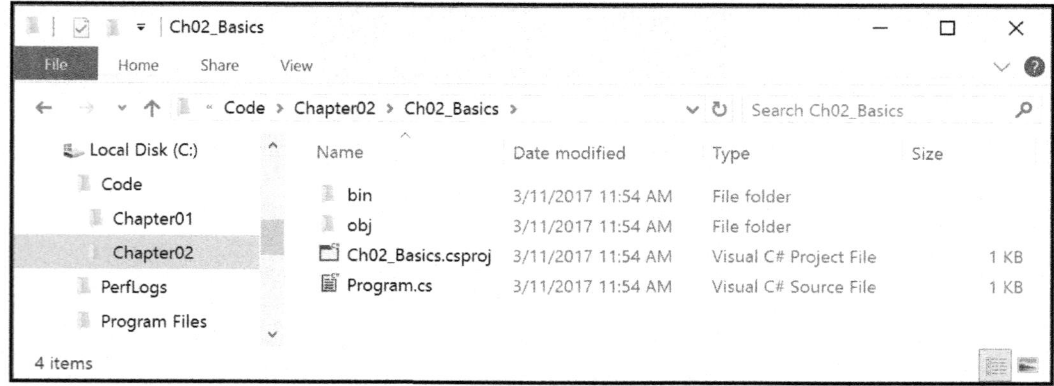

In Visual Studio, the **Solution Explorer** window shows the same files as the ones in the preceding screenshot of the file system.

Some folders and files, for example, the **bin** folder, are hidden by default in **Solution Explorer**. At the top of the window is a toolbar button named **Show All Files**. Toggle this button to show and hide folders and files, as shown in the following screenshot:

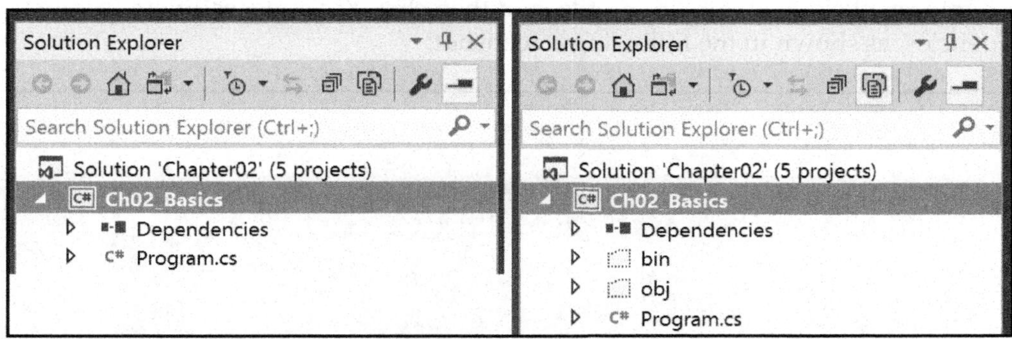

Using Visual Studio Code on macOS, Linux, or Windows

If you completed `Chapter 1`, *Hello, C#! Welcome, .NET Core!*, then you will already have a `Code` folder in your user folder. If not, create it, and then create a subfolder named `Chapter02`, and then a sub-subfolder named `Ch02_Basics`, as shown in the following screenshot:

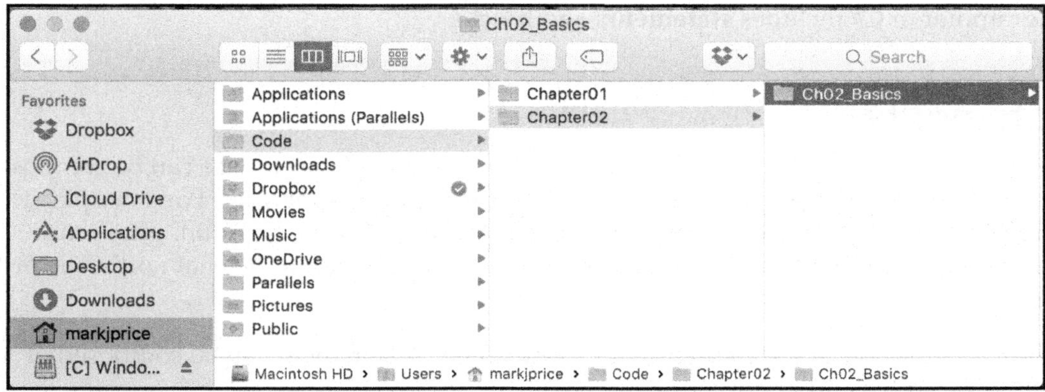

Start Visual Studio Code and open the `/Chapter02/Ch02_Basics/` folder.

In Visual Studio Code, navigate to **View** | **Integrated Terminal**, and enter the following command:

```
dotnet new console
```

In the **Explorer**, click the `Program.cs` file, and then click **Yes** and **Restore** to restore dependencies, as shown in the following screenshot:

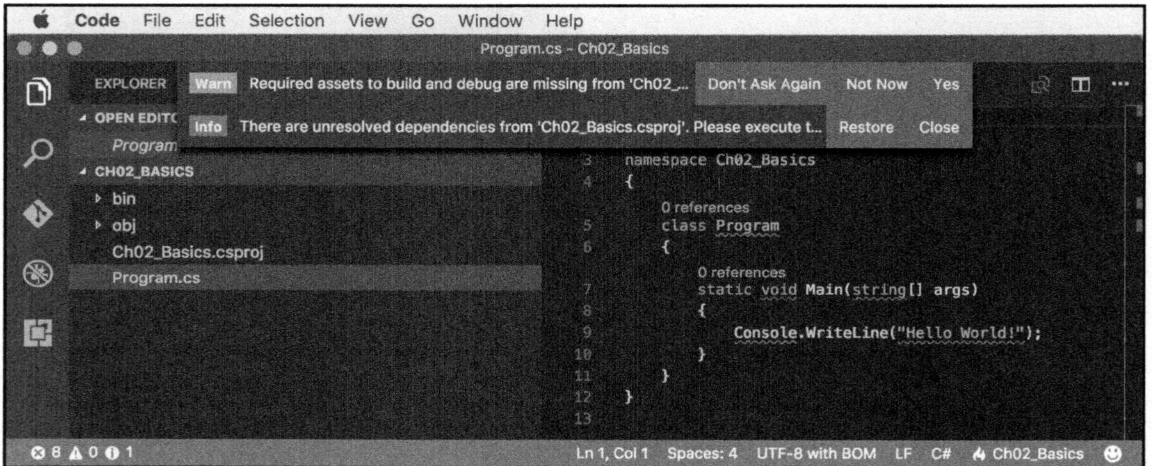

C# grammar

The grammar of C# includes **statements** and **blocks**.

Statements

In English, we indicate the end of a sentence with a full stop. A sentence can be composed of multiple words and phrases. The order of words is part of grammar. For example, in English, we say: the black cat. The adjective, black, comes before the noun, cat. French grammar has a different order; the adjective comes after the noun, “le chat noir”. The order matters.

C# indicates the end of a **statement** with a semicolon. A statement can be composed of multiple **variables** and **expressions**.

In the following statement, `FullName` is a variable and `FirstName + LastName` is an expression:

```
var FullName = FirstName + LastName;
```

The expression is made up of an **operand** (FirstName), an **operator** (+), and another operand (LastName). The order matters.

Comments

You can add comments to explain your code using a double slash `//`.

The compiler ignores everything after the `//` until the end of the line; for example:

```
var TotalPrice = Cost + Tax; // Tax is 20% of the Cost
```

Visual Studio 2017 and Visual Studio Code will add or remove the comment (double slashes) at the start of the currently selected line(s) if you press *Ctrl* + *K* + *C* or *Ctrl* + *K* + *U*. In macOS, press *Cmd* instead of *Ctrl*.

To write a multiline comment, use `/*` at the beginning and `*/` at the end of the comment, as shown in the following code:

```
/*
This is a multi-line
comment.
*/
```

Blocks

In English, we indicate a paragraph by starting a new line. C# indicates a **block** of code with curly brackets `{ }`. Blocks start with a declaration to indicate what it is defining. For example, a block can define a **namespace**, a **class**, a **method**, or a **statement**. You will learn what these are later.

In your current project, note the grammar of C# written for you by the Visual Studio template or by the `dotnet` CLI tool.

In the following example, I have added some comments to describe the code:

```
using System; // a semicolon indicates the end of a statement

class Program
```

```
    {
      static void Main(string[] args)
      { // the start of a block
        Console.WriteLine("Hello World!"); // a statement
      } // the end of a block
    }
```

C# vocabulary

Some of the 79 predefined, reserved keywords that you will see in this chapter include `using`, `namespace`, `class`, `static`, `int`, `string`, `double`, `bool`, `var`, `if`, `switch`, `break`, `while`, `do`, `for`, and `foreach`.

Visual Studio 2017 shows C# keywords in blue to make them easier to spot. In the following screenshot, `using`, `namespace`, `class`, `static`, `void`, and `string` are part of the vocabulary of C#:

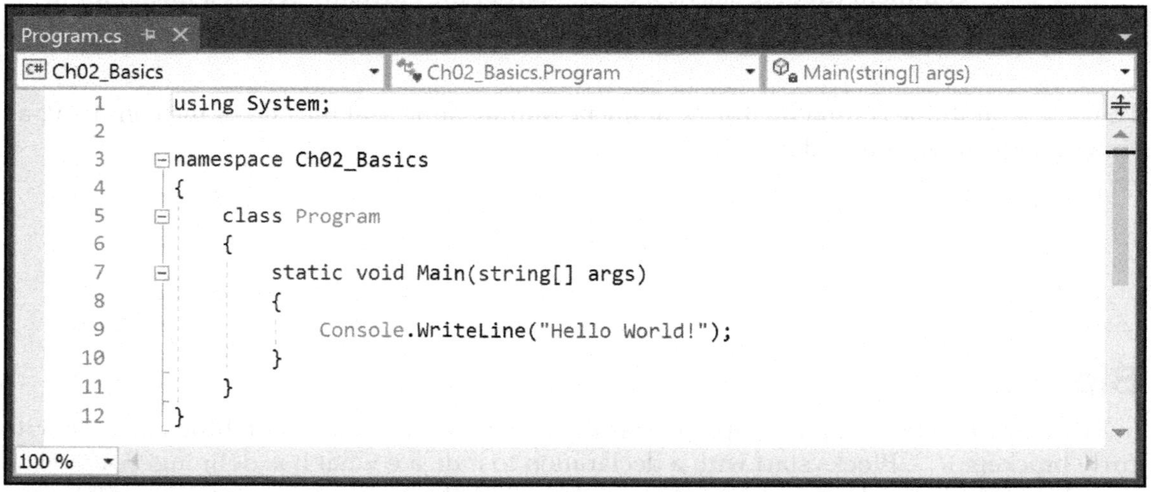

```
Program.cs
Ch02_Basics | Ch02_Basics.Program | Main(string[] args)

using System;

namespace Ch02_Basics
{
    class Program
    {
        static void Main(string[] args)
        {
            Console.WriteLine("Hello World!");
        }
    }
}

100 %
```

The equivalent for Visual Studio Code is shown in the following screenshot:

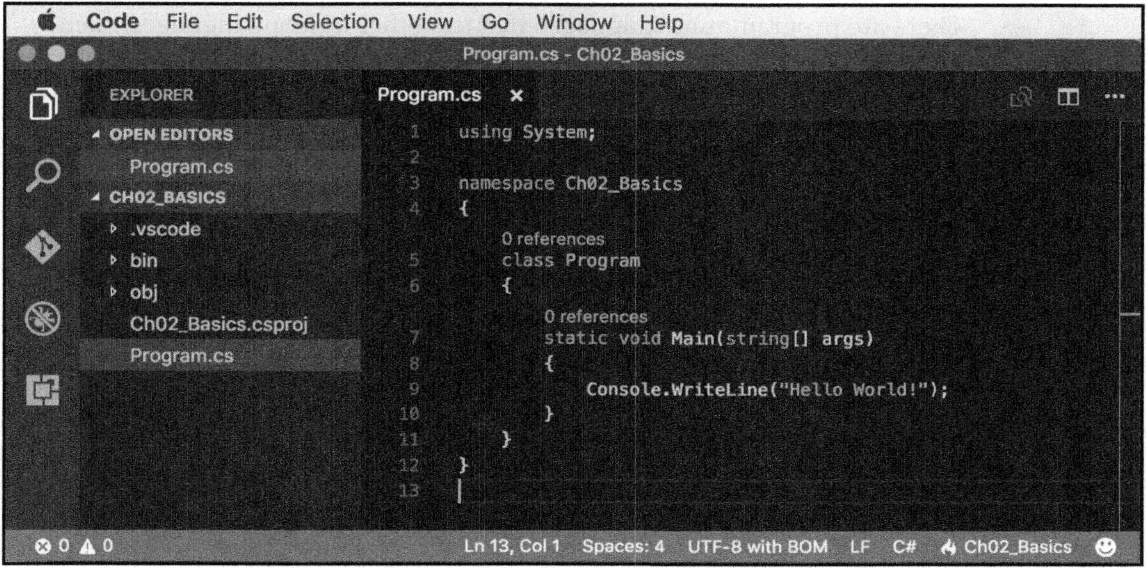

Both Visual Studio 2017 and Visual Studio Code allow you to customize the color scheme. In Visual Studio 2017, navigate to **Tools** | **Options** | **Environment** | **Fonts and Colors**. In Visual Studio Code, navigate to **Code** | **Preferences** | **Color Theme**.

C# keywords

There are another 25 contextual keywords that only have a special meaning in a specific context. However, that still means there are only 104 actual C# keywords in the language.

English has more than 250,000 distinct words. How does C# get away with only having 104 keywords? Why is C# so difficult to learn if it has so few words?

One of the key differences between a human language and a programming language is that developers need to be able to define new "words" with new meanings.

Apart from the 104 keywords in the C# language, this book will teach you about some of the hundreds of thousands of "words" that other developers have defined. You will also learn how to define your own "words".

Programmers all over the world must learn English because most programming languages use English words like `namespace` and `class`. There are programming languages that use other human languages, such as Arabic, but they are rare. This YouTube video shows a demonstration of an Arabic programming language: `https://www.youtube.com/watch?v=77KAHPZUR8g`

Writing the code

Plain text editors such as Notepad don't help you write correct English, as shown in the following screenshot:

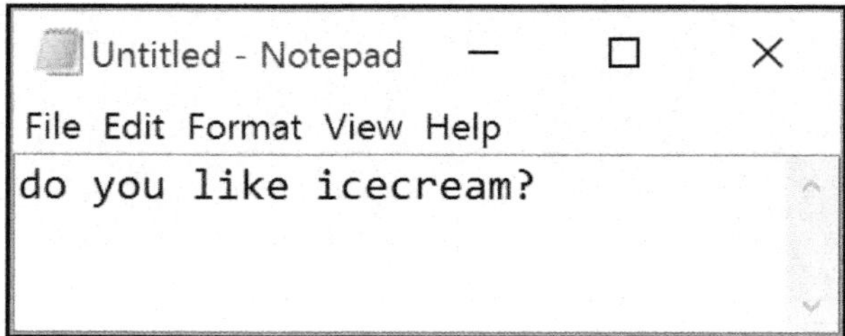

Notepad won't help you write correct C# either:

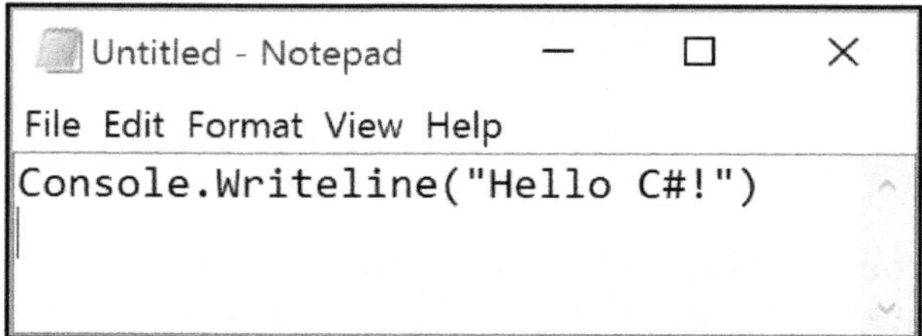

Microsoft Word helps you write English by highlighting spelling mistakes with red squiggles (it should be *ice-cream*) and grammatical errors with blue squiggles (sentences should have an uppercase first letter).

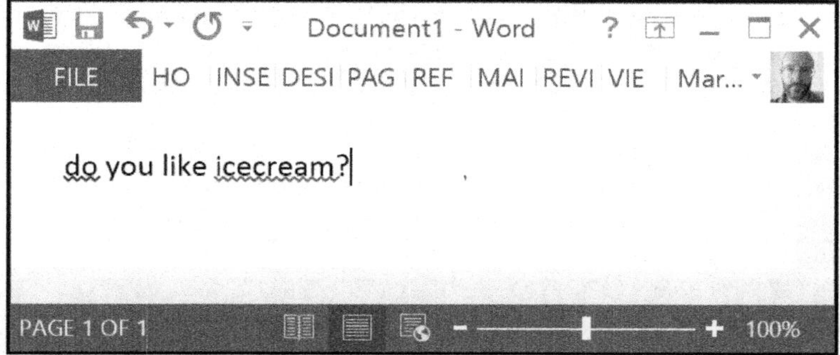

Similarly, Visual Studio 2017 and Visual Studio Code help you write C# code by highlighting spelling mistakes (the method name should be `WriteLine` with an uppercase `L`) and grammatical errors (statements must end with a semicolon).

Visual Studio 2017 constantly watches what you type and gives you feedback by highlighting problems with colored squiggly lines under your code and showing the **Error List** window (known as the Problems window in Visual Studio Code), as you can see in the following screenshot:

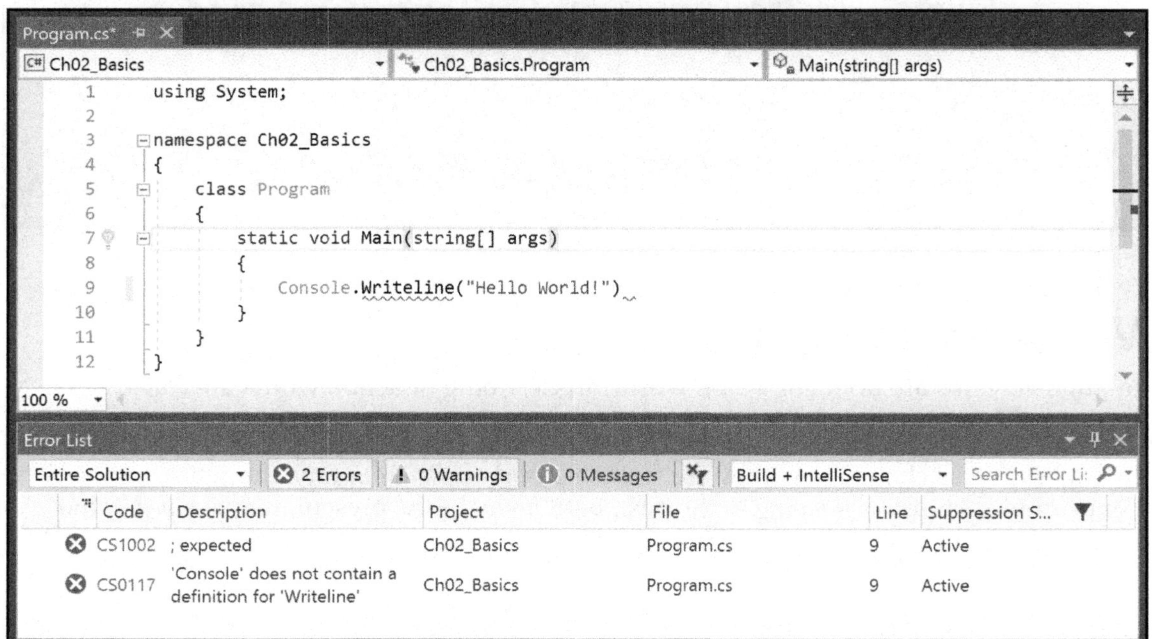

You can ask Visual Studio 2017 to do a complete check of your code by choosing **Build** | **Build Solution** or pressing *F6*.

Visual Studio Code has a similar **Problems** window, as shown in the following screenshot:

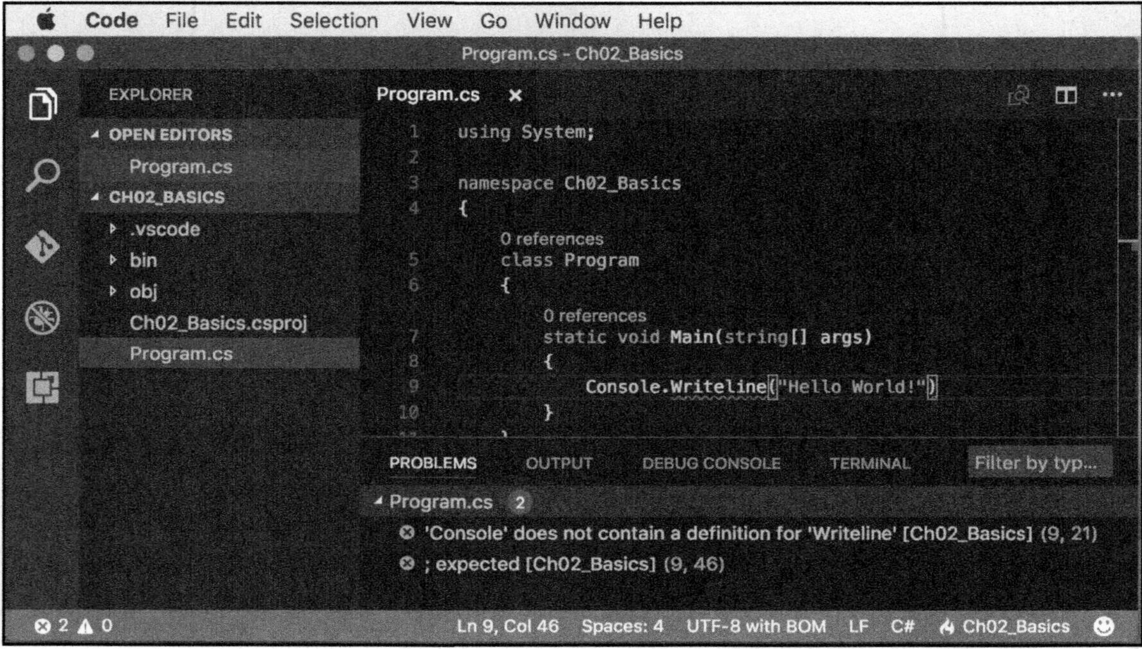

Verbs are methods

In English, verbs are doing or action words. In C#, doing or action words are called **methods**. There are literally hundreds of thousands of methods available to C#.

In English, verbs change how they are written based on when in time the action happens. For example, Amir *was jumping* in the past, Beth *jumps* in the present, they *jumped* in the past, and Charlie *will jump* in the future.

In C#, methods such as `WriteLine` change how they are called or executed based on the specifics of the action. This is called overloading, which we will cover in more detail in `Chapter 6`, *Building Your Own Types with Object-Oriented Programming*. Consider the following example:

```
// outputs a carriage-return
Console.WriteLine();
// outputs the greeting and a carriage-return
Console.WriteLine("Hello Ahmed");
// outputs a formatted number and date
Console.WriteLine("Temperature on {0:D} is {1}°C.",
  DateTime.Today, 23.4);
```

A different analogy is that some words are spelled the same but have different meanings depending on the context.

Nouns are types, fields, and variables

In English, nouns are names that refer to things. For example, Fido is the name of a dog. The word "dog" tells us the type of thing that Fido is. To order Fido to fetch a ball, we would use his name.

In C#, their equivalents are **types**, **fields**, and **variables**. There are tens of thousands of types available *to* C#. Note that I don't say, "There are tens of thousands of types *in* C#."

The difference is subtle but important. C# (the language) only has a few keywords for types, such as `string` and `int`. Strictly speaking, C# doesn't define any types. Keywords such as `string` that look like types are **aliases**. Those aliases represent types provided by the platform on which C# runs.

C# cannot exist alone. It is a language that runs on variants of .NET. In theory, someone could write a compiler for C# that uses a different platform, with different underlying types. In practice, the platform for C# is one of the .NET platforms. It is .NET that provides the tens of thousands of types to C#. Those types include `System.Int32`, which the C# keyword alias `int` maps to, as well as much more complex types, such as `System.Xml.Linq.XDocument`.

Note that the term `type` is often confused with `class`. Have you ever played the parlor game, Twenty Questions, also known as Animal, Vegetable, or Mineral? In the game, every thing can be categorized as an animal, vegetable, or mineral. In C#, every type can be categorized as a `class`, `struct`, `enum`, `interface`, or `delegate`. The C# keyword `string` is a `class`, but `int` is a `struct`. So, it is best to use the term type to include both.

Counting types and methods

Let's write some code to find out how many types and methods are available to C# in our simple console application.

Don't worry about how this code works. It uses a technique called **reflection**, which is beyond the scope of this book.

Start by adding the following statements at the top of the `Program.cs` file:

```
using System.Linq;
using System.Reflection;
```

Inside the `Main` method, delete the statement that writes Hello World!, and replace it with the following code:

```
// loop through the assemblies that this application references
foreach (var r in  Assembly.GetEntryAssembly()
  .GetReferencedAssemblies())
{
  // load the assembly so we can read its details
  var a = Assembly.Load(new AssemblyName(r.FullName));
  // declare a variable to count the total number of methods
  int methodCount = 0;
  // loop through all the types in the assembly
  foreach (var t in a.DefinedTypes)
  {
    // add up the counts of methods
    methodCount += t.GetMethods().Count();
  }
  // output the count of types and their methods
  Console.WriteLine($"{a.DefinedTypes.Count():N0} types " +
    $"with {methodCount:N0} methods in {r.Name} assembly.");
}
```

Building and running with Visual Studio 2017

Press *Ctrl* + *F5* to save, compile, and run your application without the debugger attached, or click on the **Debug** menu and then **Start Without Debugging**.

You will see the following output that shows the actual number of types and methods that are available to you in the simplest application when running on Windows:

```
23 types with 258 methods in System.Runtime assembly.
0 types with 0 methods in System.Reflection assembly.
87 types with 917 methods in System.Linq assembly.
38 types with 545 methods in System.Console assembly.
```

Building and running with Visual Studio Code

At **Integrated Terminal**, enter the following command:

```
dotnet run
```

You will see the following output that shows the actual number of types and methods that are available to you in the simplest application when running on macOS:

```
23 types with 258 methods in System.Runtime assembly.
0 types with 0 methods in System.Reflection assembly.
87 types with 917 methods in System.Linq assembly.
59 types with 721 methods in System.Console assembly.
```

The numbers of types and methods displayed may be different depending on the platform that you are using.

Add the following statements at the top of the `Main` method. By declaring variables that use types in other assemblies, those assemblies are loaded with our application. This allows our code to see all the types and methods in them:

```
static void Main(string[] args)
{
  System.Xml.XmlReader reader;
  System.Xml.Linq.XElement element;
  System.Net.Http.HttpClient client;
```

Visual Studio 2017 Error List and Visual Studio Code Problems will show three warnings about variables that are declared but never used. You can safely ignore this warning.

In Visual Studio 2017, press *Ctrl* + *F5*.

In Visual Studio Code, enter `dotnet run` in **Integrated Terminal**.

View your output, which should look similar to the following output:

```
23 types with 258 methods in System.Runtime assembly.
366 types with 3,966 methods in System.Xml.ReaderWriter assembly.
64 types with 1,121 methods in System.Xml.XDocument assembly.
223 types with 2,346 methods in System.Net.Http assembly.
0 types with 0 methods in System.Reflection assembly.
87 types with 917 methods in System.Linq assembly.
59 types with 721 methods in System.Console assembly.
```

Now, you have a better sense of why learning C# is a challenge. There are many types, with many methods to learn about, and methods are only one category of member that a type can have, and other programmers are constantly defining new members!

Declaring variables

All applications process data. Data comes in, data is processed, and data goes out.

Data usually comes into our program from files, databases, or user input. Data can be put temporarily in variables that will be stored in the memory of the running program. When the program ends, the data in memory is lost. Data is usually output to files and databases, or to the screen or a printer.

When using variables, you should think about, first, how much space it takes in memory, and, second, how fast it can be processed.

We control this by picking an appropriate type. You can think of simple common types such as `int` and `double` as being different size storage boxes. A smaller box would take less memory but may not be as fast at being processed. Some of these boxes may be stacked close by, and some may be thrown into a big heap further away.

Naming variables

There are naming conventions for variables, and it is good practice to follow them, as shown in the following table:

Naming convention	Examples	Use when naming
Camel case	`cost, orderDetail, dateOfBirth`	Local variables and private members.
Pascal/title case	`Cost, OrderDetail, DateOfBirth`	Type names and non-private members.

Good Practice
Following a consistent set of naming conventions will enable your code to be easily understood by other developers (and yourself in the future!)
Naming Guidelines:
`https://msdn.microsoft.com/en-us/library/ms229002(v=vs.110).aspx`

The following code block shows an example of declaring and initializing a local variable by assigning a value to it. Note that you can output the name of a variable using a keyword introduced in C# 6, that is, `nameof`:

```
// let the height variable become equal to the value 1.88
double heightInMetres = 1.88;
Console.WriteLine($"The variable {nameof(heightInMetres)} has the
value {heightInMetres}.");
```

The message in double quotes in the preceding code wraps onto a second line because the width of a printed page is too narrow. When entering a statement like this in your code editor, type it all in a single line.

Literal values

When you assign to a variable, you often assign a **literal** value. A literal is notation that represents a fixed value. Data types have different notations for their literal values.

Storing text

For text, a single letter, such as `A`, is stored as a `char` type and is assigned using single quotes around the literal value:

```
char letter = 'A';
```

For text, multiple letters, such as `Bob`, are stored as a `string` type and are assigned using double quotes around the literal value:

```
string name = "Bob";
```

Storing numbers

Numbers are data that we want to perform an arithmetic calculation on, for example, multiplying.

A telephone number is not a number. To decide whether a variable should be stored as a number or not, ask yourself whether you need to multiply two telephone numbers together or whether the number includes special characters such as (414)-555-1234. In these cases, the number is a sequence of characters, so it should be stored as a string.

Numbers can be natural numbers, such as 42, used for counting (also called whole numbers); they can also be negative numbers, such as -42 (called **integers**); or, they can be **real** numbers, such as 3.9 (with a fractional part), which are called **single** or **double-precision floating point** numbers in computing.

```
int myIntegerNumber = 23;
double myRealNumber = 2.3;
```

You might know that computers store everything as bits. A **bit** is either 0 or 1. This is called a **binary** number system. Humans use a **decimal** number system.

The decimal number system has ten as its base. Although it is the number base most commonly used by human civilizations, other number-base systems are popular in science, engineering, and computing.

Storing whole numbers

The following table shows how computers store the number 10. Note the 1 bits in the 8 and the 2 columns; *8 + 2 = 10*:

128	64	32	16	8	4	2	1
0	0	0	0	1	0	1	0

So, 10 in decimal is 00001010 in binary.

C# 7 improvements

Two of the improvements in C# 7 are the use of the underscore character (_) as a **digit separator** and support for **binary literals**.

You can insert underscores anywhere into a number literal, including decimal, binary, or hexadecimal notation to improve legibility. For example, you could write the value for one million in decimal notation (Base 10) as: 1_000_000.

To use binary notation (Base 2), using only 1s and 0s, start the number literal with 0b. To use hexadecimal notation (Base 16), using 0 to 9 and A to F, start the number literal with 0x, as shown in the following code:

```
int decimalNotation = 2_000_000; // 2 million
int binaryNotation = 0b_0001_1110_1000_0100_1000_0000; // 2 million
int hexadecimalNotation = 0x_001E_8480; // 2 million
```

Computers can always exactly represent integers (positive and negative whole numbers) using the `int` type or one of its sibling types such as `short`.

Storing real numbers

Computers cannot always exactly represent floating point numbers. The `float` and `double` types store real numbers using single and double precision floating points.

The following table shows how a computer stores the number 12.75. Note the 1 bits in the 8, 4, ½, and ¼ columns.

8 + 4 + ½ + ¼ = 12¾ = 12.75.

128	64	32	16	8	4	2	1	.	½	¼	1/8	1/16
0	0	0	0	1	1	0	0	.	1	1	0	0

So, 12.75 in decimal is 00001100.1100 in binary.

As you can see, the number 12.75 can be exactly represented using bits. However, some numbers can't, as you will see shortly.

Using Visual Studio 2017

In Visual Studio 2017, click on **File** | **Add** | **New Project...**. In the **Add New Project** dialog, in the **Installed** | **Templates** list, select **Visual C#**. In the list at the center, select **Console App (.NET Core)**, type the name `Ch02_Numbers`, and then click on **OK**.

In the **Solution Explorer** window, right-click on the solution and select **Properties** or press *Alt* + *Enter*. For **Startup Project**, select **Current selection**. From now on, you can simply click on a project in the **Solution Explorer** and then press *Ctrl* + *F5* to save, compile, and run that project, as shown in the following screenshot:

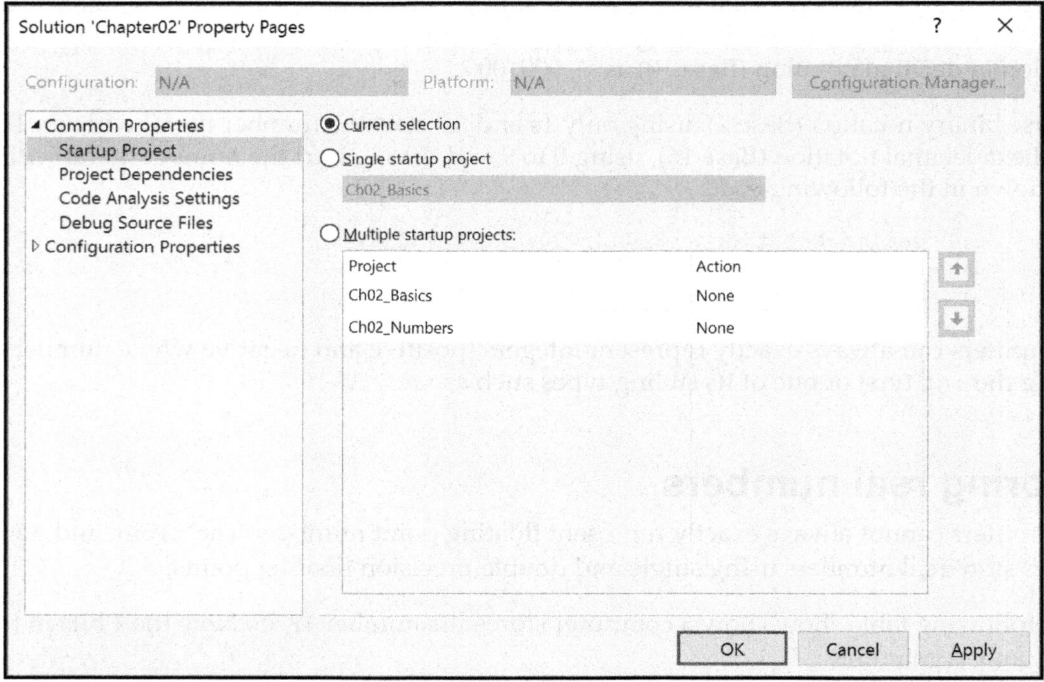

Using Visual Studio Code

Create a new folder inside the `Chapter02` folder named `Ch02_Numbers`.

In Visual Studio Code, open the `Ch02_Numbers` folder and use the **Integrated Terminal** to create a new console application using the command `dotnet new console`. When you open the `Program.cs` file, you will be prompted to restore packages.

Writing code to explore numbers

Type the following code inside the `Main` method:

```
Console.WriteLine($"int uses {sizeof(int)} bytes and can store
numbers in the range {int.MinValue:N0} to {int.MaxValue:N0}.");
Console.WriteLine($"double uses {sizeof(double)} bytes and can
store numbers in the range {double.MinValue:N0} to
{double.MaxValue:N0}.");
Console.WriteLine($"decimal uses {sizeof(decimal)} bytes and can
store numbers in the range {decimal.MinValue:N0} to
{decimal.MaxValue:N0}.");
```

Remember to enter the statements that use double-quotes in a single line.

Run the console application by pressing *Ctrl* + *F5*, or entering `dotnet run`, and view the output:

```
int uses 4 bytes and can store numbers in the range -2,147,483,648 to
2,147,483,647.
double uses 8 bytes and can store numbers in the range -
179,769,313,486,232,000,000,000,000,000,000,000,000,000,000,000,000,0
00,000,000,000,000,000,000,000,000,000,000,000,000,000,000,000,000,00
0,000,000,000,000,000,000,000,000,000,000,000,000,000,000,000,000,000
,000,000,000,000,000,000,000,000,000,000,000,000,000,000,000,000,000,
000,000,000,000,000,000,000,000,000,000,000,000,000,000,000,000,000,0
00,000,000,000,000,000,000,000,000,000,000,000,000,000,000,000,000 to
179,769,313,486,232,000,000,000,000,000,000,000,000,000,000,000,000,0
00,000,000,000,000,000,000,000,000,000,000,000,000,000,000,000,000,00
0,000,000,000,000,000,000,000,000,000,000,000,000,000,000,000,000,000
,000,000,000,000,000,000,000,000,000,000,000,000,000,000,000,000,000,
000,000,000,000,000,000,000,000,000,000,000,000,000,000,000,000,000,0
00,000,000,000,000,000,000,000,000,000,000,000,000,000,000,000,000.
decimal uses 16 bytes and can store numbers in the range -
79,228,162,514,264,337,593,543,950,335 to
79,228,162,514,264,337,593,543,950,335.
```

An `int` variable uses four bytes of memory and can store positive or negative numbers up to about 2 billion. A `double` variable uses eight bytes of memory and can store much bigger values! A `decimal` variable uses 16 bytes of memory and can store big numbers, but not as big as a `double`.

Why might a `double` variable be able to store bigger numbers than a `decimal` variable yet use half the space in memory? Let's find out!

Comparing double and decimal

Under the previous statements, enter the following code. Do not worry about understanding the syntax right now, although it isn't too hard to follow:

```
double a = 0.1;
double b = 0.2;
if (a + b == 0.3)
{
  Console.WriteLine($"{a} + {b} equals 0.3");
}
else
{
  Console.WriteLine($"{a} + {b} does NOT equal 0.3");
}
```

Run the console application and view the output:

```
0.1 + 0.2 does NOT equal 0.3
```

The `double` type is not guaranteed to be accurate. Only use `double` when accuracy, especially when comparing two numbers, is not important; for example, when measuring a person's height.

The problem with the preceding code is how the computer stores the number 0.1 or multiples of 0.1. To represent 0.1 in binary, the computer stores 1 in the 1/16 column, 1 in the 1/128 column, 1 in the 1/1024 column, and so on. The number 0.1 in decimal is 0.0001001001001 repeating forever:

4	2	1	.	½	¼	1/8	1/16	1/32	1/64	1/128	1/256	1/512	1/1024	1/2048
0	0	0	.	0	0	0	1	0	0	1	0	0	1	0

Good Practice

Never compare double values using ==. During the First Gulf War, an American Patriot missile battery used double values in its calculations. The inaccuracy caused it to fail to track and intercept an incoming Iraqi Scud missile, and 28 soldiers were killed; you can read about this at: `https://www.ima.umn.edu/~arnold/disasters/patriot.html`

Copy and paste the code you wrote before that used `double` variables and then modify it to look like the following code:

```
decimal c = 0.1M; // M indicates a decimal literal value
decimal d = 0.2M;
if (c + d == 0.3M)
{
  Console.WriteLine($"{c} + {d} equals 0.3");
}
else
{
  Console.WriteLine($"{c} + {d} does NOT equal 0.3");
}
```

Run the console application and view the output:

```
0.1 + 0.2 equals 0.3
```

The `decimal` type is accurate because it stores the number as a large integer and shifts the decimal point. For example, 0.1 is stored as 1, with a note to shift the decimal point one place to the left. 12.75 is stored as 1275, with a note to shift the decimal point two places to the left.

Good Practice

Use `int` for whole numbers and `double` for real numbers. Use `decimal` for money, CAD drawings, general engineering, and wherever accuracy of a real number is important.

The `double` type has some useful special values; `double.NaN` means not-a-number, `double.Epsilon` is the smallest positive number that can be stored in a double, and `double.Infinity` means an infinitely large value. You can use these special values when comparing `double` values.

Storing Booleans

Booleans can only contain one of the two values: `true` or `false`, as shown in the following code. They are most commonly used to branch and loop, as you will see in `Chapter 3`, *Controlling the Flow, Converting Types, and Handling Exceptions*:

```
bool happy = true;
bool sad = false;
```

The object type

There is a special type named `object` that can store any type of data, but its flexibility comes at the cost of messier code and poor performance due to boxing and unboxing operations when storing a value type. You should avoid it whenever possible.

From now on, I will assume that you know how to create a new console application using either Visual Studio 2017 or Visual Studio Code so I will only give general instructions.

Add a new console application project named `Ch02_Variables` and add the following code to the `Main` method:

```
object height = 1.88; // storing a double in an object
object name = "Amir"; // storing a string in an object
int length1 = name.Length; // gives compile error!
int length2 = ((string)name).Length; // cast to access members
```

The `object` type has been available since the first version of C#, but C# 2 and higher versions have a better alternative called **generics**, which we will cover later, that provide the flexibility we want without the performance overhead.

The dynamic type

There is another special type named `dynamic` that can also store any type of data, and like `object`, its flexibility comes at the cost of performance. Unlike object, the value stored in the variable can have its members invoked without an explicit cast, as shown in the following code:

```
// storing a string in a dynamic object
dynamic anotherName = "Ahmed";
// this compiles but might throw an exception at run-time!
int length = anotherName.Length;
```

The limitation of `dynamic` is that Visual Studio cannot show IntelliSense to help you write the code because the compiler doesn't check at build time. Instead, the CLR checks for the member at runtime. The `dynamic` keyword was introduced in C# 4.

Local variables

Local variables are declared inside methods and they only exist during the call to that method. Once the method returns, the memory allocated to any local variables is released.

Strictly speaking, value types are released while reference types must wait for a garbage collection. You will learn about the difference between value types and reference types later.

Enter the following code to declare and assign values to some local variables inside the `Main` method. Note that we specify the type before the name of each variable:

```
int population = 66_000_000; // 66 million in UK
double weight = 1.88; // in kilograms
decimal price = 4.99M; // in pounds sterling
string fruit = "Apples"; // strings use double-quotes
char letter = 'Z'; // chars use single-quotes
bool happy = true; // Booleans have value of true or false
```

Visual Studio 2017 and Visual Studio Code will show green squiggles under each of the variable names to warn you that the variable is assigned but its value is never used.

Inferring the type of a local variable

You can use the var keyword to declare local variables. The compiler will infer the type from the literal value you assign after the assignment = operator.

A literal number without a decimal point is inferred as an int variable unless you add the L suffix, in which case, it infers a long variable. A literal number with a decimal point is inferred as double unless you add the M suffix, in which case, it infers a decimal variable, or the F suffix, in which case, it infers a float variable. Double quotes indicate a string variable, single quotes indicate a char variable, and the true and false values infer a bool.

Modify your code to use var:

```
var population = 66_000_000; // 66 million in UK
var weight = 1.88; // in kilograms
var price = 4.99M; // in pounds sterling
var fruit = "Apples"; // strings use double-quotes
var letter = 'Z'; // chars use single-quotes
var happy = true; // Booleans have value of true or false
```

Good Practice
Although using var is convenient, smart developers avoid using it, to make it easier for a code reader to understand the types in use. Personally, I use it only when the type is obvious. For example, in the following code statements, the first statement is just as clear as the second in stating what the type of the xml variable is, but it is shorter. However, the third statement isn't clear, so the fourth is better. If in doubt, spell it out!

```
// good use of var
var xml1 = new XmlDocument();
// unnecessarily verbose repeating XmlDocument
XmlDocument xml2 = new XmlDocument();

// bad use of var; what data type is file1?
var file1 =
  File.CreateText(@"C:\something.txt");
// good use of a specific type declaration
StreamWriter file2 =
  File.CreateText(@"C:\something.txt");
```

Making a value type nullable

Most of the primitive types except `string` are **value types**. This means they must have a value. You can determine the default value of a type using the `default()` operator. The default value of an `int` variable is 0 (zero):

```
Console.WriteLine($"{default(int)}"); // 0
Console.WriteLine($"{default(bool)}"); // False
Console.WriteLine($"{default(DateTime)}"); // 1/01/0001 00:00:00
```

Strings are **reference types**. This means that they contain the memory address of a variable, not the value of the variable itself. A reference type variable can have a `null` value. The `null` value is a special literal value that indicates that the variable does not reference anything (yet).

You will learn more about value types and reference types in `Chapter 7`, *Implementing Interfaces and Inheriting Classes*.

Sometimes, it is convenient to allow a value type to be `null`. You can do this by adding a question mark as a suffix to the type when declaring a variable, as shown in the following code:

```
int ICannotBeNull = 4;
int? ICouldBeNull = null;
Console.WriteLine(ICouldBeNull.GetValueOrDefault()); // 0
ICouldBeNull = 4;
Console.WriteLine(ICouldBeNull.GetValueOrDefault()); // 4
```

Checking for null

It is important to check if a reference type or nullable value type variable currently contains `null` because if you do not, a `NullReferenceException` can be thrown causing an error in your code.

```
// check is myVariable is not null before using it
if (ICouldBeNull != null)
{
  // do something with ICouldBeNull
}
```

If you are trying to get a field or property from a variable that might be `null`, use the null check operator (`?.`), as shown in the following code:

```
string authorName = null;
// if authorName is null, instead of throwing an exception,
// null is returned
int? howManyLetters = authorName?.Length;
```

Sometimes you want to either assign a variable to a result, or use an alternative value, such as zero, if the variable is null. You do this using the null-coalescing operator (`??`), as shown in the following code:

```
// result will be three if howManyLetters is null
var result = howManyLetters ?? 3;
Console.WriteLine(result);
```

Storing multiple values in an array

When you need to store multiple values of the same type, you can declare an **array**. For example, you might need to store four names in a `string` array.

The following code declares an array for storing four `string` values. Then, it stores `string` values at index positions 0 to 3 (arrays count from zero, so the last item is one less than the length of the array). Finally, it loops through each item in the array using a `for` statement that we will cover in more detail in `Chapter 3`, *Controlling the Flow, Converting Types, and Handling Exceptions*.

Add the following lines of code to the end of the `Main` method:

```
// declaring the size of the array
string[] names = new string[4];
// storing items at index positions
names[0] = "Kate";
names[1] = "Jack";
names[2] = "Rebecca";
names[3] = "Tom";
for (int i = 0; i < names.Length; i++)
{
  Console.WriteLine(names[i]); // read the item at this index
}
```

Arrays are always of a fixed size, so you need to decide how many items you want to store before instantiating them. Arrays are useful for temporarily storing multiple items, but collections are more flexible when adding and removing items dynamically. We will cover collections in `Chapter 4`, *Using .NET Standard Types*.

Building console applications

Console applications are text-based and are run at the command prompt. They typically perform simple tasks that need to be scripted, such as compiling a file or encrypting a section of a configuration file. They can have arguments passed to them to control their behavior for example, to encrypt the database connection strings section in a `Web.config` file, use the following command line:

```
aspnet_regiis -pdf "connectionStrings" "c:\mywebsite"
```

Displaying output to the user

The two most common tasks that a console application performs are writing and reading data. We have already been using the `WriteLine` method to output. If we didn't want a carriage return at the end of lines, we could have used the `Write` method.

C# 6 and later has a handy feature named string interpolation. This allows us to easily output one or more variables in a nicely formatted manner. A string prefixed with `$` can use curly braces around the name of a variable to output the current value of that variable at that position in the string.

In the `Ch02_Variables` project, enter the following statements at the bottom of the `Main` method:

```
Console.WriteLine($"The UK population is {population}.");
Console.Write($"The UK population is {population:N0}. ");
Console.WriteLine($"{weight}kg of {fruit} costs {price:C}.");
```

Run the console application and view the output:

```
The population of the UK is 66000000.
The population of the UK is 66,000,000. 1.88kg of Apples costs £4.99.
```

A variable can be formatted using special pieces of code. `N0` means a number with commas for thousands and no decimal places. `C` means currency. The currency format will be determined by the current thread. If you run this code on a PC in the UK, you get pounds sterling. If you run this code on a PC in Germany, you would get Euros.

Getting input from the user

We can get input from the user using the `ReadLine` method. This method waits for the user to type some text. As soon as the user presses *Enter*, whatever the user has typed is returned as a `string`.

Let's ask the user for their name and age. Later, we will convert the age into a number, but we will leave it as a `string` for now:

```
Console.Write("Type your first name and press ENTER: ");
string firstName = Console.ReadLine();
Console.Write("Type your age and press ENTER: ");
string age = Console.ReadLine();
Console.WriteLine($"Hello {firstName}, you look good for {age}.");
```

Run the console application and view the output.

Enter a `name` and an `age`, as shown in the following output:

```
Type your name and press ENTER: Gary
Type your age and press ENTER: 34
Hello Gary, you look good for 34.
```

Importing a namespace

You might have noticed that unlike our very first application, we have not been typing `System` before `Console`.

`System` is a namespace. Namespaces are like an address for a type. To refer to someone exactly, you might use *Oxford.HighStreet.BobSmith*, which tells us to look for a person named Bob Smith on the High Street in the city of Oxford.

The line `System.Console.WriteLine` tells the compiler to look for a method named `WriteLine` in a type named `Console` in a namespace named `System`.

To simplify our code, Visual Studio 2017, or the `dotnet new console` command when using Visual Studio Code, added a statement at the top of the code file to tell the compiler to always look in the `System` namespace for types that haven't been prefixed with their namespace, as shown in the following code:

```
using System;
```

We call this **importing the namespace**.

Simplifying the usage of the console

In C# 6 and later, the `using` statement can be used to further simplify our code.

Add the following line to the top of the file:

```
using static System.Console;
```

Now, we don't need to enter the `Console` type throughout our code. We can use **Find and Replace** to remove it.

Select the first `Console.` line in your code (ensure that you select the dot after the word `Console`).

In Visual Studio 2017, press *Ctrl* + *H* to do a Quick Replace (ensure that the **Replace...** box is empty), as shown in the following screenshot:

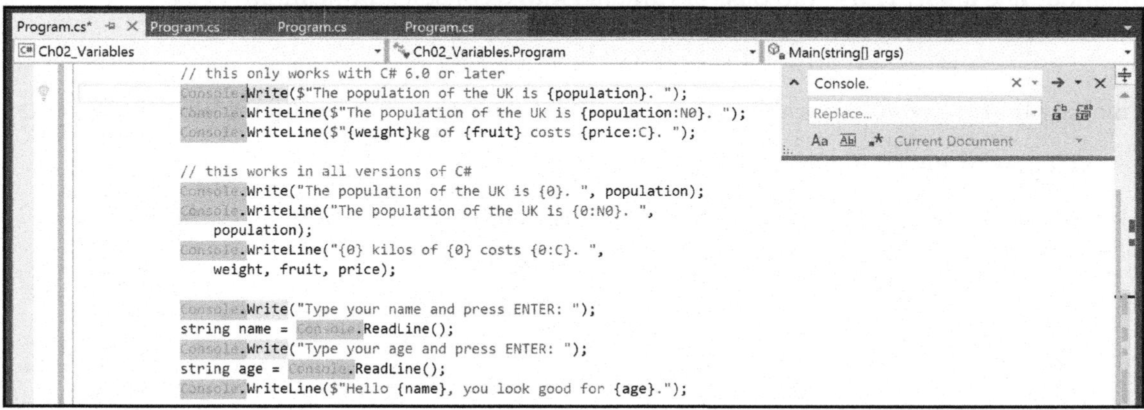

In Visual Studio Code, choose **Edit**, and then **Replace**, as shown in the following screenshot:

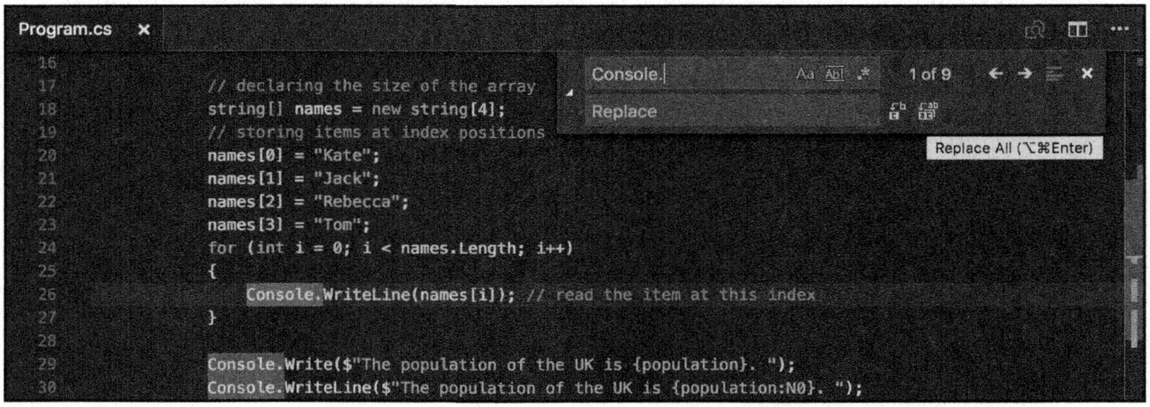

In both Visual Studio 2017 and Visual Studio Code, click the **Replace All** button or press *Alt* + *A* or *Alt* + *Cmd* + *Enter* to replace all, click on **OK**, and then close the replace box by clicking on the cross in its top-right corner.

Reading arguments and working with arrays

You have probably been wondering what the `string[] args` argument is in the `Main` method. It is an array used to pass arguments into a console application.

Add a new console application project named `Ch02_Arguments`.

Imagine that we want to be able to enter the following command at the command prompt:

```
Ch02_Arguments apples bananas cherries
```

We would be able to read the fruit names by reading them from the `args` array that is always passed into the `Main` method of a console application.

Remember that arrays use the square bracket syntax to indicate multiple values. Arrays have a property named `Length` that tells us how many items are currently in the array. If there is at least one item, then we can access it by knowing its index. Indexes start counting from zero, so the first item in an array is item 0.

Add a statement to statically import the `System.Console` type. Write a statement to output the number of arguments passed to the application. Remove the unnecessary `using` statements. Your code should now look like this:

```
using static System.Console;

namespace Ch02_Arguments
{
  class Program
  {
    static void Main(string[] args)
    {
      WriteLine($"There are {args.Length} arguments.");
    }
  }
}
```

Remember to statically import the `System.Console` type in future projects to simplify your code, as these instructions will not be repeated.

Run the console application and view the output:

```
There are 0 arguments.
```

Passing arguments with Visual Studio 2017

In **Solution Explorer**, right-click the `Ch02_Arguments` project, and choose **Properties**.

In the **Properties** window, select the **Debug** tab, and in the **Application arguments** box, enter a space-separated list of four arguments, as shown in the following code and screenshot:

```
firstarg second-arg third:arg "fourth arg"
```

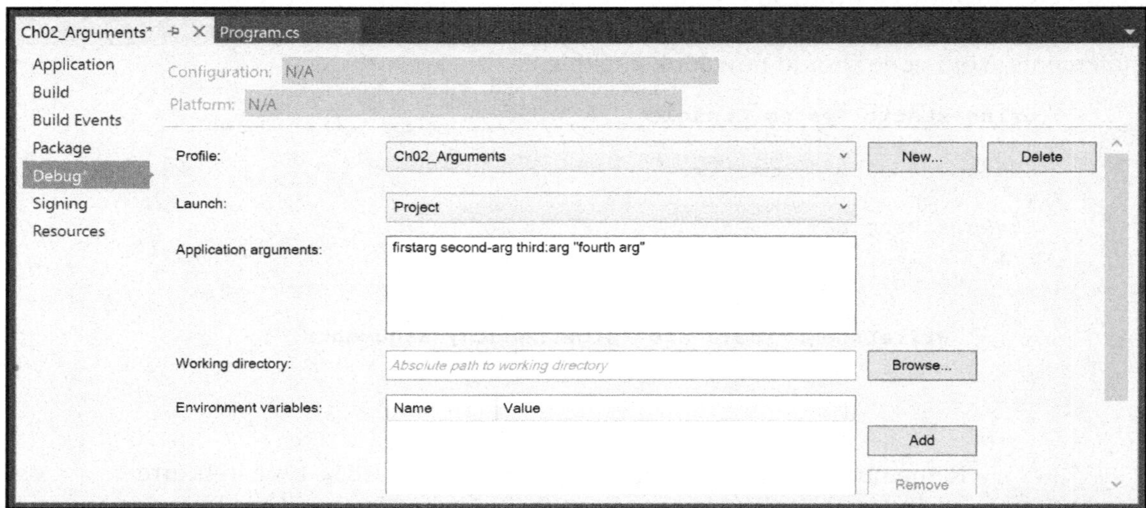

You can use almost any character in an argument, including hyphens and colons. If you need to use a space inside an argument, you must wrap it in double quotes.

Passing arguments with Visual Studio Code

Type arguments after the `dotnet run` command, as shown in the following example:

```
dotnet run firstarg second-arg third:arg "fourth arg"
```

Viewing the output

Run the console application with passed arguments, and view the output:

```
There are 4 arguments.
```

Enumerating arguments

To enumerate or iterate (that is, loop through) the values of those four arguments, add the following lines of highlighted code after outputting the length of the array:

```
WriteLine($"There are {args.Length} arguments.");
foreach (string arg in args)
{
  WriteLine(arg);
}
```

We will now use these arguments to allow the user to pick a color for the background, foreground, width, and height of the console window.

Change the argument values to the following:

```
red yellow 50 10
```

Import the `System` namespace by adding the following line to the top of the code file if it is not already there:

```
using System;
```

We need to import the `System` namespace so that the compiler knows about the `ConsoleColor` and `Enum` types. If you cannot see either of these types in the IntelliSense list, it is because you are missing the `using System;` statement.

Add the highlighted code on top of the existing code like this:

```
ForegroundColor = (ConsoleColor)Enum.Parse(typeof(ConsoleColor),
args[0], true);
BackgroundColor = (ConsoleColor)Enum.Parse(typeof(ConsoleColor),
args[1], true);
WindowWidth = int.Parse(args[2]);
WindowHeight = int.Parse(args[3]);

WriteLine($"There are {args.Length} arguments.");
foreach (var arg in args)
{
  WriteLine(arg);
}
```

Running on Windows

In Visual Studio 2017, press *Ctrl* + *F5*. The console window is now a different size and uses different colors for the foreground and background text, as shown in the following screenshot:

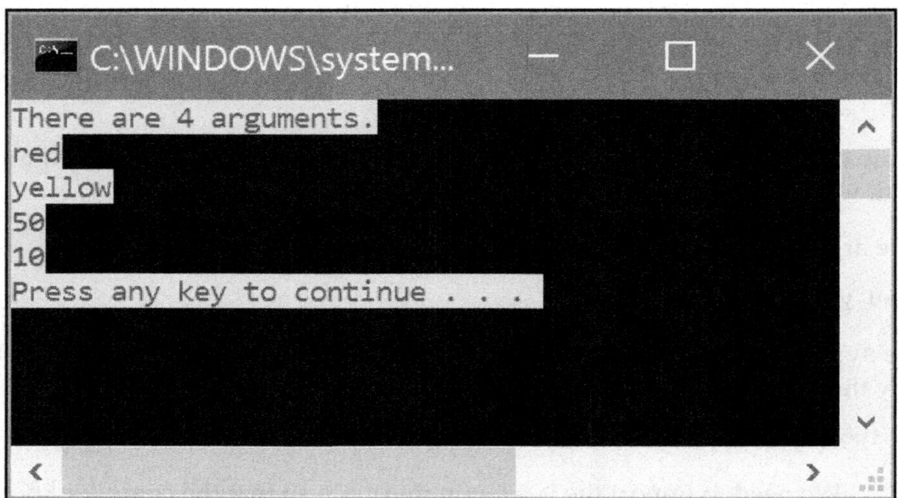

Running on macOS

In Visual Studio Code, enter the following command at the terminal:

```
dotnet run red yellow 50 10
```

You will see an error dialog, as shown in the following screenshot:

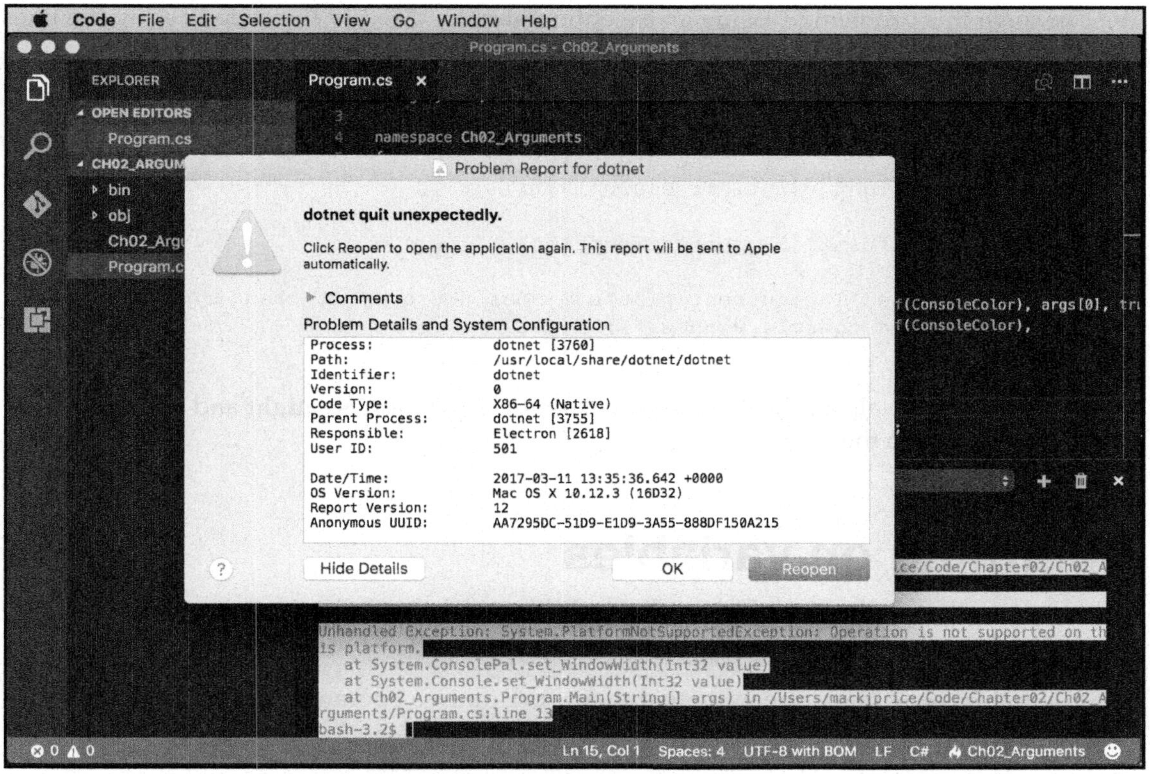

Click **OK**.

In the **Terminal**, you will see the details of the error, as shown in the following screenshot:

```
Unhandled Exception: System.PlatformNotSupportedException: Operation is not supported on this platform.
   at System.ConsolePal.set_WindowWidth(Int32 value)
   at System.Console.set_WindowWidth(Int32 value)
   at ConsoleApplication.Program.Main(String[] args) in /Users/markjprice/Code/Chapter02/Ch02_Arguments/
Program.cs:line 12
```

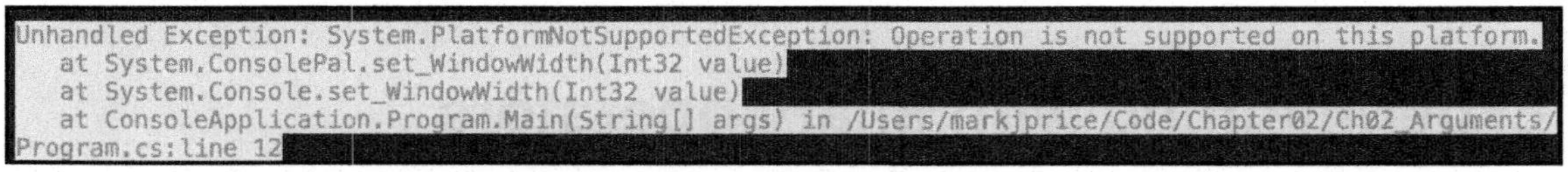

Although the compiler did not give an error or warning, at runtime some API calls may fail on some platforms. Although a console application running on Windows can change its size, on macOS it cannot.

Handling platforms that do not support an API

We can solve this problem by using an exception handler. Modify the code to wrap the lines that change the height and width in a `try` statement like this:

```
try
{
  WindowWidth = int.Parse(args[2]);
  WindowHeight = int.Parse(args[3]);
}
catch(PlatformNotSupportedException)
{
  WriteLine("The current platform does not support changing the
  size of a console window.");
}
```

If you rerun the console application, you will see the exception is caught and a friendly message is shown to the user.

Operating on variables

Operators apply simple operations such as addition and multiplication to operands such as numbers. They usually return a new value that is the result of the operation.

Most operators are **binary**, meaning that they work on two operands, as shown in the following pseudocode:

```
var resultOfOperation = FirstOperand operator SecondOperand;
```

Some operators are **unary**, meaning they work on a single operand.

A **ternary** operator works on three operands.

Experimenting with unary operators

Two common unary operators are used to increment `++` and decrement `--` a number.

In Visual Studio 2017, from the **View** menu, choose **Other Windows**, and then **C# Interactive**.

In Visual Studio Code, create a new console application and write your own statements to output the results using `Console.WriteLine()`.

Enter the following code:

```
> int i = 3;
> i
3
```

Note that when you enter a full statement ending in a semicolon, it is executed when you press *Enter*.

The first statement uses the assignment operator = to assign the value `3` to the variable `i`. When you enter a variable name at the prompt, it returns the variable's current value.

Enter the following statements, and before pressing Enter, try to guess what the value of `x` and `y` will be:

```
> int x = 3;
> int y = x++;
```

Now check the values of `x` and `y`. You might be surprised to see that `y` has the value `3`:

```
> x
4
> y
3
```

The variable `y` has the value `3` because the `++` operator executes after the assignment. This is known as **postfix**. If you need to increment before assignment, use **prefix**, as shown in the following code:

```
> int x = 3;
> int y = ++x;
> x
4
> y
4
```

You can decrement the value using the `--` operator.

Good Practice
Due to the confusion between prefix and postfix for the increment and decrement operators when combined with assignment, the Swift programming language designers plan to drop support for this operator in version 3. My recommendation for usage in C# is to never combine the use of `++` and `--` operators with an assignment `=`. Perform the operations as separate statements.

Experimenting with arithmetic operators

Arithmetic operators allow you to perform arithmetic operations on numbers.

Enter the following in the **C# Interactive** window:

```
> 11 + 3
14
> 11 - 3
8
> 11 * 3
33
> 11 / 3
3
> 11 % 3
2
> 11.0 / 3
3.6666666666666665
```

To understand the divide (`/`) and modulus (`%`) operators when applied to integers (whole numbers), you need to think back to primary school.

Imagine you have eleven sweets and three friends. How can you divide the sweets between your friends? You can give three sweets to each of your friends and there will be two left over. Those two are the modulus, also known as remainder. If you have twelve sweets, then each friend gets four of them and there are none left over. So, the remainder is 0.

If you start with a real number, such as `11.0`, then the divide operator returns a floating point value, such as `3.6666666666665`, rather than a whole number.

Comparison and Boolean operators

Comparison and Boolean operators either return `true` or `false`. In the next chapter, we will use comparison operators in the `if` and `while` statements to check for conditions.

Practicing and exploring

Test your knowledge and understanding by answering some questions, get some hands-on practice, and explore the topics covered in this chapter with deeper research.

Exercise 2.1 – test your knowledge

What type would you choose for the following "numbers"?

1. A person's telephone number.
2. A person's height.
3. A person's age.
4. A person's salary.
5. A book's ISBN.
6. A book's price.
7. A book's shipping weight.
8. A country's population.
9. The number of stars in the Universe.
10. The number of employees in each of the small or medium businesses in the UK (up to about 50,000 employees per business).

Exercise 2.2 – practice number sizes and ranges

Create a console application project named `Ch02_Exercise02` that outputs the number of bytes in memory that each of the following number types use and the minimum and maximum possible values they can have: `sbyte`, `byte`, `short`, `ushort`, `int`, `uint`, `long`, `ulong`, `float`, `double`, and `decimal`.

Read the online MSDN documentation, available at `https://msdn.microsoft.com/en-us/library/txafckwd(v=vs.110).aspx` for *Composite Formatting* to learn how to align text in a console application.

The output of your application should look something like the following screenshot:

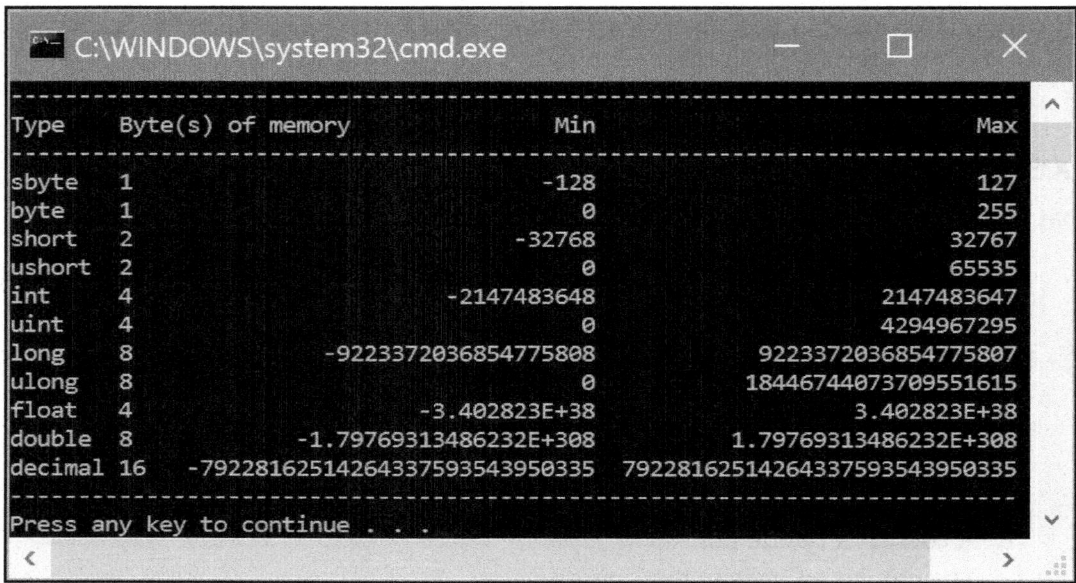

Type	Byte(s) of memory	Min	Max
sbyte	1	-128	127
byte	1	0	255
short	2	-32768	32767
ushort	2	0	65535
int	4	-2147483648	2147483647
uint	4	0	4294967295
long	8	-9223372036854775808	9223372036854775807
ulong	8	0	18446744073709551615
float	4	-3.402823E+38	3.402823E+38
double	8	-1.79769313486232E+308	1.79769313486232E+308
decimal	16	-79228162514264337593543950335	79228162514264337593543950335

Press any key to continue . . .

Exercise 2.3 – explore topics

Use the following links to read more about the topics covered in this chapter:

- **C# Keywords**: `https://docs.microsoft.com/en-us/dotnet/articles/csharp/language-reference/keywords/index`
- **Main() and Command-Line Arguments (C# Programming Guide)**: `https://docs.microsoft.com/en-us/dotnet/articles/csharp/programming-guide/main-and-command-args/`
- **Types (C# Programming Guide)**: `https://docs.microsoft.com/en-us/dotnet/articles/csharp/programming-guide/types/`
- **Statements, Expressions, and Operators (C# Programming Guide)**: `https://docs.microsoft.com/en-us/dotnet/articles/csharp/programming-guide/statements-expressions-operators/`

- **Strings (C# Programming Guide):** `https://docs.microsoft.com/en-us/dotnet/articles/csharp/programming-guide/strings/`
- **Nullable Types (C# Programming Guide):** `https://docs.microsoft.com/en-us/dotnet/articles/csharp/programming-guide/nullable-types/`
- **Console Class**: `https://msdn.microsoft.com/en-us/library/system.console(v=vs.110).aspx`
- **C# Operators**: `https://msdn.microsoft.com/en-us/library/6a71f45d.aspx`

Summary

In this chapter, you learned how to declare variables with a `type` or `var` variable; we discussed some of the built-in types for numbers, text, and Booleans; we covered how to choose between number types; and we experimented with some operators.

In the next chapter, you will learn about branching, looping, converting between types, and handling exceptions.

3

Controlling the Flow, Converting Types, and Handling Exceptions

This chapter is about writing code that makes decisions, repeats blocks of statements, converts between types, and handles errors (known as exceptions). You will also learn about some good places to look for help.

This chapter covers the following topics:

- Selection statements
- Iteration statements
- Casting and converting between types
- Handling exceptions
- Checking for overflow
- Looking for help

Selection statements

Every application needs to be able to select from choices and branch along different code paths. The two selection statements in C# are `if` and `switch`. You can use `if` for all your code but `switch` can simplify your code in some common scenarios.

Using Visual Studio 2017

Start Microsoft Visual Studio 2017. In Visual Studio, press *Ctrl* + *Shift* + *N* or choose **File** | **New** | **Project...**.

In the **New Project** dialog, in the **Installed** | **Templates** list, select **Visual C#**. In the list at the center, select **Console App (.NET Core)**, type the name `Ch03_SelectionStatements`, change the location to `C:\Code`, type the solution name `Chapter03`, and then click on **OK**.

Using Visual Studio Code on macOS, Linux, or Windows

If you completed previous chapters, then you will already have a `Code` folder in your `user` folder. If not, create it, and then create a subfolder named `Chapter03`, and then a sub-subfolder named `Ch03_SelectionStatements`.

Start Visual Studio Code and open the `/Chapter03/Ch03_SelectionStatements/` folder.

In Visual Studio Code, navigate to **View** | **Integrated Terminal**, and then enter the following command:

```
dotnet new console
```

Click the `Program.cs` file and then click **Restore** to restore dependencies.

The if statement

The `if` statement determines which branch to follow by evaluating a Boolean expression. The `else` block is optional. The `if` statement can be nested and combined. Each Boolean expression can be independent of the others.

Add the following statements inside the `Main` method to check whether this console application has any arguments passed to it:

```
if (args.Length == 0)
{
  WriteLine("There are no arguments.");
}
else
{
```

```
  WriteLine("There is at least one argument.");
}
```

As there is only a single statement inside each block, this code *can* be written without the curly braces, as shown in the following code:

```
if (args.Length == 0)
  WriteLine("There are no arguments.");
else
  WriteLine("There is at least one argument.");
```

This style of the `if` statement is not recommended because it can introduce serious bugs, for example, the infamous *#gotofail* bug in Apple's iPhone operating system. For 18 months after Apple's iOS 6 was released, it had a bug in its **Secure Sockets Layer** (**SSL**) encryption code, which meant that any user running Safari to connect to secure websites, such as their bank, were not properly secure because an important check was being accidently skipped: `https://gotofail.com/`

Just because you can leave out the curly braces, doesn't mean you should. Your code is not "more efficient" without them, instead, it is less maintainable and potentially more dangerous, as this tweet points out:

Chris Adamson @invalidname · May 26
Had a colleague remove my {} surrounding a 1-line if clause today. No, not angry. It's on his conscience now. **#gotofail**

10 15

Pattern matching with the if statement

A new feature of C# 7 is pattern matching. The `if` statement can use the `is` keyword in combination with declaring a local variable to make your code safer.

Add the following statements to the end of the `Main` method. If the value stored in the variable named `o` is an `int`, then the value is assigned to the local variable named `i`, which can then be used inside the `if` statement. This is safer than using the variable named `o` because we know for sure that `i` is an `int` and not something else:

```
object o = "3";
int j = 4;

if(o is int i)
{
```

```
    WriteLine($"{i} x {j} = {i * j}");
  }
  else
  {
    WriteLine("o is not an int so it cannot multiply!");
  }
```

Run the console application and view the output:

```
o is not an int so it cannot multiply!
```

Delete the double-quote characters around the `"3"` so that the value stored in the variable named `o` is an `int` instead of a `string` and then rerun the console application and view the output:

```
3 x 4 = 12
```

The switch statement

The `switch` statement is different from the `if` statement because it compares a single expression against a list of multiple possible cases. Every case is related to the single expression. Every case must end with the `break` keyword (like `case 1` in the following code) or the `goto case` keywords, (like `case 2` in the following code) or they should have no statements (like `case 3` in the following code).

Enter the following code after the `if` statements that you wrote previously. Note that the first line is a label that can be jumped to and the second line generates a random number. The `switch` statement branches based on the value of this random number:

```
A_label:
  var number = (new Random()).Next(1, 7);
  WriteLine($"My random number is {number}");
  switch (number)
  {
    case 1:
      WriteLine("One");
      break; // jumps to end of switch statement
    case 2:
      WriteLine("Two");
      goto case 1;
    case 3:
    case 4:
      WriteLine("Three or four");
      goto case 1;
    case 5:
```

```
        // go to sleep for half a second
        System.Threading.Thread.Sleep(500);
        goto A_label;
        default:
        WriteLine("Default");
        break;
    } // end of switch statement
```

Good Practice
You can use the `goto` keyword to jump to another case or a label. The `goto` keyword is frowned upon by most programmers but can be a good solution to code logic in some scenarios. Use it sparingly.

In Visual Studio 2017, run the program by pressing *Ctrl* + *F5*.

In Visual Studio Code, run the program by entering the following command into the **Integrated Terminal**:

```
dotnet run
```

Run the program multiple times to see what happens in various cases of random numbers, as shown in the following output from Visual Studio Code:

```
bash-3.2$ dotnet run
My random number is 4
Three or four
One
bash-3.2$ dotnet run
My random number is 2
Two
One
bash-3.2$ dotnet run
My random number is 1
One
```

Pattern matching with the switch statement

Like the `if` statement, the `switch` statement supports pattern matching in C# 7. The case values no longer need to be literal values. They can be patterns.

Add the following statement to the top of the file:

```
using System.IO;
```

Add the following statements to the end of the `Main` method:

If you are using macOS, then swap the commented statement that sets the path variable and replace my username with your user folder name:

```
// string path = "/Users/markjprice/Code/Chapter03"; // macOS
string path = @"C:\Code\Chapter03"; // Windows
Stream s = File.Open(
  Path.Combine(path, "file.txt"),
  FileMode.OpenOrCreate);

switch(s)
{
  case FileStream writeableFile when s.CanWrite:
    WriteLine("The stream is to a file that I can write to.");
    break;
  case FileStream readOnlyFile:
    WriteLine("The stream is to a read-only file.");
    break;
  case MemoryStream ms:
    WriteLine("The stream is to a memory address.");
    break;
  default: // always evaluated last despite its current position
    WriteLine("The stream is some other type.");
    break;
  case null:
    WriteLine("The stream is null.");
    break;
}
```

Note that the variable named `s` is declared as a `Stream` type.

You will learn more about the `System.IO` namespace and the `Stream` type in `Chapter 10`, *Working with Files, Streams, and Serialization*.

In .NET, there are multiple subtypes of `Stream`, including `FileStream` and `MemoryStream`. In C# 7, your code can more concisely both, branch based on the subtype of stream, and declare and assign a local variable to safely use it.

Also, note that case statements can include a `when` keyword to perform more specific pattern matching. In the first case statement in the preceding code, `s` would only be a match if the stream was both a `FileStream` and its `CanWrite` property was true.

Iteration statements

Iteration statements repeat a block either while a condition is true or for each item in a group. The choice of which statement to use is based on a combination of ease of understanding to solve the logic problem and personal preference.

Use either Visual Studio 2017 or Visual Studio Code to add a new console application project named `Ch03_IterationStatements`.

In Visual Studio 2017, you can set the solution's start up project to be the current selection so that the current project runs when you press *Ctrl* + *F5*.

The while statement

The `while` statement evaluates a Boolean expression and continues to loop while it is true.

Type the following code inside the `Main` method:

```
int x = 0;
while (x < 10)
{
  WriteLine(x);
  x++;
}
```

Run the console application and view the output:

```
0
1
2
3
4
5
6
7
8
9
```

The do statement

The `do` statement is like `while`, except the Boolean expression is checked at the bottom of the block instead of the top, which means that it always executes at least once.

Type the following code at the end of the Main method and run it:

```
string password = string.Empty;
do
{
  Write("Enter your password: ");
  password = ReadLine();
} while (password != "secret");
WriteLine("Correct!");
```

You will be prompted to enter your password repeatedly until you enter it correctly, as shown in the following output:

```
Enter your password: password
Enter your password: 12345678
Enter your password: ninja
Enter your password: asdfghjkl
Enter your password: secret
Correct!
```

As an optional exercise, add statements so that the user can only make ten attempts before an error message is displayed.

The for statement

The `for` statement is like `while`, except that it is more succinct. It combines an initializer statement that executes once at the start of the loop, a Boolean expression to check whether the loop should continue, and an incrementer that executes at the bottom of the loop. The `for` statement is commonly used with an integer counter, as shown in the following code:

```
for (int y = 1; y <= 10; y++)
{
  WriteLine(y);
}
```

Run the console application and view the output, which should be the numbers 1 to 10.

The foreach statement

The `foreach` statement is a bit different from the other three iteration statements. It is used to perform a block of statements on each item in a sequence, for example, an array or collection. Each item is read-only and if the sequence is modified during iteration, for example, by adding or removing an item, then an exception will be thrown.

Type the following code inside the `Main` method, which creates an array of string variables and then outputs the length each of them:

```
string[] names = { "Adam", "Barry", "Charlie" };
foreach (string name in names)
{
  WriteLine($"{name} has {name.Length} characters.");
}
```

Run the console application and view the output:

```
Adam has 4 characters.
Barry has 5 characters.
Charlie has 7 characters.
```

How does the foreach statement work?

Technically, the `foreach` statement will work on any type that implements an interface called `IEnumerable`, but you don't need to worry about what an interface is for now.

You will learn about interfaces in Chapter 7, *Implementing Interfaces and Inheriting Classes*.

The compiler turns the `foreach` statement in the preceding code into something like this:

```
IEnumerator e = names.GetEnumerator();
while (e.MoveNext())
{
  string name = (string)e.Current; // Current is read-only!
  WriteLine($"{name} has {name.Length} characters.");
}
```

Due to the use of an iterator, the variable declared in a `foreach` statement cannot be used to modify the value of the current item.

Casting and converting between types

You will often need to convert between different types.

Add a new console application project named `Ch03_CastingConverting`.

Casting from numbers to numbers

It is safe to implicitly cast an `int` variable into a `double` variable.

In the `Main` method, enter the following statements:

```
int a = 10;
double b = a; // an int can be stored in a double
WriteLine(b);
```

You cannot implicitly cast a `double` variable into an `int` variable because it is potentially unsafe and would lose data.

In the `Main` method, enter the following statements:

```
double c = 9.8;
int d = c; // compiler gives an error for this line
WriteLine(d);
```

In Visual Studio 2017, press *Ctrl* + *W*, *E* to view the **Error List**, as shown in the following screenshot:

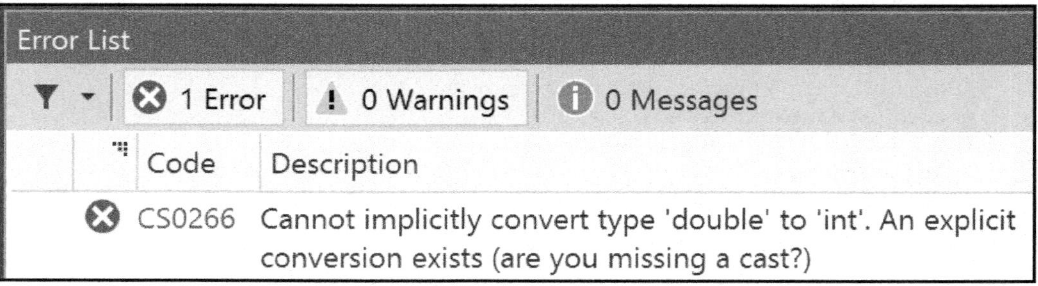

In Visual Studio Code, either view the Problems window, or when you enter the command `dotnet run`, you will see the following output:

```
Compiling Ch03_CastingConverting for .NETCoreApp,Version=v1.1
/usr/local/share/dotnet/dotnet compile-csc
@/Users/markjprice/Code/Chapter03/Ch03_CastingConverting/obj/
Debug/netcoreapp1.1/dotnet-compile.rsp returned Exit Code 1
/Users/markjprice/Code/Chapter03/Ch03_CastingConverting/Program.cs(14
,21): error CS0266: Cannot implicitly convert type 'double' to 'int'.
An explicit conversion exists (are you missing a cast?)
```

```
Compilation failed.
    0 Warning(s)
    1 Error(s)
Time elapsed 00:00:01.0461813
```

Casting explicitly

You must explicitly cast a `double` into an `int` variable using a pair of round brackets around the type you want to case the `double` into. The pair of round brackets is the **cast operator**. Even then, you must beware that the part after the decimal point will be trimmed off without warning.

Modify the assignment statement for the variable `d`, as shown in the following code:

```
double c = 9.8;
int d = (int)c;
WriteLine(d); // d is 9 losing the .8 part
```

Run the console application and view the output:

```
10
9
```

We must perform a similar operation when moving values between larger integers and smaller integers. Again, beware that you might lose information because any value too big will get set to `-1`!

Enter the following code:

```
long e = 10;
int f = (int)e;
WriteLine($"e is {e} and f is {f}");
e = long.MaxValue;
f = (int)e;
WriteLine($"e is {e} and f is {f}");
```

Run the console application and view the output:

```
e is 10 and f is 10
e is 9223372036854775807 and f is -1
```

Using the convert type

An alternative to using the casting operator is to use the `System.Convert` type.

At the top of the `Program.cs` file, type the following code:

```
using static System.Convert;
```

Add the following statements to the bottom of the `Main` method:

```
double g = 9.8;
int h = ToInt32(g);
WriteLine($"g is {g} and h is {h}");
```

Run the console application and view the output:

```
g is 9.8 and h is 10
```

One difference between casting and converting is that converting rounds the double value up to 10 instead of trimming the part after the decimal point.

The `System.Convert` type can convert to and from all the C# number types as well as Booleans, strings, and date and time values.

Rounding numbers

You have now seen that the cast operator trims the decimal part of a real number and that the convert methods round up or down. However, what is the rule for rounding?

In British primary schools, children are taught to round *up* if the decimal part is `.5` or higher and round *down* if the decimal part is less.

Enter the following code:

```
double i = 9.49;
double j = 9.5;
double k = 10.49;
double l = 10.5;
WriteLine($"i is {i}, ToInt(i) is {ToInt32(i)}");
WriteLine($"j is {j}, ToInt(j) is {ToInt32(j)}");
WriteLine($"k is {k}, ToInt(k) is {ToInt32(k)}");
WriteLine($"l is {l}, ToInt(l) is {ToInt32(l)}");
```

Run the console application and view the output:

```
i is 9.49, ToInt(i) is 9
j is 9.5, ToInt(j) is 10
k is 10.49, ToInt(k) is 10
l is 10.5, ToInt(l) is 10
```

Note that the rule for rounding in C# is subtly different. It will round *up* if the decimal part is `.5` or higher and the non-decimal part is odd, but it will round *down* if the non-decimal part is even. It always rounds *down* if the decimal part is less than `.5`.

This rule is known as **Banker's Rounding**, and it is preferred because it reduces bias. Sadly, other languages such as JavaScript use the primary school rule.

Good Practice
For every programming language that you use, check its rounding rules. They may not work the way you expect!

Converting from any type to a string

The most common conversion is from any type into a `string` variable, so all types have a method named `ToString` that they inherit from the `System.Object` class.

The `ToString` method converts the current value of any variable into a textual representation. Some types can't be sensibly represented as text so they return their namespace and type name.

Add the following statements to the bottom of the `Main` method:

```
int number = 12;
WriteLine(number.ToString());
bool boolean = true;
WriteLine(boolean.ToString());
DateTime now = DateTime.Now;
WriteLine(now.ToString());
object me = new object();
WriteLine(me.ToString());
```

Run the console application and view the output:

```
12
True
27/01/2017 13:48:54
System.Object
```

Parsing from strings to numbers or dates and times

The second most common conversion is from strings to numbers or date and time values. The opposite of `ToString` is `Parse`. Only a few types have a `Parse` method.

Add the following statements to the `Main` method:

```
int age = int.Parse("27");
DateTime birthday = DateTime.Parse("4 July 1980");
WriteLine($"I was born {age} years ago.");
WriteLine($"My birthday is {birthday}.");
WriteLine($"My birthday is {birthday:D}.");
```

Run the console application and view the output:

```
I was born 27 years ago.
My birthday is 04/07/1980 00:00:00.
My birthday is 04 July 1980.
```

By default, a date and time value outputs with the short date and time format. You can use format codes like `D` to output only the date part using long date format. There are many other format codes for common scenarios.

One problem with the `Parse` method is that it gives errors if the string cannot be converted.

Add the following statements to the bottom of the `Main` method:

```
int count = int.Parse("abc");
```

Run the console application and view the output:

```
Unhandled Exception: System.FormatException: Input string was not in
a correct format.
```

To avoid errors, you can use the `TryParse` method instead. `TryParse` attempts to convert the input string and returns `true` if it can convert it and `false` if it cannot. The `out` keyword is required to allow the `TryParse` method to set the count variable when the conversion works.

Replace the `int count` declaration with the following statements:

```
Write("How many eggs are there? ");
int count;
string input = Console.ReadLine();
```

```
if (int.TryParse(input, out count))
{
  WriteLine($"There are {count} eggs.");
}
else
{
  WriteLine("I could not parse the input.");
}
```

Run the application twice. The first time, enter `12`. You will see the following output:

```
How many eggs are there? 12
There are 12 eggs.
```

The second time, enter `twelve`. You will see the following output:

```
How many eggs are there? twelve
I could not parse the count.
```

You can also use the `Convert` type; however, like the `Parse` method, it gives an error if it cannot convert.

Handling exceptions

You've seen several scenarios when errors have occurred. C# calls where an exception has been thrown. A good practice is to avoid writing code that will throw an exception whenever possible, but sometimes you can't. In those scenarios, you must catch the exception and handle it.

As you have seen, the default behavior of a console application is to display details about the exception in the output and then stop running the application.

The default behavior of a Windows desktop application is to display details about the exception in a dialog box and allow the user to choose to either continue or stop running the application. You can take control over how to handle exceptions using the `try` statement.

The try statement

Add a new console application project named `Ch03_HandlingExceptions`.

When you know that a statement can cause an error, you should wrap that statement in a `try` block. For example, parsing from a string to a number can cause an error. We do not have to do anything inside the `catch` block. When the following code executes, the error will get caught and will not be displayed, and the console application will continue running.

In the `Main` method, add the following statements:

```
WriteLine("Before parsing");
Write("What is your age? ");
string input = Console.ReadLine();
try
{
  int age = int.Parse(input);
  WriteLine($"You are {age} years old.");
}
catch
{

}
WriteLine("After parsing");
```

Run the console application and enter a valid age, for example, `43`:

```
Before parsing
What is your age? 43
You are 43 years old.
After parsing
```

Run the console application again and enter an invalid age, for example, `kermit`;

```
Before parsing
What is your age? kermit
After parsing
```

The exception was caught, but it might be useful to see the type of error that occurred.

Catching all exceptions

Modify the `catch` statement to look like this:

```
catch(Exception ex)
{
  WriteLine($"{ex.GetType()} says {ex.Message}");
}
```

Run the console application and again enter an invalid age, for example, `kermit`:

```
Before parsing
What is your age? kermit
System.FormatException says Input string was not in a correct format.
After parsing
```

Catching specific exceptions

Now that we know which specific type of exception occurred, we can improve our code by catching just that type of exception and customizing the message that we display to the user.

Leave the existing `catch` block, but add the following code above it:

```
catch (FormatException)
{
  WriteLine("The age you entered is not a valid number format.");
}
catch (Exception ex)
{
  WriteLine($"{ex.GetType()} says {ex.Message}");
}
```

Run the program and again enter an invalid age, for example, `kermit`:

```
Before parsing
What is your age? kermit
The age you entered is not a valid number format.
After parsing
```

The reason we want to leave the more general `catch` below is because there might be other types of exceptions that can occur. For example, run the program and enter a number that is too big for an integer, for example, `9876543210`:

```
Before parsing
What is your age? 9876543210
System.OverflowException says Value was either too large or too small  for
an
Int32.
After parsing
```

Let's add another catch for this new type of exception:

```
catch(OverflowException)
{
```

```
      WriteLine("Your age is a valid number format but it is either
      too big or small.");
    }
    catch (FormatException)
    {
      WriteLine("The age you entered is not a valid number format.");
    }
```

Rerun the program one more time and enter a number that is too big:

```
Before parsing
What is your age? 9876543210
Your age is a valid number format but it is either too big or small.
After parsing
```

The order in which you catch exceptions is important. The correct order is related to the inheritance hierarchy of the exception types. You will learn about inheritance in `Chapter 6`, *Building Your Own Types with Object-Oriented Programming*. However, don't worry too much about this—the compiler will give you build errors if you get exceptions in the wrong order anyway.

The finally statement

Sometimes, we might want to ensure that some code executes regardless of whether an exception occurs or not. To do this, we use a `finally` statement.

A common scenario where you would want to use `finally` is when working with files and databases. When you open a file or a database, you are using resources outside of .NET. These are called unmanaged resources and must be disposed of when you are done working with them. To guarantee that they are disposed of, we can call the `Dispose` method inside of a `finally` block.

You will learn about files and databases in more detail in later chapters. For now, focus on the code that we write in the `finally` block.

Import the `System.IO` namespace at the top of the code file as follows:

```
using System.IO;
```

Type the following code to the end of the Main method:

If you are using macOS then swap the commented statement that sets the path variable and replace my username with your user folder name.

```
// string path = "/Users/markjprice/Code/Chapter03"; // macOS
string path = @"C:\Code\Chapter03"; // Windows

FileStream file = null;
StreamWriter writer = null;
try
{

  if (Directory.Exists(path))
  {
    file = File.OpenWrite(Path.Combine(path, "file.txt"));
    writer = new StreamWriter(file);
    writer.WriteLine("Hello, C#!");
  }
  else
  {
    WriteLine($"{path} does not exist!");
  }
}
catch (Exception ex)
{
  // if the path doesn't exist the exception will be caught
  WriteLine($"{ex.GetType()} says {ex.Message}");
}
finally
{
  if (writer != null)
  {
    writer.Dispose();
    WriteLine("The writer's unmanaged resources have been
    disposed.");
  }
  if (file != null)
  {
    file.Dispose();
    WriteLine("The file's unmanaged resources have been
    disposed.");
  }
}
```

Run the console application and view the output:

```
The writer's unmanaged resources have been disposed.
The file's unmanaged resources have been disposed.
```

If you browse to the folder specified in the path, then you will see a file has been created named `file.txt` that contains the text: `Hello, C#!`

Simplifying disposal with the using statement

If you don't need to catch any exceptions, then you can simplify the code that needs to check for a non-null object and then call its `Dispose` method by using the `using` statement.

Confusingly, there are two uses for the `using` statement: importing a namespace, and generating a `finally` statement that disposes of an object.

The compiler changes your code into a full `try` and `finally` statement, but without a `catch`. You can use nested `try` statements; so, if you do want to catch any exceptions, you can.

Add this code after the existing code. It will create a file named `file2.txt`:

```
using (FileStream file2 = File.OpenWrite(
  Path.Combine(path, "file2.txt")))
{
  using (StreamWriter writer2 = new StreamWriter(file2))
  {
    try
    {
      writer2.WriteLine("Welcome, .NET Core!");
    }
    catch (Exception ex)
    {
      WriteLine($"{ex.GetType()} says {ex.Message}");
    }
  } // automatically calls Dispose if the object is not null
} // automatically calls Dispose if the object is not null
```

Many types, including `FileStream` and `StreamWriter` mentioned earlier, provide a `Close` method as well as a `Dispose` method. In the .NET Framework, you can use either because they do the same thing. In the .NET Core, Microsoft has simplified the API, so you must use `Dispose`.

Checking for overflow

Earlier, we saw that when casting between number types, it was possible to lose information, for example, when casting from a `long` variable to an `int` variable. If the value stored in a type is too big, it will overflow.

Add a new console application project named `Ch03_CheckingForOverflow`.

The checked statement

The `checked` statement tells .NET to throw an exception when an overflow happens instead of allowing it to happen silently.

We set the initial value of an `int` variable to its maximum value minus one. Then, we increment it several times, outputting its value each time. Note that once it gets above its maximum value, it overflows to its minimum value and continues incrementing from there.

Type the following code in the `Main` method and run the program:

```
int x = int.MaxValue - 1;
WriteLine(x);
x++;
WriteLine(x);
x++;
WriteLine(x);
x++;
WriteLine(x);
```

Run the console application and view the output:

```
2147483646
2147483647
-2147483648
-2147483647
```

Now, let's get the compiler to warn us about the overflow using the `checked` statement:

```
checked
{
  int x = int.MaxValue - 1;
  WriteLine(x);
  x++;
  WriteLine(x);
  x++;
  WriteLine(x);
```

```
    x++;
    WriteLine(x);
  }
```

Run the console application and view the output:

```
2147483646
2147483647
Unhandled Exception: System.OverflowException: Arithmetic operation
resulted in an overflow.
```

Just like any other exception, we should wrap these statements in a `try` block and display a nicer error message for the user:

```
try
{
  // previous code goes here
}
catch(OverflowException)
{
  WriteLine("The code overflowed but I caught the exception.");
}
```

Run the console application and view the output:

```
2147483646
2147483647
The code overflowed but I caught the exception.
```

The unchecked statement

A related keyword is `unchecked`.

Type the following statement at the end of the previous statements. The compiler will not compile this statement because it knows it would overflow:

```
int y = int.MaxValue + 1;
```

Press *F6* or enter the command `dotnet run` to build and notice the error, as shown in the following screenshot from Visual Studio 2017:

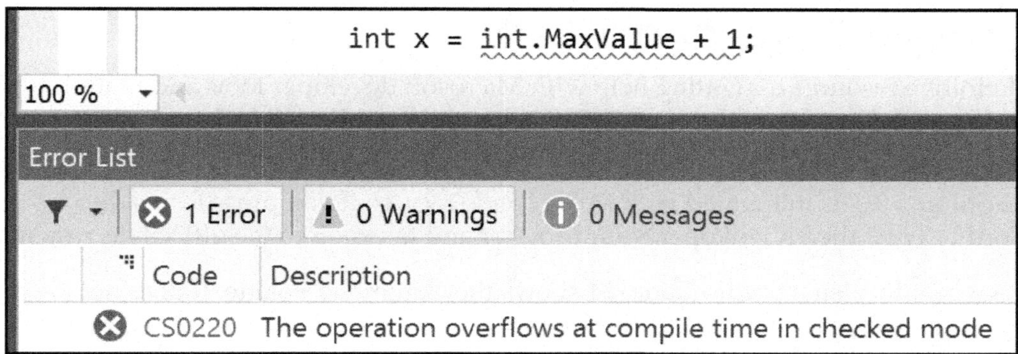

Note that this is a **compile-time** check. To disable compile-time checks, we can wrap the statement in an `unchecked` block, as shown in the following code:

```
unchecked
{
  int y = int.MaxValue + 1;
  WriteLine(y); // this will output -2147483648
  y--;
  WriteLine(y); // this will output 2147483647
  y--;
  WriteLine(y); // this will output 2147483646
}
```

Run the console application and view the output:

```
2147483646
2147483647
The code overflowed but I caught the exception.
-2147483648
2147483647
2147483646
```

Of course, it would be rare that you would want to explicitly switch off a check like this because it allows an overflow to occur. But, perhaps, you can think of a scenario where you might want that behavior.

Looking for help

This section is about how to find quality information about programming on the Web.

Microsoft Docs and MSDN

The definitive resource for getting help with Microsoft developer tools and platforms used to be **Microsoft Developer Network** (**MSDN**). Now, it is **Microsoft Docs**: `https://docs.microsoft.com/`

Visual Studio 2017 is integrated with MSDN and Docs, so if you press *F1* inside a C# keyword or type, then it will open your browser and take you to the official documentation.

In Visual Studio Code, *F1* shows the Command Palette. It does not support context sensitive help.

Go to definition

Another useful keystroke in both Visual Studio 2017 and Visual Studio Code is *F12*. This will show what the public definition of the type looks like by reading the metadata in the compiled assembly. Some tools will even reverse-engineer from the metadata and IL code back into C# for you.

Enter the following code, click inside `int`, and then press *F12* (or right-click and choose **Go To Definition**):

```
int z;
```

In the new code window that appears, you can see that `int` is in the `mscorlib.dll` assembly; it is named `Int32`; it is in the `System` namespace; and `int` is therefore an alias for `System.Int32`, as shown in the following screenshot:

```
MetadataAsSourceProject                    System.Int32
Assembly mscorlib, Version=4.0.0.0, Culture=neutral, PublicKeyToken=b77a5c561934e089

using ...

namespace System
{
    ...public struct Int32 : IComparable, IFormattable, IConvertible, IComparable<Int32>
    {
        ...public const Int32 MaxValue = 2147483647;
        ...public const Int32 MinValue = -2147483648;
```

Microsoft defined `int` using a `struct` keyword, meaning that `int` is a value type stored on the stack. You can also see that `int` implements interfaces such as `IComparable` and has constants for its maximum and minimum values.

In the code editor window, scroll down to find the `Parse` methods and in Visual Studio 2017, you will need to click on the small box with a plus symbol in them to expand the code like I have done in the following screenshot:

```
//
// Summary:
//     Converts the string representation of a number to its 32-bit signed integer equivalent.
//
// Parameters:
//   s:
//     A string containing a number to convert.
//
// Returns:
//     A 32-bit signed integer equivalent to the number contained in s.
//
// Exceptions:
//   T:System.ArgumentNullException:
//     s is null.
//
//   T:System.FormatException:
//     s is not in the correct format.
//
//   T:System.OverflowException:
//     s represents a number less than System.Int32.MinValue or greater than System.Int32.MaxValue.
public static Int32 Parse(string s);
```

In the comment, you will see that Microsoft has documented what exceptions might occur if you call this method (`ArgumentNullException`, `FormatException`, and `OverflowException`).

Now, we know that we need to wrap a call to this method in a `try` statement and which exceptions to catch.

StackOverflow

StackOverflow is the most popular third-party website for getting answers to difficult programming questions. It is so popular that search engines such as **DuckDuckGo** have a special way to write a query to search the site.

Go to DuckDuckGo.com and enter the following query:

```
!so securestring
```

You will get the following results:

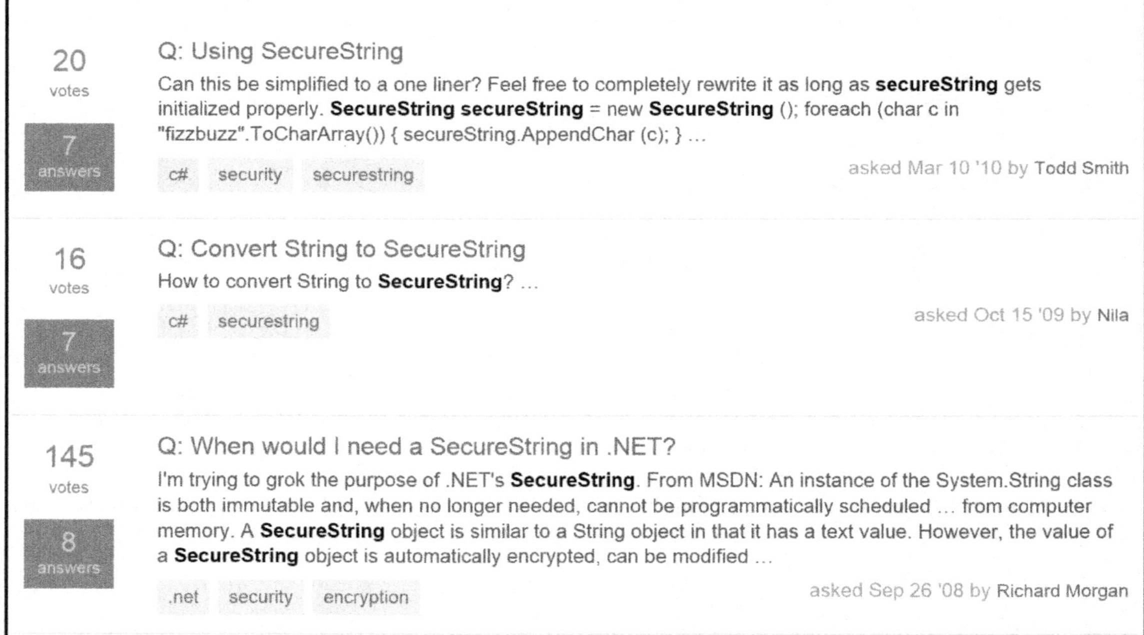

Google

You can search **Google** with advanced search options to increase the likelihood of finding what you need.

For example, if you are searching for information about **garbage collection** using a simple Google query, you will see a Wikipedia definition of garbage collection in computer science, and then a list of garbage collection services in your local area, as shown in the following screenshot:

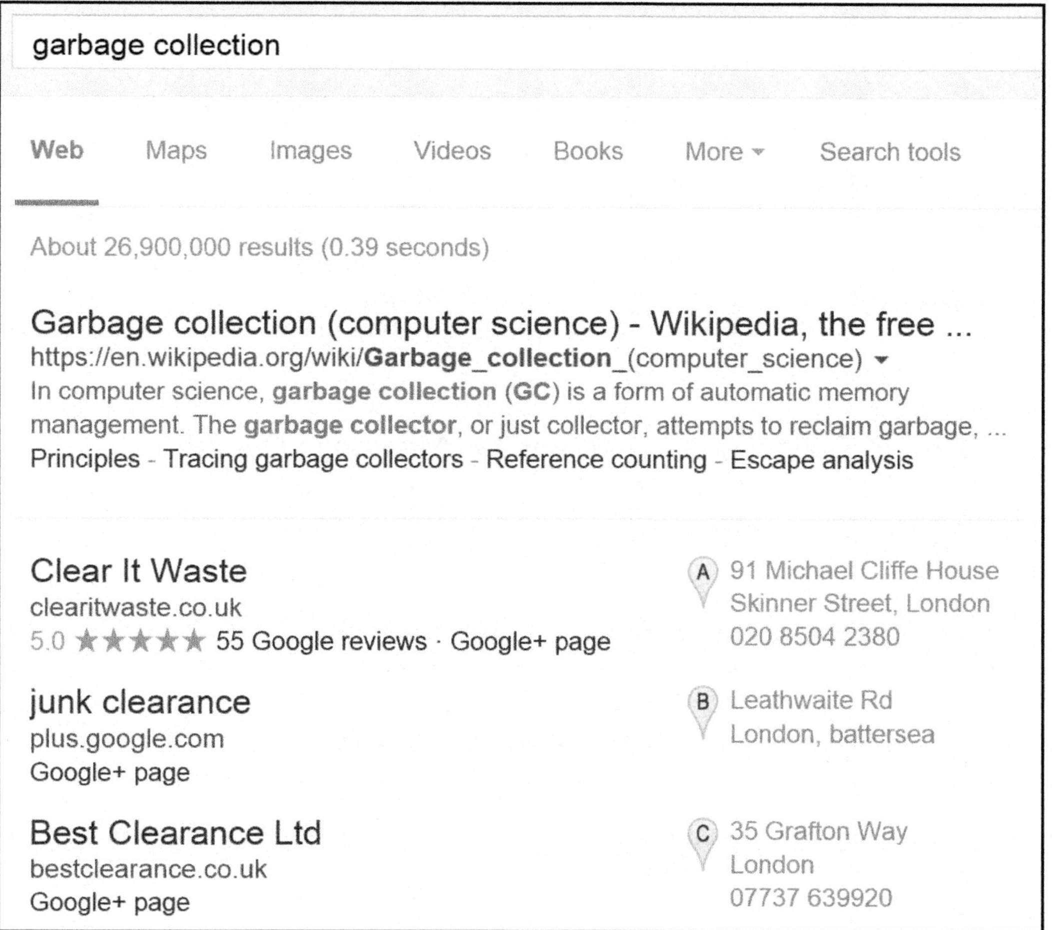

We can improve the search by restricting it to a useful site such as StackOverflow, as shown in the following screenshot:

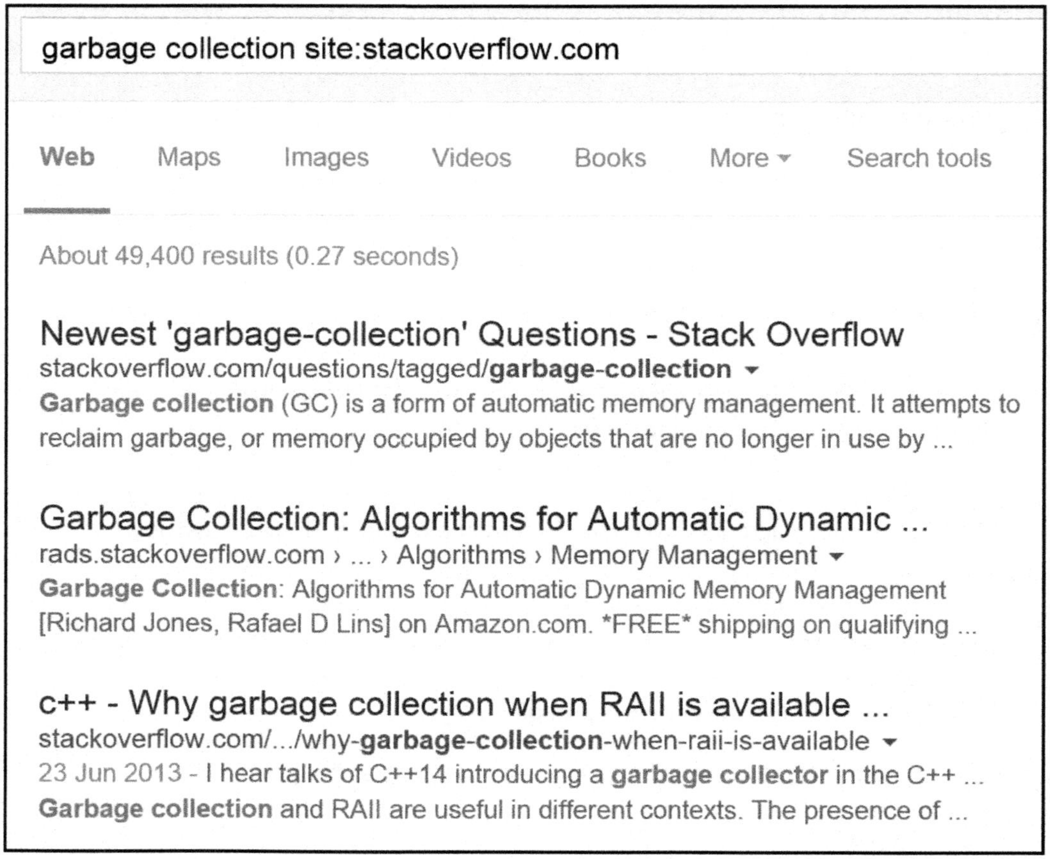

garbage collection site:stackoverflow.com

Web Maps Images Videos Books More Search tools

About 49,400 results (0.27 seconds)

Newest 'garbage-collection' Questions - Stack Overflow
stackoverflow.com/questions/tagged/**garbage-collection**
Garbage collection (GC) is a form of automatic memory management. It attempts to reclaim garbage, or memory occupied by objects that are no longer in use by ...

Garbage Collection: Algorithms for Automatic Dynamic ...
rads.stackoverflow.com › ... › Algorithms › Memory Management
Garbage Collection: Algorithms for Automatic Dynamic Memory Management [Richard Jones, Rafael D Lins] on Amazon.com. *FREE* shipping on qualifying ...

c++ - Why garbage collection when RAII is available ...
stackoverflow.com/.../why-**garbage-collection**-when-raii-is-available
23 Jun 2013 - I hear talks of C++14 introducing a **garbage collector** in the C++ ... **Garbage collection** and RAII are useful in different contexts. The presence of ...

We can improve the search even more by removing languages that we might not care about like C++, as shown in the following screenshot:

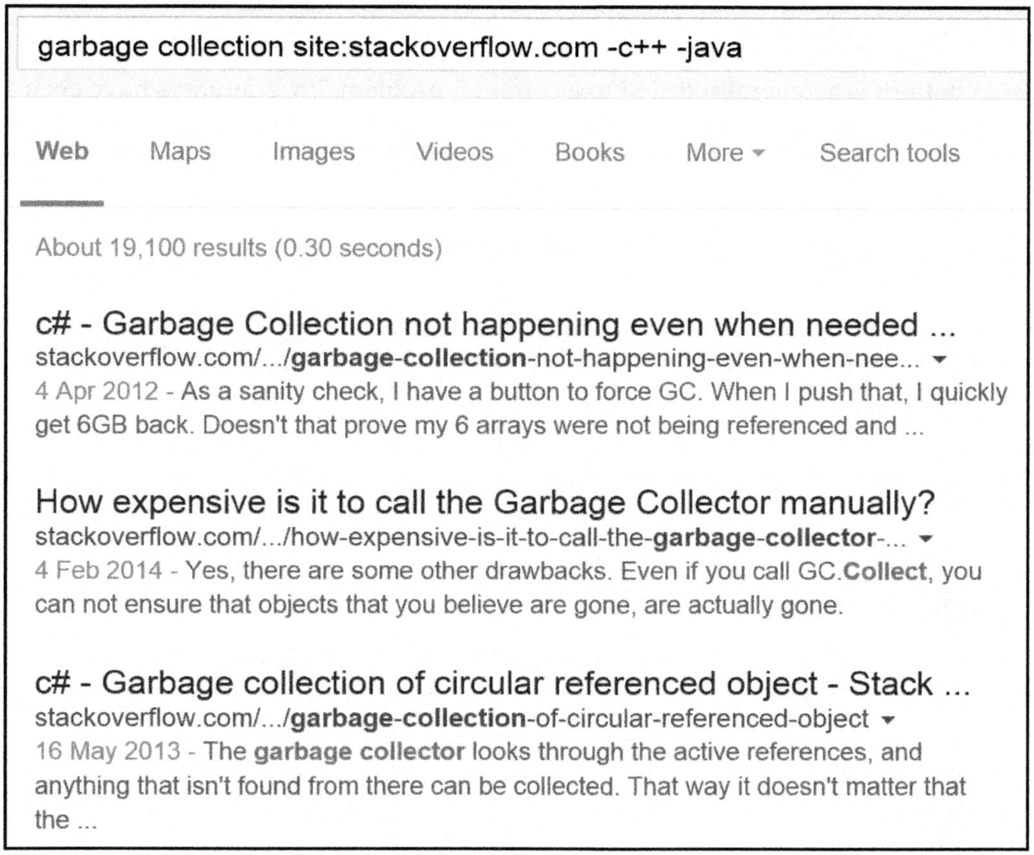

garbage collection site:stackoverflow.com -c++ -java

Web Maps Images Videos Books More Search tools

About 19,100 results (0.30 seconds)

c# - Garbage Collection not happening even when needed ...
stackoverflow.com/.../**garbage-collection**-not-happening-even-when-nee...
4 Apr 2012 - As a sanity check, I have a button to force GC. When I push that, I quickly get 6GB back. Doesn't that prove my 6 arrays were not being referenced and ...

How expensive is it to call the Garbage Collector manually?
stackoverflow.com/.../how-expensive-is-it-to-call-the-**garbage-collector**-...
4 Feb 2014 - Yes, there are some other drawbacks. Even if you call GC.**Collect**, you can not ensure that objects that you believe are gone, are actually gone.

c# - Garbage collection of circular referenced object - Stack ...
stackoverflow.com/.../**garbage-collection**-of-circular-referenced-object
16 May 2013 - The **garbage collector** looks through the active references, and anything that isn't found from there can be collected. That way it doesn't matter that the ...

Subscribing to blogs

An excellent blog to subscribe to, to keep up-to-date with .NET is the official *.NET Blog* written by the .NET engineering teams. The .NET Blog has a tag, *Week in .NET*, which is a summary of interesting news that has happened in the world of .NET in the previous week:

`https://blogs.msdn.microsoft.com/dotnet/`

Design patterns

A design pattern is a general solution to a common problem. Programmers have been solving the same problems over and over. When the community discovers a good reusable solution, we call it a design pattern. Many design patterns have been documented over the years.

Navigate to the following link to read about common design patterns: `https://en.wikipedia.org/wiki/Software_design_pattern#Classification_and_list`

Microsoft has a group called *patterns & practices* that specializes in documenting and promoting design patterns for Microsoft products.

Good Practice
Before writing new code, search to see if someone else has already solved the problem in a general way.

Singleton pattern

One of the most common patterns is the **Singleton**. Examples of Singleton in .NET are the `Console` and `Math` types.

Read more about the Singleton pattern: `https://en.wikipedia.org/wiki/Singleton_pattern`

Practice and explore

Test your knowledge and understanding by answering some questions, get some hands-on practice, and explore with deeper research into this chapter's topics.

Exercise 3.1 – test your knowledge

Answer the following questions:

1. Where would you look for help about a C# keyword?
2. Where would you look for solutions to common programming problems?
3. What happens when you divide an `int` variable by `0`?

4. What happens when you divide a `double` variable by `0`?
5. What happens when you overflow an `int` variable, that is, set it to a value beyond its range?
6. What is the difference between `x = y++;` and `x = ++y;`?
7. What is the difference between `break`, `continue`, and `return` when used inside a loop statement?
8. What are the three parts of a `for` statement and which of them are required?
9. What is the difference between the = and == operators?
10. Does the following statement compile? `for ( ; true; ) ;`

Exercise 3.2 – explore loops and overflow

What will happen if this code executes?

```
int max = 500;
for (byte i = 0; i < max; i++)
{
  WriteLine(i);
}
```

Add a new console application named `Ch03_Exercise02` and enter the preceding code. Run the console application and view the output. What happens?

What code could you add (don't change any of the preceding code) to warn us about the problem?

Exercise 3.3 – practice loops and operators

FizzBuzz is a group word game for children to teach them about division. Players take turns to count incrementally, replacing any number divisible by three with the word "fizz", any number divisible by five with the word "buzz", and any number divisible by both with "fizzbuzz".

Some interviewers give applicants simple FizzBuzz-style problems to solve during interviews. Most good programmers should be able to write out on paper or whiteboard a program to output a simulated FizzBuzz game in under a couple of minutes.

Want to know something worrisome? Many computer science graduates can't. You can even find senior programmers who take more than 10-15 minutes to write a solution.

> *"199 out of 200 applicants for every programming job can't write code at all. I repeat: they can't write any code whatsoever."*
>
> *-Reginald Braithwaite*

This quote is taken from `http://blog.codinghorror.com/why-cant-programmers-program/`.

Refer to the following link for more information:

`http://imranontech.com/2007/01/24/using-fizzbuzz-to-find-developers-who-grok-coding/`

Create a console application named `Ch03_Exercise03` that outputs a simulated FizzBuzz game counting up to 100. The output should look something like this:

```
    1, 2, Fizz, 4, Buzz, Fizz, 7, 8, Fizz, Buzz, 11, Fizz, 13, 14,
FizzBuzz, 16, 17,
    Fizz, 19, Buzz, Fizz, 22, 23, Fizz, Buzz, 26, Fizz,  28, 29, FizzBuzz,
31, 32,
    Fizz, 34, Buzz, Fizz, 37, 38, Fizz, Buzz,  41, Fizz, 43, 44, FizzBuzz,
46, 47,
    Fizz, 49, Buzz, Fizz, 52, 53,  Fizz, Buzz, 56, Fizz, 58, 59, FizzBuzz,
61, 62,
    Fizz, 64, Buzz, Fizz,  67, 68, Fizz, Buzz, 71, Fizz, 73, 74, FizzBuzz,
76, 77,
    Fizz, 79,  Buzz, Fizz, 82, 83, Fizz, Buzz, 86, Fizz, 88, 89, FizzBuzz,
91, 92,
    Fizz, 94, Buzz, Fizz, 97, 98, Fizz, Buzz
```

Exercise 3.4 – practice exception handling

Create a console application named `Ch03_Exercise04` that asks the user for two numbers in the range 0-255 and then divides the first number by the second:

```
Enter a number between 0 and 255: 100
Enter another number between 0 and 255: 8
100 divided by 8 is 12
```

Write exception handlers to catch any thrown errors:

```
Enter a number between 0 and 255: apples
Enter another number between 0 and 255: bananas
FormatException: Input string was not in a correct format.
```

Exercise 3.5 – explore topics

Use the following links to read in more detail about the topics covered in this chapter:

- **Selection Statements (C# Reference)**: `https://docs.microsoft.com/en-us/dotnet/articles/csharp/language-reference/keywords/selection-statements`
- **Iteration Statements (C# Reference)**: `https://docs.microsoft.com/en-us/dotnet/articles/csharp/language-reference/keywords/iteration-statements`
- **Jump Statements (C# Reference)**: `https://docs.microsoft.com/en-us/dotnet/articles/csharp/language-reference/keywords/jump-statements`
- **Casting and Type Conversions (C# Programming Guide)**: `https://docs.microsoft.com/en-us/dotnet/articles/csharp/programming-guide/types/casting-and-type-conversions`
- **Exception Handling Statements (C# Reference)**: `https://docs.microsoft.com/en-us/dotnet/articles/csharp/language-reference/keywords/exception-handling-statements`
- **StackOverflow**: `http://stackoverflow.com/`
- **Google Advanced Search**: `http://www.google.com/advanced_search`
- **.NET Blog:** `https://blogs.msdn.microsoft.com/dotnet/`
- **What .NET Developers ought to know to start in 2017:** `https://www.hanselman.com/blog/WhatNETDevelopersOughtToKnowToStartIn2017.aspx`
- **CoreFX README.md:** `https://github.com/dotnet/corefx/blob/master/Documentation/README.md`
- **Design Patterns**: `https://msdn.microsoft.com/en-us/library/ff649977.aspx`
- **patterns & practices**: `https://msdn.microsoft.com/en-us/library/ff921345.aspx`

Summary

In this chapter, you learned how to branch and loop, how to convert between types, how to handle exceptions, and most importantly, how to find help!

You are now ready to learn more about what is underneath C#—the .NET Core types that are included with .NET Standard.

4

Using .NET Standard Types

This chapter is about .NET Standard 1.6 types that are included with .NET Core 1.0 and 1.1. This includes common types for manipulating text, collections, and implementing internationalization. You will learn how the .NET types are related to C#.

You will learn about .NET Core and its class library assemblies and packages of types that are defined in .NET Standard that allow your applications to connect existing components together to perform common practical tasks.

This chapter covers the following topics:

- Using assemblies and namespaces
- Storing and manipulating text
- Storing data with collections
- Internationalizing an application

Using assemblies and namespaces

.NET Core is made up of several pieces, which are as follows:

- **Language compilers**: These turn your source code (written with languages such as C#, F#, Visual Basic, and others) into **intermediate language** (**IL**) code stored in assemblies (applications and class libraries). C# 6 introduced a completely rewritten compiler known as Roslyn.
- **Common Language Runtime (CoreCLR)**: The runtime loads assemblies, compiles the IL code stored in them into native code instructions for your computer's CPU, and executes the code within an environment that manages resources such as threads and memory.

- **Base Class Libraries and NuGet packages (CoreFX)**: These are prebuilt assemblies of types for performing common tasks when building applications. You can use them to quickly build anything you want, rather like combining LEGO™ pieces. .NET Core 1.0 and 1.1 are based on .NET Standard 1.6, which is a superset of all previous versions of .NET Standard.

Comparing .NET Framework with .NET Core

The .NET Framework is a superset of .NET Core.

Although .NET Core has less functionality today, once .NET Core 2.0 is released in late summer 2017, with support for .NET Standard 2.0, .NET Core will have comparable functionality to .NET Framework. Going forward, Microsoft has said that new features will be added to .NET Core first, and then ported back to .NET Framework.

Base Class Libraries and CoreFX

The .NET Framework's BCL and the .NET Core's CoreFX are libraries of prebuilt code that are divided into assemblies and namespaces that make it easier to manage the tens of thousands of types available. It is important to understand the difference between an assembly and a namespace.

Assemblies, NuGet packages, and platforms

An **assembly** is where a type is stored in the filesystem. Assemblies are a mechanism for deploying code. For example, the `System.Data.dll` assembly contains types for managing data. To use types in other assemblies, they must be referenced.

Assemblies are often distributed as **NuGet packages**, which can contain multiple assemblies and other resources. You will also hear talk about **platforms**, which are combinations of NuGet packages.

To search for useful NuGet packages, follow:

`https://www.nuget.org/packages`

When using .NET Core, you reference the dependency assemblies, NuGet packages, and platforms that your application needs in a project file.

The original project file for .NET Core was a JSON format file named `project.json`. The "newer" format is an XML file with the extension `.csproj`. I say "newer" because it is actually the old format that has been used since the beginning of .NET. Microsoft changed their mind after the release of .NET Core 1.0!

Namespaces

A **namespace** is the address of a type. Namespaces are a mechanism to uniquely identify a type by requiring a full address rather than just a short name.

In the real world, *Bob* of *34 Sycamore Street* is different from *Bob* of *12 Willow Drive*.

In .NET Core, the `IActionFilter` interface of the `System.Web.Mvc` namespace is different from the `IActionFilter` interface of the `System.Web.Http.Filters` namespace.

Referencing a dependent assembly

If an assembly is compiled as a **class library** (it provides types for other assemblies to use), then it has the file extension `.dll` (**dynamic link library**) and it cannot be executed standalone, except by the `dotnet run` command.

If an assembly is compiled as an **application**, then it has the file extension `.exe` (executable) and can be executed standalone.

Any assembly (both applications and class libraries) can reference one or more class library assemblies as dependencies, but you cannot have circular references, so assembly *B* cannot reference assembly *A* if assembly *A* already references assembly *B*. Visual Studio will warn you if you attempt to add a dependency reference that would cause a circular reference.

Every application created for .NET Core has a dependency reference to the **Microsoft .NET Core App platform**. This special platform contains thousands of types in NuGet packages that almost all applications would need, such as the `int` and `string` variables.

Browsing assemblies with Visual Studio 2017

Using Visual Studio 2017, if you open one of your previous projects, and navigate to **View** | **Object Browser**, or press *Ctrl* + *W*, *J*, then you will see that your solution has dependencies on assemblies such as `System.Collections` that you will use later in this chapter, and on `System.Console`, used in all the coding exercises so far, as shown in the following screenshot:

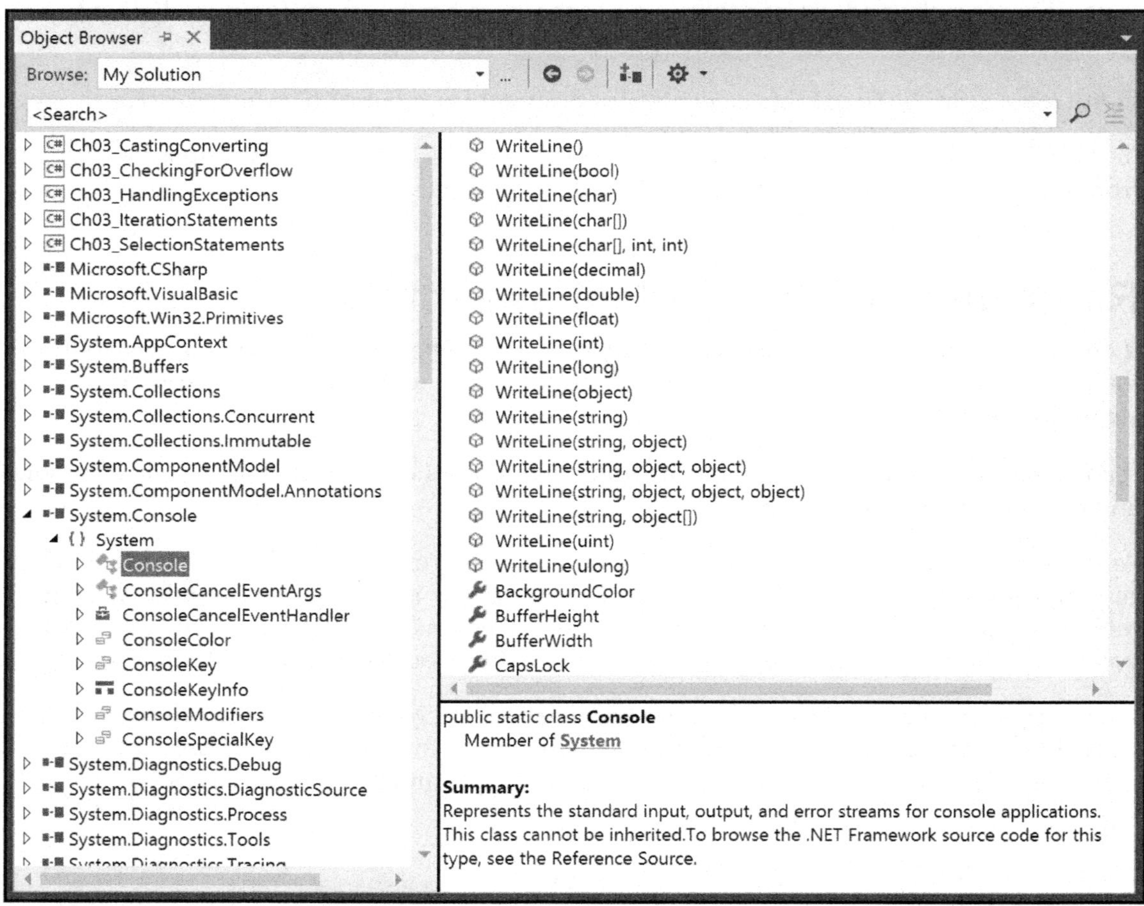

Object Browser can be used to learn about the assemblies and namespaces that .NET Core uses to logically and physically group types together.

Unfortunately, Visual Studio Code does not yet have an equivalent feature.

When you click on an assembly in **Object Browser**, you can see the version of .NET Standard that the assembly was first released with. For example, `System.Console.dll` was introduced in .NET Standard 1.3, as shown in the following screenshot:

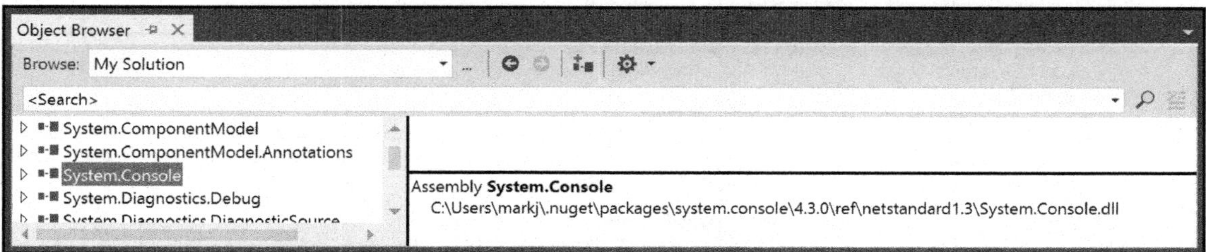

In the following screenshot, you can see that `System.IO.dll` was released as part of .NET Standard 1.5:

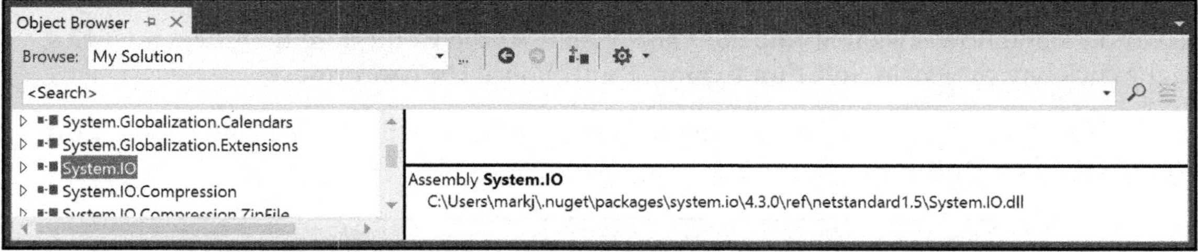

Later in this chapter, you will learn about generic collections, like `List<T>`, that are part of the `System.Collections.dll` assembly, as shown in the following screenshot:

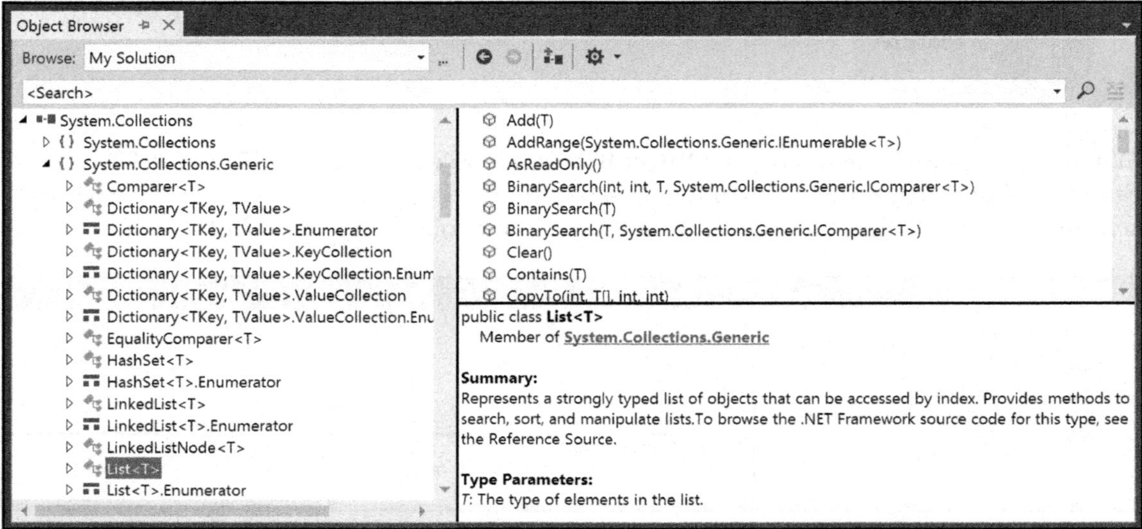

Understanding .NET Core project files

To understand how Visual Studio 2017 and Visual Studio Code store their dependencies, right-click any project in **Solution Explorer** and choose **Unload Project**.

The project will now be marked as **(unavailable)**. Right-click the project and choose **Edit <projectname>.csproj**:

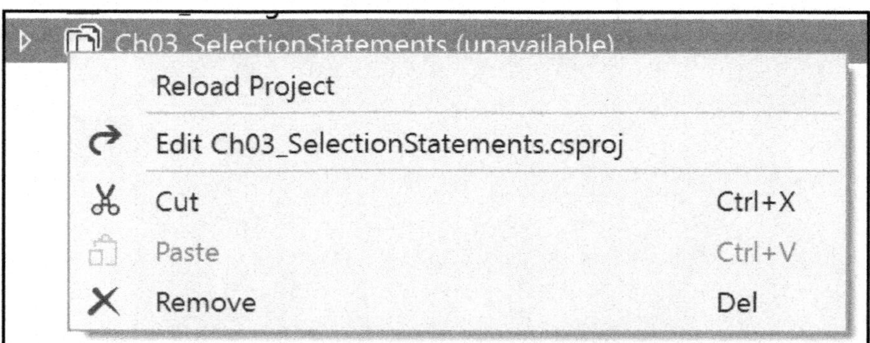

If you are using Visual Studio Code, simply open the `.csproj` file.

This action will open the project file and reveal the XML inside, as shown in the following markup:

```
<Project Sdk="Microsoft.NET.Sdk">

  <PropertyGroup>
    <OutputType>Exe</OutputType>
    <TargetFramework>netcoreapp1.1</TargetFramework>
  </PropertyGroup>

</Project>
```

Note the `<TargetFramework>` of `netcoreapp1.1`

Close the file.

In Visual Studio 2017, right-click the project, and choose **Reload Project**.

Visual Studio 2017 *should* allow you to view and modify the `.csproj` file without unloading the project first, but I have found that it works more reliably if you explicitly unload and reload.

Relating assemblies and namespaces

In Visual Studio 2017, press *Ctrl* + *Shift* + *N* or navigate to **File** | **New** | **Project...**.

In the **New Project** dialog, in the **Installed** | **Templates** list, select **Visual C#**. In the list at the center, select **Console App (.NET Core)**, type the name `Ch04_Assemblies`, change the location to `C:\Code`, type the solution name `Chapter04`, and then click on **OK**.

In Visual Studio Code, use the Integrated Terminal to create a folder named `Chapter04` with a subfolder named `Ch04_Assemblies`. Use `dotnet new console` to create a console application and restore packages.

Inside the `Main` method, type the following code:

```
var doc = new XDocument();
```

The `XDocument` type is not recognized because we have not told the compiler what the namespace of the type is. Although this project already has a reference to the assembly that contains the type, we also need to either prefix the type name with its namespace or to import the namespace. We can get Visual Studio to fix this problem for us.

Importing a namespace

Click inside the `XDocument` class name. Visual Studio 2017 and Visual Studio Code both display a light bulb showing that it recognizes the type and can automatically fix the problem for you.

Click on the light bulb, or in Visual Studio 2017 press *Ctrl* + . (dot), or in Visual Studio Code press *Cmd* + . (dot).

Visual Studio 2017 shows a nicer explanation of your choices, and a preview of its suggested changes, as shown in the following screenshot:

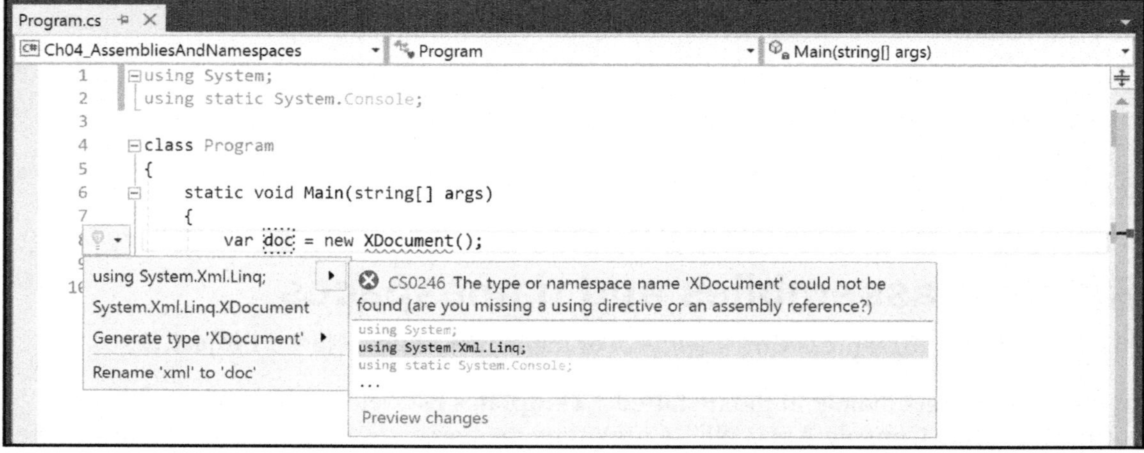

Visual Studio Code has no explanations, but it does have the same choices, as shown in the following screenshot:

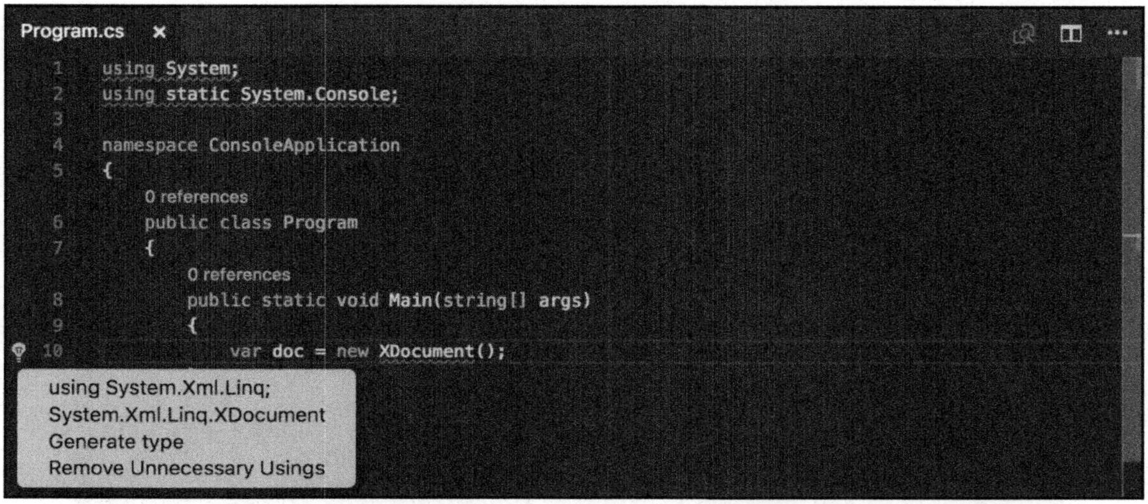

Choose `using System.Xml.Linq;` from the menu. This will **import the namespace** by adding a `using` statement to the top of the file.

Once a namespace is imported at the top of a code file, then all the types within the namespace are available for use in that code file by just typing their name.

Relating C# keywords to .NET types

One of the common questions I get from new C# programmers is, "What is the difference between `string` with a lowercase and `String` with an uppercase?"

The short answer is easy: none.

The long answer is that all C# type keywords are aliases for a .NET type in a class library assembly.

When you use the keyword `string`, the compiler turns it into a `System.String` type. When you use the type `int`, the compiler turns it into a `System.Int32` type. You can even see this if you hover your mouse over an `int` type, as follows:

Program.cs ×

```
using System;
using System.Xml.Linq;

namespace Ch04_Assemblies
{
    0 references
    class Program
    {
        Represents a 32-bit signed integer.To browse the .NET Framework source code for
        this type, see the Reference Source.
        System.Int32
            int age = 12;
        }
    }
}
```

Good Practice
Use the C# keyword instead of the actual type because the keywords do not need the namespace imported.

The following table shows the 16 C# type keywords and their actual .NET types:

Keyword	**.NET type**	**Keyword**	**.NET type**
`string`	`System.String`	`char`	`System.Char`
`sbyte`	`System.SByte`	`byte`	`System.Byte`
`short`	`System.Int16`	`ushort`	`System.UInt16`
`int`	`System.Int32`	`uint`	`System.UInt32`
`long`	`System.Int64`	`ulong`	`System.UInt64`
`float`	`System.Single`	`double`	`System.Double`
`decimal`	`System.Decimal`	`bool`	`System.Boolean`
`object`	`System.Object`	`dynamic`	`System.Dynamic.DynamicObject`

Other .NET programming language compilers can do the same thing. For example, the Visual Basic .NET language has a type named `Integer` that is its alias for `System.Int32`.

Storing and manipulating text

The most common type of data for variables is text. The most common types in .NET for working with text are show in the following table:

Namespace	Type
`System`	`Char`
`System`	`String`
`System.Text`	`StringBuilder`
`System.Text.RegularExpressions`	`Regex`

Getting the length of a string

Add a new console application project named `Ch04_ManipulatingText`.

In Visual Studio 2017, set the solution's startup project to be the current selection.

Sometimes, you need to find out the length of a piece of text stored in a `string` class. Modify the code to look like this:

```
using static System.Console;

namespace Ch04_ManipulatingText
{
  class Program
  {
    static void Main(string[] args)
    {
      string city = "London";
      WriteLine($"{city} is {city.Length} characters long.");
    }
  }
}
```

At any point during these exercises, you can see the output of your code by running the console application. In Visual Studio 2017, press *Ctrl* + *F5*. In Visual Studio Code, open the Integrated Terminal and enter the command `dotnet run`.

Getting the characters of a string

A `string` class uses an array of `char` internally to store the text. It also has an indexer, which means that we can use the array syntax to read its characters.

Add the following statement, and then run the console application:

```
WriteLine($"First char is {city[0]} and third is {city[2]}.");
```

Splitting a string

Sometimes, you need to split some text wherever there is a character, such as a comma.

Add more lines of code to define a single string with comma-separated city names. You can use the `Split` method and specify a character that you want to treat as the separator. An array of strings is then created that you can enumerate using a `foreach` statement:

```
string cities = "Paris,Berlin,Madrid,New York";
string[] citiesArray = cities.Split(',');
foreach (string item in citiesArray)
{
  WriteLine(item);
}
```

Getting part of a string

Sometimes, you need to get part of some text. For example, if you had a person's full name stored in a string with a space character between the first and last name, then you could find the position of the space and extract the first name and last name as two parts, like this:

```
string fullname = "Alan Jones";
int indexOfTheSpace = fullname.IndexOf(' ');
string firstname = fullname.Substring(0, indexOfTheSpace);
string lastname = fullname.Substring(indexOfTheSpace + 1);
WriteLine($"{lastname}, {firstname}");
```

If the format of the initial full name was different, for example, `Lastname, Firstname`, then the code would be slightly different. As an optional exercise, try writing some statements that would change the input `Jones, Alan` into `Alan Jones`.

Checking a string for content

Sometimes, you need to check whether a piece of text starts or ends with some characters or contains some characters:

```
string company = "Microsoft";
bool startsWithM = company.StartsWith("M");
bool containsN = company.Contains("N");
WriteLine($"Starts with M: {startsWithM}, contains an N:
{containsN}");
```

Other string members

Here are some other `string` members:

Member	Description
`Trim`, `TrimStart`, and `TrimEnd`	These trim whitespaces from the beginning and/or end of the `string`.
`ToUpper` and `ToLower`	These convert the `string` into uppercase or lowercase.
`Insert` and `Remove`	These insert or remove some text in the `string`.
`Replace`	This replaces some text.
`String.Concat`	This concatenates two `string` variables. The + operator calls this method when used between `string` variables.
`String.Join`	This concatenates one or more `string` variables with a character in between each one.
`String.IsEmptyOrNull`	This checks whether a `string` is empty (`""`) or null.
`String.Empty`	This can be used instead of allocating memory each time you use a literal `string` value using an empty pair of double quotes (`""`).

Note that some of the preceding methods are **static** methods. That means the method can only be called from the type, not from a variable instance.

For example, if I want to take an array of strings and combine them back together into a single `string` with a separator, I can use the `Join` method like this:

```
string recombined = string.Join(" => ", citiesArray);
WriteLine(recombined);
```

If you run the console application and view the output, it should look like this:

```
London is 6 characters long.
First char is L and third is n.
Paris
Berlin
Madrid
New York
Jones, Alan
Starts with M: True, contains an N: False
Paris => Berlin => Madrid => New York
```

Building strings efficiently

You can concatenate two strings to make a new `string` using the `String.Concat` method or simply using the + operator. But, this is a bad practice because .NET must create a completely new `string` in memory. This might not be noticeable if you are only adding two `string` variables, but if you concatenate inside a loop, it can have a significant negative impact on performance and memory use.

In `Chapter 5`, *Debugging, Monitoring, and Testing*, you will learn how to concatenate `string` variables efficiently using the `StringBuilder` type.

Pattern matching with regular expressions

Regular expressions are useful for validating input from the user. They are very powerful and can get very complicated. Almost all programming languages have support for regular expressions and use a common set of special characters to define them.

Add a new console application project named `Ch04_RegularExpressions`.

At the top of the file, import the following namespaces:

```
using System.Text.RegularExpressions;
using static System.Console;
```

In the `Main` method, add the following statements:

```
Write("Enter your age: ");
string input = ReadLine();
Regex ageChecker = new Regex(@"\d");
if(ageChecker.IsMatch(input))
{
  WriteLine("Thank you!");
}
else
{
  WriteLine($"This is not a valid age: {input}");
}
```

Good Practice
The `@` character in front of a `string` switches off the ability to use escape characters in a `string`. Escape characters are prefixed with a backslash (\). For example, `\t` means a tab and `\n` means a new line. When writing regular expressions, we need to disable this feature. To paraphrase the television show, *The West Wing*, "Let backslash be backslash."

Run the console application and view the output.

If you enter a whole number for the age, you will see `Thank you!`

```
Enter your age: 34
Thank you!
```

If you enter `carrots`, you will see the error message:

```
Enter your age: carrots
This is not a valid age: carrots
```

However, if you enter `bob30smith`, you will see `Thank you!`

```
Enter your age: bob30smith
Thank you!
```

The regular expression we used is `\d`, which means one digit. However, it does not limit what is entered *before* and *after* the digit. This regular expression could be described in English as, "Enter at least one digit character."

Change the regular expression to ^\d$, like this:

```
Regex ageChecker = new Regex(@"^\d$");
```

Rerun the application. Now, it rejects anything except a single digit.

We want to allow one or more digits. To do this, we add a + (plus) after the digit expression. Change the regular expression to look like this:

```
Regex ageChecker = new Regex(@"^\d+$");
```

Run the application and see how the regular expression now only allows positive whole numbers of any length.

The syntax of a regular expression

Here are some common symbol combinations that you can use in regular expressions:

Symbol	Meaning	Symbol	Meaning
^	Start of input	$	End of input
\d	A single digit	\D	A single NON-digit
\w	Whitespace	\W	NON-whitespace
[A-Za-z0-9]	Range(s) of characters	[AEIOU]	Set of characters
+	One or more	?	One or none
.	A single character		
{3}	Exactly three	{3,5}	Three to five
{3,}	Three or more	{,3}	Up to three

Examples of regular expressions

Here are some example regular expressions:

Expression	Meaning
\d	A single digit somewhere in the input.
a	The a character somewhere in the input.
Bob	The word Bob somewhere in the input.

`^Bob`	The word `Bob` at the start of the input.
`Bob$`	The word `Bob` at the end of the input.
`^\d{2}$`	Exactly two digits.
`^[0-9]{2}$`	Exactly two digits.
`^[A-Z]{4,}$`	At least four uppercase letters only.
`^[A-Za-z]{4,}$`	At least four upper or lowercase letters only.
`^[A-Z]{2}\d{3}$`	Two uppercase letters and three digits only.
`^d.g$`	The letter `d`, then any character, and then the letter `g`, so it would match both `dig` and `dog` or any characters between the `d` and `g`.
`^d\.g$`	The letter `d`, then a dot (`.`), and then the letter `g`, so it would match `d.g` only.

Good Practice
Use regular expressions to validate input from the user. The same regular expressions can be reused in other languages such as JavaScript.

Storing data with collections

If you need to store multiple values in a variable, then you can use a **collection**.

A **collection** is a data structure in memory that can manage multiple items in different ways, although all collections have some shared functionality.

There are three main assemblies and namespaces for collections:

- `System.Collections.dll` assembly and `System.Collections.Generic` namespace: The types in this assembly and namespace were introduced in C# 2 with .NET 2.0 and are better because they allow you to specify the type you want to store (which is safer, faster, and more efficient).
- `System.Collections.Concurrent` assembly and namespace: the types in this assembly and namespace are safe to use in multi-threaded scenarios (see `Chapter 12`, *Improving Performance and Scalability with Multitasking*).
- `System.Collections.Immutable` assembly and namespace: the types in this assembly and namespace are designed for scenarios where the contents of the collection should never change.

All collections have a `Count` property to tell you how many items are in it. For example, if we had a collection named `passengers`, we could do this:

```
int howMany = passengers.Count;
```

All collections can be iterated using the `foreach` statement. To perform some action on all the items in the passengers' collection, we can do this:

```
foreach (var passenger in passengers)
{
  // do something with each passenger
}
```

Understanding collections

There are several different collection categories: lists, dictionaries, stacks, queues, sets, and many other more specialized collections.

Lists

Lists are a good choice when you want to manually control the order of items in a collection. Each item in a list has a unique index (or position) that is automatically assigned. Items can be any type (although they should all be the same type) and items can be duplicated. Indexes are `int` types and start from **0**, so the first item in a list is at index **0**, as shown in the following table:

Index	Item
0	London
1	Paris
2	London
3	Sydney

If a new item (for example, **Santiago**) is inserted between **London** and **Sydney**, then index of **Sydney** is automatically incremented. Therefore, you must be aware that an item's index can change after inserting or removing items, as shown in the following table:

Index	Item
0	London

1	Paris
2	London
3	Santiago
4	Sydney

Dictionaries

Dictionaries are a good choice when each value (or item) has a unique subvalue (or a made-up value) that can be used as a key to quickly find the value in the collection later. The key must be unique. If you are storing a list of people, you can use a government-issued identity number as the key.

Think of the key as being like an index entry in a real-world dictionary. It allows you to quickly find the definition of a word because the words (for example, keys) are kept sorted, and if we know we're looking for the definition of *Manatee*, we would jump to the middle of the dictionary to start looking because the letter M is in the middle of the alphabet. Dictionaries in programming are similarly smart when looking something up.

Both the key and the value can be any type. This example uses strings for both:

Key	**Value**
BSA	Bob Smith
MW	Max Williams
BSB	Bob Smith
AM	Amir Mohammed

Stacks

Stacks are a good choice when you want to implement the **last-in, first-out (LIFO)** behavior. With a stack, you can only directly access the one item at the top of the stack, although you can enumerate to read through the whole stack of items. You cannot, for example, access the second item in a stack.

For example, word processors use a stack to remember the sequence of actions you have recently performed, and then when you press *Ctrl* + *Z*, it will undo the last action in the stack, and then the next last action, and so on.

Queues

Queues are a good choice when you want to implement the **first-in, first out** (**FIFO**) behavior. With a queue, you can only directly access the one item at the front of the queue, although you can enumerate to read through the whole queue of items. You cannot, for example, access the second item in a queue.

For example, background processes use a queue to process work items in the order that they arrive, just like people standing in line at the post office.

Sets

Sets are a good choice when you want to perform set operations between two collections. For example, you may have two collections of city names, and you want to know which names appear in both sets (known as the **intersect** between the sets).

Working with lists

Add a new console application project named `Ch04_Lists`.

At the top of the file, import the following namespaces:

```
using System;
using System.Collections.Generic;
using static System.Console;
```

In the `Main` method, type the following code that illustrates some of the common ways of working with lists:

The angle brackets after the `List<T>` type is a feature of C# called **generics**. It's just a fancy term for making a collection **strongly typed**, that is, the compiler knows more specifically what type of object can be stored in the collection. Generics improve the performance and correctness of your code. Strong typed is different from **statically typed**. The old `System.Collection` types are statically typed to contain weakly typed `System.Object` items. The newer `System.Collection.Generic` types are statically typed to contain strongly typed `<T>` instances. Ironically, the term "generics" means a more specific static type!

```
var cities = new List<string>();
cities.Add("London");
cities.Add("Paris");
```

```
cities.Add("Milan");
WriteLine("Initial list");
foreach (string city in cities)
{
  WriteLine($"  {city}");
}
WriteLine($"The first city is {cities[0]}.");
WriteLine($"The last city is {cities[cities.Count - 1]}.");
cities.Insert(0, "Sydney");
WriteLine("After inserting Sydney at index 0");
foreach (string city in cities)
{
  WriteLine($"  {city}");
}
cities.RemoveAt(1);
cities.Remove("Milan");
WriteLine("After removing two cities");
foreach (string city in cities)
{
  WriteLine($"  {city}");
}
```

Run the console application to see the output:

```
Initial list
  London
  Paris
  Milan
The first city is London.
The last city is Milan.
After inserting Sydney at index 0
  Sydney
  London
  Paris
  Milan
After removing two cities
  Sydney
  Paris
```

Working with dictionaries

Add a new console application project named `Ch04_Dictionaries`.

Import the same namespaces as before.

In the `Main` method, type the following code that illustrates some of the common ways of working with dictionaries:

```
var keywords = new Dictionary<string, string>();
keywords.Add("int", "32-bit integer data type");
keywords.Add("long", "64-bit integer data type");
keywords.Add("float", "Single precision floating point number");
WriteLine("Keywords and their definitions");
foreach (KeyValuePair<string, string> item in keywords)
{
  WriteLine($"  {item.Key}: {item.Value}");
}
WriteLine($"The definition of long is {keywords["long"]}");
```

Run the application to view the output:

```
Keywords and their definitions
  int: 32-bit integer data type
  long: 64-bit integer data type
  float: Single precision floating point number
The definition of long is 64-bit integer data type
```

Sorting collections

A `List<T>` class can be sorted by calling its `Sort` method (but remember that the indexes of each item will change).

Sorting a list of strings or other built-in types works automatically, but if you create a collection of your own type, then that type must implement an interface named `IComparable`. You will learn how to do this in `Chapter 7`, *Implementing Interfaces and Inheriting Classes*.

A `Dictionary<T>`, `Stack<T>`, or `Queue<T>` class cannot be sorted because you wouldn't usually want that functionality, for example, you would never sort a queue of guests checking into a hotel. But sometimes, you might want to sort a dictionary or a set.

The differences between these sorted collections are often subtle, but can have an impact on the memory requirements and performance of your application, so it is worth putting effort into picking the most appropriate for your requirements.

Collection	Description
`SortedDictionary<TKey, TValue>`	This represents a collection of key/value pairs that are sorted on the key

SortedList<TKey, TValue>	This represents a collection of key/value pairs that are sorted by key, based on the associated IComparer<T> implementation
SortedSet<T>	This represents a collection of objects that is maintained in a sorted order

Using specialized collections

There are a few other collections for special situations.

Collection	Description
System.Collections.BitArray	This manages a compact array of bit values, which are represented as Booleans, where true indicates that the bit is on (1) and false indicates the bit is off (0)
System.Collections .Generics.LinkedList<T>	This represents a doubly-linked list where every item has a reference to its previous and next item

Internationalizing an application

Internationalization is the process of enabling your application to run correctly all over the world. It has two parts: **globalization** and **localization**.

Globalization is about writing your code to accommodate multiple languages and regions. The combination of a language and a region is known as a culture. It is important for your code to know both the language and region because the date and currency formats are different in Quebec and Paris, despite them both using French.

There are **International Standards Organization** (**ISO**) codes for all culture combinations. For example, in the code da-DK, da indicates the Danish language and DK indicates the country of Denmark.

Localization is about customizing the user interface to support a language. Since localization is just about the language, it doesn't need to know about the region.

Internationalization is a huge topic on which entire books have been written. In this section, you will get a brief introduction to the basics using the CultureInfo type in the System.Globalization namespace.

.NET Core does not currently allow threads to get or set their `CurrentCulture` or `CurrentUICulture` properties. An alternative for getting these two properties (but not setting) is to use the `CultureInfo` class' static properties, but you cannot set them.

Globalizing an application

Add a new console application project named `Ch04_Internationalization`. At the top of the file, import the following types and namespaces:

```
using static System.Console;
using System;
using System.Globalization;
```

In the `Main` method, enter the following statements:

```
CultureInfo globalization = CultureInfo.CurrentCulture;
CultureInfo localization = CultureInfo.CurrentUICulture;
WriteLine($"The current globalization culture is
{globalization.Name}: {globalization.DisplayName}");
WriteLine($"The current localization culture is
{localization.Name}: {localization.DisplayName}");
WriteLine();
WriteLine("en-US: English (United States)");
WriteLine("da-DK: Danish (Denmark)");
WriteLine("fr-CA: French (Canada)");
Write("Enter an ISO culture code: ");
string newculture = ReadLine();
if (!string.IsNullOrEmpty(newculture))
{
  var ci = new CultureInfo(newculture);
  CultureInfo.CurrentCulture = ci;
  CultureInfo.CurrentUICulture = ci;
}
Write("Enter your name: ");
string name = ReadLine();
Write("Enter your date of birth: ");
string dob = ReadLine();
Write("Enter your salary: ");
string salary = ReadLine();
DateTime date = DateTime.Parse(dob);
int minutes = (int)DateTime.Today.Subtract(date).TotalMinutes;
decimal earns = decimal.Parse(salary);
WriteLine($"{name} was born on a {date:dddd} and is {minutes:N0}
minutes old and earns {earns:C}.");
```

When you run an application, it automatically sets its thread to use the culture of the operating system. I am running my code in London, UK, so the thread is already set to English (United Kingdom).

The code prompts the user to enter an alternative ISO code. This allows your applications to replace the default culture at runtime.

The application then uses standard format codes to output the day of the week, `dddd`; the number of minutes with thousand separators, `N0`; and the salary with the currency symbol, `C`. These adapt automatically, based on the thread's culture.

Run the console application and view the output. Enter `en-GB` for the ISO code and then enter some sample data. You will need to enter a date in a format valid for British English:

```
Enter an ISO culture code: en-GB
Enter your name: Alice
Enter your date of birth: 30/3/1967
Enter your salary: 23500
Alice was born on a Thursday, is 25,469,280 minutes old and earns
£23,500.00.
```

Rerun the application and try a different culture, such as Danish in Denmark (`da-DK`):

```
Enter an ISO culture code: da-DK
Enter your name: Mikkel
Enter your date of birth: 12/3/1980
Enter your salary: 34000
Mikkel was born on a onsdag, is 18.656.640 minutes old and earns kr.
34.000,00.
```

Good Practice
Consider whether your application needs to be internationalized and plan for that before you start coding! Write down all the pieces of text in the user interface that will need to be localized. Think about all the data that will need to be globalized (date formats, number formats, and sorting text behavior).

Practicing and exploring

Test your knowledge and understanding by answering some questions, get some hands-on practice, and explore with deeper research into topics of this chapter.

Exercise 4.1 – test your knowledge

Use the Web to answer the following questions:

1. What is the maximum number of characters that can be stored in a `string`?
2. When and why should you use a `SecureString`?
3. When is it appropriate to use a `StringBuilder`?
4. When should you use a `LinkedList`?
5. When should you use a `SortedDictionary` class rather than a `SortedList` class?
6. What is the ISO culture code for Welsh?
7. What is the difference between localization, globalization, and internationalization?
8. In a regular expression, what does $ mean?
9. In a regular expression, how could you represent digits?
10. Why should you *not* use the official standard for e-mail addresses to create a regular expression to validate a user's e-mail address?

Exercise 4.2 – practice regular expressions

Create a console application named `Ch04_Exercise02` that prompts the user to enter a regular expression, and then prompts the user to enter some input and compare the two for a match until the user presses *Esc*:

```
The default regular expression checks for at least one digit.
Enter a regular expression (or press ENTER to use the default): ^[a- z]+$
Enter some input: apples
apples matches ^[a-z]+$? True
Press ESC to end or any key to try again.
Enter a regular expression (or press ENTER to use the default): ^[a- z]+$
Enter some input: abc123xyz
abc123xyz matches ^[a-z]+$? False
Press ESC to end or any key to try again.
```

Exercise 4.3 – explore topics

Use the following links to read in more detail the topics covered in this chapter:

- **.NET Core API Reference**: `https://docs.microsoft.com/en-us/dotnet/core/api/index`
- **String Class**: `https://docs.microsoft.com/en-us/dotnet/core/api/system.string`
- **Regex Class**: `https://docs.microsoft.com/en-us/dotnet/core/api/system.text.regularexpressions.regex`
- **Regular expressions in .NET**: `https://docs.microsoft.com/en-us/dotnet/articles/standard/base-types/regular-expressions`
- **Regular Expression Language – Quick Reference**: `https://docs.microsoft.com/en-us/dotnet/articles/standard/base-types/quick-ref`
- **RegExr: Learn, Build, & Test RegEx**: `http://regexr.com/`
- **Collections (C# and Visual Basic)**: `https://docs.microsoft.com/en-us/dotnet/core/api/system.collections`

Summary

In this chapter, you explored the relationship between assemblies and namespaces, you learned about good choices for types to use to store and manipulate text and which collections to use for storing multiple items, and how to internationalize your code.

In the next chapter, you will learn about debugging, monitoring, and unit testing.

5
Debugging, Monitoring, and Testing

This chapter is about debugging tools, monitoring, diagnosing problems, and testing your code, to remove bugs and ensure high performance, stability, and reliability.

This chapter covers the following topics:

- Debugging tools
- Monitoring performance and resource usage
- Unit testing an application

Debugging tools

In this section, you will learn how to debug problems at design time, trace problems at runtime, and use types such as `Debug`, `Trace`, `Process`, and `Stopwatch` that are in the `System.Diagnostics` namespace.

Debugging an application

For Visual Studio 2017, press *Ctrl* + *Shift* + *N*, or navigate to **File** | **New** | **Project...**.

In the **New Project** dialog, from the **Installed** | **Templates** list, select **Visual C#**. In the list at the center, select **Console App (.NET Core)**, type the name `Ch05_Debugging`, change the location to `C:\Code`, type the solution name `Chapter05`, and then click on **OK**.

For Visual Studio Code, create a new folder named `Chapter05`, create a new subfolder named `Ch05_Debugging`, and open the folder in Visual Studio Code. In the Integrated Terminal pane, enter the `dotnet new console` command, and restore packages.

Modify the template code to look like this:

```
using static System.Console;

namespace Ch05_Debugging
{
  class Program
  {
    static double Add(double a, double b)
    {
      return a * b; // deliberate bug!
    }

    static void Main(string[] args)
    {
      double a = 4.5; // or use var
      double b = 2.5;
      double answer = Add(a, b);
      WriteLine($"{a} + {b} = {answer}");
      ReadLine(); // wait for user to press ENTER
    }
  }
}
```

Run the console application and view the output:

```
4.5 + 2.5 = 11.25
```

There is a bug: `4.5` added to `2.5` should be `7` and not `11.25`!

We will use the debugging tools in Visual Studio 2017 or Visual Studio Code to squash the bug.

Setting a breakpoint

Breakpoints allow us to mark a line of code that we want to pause at to find bugs. Click on the open curly brace at the beginning of the `Main` method and press *F9*.

A red circle will appear in the margin bar on the left-hand side to indicate that a breakpoint has been set, as shown in the following screenshot:

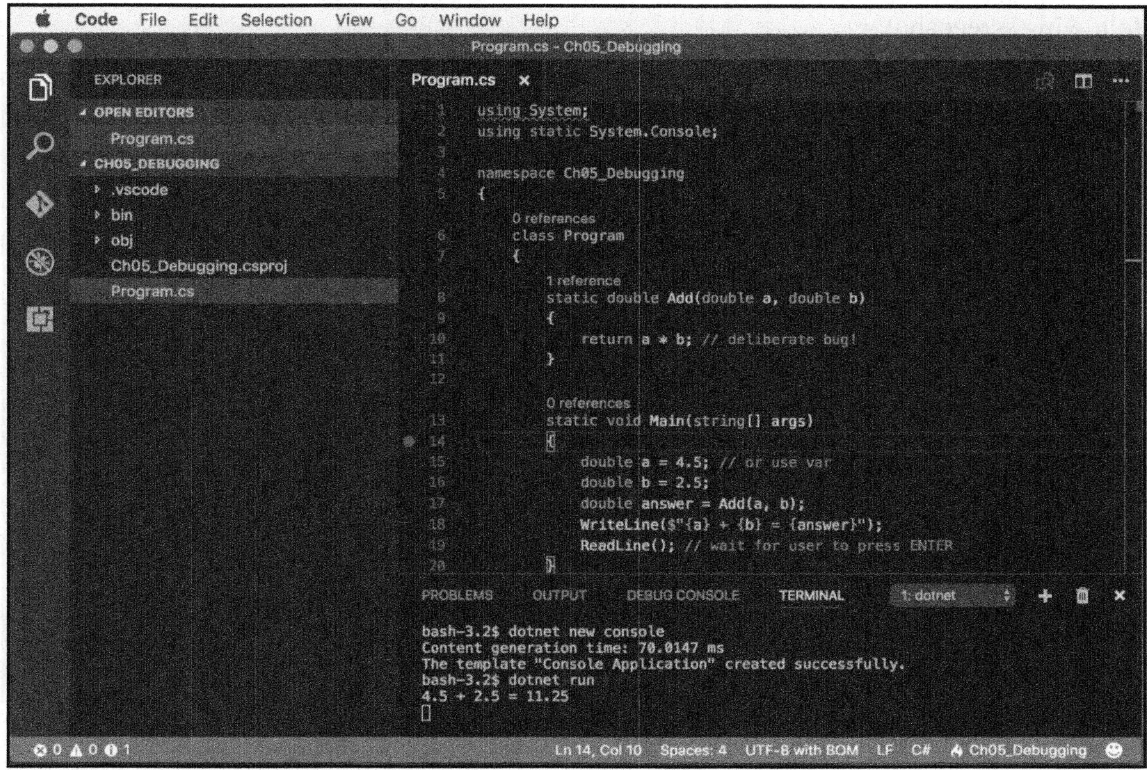

Breakpoints can be toggled with *F9*. You can also left-click in the margin to toggle the breakpoint on and off, or right-click to see more options, like remove, disable, or edit the breakpoint.

In Visual Studio 2017, go to **Debug** | **Start Debugging**, or click on the Start toolbar button, or press *F5*.

In Visual Studio Code, go to **View** | **Debug**, or press *Shift* + *Cmd* + *D*, and then click on the **Start Debugging** button, or press *F5*.

Visual Studio starts the console application executing and then pauses when it hits the breakpoint. This is known as **break mode**. The line that will be executed next is highlighted in yellow and a yellow arrow points at the line from the gray margin bar, as shown in the following screenshot:

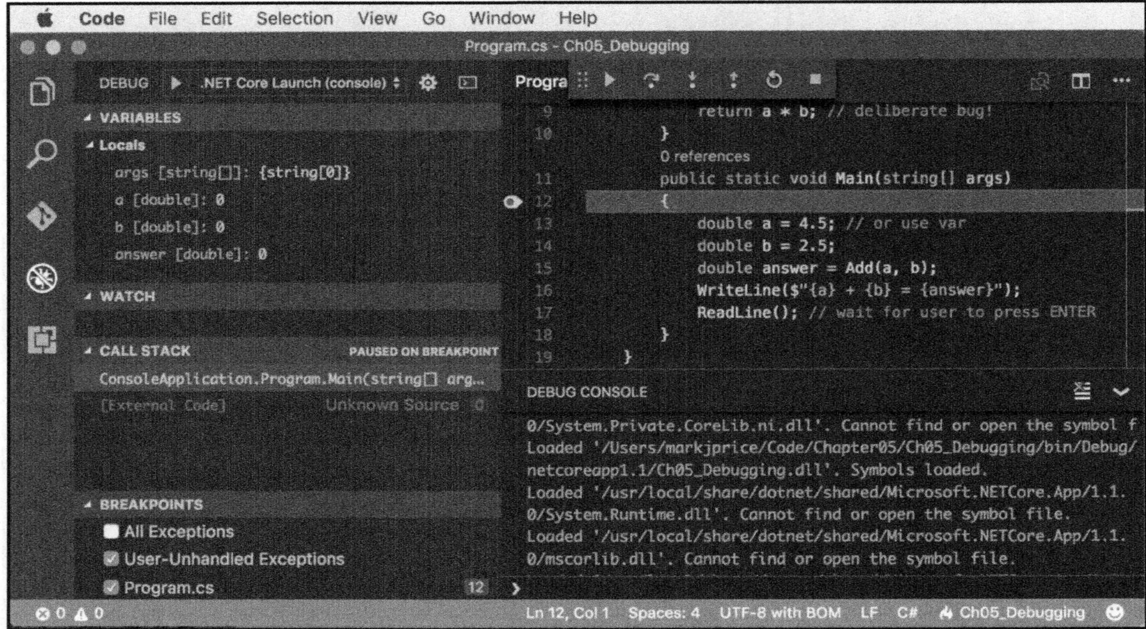

The debugging toolbar

Visual Studio 2017 enables some extra toolbar buttons to make it easy to access debugging features. Here are a few of those:

- **Continue**/*F5* (green triangle): This button will run the code at full speed from the current position
- **Stop Debugging**/*Shift* + *F5* (red square): This button will stop the program
- **Restart**/*Ctrl* or *Cmd* + *Shift* + *F5* (circular black arrow): This button will stop and then immediately restart the program
- **Step into**/*F11*, **Step over**/*F10*, and **Step out**/*Shift* + *F11* (blue arrows over dots): This button will step through the code in various ways

The following screenshot illustrates Visual Studio 2017's extra toolbar buttons:

The following screenshot illustrates Visual Studio Code's extra toolbar buttons:

Debugging windows

Visual Studio 2017 makes some extra windows visible so that you can monitor useful information, such as variables, while you step through your code. If you cannot find one of these windows, then, in Visual Studio 2017, on the **Debug** menu, choose **Windows**, and then select the window you want to view, as shown in the following screenshot:

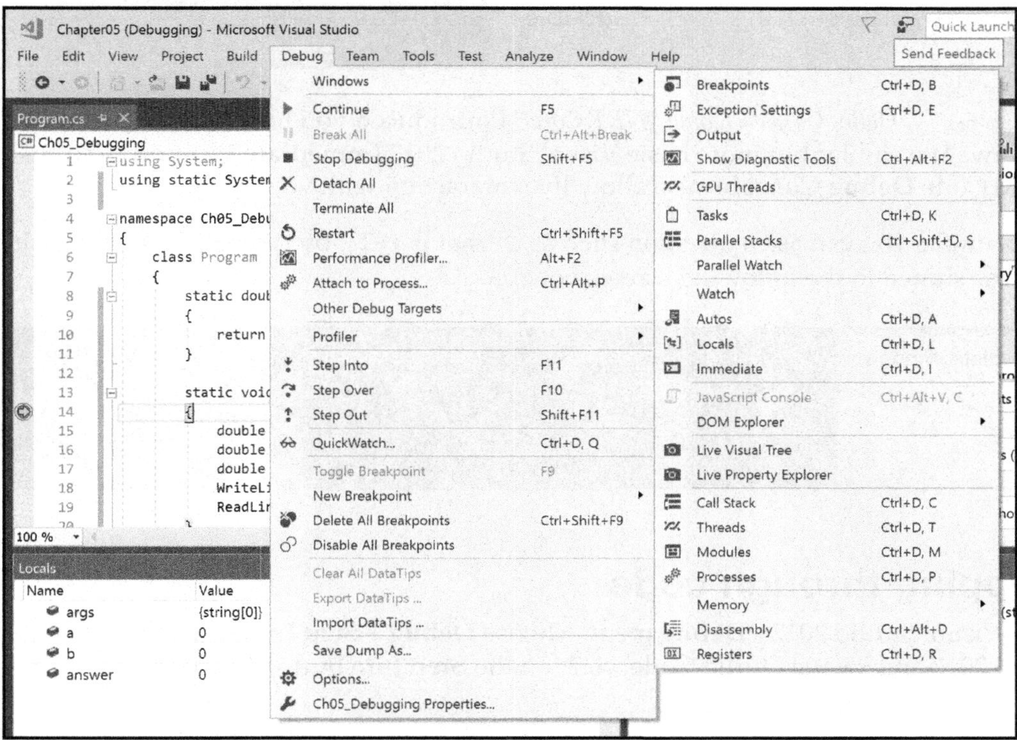

Most of the debug windows are only available when you are in the **Break** mode.

In Visual Studio Code, the windows are all in the **Debug** view on the left-hand side, as shown in the earlier screenshot.

The **Locals** windows in Visual Studio 2017 and Visual Studio Code, show the name, value, and type for any local variables. Keep an eye on this window while you step through your code, as shown in the following screenshots:

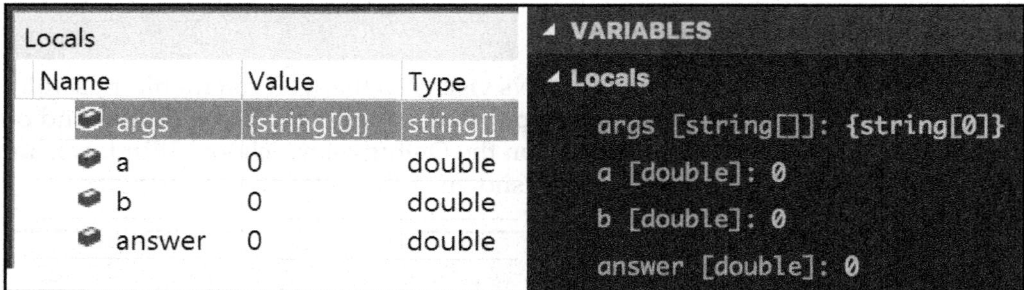

In `Chapter 1`, *Hello, C#!, Welcome, .NET Core!*, I introduced you to the **C# Interactive window**. The similar but more basic Visual Studio 2017 **Immediate Window**, and Visual Studio Code **Debug Console**, also allow live interaction with your code.

For example, you can ask a question such as, "What is 1+2?" by typing `1+2` and pressing *Enter*, as shown in the following screenshots:

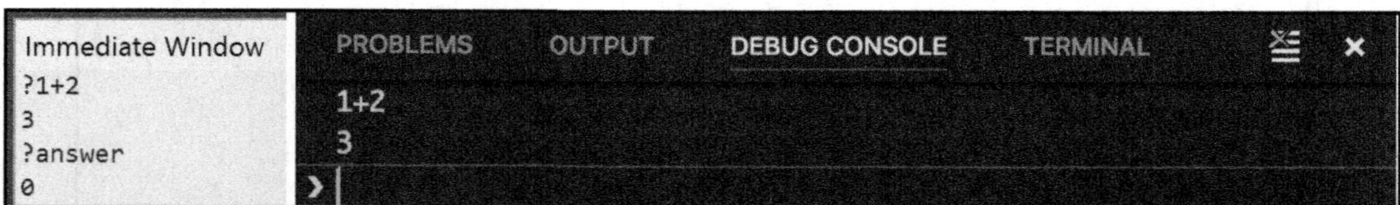

Stepping through code

From Visual Studio 2017's **Debug** menu, choose **Debug** | **Step Into**, or in both Visual Studio 2017 and Visual Studio Code, click on the **Step Into** button in the toolbar, or press *F11*.

The yellow highlight steps forward one line, as shown in the following screenshot:

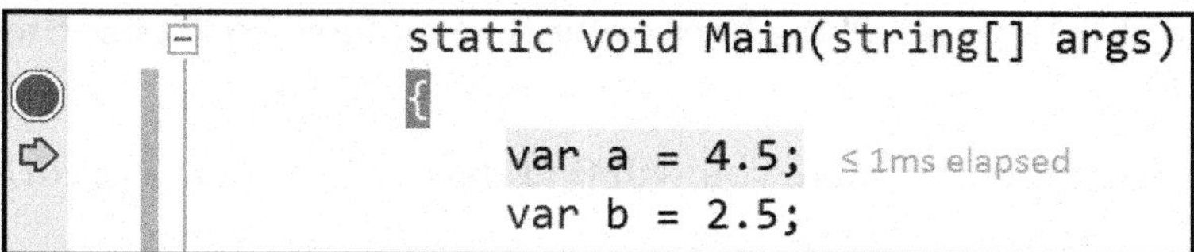

Choose **Debug** | **Step Over** or press *F10*. The yellow highlight steps forward one line. At the moment, there is no difference between using **Step Into** or **Step Over**.

Press *F10* again so that the yellow highlight is on the line that calls the `Add` method:

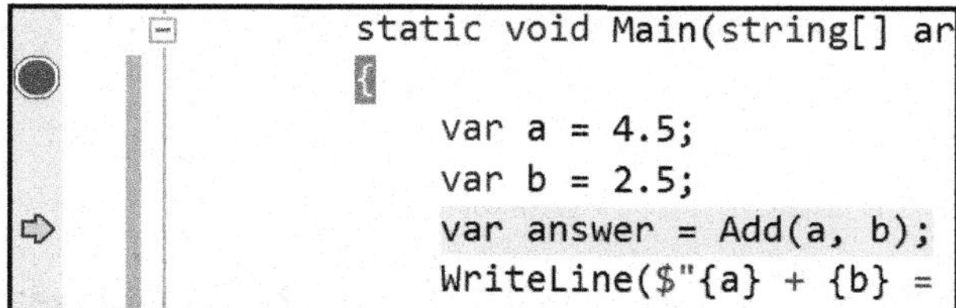

The difference between **Step Into** or **Step Over** can be seen when you are about to execute a method call. If you click on **Step Into**, the debugger steps *into* the method so that you can step through every line in that method. If you click on **Step Over**, the whole method is executed in one go; it does *not* skip over the method!

Click on **Step Into** to step inside the method. If you are using Visual Studio 2017, hover your mouse over the multiply (`*`) operator. A tooltip will appear, showing that this operator is multiplying `a` by `b` to give the result `11.25`. We can see that this is the bug. You can pin the tooltip by clicking on the pin icon as I have done here:

```
static double Add(double a, double b)
{  ≤ 20ms elapsed
    return a * b;      a * b 11.25
}
```

Visual Studio Code does not have the hover and pin features.

Fix the bug by changing the `*` to `+`.

We don't need to step through all the lines in the `Add` method, so choose **Step Out** or press *Shift* + *F11*.

If you rerun the console application, you will find that it now calculates correctly.

Customizing breakpoints

You can also right-click on a breakpoint and choose additional options, such as **Conditions...**, as shown in the following screenshot:

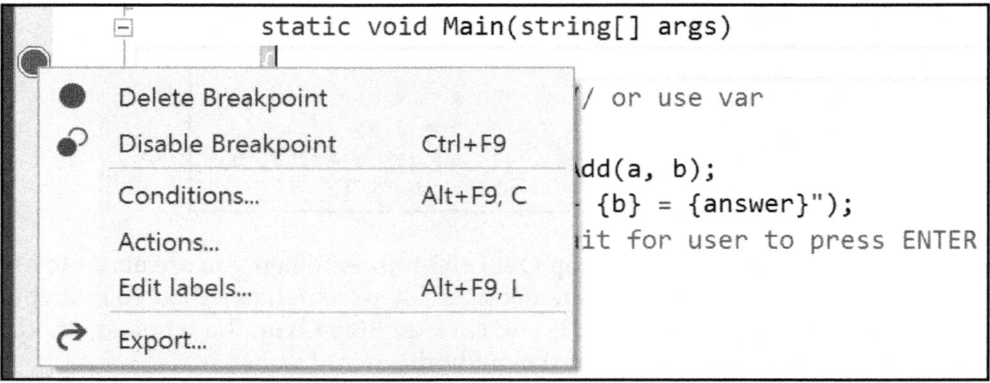

The conditions for a breakpoint include an expression that must be `true` and a hit count to reach for the breakpoint to apply.

In the example, as you can see in the following screenshot, I have set a condition to only apply the breakpoint if both the answer variable is greater than `9` and we have hit the breakpoint three times:

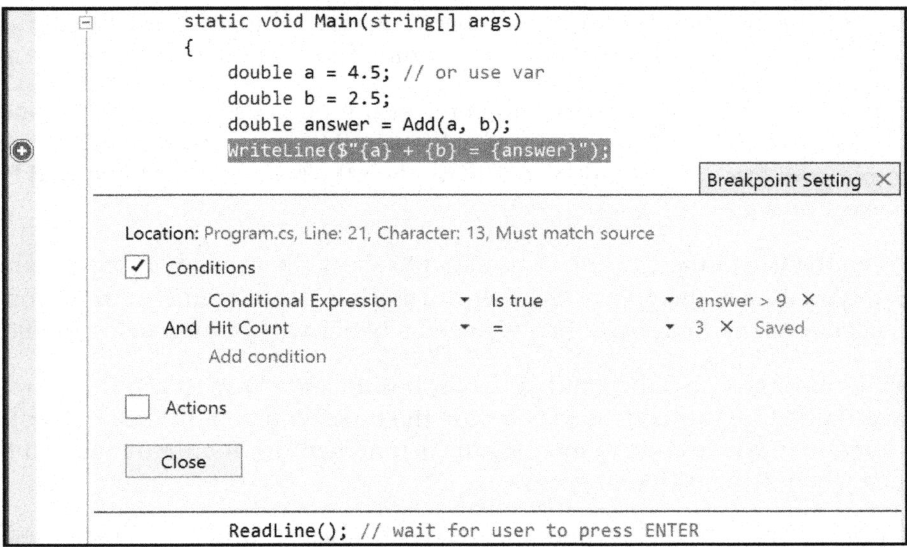

Visual Studio Code has similar, but more limited customization options.

You have now fixed a bug using some of Visual Studio's debugging features.

Monitoring performance and resource usage

To write high quality applications, we need to be able to monitor the speed and efficiency of our code.

Evaluating the efficiency of types

What is the best type to use for a scenario? To answer this question, we need to carefully consider what we mean by best. We should consider the following factors:

- **Functionality**: This can be decided by checking whether the type provides the features you need
- **Memory size**: This can be decided by the number of bytes of memory the type takes up
- **Performance**: This can be decided by how fast the type is
- **Future needs**: This depends on the changes in requirements and maintainability

There will be scenarios, such as storing numbers, where multiple types have the same functionality, so we will need to consider the memory and performance to make a choice.

If we need to store millions of numbers, then the best type to use would be the one that requires the least number of bytes of memory. If we only need to store a few numbers, but we need to perform lots of calculations on them, then the best type to use would be the one that runs fastest on a CPU.

You have seen the use of the `sizeof()` function to show the number of bytes a single instance of a type uses in memory. When we are storing lots of values in more complex data structures, such as arrays and lists, then we need a better way of measuring memory usage.

You can read lots of advice online and in books, but the only way to know for sure what the best type would be for your code is to compare the types yourself. In the next section, you will learn how to write the code to monitor the actual memory requirements and the actual performance when using different types.

Although, today a `short` variable might be the best choice, it might be a better choice to use an `int` variable even though it takes twice as much space in memory because we might need a wider range of values to be stored in the future.

There is another metric we should consider: maintenance. This is a measure of how much effort another programmer would have to put to understand and modify your code. If you use a nonobvious type choice, it might confuse the programmer who comes along later and needs to fix a bug or add a feature. There are analyzing tools that will generate a report that shows how easily maintainable your code is.

Monitoring performance and memory use

The `System.Diagnostics` namespace has lots of useful types for monitoring your code. The first one we will look at is the `Stopwatch` type.

Add a new console application project named `Ch05_Monitoring`. Set the solution's start up project to be the current selection.

Modify the code to look like this:

```
using System;
using System.Diagnostics;
using System.Linq;
using static System.Console;
using static System.Diagnostics.Process;
```

```
namespace Ch05_Monitoring
{
  class Recorder
  {
    static Stopwatch timer = new Stopwatch();
    static long bytesPhysicalBefore = 0;
    static long bytesVirtualBefore = 0;

    public static void Start()
    {
      GC.Collect();
      GC.WaitForPendingFinalizers();
      GC.Collect();
      bytesPhysicalBefore = GetCurrentProcess().WorkingSet64;
      bytesVirtualBefore =
        GetCurrentProcess().VirtualMemorySize64;
      timer.Restart();
    }

    public static void Stop()
    {
      timer.Stop();
      long bytesPhysicalAfter = GetCurrentProcess().WorkingSet64;
      long bytesVirtualAfter =
        GetCurrentProcess().VirtualMemorySize64;
      WriteLine("Stopped recording.");
      WriteLine($"{bytesPhysicalAfter - bytesPhysicalBefore:N0}
      physical bytes used.");
      WriteLine($"{bytesVirtualAfter - bytesVirtualBefore:N0}
      virtual bytes used.");
      WriteLine($"{timer.Elapsed} time span ellapsed.");
      WriteLine($"{timer.ElapsedMilliseconds:N0} total
      milliseconds ellapsed.");
    }
  }

  class Program
  {
    static void Main(string[] args)
    {
      Write("Press ENTER to start the timer: ");
      ReadLine();
      Recorder.Start();

      int[] largeArrayOfInts =
        Enumerable.Range(1, 10000).ToArray();

      Write("Press ENTER to stop the timer: ");
```

```
            ReadLine();
            Recorder.Stop();
            ReadLine();
        }
    }
}
```

The `Start` method of the `Recorder` class uses the **garbage collector** (**GC**) type to ensure that all the currently allocated memory is collected before recording the amount of used memory. This is an advanced technique that you should almost never use in production code.

You have created a class named `Recorder` with two methods to start and stop recording the time and memory used by any code you run. The `Main` method starts recording when the user presses Enter, creates an array of ten thousand `int` variables, and then stops recording when the user presses **Enter** again.

The `Stopwatch` type has some useful members, as shown in the following table:

Member	Description
The `Restart` method	This resets the elapsed time to zero and then starts the stopwatch.
The `Stop` method	This stops the stopwatch.
The `Elapsed` property	This is the elapsed time stored as a `TimeSpan` (*hours:minutes:seconds*).
The `ElapsedMilliseconds` property	This is the elapsed time in milliseconds stored as a long integer.

The `Process` type has some useful members, as shown in the following table:

Member	Description
`VirtualMemorySize64`	This displays the amount of the virtual memory, in bytes, allocated for the process.
`WorkingSet64`	This displays the amount of physical memory, in bytes, allocated for the process.

Run the console application without the debugger attached. The application will start recording the time and memory used when you press *Enter* and then stop recording when you press *Enter* again. Wait for a few seconds between pressing *Enter* twice, as you can see that I did with the following output:

```
Press ENTER to start the timer:
Press ENTER to stop the timer:
Stopped recording.
942,080 physical bytes used.
0 virtual bytes used.
00:00:03.1166037 time span ellapsed.
3,116 total milliseconds ellapsed.
```

Measuring the efficiency of processing strings

Now that you've seen how the `Stopwatch` and `Process` types can be used to monitor your code, we will use them to evaluate the best way to process string variables.

Comment out the previous code in the `Main` method by wrapping it in `/* */`.

Add the following code to the `Main` method. It creates an array of ten thousand `int` variables and then concatenates them with commas for separators using a `string` and a `StringBuilder`:

```
int[] numbers = Enumerable.Range(1, 10000).ToArray();
Recorder.Start();
WriteLine("Using string");
string s = "";
for (int i = 0; i < numbers.Length; i++)
{
  s += numbers[i] + ", ";
}
Recorder.Stop();
Recorder.Start();
WriteLine("Using StringBuilder");
var builder = new System.Text.StringBuilder();
for (int i = 0; i < numbers.Length; i++)
{
  builder.Append(numbers[i]);
  builder.Append(", ");
}
Recorder.Stop();
ReadLine();
```

Run the console application and view the output:

```
Using string
Stopped recording.
7,540,736 physical bytes used.
69,632 virtual bytes used.
00:00:00.0871730 time span ellapsed.
87 total milliseconds ellapsed.
Using StringBuilder
Stopped recording.
8,192 physical bytes used.
0 virtual bytes used.
00:00:00.0015680 time span ellapsed.
1 total milliseconds ellapsed.
```

We can summarize the results as follows:

- The `string` class used about 7.5 MB of memory and took 133 milliseconds
- The `StringBuilder` class used 8 KB of memory and took 1.5 milliseconds

In this scenario, `StringBuilder` is about one hundred times faster and about one thousand times more memory efficient when concatenating text!

Good Practice
Avoid using the `String.Concat` method or the + operator with `string` variables. Instead, use `StringBuilder` or C# `$` string interpolation to concatenate variables together, especially inside loops.

Unit testing an application

Microsoft has a proprietary unit testing framework known as MS Test, which is closely integrated with Visual Studio. However, to use a unit testing framework that is compatible with .NET Core, we will use the third-party framework: **xUnit.net**.

Creating a class library that needs testing with Visual Studio 2017

In Visual Studio 2017, add a new **Class Library (.NET Standard)** project named `Ch05_Calculator`, as shown in the following screenshot:

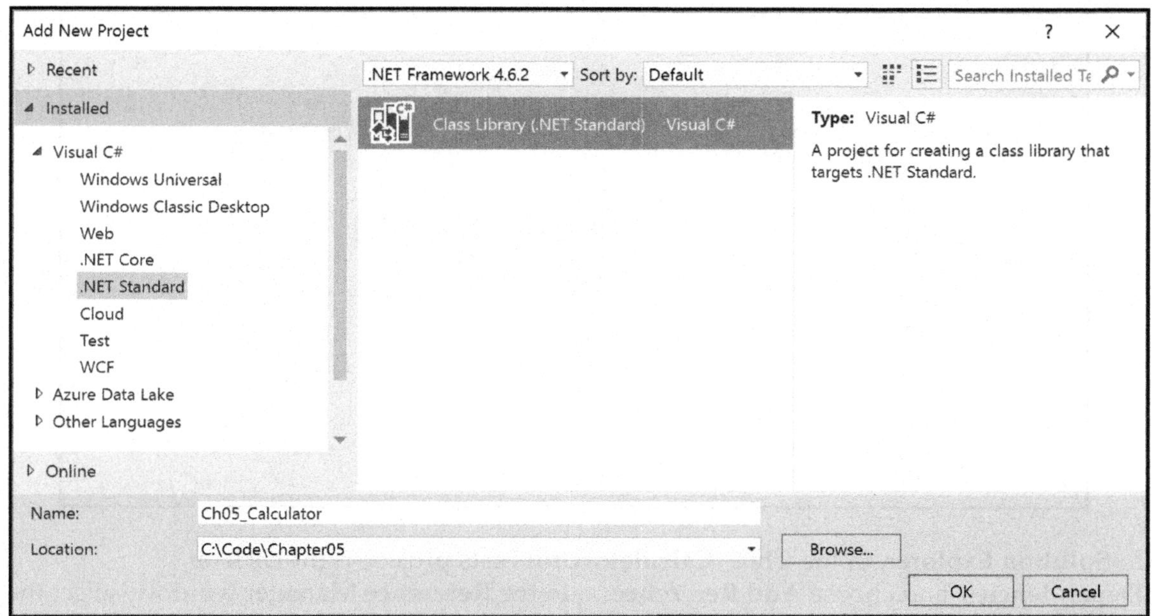

In Visual Studio 2017, in the **Solution Explorer** window, right-click on the `Class1.cs` file and choose **Rename**. Change its name to `Calculator`. You will be prompted to rename all references. Click **Yes**.

Modify the code to look like this (note the deliberate bug!):

```
namespace Ch05_Calculator
{
  public class Calculator
  {
    public double Add(double a, double b)
    {
      return a * b;
    }
  }
}
```

Creating a unit test project with Visual Studio 2017

In Visual Studio 2017, add a new **xUnit Test Project (.NET Core)** project named `Ch05_CalculatorUnitTests`, as shown in the following screenshot:

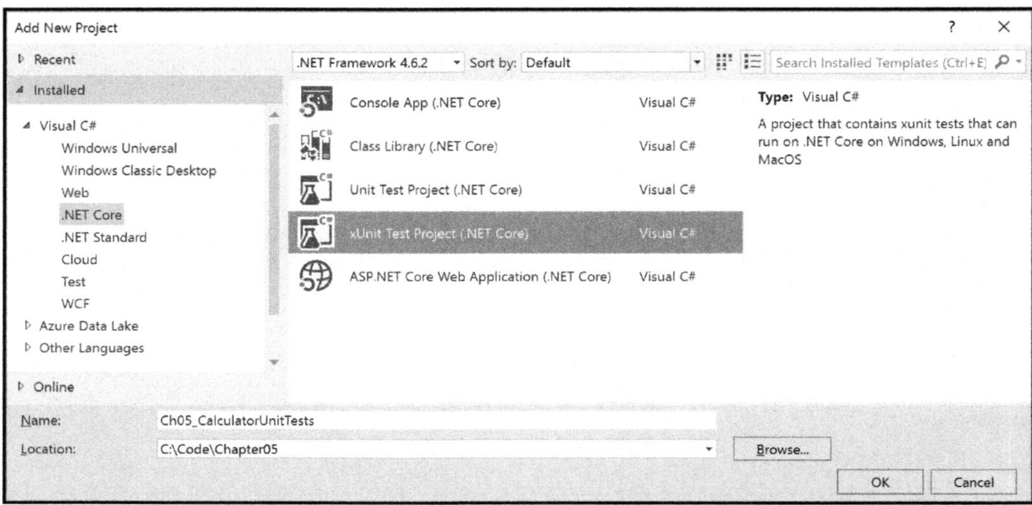

In **Solution Explorer**, in the **Ch05_CalculatorUnitTests** project, right-click on **Dependencies**, and choose **Add Reference...**. In the **Reference Manager** window, select the checkbox for `Ch05_Calculator` and then click on **OK**:

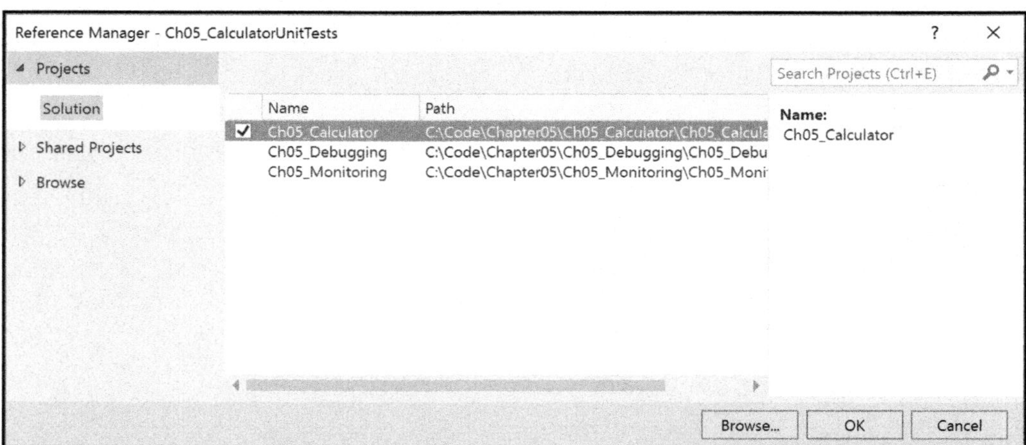

In the **Solution Explorer** window, right-click on the `UnitTest1.cs` file and choose **Rename**. Change its name to `CalculatorUnitTests`. Click **Yes** when prompted.

Creating a class library that needs testing with Visual Studio Code

Inside the `Chapter05` folder, create a subfolder named `Ch05_Calculator`, and a subfolder named `Ch05_CalculatorUnitTests`.

In Visual Studio Code, open the `Ch05_Calculator` folder, and enter the following command in the Integrated Terminal window:

```
dotnet new classlib
```

Rename the file named `Class1.cs` to `Calculator.cs`, and modify the code to look like this (note the deliberate bug!):

```
namespace Ch05_Calculator
{
  public class Calculator
  {
    public double Add(double a, double b)
    {
      return a * b;
    }
  }
}
```

Enter the following commands in the Integrated Terminal window:

```
dotnet restore
dotnet build
```

Open the `Ch05_CalculatorUnitTests` folder, and enter the following command in the Integrated Terminal window:

```
dotnet new xunit
```

Click on the file named `Ch05_CalculatorUnitTests.csproj` and modify the configuration as shown highlighted in the following markup:

```
<Project Sdk="Microsoft.NET.Sdk">

  <PropertyGroup>
    <TargetFramework>netcoreapp1.1</TargetFramework>
  </PropertyGroup>

  <ItemGroup>
    <PackageReference Include="Microsoft.NET.Test.Sdk"
                      Version="15.0.0" />
    <PackageReference Include="xunit" Version="2.2.0" />
    <PackageReference Include="xunit.runner.visualstudio"
                      Version="2.2.0" />
  </ItemGroup>

  <ItemGroup>
    <ProjectReference
      Include="..\Ch05_Calculator\Ch05_Calculator.csproj" />
  </ItemGroup>

</Project>
```

Note the project reference to the `Ch05_Calculator` class library project.

Rename the file named `UnitTest1.cs` to `CalculatorUnitTests.cs`.

Writing unit tests

In Visual Studio 2017 and Visual Studio Code, open the file named `CalculatorUnitTests.cs` and then modify the code to look like this:

```
using Ch05_Calculator;
using Xunit;

namespace Ch05_CalculatorUnitTests
{
  public class CalculatorUnitTests
  {
    [Fact]
    public void TestAdding2And2()
```

```
        {
          // arrange
          double a = 2;
          double b = 2;
          double expected = 4;
          var calc = new Calculator();
          // act
          double actual = calc.Add(a, b);
          // assert
          Assert.Equal(expected, actual);
        }
        [Fact]
        public void TestAdding2And3()
        {
          // arrange
          double a = 2;
          double b = 3;
          double expected = 5;
          var calc = new Calculator();
          // act
          double actual = calc.Add(a, b);
          // assert
          Assert.Equal(expected, actual);
        }
      }
    }
```

A well-written unit test will have three parts:

- **Arrange**: This part will declare and instantiate variables for input and output
- **Act**: This part will execute the unit that you are testing
- **Assert**: This part will make one or more assertions about the output

Running unit tests with Visual Studio 2017

Navigate to **Test** | **Windows** | **Test Explorer**.

Navigate to **Build** | **Build Solution**, or press *F6*.

In **Test Explorer**, click **Run All**.

Wait for a few seconds for the tests to complete, as shown in the following screenshot. Note that one test passed and the other failed. This is why it is good to write multiple tests for each unit:

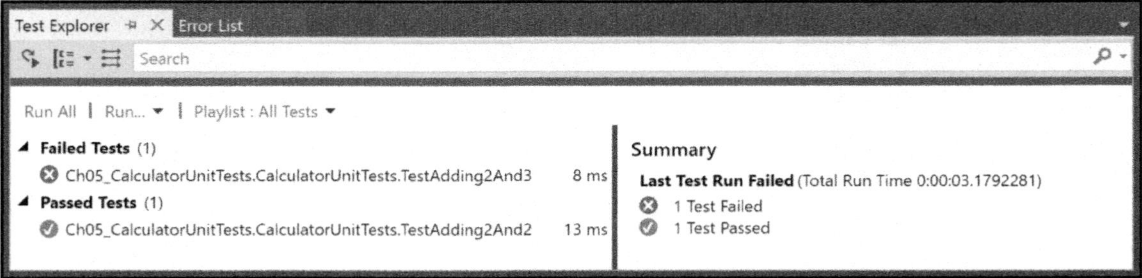

Clicking on a test shows more details and, from there, we should be able to diagnose the bug and fix it:

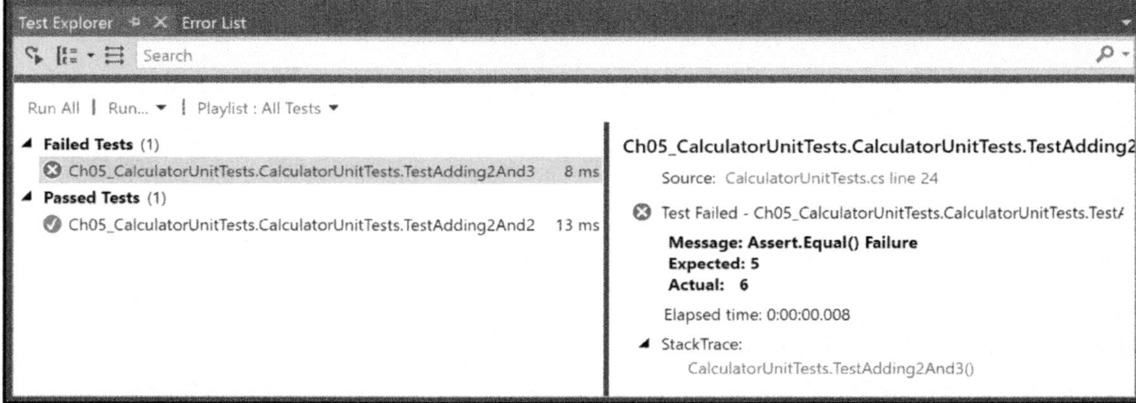

Fix the bug in the `Add` method, and then rerun the unit tests to see that the bug is now fixed, as shown in the following screenshot:

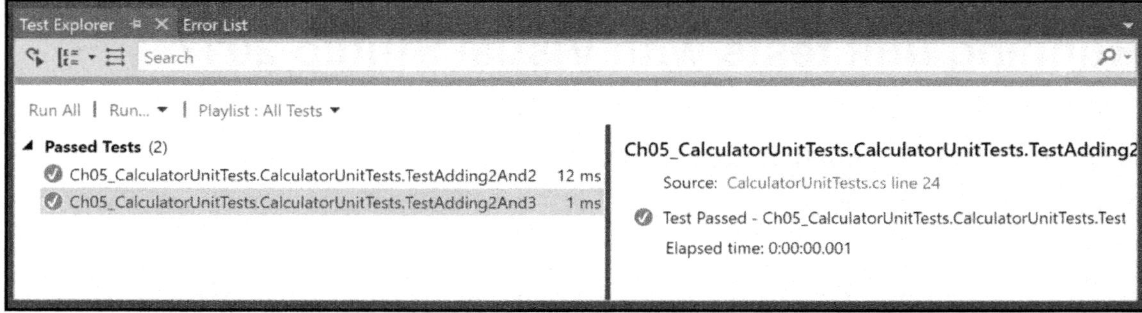

Running unit tests with Visual Studio Code

At the Integrated Terminal, enter the following command:

```
dotnet test
```

You should see the following results:

```
PROBLEMS    OUTPUT    DEBUG CONSOLE    TERMINAL    1: bash

Test run for /Users/markjprice/Code/Chapter05/Ch05_CalculatorUnitTests/bin/Debug/netc
oreapp1.1/Ch05_CalculatorUnitTests.dll(.NETCoreApp,Version=v1.1)
Microsoft (R) Test Execution Command Line Tool Version 15.0.0.0
Copyright (c) Microsoft Corporation.  All rights reserved.

Starting test execution, please wait...
[xUnit.net 00:00:00.7751594]   Discovering: Ch05_CalculatorUnitTests
[xUnit.net 00:00:00.8965400]   Discovered:  Ch05_CalculatorUnitTests
[xUnit.net 00:00:00.9499252]   Starting:    Ch05_CalculatorUnitTests
[xUnit.net 00:00:01.0906369]     Ch05_CalculatorUnitTests.CalculatorUnitTests.TestAdd
ing2And3 [FAIL]
[xUnit.net 00:00:01.0918747]       Assert.Equal() Failure
[xUnit.net 00:00:01.0919671]       Expected: 5
[xUnit.net 00:00:01.0920190]       Actual:   6
[xUnit.net 00:00:01.0931474]       Stack Trace:
[xUnit.net 00:00:01.0945452]         /Users/markjprice/Code/Chapter05/Ch05_Calculator
UnitTests/CalculatorUnitTests.cs(32,0): at Ch05_CalculatorUnitTests.CalculatorUnitTes
ts.TestAdding2And3()
[xUnit.net 00:00:01.0997456]   Finished:    Ch05_CalculatorUnitTests
Failed   Ch05_CalculatorUnitTests.CalculatorUnitTests.TestAdding2And3
Error Message:
 Assert.Equal() Failure
Expected: 5
Actual:   6
Stack Trace:
   at Ch05_CalculatorUnitTests.CalculatorUnitTests.TestAdding2And3() in /Users/markjp
rice/Code/Chapter05/Ch05_CalculatorUnitTests/CalculatorUnitTests.cs:line 32

Total tests: 2. Passed: 1. Failed: 1. Skipped: 0.
Test Run Failed.
Test execution time: 1.8676 Seconds
```

Fix the bug in the `Add` method, and then rerun the unit tests to see that the bug is now fixed.

Practicing and exploring

Test your knowledge and understanding by answering some questions, get some hands-on practice, and explore with deeper research into the topics covered in this chapter.

Exercise 5.1 – test your knowledge

Answer the following questions:

1. In Visual Studio 2017, what is the difference between pressing *F5*, *Ctrl* + *F5*, *Shift* + *F5*, and *Ctrl* + *Shift* + *F5*?
2. Which information can you find out about a process?
3. How accurate is the `Stopwatch`?
4. How do you reference another project in a `.csproj` file?
5. When writing a unit test, what are the three As?
6. What `dotnet` command executes xUnit tests?

Exercise 5.2 – practice debugging and unit testing

Create a console application named `Ch05_Exercise02` that performs some simple calculations related to your own work. Use the debugging and unit testing tools to fix any problems.

Exercise 5.3 – explore topics

Use the following links to read more about the topics covered in this chapter:

- **Debugging in Visual Studio Code:** `https://code.visualstudio.com/docs/editor/debugging`
- **System.Diagnostics Namespaces**: `https://docs.microsoft.com/en-us/dotnet/core/api/system.diagnostics`
- **Debugger Basics**: `https://docs.microsoft.com/en-us/visualstudio/debugger/debugger-basics`
- **xUnit.net**: `http://xunit.github.io/`

Summary

In this chapter, you learned how to use the Visual Studio debugging and diagnostic features, and unit test your code.

In the next chapter, you will learn how to build your own types using object-oriented programming techniques.

6

Building Your Own Types with Object-Oriented Programming

This chapter is about making your own types using **object-oriented programming** (**OOP**). You will learn about all the different categories of members that a type can have, including fields to store data and methods to perform actions. You will use OOP concepts such as aggregation and encapsulation. You will also learn about C# 7 language features, such as tuple syntax support and `out` variables.

This chapter will cover the following topics:

- Talking about OOP
- Building class libraries
- Storing data with fields
- Writing and calling methods
- Controlling how parameters are passed
- Splitting classes using partial
- Controlling access with properties and indexers

Talking about OOP

An object in the real world is a thing, such as a car or a person. An object in programming often represents something in the real world, such as a product or bank account, but can also be something more abstract.

In C#, we use `class` (usually) or `struct` (rarely) to define each type of object. You can think of a type as being a blueprint or template for an object.

- **Encapsulation** is the combination of the data and actions that are related to an object. For example, a `BankAccount` type might have data, such as `Balance` and `AccountName`, as well as actions, such as `Deposit` and `Withdraw`. When encapsulating, you often want to control what can access those actions and the data.
- **Composition** is about what an object is made of. For example, a car is composed of different parts, such as four wheels, several seats, an engine, and so on.
- **Aggregation** is about what is related to an object. For example, a person could sit in the driver's seat and then becomes the car's driver.
- **Inheritance** is about reusing code by having a subclass derive from a **base** or **super** class. All functionality in the base class becomes available in the derived class.
- **Abstraction** is about capturing the core idea of an object and ignoring the details or specifics. Abstraction is a tricky balance. If you make a class more abstract, more classes would be able to inherit from it, but there will be less functionality to share.
- **Polymorphism** is about allowing a derived class to override an inherited action to provide custom behavior.

Building class libraries

Class library assemblies group types together into easily deployable units (DLL files). Apart from when you learned about unit testing, you have only created console applications to contain your code. To make the code that you write reusable across multiple projects, you should put it in class library assemblies, just like Microsoft does.

Good Practice
Put types that you might reuse in a .NET Standard class library to enable them to be reused in .NET Core, .NET Framework, and Xamarin projects.

Creating a class library with Visual Studio 2017

Start Microsoft Visual Studio 2017. In Visual Studio, press *Ctrl* + *Shift* + *N*, or go to **File** | **New** | **Project...**.

In the **New Project** dialog, in the **Installed** | **Templates** list, expand **Visual C#** and select **.NET Standard**. In the center list, select **Class Library (.NET Standard)**, type **Name** as `Ch06_PacktLibrary`, change **Location** to `C:\Code`, type **Solution name** as `Chapter06`, and then click on **OK**.

Make sure you choose a Class Library (.NET Standard) and *not* a Console App (.NET Core)!

In **Solution Explorer**, right-click on the file named `Class1.cs` and choose **Rename**. Type the name as `Person`. When you are prompted to rename all other references to the class, click on **Yes**:

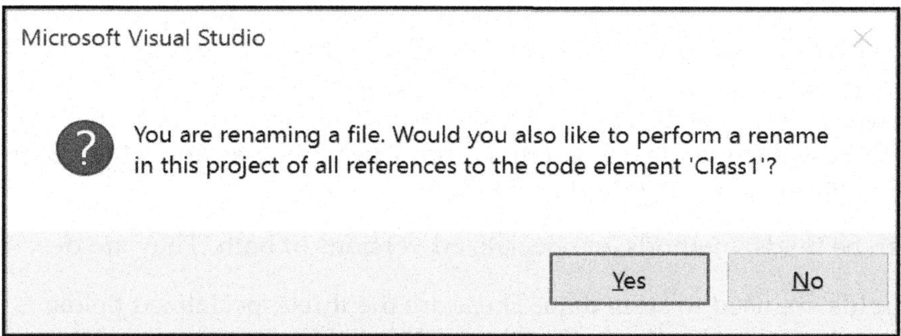
Microsoft Visual Studio
You are renaming a file. Would you also like to perform a rename in this project of all references to the code element 'Class1'?
Yes
No

Creating a class library with Visual Studio Code

Create a folder named `Chapter06` with a subfolder named `Ch06_PacktLibrary`.

Start Visual Studio Code and open the `Ch06_PacktLibrary` folder.

View **Integrated Terminal** and enter the following command:

```
dotnet new classlib
```

In the **Explorer** pane, rename the file named `Class1.cs` to `Person.cs`.

Click `Person.cs` to open it, restore packages, and change the class name to `Person`.

Defining a class

In either Visual Studio 2017 or Visual Studio Code, change the namespace to `Packt.CS7` because it is important to put your classes in a logically named namespace. In this, and the next chapter, we will learn about OOP and most of the new language features of C# 7. Your class file should now look like the following code:

```
using System;

namespace Packt.CS7
{
  public class Person
  {
  }
}
```

Note that the C# keyword, `public`, is applied before `class`. This keyword is called an **access modifier** and it allows all code to access this class. If you do not explicitly apply the `public` keyword, then it would only be accessible within the assembly that defined it. We need it to be accessible outside the assembly too. This type does not yet have any members encapsulated within it. We will create some soon.

Members can be fields, methods, or specialized versions of both. They are described here:

- **Fields** are used to store data. These are the three specialized fields:
  - **Constants**: The data in this field never changes
  - **Read-only fields**: The data in this field cannot change after the class is instantiated
  - **Events**: This refers to methods that you want to call automatically when something happens, such as clicking on a button
- **Methods** are used to execute statements. These are the four specialized methods:
  - **Constructors**: These are the methods that execute when you use the `new` keyword to allocate memory and instantiate a class
  - **Properties**: These are the methods that execute when you want to access data
  - **Indexers**: These are the methods that execute when you want to access data
  - **Operators**: These are the methods that execute when you want to apply an operator

Instantiating a class

In this section, we will make an **instance** of the `Person` class.

Referencing an assembly using Visual Studio 2017

In Visual Studio 2017, add a new console application project named `Ch06_PeopleApp` to your existing `Chapter06` solution.

Make sure you add a Console App (.NET Core) and *not* a Class Library!

Right-click the solution, choose **Properties**, and set the **Startup Project** to a single startup project, and choose **Ch06_PeopleApp**.

This project needs a reference to the class library we just made.

In **Solution Explorer**, in the **Ch06_PeopleApp** project, right-click on **Dependencies** and choose **Add Reference...**.

In the **Reference Manager** dialog box, in the list on the left-hand side, choose **Projects** | **Solution**, select the `Ch06_PacktLibrary` assembly, and then click on **OK**, as shown in the following screenshot:

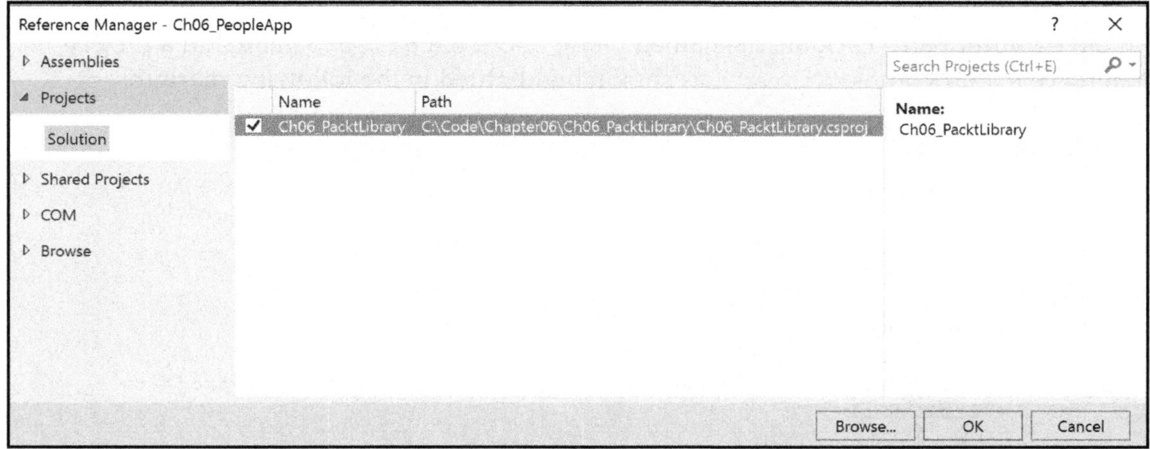

In **Solution Explorer**, expand **Dependencies** to show the reference to the **Ch06_PacktLibrary** project, as shown in the following screenshot:

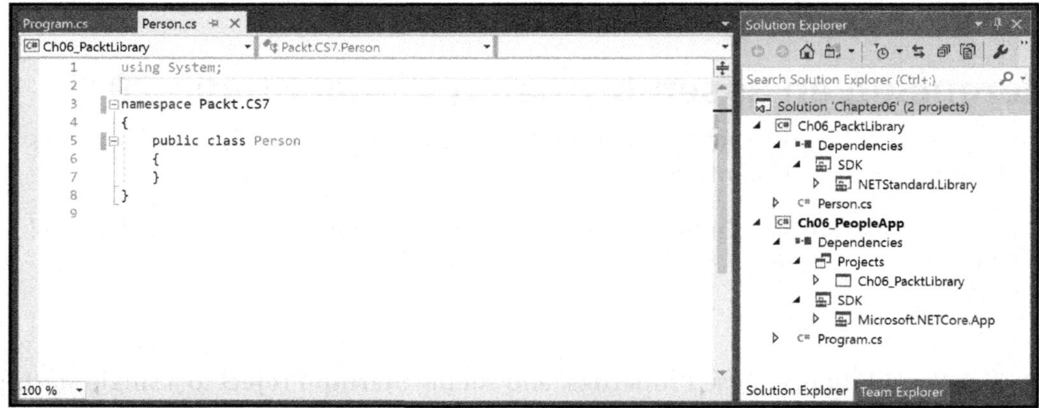

Referencing an assembly using Visual Studio Code

Create a subfolder under `Chapter06` named `Ch06_PeopleApp`.

In Visual Studio Code, open the `Ch06_PeopleApp` folder.

In Integrated Terminal, enter the following command:

```
dotnet new console
```

In the **Explorer** pane, click the file named `Ch06_PeopleApp.csproj` and add a project reference to `Ch06_PacktLibrary`, as shown highlighted in the following markup:

```
<Project Sdk="Microsoft.NET.Sdk">

  <PropertyGroup>
    <OutputType>Exe</OutputType>
    <TargetFramework>netcoreapp1.1</TargetFramework>
  </PropertyGroup>

  <ItemGroup>
    <ProjectReference
      Include="../Ch06_PacktLibrary/Ch06_PacktLibrary.csproj" />
  </ItemGroup>

</Project>
```

In Visual Studio Code, in Integrated Terminal, enter the following commands:

```
dotnet restore
dotnet build
```

Both the `Ch06_PacktLibrary` project and `Ch06_PeopleApp` project will compile into DLL assemblies, as shown in the following screenshot:

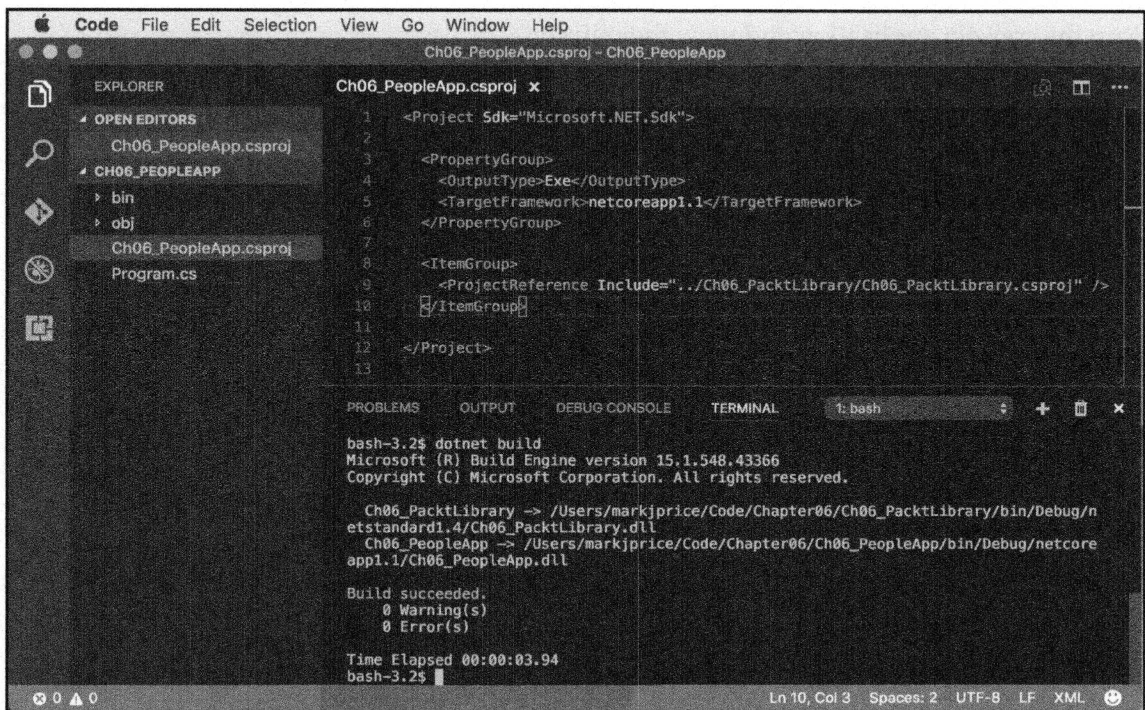

Importing a namespace

In both Visual Studio 2017 and Visual Studio Code, at the top of the `Program.cs` file, type the following code to import the namespace for our class and statically import the `Console`:

```
using Packt.CS7;
using static System.Console;
```

In the `Main` method, type the following code to create an instance of the `Person` type by using the `new` keyword. The `new` keyword allocates memory for the object and initializes any internal data. We could use `Person` in place of the `var` keyword, but the use of `var` involves less typing and is still just as clear:

```
var p1 = new Person();
WriteLine(p1.ToString());
```

Run the console application and view the output:

```
Packt.CS7.Person
```

Managing multiple projects with Visual Studio Code

If you have multiple projects that you want to work with at the same time, either open a new window by choosing **File | New Window** or press *Shift* + *Cmd* + *N*, or open a parent folder that contains the project folders that you want to work with.

If you choose to open a parent folder, be careful when executing commands in the Terminal because they will apply to whatever the current folder is.

In Visual Studio Code, open the `Chapter06` folder, and then in Terminal, enter the following command to change the directory to the console application project, as shown in the following screenshot:

```
cd Ch06_PeopleApp
```

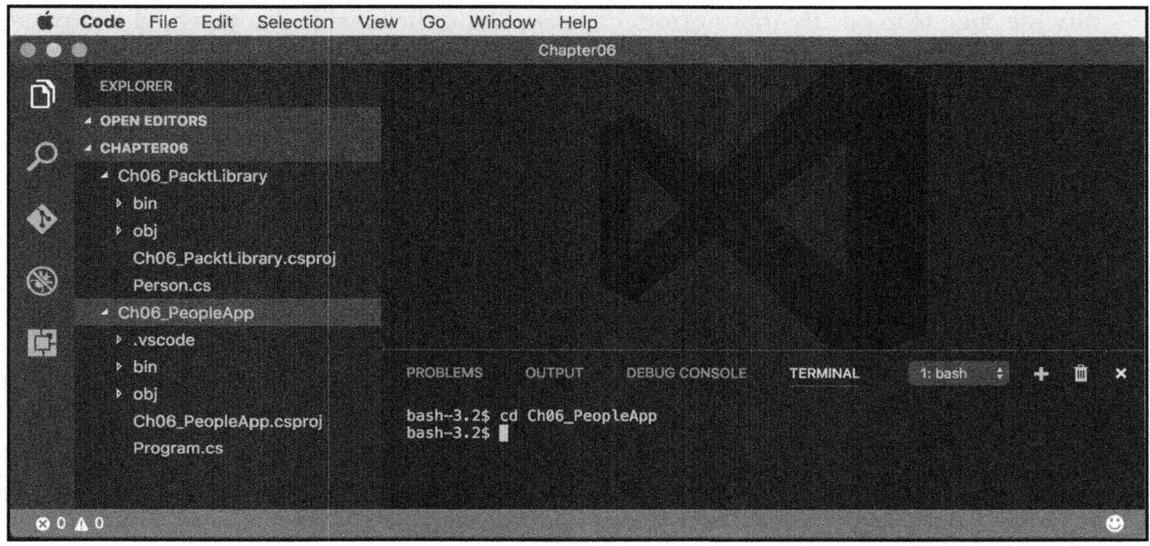

Inheriting from System.Object

Although our `Person` class did not explicitly choose to inherit from a type, all types indirectly inherit from a special type named `System.Object`. The implementation of the `ToString` method in the `System.Object` type simply outputs the full namespace and type name, as shown in the preceding output.

Back in the original `Person` class, we could have explicitly told the compiler that `Person` inherits from the `System.Object` type like this:

```
public class Person : System.Object
```

When class B **inherits** from class A, we say that A is the **base** or **super** class and B is the **derived** or **subclass**. In this case, `System.Object` is the base or super class and `Person` is the derived or subclass.

You can also use the C# type alias keyword, `object`:

```
public class Person : object
```

Modify the code to explicitly inherit from `object`. Then, click inside the keyword and press *F12*. You will see the Microsoft-defined `System.Object` type and its members. You do not need to understand any of this yet, but notice that it has a method named `ToString`, as shown in the following screenshot:

```
namespace System
{
    ...public class Object
    {
        ...public Object();

        ...~Object();

        ...public static bool Equals(Object objA, Object objB);
        ...public static bool ReferenceEquals(Object objA, Object objB);
        ...public virtual bool Equals(Object obj);
        ...public virtual int GetHashCode();
        ...public Type GetType();
        ...public virtual string ToString();
        ...protected Object MemberwiseClone();
    }
}
```

Good Practice
Assume other programmers know that if inheritance is not specified, the class will inherit from `System.Object`.

Storing data with fields

Next, we will define some fields in the class to store information about a person.

Defining fields

Inside the `Person` class, write the following code. At this point, we have decided that a person is composed of a name and a date of birth. We have encapsulated these two values inside the person. We have also made the fields public so that they are visible outside the class itself:

```
public class Person : object
{
  // fields
  public string Name;
  public DateTime DateOfBirth;
}
```

You can use any type for a field, including arrays and collections, for example, if you need to store multiple values.

In Visual Studio 2017, you might want to click, hold, and drag the tabs for one of your open files to arrange them so that you can see both `Person.cs` and `Program.cs` at the same time, as shown in the following screenshot:

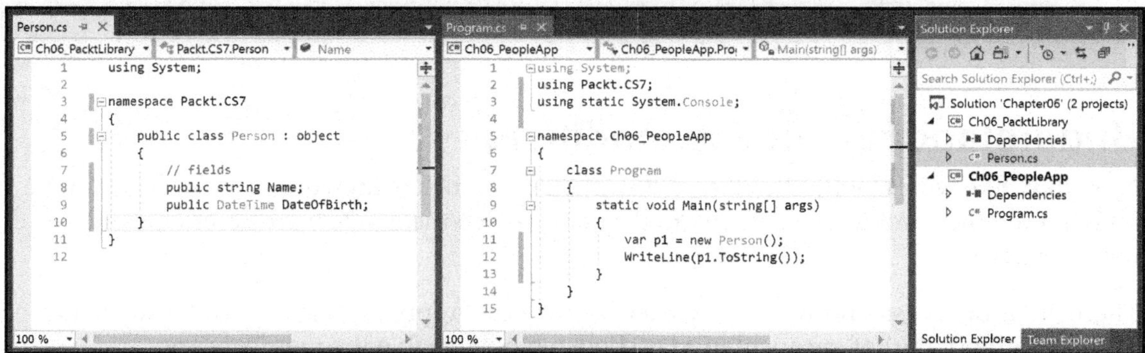

In Visual Studio Code, you can click on the Split Editor button or press *Cmd* + \ and then close one copy of the duplicated file editor so that you have two files open side by side, as shown in the following screenshot:

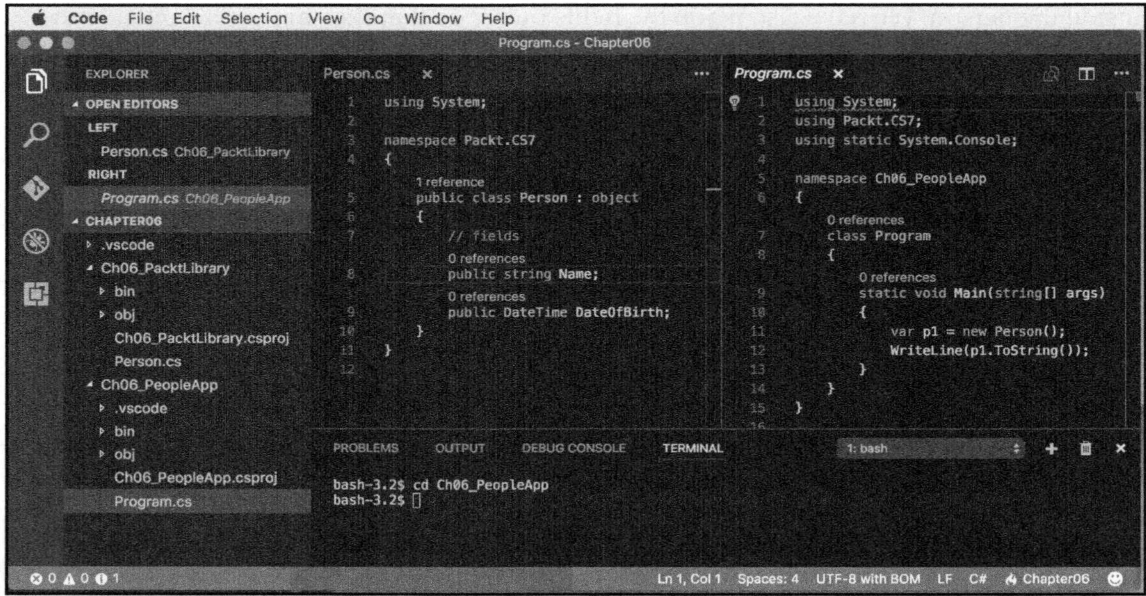

Understanding access modifiers

Note that, like we did with the class, we applied the `public` keyword to these fields. If we hadn't, then they would be `private` to the class, which means they are accessible only inside the class.

There are four **access modifier** keywords that you can apply to a class member, such as a field or method. Part of encapsulation is choosing how visible the members are:

Access Modifier	Description
`private`	Member is accessible inside the type only. This is the default.
`internal`	Member is accessible inside the type and any type in the same assembly.
`protected`	Member is accessible inside the type and any type that inherits from the type.

`internal protected`	Member is accessible inside the type, any type in the same assembly, and any type that inherits from the type.
`public`	Member is accessible everywhere.

Good Practice
Explicitly apply one of the access modifiers to all type members even if you want to use the default, which is `private`.

Inside the `Main` method, change the code to look like this:

```
var p1 = new Person();
p1.Name = "Bob Smith";
p1.DateOfBirth = new DateTime(1965, 12, 22);
WriteLine($"{p1.Name} was born on {p1.DateOfBirth:dddd, d MMMM
yyyy}");
```

Run the application and view the output:

```
Bob Smith was born on Wednesday, 22 December 1965
```

You can also initialize fields using a short-hand object initializer syntax using curly braces.

Add the following code underneath the existing code to create another new person. Notice the different format code for the date of birth when writing to the console:

```
var p2 = new Person { Name = "Alice Jones", DateOfBirth = new
DateTime(1998, 3, 17) };
WriteLine($"{p2.Name} was born on {p2.DateOfBirth:d MMM yy}");
```

Run the application and view the output:

```
Bob Smith was born on Wednesday, 22 December 1965
Alice Jones was born on 17 Mar 98
```

Storing a value using the enum keyword

Sometimes, a value needs to be one of a limited list of options. For example, a person may have a favorite ancient world wonder. Sometimes, a value needs to be combination of a limited list of options. For example, a person may have a bucket list of ancient world wonders they want to visit. We can store this data using an `enum` type.

An `enum` is a very efficient way of storing one or more choices because, internally, it uses `int` values in combination with a lookup table of string descriptions.

In Visual Studio 2017, add a new class to the `Ch06_PacktLibrary` project named `WondersOfTheAncientWorld` by pressing *Shift* + *Alt* + *C* or going to **Project** | **Add Class...**.

In Visual Studio Code, add a new class to the project by selecting `Ch06_PacktLibrary`, clicking the New File button in the mini toolbar, and entering the name `WondersOfTheAncientWorld.cs`, as shown in the following screenshot:

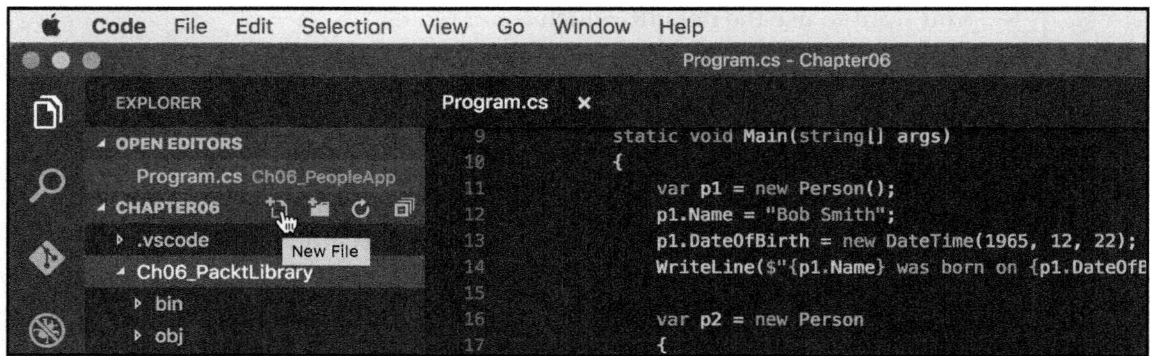

Modify the `WondersOfTheAncientWorld.cs` class file to make it look like this:

```
namespace Packt.CS7
{
  public enum WondersOfTheAncientWorld
  {
    GreatPyramidOfGiza,
    HangingGardensOfBabylon,
    StatueOfZeusAtOlympia,
    TempleOfArtemisAtEphesus,
    MausoleumAtHalicarnassus,
    ColossusOfRhodes,
    LighthouseOfAlexandria
  }
}
```

In the `Person` class, add the following statement to your list of fields:

```
public WondersOfTheAncientWorld FavouriteAncientWonder;
```

Back in the `Main` method of `Program.cs`, add the following statements:

```
p1.FavouriteAncientWonder =
  WondersOfTheAncientWorld.StatueOfZeusAtOlympia;
WriteLine($"{p1.Name}'s favourite wonder is
{p1.FavouriteAncientWonder}");
```

Run the application and view the additional output:

```
Bob Smith's favourite wonder is StatueOfZeusAtOlympia
```

For the bucket list, we could create a collection of instances of the `enum`, but there is a better way. We can combine multiple choices into a single value using **flags**.

Modify the `enum` to look as shown in the following code. Note that I have used the left shift operator (<<) to set individual bits within the flag. I could also have set the values to 1, 2, 4, 8, 16, 32, and so on:

```
namespace Packt.CS7
{
  [System.Flags]
  public enum WondersOfTheAncientWorld : byte
  {
    None = 0,
    GreatPyramidOfGiza = 1,
    HangingGardensOfBabylon = 1 << 1,
    StatueOfZeusAtOlympia = 1 << 2,
    TempleOfArtemisAtEphesus = 1 << 3,
    MausoleumAtHalicarnassus = 1 << 4,
    ColossusOfRhodes = 1 << 5,
    LighthouseOfAlexandria = 1 << 6
  }
}
```

We are assigning explicit values for each choice that would not overlap when looking at the bits stored in memory. We must also mark the `enum` with the `System.Flags` attribute. Normally, an `enum` uses an `int` variable internally, but since we don't need values that big, we can make it more efficient by telling it to use a `byte` variable.

If we want to indicate that our bucket list includes the *Hanging Gardens* and the *Mausoleum at Halicarnassus*, then we would want the **16** and **2** bits set to `1`. In other words, we would store the value `18`:

64	32	16	8	4	2	1	0
0	0	1	0	0	1	0	0

In the `Person` class, add the following statement to your list of fields:

```
public WondersOfTheAncientWorld BucketList;
```

Back in the Main method of Ch06_PeopleApp, add the following statements to set the bucket list using the | operator (logical OR) to combine enum values. We could also set the value using the number 18 cast into the enum type as in the comment:

```
p1.BucketList = WondersOfTheAncientWorld.HangingGardensOfBabylon |
WondersOfTheAncientWorld.MausoleumAtHalicarnassus;
// p1.BucketList = (WondersOfTheAncientWorld)18;
WriteLine($"{p1.Name}'s bucket list is {p1.BucketList}");
```

Run the application and view the additional output:

```
Bob Smith's bucket list is HangingGardensOfBabylon,
MausoleumAtHalicarnassus
```

Good Practice
Use enum values to store combinations of discreet options. Derive an enum from byte if there are up to eight options, from short if there are up to 16 options, from int if there are up to 32 options, and from long if there are up to 64 options.

Storing multiple values using collections

Let's add a field to store a person's children. This is an example of aggregation because children are instances of a class that is related to the current person, but are not part of the person itself.

We will use a generic List<T> collection type, so we need to import the System.Collections.Generic namespace:

```
using System.Collections.Generic;
```

Then we can declare a new field in the Person class:

```
public List<Person> Children = new List<Person>();
```

Notice that we need to ensure the collection is initialized to a new instance of a collection before we can add items to the collection.

In the Main method, add the following code:

```
p1.Children.Add(new Person());
p1.Children.Add(new Person());
WriteLine($"{p1.Name} has {p1.Children.Count} children.");
```

Run the application and view the output:

```
Bob Smith has 2 children.
```

Making a field static

The fields that we have created so far have all been instance members, meaning that a copy of each field exists for each instance of the class that is created.

Sometimes, you want to define a field that only has one copy that is shared across all instances. These are called **static** members.

In the `Ch06_PacktLibrary` project, add a new class named `BankAccount`. Modify the class as shown in the following code:

```
namespace Packt.CS7
{
  public class BankAccount
  {
    public string AccountName;
    public decimal Balance;
    public static decimal InterestRate;
  }
}
```

Each instance of `BankAccount` will have its own `AccountName` and `Balance`, but all instances will share a single `InterestRate` value.

In `Program.cs` and its `Main` method, add the following code where we will set the shared interest rate and then create two instances of the `BankAccount` type:

```
BankAccount.InterestRate = 0.012M;
var ba1 = new BankAccount();
ba1.AccountName = "Mrs. Jones";
ba1.Balance = 2400;
WriteLine($"{ba1.AccountName} earned {ba1.Balance *
BankAccount.InterestRate:C} interest.");
var ba2 = new BankAccount();
ba2.AccountName = "Ms. Gerrier";
ba2.Balance = 98;
WriteLine($"{ba2.AccountName} earned {ba2.Balance *
BankAccount.InterestRate:C} interest.");
```

Run the application and view the additional output:

```
Mrs. Jones earned £28.80 interest.
Ms. Gerrier earned £1.18 interest.
```

`:C` is a format code that tells .NET to use the currency format for the numbers. In `Chapter 4`, *Using .NET Standard Types*, you learned how to control the culture that determines the currency symbol.

Making a field constant

If the value of a field will never *ever* change, you can use the `const` keyword and assign the value at compile time.

Inside the `Person` class, add the following code:

```
// constants
public const string Species = "Homo Sapien";
```

Inside the `Main` method, change the code to look like this. Note that, to read a constant field, you must write the name of the class, not the name of an instance of the class:

```
WriteLine($"{p1.Name} is a {Person.Species}");
```

Run the application and view the additional output:

```
Bob Smith is a Homo Sapien
```

Examples of `const` fields in Microsoft types include `System.Int32.MaxValue` and `System.Math.PI` because neither value will ever change, as you can see in the following screenshot:

(constant) int int.MaxValue = 2147483647
Represents the largest possible value of an int. This field is constant.

(constant) double Math.PI = 3.1415926535897931
Represents the ratio of the circumference of a circle to its diameter, specified by the constant, π.

Good Practice
Constants should be avoided for two important reasons:
The value must be known at compile time, and it must be expressible as a literal string, Boolean, or number value.
Every reference to the `const` field is replaced with the literal value at compile time, which will, therefore, not be reflected if the value changes in a future version.

Making a field read-only

A better choice for fields that should not change is to mark them as read-only.

Inside the `Person` class, write the following code:

```
// read-only fields
public readonly string HomePlanet = "Earth";
```

Inside the `Main` method, add the following code statement. Notice that, to get a read-only field, you must write the name of an instance of the class, not the type name, unlike `const`:

```
WriteLine($"{p1.Name} was born on {p1.HomePlanet}");
```

Run the application and view the output:

```
Bob Smith was born on Earth
```

Good Practice
Use read-only fields over `const` fields for two important reasons:
The value can be calculated or loaded at runtime and can be expressed using any executable statement. So, a read-only field can be set using a constructor.
Every reference to the field is a live reference, so any future changes will be correctly reflected by calling code.

Initializing fields with constructors

Fields often need to be initialized at runtime. You do this in a constructor that will be called when you make an instance of the class using the `new` keyword. Constructors execute before any fields are set by the code that is using the type.

Inside the Person class, add the following highlighted code after the existing read-only HomePlanet field:

```
// read-only fields
public readonly string HomePlanet = "Earth";
public readonly DateTime Instantiated;

// constructors
public Person()
{
  // set default values for fields
  // including read-only fields
  Name = "Unknown";
  Instantiated = DateTime.Now;
}
```

Inside the Main method, add the following code:

```
    var p3 = new Person();
    WriteLine($"{p3.Name} was instantiated at  {p3.Instantiated:hh:mm:ss}
on
    {p3.Instantiated:dddd, d MMMM  yyyy}");
```

Run the application and view the output:

```
Unknown was instantiated at 11:58:12 on Sunday, 12 March 2017
```

You can have multiple constructors in a type.

Inside the Person class, add the following code:

```
public Person(string initialName)
{
  Name = initialName;
  Instantiated = DateTime.Now;
}
```

Inside the Main method, add the following code:

```
var p4 = new Person("Aziz");
WriteLine($"{p4.Name} was instantiated at
{p4.Instantiated:hh:mm:ss} on {p4.Instantiated:dddd, d MMMM
yyyy}");
```

Run the application and view the output:

```
Aziz was instantiated at 11:59:25 on Sunday, 4 June 2017
```

Constructors are a special category of **method**. Let's look at methods in more detail.

Writing and calling methods

Methods are type members that execute a block of statements.

A method that performs some actions but does not return a value shows this by showing that it returns the `void` type before the name of the method. A method that performs some actions and returns a value shows this by showing that it returns the type of that value before the name of the method.

For example, you will create two methods:

- `WriteToConsole`: This will perform an action (writing a line), but it will return nothing from the method, indicated by the `void` keyword
- `GetOrigin`: This will return a string value, indicated by the `string` keyword

Inside the `Person` class, statically import `System.Console`, and then add the following code:

```
// methods
public void WriteToConsole()
{
  WriteLine($"{Name} was born on {DateOfBirth:dddd, d MMMM
  yyyy}");
}

public string GetOrigin()
{
  return $"{Name} was born on {HomePlanet}";
}
```

Inside the `Main` method, add the following code:

```
p1.WriteToConsole();
WriteLine(p1.GetOrigin());
```

Run the application and view the output:

```
Bob Smith was born on Wednesday, 22 December 1965
Bob Smith was born on Earth
```

Combining multiple values with tuples

Each method can only return a single value that has a single type. That type could be a simple type, such as `string` in the previous example, a complex type, such as `Person`, or a collection type, such as `List<Person>`.

Imagine that we want to define a method that returns both a `string` and an `int` value. We could define a new type with a `string` field and an `int` field and return an instance of that complex type. Or we could use tuples.

Tuples have been a part of some languages such as F# since their first version, but .NET only added support for them in .NET 4.0 with the `System.Tuple` type, and it was only in C# 7 that the C# language added syntax support for tuples.

While adding tuple support to the C# 7 language, .NET also added a new `System.ValueTuple` type that is more efficient in some common scenarios than the old .NET 4.0 `System.Tuple` type.

System.ValueTuple is not part of .NET Standard 1.6, and therefore not available by default in .NET Core 1.0 or 1.1 projects.

Referencing the System.ValueTuple package with Visual Studio 2017

In Visual Studio 2017, in **Solution Explorer**, in the **Ch06_PacktLibrary** project, right-click on **Dependencies** and choose **Manage NuGet Packages...**

Click the **Browse** tab, search for `System.ValueTuple`, select the package, and click **Install**, as shown in the following screenshot:

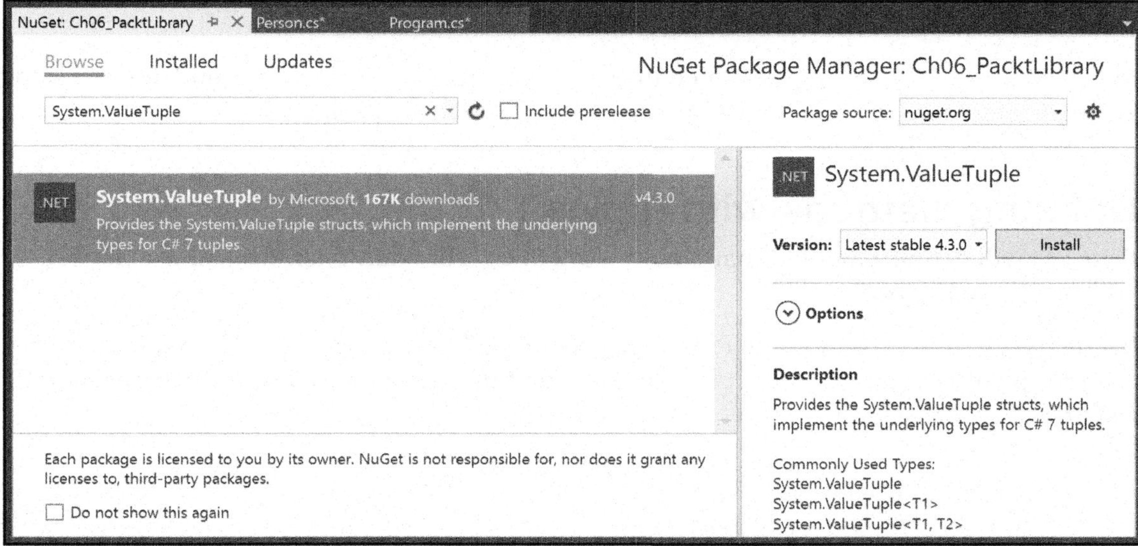

In the **Review Changes** dialog, click **OK**.

In the **License Agreement** dialog, click **I Accept**.

Referencing the System.ValueTuple package with Visual Studio Code

In Visual Studio Code, in the `Ch06_PacktLibrary` project, open the `Ch06_PacktLibrary.csproj` file and add a package reference, as shown in the following markup:

```
<Project Sdk="Microsoft.NET.Sdk">

  <PropertyGroup>
    <TargetFramework>netstandard1.4</TargetFramework>
  </PropertyGroup>

  <ItemGroup>
    <PackageReference Include="System.ValueTuple"
                      Version="4.3.0" />
  </ItemGroup>

</Project>
```

When prompted, restore dependency packages.

In the `Ch06_PeopleApp` project, open the `Ch06_PeopleApp.csproj` file, and add the same package reference, and when prompted, restore dependency packages.

Defining methods with tuples

First, we will define a method that would work in C# 4 or later. Then we will use the new C# 7 language support.

Inside the `Person` class, add the following code to define two methods, the first with a return type of `System.Tuple<string, int>` and the second with a `return` type using C# 7 syntax:

```
// the old C# 4 and .NET 4.0 System.Tuple type
public Tuple<string, int> GetFruitCS4()
{
  return Tuple.Create("Apples", 5);
}

// the new C# 7 syntax and new System.ValueTuple type
public (string, int) GetFruitCS7()
{
  return ("Apples", 5);
}
```

Inside the `Main` method, add the following code:

```
Tuple<string, int> fruit4 = p1.GetFruitCS4();
WriteLine($"There are {fruit4.Item2} {fruit4.Item1}.");

(string, int) fruit7 = p1.GetFruitCS7();
WriteLine($"{fruit7.Item1}, {fruit7.Item2} there are.");
```

Run the application and view the output:

```
There are 5 Apples.
Apples, 5 there are.
```

Naming the fields of a tuple

To access the fields of a tuple, the default names are **Item1**, **Item2**, and so on.

You can explicitly specify the field names. Inside the `Person` class, add the following code to define a method:

```
public (string Name, int Number) GetNamedFruit()
{
  return (Name: "Apples", Number: 5);
}
```

Inside the `Main` method, add the following code:

```
var fruitNamed = p1.GetNamedFruit();
WriteLine($"Are there {fruitNamed.Number} {fruitNamed.Name}?");
```

Run the application and view the output:

```
Are there 5 Apples?
```

Deconstructing tuples

You can also deconstruct tuples into separate variables. The deconstructing declaration has the same syntax as named field tuples, but without a variable name for the whole tuple. This has the effect of splitting the tuple into its parts and assigning those parts to new variables.

Inside the `Main` method, add the following code:

```
(string fruitName, int fruitNumber) = p1.GetFruitCS7();
WriteLine($"Deconstructed: {fruitName}, {fruitNumber}");
```

Run the application and view the output:

```
Deconstructed: Apples, 5
```

Deconstruction is not just for tuples. Any type can be deconstructed if it has a **Deconstructor** method. You can read about this at the following link: `https://docs.microsoft.com/en-us/dotnet/articles/csharp/tuples#deconstruction`.

Defining and passing parameters to methods

Methods can have parameters passed to them to change their behavior. Parameters are defined a bit like variable declarations, but inside the parentheses of the method.

Inside the `Person` class, add the following code to define two methods, the first without parameters and the second with one parameter:

```
public string SayHello()
{
  return $"{Name} says 'Hello!'";
}

public string SayHelloTo(string name)
{
  return $"{Name} says 'Hello {name}!'";
}
```

Inside the `Main` method, add the following code:

```
WriteLine(p1.SayHello());
WriteLine(p1.SayHelloTo("Emily"));
```

Run the application and view the output:

```
Bob Smith says 'Hello!'
Bob Smith says 'Hello Emily!'
```

Overloading methods

When typing a statement that calls a method, IntelliSense, in both Visual Studio 2017 and Visual Studio Code with the appropriate language extension installed, should show useful tooltips.

In Visual Studio 2017, you can press *Ctrl* + *K*, *I* or go to **Edit** | **IntelliSense** | **Quick Info** to see **Quick Info** of a method, as shown in the following screenshot:

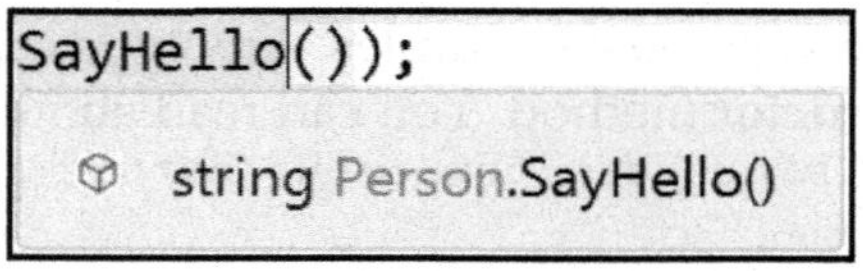

```
SayHello());
  string Person.SayHello()
```

Here is the `SayHelloTo` method's quick info:

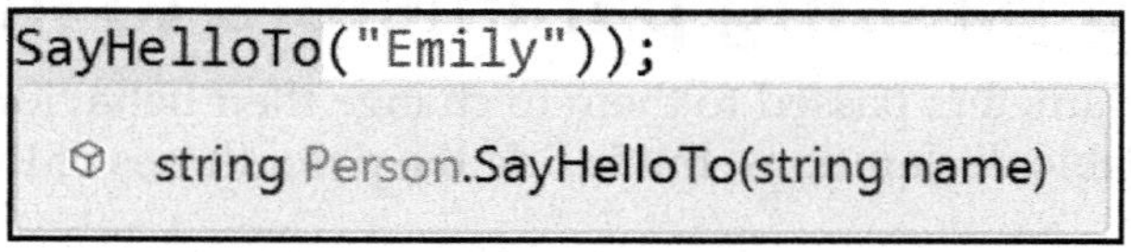

```
SayHelloTo("Emily"));
  string Person.SayHelloTo(string name)
```

Instead of having two different method names, we could give both methods the same name. This is allowed because the methods each have a different signature. A method signature is a list of parameter types that can be passed when calling the method.

In the `Person` class, change the name of the `SayHelloTo` method to `SayHello`. Now, when you view the quick info for the method, it tells you that it has one additional overload:

```
SayHello("Emily"));
   string Person.SayHello(string name) (+ 1 overload)
```

Good Practice
Use overloaded methods to simplify your class by making it appear to have fewer methods.

Optional parameters and named arguments

Another way to simplify methods is to make parameters optional. You make a parameter optional by assigning a default value inside the method parameter list. Optional parameters must always come last in the list of parameters.

You will now create a method with three optional parameters.

Inside the `Person` class, add the following code:

```
public void OptionalParameters(string command = "Run!",
  double number = 0.0, bool active = true)
{
  WriteLine($"command is {command}, number is {number}, active is
  {active}");
}
```

Inside the `Main` method, add the following code:

```
p1.OptionalParameters();
```

Watch IntelliSense's **Quick Info** appear as you type the code, and you will see a tooltip, showing the three optional parameters with default values, as shown in the following screenshot:

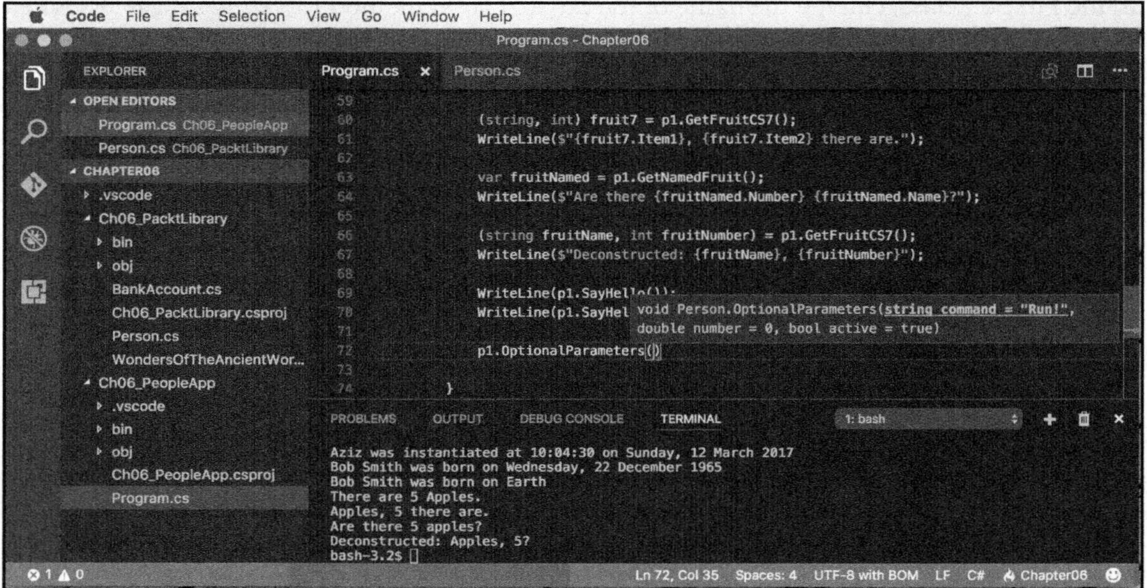

When you run the application, you will see the following output:

```
command is Run!, number is 0, active is True
```

In the `Main` method, add the following line, which passes a string for the command and a double for the number parameters:

```
p1.OptionalParameters("Jump!", 98.5);
```

Run the application and see the output:

```
command is Jump!, number is 98.5, active is True
```

The default values for command and number have been replaced, but the default for active is still true.

Optional parameters are often combined with naming parameters when you call the method, because naming a parameter allows the values to be passed in a different order than how they were declared.

In the `Main` method, add the following line, which passes a string for the command and a double for the number parameters but using named parameters, so that the order they are passed can be swapped around:

```
p1.OptionalParameters(number: 52.7, command: "Hide!");
```

Run the application and see the output:

```
command is Hide!, number is 52.7, active is True
```

You can even use named parameters to skip over optional parameters.

In the `Main` method, add the following line that passes a string for the command using positional order, skips the number parameter, and uses the named active parameter:

```
p1.OptionalParameters("Poke!", active: false);
```

Run the application and see the output:

```
command is Poke!, number is 0, active is False
```

Controlling how parameters are passed

When a parameter is passed into a method, it can be passed in one of three ways:

- By **value** (this is the default): think of these as being **in-only**
- By **reference** as a `ref` parameter: think of these as being **in-and-out**
- As an `out` parameter: think of these as being **out-only**

In the `Person` class, add the following method:

```
public void PassingParameters(int x, ref int y, out int z)
{
  // out parameters cannot have a default
  // AND must be initialized inside the method
  z = 99;

  // increment each parameter
  x++;
  y++;
  z++;
}
```

In the `Main` method, add the following statements to declare some `int` variables and pass them into the method:

```
int a = 10;
int b = 20;
int c = 30;
WriteLine($"Before: a = {a}, b = {b}, c = {c}");
p1.PassingParameters(a, ref b, out c);
WriteLine($"After: a = {a}, b = {b}, c = {c}");
```

Run the application and see the output:

```
Before: a = 10, b = 20, c = 30
After: a = 10, b = 21, c = 100
```

When passing a variable as a parameter by default, its current *value* gets passed, *not* the variable itself. Therefore, `x` is a copy of the variable `a`. Variable `a` retains its original value of 10.
When passing a variable as a `ref` parameter, a *reference* to the variable gets passed into the method. Therefore, `y` is a reference to `b`. Variable `b` gets incremented when parameter `y` gets incremented.
When passing a variable as an `out` parameter, a *reference* to the variable gets passed into the method. Therefore, `z` is a reference to `c`. Variable `c` gets replaced by whatever code executes inside the method. We could simplify the code in the `Main` method by not assigning the value `30` to the variable `c` since it will always be replaced anyway.

In C# 7, we can simplify code that uses `out` variables.

Add the following statements to the `Main` method:

```
// simplified C# 7 syntax for out parameters
int d = 10;
int e = 20;
WriteLine($"Before: d = {d}, e = {e}, f doesn't exist yet!");
p1.PassingParameters(d, ref e, out int f);
WriteLine($"After: d = {d}, e = {e}, f = {f}");
```

In C# 7, the `ref` keyword is not just for passing parameters into a method, it can also be applied to the return value. This allows an external variable to reference an internal variable and modify its value after the method call. This might be useful in advanced scenarios, for example, passing around placeholders into big data structures, but it's beyond the scope of this book.

Splitting classes using partial

When working on large projects with multiple team members, it is useful to be able to split the definition of a complex class across multiple files. You do this using the `partial` keyword.

Imagine we want to add a new method to the `Person` class without having to ask another programmer to close the `Person.cs` file. If the class is defined as `partial`, then we can split it over as many separate files as we like.

In the `Person` class, add the `partial` keyword, as shown highlighted in the following code:

```
namespace Packt.CS7
{
  public partial class Person
  {
```

In Visual Studio 2017, on the **Project** menu, go to **Add Class...** or press *Shift* + *Alt* + *C*. Enter the name `Person2`. We cannot enter `Person` because Visual Studio 2017 isn't smart enough to understand what we want to do. Instead, we must now rename the new class to `Person`, change the namespace, and add the `public partial` keywords, as shown in the following code:

```
namespace Packt.CS7
{
  public partial class Person
  {
```

In Visual Studio Code, click the New File button in the `Ch06_PacktLibrary` folder in the **Explorer** pane and enter a name of `Person2.cs`. Add the following statements to the new file:

```
namespace Packt.CS7
{
  public partial class Person
  {
  }
}
```

The rest of the code we write for this chapter will be written in the `Person2.cs` file.

Controlling access with properties and indexers

Earlier, you created a method named `GetOrigin` that returned a `string` containing the name and origin of the person. Languages such as Java do this a lot. C# has a better way: **properties**.

A property is simply a method (or pair of methods) that act look and like a field when you want to get or set a value, thereby simplifying the syntax.

Defining read-only properties

In the `Person2.cs` file, inside the `Person` class, add the following code to define three properties:

- The first property will perform the same role as the `GetOrigin` method using the `property` syntax that works with all versions of C# (although, it uses the C# 6 and later string interpolation syntax).
- The second property will return a greeting message using the C# 6 and later lambda expression (=>) syntax.
- The third property will calculate the person's age.

Here is the code:

```
// property defined using C# 1 - 5 syntax
public string Origin
{
  get
  {
    return $"{Name} was born on {HomePlanet}";
  }
}

// two properties defined using C# 6+ lambda expression syntax
public string Greeting => $"{Name} says 'Hello!'";

public int Age => (int)(System.DateTime.Today
  .Subtract(DateOfBirth).TotalDays / 365.25);
```

In the `Main` method, add the following code. You can see that, to set or get a property, you treat it like a field:

```
var max = new Person
{
  Name = "Max",
  DateOfBirth = new DateTime(1972, 1, 27)
};
WriteLine(max.Origin);
WriteLine(max.Greeting);
WriteLine(max.Age);
```

Run the application and view the output:

```
Max was born on Earth
Max says 'Hello!'
43
```

Defining settable properties

To create a settable property, you must use the older syntax and provide a pair of methods- not just a `get` part, but also a `set` part.

In the `Person2.cs` file, add the following code to define a `string` property that has both a `get` and `set` method (aka *getter* and *setter*). Although, you have not manually created a field to store the person's favorite ice cream, it is there, automatically created by the compiler for you:

```
public string FavoriteIceCream { get; set; } // auto-syntax
```

Sometimes, you need more control over what happens when a property is set. In this scenario, you must use a more detailed syntax and manually create a `private` field to store the value for the property:

```
private string favoritePrimaryColor;
public string FavoritePrimaryColor
{
  get
  {
    return favoritePrimaryColor;
  }
  set
  {
    switch (value.ToLower())
    {
      case "red":
      case "green":
      case "blue":
      favoritePrimaryColor = value;
      break;
      default:
      throw new System.ArgumentException($"{value} is not a
      primary color. Choose from: red, green, blue.");
    }
  }
}
```

In the `Main` method, add the following code:

```
    max.FavoriteIceCream = "Chocolate Fudge";
    WriteLine($"Max's favorite ice-cream flavor is
{max.FavoriteIceCream}.");
    max.FavoritePrimaryColor = "Red";
    WriteLine($"Max's favorite primary color is
{max.FavoritePrimaryColor}.");
```

Run the application and view the output:

```
Max's favorite ice-cream flavor is Chocolate Fudge.
Max's favorite primary color is Red.
```

If you try to set the color to any value other than red, green, or blue, then the code will throw an exception. The calling code could then use a `try` statement to display the error message.

Good Practice
Use properties instead of fields when you want to validate what value can be stored, when you want to data bind in XAML (we will cover this in Chapter 13, *Building Universal Windows Platform Apps Using XAML*), and when you want to read and write to fields without using methods.

Defining indexers

Indexers allow the calling code to use the array syntax to access a property. For example, the `string` type defines an **indexer** so that the calling code can access individual characters in the string individually. We will define an indexer to simplify access to the children of a person.

In the `Person2.cs` file, add the following code to define an indexer to get and set a child using the index (position) of the child:

```
// indexers
public Person this[int index]
{
  get
  {
    return Children[index];
  }
  set
  {
    Children[index] = value;
  }
}
```

You can overload indexers so that different types can be used to call them. For example, as well as passing an `int`, you could also pass a `string`.

In the `Main` method, add the following code. After adding to the children, we will access the first and second child using the longer `Children` field and the shorter indexer syntax:

```
max.Children.Add(new Person { Name = "Charlie" });
max.Children.Add(new Person { Name = "Ella" });
WriteLine($"Max's first child is {max.Children[0].Name}");
WriteLine($"Max's second child is {max.Children[1].Name}");
WriteLine($"Max's first child is {max[0].Name}");
WriteLine($"Max's second child is {max[1].Name}");
```

Run the application and view the output:

```
Max's first child is Charlie
Max's second child is Ella
Max's first child is Charlie
Max's second child is Ella
```

Good Practice
Only use indexers if it makes sense to use the square bracket/array syntax. As you can see from the preceding example, indexers rarely add much value.

Practicing and exploring

Test your knowledge and understanding by answering some questions, get some hands-on practice, and explore this chapter's topics with deeper research.

Exercise 6.1 – test your knowledge

Answer the following questions:

1. What are the four access modifiers and what do they do?
2. What is the difference between the `static`, `const`, and `readonly` keywords?
3. How many parameters can a method have?
4. What does a constructor do?
5. Why do you need to apply the `[Flags]` attribute to an `enum` keyword when you want to store combined values?
6. Why is the `partial` keyword useful?

Exercise 6.2 – practice writing mathematical methods

Create a console application named `Ch06_Exercise02` and add three static methods to the `Program` class to perform the following tasks:

- Numbers used to count are called "cardinal" numbers, for example, 1, 2, 3. Numbers used to order are "ordinal" numbers, for example, 1st, 2nd, 3rd. Write a method named `CardinalToOrdinal` that converts a cardinal `int` into an ordinal `string`, for example, it converts 1 into 1st, 2 into 2nd, and so on.
- The factorial of 5 is 120, because factorials are calculated by multiplying the number by one less than itself and so on, like this: 5 x 4 x 3 x 2 x 1 = 120. The factorial of 3 is 6 because it is 3 x 2 x 1 = 6. Write a method named `Factorial` that calculates the factorial for an `int` variable passed to it as a parameter. You could either use a loop or a technique called **recursion**, which means a method that calls itself.
- Prime factors are the combination of the smallest prime numbers, that, when multiplied together, will produce the original number. For example, the prime factors of 30 are 2 x 3 x 5. The prime factors of 4 are 2 x 2. Write a method named `PrimeFactors` that, when passed an `int` variable as a parameter, returns a `string` showing the prime factors as stated earlier.

In the `Main` method, prompt the user to press A, B, or C to choose between the three mathematical functions. Then, prompt the user to enter a number as input and then show the output.

Exercise 6.3 – explore topics

Use the following links to read more about this chapter's topics:

- **Fields (C# programming guide)**: `https://docs.microsoft.com/en-us/dotnet/articles/csharp/programming-guide/classes-and-structs/fields`
- **Access modifiers (C# programming guide)**: `https://docs.microsoft.com/en-us/dotnet/articles/csharp/language-reference/keywords/access-modifiers`

- **Constructors (C# programming guide)**: `https://docs.microsoft.com/en-us/dotnet/articles/csharp/programming-guide/classes-and-structs/constructors`
- **Methods (C# programming guide)**: `https://docs.microsoft.com/en-us/dotnet/articles/csharp/methods`
- **Properties (C# programming guide)**: `https://docs.microsoft.com/en-us/dotnet/articles/csharp/properties`

Summary

In this chapter, you learned about making your own types using OOP. You learned about some of the different categories of members that a type can have, including fields to store data and methods to perform actions. You used OOP concepts, such as aggregation and encapsulation, and explored some of the new language syntax features in C# 7.

In the next chapter, you will take these concepts further by defining delegates and events, implementing interfaces, and inheriting from existing classes.

7
Implementing Interfaces and Inheriting Classes

This chapter is about deriving new types from existing ones using **object-oriented programming** (OOP). You will learn how to define operators and local functions, delegates and events, implement interfaces about base and derived classes, override a type member, use polymorphism, create extension methods, and cast between classes in an inheritance hierarchy.

This chapter covers the following topics:

- Setting up a class library and console application
- Simplifying methods with operators
- Defining local functions
- Raising and handling events
- Implementing interfaces
- Managing memory with reference and value types
- Inheriting from classes
- Casting within inheritance hierarchies
- Inheriting and extending .NET types

Setting up a class library and console application

We will start by defining a solution/project like the one created in `Chapter 6`, *Building Your Own Types with Object-Oriented Programming*. If you completed all the exercises in that chapter, then you can open it and continue with it. Otherwise, follow the instructions for your preferred development tool below.

Using Visual Studio 2017

In Visual Studio 2017, press *Ctrl* + *Shift* + *N* or go to **File** | **New** | **Project...**.

In the **New Project** dialog, in the **Installed** | **Templates** list, expand **Visual C#**, and select **.NET Standard**. In the center list, select **Class Library (.NET Standard)**, type **Name** as `Ch07_PacktLibrary`, change **Location** to `C:\Code`, type **Solution name** as `Chapter07`, and then click on **OK**.

In **Solution Explorer**, right-click on the file named `Class1.cs` and choose **Rename**. Type the name as `Person`. Modify the contents like this:

```
namespace Packt.CS7
{
  public class Person
  {
  }
}
```

Add a new console application project named `Ch07_PeopleApp`.

In the solution's properties, set the startup project to be the `Ch07_PeopleApp` project.

In **Solution Explorer**, in the `Ch07_PeopleApp` project, right-click on **Dependencies** and choose **Add Reference...**.

In the **Reference Manager** dialog box, in the list on the left-hand side, choose **Projects**, select the `Ch07_PacktLibrary` assembly, and then click on **OK**.

Using Visual Studio Code

Create a folder named `Chapter07` with two subfolders named `Ch07_PacktLibrary` and `Ch07_PeopleApp`.

Start Visual Studio Code and open the `Chapter07` folder.

In **Integrated Terminal**, enter the following commands:

```
cd Ch07_PacktLibrary
dotnet new classlib
cd ..
cd Ch07_PeopleApp
dotnet new console
```

In the **Explorer** pane, in the Ch07_PacktLibrary project, rename the file named `Class1.cs` to `Person.cs`. Modify the contents like this:

```
namespace Packt.CS7
{
  public class Person
  {
  }
}
```

In the **Explorer** pane, expand the folder named `Ch07_PeopleApp` and click on the file named `Ch07_PeopleApp.csproj`. Add a project reference to `Ch07_PacktLibrary`, as shown in the following markup:

```
<Project Sdk="Microsoft.NET.Sdk">

  <PropertyGroup>
    <OutputType>Exe</OutputType>
    <TargetFramework>netcoreapp1.1</TargetFramework>
  </PropertyGroup>

  <ItemGroup>
    <ProjectReference
Include="..\Ch07_PacktLibrary\Ch07_PacktLibrary.csproj" />
  </ItemGroup>

</Project>
```

In **Integrated Terminal**, enter the following commands:

```
dotnet restore
dotnet build
```

Defining the classes

In either **Visual Studio 2017** or **Visual Studio Code**, add the following code to the `Person` class in the class library named `Ch07_PacktLibrary`:

```
using System;
using System.Collections.Generic;
using static System.Console;

namespace Packt.CS7
{
  public partial class Person
  {
    // fields
    public string Name;
    public DateTime DateOfBirth;
    public List<Person> Children = new List<Person>();

    // methods
    public void WriteToConsole()
    {
      WriteLine(
        $"{Name} was born on {DateOfBirth:dddd, d MMMM yyyy}");
    }
  }
}
```

Simplifying methods with operators

We might want two instances of a person to be able to procreate.

Implementing some functionality with a method

Add the following method to the `Person` class:

```
// method to "multiply"
public Person Procreate(Person partner)
{
  var baby = new Person
  {
    Name = $"Baby of {this.Name} and {partner.Name}"
  };
  this.Children.Add(baby);
  partner.Children.Add(baby);
```

```
    return baby;
  }
```

At the top of the Program.cs file, type the following code to import the namespace for our class and statically import the Console type:

```
using Packt.CS7;
using static System.Console;
```

Now, we can get two people to make a baby by adding the following to the Main method of the Program.cs file:

```
var harry = new Person { Name = "Harry" };
var mary = new Person { Name = "Mary" };
var baby1 = harry.Procreate(mary);
WriteLine($"{mary.Name} has {mary.Children.Count} children.");
WriteLine($"{harry.Name} has {harry.Children.Count} children.");
WriteLine($"{harry.Name}'s first child is named
\"{harry.Children[0].Name}\".");
```

Run the console application and view the output:

```
Mary has 1 children.
Harry has 1 children.
Harry's first child is named "Baby of Harry and Mary".
```

Implementing some functionality with an operator

An alternative would be to define an operator to allow two people to **multiply**. To allow this, we need to define a static operator for the * symbol inside the Person class:

```
// operator to "multiply"
public static Person operator *(Person p1, Person p2)
{
  return p1.Procreate(p2);
}
```

Add the following code at the end of the Main method, but before writing the children, count to the console:

```
var baby1 = harry.Procreate(mary);
var baby2 = harry * mary;
WriteLine($"{mary.Name} has {mary.Children.Count} children.");
```

Run the application and view the output:

```
Mary has 2 children.
Harry has 2 children.
Harry's first child is named "Baby of Harry and Mary".
```

Good Practice
Since it may not be obvious to a programmer who is using your class that instances of the class can use an operator, it's best to have both a method and an operator that perform the same function. For example, the `string` type has both a `Concat` method and can use the `+` operator to concatenate two strings together.

Defining local functions

A new language feature in C# 7 is the ability to define a local function. They are the method equivalent to local variables. In other words, they are methods that are only visible and callable from within the containing method in which they have been defined. In other languages, they are sometimes called *nested* or *inner* functions.

We will use a local function to implement a factorial calculation.

Add the following code to the `Person` class:

```
// method with a local function
public int Factorial(int number)
{
  if (number < 0)
  {
    throw new ArgumentException(
      $"{nameof(number)} cannot be less than zero.");
  }

  int localFactorial(int localNumber)
  {
    if (localNumber < 1) return 1;
    return localNumber * localFactorial(localNumber - 1);
  }

  return localFactorial(number);
}
```

In the `Program.cs` file, in the `Main` method, add the following statement:

```
WriteLine($"5! is {harry.Factorial(5)}");
```

Run the console application and view the output:

```
5! is 120
```

Raising and handling events

Methods are often described as *actions that an object can do*. For example, a `List` class can add an item to itself or clear itself.

Events are often described as *actions that happen to an object*. For example, in a user interface, `Button` has a `Click` event, click being something that happens to a button.

Another way of thinking of events is a way of exchanging messages between two objects.

Calling methods using delegates

You have already seen the most common way to call or execute a method: use the **dot** syntax to access the method using its name. For example, `Console.WriteLine` tells the `Console` type to write out the message to the console window or terminal.

The other way to call or execute a method is to use a delegate. If you have used languages that support function pointers, then think of a delegate as being a type-safe method pointer. In other words, a delegate is the memory address of a method that matches the same signature as the delegate so that it can be safely called.

For example, imagine there is a method that must have a `string` passed as its only parameter and it returns an `int`:

```
public int MethodIWantToCall(string input)
{
  return input.Length; // it doesn't matter what this does
}
```

I could call this method directly like this:

```
int answer = p1.MethodIWantToCall("Frog");
```

Alternatively, I could define a delegate with a matching signature to call the method indirectly. Notice that the names of parameters do not have to match. Only the types of parameters and return values must match:

```
delegate int DelegateWithMatchingSignature(string s);
```

Now, I can create an instance of the delegate, point it at the method, and finally call the delegate (which calls the method!):

```
var d = new DelegateWithMatchingSignature(p1.MethodIWantToCall);
int answer2 = d("Frog");
```

You are probably thinking, “What's the point of that?” Well, it provides flexibility.

We could use delegates to create a queue of methods that need to be called in order. Delegates have built-in support for asynchronous operations that run on a different thread for better performance. Most importantly, delegates allow us to create events.

Delegates and events are one of the most advanced features of C# and can take a few attempts to understand, so don't worry if you're feeling lost!

Defining events

Microsoft has two predefined delegates for use as events. They look like this:

```
public delegate void EventHandler(object sender, EventArgs e);
public delegate void EventHandler<TEventArgs>(object sender,
TEventArgs e);
```

Good Practice
When you want to define an event in your own type, you should use one of these two predefined delegates.

Add the following code to the `Person` class. The code defines an event named `Shout`. It also defines a field to store `AngerLevel` and a method named `Poke`. Each time a person is poked, their anger level increments. Once their anger level reaches three, they raise the `Shout` event, but only if the event delegate is pointing at a method defined somewhere else in code, that is, not null:

```
// event
public event EventHandler Shout;
```

```
// field
public int AngerLevel;

// method
public void Poke()
{
  AngerLevel++;
  if (AngerLevel >= 3)
  {
    // if something is listening...
    if (Shout != null)
    {
      // ...then raise the event
      Shout(this, EventArgs.Empty);
    }
  }
}
```

Checking if an object is null before calling one of its methods is very common. C# allows these statements to be simplified like this: `Shout?.Invoke(this, EventArgs.Empty);`

In Visual Studio 2017, in the `Main` method, start typing the following code to assign an event handler:

```
harry.Shout +=
```

Notice the IntelliSense that appears when you enter the += operator, as shown in the following screenshot:

harry.Shout+=
Harry_Shout;
(Press TAB to insert)

Press Tab. You will now see a preview of what Visual Studio would like to do for you, as shown in the following screenshot:

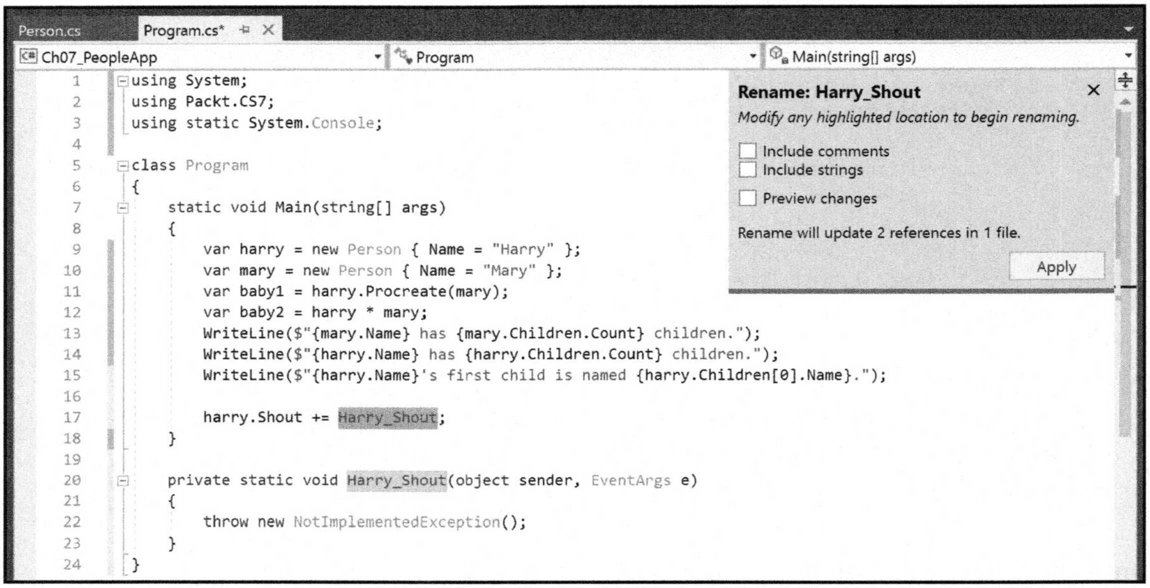

Person.cs Program.cs*

Ch07_PeopleApp Program Main(string[] args)

```
using System;
using Packt.CS7;
using static System.Console;

class Program
{
    static void Main(string[] args)
    {
        var harry = new Person { Name = "Harry" };
        var mary = new Person { Name = "Mary" };
        var baby1 = harry.Procreate(mary);
        var baby2 = harry * mary;
        WriteLine($"{mary.Name} has {mary.Children.Count} children.");
        WriteLine($"{harry.Name} has {harry.Children.Count} children.");
        WriteLine($"{harry.Name}'s first child is named {harry.Children[0].Name}.");

        harry.Shout += Harry_Shout;
    }

    private static void Harry_Shout(object sender, EventArgs e)
    {
        throw new NotImplementedException();
    }
}
```

Rename: Harry_Shout

Modify any highlighted location to begin renaming.

Include comments

Include strings

Preview changes

Rename will update 2 references in 1 file.

Apply

Press *Enter* to accept the name of the method.

Visual Studio 2017 inserts a method that correctly matches the signature of the event delegate. This method will be automatically called when the event is raised.

Scroll down to find the method Visual Studio 2017 created for you and delete the statement that throws `NotImplementedException`.

In Visual Studio Code, you must write the method and assign its name yourself. The method should look like this. The name can be anything, but `Harry_Shout` is sensible:

```
private static void Harry_Shout(object sender, EventArgs e)
{
}
```

In Visual Studio Code, in the `Main` method, add the following statement to assign the method to the event:

```
harry.Shout += Harry_Shout;
```

In both Visual Studio 2017 and Visual Studio Code, add statements to the `Harry_Shout` method to get a reference to the `Person` object and output some information about them, as shown in the following code:

```
private static void Harry_Shout(object sender, EventArgs e)
{
  Person p = (Person)sender;
  WriteLine($"{p.Name} is this angry: {p.AngerLevel}.");
}
```

Back in the `Main` method, add the following statements to call the `Poke` method four times, after assigning the method to the `Shout` event:

```
harry.Shout += harry_Shout;
harry.Poke();
harry.Poke();
harry.Poke();
harry.Poke();
```

Run the application. Note that Harry only gets angry enough to shout once he's been poked at least three times:

```
Harry is this angry: 3.
Harry is this angry: 4.
```

Implementing interfaces

Interfaces are a way of connecting different types together to make new things. Think of them like the studs on top of LEGO™ bricks that allow them to "stick" together, or electrical standards for plugs and sockets.

If a type implements an interface, then it is making a promise to the rest of .NET that it supports a certain feature.

Common interfaces

Here are some common interfaces that your types might want to implement:

Interface	Method(s)	Description
`IComparable`	`CompareTo`(other)	This defines a comparison method that a type implements to order or sort its instances.
`IComparer`	`Compare`(first, second)	This defines a comparison method that a secondary type implements to order or sort instances of a primary type.
`IDisposable`	`Dispose()`	This defines a disposal method to release unmanaged resources more efficiently than waiting for a finalizer.
`IFormattable`	`ToString`(format, culture)	This defines a culture-aware method to format the value of an object into a string representation.
`IFormatter`	`Serialize`(stream, object), `Deserialize`(stream)	This defines methods to convert an object to and from a stream of bytes for storage or transfer.

Comparing objects when sorting

One of the most common interfaces that you will want to implement is `IComparable`. It allows arrays and collections of your type to be sorted.

Add the following code to the `Main` method, which creates an array of `Person` instances, outputs the array, attempts to sort it, and then outputs the sorted array:

```
Person[] people =
{
  new Person { Name = "Simon" },
  new Person { Name = "Jenny" },
  new Person { Name = "Adam" },
  new Person { Name = "Richard" }
};

WriteLine("Initial list of people:");
foreach (var person in people)
{
  WriteLine($"{person.Name}");
```

```
}

WriteLine("Use Person's sort implementation:");
Array.Sort(people);
foreach (var person in people)
{
  WriteLine($"{person.Name}");
}
```

Run the application, and you will see this runtime error:

```
Unhandled Exception: System.InvalidOperationException: Failed to
compare two elements in the array. ---> System.ArgumentException: At
least one object must implement IComparable.
```

As the error explains, to fix the problem, our type must implement `IComparable`.

In the `Ch07_PacktLibrary` project, in the `Person` class, add the following code to the end of the class definition:

```
public partial class Person : IComparable<Person>
```

Visual Studio 2017 and Visual Studio Code will draw a red squiggle under the new code to warn you that you have not yet implemented the method you have promised to.

Visual Studio 2017 and Visual Studio Code can write the skeleton implementation for you if you click on the lightbulb and choose the option **Implement interface**, as shown in the following screenshot:

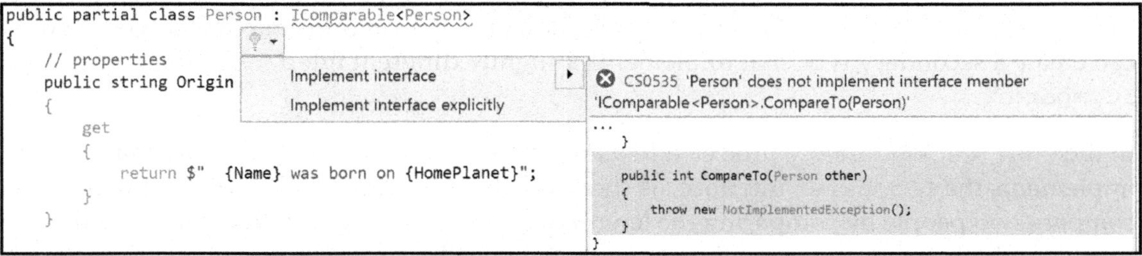

Visual Studio 2017 shows a preview of the change that it will make. Visual Studio Code does not.

Scroll down to find the method that was written for you and delete the statement that throws the `NotImplementedException` error. Modify the method to look like this. Visual Studio Code users must write the whole method themselves:

```
public int CompareTo(Person other)
{
  return Name.CompareTo(other.Name);
}
```

I have chosen to compare two `Person` instances by comparing their name fields. People will, therefore, be sorted alphabetically by their name.

Run the application. This time it works:

```
Initial list of people:
Simon
Jenny
Adam
Richard
Use Person's sort implementation:
Adam
Jenny
Richard
Simon
```

Defining a separate comparer

Sometimes, you won't have access to the source code for a type, and it might not implement the `IComparable` interface. Luckily, there is another way to sort instances of a type. You can create a secondary type that implements a slightly different interface, named `IComparer`.

In the `Ch07_PacktLibrary` project, add a new class named `PersonComparer` that implements the `IComparer` interface, as shown in the following block of code. It will compare two people by comparing the length of their `Name` field, or if the names are the same length, then by comparing the names alphabetically:

```
using System.Collections.Generic;

namespace Packt.CS7
{
  public class PersonComparer : IComparer<Person>
  {
    public int Compare(Person x, Person y)
    {
```

```
            int temp = x.Name.Length.CompareTo(y.Name.Length);
            if (temp == 0)
            {
              return x.Name.CompareTo(y.Name);
            }
            else
            {
              return temp;
            }
          }
        }
      }
```

In the `Main` method, add the following code:

```
      WriteLine("Use PersonComparer's sort implementation:");
      Array.Sort(people, new PersonComparer());
      foreach (var person in people)
      {
        WriteLine($"{person.Name}");
      }
```

Run the application. This time, when we sort the people array, we explicitly ask the sorting algorithm to use the `PersonComparer` type instead, so the people are sorted with the shortest names first, and when the lengths of two or more names are equal, to sort them alphabetically:

```
Use Person's sort implementation:
Adam
Jenny
Richard
Simon
Use PersonComparer's sort implementation:
Adam
Jenny
Simon
Richard
```

Good Practice
If anyone would want to sort an array or collection of instances of your type, then implement the `IComparable` interface.

Managing memory with reference and value types

There are two categories of memory: **stack** memory and **heap** memory. Stack memory is fast but limited and heap memory is slow but plentiful.

There are two C# keywords that you use to create object types: `class` and `struct`. Both can have the same members. The difference between the two is how memory is allocated.

When you define a type using class, you are defining a reference type. This means that the memory for the object itself is allocated on the heap, and only the memory address of the object (and a little overhead) is stored on the stack.

When you define a type using `struct`, you are defining a value type. This means that the memory for the object itself is allocated on the stack.

If a `struct` uses types that are not of the `struct` type for any of its fields, then those fields will be stored on the heap!

These are the most common `struct` types in .NET Core:

- **Numbers**: `byte`, `sbyte`, `short`, `ushort`, `int`, `uint`, `long`, `ulong`, `float`, `double`, `decimal`
- **Miscellaneous**: `char`, `bool`
- **System.Drawing**: `Color`, `Point`, `Rectangle`

Almost all the other types in .NET Core are `class` types, including `string`.

You cannot inherit from `struct`.

Defining a struct type

Add a class file named `DisplacementVector.cs` to the `Ch07_PacktLibrary` project.

There isn't an item template in Visual Studio 2017 for `struct`, so you must use class and then change it manually.

Modify the file as shown in the following code:

```
namespace Packt.CS7
{
  public struct DisplacementVector
  {
    public int X;
    public int Y;

    public DisplacementVector(int initialX, int initialY)
    {
      X = initialX;
      Y = initialY;
    }

    public static DisplacementVector operator +(
      DisplacementVector vector1, DisplacementVector vector2)
    {
      return new DisplacementVector(vector1.X + vector2.X,
      vector1.Y + vector2.Y);
    }
  }
}
```

In the `Ch07_PeopleApp` project, in the `Main` method, add the following code:

```
var dv1 = new DisplacementVector(3, 5);
var dv2 = new DisplacementVector(-2, 7);
var dv3 = dv1 + dv2;
WriteLine($"({dv1.X}, {dv1.Y}) + ({dv2.X}, {dv2.Y}) = ({dv3.X},
{dv3.Y})");
```

Run the application and view the output:

```
(3, 5) + (-2, 7) = (1, 12)
```

Good Practice
If all the fields in your type use 16 bytes or less of stack memory, your type only uses `struct` types for its fields, and you will never want to derive from your type, then Microsoft recommends that you use a `struct`. If your type uses more than 16 bytes of stack memory, or if it uses class types for its fields, or if you might want to inherit from it, then use `class`.

Releasing unmanaged resources

In the previous chapter, we saw that constructors can be used to initialize fields and that a type may have multiple constructors.

Imagine that a constructor allocates an unmanaged resource, that is, anything that is not controlled by .NET. The unmanaged resource must be manually released because .NET cannot do it for us.

For this topic, I will show some code examples, but you do not need to create them in your current project.

Each type can have a single **finalizer** (aka destructor) that will be called by the CLR when the resources need to be released. A finalizer has the same name as a constructor, that is, the type name, but it is prefixed with a tilde (~), as shown in the following example:

```
public class Animal
{
  public Animal()
  {
    // allocate an unmanaged resource
  }
  ~Animal() // Finalizer aka destructor
  {
    // deallocate the unmanaged resource
  }
}
```

Do not confuse a finalizer aka **destructor** with a **deconstructor**. A destructor releases resources, that is, it destroys an object. A deconstructor returns an object split up into its constituent parts and uses the new C# 7 deconstruction syntax.

This is the minimum you should do in this scenario. The problem with just providing a finalizer is that the .NET garbage collector requires two garbage collections to completely release the allocated resources for this type.

Though optional, it is recommended to also provide a method to allow a developer who uses your type to explicitly release resources so that the garbage collector can then release the object in a single collection.

There is a standard mechanism to do this in .NET by implementing the `IDisposable` interface, as shown in the following example:

```
public class Animal : IDisposable
{
  public Animal()
  {
    // allocate unmanaged resource
  }

  ~Animal() // Finalizer
  {
    if (disposed) return;
    Dispose(false);
  }

  bool disposed = false; // have resources been released?

  public void Dispose()
  {
    Dispose(true);
    GC.SuppressFinalize(this);
  }

  protected virtual void Dispose(bool disposing)
  {
    if (disposed) return;
    // deallocate the *unmanaged* resource
    // ...
    if (disposing)
    {
      // deallocate any other *managed* resources
      // ...
    }
    disposed = true;
  }
}
```

There are two `Dispose` methods. The `public` method will be called by a developer using your type. The `Dispose` method with a `bool` parameter is used internally to implement the deallocation of resources, both unmanaged and managed. When the public `Dispose` method is called, both unmanaged and managed resources need to be deallocated, but when the finalizer runs, only unmanaged resources need to be deallocated.

Also, note the call to `GC.SuppressFinalize(this)`—this is what notifies the garbage collector that it no longer needs to run the finalizer and removes the need for a second collection.

Ensuring that dispose is called

When someone uses a type that implements `IDisposable`, they can ensure that the public `Dispose` method is called with the `using` statement, as shown in the following code:

```
using(Animal a = new Animal())
{
  // code that uses the Animal instance
}
```

The compiler converts your code into something like the following, which guarantees that even if an exception occurs, the `Dispose` method will still be called:

```
Animal a = new Animal();
try
{
  // code that uses the Animal instance
}
finally
{
  if (a != null) a.Dispose();
}
```

Inheriting from classes

The `Person` type we created earlier implicitly derived (inherited) from `System.Object`. Now, we will create a new class that inherits from `Person`.

Add a new class named `Employee.cs` to the `Ch07_PacktLibrary` project.

Modify its code as shown in the following code:

```
using System;

namespace Packt.CS7
{
  public class Employee : Person
  {
  }
}
```

Add statements to the `Main` method to create an instance of the `Employee` class:

```
Employee e1 = new Employee
{
  Name = "John Jones",
  DateOfBirth = new DateTime(1990, 7, 28)
};
e1.WriteToConsole();
```

Run the console application and view the output:

```
John Jones was born on Saturday, 28 July 1990
```

Note that the `Employee` class has inherited all the members of `Person`.

Extending classes

Now, we will add some employee-specific members to extend the class.

In the `Employee` class, add the following code to define two properties:

```
public string EmployeeCode { get; set; }
public DateTime HireDate { get; set; }
```

Back in the `Main` method, add the following code:

```
e1.EmployeeCode = "JJ001";
e1.HireDate = new DateTime(2014, 11, 23);
WriteLine($"{e1.Name} was hired on {e1.HireDate:dd/MM/yy}");
```

Run the console application and view the output:

```
John Jones was hired on 23/11/14
```

Hiding members

So far, the `WriteToConsole` method is being inherited from `Person`, and it only outputs the employee's name and date of birth. We might want to change what this method does for an employee.

In the `Employee` class, add the following code to redefine the `WriteToConsole` method:

```
using System;
using static System.Console;

namespace Packt.CS6
{
  public class Employee : Person
  {
    public string EmployeeCode { get; set; }
    public DateTime HireDate { get; set; }

    public void WriteToConsole()
    {
      WriteLine($"{Name}'s birth date is {DateOfBirth:dd/MM/yy} and
      hire date was {HireDate:dd/MM/yy}");
    }
  }
}
```

Run the application and view the output:

```
John Jones's birth date is 28/07/90 and hire date was 01/01/01
John Jones was hired on 23/11/14
```

Both Visual Studio 2017 and Visual Studio Code warn you that your method now hides the method with the same name that you inherited from the `Person` class by drawing a green squiggle under the method name.

Visual Studio Code also warns you in the output, as shown in the following screenshot:

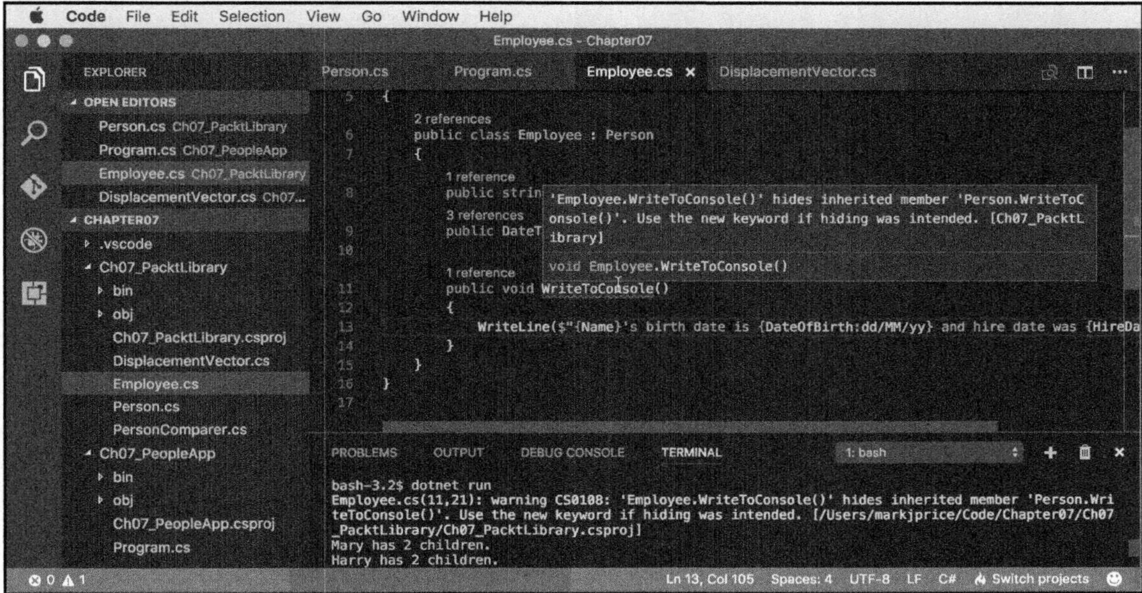

You can remove this warning by applying the `new` keyword to the method, to indicate that you are deliberately replacing the old method, as shown in the following code:

```
public new void WriteToConsole()
```

Overriding members

Rather than hiding a method, it is usually better to override it. You can only override members if the base class chooses to allow overriding, by applying the `virtual` keyword.

In the `Main` method, add the following statement:

```
WriteLine(e1.ToString());
```

Run the application. The `ToString` method is inherited from `System.Object`. The implementation outputs the namespace and type name, as follows:

```
Packt.CS7.Employee
```

Let's override this behavior for the `Person` class.

Make this change to the `Person` class, not the `Employee` class.

In Visual Studio 2017, open the `Person.cs` file, and at the bottom (but inside the class brackets), type the keyword `override` and enter a space after the word. You will see that Visual Studio shows a list of methods that have been marked as `virtual` so that they can be overridden, as shown in the following screenshot:

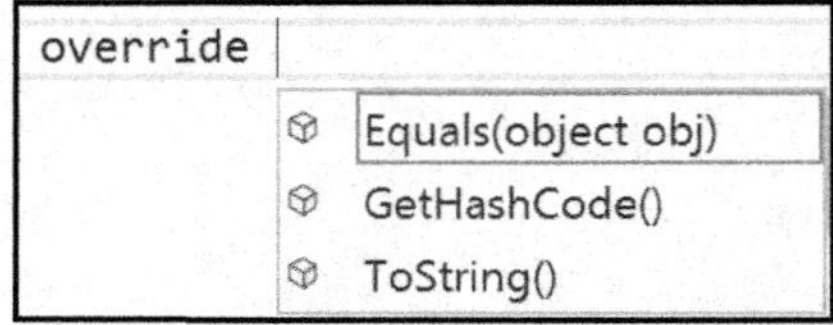

Use the arrow keys on your keyboard to choose `ToString` and then press *Enter*.

Modify the code to look like the following statements:

```
// overridden methods
public override string ToString()
{
  return $"{Name} is a {base.ToString()}";
}
```

In Visual Studio Code, you must type the whole method yourself.

Run the console application and view the output. Now, when the `ToString` method is called, it outputs the person's name, as well as the base class's implementation of `ToString`, as shown in the following output:

```
John Jones is a Packt.CS7.Employee
```

Good Practice
Many real-world APIs, for example, Microsoft's Entity Framework, Castle's Windsor proxies, and Episerver's content models, require the properties that you define in your classes to be marked as `virtual`. Unless you have a good reason, mark your method and property members as `virtual`.

Preventing inheritance and overriding

You can prevent someone from inheriting from your class by applying the `sealed` keyword to its definition. No one can inherit from Scrooge McDuck:

```
public sealed class ScroogeMcDuck
{
}
```

An example of `sealed` in the real world is the `string` class. Microsoft has implemented some extreme optimizations inside the `string` class that could be negatively affected by your inheritance; so, Microsoft prevents that.

You can prevent someone from overriding a method in your class by applying the `sealed` keyword to the method. No one can change the way Lady Gaga sings:

```
public class LadyGaga
{
  public sealed void Sing()
  {
  }
}
```

Polymorphism

You have now seen two ways to change the behavior of an inherited method. We can hide it using `new` (known as nonpolymorphic inheritance), or we can override it (polymorphic inheritance).

Both ways can call the base class using the `base` keyword, so what is the difference?

It all depends on the type of the variable holding a reference to the object. For example, a variable of the `Person` type can hold a reference to a `Person` class, *or any type that derives from* `Person`.

In the `Employee` class, add the following code:

```
public override string ToString()
{
  return $"{Name}'s code is {EmployeeCode}";
}
```

In the `Main` method, write the following code:

```
Employee aliceInEmployee = new Employee
  { Name = "Alice", EmployeeCode = "AA123" };
Person aliceInPerson = aliceInEmployee;
aliceInEmployee.WriteToConsole();
aliceInPerson.WriteToConsole();
WriteLine(aliceInEmployee.ToString());
WriteLine(aliceInPerson.ToString());
```

Run the console application and view the output:

```
Alice's birth date is 01/01/01 and hire date was 01/01/01
Alice was born on Monday, 1 January 0001
Alice's code is AA123
Alice's code is AA123
```

Note that when a method is hidden with `new`, the compiler is not smart enough to know that the object is an employee, so it calls the `WriteToConsole` method in `Person`.

When a method is overridden with `virtual` and `override`, the compiler is smart enough to know that although the variable is declared as a `Person` class, the object itself is an `Employee` and, therefore, the `Employee` implementation of `ToString` is called.

Variable type	Access modifier	Method executed	In class
`Person`		`WriteToConsole`	`Person`
`Employee`	`new`	`WriteToConsole`	`Employee`
`Person`	`virtual`	`ToString`	`Employee`
`Employee`	`override`	`ToString`	`Employee`

Polymorphism is literally academic to most programmers. If you get the concept, that's fine; but, if not, I suggest that you don't worry about it. Some people like to make others feel inferior by saying understanding polymorphism is important, but IMHO it's not. You can have a successful career with C# and never need to be able to explain polymorphism, just as a racing car driver doesn't need to be able to explain the engineering behind fuel injection.

Casting within inheritance hierarchies

Casting is subtly different from converting between types.

Implicit casting

In the previous example, you saw how an instance of a derived type can be stored in a variable of its base type (or its base's base type and so on). When we do this, it is called implicit casting.

Explicit casting

Going the other way is an explicit cast, and you must use parentheses to do it.

In the `Main` method, add the following code:

```
Employee e2 = aliceInPerson;
```

Visual Studio 2017 and Visual Studio Code display a red squiggle and a compile error in the Error List and Problems window, as shown in the following screenshot:

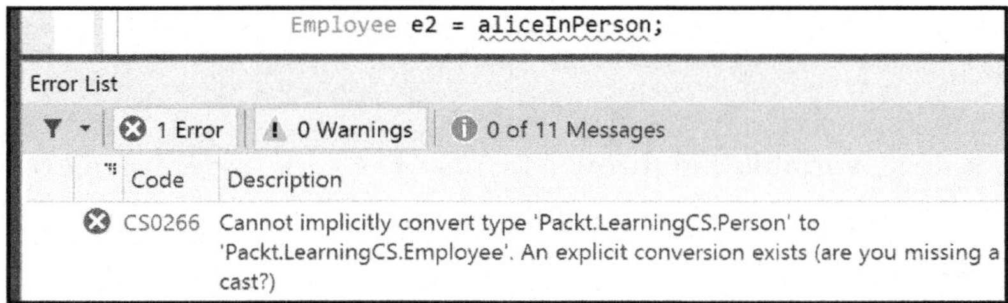

Change the code as follows:

```
Employee e2 = (Employee)aliceInPerson;
```

Handling casting exceptions

The compiler is now happy; *but*, because `aliceInPerson` might be a different derived type, like a `Student` instead of an `Employee`, we need to be careful. This statement might throw an `InvalidCastException` error.

We can handle this by writing a `try` statement, but there is a better way. We can check the current type of the object using the `is` keyword.

Wrap the explicit cast statement in an `if` statement, as follows:

```
if (aliceInPerson is Employee)
{
  WriteLine($"{nameof(aliceInPerson)} IS an Employee");
  Employee e2 = (Employee)aliceInPerson;
  // do something with e2
}
```

Run the console application and view the output:

```
aliceInPerson IS an Employee
```

Alternatively, you can use the `as` keyword to cast. Instead of throwing an exception, the `as` keyword returns `null` if the type cannot be cast.

Add the following statements to the end of the `Main` method:

```
Employee e3 = aliceInPerson as Employee;
if (e3 != null)
{
  WriteLine($"{nameof(aliceInPerson)} AS an Employee");
  // do something with e3
}
```

Since accessing a `null` variable can throw a `NullReferenceException` error, you should always check for `null` before using the result.

Run the console application and view the output:

```
aliceInPerson AS an Employee
```

Good Practice
Use the `is` and `as` keywords to avoid throwing exceptions when casting between derived types.

Inheriting and extending .NET types

.NET has prebuilt class libraries containing hundreds of thousands of types. Rather than creating your own completely new types, you can often start by inheriting from one of Microsoft's.

Inheriting from an exception

In the `Ch07_PacktLibrary` project, add a new class named `PersonException`, as shown in the following code:

```
using System;

namespace Packt.CS7
{
  public class PersonException : Exception
  {
    public PersonException() : base() { }
    public PersonException(string message) : base(message) { }
    public PersonException(string message,
      Exception innerException) : base(
      message, innerException) { }
  }
}
```

In the `Person` class, add the following method:

```
public void TimeTravel(DateTime when)
{
  if (when <= DateOfBirth)
  {
    throw new PersonException("If you travel back in time to a
    date earlier than your own birth then the universe will
    explode!");
```

```
    }
    else
    {
      WriteLine($"Welcome to {when:yyyy}!");
    }
  }
```

In the `Main` method, add the following statements to test what happens when we try to time travel too far back:

```
try
{
  e1.TimeTravel(new DateTime(1999, 12, 31));
  e1.TimeTravel(new DateTime(1950, 12, 25));
}
catch (PersonException ex)
{
  WriteLine(ex.Message);
}
```

Run the console application and view the output:

```
Welcome to 1999!
If you travel back in time to a date earlier than your own birth then
the universe will explode!
```

Good Practice
When defining your own exceptions, give them the same three constructors.

Extending types when you can't inherit

Earlier, we saw how the `sealed` modifier can be used to prevent inheritance.

Microsoft has applied the `sealed` keyword to the `System.String` class so that no one can inherit and potentially break the behavior of strings.

Can we still add new methods to strings? Yes, if we use a language feature named **extension methods**, which was introduced with C# 3.

Using static methods to reuse functionality

Since the first version of C#, we could create `static` methods to reuse functionality, such as the ability to validate that a string contains an e-mail address.

In the `Ch07_PacktLibrary` project, add a new class named `MyExtensions.cs`, as shown in the following code:

```
using System.Text.RegularExpressions;

namespace Packt.CS7
{
  public class MyExtensions
  {
    public static bool IsValidEmail(string input)
    {
      // use simple regular expression to check
      // that the input string is a valid email
      return Regex.IsMatch(input,
        @"[a-zA-Z0-9\.-_]+@[a-zA-Z0-9\.-_]+");
    }
  }
}
```

Add the following statements to the bottom of the `Main` method to validate two examples of e-mail addresses:

```
string email1 = "pamela@test.com";
string email2 = "ian&test.com";

WriteLine($"{email1} is a valid e-mail address:
{MyExtensions.IsValidEmail(email1)}.");
WriteLine($"{email2} is a valid e-mail address:
{MyExtensions.IsValidEmail(email2)}.");
```

Run the application and view the output:

```
pamela@test.com is a valid e-mail address: True.
ian&test.com is a valid e-mail address: False.
```

This works, but extension methods can reduce the amount of code we must type and simplify the usage of this function.

Using extension methods to reuse functionality

In the `MyExtensions` class, add the `static` modifier before the class, and add the `this` modifier before the `string` type, like this:

```
public static class MyExtensions
{
  public static bool IsValidEmail(this string input)
  {
```

These two changes inform the compiler that it should treat the method as a method that extends the `System.String` type.

Back in the `Program` class, add some new statements to use the method as an extension method for strings:

```
WriteLine($"{email1} is a valid e-mail address:
{email1.IsValidEmail()}.");
WriteLine($"{email2} is a valid e-mail address:
{email2.IsValidEmail()}.");
```

Note the subtle change in the syntax. The `IsValidEmail` method now appears to be an instance member of the `string` type:

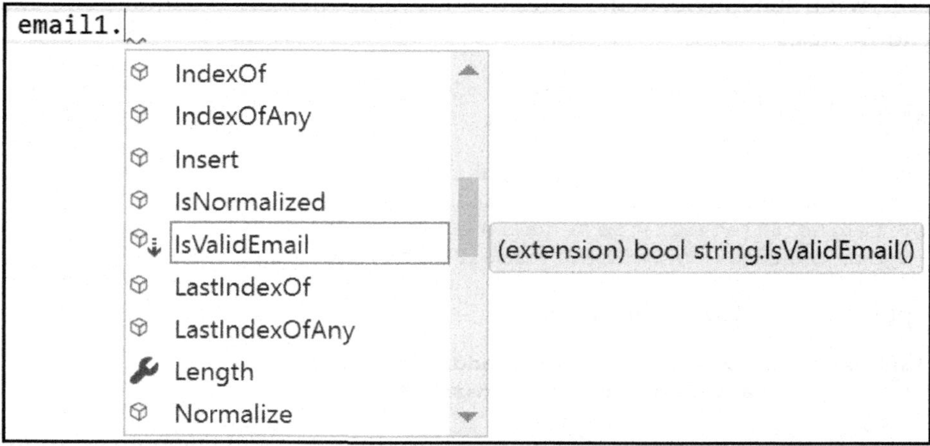

Extension methods cannot replace or override existing instance methods, so you cannot, for example, redefine the `Insert` method of a `string` variable. The extension method will appear as an overload, but the instance method will be called in preference to the extension method with the same name and signature.

Although extension methods don't seem to give a big benefit compared to simply using `static` methods, in `Chapter 9`, *Querying and Manipulating Data with LINQ*, you will see some extremely powerful uses of extension methods.

Practice and explore

Test your knowledge and understanding by answering some questions. Get some hands-on practice and explore with deeper research into this chapter's topics.

Exercise 7.1 – test your knowledge

Answer the following questions:

1. What is a delegate?
2. What is an event?
3. How are a base class and a derived class related?
4. What is the difference between `is` and `as`?
5. Which keyword is used to prevent a class from being derived from or a method from being overridden?
6. Which keyword is used to prevent a class from being instantiated with the `new` keyword?
7. Which keyword is used to allow a member to be overridden?
8. What's the difference between a destructor and a deconstructor?
9. What are the signatures of the constructors that all exceptions should have?
10. What is an extension method and how do you define one?

Exercise 7.2 – practice creating an inheritance hierarchy

Add a new console application named `Ch07_Exercise02`.

Create a class named `Shape` with properties named `Height`, `Width`, and `Area`.

Add three classes that derive from it—`Rectangle`, `Square`, and `Circle`-with any additional members you feel are appropriate and that override and implement the `Area` property correctly.

Exercise 7.3 – explore topics

Use the following links to read more about the topics covered in this chapter:

- **Operator (C# reference)**: `https://docs.microsoft.com/en-us/dotnet/articles/csharp/language-reference/keywords/operator`
- **Delegates**: `https://docs.microsoft.com/en-us/dotnet/articles/csharp/tour-of-csharp/delegates`
- **Events (C# programming guide)**: `https://docs.microsoft.com/en-us/dotnet/articles/csharp/language-reference/keywords/event`
- **Interfaces**: `https://docs.microsoft.com/en-us/dotnet/articles/csharp/tour-of-csharp/interfaces`
- **Reference Types (C# Reference)**: `https://docs.microsoft.com/en-us/dotnet/articles/csharp/language-reference/keywords/reference-types`
- **Value Types (C# Reference)**: `https://docs.microsoft.com/en-us/dotnet/articles/csharp/language-reference/keywords/value-types`
- **Inheritance (C# Programming Guide)**: `https://docs.microsoft.com/en-us/dotnet/articles/csharp/programming-guide/classes-and-structs/inheritance`
- **Destructors (C# Programming Guide)**: `https://docs.microsoft.com/en-us/dotnet/articles/csharp/programming-guide/classes-and-structs/destructors`

Summary

In this chapter, you learned about delegates and events, implementing interfaces, and deriving types using inheritance and OOP. You learned about base and derived classes, how to override a type member, how to use polymorphism, and how to cast between types.

In the next chapter, you will learn about working with databases using the Entity Framework Core.

8

Working with Databases Using the Entity Framework Core

This chapter is about reading and writing to databases, such as Microsoft SQL Server and SQLite, using the object-relational mapping technology known as the Entity Framework Core.

This chapter will cover the following topics:

- Relational Database Management Systems
- Using Microsoft SQL Server on Windows
- Using SQLite on macOS and mobile platforms
- Setting up Entity Framework Core
- Querying an EF Core model
- Manipulating data with EF Core

Relational Database Management Systems

One of the most common places to store data is in a **Relational Database Management System (RDBMS)**. Common ones include Microsoft SQL Server, Oracle, and SQLite.

Using a sample database

To learn how to manage a database using .NET Core, it would be useful to have a sample one to practice on that has a medium complexity and a decent amount of sample records. Microsoft offers several sample databases, most of which are too complex for our needs. So, we will use a database that was first created in the early 1990s known as **Northwind**.

Use the link `https://github.com/markjprice/cs7dotnetcore/tree/master/VSCode/Chapter08` to download the `Northwind.sql` file for use with Microsoft SQL Server on Windows, or the `NorthwindSQLite.sql` file for use with SQLite on macOS or mobile platforms.

Here is a diagram of the Northwind database that you can refer to as we write queries:

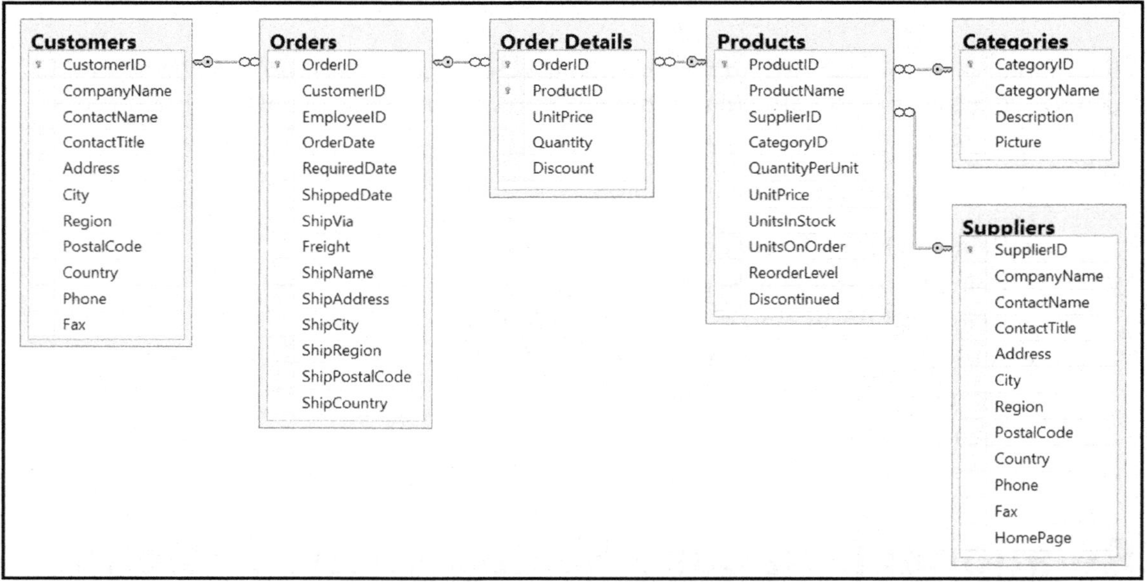

Using Microsoft SQL Server on Windows

Microsoft offers various editions of its SQL Server product. We will use a free version that can run stand-alone, known as **LocalDb**. The latest version of LocalDb is installed as part of Visual Studio 2017.

Microsoft SQL Server used to be a Windows-only RDBMS. In 2017, Microsoft plans to release a version for Linux that will be great for cross-platform .NET Core developers. A preview is available, but we will not cover it in this book.

Connecting to Microsoft SQL Server LocalDb

When you write code to connect to a SQL Server database, you need to know its **server name**. The name depends on the version you choose to use. Here are some examples:

- **Visual Studio 2017 installs SQL Server 2016**: `(localdb)\mssqllocaldb`
- **Visual Studio 2015 installs SQL Server 2014**: `(localdb)\mssqllocaldb`
- **Visual Studio 2012/2013 installs SQL Server 2012**: `(localdb)\v11.0`
- **If you install SQL Server Express**: `.\sqlexpress`

Creating the Northwind sample database

In Visual Studio 2017, go to **File** | **Open** | **File...** or press *Ctrl* + *O*.

Browse to select the `Northwind.sql` file and choose **Open**.

In the editor window, right-click and choose **Execute...** or press *Ctrl* + *Shift* + *E*.

In the dialog box, enter the server name as `(localdb)\mssqllocaldb` and click on **Connect**, as shown in the following screenshot:

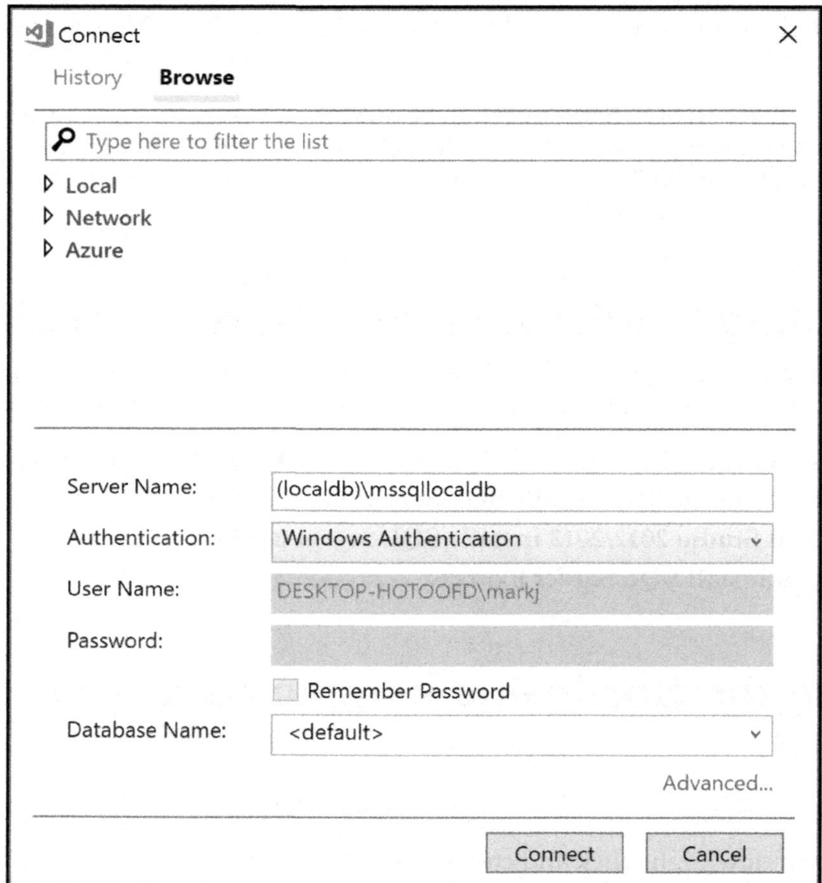

When you see the **Command(s) completed successfully** message, then the Northwind database has been created, and we can connect to it.

LocalDb, sometimes, takes too long to start the first time, and you might see a timeout error. Simply click on **Connect** again, and it should work.

Managing the Northwind sample database

In Visual Studio 2017, choose **View** | **Server Explorer...** or press *Ctrl* + *W*, *L*.

In the **Server Explorer** window, right-click on **Data Connections** and choose **Add Connection**...

If you see the **Choose Data Source** dialog, as shown in the following screenshot, then select **Microsoft SQL Server** and click on **Continue**:

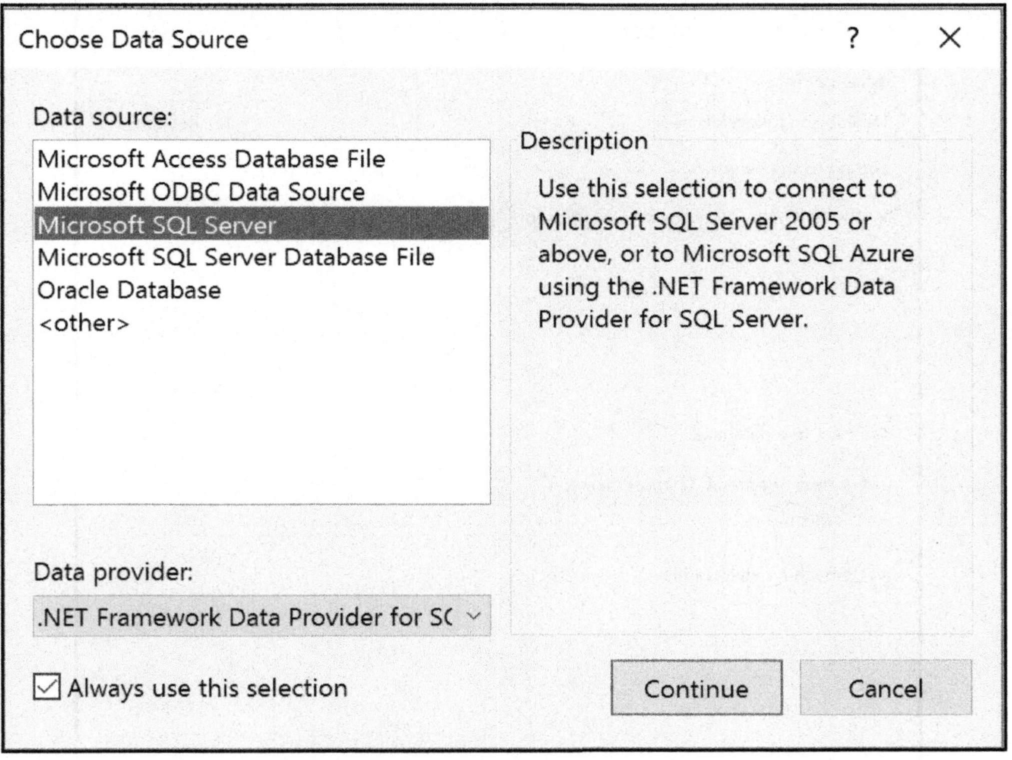

In the **Add Connection** dialog box, enter the server name as `(localdb)\mssqllocaldb`, enter the database name as `Northwind`, and click on **OK**, as shown in the following screenshot:

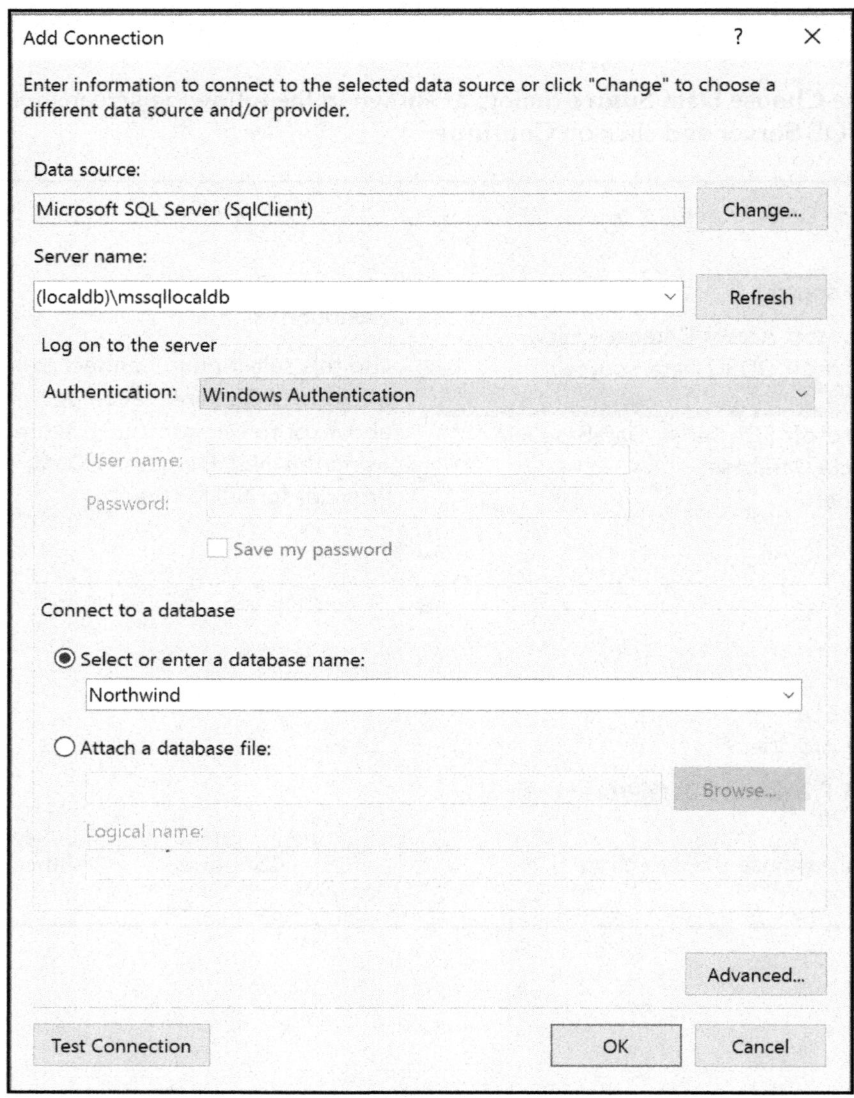

In the **Server Explorer** window, expand the data connection and its tables. You should see a dozen tables, including the **Products** table, as shown in the following screenshot:

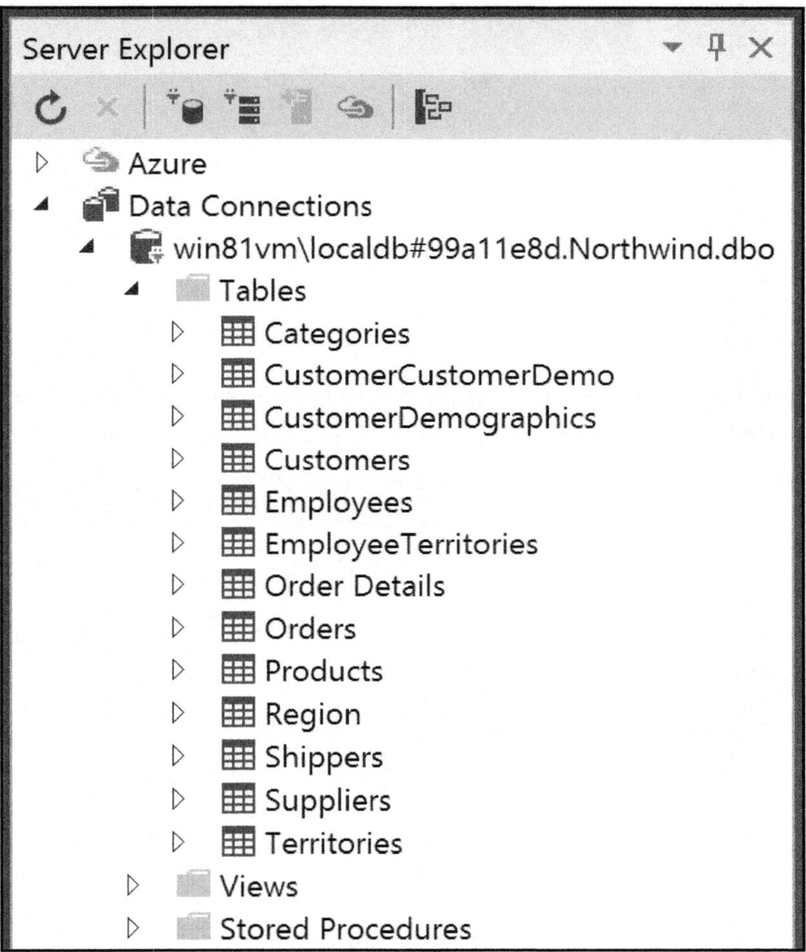

Right-click on the **Products** table and choose **Show Table Data**, as shown in the following screenshot:

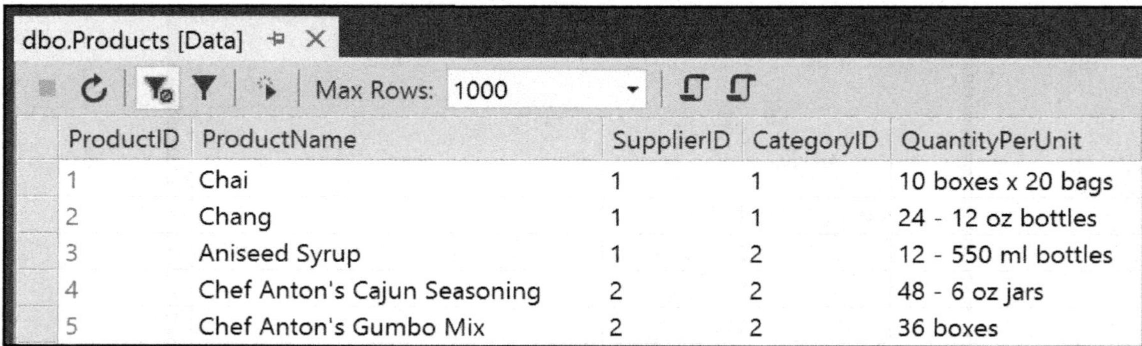

dbo.Products [Data]

Max Rows: 1000

ProductID	ProductName	SupplierID	CategoryID	QuantityPerUnit
1	Chai	1	1	10 boxes x 20 bags
2	Chang	1	1	24 - 12 oz bottles
3	Aniseed Syrup	1	2	12 - 550 ml bottles
4	Chef Anton's Cajun Seasoning	2	2	48 - 6 oz jars
5	Chef Anton's Gumbo Mix	2	2	36 boxes

To see the details of the **Products** table columns and types, right-click on **Products** and choose **Show Table Definition**, as shown in the following screenshot:

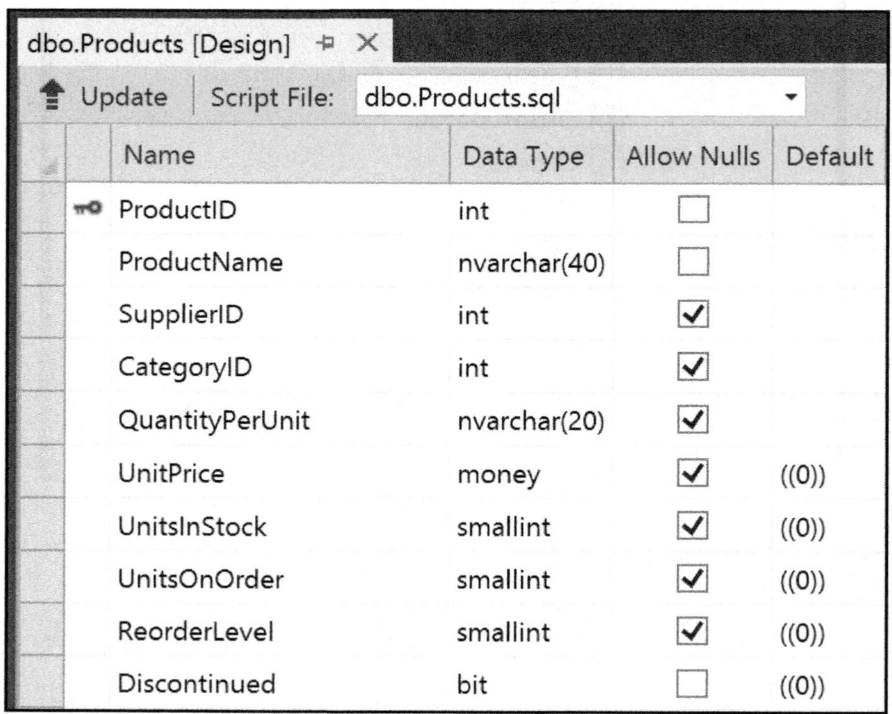

dbo.Products [Design]

Update Script File: dbo.Products.sql

Name	Data Type	Allow Nulls	Default
ProductID	int	☐	
ProductName	nvarchar(40)	☐	
SupplierID	int	☑	
CategoryID	int	☑	
QuantityPerUnit	nvarchar(20)	☑	
UnitPrice	money	☑	((0))
UnitsInStock	smallint	☑	((0))
UnitsOnOrder	smallint	☑	((0))
ReorderLevel	smallint	☑	((0))
Discontinued	bit	☐	((0))

Using SQLite on macOS and mobile platforms

SQLite is a small, cross-platform, self-contained RDBMS that is available in the public domain. It is the most common RDBMS for mobile platforms such as iOS (iPhone and iPad) and Android.

SQLite is included in macOS in the `/usr/bin/` directory as a command-line application named sqlite3.

You can download a graphical database manager named SQLiteStudio for SQLite here:

`http://sqlitestudio.pl`

You can read about the SQL statements supported by SQLite here:

`https://sqlite.org/lang.html`

Running a script for SQLite

Create a folder named `Chapter08` with a subfolder named `Ch08_EFCore`.

Download the `NorthwindSQLite.sql` file into the `Chapter08` folder.

Start **Terminal**. Enter commands to change to the `Code` folder, change to the directory named `Chapter08`, and run the SQLite script to create the `Northwind.db` database:

```
cd Code
cd Chapter08
sqlite3 Northwind.db < NorthwindSQLite.sql
```

Quit **Terminal** and launch SQLiteStudio.

If you see a warning about not being able to run the application, hold down *Shift* while opening it, and then click **Open**.

In SQLiteStudio, on the **Database** menu, choose **Add a database** or press *Cmd* + *O*.

In the **Database** dialog, click the folder button to browse for existing database file on local computer. Select the `Northwind.db` file. Click on **Test connection** to see the green tick, as shown in the following screenshot, and then click on **OK**:

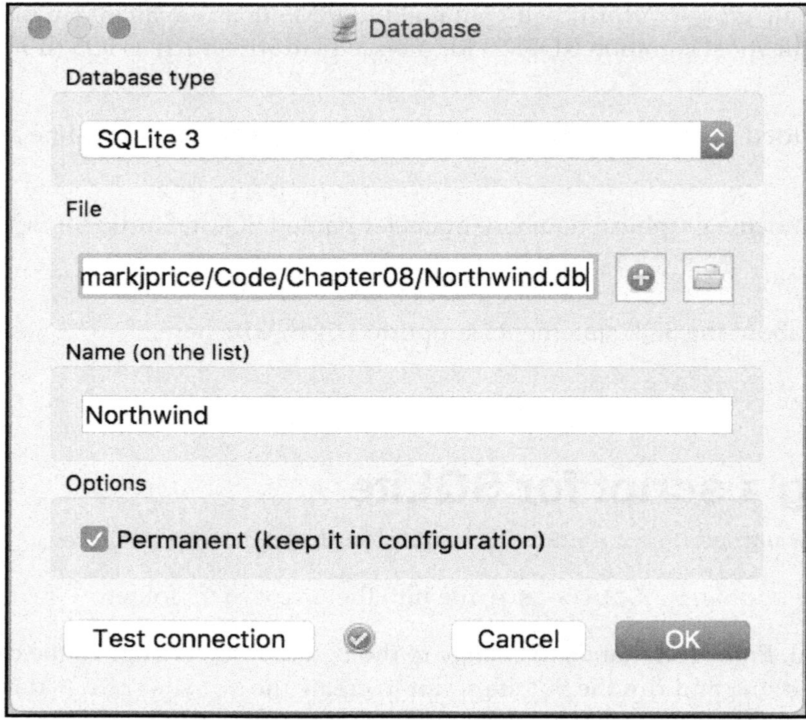

Right-click the `Northwind` database and choose **Connect to the database**, as shown in the following screenshot:

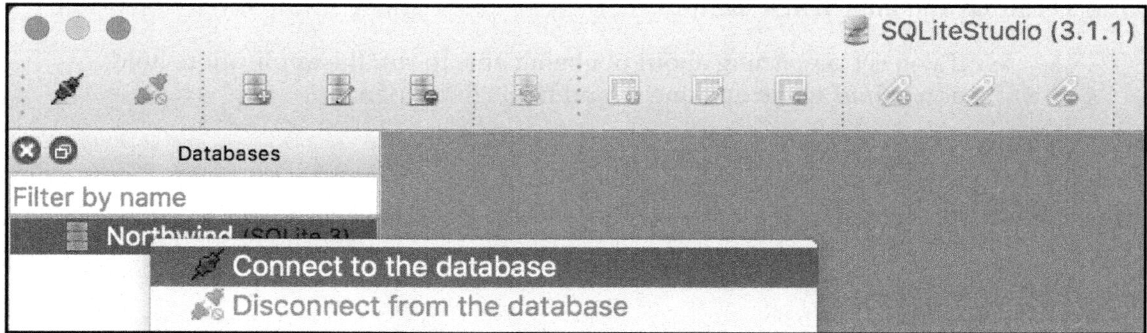

You will see the tables that were created by the script, as shown in the following screenshot:

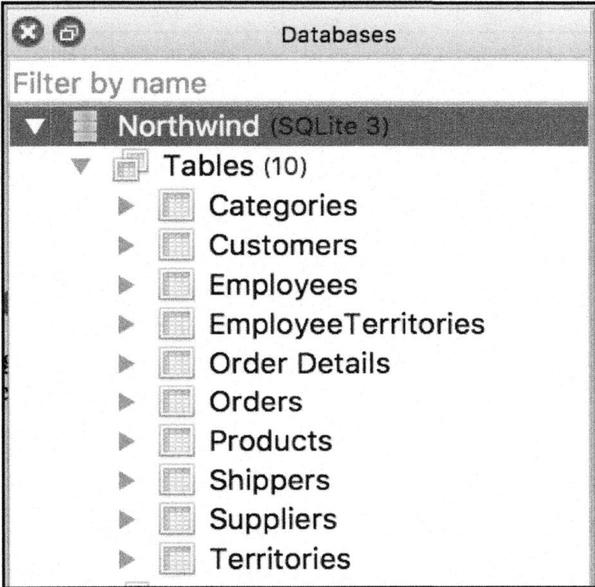

Right-click the **Products** table and choose **Edit the table**, as shown in the following screenshot:

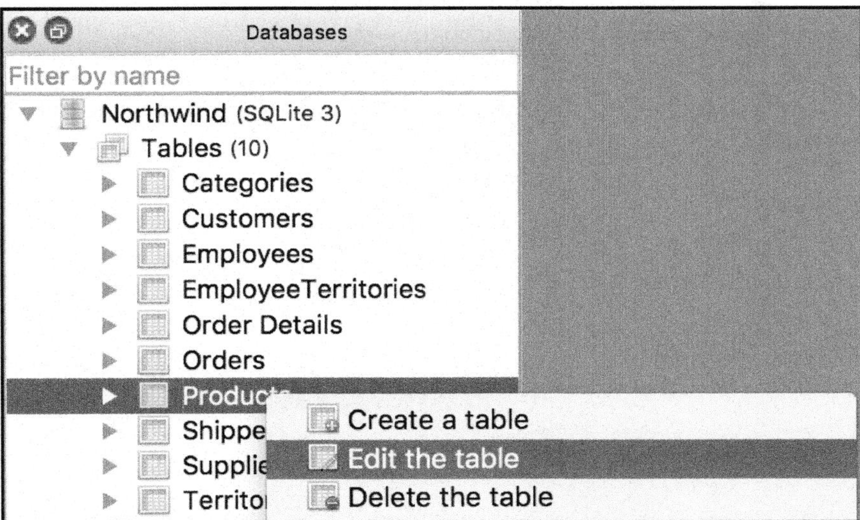

In the table editor window, you will see the structure of the **Products** table, including column names, data types, keys, and constraints, as shown in the following screenshot:

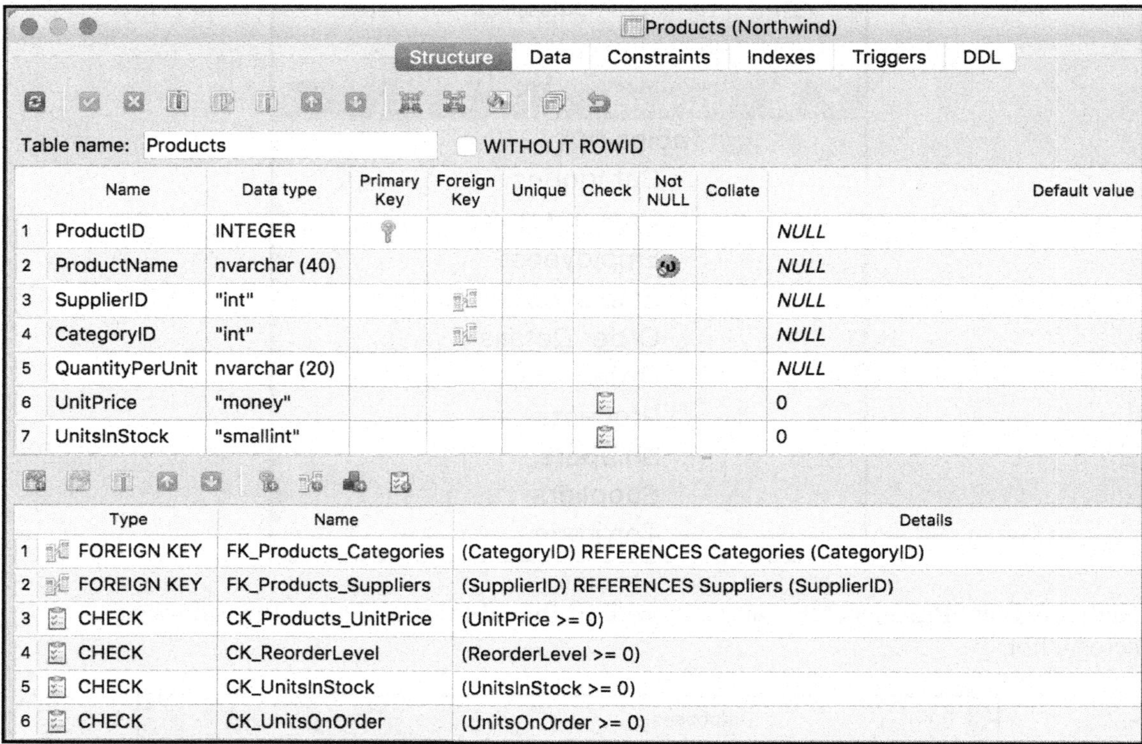

In the table editor window, click the **Data** tab. You will see 77 products, as shown in the following screenshot:

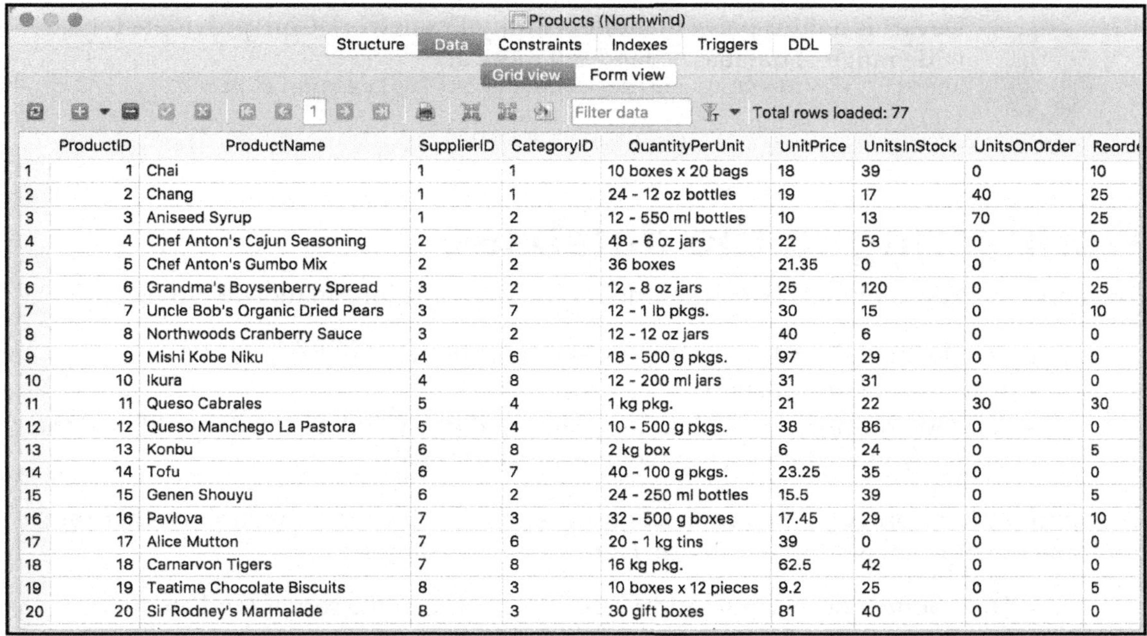

You will write code to work with these products later in this chapter.

Choosing a .NET data provider

Before we dive into the practicalities of managing data in a RDBMS, let's briefly talk about choosing between **.NET data providers**.

To manage data, we need classes that know how to efficiently "talk" to the database. .NET data providers are sets of classes that are optimized for a specific RDBMS. They are distributed as NuGet packages.

To manage this RDBMS	NuGet package
Microsoft SQL Server 2008 or later	`Microsoft.EntityFrameworkCore.SqlServer`
SQLite 3.7 or later	`Microsoft.EntityFrameworkCore.SQLite`
MySQL	`MySQL.Data.EntityFrameworkCore`
In-memory (for unit testing)	`Microsoft.EntityFrameworkCore.InMemory`

Devart is a third party that offers Entity Framework Core providers for a wide range of databases. Find out more at `https://www.devart.com/dotconnect/entityframework.html`

Connecting to the database

To connect to Microsoft SQL Server, we need to know some information about it:

- The name of the server computer that is running the RDBMS
- The name of the database
- Security information, such as username and password, or if we should pass the currently logged-on user's credentials automatically

We specify this information in a connection string. For backward compatibility, there are multiple possible keywords we can use. Here are some examples:

- **Data Source or server or addr**: This is the name of the server (and an optional instance).
- **Initial Catalog or database**: This is the name of the database.
- **Integrated Security or trusted_connection**: This keyword is set to true or SSPI to pass the thread's current user credentials.

To connect to SQLite, we just need to know the database filename.

Setting up Entity Framework Core

The **Entity Framework** (**EF**) was first released as part of **.NET Framework 3.5 with Service Pack 1** back in late 2008. Since then, it has evolved, as Microsoft has observed how programmers use an **object-relational mapping** (**ORM**) tool in the real world.

The version included with .NET Framework 4.6 is **Entity Framework 6.1.3 (EF6)**. It is mature, stable, and supports the old EDMX design-time way of defining the model as well as complex inheritance models, and a few other advanced features. However, EF6 is only supported by the .NET Framework, not by the .NET Core.

The cross-platform version, **Entity Framework Core** (**EF Core**), is different. Microsoft has named it that way to emphasize that it is a reset of functionality. Although EF Core has a similar name, you should be aware that it currently varies from EF6.

Look at its pros and cons:

- Pros
    - EF Core is available for the .NET Core as well as the .NET Framework, which means it can be used cross-platform on Linux and macOS as well as Windows.
    - EF Core supports modern cloud-based, non-relational, schema-less data stores, such as Microsoft Azure Table Storage and Redis.
- Cons
    - EF Core will never support the EDMX design-time XML file format.
    - EF Core does not (yet) support lazy loading or complex inheritance models and other advanced features of EF6.

Using Visual Studio 2017

In Visual Studio 2017, press *Ctrl* + *Shift* + *N* or go to **File** | **New** | **Project...**.

In the **New Project** dialog, in the **Installed** | **Templates** list, expand **Visual C#**, and select **.NET Core**. In the center list, select **Console App (.NET Core)**, type name as `Ch08_EFCore`, change the location to `C:\Code`, type solution name as `Chapter08`, and then click on **OK**.

Right-click on **Dependencies** and choose **Manage NuGet packages**. In **Package Manager**, click on the **Browse** tab and, in the search box, enter `Microsoft.EntityFrameworkCore.SqlServer`, and click on **Install**:

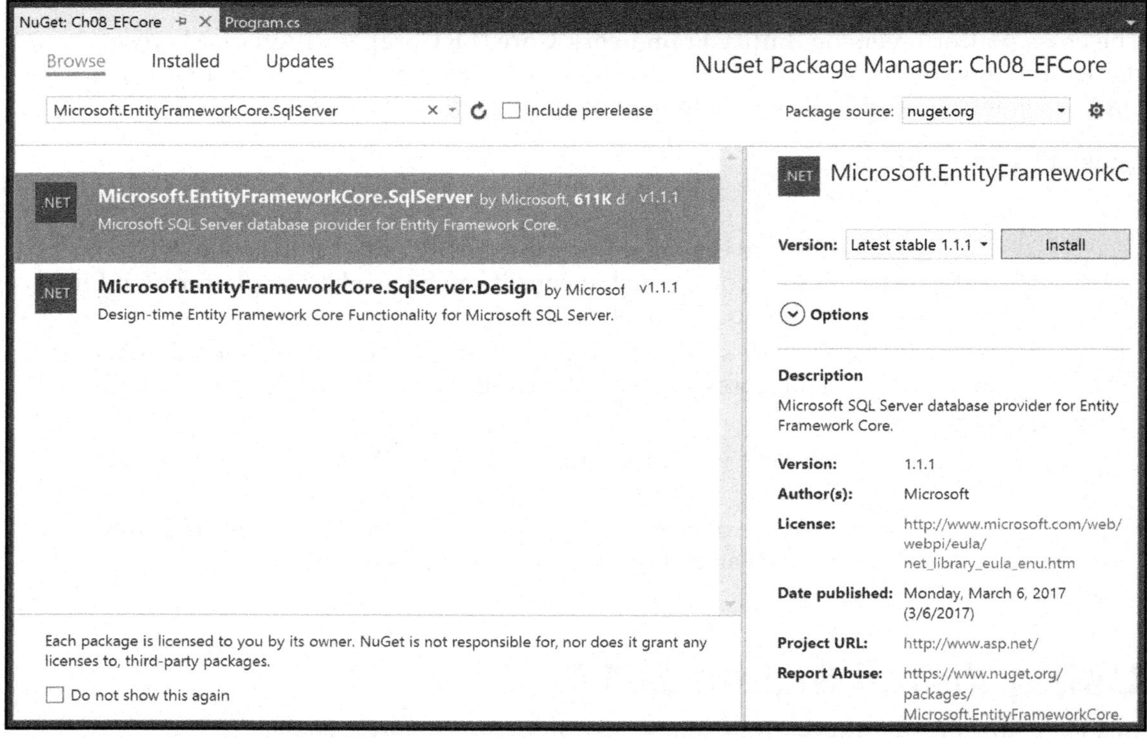

Review the changes, as shown in the following screenshot, and accept the license agreement:

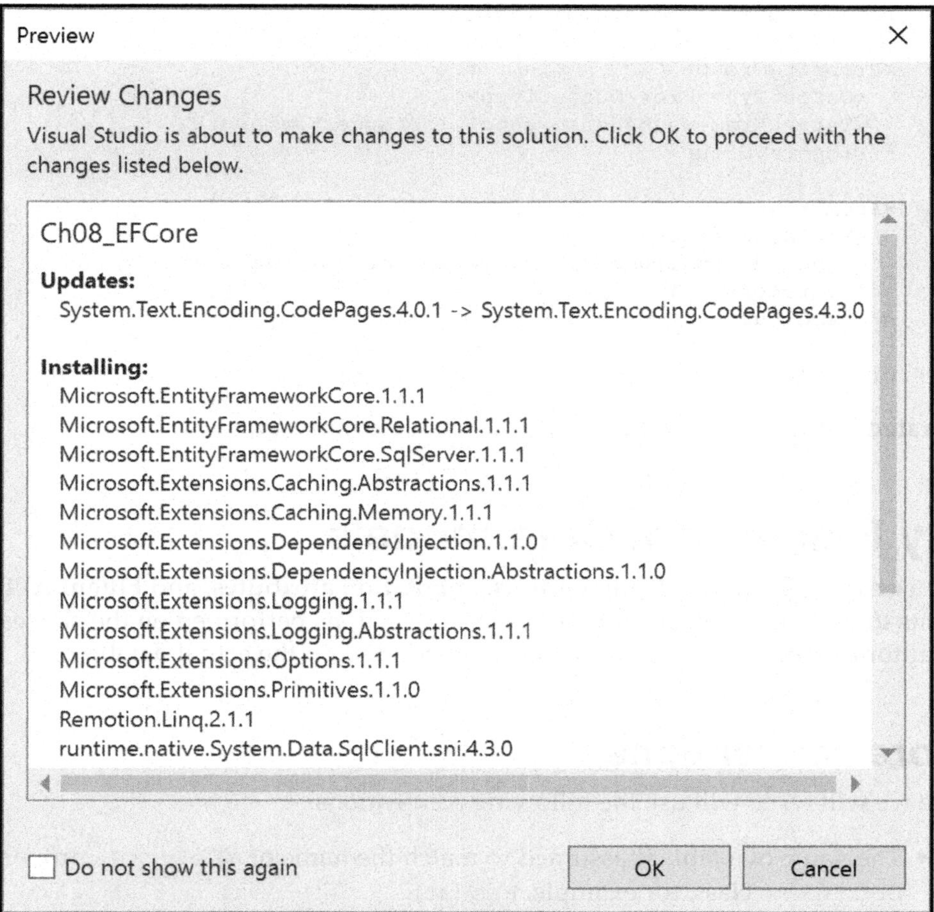

Using Visual Studio Code

Use Visual Studio Code to open the `Ch08_EFCore` folder that you created earlier.

In Integrated Terminal, enter the `dotnet new console` command.

In the **Explorer** pane, click on the `Ch08_EFCore.csproj` file.

Add a package reference to EF Core for SQLite, as shown highlighted in the following markup:

```
<Project Sdk="Microsoft.NET.Sdk">

  <PropertyGroup>
    <OutputType>Exe</OutputType>
    <TargetFramework>netcoreapp1.1</TargetFramework>
  </PropertyGroup>

  <ItemGroup>
    <PackageReference
      Include="Microsoft.EntityFrameworkCore.Sqlite"
      Version="1.1.1" />
  </ItemGroup>

</Project>
```

In **Integrated Terminal**, enter the `dotnet restore` command.

Entity Framework Core models

EF Core uses a combination of **conventions**, **annotation attributes**, and **Fluent API** statements to build a model at runtime so that any actions performed on the classes can later be automatically translated into actions performed on the actual database.

EF Core conventions

The code we will write will use the following conventions:

- The name of a table is assumed to match the name of a `DbSet<T>` property in the `DbContext` class, for example, `Products`.
- The names of the columns are assumed to match the names of properties in the class, for example, `ProductID`.
- The string .NET type is assumed to be an `nvarchar` type in the database.
- The `int` .NET type is assumed to be an `int` type in the database.
- A property that is named `ID` or the name of the class with `ID` as the suffix is assumed to be a primary key. If this property is any integer type or the `Guid` type, then it is also assumed to be `IDENTITY` (automatically assigned value when inserting).

There are many other conventions, and you can even define your own, but that is beyond the scope of this book, and you can read about them at the following link: `https://docs.microsoft.com/en-us/ef/core/modeling/`

EF Core annotation attributes

Conventions often aren't enough to completely map the classes to the database objects. A simple way of adding more smarts to your model is to apply annotation attributes.

For example, in the database, the maximum length of a product name is `40`, and the value cannot be null (empty). In a `Product` class, we could apply attributes to specify this:

```
[Required]
[StringLength(40)]
public string ProductName { get; set; }
```

When there isn't an obvious map between .NET types and database types, an attribute can be used. For example, in the database, the column type of `UnitPrice` for the `Products` table is money. .NET does not have a `money` type, so it should use `decimal` instead:

```
[Column(TypeName = "money")]
public decimal? UnitPrice { get; set; }
```

In the `Category` table, the `Description` column can be longer than the 8,000 characters that can be stored in an `nvarchar` variable, so it needs to map to `ntext` instead:

```
[Column(TypeName = "ntext")]
public string Description { get; set; }
```

There are many other attributes, but they are beyond the scope of this book.

EF Core Fluent API

The last way that the model can be defined is using the **Fluent API**. It can be used instead of attributes or in addition to them. For example, look at the following two attributes in a `Product` class:

```
[Required]
[StringLength(40)]
public string ProductName { get; set; }
```

They could be deleted and replaced with this Fluent API statement in the `Northwind` class' `OnModelBuilding` method:

```
modelBuilder.Entity<Product>()
  .Property(product => product.ProductName)
  .IsRequired()
  .HasMaxLength(40);
```

Building an EF Core Model

In both Visual Studio 2017 and Visual Studio Code, add three class files to the project named `Northwind.cs`, `Category.cs`, and `Product.cs`.

`Northwind.cs` should look like this:

```
using Microsoft.EntityFrameworkCore;

namespace Packt.CS7
{
  // this manages the connection to the database
  public class Northwind : DbContext
  {
    // these properties map to tables in the database
    public DbSet<Category> Categories { get; set; }
    public DbSet<Product> Products { get; set; }

    protected override void OnConfiguring(
      DbContextOptionsBuilder optionsBuilder)
    {
      // for Microsoft SQL Server
      // optionsBuilder.UseSqlServer(
      // @"Data Source=(localdb)\mssqllocaldb;" +
      // "Initial Catalog=Northwind;" +
      // "Integrated Security=true;");

      // for SQLite
      optionsBuilder.UseSqlite(
        "Filename=../../../../Northwind.db");
    }

    protected override void OnModelCreating(
      ModelBuilder modelBuilder)
    {
      // example of using Fluent API instead of attributes
      modelBuilder.Entity<Category>()
      .Property(category => category.CategoryName)
```

```
        .IsRequired()
        .HasMaxLength(40);
      }
    }
  }
```

`Category.cs` should look like this:

```
using System.Collections.Generic;
using System.ComponentModel.DataAnnotations.Schema;

namespace Packt.CS7
{
  public class Category
  {
    public int CategoryID { get; set; }
    public string CategoryName { get; set; }

    [Column(TypeName = "ntext")]
    public string Description { get; set; }

    // defines a navigation property for related rows
    public virtual ICollection<Product> Products { get; set; }

    public Category()
    {
      this.Products = new List<Product>();
    }
  }
}
```

`Product.cs` should look like this:

```
using System.ComponentModel.DataAnnotations;
using System.ComponentModel.DataAnnotations.Schema;

namespace Packt.CS7
{
  public class Product
  {
    public int ProductID { get; set; }

    [Required]
    [StringLength(40)]
    public string ProductName { get; set; }

    [Column(TypeName = "money")]
    public decimal? UnitPrice { get; set; }
```

```
        // these two define the foreign key relationship
        // to the Categories table
        public int CategoryID { get; set; }
        public virtual Category Category { get; set; }
    }
}
```

Note that you did not need to include all columns from a table as properties on a class.

The two properties that relate the two entities, `Category.Products` and `Product.Category`, are both marked as `virtual`. This allows EF to inherit and override them to provide extra features, such as lazy loading. Currently, EF Core does not support lazy loading, but EF6 does. Microsoft intends to add lazy loading support into EF Core soon.

Querying an EF Core model

Open the `Program.cs` file and import the following namespaces:

```
using static System.Console;
using Packt.CS7;
using Microsoft.EntityFrameworkCore;
using System.Linq;
```

In the `Main` method, add the following statements to:

- Create an instance of the `Northwind` class that will manage the database
- Create a query for all categories that includes their related products
- Enumerates through the categories, outputting the name and number of products for each one
- Prompt the user for a price for products
- Create a query for products that cost more than the price by using LINQ
- Loop through the results

```
using(var db = new Northwind())
{
  WriteLine("List of categories and the number of products:");

  IQueryable<Category> cats =
    db.Categories.Include(c => c.Products);

  foreach(Category c in cats)
  {
```

```
        WriteLine(
          $"{c.CategoryName} has {c.Products.Count} products.");
      }

      WriteLine("List of products that cost more than a given price
      with most expensive first.");
      string input;
      decimal price;
      do
      {
        Write("Enter a product price: ");
        input = ReadLine();
      } while (!decimal.TryParse(input, out price));

      IQueryable<Product> prods = db.Products
      .Where(product => product.UnitPrice > price)
      .OrderByDescending(product => product.UnitPrice);

      foreach (Product item in prods)
      {
        WriteLine($"{item.ProductID}: {item.ProductName} costs
        {item.UnitPrice:$#,##0.00}");
      }
    }
```

You will learn much more about LINQ in `Chapter 9`, *Querying and Manipulating Data with LINQ.*

Run the console program, and enter `50` when prompted to enter a product price:

```
List of categories and the number of products:
Beverages has 12 products.
Condiments has 12 products.
Confections has 13 products.
Dairy Products has 10 products.
Grains/Cereals has 7 products.
Meat/Poultry has 6 products.
Produce has 5 products.
Seafood has 12 products.
List of products that cost more than a given price with most
expensive first.
Enter a product price: 50
38: Côte de Blaye costs $263.50
29: Thüringer Rostbratwurst costs $123.79
9: Mishi Kobe Niku costs $97.00
20: Sir Rodney's Marmalade costs $81.00
```

```
18: Carnarvon Tigers costs $62.50
59: Raclette Courdavault costs $55.00
51: Manjimup Dried Apples costs $53.00
```

Logging EF Core

To monitor the interaction between EF Core and the database, we need to enable logging. This requires the registering of a **logging provider** and the implementation of a **logger**.

In Visual Studio 2017 or Visual Studio Code, add a class to your project named `ConsoleLogger.cs`.

Modify it to look like this:

```
using Microsoft.Extensions.Logging;
using System;
using static System.Console;

namespace Packt.CS7
{
  public class ConsoleLogProvider : ILoggerProvider
  {
    public ILogger CreateLogger(string categoryName)
    {
      return new ConsoleLogger();
    }

    // if your logger uses unmanaged resources,
    // you can release the memory here
    public void Dispose() { }
  }

  public class ConsoleLogger : ILogger
  {
    // if your logger uses unmanaged resources, you can
    // return the class that implements IDisposable here
    public IDisposable BeginScope<TState>(TState state)
    {
      return null;
    }

    public bool IsEnabled(LogLevel logLevel)
    {
      // to avoid overlogging, you can filter
      // on the log level
      switch (logLevel)
```

```
        {
          case LogLevel.Trace:
          case LogLevel.Information:
          case LogLevel.None:
          return false;
          case LogLevel.Debug:
          case LogLevel.Warning:
          case LogLevel.Error:
          case LogLevel.Critical:
          default:
          return true;
        };
      }

      public void Log<TState>(LogLevel logLevel,
      EventId eventId, TState state, Exception exception,
      Func<TState, Exception, string> formatter)
      {
        // log the level and event identifier
        Write($"Level: {logLevel}, Event ID: {eventId}");

        // only output the state or exception if it exists
        if (state != null)
        {
          Write($", State: {state}");
        }
        if (exception != null)
        {
          Write($", Exception: {exception.Message}");
        }
        WriteLine();
      }
    }
  }
```

At the top of the `Program.cs` file, add the following statements to import namespaces:

```
using System;
using Microsoft.EntityFrameworkCore.Infrastructure;
using Microsoft.Extensions.DependencyInjection;
using Microsoft.Extensions.Logging;
```

In the `Main` method, add the following statements immediately inside the `using` block for the Northwind database context:

```
using (var db = new Northwind())
{
  var loggerFactory = db.GetService<ILoggerFactory>();
  loggerFactory.AddProvider(new ConsoleLogProvider());
```

Run the console application and view the output:

```
List of categories and the number of products:
Level: Debug, Event ID: 2
Level: Debug, Event ID: 3
Level: Debug, Event ID: 4
Level: Debug, Event ID: 5
Level: Debug, Event ID: 3, State: { Database = main, DataSource =
../../../../North
wind.db }
Beverages has 12 products.
Condiments has 12 products.
Confections has 13 products.
```

The event ID values and what they mean will be specific to the .NET data provider.

Loading patterns with EF Core

There are three **loading patterns** that are commonly used with the Entity Framework: **lazy loading**, **eager loading**, and **explicit loading**.

Unfortunately, although EF6 supports all three, EF Core does not currently support lazy loading. This feature is a high priority for the EF Core team so, hopefully, it will be implemented soon.

Eager and lazy loading entities

In the `Main` method, the code currently uses the `Categories DbSet` (equivalent to a table) to loop through each category, outputting the category name and the number of products in that category. This only works because when we wrote the query, we used the Include method to use eager loading (aka early loading) for the related products.

Modify the query to comment out the `Include` method call, like this:

```
IQueryable<Categories> cats =
  db.Categories; //.Include(c => c.Products);
```

Run the console application and view the output:

```
Beverages has 0 products.
Condiments has 0 products.
Confections has 0 products.
Dairy Products has 0 products.
Grains/Cereals has 0 products.
Meat/Poultry has 0 products.
Produce has 0 products.
Seafood has 0 products.
```

Each item in `foreach` is an instance of the `Category` class, which has a property named `Products`, that is, the list of products in that category. Since the original query is only selected from the `Categories` table, this property is empty for each category.

When lazy loading is finally implemented in EF Core, every time the loop enumerates and an attempt is made to read the `Products`, EF Core will automatically check if they are loaded. If not, EF Core will load them for us "lazily" by executing a `SELECT` statement to load just that set of products for the current category, and then the correct count would be returned to the output.

The problem with lazy loading is that multiple round trips to the database server are required to eventually fetch all the data. Therefore, it has not been a priority for the EF Core team.

Explicit loading entities

Another type of loading is explicit loading. It works like lazy loading, but you are in control of exactly which related data is loaded and when.

Modify your query definition code to make it look like this:

```
IQueryable<Category> cats;
  // = db.Categories.Include(c => c.Products);

Write("Enable eager loading? (Y/N): ");
bool eagerloading = (ReadKey().Key == ConsoleKey.Y);
bool explicitloading = false;
WriteLine();
if (eagerloading)
```

```
{
  cats = db.Categories.Include(c => c.Products);
}
else
{
  cats = db.Categories;
  Write("Enable explicit loading? (Y/N): ");
  explicitloading = (ReadKey().Key == ConsoleKey.Y);
  WriteLine();
}
```

Inside the `foreach` loop, before the `WriteLine` method call, add the following statements:

```
if (explicitloading)
{
  Write($"Explicitly load products for {c.CategoryName}? (Y/N):
  ");
  if (ReadKey().Key == ConsoleKey.Y)
  {
    var products = db.Entry(c).Collection(c2 => c2.Products);
    if (!products.IsLoaded) products.Load();
  }
  WriteLine();
}
```

Run the console application, disable eager loading, and enable explicit loading. For each category, press `Y` or `N` to load its products as you wish.

For example, this is the output when I ran it. I chose to load products for only four of the eight categories:

```
List of categories and the number of products:
Enable eager loading? (Y/N): n
Enable explicit loading? (Y/N): y
Level: Debug, Event ID: 2
Level: Debug, Event ID: 3
Level: Debug, Event ID: 5
Level: Debug, Event ID: 3, State: { Database = main, DataSource =
../../../../North
wind.db }
Explicitly load products for Beverages? (Y/N): n
Beverages has 0 products.
Explicitly load products for Condiments? (Y/N): y
Level: Debug, Event ID: 2
Level: Debug, Event ID: 3
Level: Debug, Event ID: 5
Condiments has 12 products.
Explicitly load products for Confections? (Y/N): y
```

```
Confections has 13 products.
Explicitly load products for Dairy Products? (Y/N): y
Dairy Products has 10 products.
Explicitly load products for Grains/Cereals? (Y/N): n
Grains/Cereals has 0 products.
Explicitly load products for Meat/Poultry? (Y/N): y
Meat/Poultry has 6 products.
Explicitly load products for Produce? (Y/N): n
Produce has 0 products.
Explicitly load products for Seafood? (Y/N): n
Seafood has 0 products.
Level: Debug, Event ID: 4, State: { Database = main, DataSource =
/Users/markjprice
/Code/Chapter08/Northwind.db }
```

Good Practice
Carefully consider which loading pattern is best for your code. In the future, the default of lazy loading could literally make you a lazy database developer!

Manipulating data with EF Core

It is easy to insert, update, and delete entities using EF Core.

Inserting entities

At the bottom of the `Main` method, after the `foreach` statement, add the following code to insert a new product and relist all products:

```
var newProduct = new Product
{
  CategoryID = 6, // Meat & Poultry
  ProductName = "Bob's Burger",
  UnitPrice = 500M
};
// mark product as added in change tracking
db.Products.Add(newProduct);
// save tracked changes to database
db.SaveChanges();
foreach (var item in db.Products)
{
  WriteLine($"{item.ProductID}: {item.ProductName} costs
  {item.UnitPrice:$#,##0.00}");
}
```

Rerun the application and enter 50. You will see that the product has been inserted:

```
78: Bob's Burger costs $500.00
```

Updating entities

Add the following code to increase the price of the first product with a name that begins with "Bob" by $20 and then relist the products:

```
Product updateProduct = db.Products.First(
  p => p.ProductName.StartsWith("Bob"));
updateProduct.UnitPrice += 20M;
db.SaveChanges();
foreach (var item in db.Products)
{
  WriteLine($"{item.ProductID}: {item.ProductName} costs
  {item.UnitPrice:$#,##0.00}");
}
```

Rerun the application and notice that the existing entity for Bob's Burgers has increased in price by $20:

```
78: Bob's Burger costs $520.00
```

Deleting entities

Add the following code to delete the first product with a name that begins with "Bob" and then relist the products:

```
Product deleteProduct = db.Products.First(
  p => p.ProductName.StartsWith("Bob"));
db.Products.Remove(deleteProduct);
db.SaveChanges();
foreach (var item in db.Products)
{
  WriteLine($"{item.ProductID}: {item.ProductName} costs
  {item.UnitPrice:$#,##0.00}");
}
```

Transactions

Every time you call the `SaveChanges` method, an **implicit transaction** is started so that if something goes wrong, it would automatically rollback all the changes. If every operation succeeds, then the transaction is committed.

Transactions maintain the integrity of your database by applying locks to prevent reads and writes while a sequence of operations is occurring.

Transactions are ACID, which is explained here:

- **A** is for atomic. Either all the operations in the transaction commit or none of them do.
- **C** is for consistent. The state of the database before and after a transaction is consistent. This is dependent on your code logic.
- **I** is for isolated. During a transaction, changes are hidden from other processes. There are multiple isolation levels that you can pick from (see the following table). The stronger the level, the better the integrity of the data. However, more locks must be applied, which will negatively affect other processes. Snapshot is a special case because it creates multiple copies of rows to avoid locks, but this will increase the size of your database while transactions occur.
- **D** is for durable. If a failure occurs during a transaction, it can be recovered. The opposite of durable is volatile.

Isolation level	**Lock(s)**	**Integrity problems allowed**
`ReadUncommitted`	None	Dirty reads, non-repeatable reads, and phantom data
`ReadCommitted`	When editing, it applies read lock(s) to block other users from reading the record(s) until the transaction ends	Non-repeatable reads and phantom data
`RepeatableRead`	When reading, it applies edit lock(s) to block other users from editing the record(s) until the transaction ends	Phantom data
`Serializable`	Applies key-range locks to prevent any action that would affect the results, including inserts and deletes	None
`Snapshot`	None	None

Defining an explicit transaction

You can control explicit transactions using the `Database` property of the database context.

Import the following namespace to use the `IDbContextTransaction` interface:

```
using Microsoft.EntityFrameworkCore.Storage;
```

After the instantiation of the `db` variable, add the following statements to start an explicit transaction and output its isolation level:

```
using(var db = new Northwind())
{
  using(IDbContextTransaction t =
    db.Database.BeginTransaction())
  {
    WriteLine($"Transaction started with this isolation level:
    {t.GetDbTransaction().IsolationLevel}");
```

At the bottom of the `Main` method, commit the transaction, and close the brace, as shown in the following code:

```
  t.Commit();
}
```

When using Microsoft SQL Server, you will see the following isolation level:

```
Transaction started with this isolation level: ReadCommitted
```

When using SQLite, you will see the following isolation level:

```
Transaction started with this isolation level: Serializable
```

Practicing and exploring

Test your knowledge and understanding by answering some questions, get some hands-on practice, and explore this chapter's topics with deeper research.

Exercise 8.1 – test your knowledge

Answer the following questions:

1. Which .NET data provider would you use to work with Microsoft SQL Server 2012 Express Edition?
2. When defining a `DbContext` class, what type would you use for the property that represents a table, for example, the `Products` property of a `Category` entity?
3. What is the EF convention for primary keys?
4. When would you use an annotation attribute in an entity class?
5. Why might you choose the Fluent API in preference to annotation attributes?

Exercise 8.2 – explore the EF Core documentation

Go to the following website and read the official Entity Framework Core documentation. Follow the tutorials to create Windows desktop, and web applications and services. If you have a macOS or a Linux virtual machine, follow the tutorials to use EF Core on those alternative platforms.

`https://docs.microsoft.com/en-us/ef/core/index`

Summary

In this chapter, you learned how to connect to a database, how to execute a simple LINQ query and process the results, and how to build Code First entity data models for an existing database, such as Northwind.

In the next chapter, you will learn how to write more advanced LINQ queries to select, filter, sort, join, and group.

9
Querying and Manipulating Data with LINQ

This chapter is about **Language Integrated Query** (**LINQ**), a set of language extensions that add the ability to work with sequences of items and then filter, sort, and project them into different outputs.

This chapter covers the following topics:

- Writing LINQ queries
- Working with sets
- Projecting entities with Select
- Sweetening the syntax with syntactic sugar
- Using multiple threads with parallel LINQ
- Creating your own LINQ extension methods
- Working with LINQ to XML

Writing LINQ queries

Although we wrote a few LINQ queries in `Chapter 8`, *Working with Databases Using the Entity Framework Core*, I didn't properly explain how LINQ works.

LINQ has several parts; some are required and some are optional:

- **Extension methods (required)**: These include examples like `Where`, `OrderBy`, `Select`, and so on. These are what provide the functionality of LINQ.
- **LINQ providers (required)**: These include LINQ to Objects, LINQ to Entities, LINQ to XML, LINQ to OData, LINQ to Amazon, and so on are LINQ providers. These are what convert standard LINQ operations into specific commands for different types of data.
- **Lambda expressions (optional)**: These can be used instead of named methods to simplify LINQ extension method calls.
- **LINQ query comprehension syntax (optional)**: These include `from`, `in`, `where`, `orderby`, `descending`, `select`, and so on. These are C# keywords that are an alias for some of the LINQ extension methods, and their use can simplify the queries you write, especially if you already have experience with other query languages, such as **Structured Query Language** (**SQL**).

When programmers are first introduced to LINQ, they often believe that the query comprehension syntax is LINQ but, ironically, that is one of the parts of LINQ that is optional!

Extending sequences with the enumerable class

The extension methods, such as `Where` and `Select`, are appended by the `Enumerable` static class to any type, known as a **sequence**, that implements `IEnumerable<T>`.

For example, an array of any type automatically implements the `IEnumerable<T>` class, where `T` is the type of item in the array, so all arrays support LINQ to query and manipulate them.

All generic collections, such as `List<T>`, `Dictionary<TKey, TValue>`, `Stack<T>`, and `Queue<T>`, implement `IEnumerable<T>` so they can be queried and manipulated with LINQ.

Filtering entities with Where

The most common reason for using LINQ is to filter items in a sequence using the `Where` extension method.

In **Visual Studio 2017**, press *Ctrl* + *Shift* + *N* or navigate to **File** | **New** | **Project...**. In the **New Project** dialog, in the **Installed** | **Templates** list, expand **Visual C#**, and select **.NET Core**. In the list at the center, select **Console App (.NET Core)**, type the name `Ch09_LinqToObjects`, change the location to `C:\Code`, type the solution name `Chapter09`, and then click on **OK**.

In **Visual Studio Code**, make a directory named `Chapter09` with a subfolder named `Ch09_LinqToObjects`. Open the `Ch09_LinqToObjects` folder and execute the `dotnet new console` command in the Terminal.

In the `Main` method, add the following statements:

```
var names = new string[] { "Michael", "Pam", "Jim",
  "Dwight", "Angela", "Kevin", "Toby", "Creed" };
var query = names.Where(
```

As you type the `Where` method, note that it is missing from the IntelliSense list of members of a `string` array, as shown in the following screenshot:

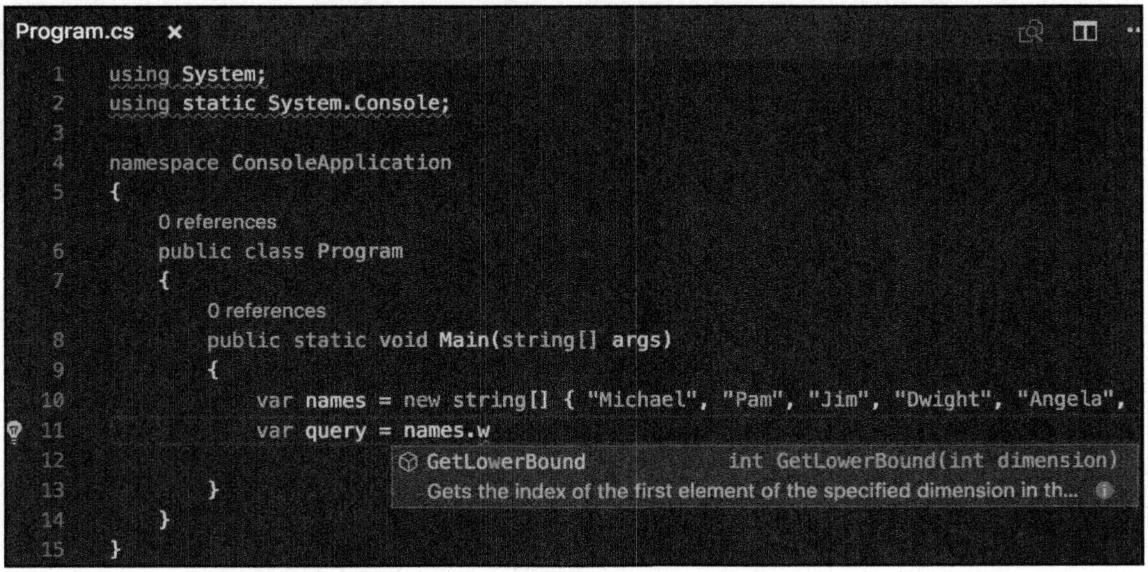

This is because the `Where` method is an **extension method**. It does not exist on the array type. It exists in a separate assembly and namespace. To make the `Where` extension method available, we must import the `System.Linq` namespace.

Add the following statement to the top of the `Program.cs` file:

```
using System.Linq;
```

Now, as you type the open parenthesis after `Where`, note the IntelliSense. It tells us that to call `Where`, we must pass in an instance of a `Func<string, bool>` delegate. This delegate must target a method with a matching signature:

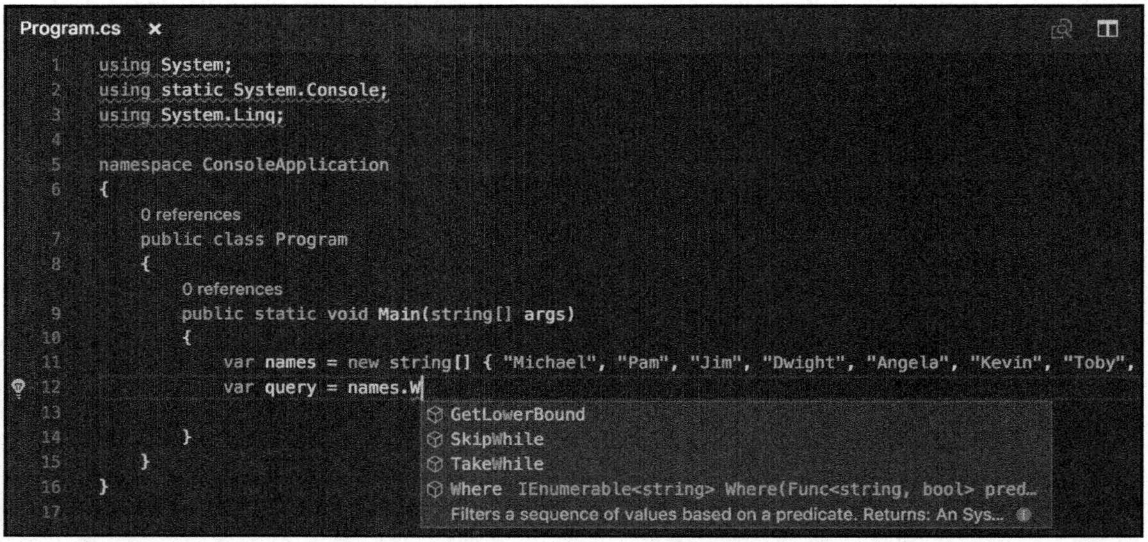

```
Program.cs  ×
using System;
using static System.Console;
using System.Linq;

namespace ConsoleApplication
{
    0 references
    public class Program
    {
        0 references
        public static void Main(string[] args)
        {
            var names = new string[] { "Michael", "Pam", "Jim", "Dwight", "Angela", "Kevin", "Toby",
            var query = names.W
                               GetLowerBound
        }                      SkipWhile
    }                          TakeWhile
}                              Where  IEnumerable<string> Where(Func<string, bool> pred…
                               Filters a sequence of values based on a predicate. Returns: An Sys…
```

Enter the following code to create a new delegate instance:

```
var query = names.Where(new Func<string, bool>())
```

Note the IntelliSense shown in Visual Studio 2017 (but not in Visual Studio Code). This tells us that the `target` method must have a single input parameter of type `string`, and a return of type `bool`, as shown in the following screenshot:

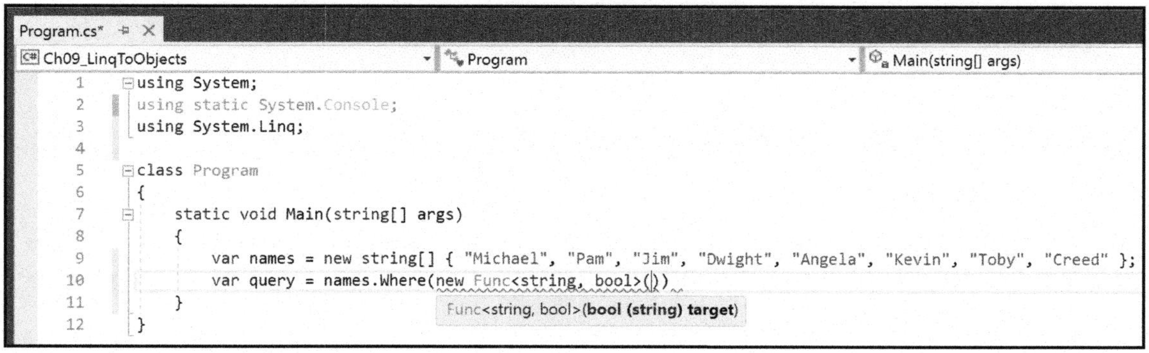

Program.cs* Ch09_LinqToObjects Program Main(string[] args)

```
using System;
using static System.Console;
using System.Linq;

class Program
{
    static void Main(string[] args)
    {
        var names = new string[] { "Michael", "Pam", "Jim", "Dwight", "Angela", "Kevin", "Toby", "Creed" };
        var query = names.Where(new Func<string, bool>())
    }
}
```

Func<string, bool>(**bool (string) target**)

For each `string` variable passed to the method, the method must return a Boolean value. If the method returns `true`, it indicates that we should include the `string` in the results, and if the method returns `false`, it indicates that we should exclude it.

Targeting a named method

Let's define a method that only includes names that are longer than four characters.

Add the following method under the `Main` method:

```
static bool NameLongerThanFour(string name)
{
  return name.Length > 4;
}
```

Modify the `Where` call and loop through the query items, as shown in the following code:

```
var query = names.Where(
  new Func<string, bool>(NameLongerThanFour));
foreach (var item in query)
{
  WriteLine(item);
}
```

In **Visual Studio 2017**, run the console application by pressing *Ctrl* + *F5*.

In **Visual Studio Code**, run the console application by entering `dotnet run`.

View the following output:

```
Michael
Dwight
Angela
```

```
Kevin
Creed
```

Simplifying the code by removing the explicit delegate instantiation

We can simplify the code by deleting the explicit instantiation of the `Func<string, bool>` delegate. The C# compiler will instantiate the `Func<string, bool>` delegate for us, so you never need to explicitly do it.

Modify the query to look like this:

```
var query = names.Where(NameLongerThanFour);
```

Rerun the application and note that it has the same behavior.

Targeting a lambda expression

We can simplify our code even further using a **lambda expression** in place of the named method.

Although it can look complicated at first, a lambda expression is simply a *nameless function.* It uses the => (read as "goes to") symbol to indicate the return value.

Modify the query to look like the following statement:

```
var query = names.Where(name => name.Length > 4);
```

Note that the syntax for a lambda expression includes all the important parts of the `NameLongerThanFour` method, but nothing more. A lambda expression only needs to define the following:

- The names of input parameters
- A return value expression

The type of the `name` input parameter is inferred from the fact that the sequence contains `string` values, and the return type must be a `bool` value for `Where` to work, so the expression after the => symbol must return a `bool` value.

The compiler does most of the work for us, so our code can be as concise as possible.

Rerun the application and note that it has the same behavior.

Sorting entities with OrderBy

`Where` is just one of about 30 extension methods provided by the `Enumerable` type. Extension methods can be chained if the previous method returns another sequence, that is, a type that implements the `IEnumerable<T>` class.

Append a call to `OrderBy` to the end of the existing query, as shown here:

```
var query = names
  .Where(name => name.Length > 4)
  .OrderBy(name => name.Length);
```

Good Practice
Format the LINQ statement so that each extension method call happens on its own line to make them easier to read.

Rerun the application and note that the names are now sorted with shortest first:

```
Kevin
Creed
Dwight
Angela
Michael
```

To put the longest name first, you will use `OrderByDescending`.

Sorting by multiple properties with the ThenBy method

We might want to sort by more than one property.

Append a call to `ThenBy` to the end of the existing query, as shown here:

```
var query = names
  .Where(name => name.Length > 4)
  .OrderBy(name => name.Length)
  .ThenBy(name => name);
```

Rerun the application and note the slight difference in the following sort order. Within a group of names of the same length, the names are sorted alphabetically by the full value of the string, so `Creed` comes before `Kevin`, and `Angela` comes before `Dwight`:

```
Creed
Kevin
Angela
Dwight
Michael
```

Working with sets

Sets are one of the most fundamental concepts in mathematics. A set is a collection of one or more objects. You might remember being taught about Venn diagrams in school. Common set operations include the **intersect** or **union** between sets.

Add a new console application project named `Ch09_Sets` in either Visual Studio 2017 or Visual Studio Code.

In Visual Studio 2017, set the solution's start up project to be the current selection.

This application will define three arrays of strings for cohorts of apprentices and then perform some common set operations.

Import the following additional namespaces:

```
using System.Collections.Generic; // for IEnumerable<T>
using System.Linq; // for LINQ extension methods
```

Inside the `Program` class, before the `Main` method, add the following method that outputs any sequence of `string` variables as a comma-separated single `string` to the console output along with an optional description:

```
private static void Output(
  IEnumerable<string> cohort, string description = "")
  {
    if (!string.IsNullOrEmpty(description))
    {
      WriteLine(description);
    }
    Write("  ");
    WriteLine(string.Join(", ", cohort.ToArray()));
  }
```

In the `Main` method, write the following statements:

```
var cohort1 = new string[]
  { "Rachel", "Gareth", "Jonathan", "George" };
var cohort2 = new string[]
  { "Jack", "Stephen", "Daniel", "Jack", "Jared" };
var cohort3 = new string[]
  { "Declan", "Jack", "Jack", "Jasmine", "Conor" };

Output(cohort1, "Cohort 1");
Output(cohort2, "Cohort 2");
Output(cohort3, "Cohort 3");
WriteLine();

Output(cohort2.Distinct(), "cohort2.Distinct(): removes
duplicates");
Output(cohort2.Union(cohort3), "cohort2.Union(cohort3): combines
two sequences and removes any duplicates");
Output(cohort2.Concat(cohort3), "cohort2.Concat(cohort3): combines
two sequences but leaves in any duplicates");
Output(cohort2.Intersect(cohort3), "cohort2.Intersect(cohort3):
returns items that are in both sequences");
Output(cohort2.Except(cohort3), "cohort2.Except(cohort3): removes
items from the first sequence that are in the second sequence");
Output(cohort1.Zip(cohort2, (c1, c2) => $"{c1} matched with
{c2}"), "cohort1.Zip(cohort2, (c1, c2) => $"{c1} matched with
{c2}"): matches items based on position in the sequence");
```

Run the console application and view the output:

```
Cohort 1
  Rachel, Gareth, Jonathan, George
Cohort 2
  Jack, Stephen, Daniel, Jack, Jared
Cohort 3
  Declan, Jack, Jack, Jasmine, Conor
cohort2.Distinct(): removes duplicates
  Jack, Stephen, Daniel, Jared
cohort2.Union(cohort3): combines two sequences and removes any
duplicates
  Jack, Stephen, Daniel, Jared, Declan, Jasmine, Conor
cohort2.Concat(cohort3): combines two sequences but leaves in any
duplicates
  Jack, Stephen, Daniel, Jack, Jared, Declan, Jack, Jack, Jasmine,
  Conor
cohort2.Intersect(cohort3): returns items that are in both sequences
  Jack
cohort2.Except(cohort3): removes items from the first sequence that
```

```
are in the second sequence
  Stephen, Daniel, Jared
cohort1.Zip(cohort2, (c1, c2) => $"{c1} matched with {c2}"): matches
items based on position in the sequence
  Rachel matched with Jack, Gareth matched with Stephen, Jonathan
  matched with Daniel, George matched with Jack
```

With `Zip`, if there are unequal numbers of items in the two sequences, then some items will not have a matching partner.

Projecting entities with Select

To learn about **projection**, it is best to have some more complex sequences to work with; so, in the next project, we will use the `Northwind` sample database.

Add a new console application project named `Ch09_Projection`.

In **Visual Studio 2017**, in the **Ch09_Projection** project, right-click **Dependencies** and choose **Manage NuGet Packages**. Search for the `Microsoft.EntityFrameworkCore.SqlServer` package and install it.

If you did not complete `Chapter 8`, *Working with Databases Using the Entity Framework Core*, then open the `Northwind.sql` file and right-click and choose **Execute** to create the `Northwind` database on the server named `(localdb)\mssqllocaldb`.

In **Visual Studio Code**, modify the `Ch09_Projection.csproj` file as highlighted in the following markup:

```
<Project Sdk="Microsoft.NET.Sdk">

  <PropertyGroup>
    <OutputType>Exe</OutputType>
    <TargetFramework>netcoreapp1.1</TargetFramework>
  </PropertyGroup>

  <ItemGroup>
    <PackageReference
     Include="Microsoft.EntityFrameworkCore.Sqlite"
     Version="1.1.1" />
  </ItemGroup>

</Project>
```

Copy the `NorthwindSQLite.sql` file into the `Ch09_Projection` folder, and then use **Integrated Terminal** to create the `Northwind` database by executing the following command:

```
sqlite3 Northwind.db < NorthwindSQLite.sql
```

Building an EF Core model

In both Visual Studio 2017 and Visual Studio Code, add three class files to the project named `Northwind.cs`, `Category.cs`, and `Product.cs`.

`Northwind.cs` should look like this:

```
using Microsoft.EntityFrameworkCore;

namespace Packt.CS7
{
  public class Northwind : DbContext
  {
    public DbSet<Category> Categories { get; set; }
    public DbSet<Product> Products { get; set; }

    protected override void OnConfiguring(
      DbContextOptionsBuilder optionsBuilder)
    {
      // for Microsoft SQL Server
      // optionsBuilder.UseSqlServer(
      //     @"Data Source=(localdb)\mssqllocaldb;" +
      //     "Initial Catalog=Northwind;" +
      //     "Integrated Security=true;");

      // for SQLite
      optionsBuilder.UseSqlite(
      "Filename=../../../Northwind.db");
    }
  }
}
```

`Category.cs` should look like this:

```
using System.ComponentModel.DataAnnotations;

namespace Packt.CS7
{
  public class Category
  {
```

```
    public int CategoryID { get; set; }
    [Required]
    [StringLength(15)]
    public string CategoryName { get; set; }
    public string Description { get; set; }
  }
}
```

`Product.cs` should look like this:

```
using System.ComponentModel.DataAnnotations;

namespace Packt.CS7
{
  public class Product
  {
    public int ProductID { get; set; }
    [Required]
    [StringLength(40)]
    public string ProductName { get; set; }
    public int? SupplierID { get; set; }
    public int? CategoryID { get; set; }
    [StringLength(20)]
    public string QuantityPerUnit { get; set; }
    public decimal? UnitPrice { get; set; }
    public short? UnitsInStock { get; set; }
    public short? UnitsOnOrder { get; set; }
    public short? ReorderLevel { get; set; }
    public bool Discontinued { get; set; }
  }
}
```

Open the `Program.cs` file and import the following namespaces:

```
using static System.Console;
using Packt.CS7;
using Microsoft.EntityFrameworkCore;
using System.Linq;
```

In the `Main` method, write the following statements:

```
var db = new Northwind();

var query = db.Products
  .Where(product => product.UnitPrice < 10M)
  .OrderByDescending(product => product.UnitPrice);

WriteLine("Products that cost less than $10.");
```

```
foreach (var item in query)
{
  WriteLine($"{item.ProductID}: {item.ProductName} costs
  {item.UnitPrice:$#,##0.00}");
}
WriteLine();
```

Run the console application and view the output:

```
41: Jack's New England Clam Chowder costs $9.65
45: Rogede sild costs $9.50
47: Zaanse koeken costs $9.50
19: Teatime Chocolate Biscuits costs $9.20
23: Tunnbröd costs $9.00
75: Rhönbräu Klosterbier costs $7.75
54: Tourtière costs $7.45
52: Filo Mix costs $7.00
13: Konbu costs $6.00
24: Guaraná Fantástica costs $4.50
33: Geitost costs $2.50
```

Although this query outputs the information we want, it does so inefficiently because it returns all columns from the `Products` table instead of just the three columns we need, which is the equivalent of the following SQL statement:

```
SELECT * FROM Products;
```

> You might have also noticed that the sequences implement `IQueryable<T>` and `IOrderedQueryable<T>` instead of `IEnumerable<T>` or `IOrderedEnumerable<T>`. This is an indication that we are using a LINQ provider that uses deferred execution and builds the query in memory using expression trees. The query will not be executed until the last possible moment and only then will it be converted into another query language, such as Transact-SQL for Microsoft SQL Server. Enumerating the query with `foreach` or calling a method such as `ToArray` will force immediate execution of the query.

In the `Main` method, modify the LINQ query to use the `Select` method to return only the three properties (table columns) that we need, as shown in the following statements:

```
var query = db.Products
  .Where(product => product.UnitPrice < 10M)
  .OrderByDescending(product => product.UnitPrice);
  .Select(product => new
  {
    product.ProductID,
```

```
        product.ProductName,
        product.UnitPrice
      });
```

Run the console application and confirm that the output is the same as before.

Joining and grouping

There are two extension methods for joining and grouping:

- `Join`: This method has four parameters: the sequence that you want to join with, the property or properties on the *left* sequence to match on, the property or properties on the *right* sequence to match on, and a projection
- `GroupJoin`: This method has the same parameters, but it combines the matches into a group object with a `Key` for the matching value and an `IEnumerable<T>` for the multiple matches

In the `Main` method, write the following statements:

```
// create two sequences that we want to join together
var categories = db.Categories.Select(c => new { c.CategoryID,
c.CategoryName }).ToArray();

var products = db.Products.Select(p => new { p.ProductID,
p.ProductName, p.CategoryID }).ToArray();

// join every product to its category to return 77 matches
var queryJoin = categories.Join(products,
  category => category.CategoryID,
  product => product.CategoryID,
  (c, p) => new { c.CategoryName, p.ProductName, p.ProductID });

foreach (var item in queryJoin)
{
  WriteLine($"{item.ProductID}: {item.ProductName} is in
  {item.CategoryName}.");
}
```

Run the console application and view the output.

Note that there is a single line output for each of the 77 products, and the results show all products in the `Beverages` category first, then the `Condiments` category, and so on:

```
1: Chai is in Beverages.
2: Chang is in Beverages.
```

```
24: Guaraná Fantástica is in Beverages.
34: Sasquatch Ale is in Beverages.
35: Steeleye Stout is in Beverages.
38: Côte de Blaye is in Beverages.
39: Chartreuse verte is in Beverages.
43: Ipoh Coffee is in Beverages.
67: Laughing Lumberjack Lager is in Beverages.
70: Outback Lager is in Beverages.
75: Rhönbräu Klosterbier is in Beverages.
76: Lakkalikööri is in Beverages.
3: Aniseed Syrup is in Condiments.
4: Chef Anton's Cajun Seasoning is in Condiments.
```

Change the query to sort by `ProductID`:

```
var queryJoin = categories.Join(products,
  category => category.CategoryID,
  product => product.CategoryID,
  (c, p) => new { c.CategoryName, p.ProductName, p.ProductID })
  .OrderBy(cp => cp.ProductID);
```

Rerun the application and view the output:

```
1: Chai is in Beverages.
2: Chang is in Beverages.
3: Aniseed Syrup is in Condiments.
4: Chef Anton's Cajun Seasoning is in Condiments.
5: Chef Anton's Gumbo Mix is in Condiments.
6: Grandma's Boysenberry Spread is in Condiments.
7: Uncle Bob's Organic Dried Pears is in Produce.
8: Northwoods Cranberry Sauce is in Condiments.
9: Mishi Kobe Niku is in Meat/Poultry.
10: Ikura is in Seafood.
11: Queso Cabrales is in Dairy Products.
12: Queso Manchego La Pastora is in Dairy Products.
13: Konbu is in Seafood.
14: Tofu is in Produce.
15: Genen Shouyu is in Condiments.
```

Add some new statements, as shown in the following code, to the bottom of the `Main` method to show the use of the `GroupJoin` method, and in the output, show the group name and then all the items within each group:

```
// group all products by their category to return 8 matches
var queryGroup = categories.GroupJoin(products,
  category => category.CategoryID,
  product => product.CategoryID,
  (c, Products) => new { c.CategoryName,
```

```
            Products = Products.OrderBy(p => p.ProductName) });

        foreach (var item in queryGroup)
        {
          WriteLine(
          $"{item.CategoryName} has {item.Products.Count()} products.");
          foreach (var product in item.Products)
          {
            WriteLine($"  {product.ProductName}");
          }
        }
```

Rerun the console application and view the output.

Note that the products inside each category have been sorted by their name as the query asked:

```
Beverages has 12 products.
  Chai
  Chang
  Chartreuse verte
  Côte de Blaye
  Guaraná Fantástica
  Ipoh Coffee
  Lakkalikööri
  Laughing Lumberjack Lager
  Outback Lager
  Rhönbräu Klosterbier
  Sasquatch Ale
  Steeleye Stout
Condiments has 12 products.
  Aniseed Syrup
  Chef Anton's Cajun Seasoning
  Chef Anton's Gumbo Mix
```

Sweetening the syntax with syntactic sugar

C# 3 introduced some new keywords in 2008 to make it easier for programmers with experience in SQL to write LINQ queries. This *syntactic sugar* is sometimes called the **LINQ query comprehension syntax**.

The LINQ query comprehension syntax is limited in functionality. You must use extension methods to access all the features of LINQ.

Consider the following code:

```
var names = new string[] { "Michael", "Pam", "Jim",
  "Dwight", "Angela", "Kevin", "Toby", "Creed" };

var query = names
  .Where(name => name.Length > 4)
  .OrderBy(name => name.Length)
  .ThenBy(name => name);
```

Instead of writing the preceding code using **extension methods** and **lambda expressions**, you can write the following code using **query comprehension syntax**:

```
var query = from name in names
            where name.Length > 4
            orderby name.Length, name
            select name;
```

The compiler changes the query comprehension syntax to the extension method and lambda expression equivalent for you.

The `select` keyword is always required for LINQ query comprehension syntax. The `Select` extension method is optional when using extension methods and lambda expressions.

Not all extension methods have a C# keyword equivalent, for example, the `Skip` and `Take` extension methods that are commonly used to implement paging for lots of data. The following query cannot be written using only the query syntax:

```
var query = names
  .Where(name => name.Length > 4)
  .OrderBy(name => name.Length)
  .ThenBy(name => name)
  .Skip(80)
  .Take(10);
```

Luckily, you can wrap query comprehension syntax in parentheses and then switch to using extension methods, as shown in the following code:

```
var query = (from name in names
            where name.Length > 4
            orderby name.Length, name
            select name)
            .Skip(80)
            .Take(10);
```

Good Practice
Learn both extension methods with lambda expressions and the query comprehension syntax ways of writing LINQ queries because you are likely to have to maintain code that uses both.

Using multiple threads with parallel LINQ

By default, only one thread is used to execute a LINQ query. **Parallel LINQ (PLINQ)** is an easy way to enable multiple threads to execute a LINQ query.

Good Practice
Do not assume that using parallel threads will improve the performance of your applications. Always measure real-world timings and resource usage.

To see it in action, we will start with some code that only uses a single thread to double 200 million integers. We will use the `StopWatch` type to measure the change in performance. We will use operating system tools to monitor CPU and CPU core usage.

Use either Visual Studio 2017 or Visual Studio Code to add a new console application project named `Ch09_PLINQ`.

Import the `System.Diagnostics` namespace so that we can use the `StopWatch` type; `System.Collections.Generic` so that we can use the `IEnumerable<T>` type, `System.Linq`; and statically import the `System.Console` type.

Add the following statements to the `Main` method:

```
var watch = Stopwatch.StartNew();
Write("Press ENTER to start. ");
ReadLine();
watch.Start();
IEnumerable<int> numbers = Enumerable.Range(1, 200_000_000);
var squares = numbers.Select(number => number * 2).ToArray();
// var squares = numbers.AsParallel()
//    .Select(number => number * 2).ToArray();
watch.Stop();
WriteLine($"{watch.ElapsedMilliseconds:#,##0} elapsed
milliseconds.");
```

Run the console application, but *do not* press *Enter* to start yet.

In Windows 10, right-click on the Windows Start button or press *Ctrl* + *Alt* + *Delete*, and then click on **Task Manager**.

At the bottom of the **Task Manager** window, click on the **More details** button. At the top of the **Task Manager** window, click on the **Performance** tab.

Right-click on the **CPU Utilization** graph, choose **Change graph to**, and then **Logical processors**, as you can see in the following screenshot:

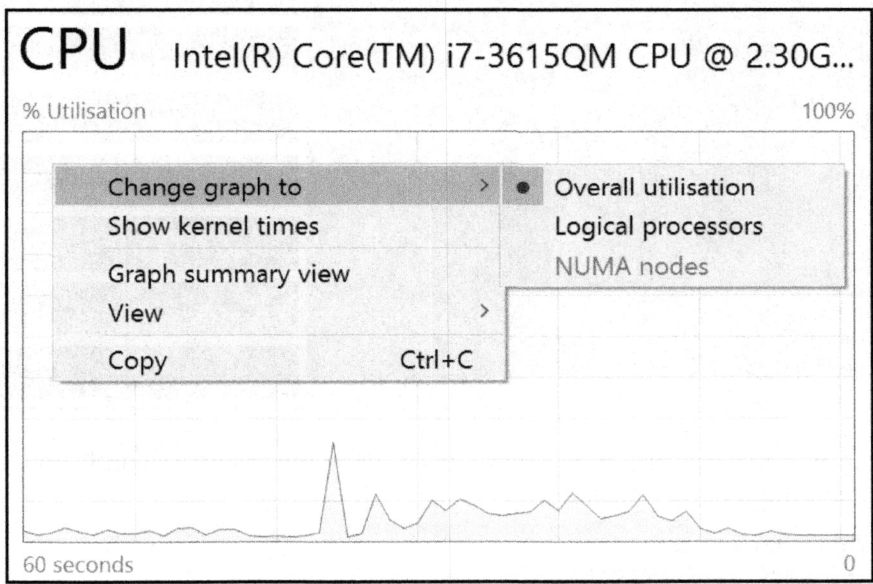

In macOS, run **Activity Monitor**. Increase the frequency of CPU measurements by navigating to **View** | **Update Frequency** | **Very often (1 sec)**. To see the CPU graphs, navigate to **Window** | **CPU History**.

If you do not have multiple CPUs, then this exercise won't show much!

Rearrange **Task Manager** and your console application, or **CPU History** and Visual Studio Code Integrated Terminal so that they are side by side, as shown in the following screenshot:

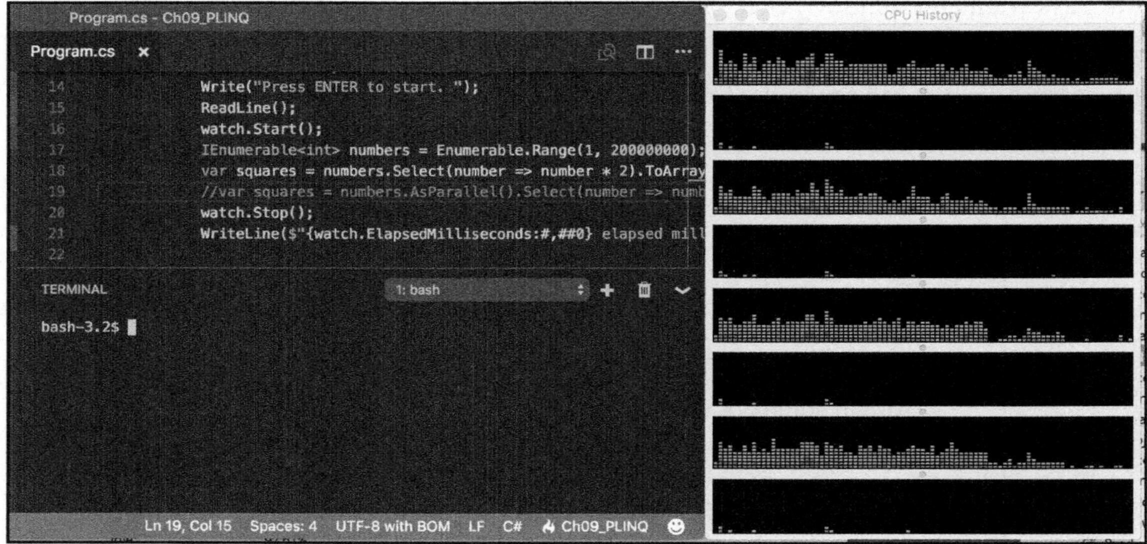

Wait for the CPUs to settle and then press *Enter* to start the stopwatch and run the query. Your output should look like this:

```
Press ENTER to start.
31,230 elapsed milliseconds.
```

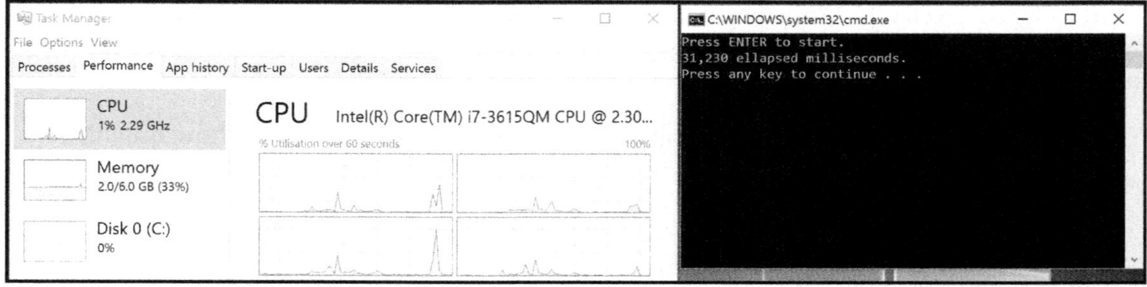

On macOS, it'll look something like this:

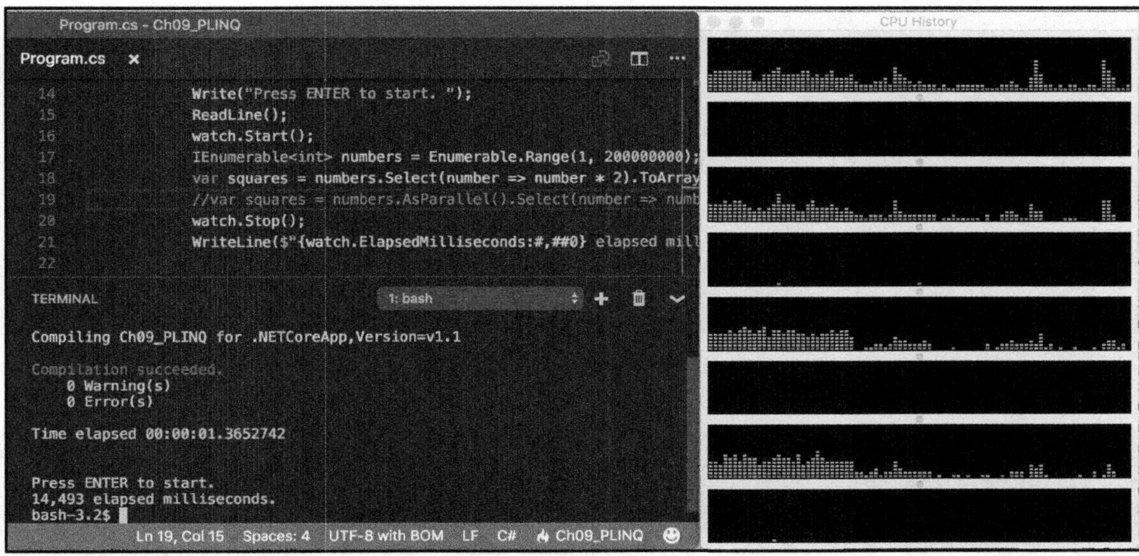

Task Manager or **CPU History** windows should show that one or two CPUs were used the most. Others may execute background tasks at the same time, such as the garbage collector, so the others CPUs won't be completely flat, but the work certainly is not being evenly spread amongst all possible CPUs.

Back in the `Main` method, modify the query to make a call to the `AsParallel` extension method as follows:

```
var squares = numbers.AsParallel()
  .Select(number => number * 2).ToArray();
```

Run the application again. Wait for the **Task Manager** or **CPU History** windows to settle and then press *Enter* to start the stopwatch and run the query.

This time, the application should complete in less time (although it might not be as less as you might hope for-managing those multiple threads takes extra effort!).

```
Press ENTER to start.
26,830 elapsed milliseconds.
```

The **Task Manager** or **CPU History** windows should show that all CPUs were used equally to execute the LINQ query, as shown in the following screenshot for Windows 10:

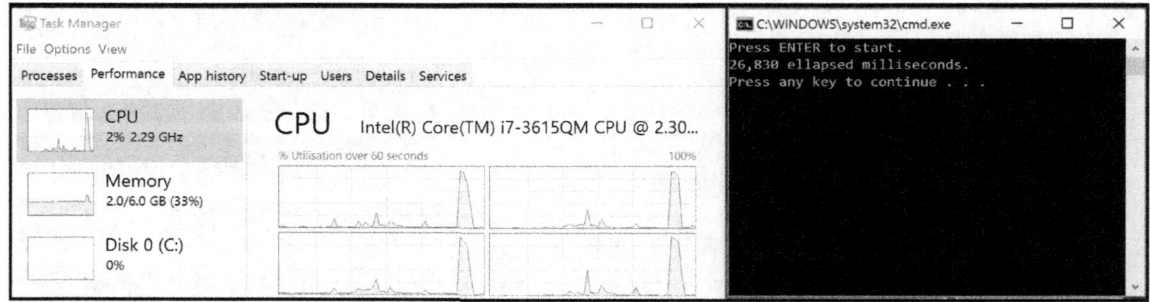

And, in this screenshot for macOS:

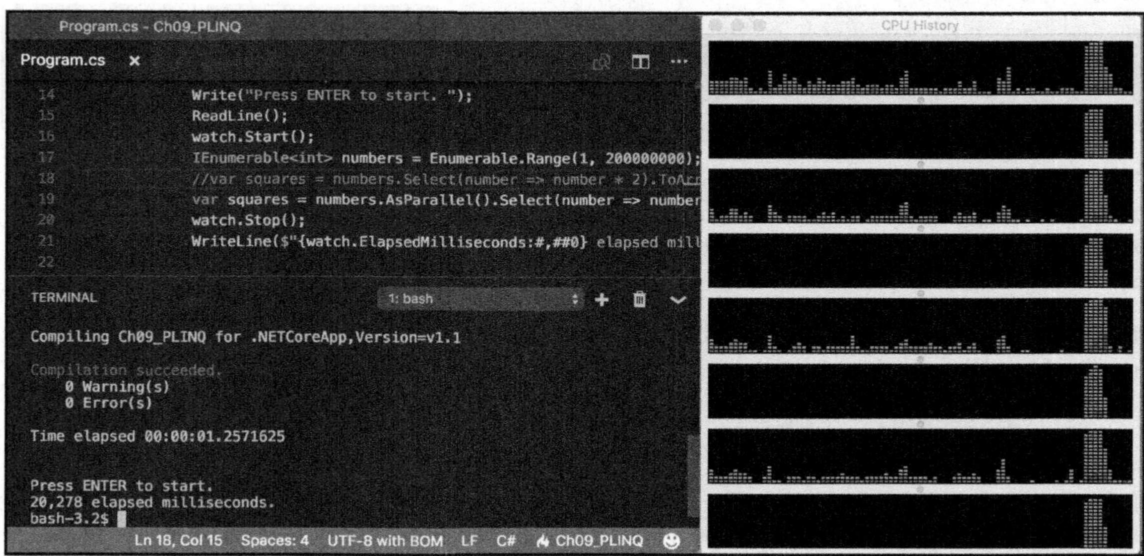

You will learn more about managing multiple threads in `Chapter 12`, *Improving Performance and Scalability with Multitasking*.

Creating your own LINQ extension methods

In `Chapter 7`, *Implementing Interfaces and Inheriting Classes*, you learned how to create your own extension methods. To create LINQ extension methods, all you must do is extend the `IEnumerable<T>` type.

Good Practice
Put your own extension methods in a separate class library so that they can be easily deployed as their own assembly or NuGet package.

In either Visual Studio 2017 or Visual Studio Code, open the `Ch09_LinqToObjects` project or folder, and add a new class file named `MyLINQExtensions.cs`.

Modify the class to look like the following code. Note that the `ProcessSequence` extension method doesn't modify the sequence because it exists only as an example. It would be up to you to process the sequence in whatever manner you want. The `SummariseSequence` extension method also doesn't do anything especially useful. It simply returns a `long` count of the number of items in the sequence using the built-in `LongCount` extension method. Again, it would be up to you to decide exactly what this method should do and what type it should return:

```
using System.Collections.Generic;

namespace System.Linq
{
  public static class MyLINQExtensions
  {
    // this is a chainable LINQ extension method
    public static IEnumerable<T> ProcessSequence<T>(
    this IEnumerable<T> sequence)
    {
      return sequence;
    }

    // this is a scalar LINQ extension method
    public static long SummariseSequence<T>(
    this IEnumerable<T> sequence)
    {
      return sequence.LongCount();
    }
  }
}
```

To use your LINQ extension methods, you would simply need to reference the class library assembly because the `System.Linq` namespace is usually already imported.

Modify the LINQ query to call your chainable extension method as follows:

```
var query = names
  .ProcessSequence()
  .Where(name => name.Length > 4)
  .OrderBy(name => name.Length)
  .ThenBy(name => name);
```

If you run the console application, then you will see the same output as before because your method doesn't modify the sequence. But, you now know how to extend LINQ with your own functionality.

Working with LINQ to XML

LINQ to XML is a LINQ provider that allows you to query and manipulate XML.

Generating XML using LINQ to XML

Open the console application project or folder named `Ch09_Projection`.

In the `Program.cs` file, import the `System.Xml.Linq` namespace.

In the `Main` method, at the bottom, write the following statements:

```
var productsForXml = db.Products.ToArray();

var xml = new XElement("products",
  from p in productsForXml
  select new XElement("product",
    new XAttribute("id", p.ProductID),
    new XAttribute("price", p.UnitPrice),
    new XElement("name", p.ProductName)));

WriteLine(xml.ToString());
```

Run the console application and view the output.

Note the structure of the XML generated matches the elements and attributes that the LINQ to XML statement declaratively described in the preceding code:

```
<products>
  <product id="1" price="18.0000">
    <name>Chai</name>
  </product>
  <product id="2" price="19.0000">
    <name>Chang</name>
  </product>
  <product id="3" price="10.0000">
    <name>Aniseed Syrup</name>
  </product>
```

Reading XML by using LINQ to XML

You might want to use LINQ to XML to easily query XML files.

In the `Ch09_Projection` project, add an XML file named `settings.xml`. Modify its contents to look like this:

```
<?xml version="1.0" encoding="utf-8" ?>
<appSettings>
  <add key="color" value="red" />
  <add key="size" value="large" />
  <add key="price" value="23.99" />
</appSettings>
```

Back in the `Program` class, add the following statements to:

- Load the XML file.
- Use LINQ to XML to search for an element named `appSettings`, and its descendants named `add`.
- Project the XML into an array of an anonymous type with a `Key` and `Value` property.
- Enumerate through the array to show the results.

```
XDocument doc = XDocument.Load("settings.xml");

var appSettings = doc.Descendants(
  "appSettings").Descendants("add")
  .Select(node => new
  {
    Key = node.Attribute("key").Value,
```

```
      Value = node.Attribute("value").Value
    })
    .ToArray();

  foreach (var item in appSettings)
  {
    WriteLine($"{item.Key}: {item.Value}");
  }
```

Run the console application and view the output:

```
color: red
size: large
price: 23.99
```

Practicing and exploring

Test your knowledge and understanding by answering some questions, get some hands-on practice, and explore with deeper research into the topics covered in this chapter.

Exercise 9.1 – test your knowledge

Answer the following questions:

1. What are the two required parts of LINQ?
2. Which LINQ extension method would you use to return a subset of properties from a type?
3. Which LINQ extension method would you use to filter a sequence?
4. List five LINQ extension methods that perform aggregation.
5. What is the difference between the `Select` and `SelectMany` extension methods?

Exercise 9.2 – practice querying with LINQ

Create a console application, named `Ch09_Exercise02`, that prompts the user for a city and then lists the company names for Northwind customers in that city:

```
Enter the name of a city: London
There are 6 customers in London:
Around the Horn
B's Beverages
```

```
Consolidated Holdings
Eastern Connection
North/South
Seven Seas Imports
```

Enhance the application by displaying a list of all unique cities that customers already reside in as a prompt to the user before they enter their preferred city:

```
Aachen, Albuquerque, Anchorage, Århus, Barcelona, Barquisimeto,
Bergamo, Berlin, Bern, Boise, Bräcke, Brandenburg, Bruxelles, Buenos
Aires, Butte, Campinas, Caracas, Charleroi, Cork, Cowes, Cunewalde,
Elgin, Eugene, Frankfurt a.M., Genève, Graz, Helsinki, I. de
Margarita, Kirkland, Kobenhavn, Köln, Lander, Leipzig, Lille, Lisboa,
London, Luleå, Lyon, Madrid, Mannheim, Marseille, México D.F.,
Montréal, München, Münster, Nantes, Oulu, Paris, Portland, Reggio
Emilia, Reims, Resende, Rio de Janeiro, Salzburg, San Cristóbal, San
Francisco, Sao Paulo, Seattle, Sevilla, Stavern, Strasbourg,
Stuttgart, Torino, Toulouse, Tsawassen, Vancouver, Versailles, Walla
Walla, Warszawa
```

Exercise 9.3 – explore topics

Use the following links to read more details about the topics covered in this chapter:

- **LINQ in C#**: `https://docs.microsoft.com/en-us/dotnet/articles/csharp/linq/linq-in-csharp`
- **101 LINQ Samples**: `https://code.msdn.microsoft.com/101-LINQ-Samples-3fb9811b`
- **Parallel LINQ (PLINQ)**: `https://msdn.microsoft.com/en-us/library/dd460688(v=vs.110).aspx`
- **LINQ to XML (C#)**: `https://docs.microsoft.com/en-us/dotnet/articles/csharp/programming-guide/concepts/linq/linq-to-xml`
- **LINQPad – The .NET Programmer's Playground**: `https://www.linqpad.net/`

Summary

In this chapter, you learned how to write LINQ queries to select, project, filter, sort, join, and group data in many different formats, including XML, which are tasks you will perform every day.

In the next chapter, we will manage files and streams, encode and decode text, and perform serialization.

10
Working with Files, Streams, and Serialization

This chapter is about reading and writing to files and streams, text encoding, and serialization.

This chapter will cover the following topics:

- Managing the filesystem
- Reading and writing with streams
- Encoding text
- Serializing object graphs

Managing the filesystem

Your applications will often need to perform input and output with files and directories. The `System.IO` namespace contains classes for this purpose.

Managing directories

In Visual Studio 2017, press *Ctrl* + *Shift* + *N* or choose **File** | **New** | **Project...**.

In the **New Project** dialog, in the **Installed** | **Templates** list, select **.NET Core**. In the center list, select **Console App (.NET Core)**, type **Name** as `Ch10_FileSystem`, change the location to `C:\Code`, type the solution name as `Chapter10`, and then click on **OK**.

In Visual Studio Code, in the Integrated Terminal, make a new directory named `Chapter10`, and a subdirectory named `Ch10_FileSystem`. Open the folder and enter the command `dotnet new console`.

At the top of the `Program.cs` file, add the following import statements. Note that we will statically import the `Directory` type to simplify our code:

```
using static System.Console;
using System.IO;
using static System.IO.Directory;
```

In the `Main` method, write the following statements to check for the existence of a directory. Then, create and delete it. Note that the path is different for Windows and macOS:

```
// define a directory path
// string dir = @"C:\Code\Ch10_Example"; // Windows
string dir = @"/Users/markjprice/Code/Ch10_Example/"; // macOS

// check if it exists
WriteLine($"Does {dir} exist? {Exists(dir)}");
// create a directory
CreateDirectory(dir);
WriteLine($"Does {dir} exist? {Exists(dir)}");
// delete a directory
Delete(dir);
WriteLine($"Does {dir} exist? {Exists(dir)}");
```

Run the console application and view the output:

```
Does /Users/markjprice/Code/Ch10_Example/ exist? False
Does /Users/markjprice/Code/Ch10_Example/ exist? True
Does /Users/markjprice/Code/Ch10_Example/ exist? False
```

Managing files

Note that, this time we will not statically import the `File` type, because it has some of the same methods as the `Directory` type and they would conflict. The `File` type has a short enough name not to matter in this case.

In the `Main` method, add the following statements to:

- Check for the existence of a file
- Create a text file
- Write a line of text to the file

- Copy the file to a backup
- Delete the original file
- Read the backup file's contents

```
// string textFile = @"C:\Code\Ch10.txt"; // Windows
// string backupFile = @"C:\Code\Ch10.bak"; // Windows
string textFile = @"/Users/markjprice/Code/Ch10.txt"; // macOS
string backupFile = @"/Users/markjprice/Code/Ch10.bak"; // macOS

// check if a file exists
WriteLine($"Does {textFile} exist? {File.Exists(textFile)}");

// create a new text file and write a line to it
StreamWriter textWriter = File.CreateText(textFile);
textWriter.WriteLine("Hello, C#!");
textWriter.Dispose();
WriteLine($"Does {textFile} exist? {File.Exists(textFile)}");

// copy a file and overwrite if it already exists
File.Copy(textFile, backupFile, true);
WriteLine($"Does {backupFile} exist? {File.Exists(backupFile)}");

// delete a file
File.Delete(textFile);
WriteLine($"Does {textFile} exist? {File.Exists(textFile)}");

// read from a text file
StreamReader textReader = File.OpenText(backupFile);
WriteLine(textReader.ReadToEnd());
textReader.Dispose();
```

Run the console application and view the output:

```
Does C:\Code\Ch10.txt exist? False
Does C:\Code\Ch10.txt exist? True
Does C:\Code\Ch10.bak exist? True
Does C:\Code\Ch10.txt exist? False
Hello, C#!
```

In .NET Framework, you can use either the `Close` or `Dispose` method when you are finished with `StreamReader` or `StreamWriter`. In .NET Core, you can only use `Dispose`, because Microsoft has simplified the API.

Managing paths

Sometimes, you need to work with paths, for example, you might want to extract just the folder name, the file name, or the extension. Sometimes, you need to generate temporary folders and file names. You can do this with the `Path` class.

Add the following statements to the `Main` method:

```
WriteLine($"File Name: {Path.GetFileName(textFile)}");
WriteLine($"File Name without Extension:
{Path.GetFileNameWithoutExtension(textFile)}");
WriteLine($"File Extension: {Path.GetExtension(textFile)}");
WriteLine($"Random File Name: {Path.GetRandomFileName()}");
WriteLine($"Temporary File Name: {Path.GetTempFileName()}");
```

Run the console application and view the output:

```
File Name: Ch10.txt
File Name without Extension: Ch10
File Extension: .txt
Random File Name: u45w1zki.co3
Temporary File Name:
/var/folders/tz/xx0y_w1d5sx0nv0fjtq4tnpc0000gn/T/tmpyqrepP.
tmp
```

The `GetTempFileName` method creates a zero-byte file and returns its name, ready for you to use. `GetRandomFileName` just returns a filename; it doesn't create the file.

Getting file information

To get more information about a file or directory, you can create an instance of the `FileInfo` or `DirectoryInfo` class.

Add the following statements to the end of the `Main` method:

```
string backup = @"/Users/markjprice/Code/Ch10.bak"; // macOS
// string backup = @"C:\Code\Ch10.bak"; // Windows
var info = new FileInfo(backup);
WriteLine($"{backup} contains {info.Length} bytes.");
WriteLine($"{backup} was last accessed {info.LastAccessTime}.");
WriteLine($"{backup} has readonly set to {info.IsReadOnly}.");
```

Run the console application and view the output:

```
C:\Code\Ch10.bak contains 11 bytes.
C:\Code\Ch10.bak was last accessed 29/08/2015 16:25:47.
C:\Code\Ch10.bak has readonly set to False.
```

Reading and writing with streams

A **stream** is a sequence of bytes.

There is an abstract class named `Stream` that represents a stream. There are many classes that inherit from this base class, so they all work the same way. In the following table are some of the common members of the `Stream` class:

Member	**Description**
`CanRead`, `CanWrite`	This determines whether you can read from and write to the stream
`Length`, `Position`	This determines the total number of bytes and the current position within the stream
`Dispose()`	This closes the stream and releases its resources
`Flush()`	If the stream has a buffer, then it is cleared and written to the underlying stream
`Read()`, `ReadAsync()`	This reads a specified number of bytes from the stream into a byte array and advances the position
`ReadByte()`	This reads the next byte from the stream and advances the position
`Seek()`	This moves the position to the specified position (if CanSeek is true)
`Write()`, `WriteAsync()`	This writes the contents of a byte array into the stream
`WriteByte()`	This writes a byte to the stream

Storage streams can be read and written to, and the bytes will be stored in that location.

Namespace	Class	Description
`System.IO`	`FileStream`	This is stored in the filesystem
	`MemoryStream`	This is stored in memory in the current process
`System.Net.Sockets`	`NetworkStream`	This is stored at a network location

Function streams can only be "plugged onto" other streams to add functionality.

Namespace	Class	Description
`System.Security.Cryptography`	`CryptoStream`	This encrypts and decrypts the stream
`System.IO.Compression`	`GZipStream`, `DeflateStream`	This compresses and decompresses the stream
`System.Net.Security`	`AuthenticatedStream`	This sends credentials across the stream

Although there will be occasions where you need to work with streams at a low level, most often, you can plug helper classes into the chain to make things easier. Here are some helper classes to handle common scenarios:

Namespace	Class	Description
`System.IO`	`StreamReader`	This reads from streams as text
	`StreamWriter`	This writes to streams as text
	`BinaryReader`	This reads from streams as .NET types
	`BinaryWriter`	This writes to streams as .NET types
`System.Xml`	`XmlReader`	This reads from streams as XML
	`XmlWriter`	This writes to streams as XML

Writing to text and XML streams

Add a new console application project named Ch10_Streams.

In Visual Studio 2017, set the solution's start-up project to be the current selection.

Import the System.IO and System.Xml namespaces, statically import the System.Console type, and add the following statement to the Main method:

```
// define an array of strings
string[] callsigns = new string[] { "Husker", "Starbuck",
"Apollo", "Boomer", "Bulldog", "Athena", "Helo", "Racetrack" };

// define a file to write to using a text writer helper
string textFile = @"/Users/markjprice/Code/Ch10_Streams.txt";
// string textFile = @"C:\Code\Ch10_Streams.txt"; // Windows
StreamWriter text = File.CreateText(textFile);

// enumerate the strings writing each one to the stream
foreach (string item in callsigns)
{
  text.WriteLine(item);
}
text.Dispose(); // close the stream

// output all the contents of the file to the Console
WriteLine($"{textFile} contains {new FileInfo(textFile).Length}
bytes.");
WriteLine(File.ReadAllText(textFile));

// define a file to write to using the XML writer helper
string xmlFile = @"/Users/markjprice/Code/Ch10_Streams.xml";
// string xmlFile = @"C:\Code\Ch10_Streams.xml";

FileStream xmlFileStream = File.Create(xmlFile);
XmlWriter xml = XmlWriter.Create(xmlFileStream,
  new XmlWriterSettings { Indent = true });

// write the XML declaration
xml.WriteStartDocument();
// write a root element
xml.WriteStartElement("callsigns");

// enumerate the strings writing each one to the stream
foreach (string item in callsigns)
{
  xml.WriteElementString("callsign", item);
```

```
    }

    // write the close root element
    xml.WriteEndElement();
    xml.Dispose();
    xmlFileStream.Dispose();

    // output all the contents of the file to the Console
    WriteLine($"{xmlFile} contains {new FileInfo(xmlFile).Length}
    bytes.");
    WriteLine(File.ReadAllText(xmlFile));
```

Run the console application and view the output:

```
C:\Code\Ch10_Streams.txt contains 68 bytes.
Husker
Starbuck
Apollo
Boomer
Bulldog
Athena
Helo
Racetrack
C:\Code\Ch10_Streams.xml contains 320 bytes.
<?xml version="1.0" encoding="utf-8"?>
<callsigns>
  <callsign>Husker</callsign>
  <callsign>Starbuck</callsign>
  <callsign>Apollo</callsign>
  <callsign>Boomer</callsign>
  <callsign>Bulldog</callsign>
  <callsign>Athena</callsign>
  <callsign>Helo</callsign>
  <callsign>Racetrack</callsign>
</callsigns>
```

Compressing streams

XML is relatively verbose, so it takes up more space in bytes than plain text. We can squeeze the XML using a common compression algorithm known as **GZIP**.

Import the following namespace:

```
using System.IO.Compression;
```

Add the following code to the end of the `Main` method:

```
// compress the XML output
string gzipFilePath = @"/Users/markjprice/Code/Ch10.gzip";
// string gzipFilePath = @"C:\Code\Ch10.gzip"; // Windows

FileStream gzipFile = File.Create(gzipFilePath);
GZipStream compressor = new GZipStream(gzipFile,
CompressionMode.Compress);
XmlWriter xmlGzip = XmlWriter.Create(compressor);
xmlGzip.WriteStartDocument();
xmlGzip.WriteStartElement("callsigns");
foreach (string item in callsigns)
{
  xmlGzip.WriteElementString("callsign", item);
}
xmlGzip.Dispose();
compressor.Dispose(); // also closes the underlying stream

// output all the contents of the compressed file to the Console
WriteLine($"{gzipFilePath} contains {new
FileInfo(gzipFilePath).Length} bytes.");
WriteLine(File.ReadAllText(gzipFilePath));

// read a compressed file
WriteLine("Reading the compressed XML file:");
gzipFile = File.Open(gzipFilePath, FileMode.Open);
GZipStream decompressor = new GZipStream(gzipFile,
CompressionMode.Decompress);
XmlReader reader = XmlReader.Create(decompressor);
while (reader.Read())
{
  // check if we are currently on an element node named callsign
  if ((reader.NodeType == XmlNodeType.Element) && (reader.Name ==
  "callsign"))
  {
    reader.Read(); // move to the Text node inside the element
    WriteLine($"{reader.Value}"); // read its value
  }
}
reader.Dispose();
decompressor.Dispose();
```

Rerun the application and notice that the compressed XML is less than half the size of the same XML without compression:

```
C:\Code\Ch10.gzip contains 150 bytes.
▼     ♦
```

```
{?{??}En?BYjQqf~???????Bj^r~Jf^??RiI??????MrbNNqfz^1?i?QZ??Zd?☼↨@H♣?$
▬%?
&gc?t,?????*????H?????t?&?d??%b??H?aUPbrjIQ"?←?◄?♦ ??9→∟:)
Reading the compressed XML file:
Husker
Starbuck
Apollo
Boomer
Bulldog
Athena
Helo
Racetrack
```

Encoding text

Text characters can be represented in different ways. For example, the alphabet can be encoded using Morse code into a series of dots and dashes for transmission over a telegraph line.

In a similar way, text inside a computer is stored as bits (ones and zeros). .NET Core uses a standard called **Unicode** to encode text internally. Sometimes, you will need to move text outside .NET Core for use by systems that do not use Unicode or use a variation of Unicode.

The following table lists some alternative text encodings commonly used by computers:

Encoding	**Description**
ASCII	This encodes a limited range of characters using the lower seven bits of a byte
UTF-8	This represents each Unicode code point as a sequence of one to four bytes
UTF-16	This represents each Unicode code point as a sequence of one or two 16-bit integers
ANSI/ISO encodings	This provides support for a variety of code pages that are used to support a specific language or group of languages

Encoding strings as byte arrays

Add a new console application project named `Ch10_Encoding`.

Import the `System.Text` namespace and add the following statements to the `Main` method. The code encodes a string using the chosen encoding, loops through each byte, and then decodes back into a string and outputs it:

```
WriteLine("Encodings");
WriteLine("[1] ASCII");
WriteLine("[2] UTF-7");
WriteLine("[3] UTF-8");
WriteLine("[4] UTF-16 (Unicode)");
WriteLine("[5] UTF-32");
WriteLine("[any other key] Default");

// choose an encoding
Write("Press a number to choose an encoding: ");
ConsoleKey number = ReadKey(false).Key;
WriteLine();
WriteLine();

Encoding encoder;
switch (number)
{
  case ConsoleKey.D1:
    encoder = Encoding.ASCII;
    break;
  case ConsoleKey.D2:
    encoder = Encoding.UTF7;
    break;
  case ConsoleKey.D3:
    encoder = Encoding.UTF8;
    break;
  case ConsoleKey.D4:
    encoder = Encoding.Unicode;
    break;
  case ConsoleKey.D5:
    encoder = Encoding.UTF32;
    break;
  default:
    encoder = Encoding.GetEncoding(0);
    break;
}

// define a string to encode
string message = "A pint of milk is £1.99";

// encode the string into a byte array
byte[] encoded = encoder.GetBytes(message);

// check how many bytes the encoding needed
```

```
WriteLine($"{encoder.GetType().Name} uses {encoded.Length}
bytes.");

// enumerate each byte
WriteLine($"Byte  Hex  Char");
foreach (byte b in encoded)
{
  WriteLine($"{b,4} {b.ToString("X"),4} {(char)b,5}");
}

// decode the byte array back into a string and display it
string decoded = encoder.GetString(encoded);
WriteLine(decoded);
```

Run the application and press `1` to choose ASCII. Notice that when outputting the bytes, the pound sign (`£`) cannot be represented in ASCII, so it uses a question mark (`?`) instead:

```
Encodings
[1] ASCII
[2] UTF-7
[3] UTF-8
[4] UTF-16 (Unicode)
[5] UTF-32
[any other key] Default
Press a number to choose an encoding: 1
ASCIIEncoding uses 23 bytes.
Byte  Hex  Char
  65   41     A
  32   20
 112   70     p
 105   69     i
 110   6E     n
 116   74     t
 32   20
 111   6F     o
 102   66     f
  32   20
 109   6D     m
 105   69     i
 108   6C     l
 107   6B     k
  32   20
 105   69     i
 115   73     s
  32   20
  63   3F     ?
  49   31     1
  46   2E     .
```

```
   57   39      9
   57   39      9
A pint of milk is ?1.99
```

Rerun the application and press `3` to choose UTF-8. Notice that, UTF-8 requires one extra byte (24 bytes instead of 23 bytes), but it can store the `£`:

```
UTF8Encoding uses 24 bytes.
Byte  Hex  Char
  65   41     A
  32   20
 112   70     p
 105   69     i
 110   6E     n
 116   74     t
  32   20
 111   6F     o
 102   66     f
  32   20
 109   6D     m
 105   69     i
 108   6C     l
 107   6B     k
  32   20
 105   69     i
 115   73     s
  32   20
 194   C2     Â
 163   A3     £
  49   31     1
  46   2E     .
  57   39     9
  57   39     9
A pint of milk is £1.99
```

Rerun the application and press `4` to choose Unicode (UTF-16). Notice that UTF-16 requires two bytes for every character, but it can store the `£`:

```
UnicodeEncoding uses 46 bytes.
```

Encoding and decoding text in files

When using stream helper classes, such as `StreamReader` and `StreamWriter`, you can specify the encoding you want to use. As you write to the helper, the strings will automatically be encoded, and as you read from the helper, the bytes will be automatically decoded. This is how you can specify the encoding:

```
var reader = new StreamReader(stream, Encoding.UTF7);
var writer = new StreamWriter(stream, Encoding.UTF7);
```

Good Practice
Often, you won't have a choice of encoding to use, because you will be generating a file for use by another system. However, if you do, pick one that uses the least number of bytes but can store every character you need.

Serializing object graphs

Serialization is the process of converting a live object into a sequence of bytes using a specified format. **Deserialization** is the reverse process.

There are dozens of formats you can choose, but the two most common ones are **eXtensible Markup Language** (XML) and **JavaScript Object Notation** (JSON).

Good Practice
JSON is more compact and is best for web and mobile applications. XML is more verbose, but is better supported in older systems.
Ironically, Microsoft originally chose JSON for the `project.json` file format in .NET Core 1.0, but then changed their mind and went back to XML with the C# project `.csproj` file format!

.NET Core has multiple classes that will serialize to and from XML and JSON. We will start by looking at `XmlSerializer` and `JsonSerializer`.

Serializing with XML

Add a new console application project named `Ch10_Serialization`.

In Visual Studio 2017, in the **Solution Explorer**, right-click **Dependencies** and choose **Manage NuGet Packages**. Search for `System.Xml.XmlSerializer`, select the found item, and then click on **Install**, as shown in the following screenshot:

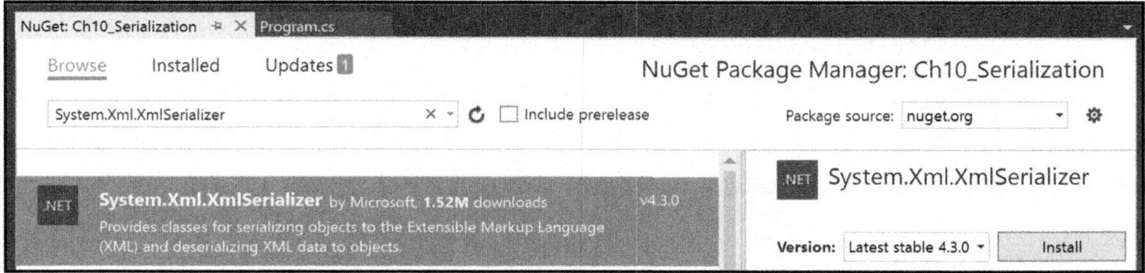

Good Practice
If there are updates to other packages found, then install those too.

In Visual Studio Code, edit the `Ch10_Serialization.csproj` file to add a package reference for `System.Xml.XmlSerializer` version `4.3.0`, as highlighted in the following markup:

```
<Project Sdk="Microsoft.NET.Sdk">

  <PropertyGroup>
    <OutputType>Exe</OutputType>
    <TargetFramework>netcoreapp1.1</TargetFramework>
  </PropertyGroup>

  <ItemGroup>
    <PackageReference Include="System.Xml.XmlSerializer"
                      Version="4.3.0" />
  </ItemGroup>

</Project>
```

To show a common example, we will define a custom class to store information about a person and then create an object graph using a list of `Person` instances with nesting.

Add a class named `Person` with the following definition. Notice that the `Salary` property is protected, meaning it is only accessible to itself and derived classes. To populate the salary, the class has a constructor with a single parameter to set the initial salary:

```
using System;
using System.Collections.Generic;

namespace Ch10_Serialization
{
  public class Person
```

```
    {
      public Person(decimal initialSalary)
      {
        Salary = initialSalary;
      }
      public string FirstName { get; set; }
      public string LastName { get; set; }
      public DateTime DateOfBirth { get; set; }
      public HashSet<Person> Children { get; set; }
      protected decimal Salary { get; set; }
    }
  }
```

Back in `Program.cs`, import the following namespaces:

```
using System;
using System.Collections.Generic;
using System.Xml.Serialization;
using System.IO;
using static System.Console;
```

Add the following statements to the `Main` method:

```
// create an object graph
var people = new List<Person>
{
  new Person(30000M) { FirstName = "Alice", LastName = "Smith",
    DateOfBirth = new DateTime(1974, 3, 14) },
  new Person(40000M) { FirstName = "Bob", LastName = "Jones",
    DateOfBirth = new DateTime(1969, 11, 23) },
  new Person(20000M) { FirstName = "Charlie", LastName = "Rose",
    DateOfBirth = new DateTime(1964, 5, 4),
    Children = new HashSet<Person>
    { new Person(0M) { FirstName = "Sally", LastName = "Rose",
    DateOfBirth = new DateTime(1990, 7, 12) } } }
};

// create a file to write to
string xmlFilepath = @"/Users/markjprice/Code/Ch10_People.xml";
// string xmlFilepath = @"C:\Code\Ch10_People.xml"; // Windows
FileStream xmlStream = File.Create(xmlFilepath);

// create an object that will format as List of Persons as XML
var xs = new XmlSerializer(typeof(List<Person>));

// serialize the object graph to the stream
xs.Serialize(xmlStream, people);
```

```
// you must close the stream to release the file lock
xmlStream.Dispose();

WriteLine($"Written {new FileInfo(xmlFilepath).Length} bytes of
XML to {xmlFilepath}");
WriteLine();

// Display the serialized object graph
WriteLine(File.ReadAllText(xmlFilepath));
```

Run the console application and view the output.

Note that an exception is thrown:

```
Unhandled Exception: System.InvalidOperationException:
Ch10_Serialization.Person cannot be serialized because it does not
have a parameterless constructor.
```

Back in the `Person.cs` file, add the following statement to define a parameter-less constructor. Note that the constructor does not need to do anything, but it must exist so that the `XmlSerializer` can call it to instantiate new `Person` instances during the deserialization process:

```
public Person() { }
```

Rerun the console application and view the output.

Note that the object graph is serialized as XML and the `Salary` property is not included:

```
Written 778 bytes of XML to C:\Code\Ch10_People.xml
<?xml version="1.0"?>
<ArrayOfPerson xmlns:xsi="http://www.w3.org/2001/XMLSchema-instance"
xmlns:xsd="http://www.w3.org/2001/XMLSchema">
  <Person>
    <FirstName>Alice</FirstName>
    <LastName>Smith</LastName>
    <DateOfBirth>1974-03-14T00:00:00</DateOfBirth>
  </Person>
  <Person>
    <FirstName>Bob</FirstName>
    <LastName>Jones</LastName>
    <DateOfBirth>1969-11-23T00:00:00</DateOfBirth>
  </Person>
  <Person>
    <FirstName>Charlie</FirstName>
    <LastName>Rose</LastName>
    <DateOfBirth>1964-05-04T00:00:00</DateOfBirth>
    <Children>
```

```
    <Person>
      <FirstName>Sally</FirstName>
      <LastName>Rose</LastName>
      <DateOfBirth>1990-07-12T00:00:00</DateOfBirth>
    </Person>
  </Children>
</Person>
</ArrayOfPerson>
```

We could make the XML more efficient using attributes instead of elements for some fields.

In the `Person.cs` file, import the `System.Xml.Serialization` namespace and modify all the properties, except `Children`, with the `[XmlAttribute]` attribute:

```
[XmlAttribute("fname")]
public string FirstName { get; set; }
[XmlAttribute("lname")]
public string LastName { get; set; }
[XmlAttribute("dob")]
public DateTime DateOfBirth { get; set; }
```

Rerun the application and notice that the XML is now more efficient:

```
Written 473 bytes of XML to C:\Code\Ch10_People.xml
<?xml version="1.0"?>
<ArrayOfPerson xmlns:xsi="http://www.w3.org/2001/XMLSchema-instance"
xmlns:xsd="
http://www.w3.org/2001/XMLSchema">
  <Person fname="Alice" lname="Smith" dob="1974-03-14T00:00:00" />
  <Person fname="Bob" lname="Jones" dob="1969-11-23T00:00:00" />
  <Person fname="Charlie" lname="Rose" dob="1964-05-04T00:00:00">
    <Children>
      <Person fname="Sally" lname="Rose" dob="1990-07-12T00:00:00" />
    </Children>
  </Person>
</ArrayOfPerson>
```

Deserializing with XML

Add the following statements to the end of the `Main` method:

```
FileStream xmlLoad = File.Open(xmlFilepath, FileMode.Open);
// deserialize and cast the object graph into a List of Person
var loadedPeople = (List<Person>)xs.Deserialize(xmlLoad);
foreach (var item in loadedPeople)
{
```

```
        WriteLine($"{item.LastName} has {item.Children.Count}
        children.");
      }
      xmlLoad.Dispose();
```

Rerun the application and notice that the people are loaded successfully from the XML file:

```
Smith has 0 children.
Jones has 0 children.
Rose has 1 children.
```

Customizing the XML

There are many other attributes that can be used to control the XML generated. See the references at the end of this chapter for more information.

Good Practice
When using `XmlSerializer`, remember that only `public` fields and properties are included, and the type must have a parameter-less constructor. You can customize the output with attributes.

Serializing with JSON

In Visual Studio 2017, in the **Solution Explorer**, in the `Ch10_Serialization` project, right-click on **Dependencies** and choose **Manage NuGet Packages**. Search for `Newtonsoft.Json`, select the found item, and then click on **Install**.

In Visual Studio Code, edit the `Ch10_Serialization.csproj` file to add a package reference for the `Newtonsoft.Json` version `9.0.1`, as shown in the following markup:

```
<PackageReference Include="Newtonsoft.Json"
                  Version="9.0.1" />
```

Import the following namespace at the top of the `Program.cs` file:

```
using Newtonsoft.Json;
```

Add the following statements to the end of the `Main` method:

```
// create a file to write to
string jsonFilepath = @"/Users/markjprice/Code/Ch10_People.json";
// string jsonFilepath = @"C:\Code\Ch10_People.json"; // Windows
StreamWriter jsonStream = File.CreateText(jsonFilepath);
```

```
// create an object that will format as JSON
var jss = new JsonSerializer();

// serialize the object graph into a string
jss.Serialize(jsonStream, people);

// you must dispose the stream to release the file lock
jsonStream.Dispose();

WriteLine();
WriteLine($"Written {new FileInfo(jsonFilepath).Length} bytes of
JSON to: {jsonFilepath}");

// Display the serialized object graph
WriteLine(File.ReadAllText(jsonFilepath));
```

Rerun the application and notice that JSON requires less than half the number of bytes compared to XML with elements. It's even smaller than XML, which uses attributes:

```
Written 368 bytes of JSON to: C:\Code\Ch10_People.json
[{"FirstName":"Alice","LastName":"Smith","DateOfBirth":"\/Date(132451
200000)\/",
"Children":null},{"FirstName":"Bob","LastName":"Jones","DateOfBirth":
"\/Date(-
3369600000)\/","Children":null},{"FirstName":"Charlie","LastName":"Ro
se","DateOfBirth":"\/Date(-
178678800000)\/","Children":[{"FirstName":"Sally","LastName":"Rose","
DateOfBirth":"\/Date(647737200000)\/","Children":null}]}]
```

Good Practice
Use JSON to minimize the size of serialized object graphs. JSON is also a good choice when sending object graphs to web applications and mobile applications because JSON is the native serialization format for JavaScript.

Serializing with other formats

There are many other formats available as NuGet packages that you can use for serialization. A commonly used pair are: `DataContractSerializer` (for XML) and `DataContractJsonSerializer` (for JSON), which are both in the `System.Runtime.Serialization` namespace.

The main serializer that is available for .NET Framework but was not ported to .NET Core are the `System.Runtime.Serialization` formatters, especially the `BinaryFormatter`.

Practice and explore

Test your knowledge and understanding by answering some questions, get some hands-on practice, and explore this chapter's topics with deeper research.

Exercise 10.1 – test your knowledge

Answer the following questions:

1. What is the difference between using the `File` class and the `FileInfo` class?
2. What is the difference between the `ReadByte` method and the `Read` method of a stream?
3. When would you use the `StringReader`, `TextReader`, and `StreamReader` classes?
4. What does the `DeflateStream` type do?
5. How many bytes per character does the UTF-8 encoding use?
6. What is an object graph?
7. What is the best serialization format to choose for minimizing space requirements?
8. What is the best serialization format to choose for cross-platform compatibility?

Exercise 10.2 – practice serializing as XML

Create a console application named `Ch10_Exercise02` that creates a list of shapes, uses serialization to save it to the filesystem using XML, and then deserializes it back:

```
// create a list of Shapes to serialize
var listOfShapes = new List<Shape>
{
  new Circle { Colour = "Red", Radius = 2.5 },
  new Rectangle { Colour = "Blue", Height = 20.0, Width = 10.0 },
  new Circle { Colour = "Green", Radius = 8 },
  new Circle { Colour = "Purple", Radius = 12.3 },
  new Rectangle { Colour = "Blue", Height = 45.0, Width = 18.0  }
};
```

Shapes should have a read-only property named `Area` so that, when you deserialize, you can output a list of shapes, including their areas, as shown here:

```
List<Shape> loadedShapesXml = serializerXml.Deserialize(fileXml)
as List<Shape>;
foreach (Shape item in loadedShapesXml)
{
  WriteLine($"{item.GetType().Name} is {item.Colour} and has an
  area of {item.Area}");
}
```

This is what your output should look like when you run the application:

```
Loading shapes from XML:
Circle is Red and has an area of 19.6349540849362
Rectangle is Blue and has an area of 200
Circle is Green and has an area of 201.061929829747
Circle is Purple and has an area of 475.2915525616
Rectangle is Blue and has an area of 810
```

Exercise 10.3 – explore serialization formats

Create a console application named `Ch10_Exercise03` that queries the Northwind database for all the categories and products and then serializes the data using at least three formats of serialization available to .NET Core.

Which uses the least number of bytes?

Exercise 10.4 – explore topics

Use the following links to read more on this chapter's topics:

- **File System and the Registry (C# Programming Guide)**: `https://docs.microsoft.com/en-us/dotnet/articles/csharp/programming-guide/file-system/`
- **Character encoding in .NET**: `https://docs.microsoft.com/en-us/dotnet/articles/standard/base-types/character-encoding`
- **Serialization (C#)**: `https://docs.microsoft.com/en-us/dotnet/articles/csharp/programming-guide/concepts/serialization/`

- **Serializing to Files, TextWriters, and XmlWriters**: `https://docs.microsoft.com/en-us/dotnet/articles/csharp/programming-guide/concepts/linq/serializing-to-files-textwriters-and-xmlwriters`
- **Newtonsoft Json.NET**: `http://www.newtonsoft.com/json`

Summary

In this chapter, you learned how to read from and write to text files and XML files, how to compress and decompress files, how to encode and decode text, and how to serialize an object into JSON and XML (and deserialize it back again).

In the next chapter, you will learn how to protect data and files.

11

Protecting Your Data

This chapter is about protecting your data from being viewed by malicious users using encryption, and from being manipulated or corrupted using hashing and signing.

This chapter covers the following topics:

- Understanding the vocabulary of protection
- Encrypting and decrypting data
- Hashing data
- Signing data

Understanding the vocabulary of protection

There are many techniques to protect your data; some of them are as follows:

- **Encryption and decryption**: This is a two-way process to convert your data from clear-text into crypto-text and back again.
- **Hashes**: This is a one-way process to generate a hash value to securely store passwords or that can be used to detect malicious changes or corruption of your data.
- **Signatures**: This technique is used to ensure that data has come from someone you trust by validating a signature that has been applied to some data against someone's public key.
- **Authentication**: This technique is used to identify someone by checking their credentials.
- **Authorization**: This technique is used to ensure that someone has permission to perform an action or work with some data by checking the roles or groups they belong to.

Authentication and authorization will be covered in Chapter 14, *Building Web Applications Using ASP.NET Core MVC*.

Good Practice
If security is important to you (and it should be!) then hire an experienced security expert for guidance rather than relying on advice found online. It is very easy to make small mistakes and leave your applications and data vulnerable without realizing until it is too late!

Keys and key sizes

Protection algorithms often use a **key**. Keys can be **symmetric** (also known as shared or secret because the same key is used to encrypt and decrypt) or **asymmetric** (a public-private key pair where the public key is used to encrypt and only the private key can be used to decrypt).

Good Practice
Symmetric key encryption algorithms are fast and can encrypt large amounts of data using a stream. Asymmetric key encryption algorithms are slow and can only encrypt small byte arrays. In the real world, use the best of both worlds by using symmetric to encrypt your data, and asymmetric to share the symmetric key. For example, this is how **Secure Sockets Layer** (**SSL**) encryption on the Internet works.

Keys are represented by byte arrays of varying sizes.

Good Practice
Choose a bigger key size for stronger protection.

IVs and block sizes

When encrypting large amounts of data, there are likely to be repeating sequences. For example, in an English document, the sequence of characters "the" would appear frequently. A good cracker would use this knowledge to make it easier to crack the encryption:

```
When the wind blew hard the umbrella broke.
5:s4&hQ2aj#D f9d1d£8fh"&hQ2s0)an DF8SFd#][1
```

We can avoid repeating sequences by dividing data into **blocks**. After encrypting a block, a byte array value is generated from that block and this value is fed into the next block to adjust the algorithm so that "the" isn't encrypted in the same way. To encrypt the first block, we need a byte array to feed in. This is called the **initialization vector** (**IV**).

Good Practice
Choose a small block size for stronger encryption.

Salts

A salt is a random byte array that is used as an additional input to a one-way hash function. If you do not use a salt when generating hashes, then when many of your users register with **123456** as their password (about 8% of users still do this!), they all have the same hashed value, and their account will be vulnerable to a dictionary attack.

When a user registers, a salt should be randomly generated and concatenated with their chosen password before being hashed. The output (but not the original password) is stored with the salt in the database.

When the user next logs in and enters their password, you look up their salt, concatenate it with the entered password, regenerate a hash, and then compare its value with the hash stored in the database. If they are the same, you know they entered the correct password.

Generating keys and IVs

Keys and IVs are byte arrays. You can reliably generate a key or IV using a **password-based key derivation function** (**PBKDF2**). A good one is the `Rfc2898DeriveBytes` class, which takes a password, a salt, and an iteration count, and then generates keys and IVs by making calls to its `GetBytes` method.

Good Practice
The salt size should be 8 bytes or larger and the iteration count should be greater than zero. The minimum recommended number of iterations is 1,000.

Encrypting and decrypting data

There are multiple encryption algorithms you can choose from in .NET Core. Some algorithms are implemented by the operating system and their names are suffixed with the `CryptoServiceProvider` class, some are implemented entirely in .NET, some use symmetric keys, and some use asymmetric keys.

Best Practice
Choose AES for symmetric encryption and RSA for asymmetric encryption.

Encrypting symmetrically with AES

To make it easier to reuse your protection code in the future, we will create a static class named `Protector` in its own class library.

Using Visual Studio 2017

In Visual Studio 2017, press *Ctrl* + *Shift* + *N* or navigate to **File** | **New** | **Project...**.

In the **New Project** dialog, in the **Installed** | **Templates** list, expand **Visual C#** and select **.NET Standard**. In the list at the center, select **Class Library (.NET Standard)**, type the name `Ch11_CryptographyLib`, change the location to `C:\Code`, type the solution name as `Chapter11`, and then click on **OK**. Rename `Class1.cs` to `Protector.cs`.

In Visual Studio 2017, add a new console application project named `Ch11_EncryptionApp`.

Make sure that you add **Console App (.NET Core)** and not **Class Library (.NET Standard)**!

Set your solution's startup project as the current selection.

In **Solution Explorer**, in the `Ch11_EncryptionApp` project, right-click on **Dependencies** and choose **Add Reference...**, select the `Ch11_CryptographyLib` project, and then click on **OK**.

Using Visual Studio Code

In macOS, in the `Code` folder, create a folder named `Chapter11`, with two subfolders named `Ch11_CryptographyLib` and `Ch11_EncryptionApp`.

In Visual Studio Code, open the folder named `Ch11_CryptographyLib`.

In the **Integrated Terminal**, enter the following command:

```
dotnet new classlib
```

Open the folder named `Ch11_EncryptionApp`.

In the **Integrated Terminal**, enter the following command:

```
dotnet new console
```

Open the folder named `Chapter11`.

In the **Explorer** window, expand `Ch11_CryptographyLib` and rename the `Class1.cs` file to `Protector.cs`.

In the `Ch11_EncryptionApp` project folder, open the file named `Ch11_EncryptionApp.csproj`, and add a package reference to the `Ch11_CryptographyLib` library, as shown highlighted in the following markup:

```
<Project Sdk="Microsoft.NET.Sdk">

  <PropertyGroup>
    <OutputType>Exe</OutputType>
    <TargetFramework>netcoreapp1.1</TargetFramework>
  </PropertyGroup>

  <ItemGroup>
    <ProjectReference
Include="..\Ch11_CryptographyLib\Ch11_CryptographyLib.csproj"
    />
  </ItemGroup>

</Project>
```

In the **Integrated Terminal**, enter the following commands:

```
cd Ch11_EncryptionApp
dotnet restore
dotnet build
```

Creating the Protector class

In both Visual Studio 2017 and Visual Studio Code, open the `Protector.cs` file and change its contents to look like this:

```
using System;
using System.Collections.Generic;
using System.IO;
using System.Security.Cryptography;
using System.Text;
using System.Xml.Linq;

namespace Packt.CS7
{
  public static class Protector
  {
    // salt size must be at least 8 bytes, we will use 16 bytes
    private static readonly byte[] salt =
      Encoding.Unicode.GetBytes("7BANANAS");

    // iterations must be at least 1000, we will use 2000
    private static readonly int iterations = 2000;

    public static string Encrypt(
      string plainText, string password)
    {
      byte[] plainBytes = Encoding.Unicode.GetBytes(plainText);
      var aes = Aes.Create();
      var pbkdf2 = new Rfc2898DeriveBytes(
        password, salt, iterations);
      aes.Key = pbkdf2.GetBytes(32); // set a 256-bit key
      aes.IV = pbkdf2.GetBytes(16); // set a 128-bit IV
      var ms = new MemoryStream();
      using (var cs = new CryptoStream(
        ms, aes.CreateEncryptor(), CryptoStreamMode.Write))
      {
        cs.Write(plainBytes, 0, plainBytes.Length);
      }
      return Convert.ToBase64String(ms.ToArray());
    }
```

```
        public static string Decrypt(
          string cryptoText, string password)
        {
          byte[] cryptoBytes = Convert.FromBase64String(cryptoText);
          var aes = Aes.Create();
          var pbkdf2 = new Rfc2898DeriveBytes(
            password, salt, iterations);
          aes.Key = pbkdf2.GetBytes(32);
          aes.IV = pbkdf2.GetBytes(16);
          var ms = new MemoryStream();
          using (var cs = new CryptoStream(
            ms, aes.CreateDecryptor(), CryptoStreamMode.Write))
          {
            cs.Write(cryptoBytes, 0, cryptoBytes.Length);
          }
          return Encoding.Unicode.GetString(ms.ToArray());
        }
      }
    }
```

Note the following points:

- We used double the recommended salt size and iteration count
- Although the salt and iteration count can be hardcoded, the password *must* be passed at runtime when calling `Encrypt` and `Decrypt`
- We use a temporary `MemoryStream` type to store the results of encrypting and decrypting and then call `ToArray` to turn the stream into a byte array
- We convert the encrypted byte arrays to and from a Base64 encoding to make them easier to read

Good Practice
Never hardcode a password in your source code because, even after compilation, the password can be read in the assembly by using disassembler tools.

In the `Ch11_EncryptionApp` project, open the `Program.cs` file and then import the following namespace and type:

```
using Packt.CS7;
using static System.Console;
```

In the `Main` method, add the following statements to prompt the user for a message and a password and then encrypt and decrypt:

```
Write("Enter a message that you want to encrypt: ");
string message = ReadLine();
Write("Enter a password: ");
string password = ReadLine();
string cryptoText = Protector.Encrypt(message, password);
WriteLine($"Encrypted text: {cryptoText}");
Write("Enter the password: ");
string password2 = ReadLine();
try
{
  string clearText = Protector.Decrypt(cryptoText, password2);
  WriteLine($"Decrypted text: {clearText}");
}
catch
{
  WriteLine(
    "Enable to decrypt because you entered the wrong password!");
}
```

Run the console application.

In Visual Studio 2017, press *Ctrl* + *F5*. In Visual Studio Code, in the Integrated Terminal, enter the command: `dotnet run`

Try entering a message and password, and view the output:

```
Enter a message that you want to encrypt: Hello Bob
Enter a password: secret
Encrypted text: pV5qPDf1CCZmGzUMH2gapFSkn573lg7tMj5ajice3cQ=
Enter the password: secret
Decrypted text: Hello Bob
```

Rerun the application and try entering a message and password, but this time enter the password incorrectly after encrypting and view the output:

```
Enter a message that you want to encrypt: Hello Bob
Enter a password: secret
Encrypted text: pV5qPDf1CCZmGzUMH2gapFSkn573lg7tMj5ajice3cQ=
Enter the password: 123456
Enable to decrypt because you entered the wrong password!
```

Hashing data

There are multiple hash algorithms you can choose from in .NET Core. Some do not use any key, some use symmetric keys, and some use asymmetric keys.

There are two important factors to consider when choosing a hash algorithm:

- **Collision resistance**: How rare is it to find two inputs that share the same hash?
- **Preimage resistance**: For a hash, how difficult would it be to find another input that shares the same hash?

Here are some common hashing algorithms:

Algorithm	Hash size	Description
MD5	16 bytes	This is commonly used because it is fast, but it is not collision-resistant.
SHA1, SHA256, SHA384, SHA512	20 bytes, 32 bytes, 48 bytes, 64 bytes	These are Secure Hashing Algorithm 2nd generation algorithms (SHA2) with different hash sizes. The use of SHA1s on the Internet has been deprecated since 2011.

Good Practice
Avoid MD5 and SHA1 because they have known weaknesses. Choose a larger hash size to reduce the possibility of repeated hashes.

Hashing with SHA256

In the `Ch11_CryptographyLib` class library project, add a new class named `User`. This will represent a user stored in memory, a file, or a database:

```
namespace Packt.CS7
{
  public class User
  {
    public string Name { get; set; }
    public string Salt { get; set; }
    public string SaltedHashedPassword { get; set; }
  }
}
```

Add the following code to the `Protector` class. We will use a dictionary to store multiple users in memory. There are two methods, one to register a new user and one to validate their password when they subsequently log in:

```
private static Dictionary<string, User> Users =
  new Dictionary<string, User>();

public static User Register(string username, string password)
{
  // generate a random salt
  var rng = RandomNumberGenerator.Create();
  var saltBytes = new byte[16];
  rng.GetBytes(saltBytes);
  var saltText = Convert.ToBase64String(saltBytes);

  // generate the salted and hashed password
  var sha = SHA256.Create();
  var saltedPassword = password + saltText;
  var saltedhashedPassword = Convert.ToBase64String(
    sha.ComputeHash(Encoding.Unicode.GetBytes(saltedPassword)));

  var user = new User
  {
    Name = username,
    Salt = saltText,
    SaltedHashedPassword = saltedhashedPassword
  };
  Users.Add(user.Name, user);

  return user;
}

public static bool CheckPassword(string username, string password)
{
  if (!Users.ContainsKey(username))
  {
    return false;
  }
  var user = Users[username];

  // re-generate the salted and hashed password
  var sha = SHA256.Create();
  var saltedPassword = password + user.Salt;
  var saltedhashedPassword = Convert.ToBase64String(
    sha.ComputeHash(Encoding.Unicode.GetBytes(saltedPassword)));

  return (saltedhashedPassword == user.SaltedHashedPassword);
}
```

Add a new console application project named `Ch11_HashingApp`. Add a reference to the `Ch11_CryptographyLib` assembly as you did before, and then import the following namespace and type:

```
using Packt.CS7;
using static System.Console;
```

In the `Main` method, add the following statements to register a user and prompt to register a second user, and then prompt to log in as one of those users and validate the password:

```
WriteLine("A user named Alice has been registered with Pa$$w0rd as
her password.");
var alice = Protector.Register("Alice", "Pa$$w0rd");
WriteLine($"Name: {alice.Name}");
WriteLine($"Salt: {alice.Salt}");
WriteLine(
  $"Salted and hashed password: {alice.SaltedHashedPassword}");
WriteLine();
Write("Enter a different username to register: ");
string username = ReadLine();
Write("Enter a password to register: ");
string password = ReadLine();
var user = Protector.Register(username, password);
WriteLine($"Name: {user.Name}");
WriteLine($"Salt: {user.Salt}");
WriteLine(
  $"Salted and hashed password: {user.SaltedHashedPassword}");

bool correctPassword = false;
while (!correctPassword)
{
  Write("Enter a username to log in: ");
  string loginUsername = ReadLine();
  Write("Enter a password to log in: ");
  string loginPassword = ReadLine();
  correctPassword = Protector.CheckPassword(
    loginUsername, loginPassword);
     if (correctPassword)
  {
    WriteLine(
      $"Correct! {loginUsername} has been logged in.");
  }
  else
  {
    WriteLine("Invalid username or password. Try again.");
  }
}
```

When using multiple projects in Visual Studio Code, remember to manually restore dependencies by entering the `dotnet restore` command before entering the `dotnet run` command.

Run the console application and view the output:

```
A user named Alice has been registered with Pa$$w0rd as her password.
Name: Alice
Salt: tLn3gRn9DXmp2oeuvBSxTg==
Salted and hashed password:
  w8Ub2aH5NNQ8MJarYsUgm29bbb101V/9dlozjWs2Ipk=
Enter a different username to register: Bob
Enter a password to register: Pa$$w0rd
Name: Bob
Salt: zPU9YyFLaz0idhQkKpzY+g==
Salted and hashed password:
  8w14w8WNHoZddEeIx2+UJhpHQqSs4EmyoazqjbmmEz0=
Enter a username to log in: Bob
Enter a password to log in: secret
Invalid username or password. Try again.
Enter a username to log in: Alice
Enter a password to log in: secret
Invalid username or password. Try again.
Enter a username to log in: Bob
Enter a password to log in: Pa$$w0rd
Correct! Bob has been logged in.
```

Even if two users register with the same password, they have randomly generated salts so that their salted and hashed passwords are different.

Signing data

To prove that some data has come from someone we trust, it can be signed. Actually, you don't sign the data itself; instead, you sign a hash of the data. We will use the RSA algorithm combined with the SHA256 algorithm.

Signing with SHA256 and RSA

In the `Ch11_CryptographyLib` class library project, add the following code to the `Protector` class:

```
public static string PublicKey;

public static string ToXmlString(
  this RSA rsa, bool includePrivateParameters)
{
  var p = rsa.ExportParameters(includePrivateParameters);
  XElement xml;
  if (includePrivateParameters)
  {
    xml = new XElement("RSAKeyValue"
      , new XElement("Modulus", Convert.ToBase64String(p.Modulus))
      , new XElement("Exponent",
        Convert.ToBase64String(p.Exponent))
      , new XElement("P", Convert.ToBase64String(p.P))
      , new XElement("Q", Convert.ToBase64String(p.Q))
      , new XElement("DP", Convert.ToBase64String(p.DP))
      , new XElement("DQ", Convert.ToBase64String(p.DQ))
      , new XElement("InverseQ",
        Convert.ToBase64String(p.InverseQ))
    );
  }
  else
  {
    xml = new XElement("RSAKeyValue"
      , new XElement("Modulus", Convert.ToBase64String(p.Modulus))
      , new XElement("Exponent",
        Convert.ToBase64String(p.Exponent))
    );
  }
  return xml?.ToString();
}

public static void FromXmlString(
  this RSA rsa, string parametersAsXml)
{
  var xml = XDocument.Parse(parametersAsXml);
  var root = xml.Element("RSAKeyValue");
  var p = new RSAParameters
  {
    Modulus = Convert.FromBase64String(
      root.Element("Modulus").Value),
    Exponent = Convert.FromBase64String(
      root.Element("Exponent").Value)
  };
  if(root.Element("P") != null)
  {
    p.P = Convert.FromBase64String(root.Element("P").Value);
    p.Q = Convert.FromBase64String(root.Element("Q").Value);
```

```
            p.DP = Convert.FromBase64String(root.Element("DP").Value);
            p.DQ = Convert.FromBase64String(root.Element("DQ").Value);
            p.InverseQ = Convert.FromBase64String(
              root.Element("InverseQ").Value);
          }
          rsa.ImportParameters(p);
        }

        public static string GenerateSignature(string data)
        {
          byte[] dataBytes = Encoding.Unicode.GetBytes(data);
          var sha = SHA256.Create();
          var hashedData = sha.ComputeHash(dataBytes);

          var rsa = RSA.Create();
          PublicKey = rsa.ToXmlString(false); // exclude private key

          return Convert.ToBase64String(rsa.SignHash(hashedData,
            HashAlgorithmName.SHA256, RSASignaturePadding.Pkcs1));
        }

        public static bool ValidateSignature(
          string data, string signature)
        {
          byte[] dataBytes = Encoding.Unicode.GetBytes(data);
          var sha = SHA256.Create();
          var hashedData = sha.ComputeHash(dataBytes);

          byte[] signatureBytes = Convert.FromBase64String(signature);

          var rsa = RSA.Create();
          rsa.FromXmlString(PublicKey);

          return rsa.VerifyHash(hashedData, signatureBytes,
            HashAlgorithmName.SHA256, RSASignaturePadding.Pkcs1);
        }
```

Note the following:

- I have recreated two useful methods that exist on the RSA type in the .NET Framework: `ToXmlString` and `FromXmlString`. These serialize and deserialize the `RSAParameters` structure that contains the public and private keys. .NET Core's implementation of RSA does not include them.
- Only the public part of the public-private key pair needs to be made available to the code that is checking the signature so that we can pass the value `false` when we call the `ToXmlString` method.

- The hash algorithm used to generate the hash from the data must match the hash algorithm set on the signer and checker. In the preceding code, we used `SHA256`.

Add a new console application project named `Ch11_SigningApp`. Add a reference to the `Ch11_CryptographyLib` assembly, and then import the following namespaces:

```
using static System.Console;
using Packt.CS7;
```

In the `Main` method, add the following code:

```
Write("Enter some text to sign: ");
string data = ReadLine();
var signature = Protector.GenerateSignature(data);
WriteLine($"Signature: {signature}");
WriteLine("Public key used to check signature:");
WriteLine(Protector.PublicKey);

if (Protector.ValidateSignature(data, signature))
{
  WriteLine("Correct! Signature is valid.");
}
else
{
  WriteLine("Invalid signature.");
}

// create a fake signature by replacing the
// first character with an X
var fakeSignature = signature.Replace(signature[0], 'X');
if (Protector.ValidateSignature(data, fakeSignature))
{
  WriteLine("Correct! Signature is valid.");
}
else
{
  WriteLine($"Invalid signature: {fakeSignature}");
}
```

Run the console application and enter some text:

```
Enter some text to sign: The cat sat on the mat.
Signature:
LSmfgRuRRvYzM1/jg7U7jkKINCU4KKGpFUCvCB87hmWpa3gDVLjLj0Wift+CktZuPSkc/
gAnIzC1bQCOyELsrNWzATnPDFa/B0Gpy0vAJ8VJ9FPs1vFy353mMnGcnQU8fOummKgEv4
r1JpsnkJQ41MGUMNCH9YVodO6Bn6o81g0=
Public key used to check signature:
<RSAKeyValue><Modulus>qPnY4UHIqJMuUJ0CQ4F0Xy/fxaugNFFe/QNikGsufdKrwa1
```

```
t+CcQqCmWso4zUDW3NTFCWFGilisJ4SqTBgYee/VT9UGuFng68TrZXNiNJO8dP8OZHNBi
rWkhtsNQx9A6rq9bZ/9dsjY1hYsWpGKCw4WhxsHjmGuevQew8C+I2z0=</Modulus><Ex
ponent>AQAB</Exponent></RSAKeyValue>
Correct! Signature is valid.
Invalid signature:
X1uDRfCDXvOyhMtqXlxqzSljhADD/81E0UonuVs9VfZ7ceuyFWh4O7rwkdc1+l25DzGf6
4swtbXZsukpSupFqvkAOIJ6XqMlD92vlG1nquereiWkshYnxxVts30QJIFKKyOTBTfN/V
OljlZVMxT/RA6pggPtESlv+urDJT4z/PEtR5jdx+CTZHQc9WiceFbpuybyf/vEdddtF0T
7g8NeLKEPbT6b7CHGDM1HKbRqnSecv456QNfHNmEXxRk9MpI0DgQLnXpOhHcVwEFc6+dY
6kdNnWd6NIOY3qX6FT782t01Q2swcWxF9fUcvWVSeC84EgVK447X9Xewkrf6CF7jxg==
```

Practicing and exploring

Test your knowledge and understanding by answering some questions, get some hands-on practice, and explore the topics covered in this chapter with deeper research.

Exercise 11.1 – test your knowledge

Answer the following questions:

1. Of the encryption algorithms provided by .NET, which is the best choice for symmetric encryption?
2. Of the encryption algorithms provided by .NET, which is the best choice for asymmetric encryption?
3. For encryption algorithms, is it better to have a larger or smaller block size?

Exercise 11.2 – practice protecting data with encryption and hashing

Create a console application named `Ch11_Exercise02` that protects an XML file, such as the following example. Note that the customer's credit card number and password are currently stored in clear text. The credit card must be encrypted so that it can be decrypted and used later, and the password must be salted and hashed:

```
<?xml version="1.0" encoding="utf-8" ?>
<customers>
  <customer>
    <name>Bob Smith</name>
    <creditcard>1234-5678-9012-3456</creditcard>
    <password>Pa$$w0rd</password>
```

```
    </customer>
</customers>
```

Exercise 11.3 – practice protecting data with decryption

Create a console application named `Ch11_Exercise03` that opens the XML file that you protected in the preceding code and decrypts the credit card number.

Exercise 11.4 – explore topics

Use the following links to read more about the topics covered in this chapter:

- **Key Security Concepts**: `https://msdn.microsoft.com/en-us/library/z164t8hs(v=vs.110).aspx`
- **Encrypting Data**: `https://msdn.microsoft.com/en-us/library/as0w18af(v=vs.110).aspx`
- **Cryptographic Signatures**: `https://msdn.microsoft.com/en-us/library/hk8wx38z(v=vs.110).aspx`

Summary

In this chapter, you learned how to encrypt and decrypt using symmetric encryption, how to generate a salted hash, and how to sign data and check that signature.

In the next chapter, you will use the `Task` type to improve the performance of your applications.

12
Improving Performance and Scalability with Multitasking

This chapter is about allowing multiple actions to occur at the same time to improve performance, scalability, and user productivity.

In this chapter, we will cover the following topics:

- Understanding processes, threads, and tasks
- Running tasks asynchronously
- Synchronizing access to shared resources
- Implementing multitasking for a GUI

The *Implementing multitasking for a GUI* section requires Visual Studio 2017 on Windows 7 or later.

Understanding processes, threads, and tasks

A **process**, for example, each of the console applications we have created has resources allocated to it, such as memory and threads. A **thread** executes your code, statement by statement. By default, each process only has one thread, and this can cause problems when we need to do more than one **task** at the same time.

Windows and most other modern operating systems use preemptive multitasking, which simulates the parallel execution of tasks. It divides the processor time among the threads, allocating a "time slice" to each thread one after another. The current thread is suspended when its time slice finishes. The processor allows another thread to run for a time slice.

When Windows switches from one thread to another, it saves the context of the thread and reloads the previously saved context of the next thread in the thread queue. This takes time and resources.

Threads may have to compete for, and wait for access to, shared resources, such as variables, files, and database objects.

Depending on the task, doubling the number of threads (workers) to perform a task does not halve the number of seconds the task will take. In fact, it can *increase* the duration of the task, as pointed out by the following tweet:

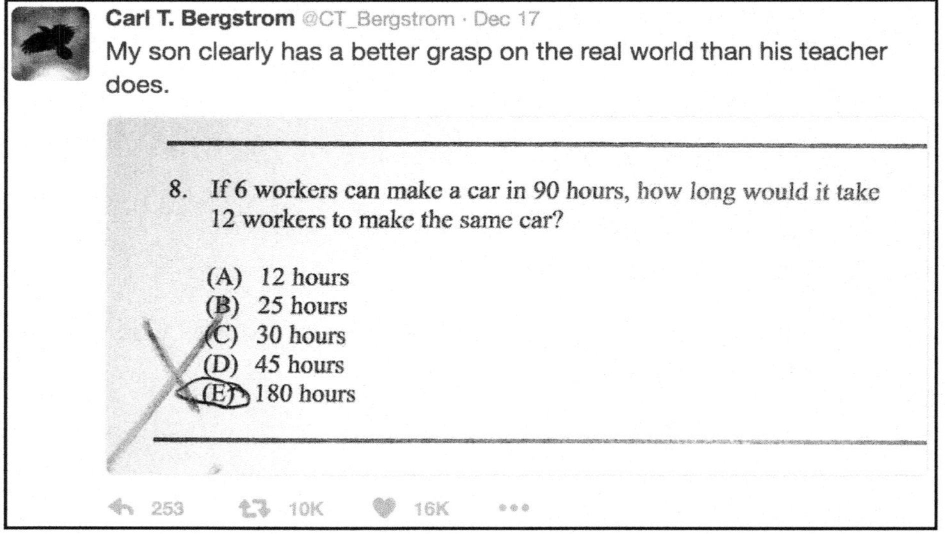

Good Practice
Never assume that more threads (workers) will improve performance. Run performance tests on a base line code implementation *without* multiple threads, and then again on a code implementation *with* multiple threads.
Run performance tests in a staging environment that is as close as possible to the production environment.

Running tasks asynchronously

First, we will write a simple console application that needs to execute three methods, and execute them synchronously (one after the other).

Running multiple actions synchronously

In Visual Studio 2017, press *Ctrl* + *Shift* + *N* or go to **File** | **New** | **Project...**.

In the **New Project** dialog, in the **Installed** | **Templates** list, expand **Visual C#**, and select **.NET Core**. In the center list, select **Console App (.NET Core)**, type the name as `Ch12_Tasks`, change the location to `C:\Code`, type the solution name as `Chapter12`, and then click on **OK**.

In Visual Studio Code, create a directory named `Chapter12` with a subfolder named `Ch12_Tasks`, and open the `Ch12_Tasks` folder. In the Integrated Terminal, execute the command: `dotnet new console`.

In both Visual Studio 2017 and Visual Studio Code, ensure that the following namespaces have been imported:

```
using System;
using System.Threading;
using System.Threading.Tasks;
using System.Diagnostics;
using static System.Console;
```

There will be three methods that need to be executed: the first takes three seconds, the second takes two seconds, and the third takes one second. To simulate that work, we can use the `Thread` class to tell the current thread to go to sleep for a specified number of milliseconds.

Inside the `Program` class, add the following code:

```
static void MethodA()
{
  WriteLine("Starting Method A...");
  Thread.Sleep(3000); // simulate three seconds of work
  WriteLine("Finished Method A.");
}

static void MethodB()
{
  WriteLine("Starting Method B...");
```

```
    Thread.Sleep(2000); // simulate two seconds of work
    WriteLine("Finished Method B.");
  }

  static void MethodC()
  {
    WriteLine("Starting Method C...");
    Thread.Sleep(1000); // simulate one second of work
    WriteLine("Finished Method C.");
  }
```

In the `Main` method, add the following statements:

```
  static void Main(string[] args)
  {
    var timer = Stopwatch.StartNew();
    WriteLine("Running methods synchronously on one thread.");
    MethodA();
    MethodB();
    MethodC();
    WriteLine($"{timer.ElapsedMilliseconds:#,##0}ms elapsed.");
    WriteLine("Press ENTER to end.");
    ReadLine();
  }
```

Run the console application and view the output.

In Visual Studio 2017, press *Ctrl* + *F5*. In Visual Studio Code, in Integrated Terminal, enter the command: `dotnet run`

As there is only one thread, the total time required is just over six seconds:

```
Running methods synchronously on one thread.
Starting Method A...
Finished Method A.
Starting Method B...
Finished Method B.
Starting Method C...
Finished Method C.
6,047ms elapsed.
Press ENTER to end.
```

Running multiple actions asynchronously using tasks

The Thread class has been available since the first version of C# and can be used to create new threads and manage them, but it can be tricky to work with directly.

C# 4 introduced the Task class, which is a wrapper around a thread that enables easier creating and management. Creating multiple threads wrapped in tasks will allow our code to execute asynchronously (at the same time).

We will look at three ways to start the methods using Task instances. Each has a slightly different syntax, but they all define a Task and start it.

Comment out the calls to the three methods and the associated console message, and then add the new statements, as shown highlighted in the following code:

```
static void Main(string[] args)
{
  var timer = Stopwatch.StartNew();
  //WriteLine("Running methods synchronously on one thread.");
  //MethodA();
  //MethodB();
  //MethodC();
  WriteLine("Running methods asynchronously on multiple threads.");
  Task taskA = new Task(MethodA);
  taskA.Start();
  Task taskB = Task.Factory.StartNew(MethodB);
  Task taskC = Task.Run(new Action(MethodC));
  WriteLine($"{timer.ElapsedMilliseconds:#,##0}ms elapsed.");
  WriteLine("Press ENTER to end.");
  ReadLine();
}
```

Rerun the console application and view the output.

The actual elapsed milliseconds will depend on the performance of your CPU, so you are likely to see a different value than shown in the following example output:

```
Running methods asynchronously on multiple threads.
10 milliseconds elapsed.
Press ENTER to end.
Starting Method C...
Starting Method A...
Starting Method B...
Finished Method C.
Finished Method B.
Finished Method A.
```

Note the elapsed time is output almost immediately, because each of the three methods are now being executed by three *new* threads. The *original* thread continues executing until it reaches the `ReadLine` call at the end of the `Main` method.

Meanwhile, the three new threads execute their code simultaneously, and they start in any order. `MethodC` will usually finish first, because it takes only one second, then `MethodB`, and finally `MethodA`, because it takes three seconds.

However, the actual CPU used has a big effect on the results. It is the CPU that allocates time slices to each process to allow them to execute their threads. You have no control over when the methods run.

Waiting for tasks

Sometimes, you need to wait for a task to complete before continuing. To do this, you can use the `Wait` method on a `Task` instance, or the `WaitAll` or `WaitAny` static methods on an array of tasks.

Method	Description
`t.Wait()`	Waits for the task instance named `t` to complete execution.
`Task.WaitAny(Task[])`	Waits for any of the tasks in the array to complete execution.
`Task.WaitAll(Task[])`	Waits for all the tasks in the array to complete execution.

Add the following statements to the `Main` method immediately after creating the three tasks. This will combine references to the three tasks into an array and pass them to the `WaitAll` method. Now, the original thread will pause on that statement, waiting for all three tasks to finish before outputting the elapsed time:

```
Task[] tasks = { taskA, taskB, taskC };
Task.WaitAll(tasks);
```

Rerun the console application and view the output:

```
Running methods asynchronously on multiple threads.
Starting Method B...
Starting Method C...
Starting Method A...
Finished Method C.
Finished Method B.
Finished Method A.
3,024 milliseconds elapsed.
Press ENTER to end.
```

Notice that the total time is now slightly more than the time to run the longest method. If all three tasks can be performed at the same time, then this will be all we need to do.

However, often a task is dependent on the output from another task. To handle this scenario, we need to define **continuation tasks**.

Continuing with another task

Add the following methods to the `Program` class:

```
static decimal CallWebService()
{
  WriteLine("Starting call to web service...");
  Thread.Sleep((new Random()).Next(2000, 4000));
  WriteLine("Finished call to web service.");
  return 89.99M;
}

static string CallStoredProcedure(decimal amount)
{
  WriteLine("Starting call to stored procedure...");
  Thread.Sleep((new Random()).Next(2000, 4000));
  WriteLine("Finished call to stored procedure.");
  return $"12 products cost more than {amount:C}.";
}
```

These methods simulate a call to a web service that returns a monetary amount that then needs to be used to retrieve how many products cost more than that amount in a database. The result returned from the first method needs to be fed into the input of the second method.

I used the `Random` class to wait for a random interval of between two and four seconds for each method call to simulate the work.

Inside the `Main` method, comment out the previous tasks by highlighting the statements and, in Visual Studio Code, press *Cmd* + *K*, *C*, or in Visual Studio 2017 press *Ctrl* + *K*, *C*.

Then, add the following statements before the existing statement that outputs the total time elapsed and then calls `ReadLine` to wait for the user to press *Enter*:

```
WriteLine("Passing the result of one task as an input into
another.");

var taskCallWebServiceAndThenStoredProcedure =
  Task.Factory.StartNew(CallWebService)
  .ContinueWith(previousTask =>
    CallStoredProcedure(previousTask.Result));

WriteLine($"{taskCallWebServiceAndThenStoredProcedure.Result}");
```

Run the console application and view the output:

```
Passing the result of one task as an input into another.
Starting call to web service...
Finished call to web service.
Starting call to stored procedure...
Finished call to stored procedure.
12 products cost more than £89.99.
5,971 milliseconds elapsed.
Press ENTER to end.
```

Nested and child tasks

Add a new console application project named `Ch12_NestedAndChildTasks`.

In Visual Studio 2017, in the solution's **Properties**, remember to change **Startup Project** to **Current selection**.

Ensure the following namespaces have been imported:

```
using System;
using System.Threading;
using System.Threading.Tasks;
using System.Diagnostics;
using static System.Console;
```

Inside the `Main` method, add the following statements:

```
var outer = Task.Factory.StartNew(() =>
{
  WriteLine("Outer task starting...");
  var inner = Task.Factory.StartNew(() =>
  {
    WriteLine("Inner task starting...");
    Thread.Sleep(2000);
    WriteLine("Inner task finished.");
  });
});
outer.Wait();
WriteLine("Outer task finished.");
WriteLine("Press ENTER to end.");
ReadLine();
```

Run the console application and view the output:

```
Outer task starting...
Outer task finished.
Inner task starting...
Inner task finished.
Press ENTER to end.
```

Note that, although we wait for the outer task to finish, its inner task does not have to finish as well. To link the two tasks, we must use a special option.

Modify the existing code that defines the inner task to add a `TaskCreationOption` value of `AttachedToParent`:

```
var inner = Task.Factory.StartNew(() =>
{
  WriteLine("Inner task starting...");
  Thread.Sleep(2000);
  WriteLine("Inner task finished.");
}, TaskCreationOptions.AttachedToParent);
```

Rerun the console application and view the output. Note that the inner task must finish before the outer task can:

```
Outer task starting...
Inner task starting...
Inner task finished.
Outer task finished.
Press ENTER to end.
```

Synchronizing access to shared resources

When you have multiple threads executing at the same time, there is a possibility that two or more threads may access the same variable or other resource at the same time and cause a problem.

For this reason, you should carefully consider how to make your code "thread safe".

The simplest mechanism for implementing thread safety is to use an object variable as a "flag" or "traffic light" to indicate when a shared resource has an exclusive lock applied.

In William Golding's *Lord of the Flies*, Piggy and Ralph spot a conch shell and use it to call a meeting. The boys impose a "rule of the conch" on themselves, deciding that no one can speak unless he's holding the conch. I like to name the object variable I use the "conch." When a thread has the conch, no other thread can access the shared resource(s) represented by that conch.

Accessing a resource from multiple threads

Add a new console application project named `Ch12_LockAndMonitor`.

Ensure that the following namespaces have been imported:

```
using System;
using System.Threading;
using System.Threading.Tasks;
using System.Diagnostics;
using static System.Console;
```

Inside the `Program` class, add the following statements to:

- Declare and instantiate an object to generate random wait times

- Declare a `string` variable to store a message (this is the shared resource)
- Declare two methods that add a letter, `A` or `B`, to the shared `string` five times in a loop, and wait for a random interval of up to two seconds for each iteration
- A `Main` method that executes both methods on separate threads using a pair of tasks and waits for them to complete before outputting the elapsed milliseconds it took

```
static Random r = new Random();
static string Message; // a shared resource

static void MethodA()
{
  for (int i = 0; i < 5; i++)
  {
    Thread.Sleep(r.Next(2000));
    Message += "A";
    Write(".");
  }
}

static void MethodB()
{
  for (int i = 0; i < 5; i++)
  {
    Thread.Sleep(r.Next(2000));
    Message += "B";
    Write(".");
  }
}

static void Main(string[] args)
{
  WriteLine("Please wait for the tasks to complete.");
  Stopwatch watch = Stopwatch.StartNew();

  Task a = Task.Factory.StartNew(MethodA);
  Task b = Task.Factory.StartNew(MethodB);

  Task.WaitAll(new Task[] { a, b });
  WriteLine();
  WriteLine($"Results: {Message}.");
  WriteLine($"{watch.ElapsedMilliseconds:#,##0} elapsed
  milliseconds.");
}
```

Run the console application and view the output:

```
Please wait for the tasks to complete.
..........
Results: BABBABBAAA.
6,099 elapsed milliseconds.
```

Note that the results show that both threads were modifying the message concurrently. In an actual application, this could be a problem. We could prevent concurrent access by applying a mutually exclusive lock.

Applying a mutually exclusive lock to a resource

In the `Program` class, add an object variable instance to act as a "conch":

```
static object conch = new object();
```

In both `MethodA` and `MethodB`, add a `lock` statement around the `for` statement:

```
lock(conch)
{
  for (int i = 0; i < 5; i++)
  {
    Thread.Sleep(r.Next(2000));
    Message += "A";
    Write(".");
  }
}
```

Rerun the console application and view the output:

```
Please wait for the tasks to complete.
..........
Results: AAAAABBBBB.
9,751 elapsed milliseconds.
```

Although the time elapsed was longer, only one method at a time could access the shared resource. Only once a method has finished its work on the shared resource, does the conch get released and the other method has a chance to do its work.

Either `MethodA` or `MethodB` could start first.

Understanding the lock statement

The compiler changes this:

```
lock(conch)
{
  // access shared resource
}
```

Into this:

```
try
{
  Monitor.Enter(conch);
  // access shared resource
}
finally
{
  Monitor.Exit(conch);
}
```

Knowing how the `lock` statement works internally is important because using the `lock` statement can cause a deadlock.

Deadlocks occur when there are two or more shared resources (and therefore conches) and the following sequence of events happen:

- Thread X locks conch A
- Thread Y locks conch B
- Thread X attempts to lock conch B but is blocked because thread Y already has it
- Thread Y attempts to lock conch A but is blocked because thread X already has it

A proven way to prevent deadlocks is to specify a timeout when attempting to get a lock. To do this, you must manually use the `Monitor` class instead of using the `lock` statement.

Modify your code to replace the `lock` statements with code that tries to enter the conch with a timeout like this:

```
try
{
  Monitor.TryEnter(conch, TimeSpan.FromSeconds(15));
  for (int i = 0; i < 5; i++)
  {
    Thread.Sleep(r.Next(2000));
    Message += "A";
    Write(".");
```

```
    }
  }
  finally
  {
    Monitor.Exit(conch);
  }
```

Rerun the console application and view the output. It should return the same results as before, but is better code because it would avoid potential deadlocks.

Good Practice
Never use the `lock` keyword. Always use the `Monitor.TryEnter` method instead, in combination with a `try` statement, so that you can supply a timeout and avoid a potential deadlock scenario.

Making operations atomic

Look at the following increment operation:

```
int x = 3;
x++; // is this an atomic CPU operation?
```

Atomic: from Greek *atomos, undividable.*

It is not atomic! Incrementing an integer requires the following three CPU operations:

1. Load a value from an instance variable into a register.
2. Increment the value.
3. Store the value in the instance variable.

A thread could be preempted after executing the first two steps. A second thread could then execute all three steps. When the first thread resumes execution, it will overwrite the value in the variable, and the effect of the increment or decrement performed by the second thread will be lost!

There is a type named `Interlocked` that can perform atomic actions on value types, such as integers and floats.

Declare another shared resource that will count how many operations have occurred:

```
static int Counter; // another shared resource
```

In both methods, inside the `for` statement, after modifying `string`, add the following statement to safely increment the counter:

```
Interlocked.Increment(ref Counter);
```

After outputting the elapsed time, output the counter:

```
WriteLine($"{Counter} string modifications.");
```

Rerun the console application and view the output:

```
10 string modifications.
```

Applying other types of synchronization

`Monitor` and `Interlocked` are mutually exclusive locks that are simple and effective but, sometimes, you need more advanced options to synchronize access to shared resources.

Type	Description
`ReaderWriterLock` and `ReaderWriterLockSlim` (recommended)	This allows multiple threads to be in **read mode**, one thread to be in the **write mode** with exclusive ownership of the lock, and one thread that has read access to be in the **upgradeable read mode**, from which the thread can upgrade to the write mode without having to relinquish its read access to the resource.
`Mutex`	Like `Monitor`, this provides exclusive access to a shared resource, except it is used for **inter-process** synchronization
`Semaphore` and `SemaphoreSlim`	This limits the number of threads that can access a resource or pool of resources concurrently by defining **slots**
`AutoResetEvent` and `ManualResetEvent`	Event wait handles allow threads to synchronize activities by **signaling** each other and by waiting for each other's signals

Implementing multitasking for a GUI

In this section, you will use threads to improve multitasking in a graphical app.

Visual Studio Code cannot be used to create GUI applications, so you will need Visual Studio 2017 on Windows 7 or later to complete this last section of the chapter. In `Chapter 13`, *Building Universal Windows Platform Apps Using XAML*, you will learn about Universal Windows Platform apps; however, these can only be created on Windows 10. So, if you only have Visual Studio Code on a non-Windows OS, at this point, you might want to jump ahead to `Chapter 14`, *Building Web Applications Using ASP.NET Core MVC*.

C# 5 introduced two keywords to simplify working with the `Task` type. They are especially useful for:

- Implementing multitasking for a **graphical user interface** (GUI)
- Improving the scalability of web applications and services

In this chapter, we will explore how the `async` and `await` keywords can implement multitasking with a GUI running on Windows 7 or later.

In `Chapter 14`, *Building Web Applications Using ASP.NET Core MVC*, we will explore how the `async` and `await` keywords can improve scalability in web applications.

In `Chapter 15`, *Building Mobile Apps Using Xamarin.Forms and ASP.NET Core Web API*, we will explore how the `async` and `await` keywords can implement multitasking with a mobile GUI and improve scalability in a web service.

Creating a GUI that blocks

In Visual Studio 2017, go to **File** | **Add** | **New Project...**. In the **Add New Project** dialog, in the **Installed** | **Templates** list, select **Visual C#**. In the center list, select **WPF App (.NET Framework)**, type the name as `Ch12_GUITasks`, and then click on **OK**.

You will learn more about XAML in the next chapter, but for now, just enter the following markup in the XAML view inside the `<Grid>` element:

```
<StackPanel>
  <Button Name="GetProductsButton">Get Products</Button>
  <TextBox>Type in here while the products load...</TextBox>
  <ListBox Name="ProductsListBox"></ListBox>
</StackPanel>
```

Your main editor window should now look like the following screenshot:

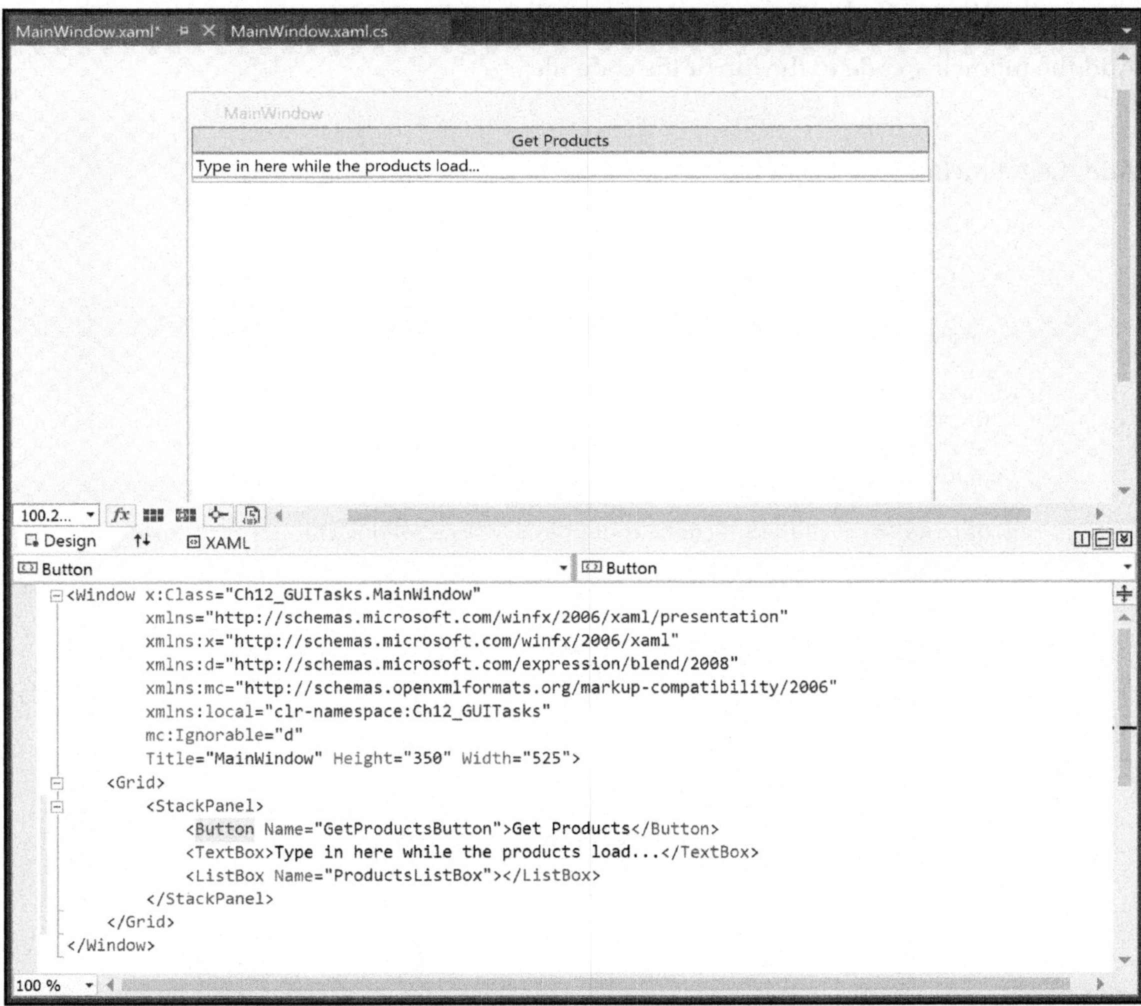

Inside the `Button` element, after setting the `Name`, enter an attribute named `Click`, as shown in the following screenshot, and when the IntelliSense appears, press *Enter* to insert a new event handler:

```
<Grid>
    <StackPanel>                                   <New Event Handler>
        <Button Name="GetProductsButton" Click="">Get Products</Button>
        <TextBox>Type in here while the products load...</TextBox>
```

Choose the **View** | **Code** menu, or press *F7*, or click on the `MainWindow.xaml.cs` tab.

Add the following code to the top of the code file:

```
using System.Data.SqlClient;
```

Add the following code inside the `GetProductsButton_Click` method:

```
var connection = new SqlConnection(
  @"Data Source=(localdb)\mssqllocaldb;" +
  "Initial Catalog=Northwind;Integrated Security=true;");

connection.Open();

var getProducts = new SqlCommand(
  "WAITFOR DELAY '00:00:05';" +
  "SELECT ProductID, ProductName, UnitPrice FROM Products",
  connection);

SqlDataReader reader = getProducts.ExecuteReader();

int indexOfID = reader.GetOrdinal("ProductID");
int indexOfName = reader.GetOrdinal("ProductName");
int indexOfPrice = reader.GetOrdinal("UnitPrice");

while (reader.Read())
{
  ProductsListBox.Items.Add(
    string.Format("{0}: {1} costs {2:c}",
    reader.GetInt32(indexOfID),
    reader.GetString(indexOfName),
    reader.GetDecimal(indexOfPrice)));
}
reader.Dispose();
connection.Dispose();
```

The database connection string uses Microsoft SQL Server LocalDb and connects to the Northwind sample database
The SQL statement waits for five seconds before returning four columns from the `Products` table

Run the WPF app by pressing *Ctrl* + *F5*.

Click inside the text box and enter some text. The user interface is responsive.

Click on the **Get Products** button and then try to enter some text in the text box again.

The user interface is blocked because the thread is busy running the SQL command, as shown in the following screenshot. Only once the list of products has been populated does the UI become responsive and you can type into the text box again.

MainWindow

Get Products

Type in here while the products load...hjhhkhhk

Creating a GUI that doesn't block

The types in the `SqlClient` namespace have been improved in .NET Framework 4.5 and later by giving any method that might take a long time an asynchronous equivalent that returns a `Task`.

For example, the `SqlConnection` class has both an `Open` method that returns `void` and an `OpenAsync` method that returns `Task`. `SqlCommand` has both an `ExecuteReader` method that returns `SqlDataReader` and an `ExecuteReaderAsync` method that returns `Task<SqlDataReader>`.

We can use these `Task` objects as we did earlier, but that would still block the user interface when we call any of the `Wait` methods.

Instead, we can use the `await` keyword for any `Task`. This means that the main thread will not be blocked while we wait, but will remember its current position within the statements so that, once the `Task` has completed, the main thread continues executing from that same point. This allows us to write code that looks as simple as synchronous, but underneath, it is much more complex.

Internally, `await` creates a state machine to manage the complexity of passing state between any worker threads and the user interface thread.

Modify the statements as shown in the following code. Note that, to use the `await` keyword, we must mark the containing method `await` with the `async` keyword. They always work as a pair:

```
private async void GetProductsButton_Click(
  object sender, RoutedEventArgs e)
{
  var connection = new SqlConnection(
    @"Data Source=(localdb)\mssqllocaldb;" +
    "Initial Catalog=Northwind;Integrated Security=true;");
  await connection.OpenAsync();
  var getProducts = new SqlCommand(
    "WAITFOR DELAY '00:00:05';" +
    "SELECT ProductID, ProductName, UnitPrice FROM Products",
    connection);
  SqlDataReader reader = await getProducts.ExecuteReaderAsync();
  int indexOfID = reader.GetOrdinal("ProductID");
  int indexOfName = reader.GetOrdinal("ProductName");
  int indexOfPrice = reader.GetOrdinal("UnitPrice");
  while (await reader.ReadAsync())
  {
    ProductsListBox.Items.Add(
      string.Format("{0}: {1} costs {2:c}",
      await reader.GetFieldValueAsync<int>(indexOfID),
      await reader.GetFieldValueAsync<string>(indexOfName),
      await reader.GetFieldValueAsync<decimal>(indexOfPrice)));
  }
  reader.Dispose();
  connection.Dispose();
}
```

Rerun the application by pressing *Ctrl* + *F5*.

This time, after clicking on the **Get Products** button, you will be able to enter text in the text box while the command executes:

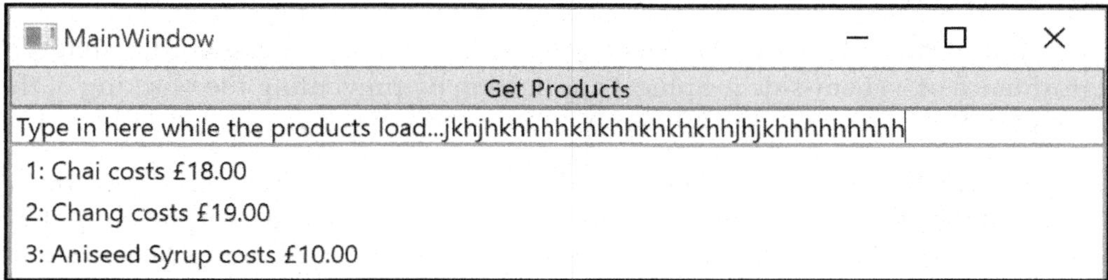

Other types with Async methods

Here are some of the other types that have an asynchronous method support:

Type	Methods
`HttpClient`	`GetAsync`, `PostAsync`, `PutAsync`, `DeleteAsync`, `SendAsync`
`StreamReader`	`ReadAsync`, `ReadLineAsync`, `ReadToEndAsync`
`StreamWriter`	`WriteAsync`, `WriteLineAsync`, `FlushAsync`

Good Practice
Any time you see a method that ends in the suffix `Async`, check to see whether it returns `Task` or `Task<T>`. If it does, then you should use it instead of the synchronous non-Async suffixed method. Remember to call it using `await` and decorate your method with `async`.

await in catch blocks

In C# 5, it was only possible to use the `await` keyword in a `try` exception handling block, but not in a `catch` block.

In C# 6 or later, it is now possible to use `await` in both `try` and `catch` blocks.

Improving scalability for client-server applications

In the previous example, we saw how using the `async` and `await` keywords can improve the performance of a client-side graphical application by preventing the blocking of the user interface thread.

The same keywords can be applied on the server side when building web applications and services. From the client application's point of view, nothing changes (or they might even notice a small increase in the time for a request to return). So, from a single client's point of view, the use of `async` on the server side makes their experience worse!

On the server side, additional, cheaper worker threads are created to wait for long-running tasks to finish so that expensive IO threads can handle other client's requests instead of being blocked. This improves the overall scalability of a web application or service. More clients can be supported simultaneously.

You will create asynchronous operations on the server side in `Chapter 14`, *Building Web Applications Using ASP.NET Core MVC*.

Practicing and exploring

Test your knowledge and understanding by answering some questions, get some hands-on practice, and explore this chapter's topics with deeper research.

Exercise 12.1 – test your knowledge

Answer the following questions:

1. By convention, what suffix should be applied to a method that returns `Task` or `Task<T>`?
2. To use the `await` keyword inside a method, what keyword must be applied to the method declaration?
3. How do you create a child task?
4. Why should you avoid the `lock` keyword?
5. When should you use the `Interlocked` class?

Exercise 12.2 – explore topics

Use the following links to read more about this chapter's topics:

- **Threads and threading**: `https://msdn.microsoft.com/en-us/library/6kac2kdh(v=vs.110).aspx`
- **Task parallelism (task parallel library)**: `https://msdn.microsoft.com/en-us/library/dd537609(v=vs.110).aspx`
- **await (C# reference)**: `https://msdn.microsoft.com/en-GB/library/hh156528.aspx`
- **Asynchronous Programming with Async and Await (C# and Visual Basic)**: `https://msdn.microsoft.com/en-us/library/vstudio/hh191443.aspx`
- **Interlocked Operations**: `https://msdn.microsoft.com/en-us/library/sbhbke0y(v=vs.110).aspx`
- **EventWaitHandle, AutoResetEvent, CountdownEvent, ManualResetEvent**: `https://msdn.microsoft.com/en-us/library/ksb7zs2x(v=vs.110).aspx`

Summary

In this chapter, you learned how to define and start a task, how to wait for one or more tasks to finish, and how to control task completion order. You also learned how to use `async` and `await` to prevent the user interface thread from being blocked and how to synchronize access to shared resources.

In the next chapter, you will learn how to create apps for the Universal Windows Platform.

13
Building Universal Windows Platform Apps Using XAML

This chapter is about seeing what can be achieved with XAML when defining the user interface for a graphical app, in particular, for **Universal Windows Platform** (**UWP**).

In a single chapter, we will only be able to scratch the surface of everything that can be done with UWP. However, I hope to excite you into wanting to learn more about this cool technology and platform.

Think of this chapter as a whistle-stop tour of the coolest parts of UWP and XAML, including template-able controls, data binding, and animation!

Some important points about this chapter
UWP apps are not cross-platform, but they are cross-device if those devices run a modern flavor of Windows.
You will need Windows 10 and Visual Studio 2017 to create the examples in this chapter.
UWP apps use a custom forked implementation of .NET Core.
UWP supports .NET Native, which means that your code is compiled to native CPU instructions for a smaller memory footprint and faster execution.

In this chapter, we will cover the following topics:

- Understanding Universal Windows Platform
- Understanding XAML
- Creating an app for Universal Windows Platform
- Using resources and templates
- Data binding

- Animating with storyboards
- Testing in emulators

Understanding Universal Windows Platform

UWP is Microsoft's latest technology solution to build applications for its Windows suite of operating systems.

UWP provides a guaranteed API layer across multiple device types. You can create a single app package that can be uploaded to a single Store to be distributed to reach all the device types your app can run on. These devices include Windows 10, Windows 10 Mobile, Xbox One, and Microsoft HoloLens.

Adapting your app's layout

XAML and UWP provide layout panels that adapt how they display their child controls to make the most of the device they are currently running on. It is the Windows app equivalent of web page responsive design.

XAML and UWP provide visual state triggers to alter the layout based on dynamic changes, such as the horizontal or vertical orientation of a tablet.

Taking advantage of unique device capabilities

UWP provides standard mechanisms to detect the capabilities of the current device and then activate additional features of your app to fully take advantage of them.

Understanding XAML

In 2006, Microsoft released WPF, which was the first technology to use XAML. It is used even today to create desktop applications.

Microsoft Visual Studio 2017 is a WPF application.

XAML can be used to create:

- **UWP apps** for Windows 10, Windows 10 Mobile, Xbox One, and Microsoft HoloLens
- **Windows Store apps** for Windows 8 and 8.1
- **Windows Presentation Foundation** (**WPF**) applications for the Windows desktop, including Windows 7 and later
- **Silverlight applications** for web browsers, Windows Phone, and desktop

Although Silverlight is still supported by Microsoft, it is not being actively developed, so it should be avoided.

Simplifying code using XAML

XAML simplifies C# code, especially when building a user interface.

Imagine that you need two or more buttons laid out horizontally to create a toolbar. In C#, you would write this code:

```
var toolbar = new StackPanel();
toolbar.Orientation = Orientation.Horizontal;
var newButton = new Button();
newButton.Content = "New";
newButton.Background = new SolidColorBrush(Colors.Pink);
toolbar.Children.Add(newButton);
var openButton = new Button();
openButton.Content = "Open";
openButton.Background = new SolidColorBrush(Colors.Pink);
toolbar.Children.Add(openButton);
```

In XAML, this would be simplified to the following lines of code. When this XAML is processed, the equivalent properties are set, and methods are called to achieve the same goal as the preceding C# code:

```
<StackPanel Name="toolbar" Orientation="Horizontal">
  <Button Name="newButton" Background="Pink">New</Button>
  <Button Name="OpenButton" Background="Pink">Open</Button>
</StackPanel>
```

XAML is an alternative (better) way of declaring and instantiating .NET types.

Choosing common controls

There are lots of predefined controls that you can choose from for common user interface scenarios. Almost all versions of XAML support these controls.

Control(s)	**Description**
`Button`, `Menu`, `Toolbar`	Executing actions
`CheckBox`, `RadioButton`	Choosing options
`Calendar`, `DatePicker`	Choosing dates
`ComboBox`, `ListBox`, `ListView`, `TreeView`	Choosing items from lists and hierarchical trees
`Canvas`, `DockPanel`, `Grid`, `StackPanel`, `WrapPanel`	Layout containers that affect their children in different ways
`Label`, `TextBlock`	Displaying read-only text
`RichTextBox`, `TextBox`	Editing text
`Image`, `MediaElement`	Embedding images, videos, and audio files
`DataGrid`	Viewing and editing bound data
`Scrollbar`, `Slider`, `StatusBar`	Miscellaneous user interface elements

Creating an app for Universal Windows Platform

To be able to create apps for UWP, you must enable developer mode in Windows 10.

Go to **Start Menu** | **Settings** | **Update & security** | **For developers**, and then click on **Developer mode**, as shown in the following screenshot. Accept the warning about how it "could expose your device and personal data to security risk or harm your device," and then close the **Settings** app. You might need to restart your PC.

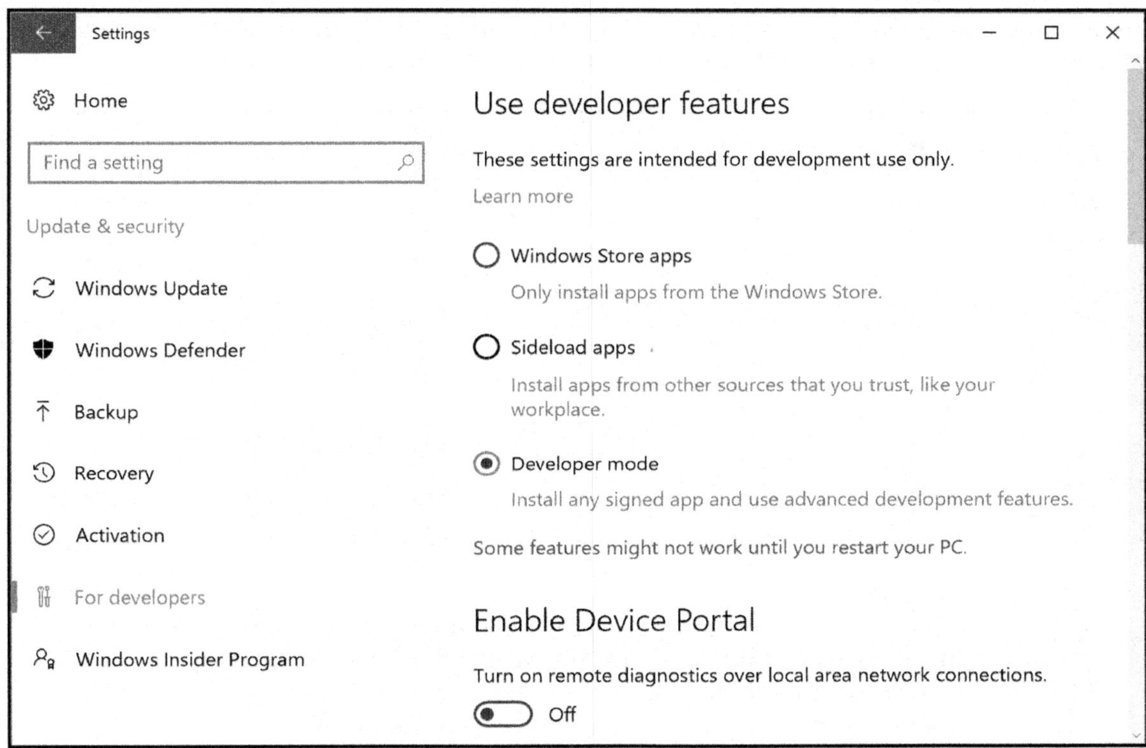

In Visual Studio 2017, press *Ctrl* + *Shift* + *N* or choose **File** | **New** | **Project...**.

In the **New Project** dialog, in the **Installed** | **Templates** list, select **Visual C#**. In the center list, select **Blank App (Universal Windows)**, type the name as `Ch13_UWP`, change the location to `C:\Code`, type the solution name as `Chapter13`, and then click on **OK**.

In the **New Universal Windows Project** dialog box, as shown in the following screenshot, choose **Minimum Version** of **Windows 10 (10.0; Build 10240)** and click **OK**.

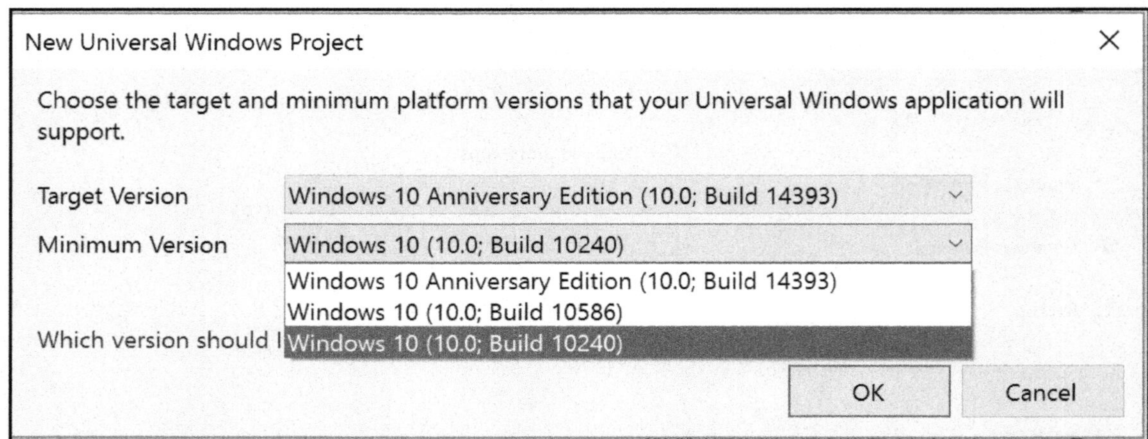

Good Practice
Developers writing UWP apps for a general audience should choose the latest build of Windows 10 for the **Minimum Version**. Developers writing Enterprise apps should choose an older **Minimum Version**. Build 10240 was released in July 2015 and is the best choice for maximum compatibility.

In the **Solution Explorer** window, double-click on the `MainPage.xaml` file to open it for editing. You will see the XAML design window showing a graphical view and an XAML view of the `MainWindow.xaml` file. You will be able to make the following observations:

- The XAML designer is split horizontally, but you can toggle to a vertical split and collapse one side by clicking the buttons on the right edge of the divider

- You can swap views by clicking the double-arrow button in the divider
- You can scroll and zoom both views

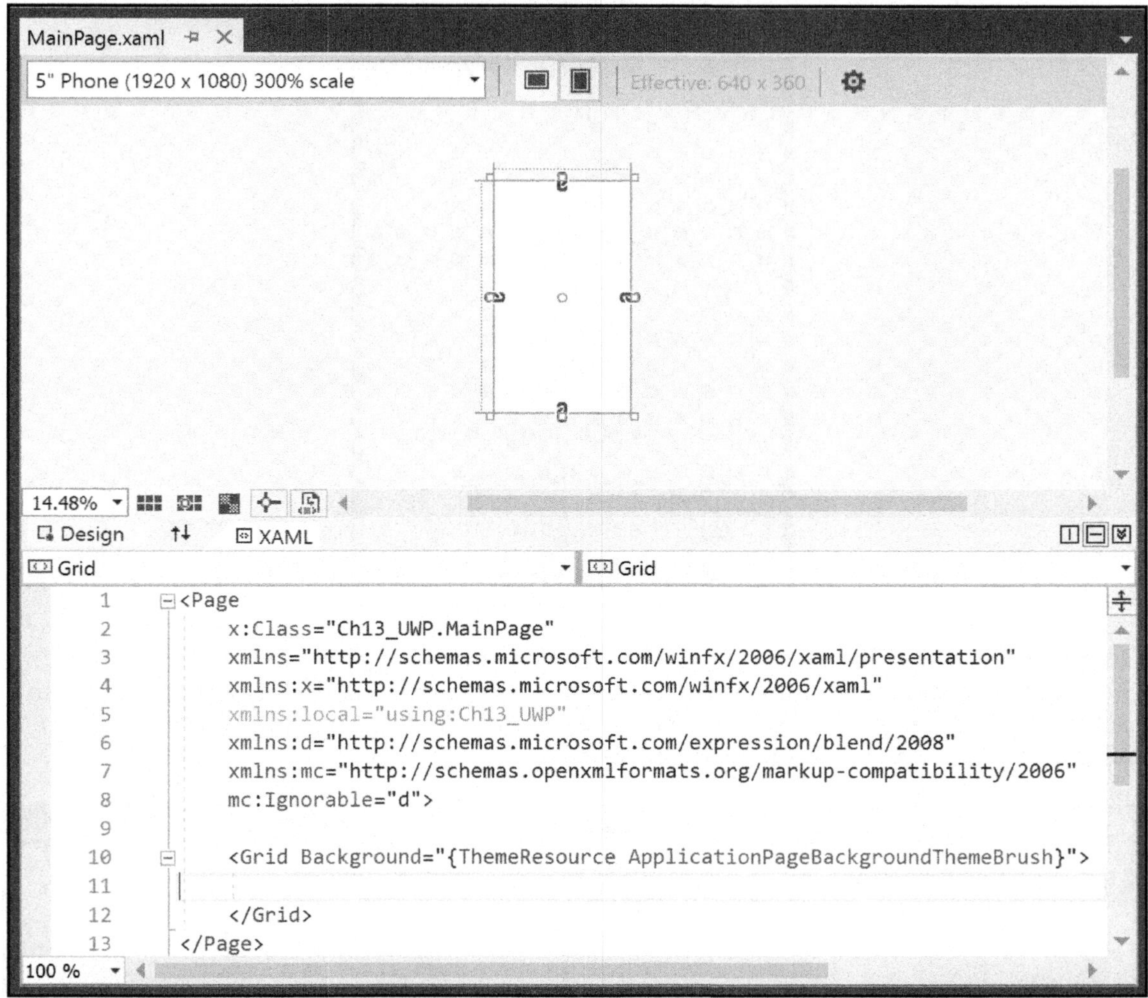

On the **View** menu, choose **Toolbox** or press *Ctrl + W, X*. Note that the toolbox has sections for **Common XAML Controls**, **All XAML Controls**, and **General**. At the top of the toolbox is a search box. Enter the letters `bu`, as shown in the following screenshot. Note that the list of controls is filtered:

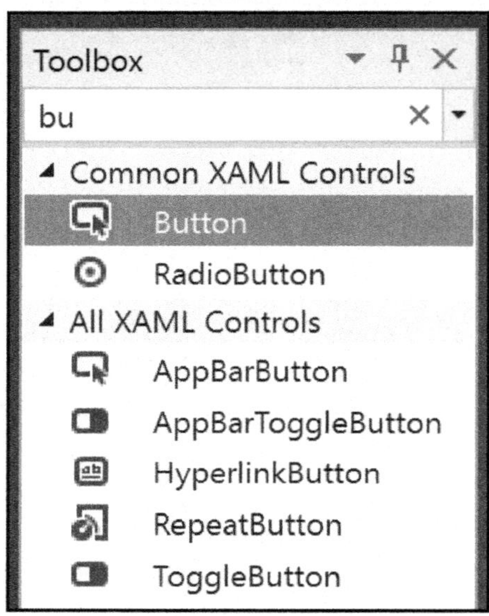

Drag and drop the **Button** control from the toolbox onto the graphical view. Resize it by clicking, holding, and dragging any of the eight square resize handles on each edge and in each corner. Note that the button is given a fixed width and height, and fixed left and top margins, to position and size it inside the grid.

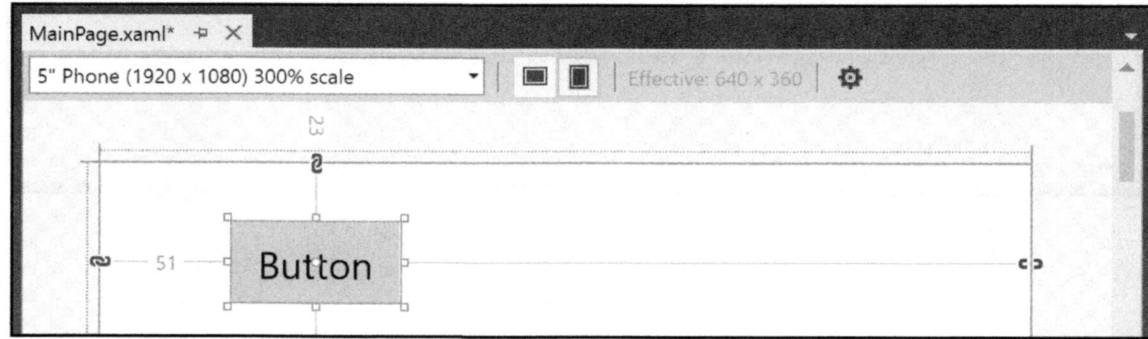

Although you can drag and drop controls, it is better to use the XAML view for layout.

In the XAML view, find the `Button` element and delete it.

In the XAML view, inside the `Grid` element, enter the following markup:

```
<Button Margin="6" Padding="6" Name="clickMeButton">
  Click Me
</Button>
```

Note that the button is automatically sized to its content, `Click Me`, aligned vertically in the center and aligned horizontally to the left, as shown in the following screenshot:

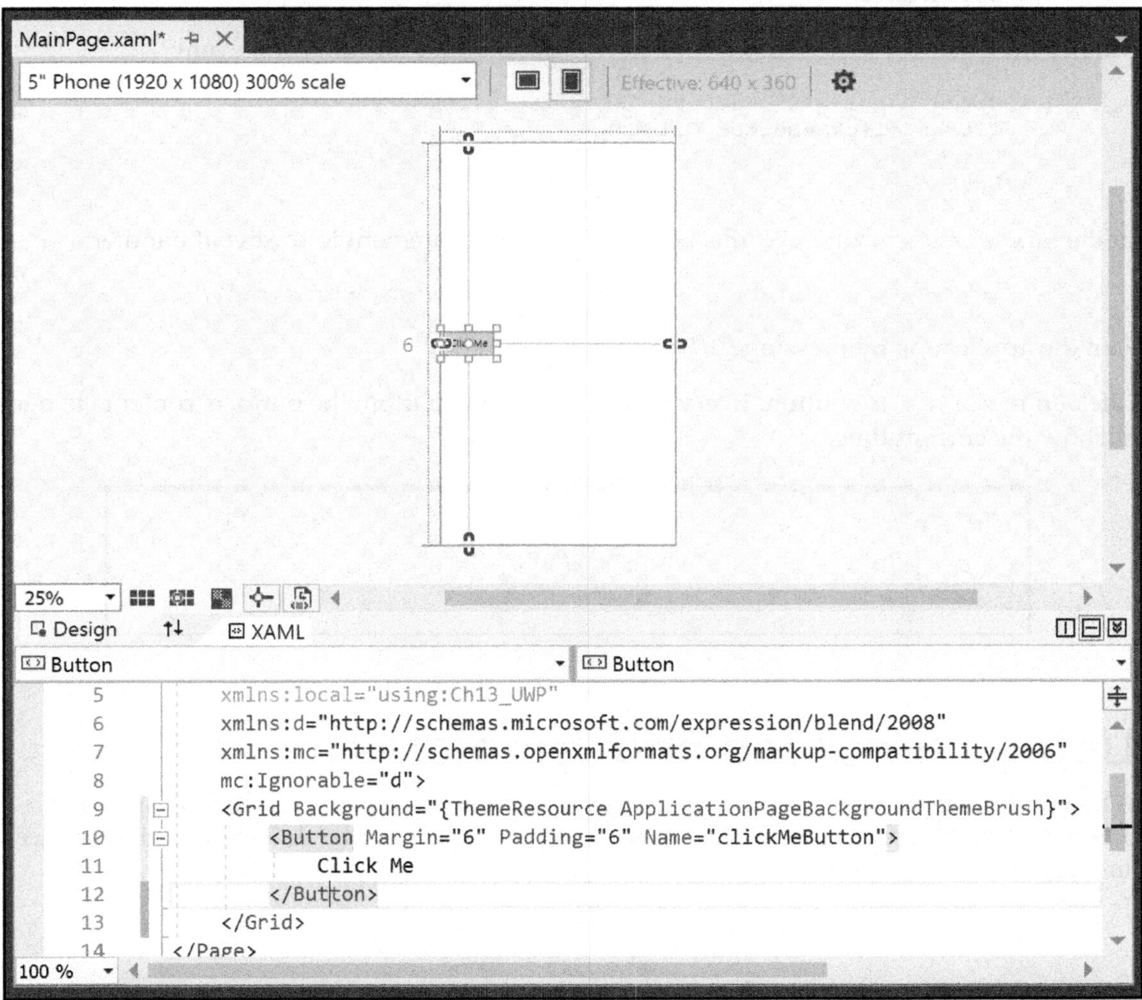

Modify the XAML to wrap the `Button` element inside a horizontally orientated `StackPanel` that is inside a vertically orientated, by default, `StackPanel`, and note the change in its layout:

```
<StackPanel>
  <StackPanel Orientation="Horizontal">
    <Button Margin="6" Padding="6" Name="clickMeButton">
      Click Me
    </Button>
  </StackPanel>
</StackPanel>
```

Modify the `Button` element to give it a new event handler for its `Click` event:

```
<Button Margin="6" Padding="6" Name="clickMeButton"
  Click="clickMeButton_Click">
  Click Me
</Button>
```

In the `MainWindows.xaml.cs` file, add the following statement to the event handler:

```
clickMeButton.Content = DateTime.Now.ToString("hh:mm:ss");
```

Run the application by pressing *Ctrl* + *F5*.

Click on the `Click Me` button. Every time you click the button, the button's content changes to show the current time:

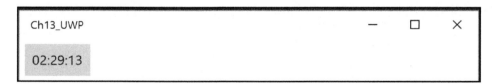

Using resources and templates

When building graphical user interfaces, you will often want to use a resource, such as a brush, to paint the background of controls. These resources can be defined in a single place and shared throughout the app.

Sharing resources

In the**Solution Explorer** window, double-click on the `App.xaml` file.

Add the following markup inside the existing `<Application>` element:

```
<Application.Resources>
  <LinearGradientBrush x:Key="rainbow">
    <GradientStop Color="Red" Offset="0" />
    <GradientStop Color="Orange" Offset="0.1" />
    <GradientStop Color="Yellow" Offset="0.3" />
    <GradientStop Color="Green" Offset="0.5" />
    <GradientStop Color="Blue" Offset="0.7" />
    <GradientStop Color="Indigo" Offset="0.9" />
    <GradientStop Color="Violet" Offset="1" />
  </LinearGradientBrush>
</Application.Resources>
```

In the `MainPage.xaml` file, modify the `Grid` element to have its background set to the rainbow brush that you just defined, like this:

```
<Grid Background="{StaticResource rainbow}">
```

Rerun the application and view the result:

Good Practice
A resource can be an instance of any object. To share it within an application, define it in the `App.xaml` file and give it a unique `Key`. To set an element's property to apply the resource, use `StaticResource` with the `Key`.

Replacing a control template

You can redefine how a control looks by replacing its default template.

One of the most common resources is a `Style` that can set multiple properties at once. If a style has a unique `Key`, then it must be explicitly set, like we did earlier with the linear gradient. If it doesn't have a `Key`, then it will be automatically applied based on the `TargetType`.

In the `App.xaml` file, add the following markup inside the `<Application.Resources>` element:

```
<ControlTemplate x:Key="DarkGlassButton" TargetType="Button">
  <Border BorderBrush="#FFFFFFFF"
    BorderThickness="1,1,1,1" CornerRadius="4,4,4,4">
    <Border x:Name="border" Background="#7F000000"
      BorderBrush="#FF000000" BorderThickness="1,1,1,1"
      CornerRadius="4,4,4,4">
      <Grid>
        <Grid.RowDefinitions>
          <RowDefinition Height="*"/>
          <RowDefinition Height="*"/>
        </Grid.RowDefinitions>
        <Border Opacity="0" HorizontalAlignment="Stretch"
          x:Name="glow" Width="Auto" Grid.RowSpan="2"
          CornerRadius="4,4,4,4">
        </Border>
        <ContentPresenter HorizontalAlignment="Center"
          VerticalAlignment="Center" Width="Auto"
          Grid.RowSpan="2" Padding="4"/>
        <Border HorizontalAlignment="Stretch" Margin="0,0,0,0"
          x:Name="shine" Width="Auto"
          CornerRadius="4,4,0,0">
          <Border.Background>
            <LinearGradientBrush EndPoint="0.5,0.9"
              StartPoint="0.5,0.03">
              <GradientStop Color="#99FFFFFF" Offset="0"/>
              <GradientStop Color="#33FFFFFF" Offset="1"/>
            </LinearGradientBrush>
          </Border.Background>
        </Border>
      </Grid>
    </Border>
  </Border>
</ControlTemplate>
<Style TargetType="Button">
  <Setter Property="Template"
    Value="{StaticResource DarkGlassButton}" />
  <Setter Property="Foreground" Value="White" />
</Style>
```

Rerun the application and view the results. Note the "black glass" effect on the button:

Data binding

When building graphical user interfaces, you will often want to bind a property of one control to another or to some data.

Binding to elements

In the `MainWindow.xaml` file, add the following markup after the `Button` element inside the horizontally orientated `StackPanel`:

```
<Slider Value="50" Maximum="100" Minimum="0"
  Width="200" Name="slider"/>
<TextBlock Text="{Binding ElementName=slider, Path=Value}"
  VerticalAlignment="Center" Margin="10"/>
```

Rerun the app. Click, hold, and drag the slider, and notice that the text block shown to the right of the slider always shows the current value of the slider:

Under the horizontally orientated stack panel, but inside the outer stack panel, add the following markup to define some instructions to the user, a slider for values between `0` and `360` degrees, and a red square with a rotation transformation:

```
<TextBlock>Use the slider below to rotate the square:</TextBlock>
<Slider Value="0" Minimum="0" Maximum="360"
  Name="sliderRotation"/>
<Rectangle Height="100" Width="100" Fill="Red">
```

```
      <Rectangle.RenderTransform>
        <RotateTransform
          Angle="{Binding ElementName=sliderRotation, Path=Value}" />
      </Rectangle.RenderTransform>
    </Rectangle>
```

Note that the angle of the rotation transform is data bound to the slider's value.

Rerun the app and click, hold, and drag the slider to rotate the red square:

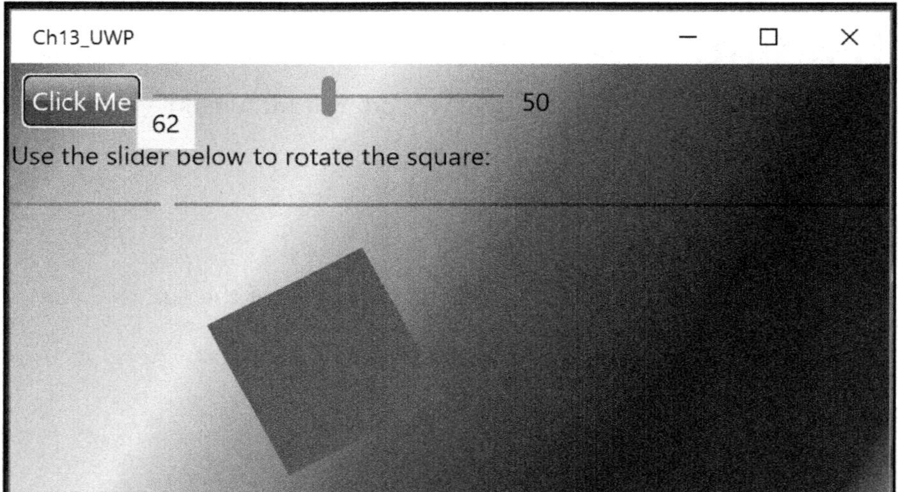

Binding to data

Add a new **Blank App (Universal Windows)** project named `Ch13_DataBinding`.

Set the solution's startup project to be the current selection.

In the **Solution Explorer** window, right-click on the new project and add a new folder named `Models`.

Right-click on the `Models` folder and add a new class named `Employee`. Add the following statements to it:

```
public class Employee
{
  public int EmployeeID { get; set; }
  public string FirstName { get; set; }
  public string LastName { get; set; }
```

```
    public DateTime DOB { get; set; }
    public decimal Salary { get; set; }
  }
```

Add another class named `EmployeesViewModel`:

```
  public class EmployeesViewModel
  {
    public HashSet<Employee> Employees { get; set; }

    public EmployeesViewModel()
    {
      Employees = new HashSet<Employee>();
      Employees.Add(new Employee
        { EmployeeID = 1, FirstName = "Alice", LastName = "Smith",
          DOB = new DateTime(1972, 1, 27), Salary = 34000M });
      Employees.Add(new Employee
        { EmployeeID = 2, FirstName = "Bob", LastName = "Jones",
          DOB = new DateTime(1965, 4, 13), Salary = 64000M });
    }
  }
```

Open `MainPage.xaml`. Add the following `ListBox` element whose items are bound to each employee instance in the `Employees` hash set of the view model:

```
  <ListBox ItemsSource="{Binding Employees}">
    <ListBox.ItemTemplate>
      <DataTemplate>
        <StackPanel Orientation="Horizontal">
          <TextBlock Text="{Binding EmployeeID}" FontSize="30" />
          <TextBox Text="{Binding FirstName}"
            Header="First Name" Margin="10" />
          <TextBox Text="{Binding LastName}"
            Header="Last Name" Margin="10" />
          <DatePicker Date="{Binding DOB}"
            Header="DOB" Margin="10" />
          <TextBox Text="{Binding Salary}"
            Header="Salary" Margin="10" />
        </StackPanel>
      </DataTemplate>
    </ListBox.ItemTemplate>
  </ListBox>
```

Since the data won't be loaded until runtime, you won't see a preview of the layout in the design window. You *can* configure a UWP project with sample data for use at design time, but that is beyond the scope of this book.

In the XAML for the `Page` element, insert a new event handler for the `Load` event:

```
Loading="Page_Loading"
```

Press *F7* to view the code.

Add the following statement to the event handler for `Page_Loading`. The `DataContext` method is inherited by all controls, so the instance of the view model can be easily bound to by everything on the page:

```
DataContext = new Models.EmployeesViewModel();
```

Run the application. The user can click inside each box to modify the data values:

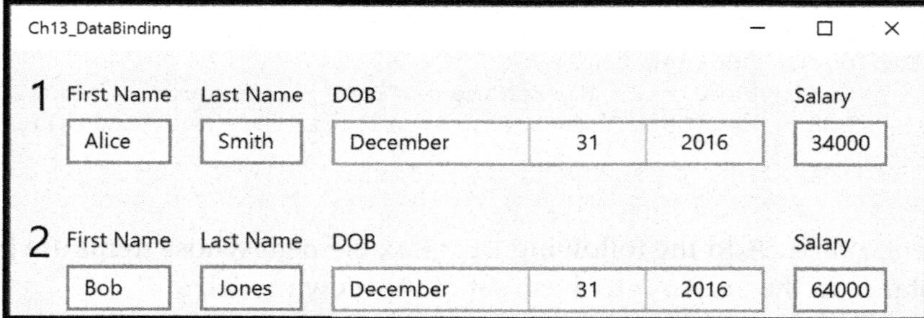

Note the date picker. This will look different and is optimized for input on different devices:

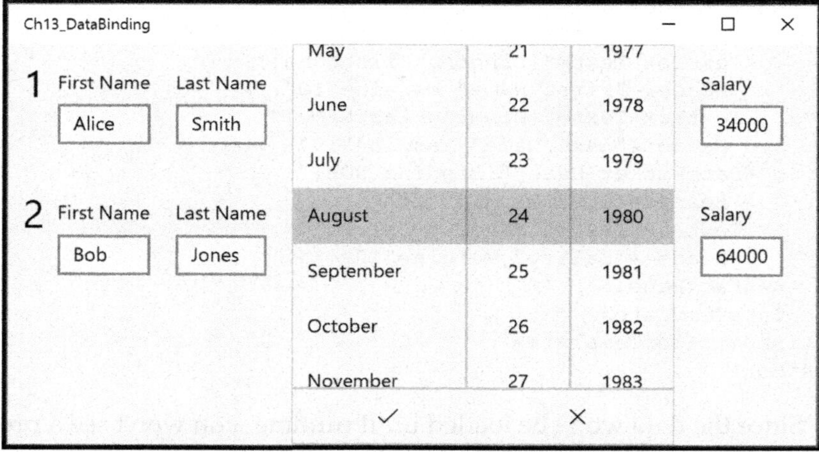

In the real world, you would load the data from a file or service. You will learn how to build services in Chapter 15, *Building Mobile Apps Using Xamarin.Forms and ASP.NET Core Web API.*

Animating with storyboards

You can make your application feel more natural and organic (and fun) using storyboard animations.

Add a new **Blank App (Universal Windows)** project named `Ch13_BouncingBall`.

Open the `MainPage.xaml` file, change `Grid` into `Canvas`, and add an ellipse to make a red ball. Save your changes:

```
<Canvas Background=
  "{ThemeResource ApplicationPageBackgroundThemeBrush}">
  <Ellipse Fill="Red" Height="100" Width="100"/>
</Canvas>
```

In the **Solution Explorer** window, right-click on the `Ch13_BouncingBall` project and choose **Design in Blend...**

Be patient. The first time you start Blend, it can take a few minutes.

The project will open in the **Microsoft Blend for Visual Studio** tool, which is used by designers because it has better support for graphical effects and animation than Visual Studio does.

On the drawing surface, click on the red ellipse to select it, as shown in the following screenshot.

In the **Objects and Timeline** window on the left, click on the small green **+** button, or click on the down triangle to drop down a menu, to create a **New Storyboard** resource:

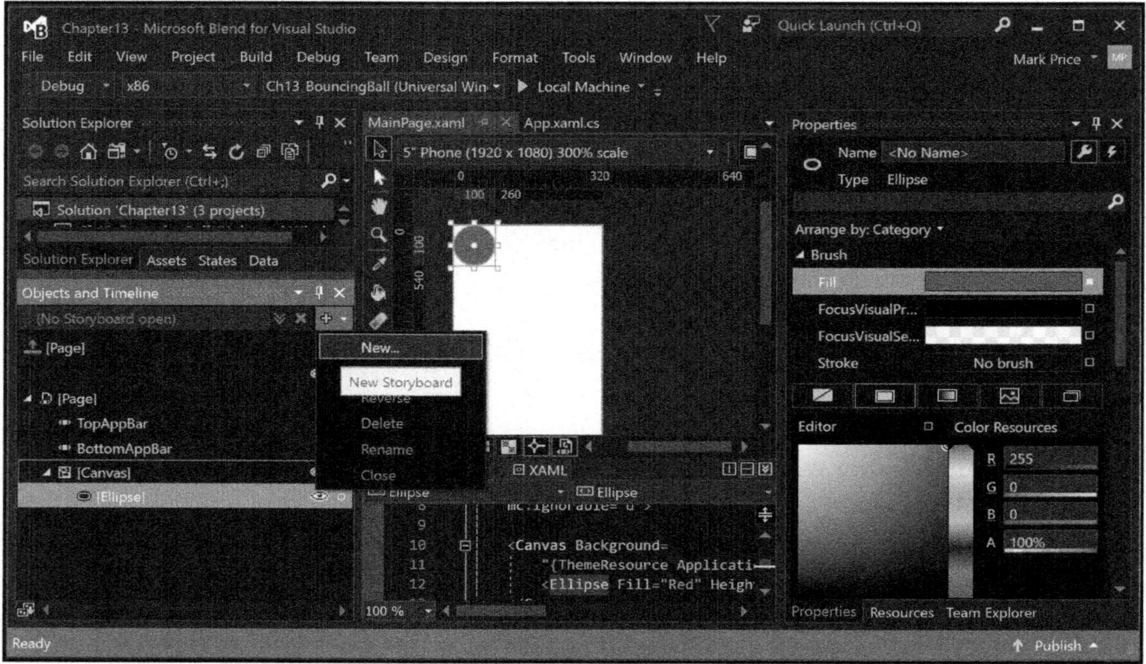

Change the name of the storyboard resource to **BounceBall** and click on **OK**:

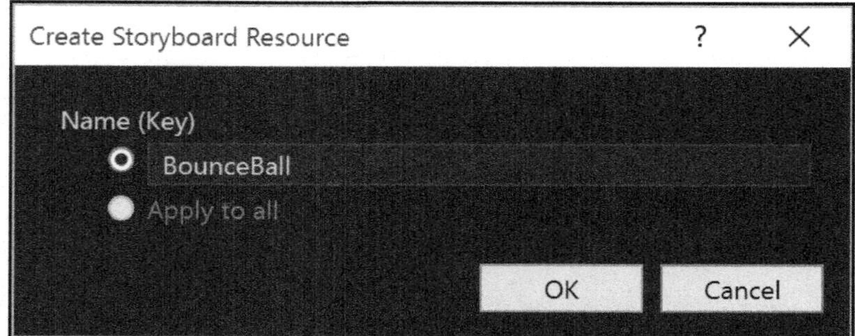

A red box appears around the drawing surface, and you will see in the top-right corner that timeline recording is on. Later, you will click on the red dot to stop recording:

BounceBall timeline recording is on.

In the **Objects and Timeline** window, click on the Record Keyframe button—it looks like a green **+** symbol combined with a small diamond, and is to the left of the current time indicator. This will record the current properties of the ball at time **0:00.000**:

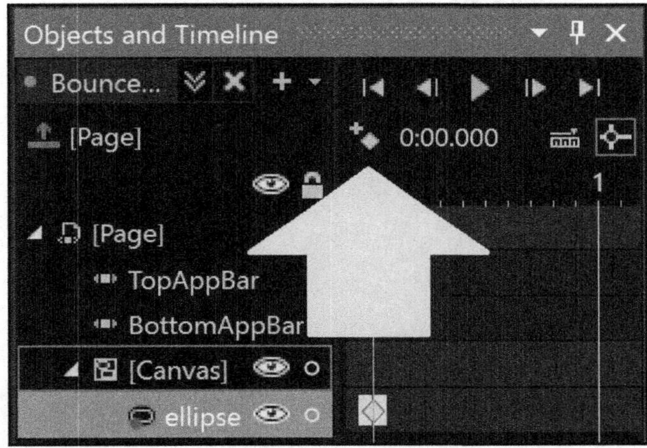

On the timeline, drag the down-pointing orange triangle and its vertical orange line to time position **0:00.800**. This means 0.8 seconds later:

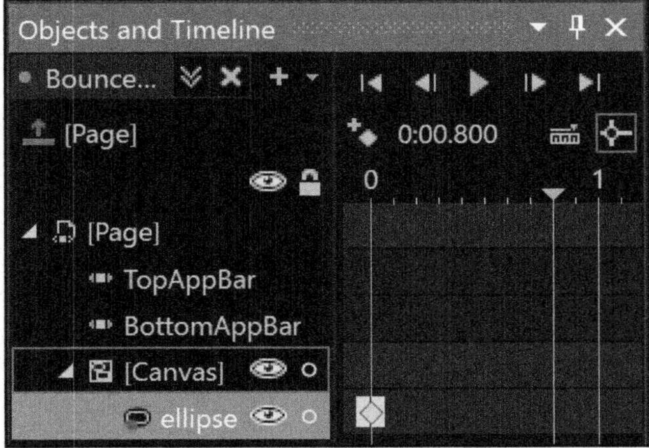

On the drawing surface, drag the red ellipse down and a little to the right. This change will be recorded automatically:

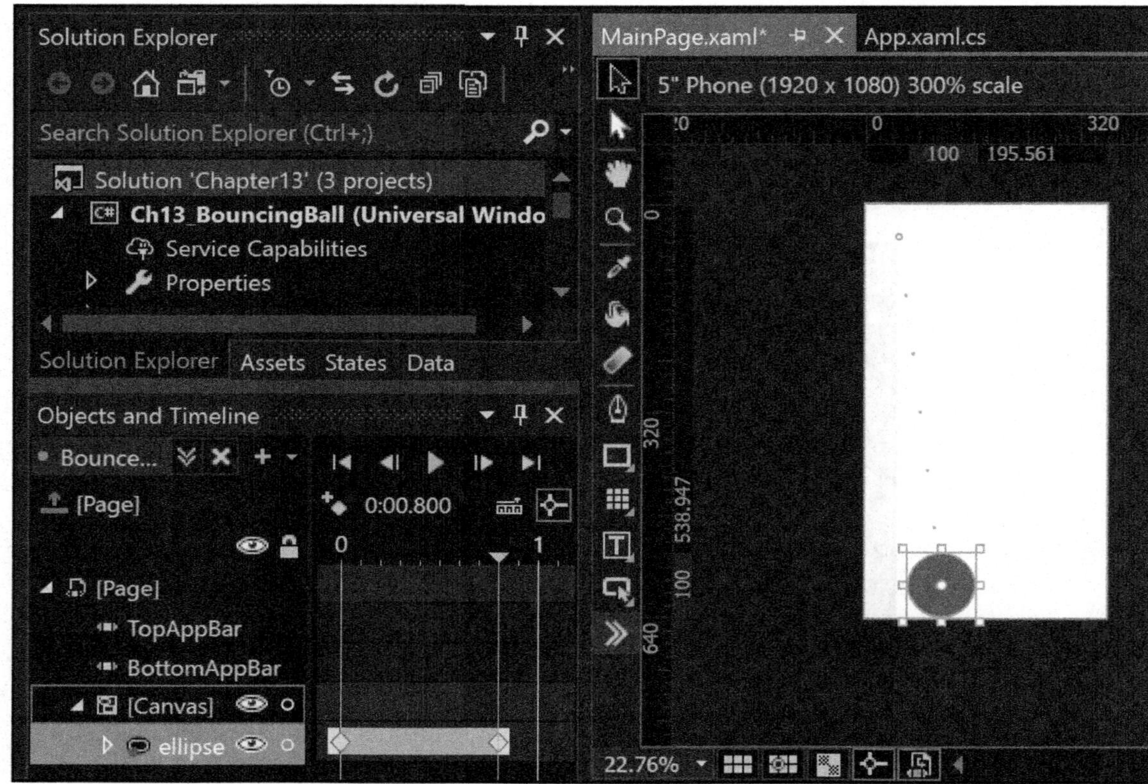

Drag the orange triangle to time position **0:01.000**. Click and drag the resize handle at the top of the ball to squash it down a little:

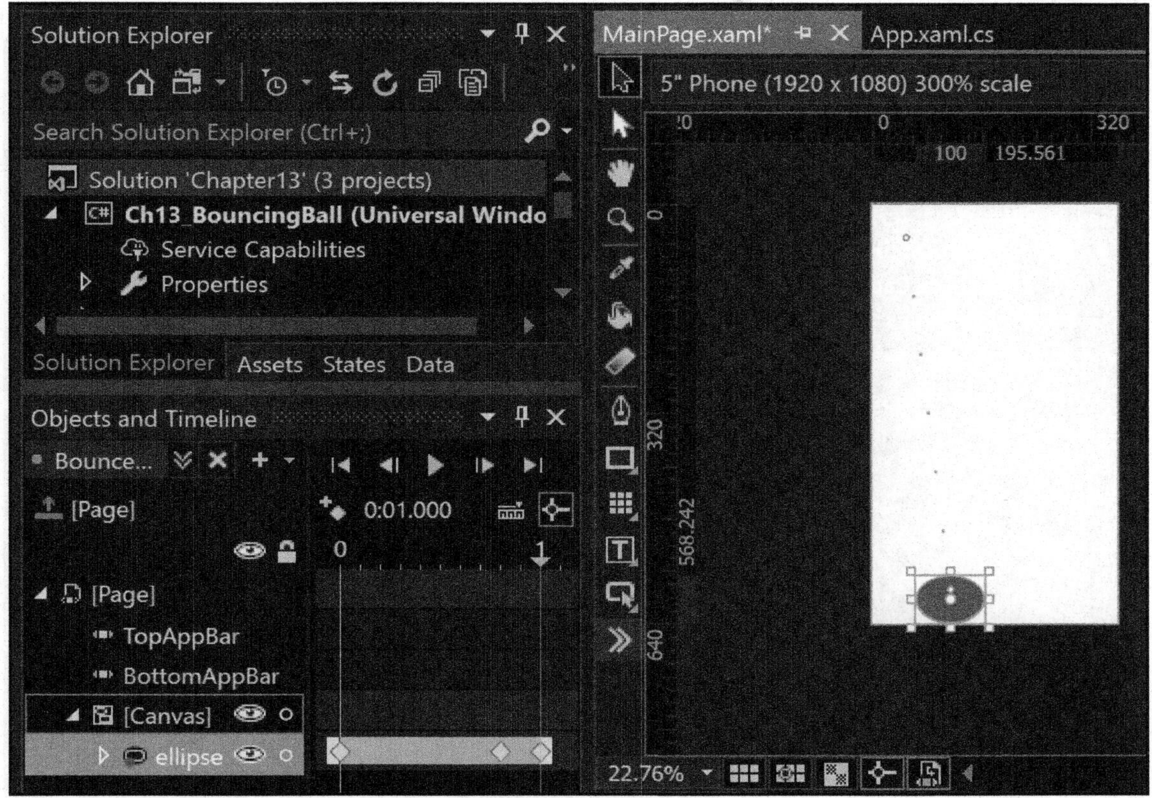

Drag the orange triangle to time position **0:01.200**. Resize the ball to stretch it back to its original height. Don't worry about accuracy. You will modify the recorded values later.

Drag the orange triangle to time position **0:02.000**. Click near the middle of the ball when the mouse pointer has a four-pointed arrow next to it, and drag it back up to near the top of the window and a little to the right:

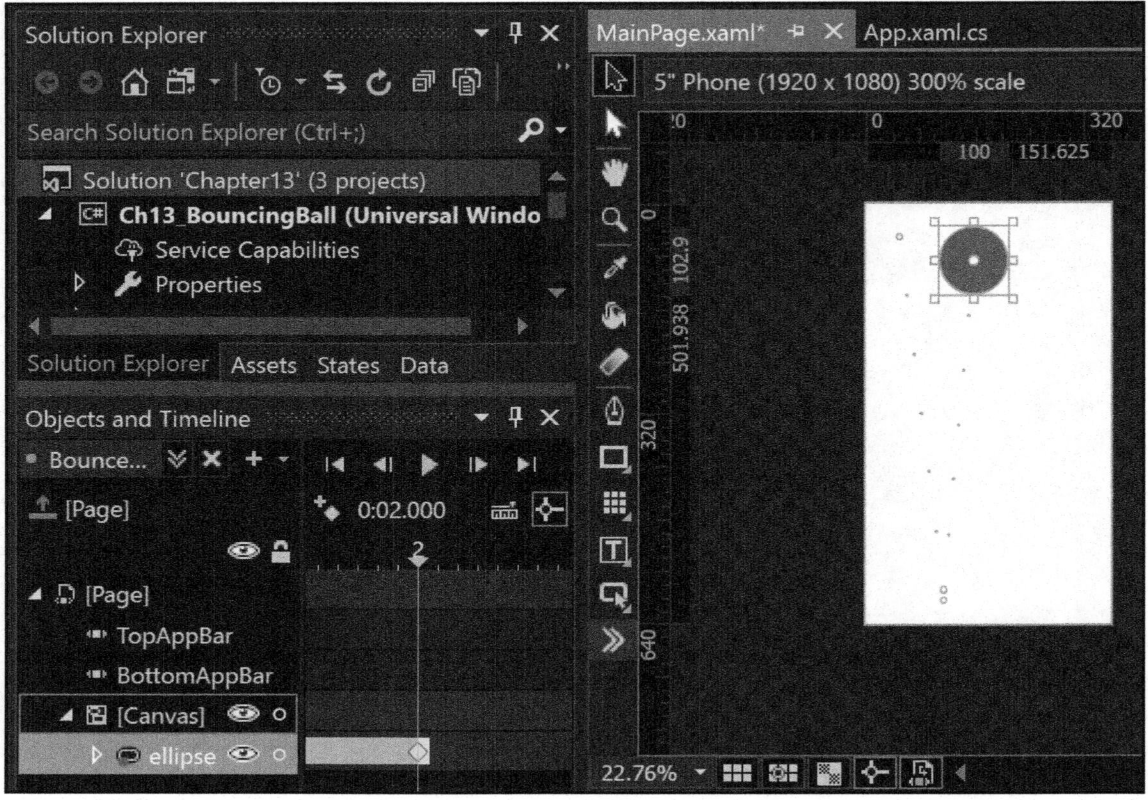

Click the red dot to stop recording:

BounceBall timeline recording is off.

In the **Objects and Timeline** window, click on the small green triangle **Play** button.

You should see the red ball smoothly drop down. When it hits the bottom, it squashes slightly, as a rubber ball would in real life, before bouncing back up to the top.

Save your work and exit from Blend.

When you return to Visual Studio 2017, it should warn you that the file has changes and prompts you to reload it. Click on **Yes**.

Notice that Blend created some XAML elements to define a storyboard named `BounceBall` that animates properties of the `Ellipse` object.

Three properties were animated, and are listed as follows:

- **TranslateY**: This property moves the ball vertically
- **ScaleY**: This property squashes the ball vertically
- **TranslateX**: This property moves the ball horizontally

Modify the squashing effect by changing the value of ScaleY to be 0.666 (that is, 66.6%) of its normal height at time position 1s, and return to exactly 1 at time position 1.2s:

```
<DoubleAnimationUsingKeyFrames Storyboard.TargetProperty=
    "(UIElement.RenderTransform).(CompositeTransform.ScaleY)"
    Storyboard.TargetName="ellipse">
  <EasingDoubleKeyFrame KeyTime="0:0:0.8" Value="1"/>
  <EasingDoubleKeyFrame KeyTime="0:0:1" Value="0.666"/>
  <EasingDoubleKeyFrame KeyTime="0:0:1.2" Value="1"/>
</DoubleAnimationUsingKeyFrames>
```

In the toolbox, choose `Button` and draw one on the canvas named `BounceBallButton`. Change its contents to `Bounce Ball`. Give it a `Click` event handler:

```
<Button Name="BounceBallButton" Content="Bounce Ball"
  Canvas.Left="154" Canvas.Top="45"
  Click="BounceBallButton_Click"/>
```

In the code behind file, add the following statement to the event handler method:

```
BounceBall.Begin();
```

Run the application. Click on the `Bounce Ball` button to run the animation:

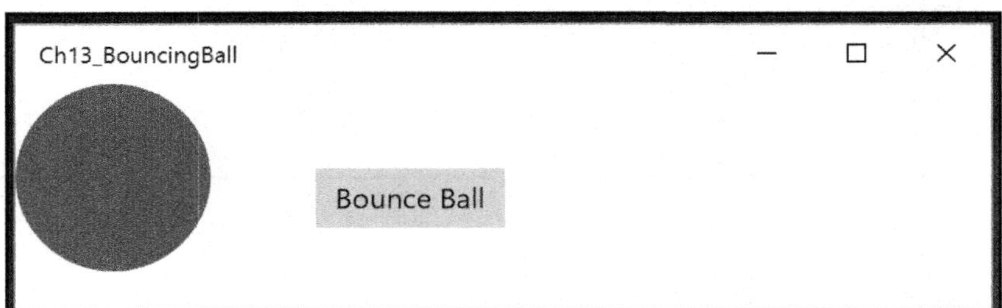

Testing in emulators

While developing a UWP app, you can quickly see what it would look like on various devices in the XAML design window.

The following screenshot shows the **23" Desktop (1920 x 1080) 100% scale** emulator:

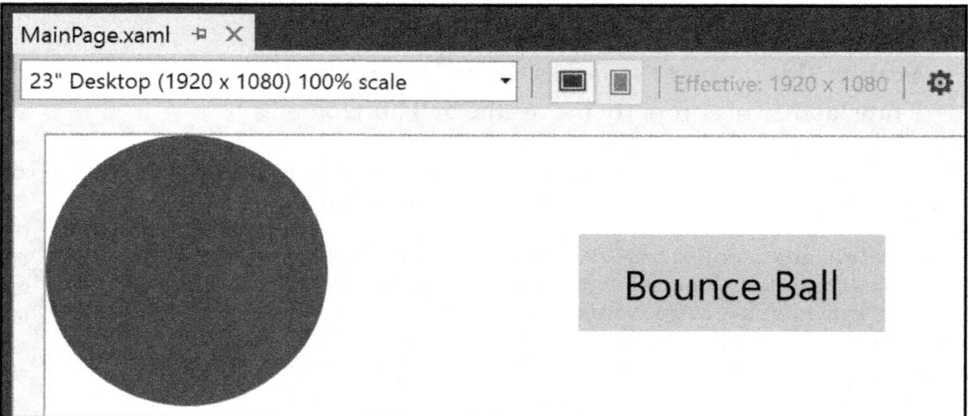

The following screenshot shows the **57" HoloLens 2D App (1280 x 720) 150% scale** emulator:

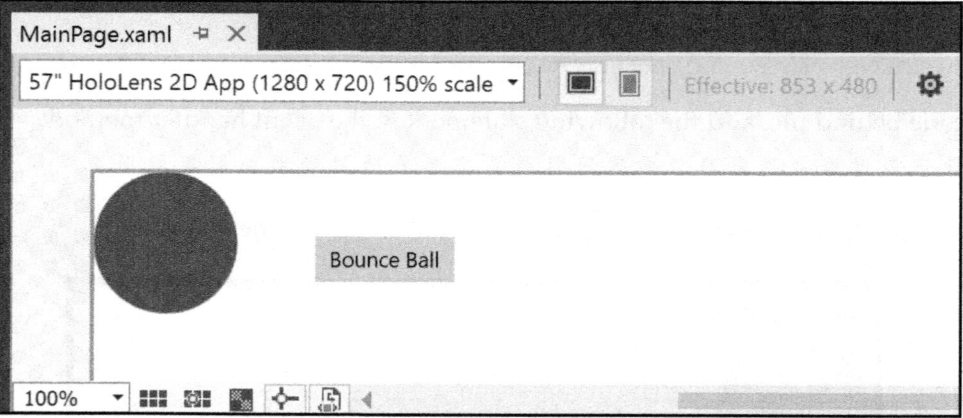

You can also run the app in a **Simulator** rather than on your **Local Machine**. You can also choose **Remote Machine** or **Device**:

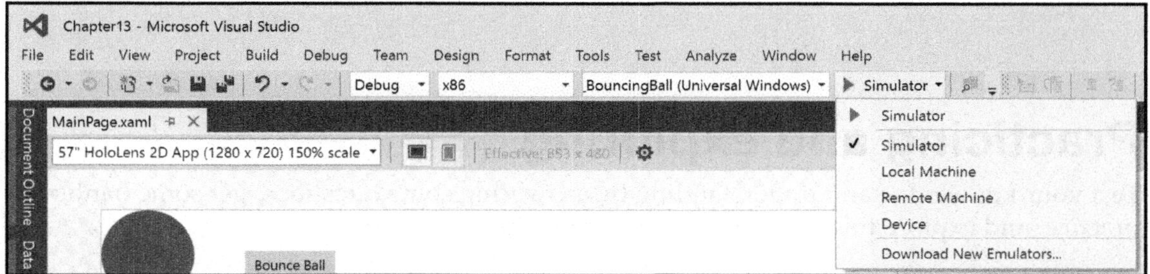

Simulator can rotate and change input modes and the screen resolution using the buttons in the toolbar on the right edge of the **Simulator** window:

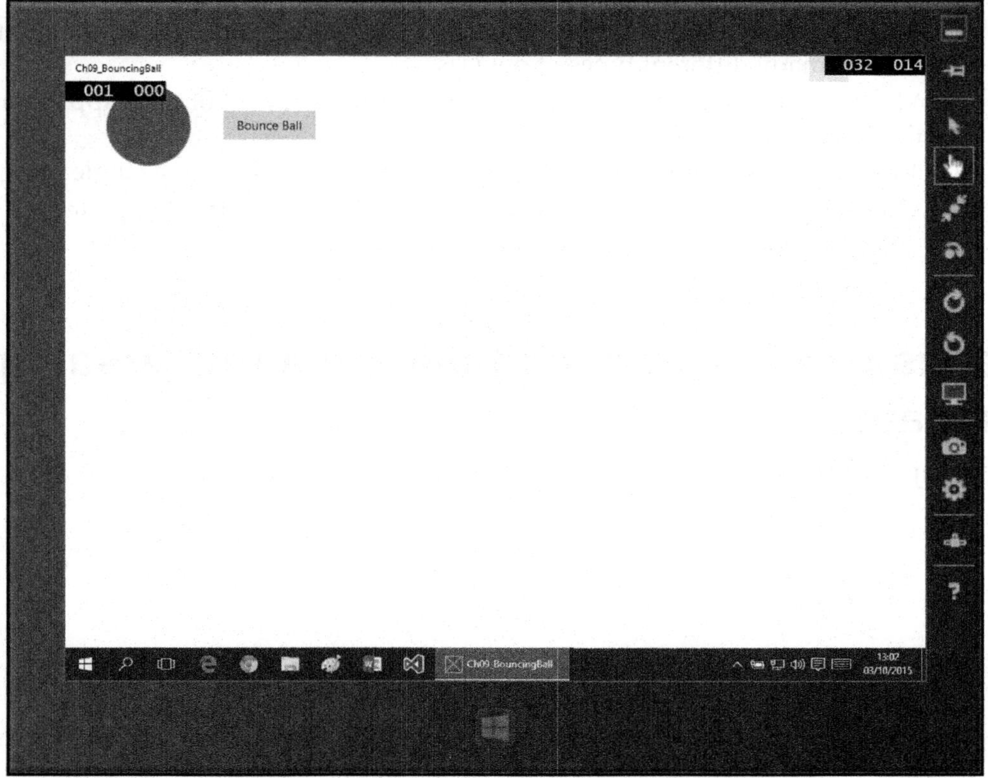

Good Practice
Test your apps with **Simulator**, and then also test on all the actual devices that your users will deploy your app to.

Practicing and exploring

Test your knowledge and understanding by answering some questions, get some hands-on practice, and explore this chapter's topics with deeper research.

Exercise 13.1 – test your knowledge

Answer the following questions:

1. Which control would you choose to allow the user to easily choose their date of birth on many different types of devices?
2. Which XAML element would you use to adapt the layout of your app to handle different device families?
3. How can you set multiple properties on an XAML element as a single group?
4. What is the difference between a control template and a data template?
5. Can XAML bindings be two-ways or just one-way?

Exercise 13.2 – practice building a universal tip calculator

Create an app for UWP that calculates a tip for common percentages.

Exercise 13.3 – explore topics

Use the following links to read more about this chapter's topics.

- **Enable your device for development**: https://docs.microsoft.com/en-us/windows/uwp/get-started/enable-your-device-for-development
- **Intro to the Universal Windows Platform:** https://docs.microsoft.com/en-us/windows/uwp/get-started/universal-application-platform-guide
- **Design and UI**: https://developer.microsoft.com/en-us/windows/apps/design
- **How-to articles for UWP apps on Windows 10**: https://developer.microsoft.com/en-us/windows/apps/develop

Summary

In this chapter, you learned how to build a graphical user interface using XAML, how to share resources in a central location, how to replace a control's template, how to bind to data and controls, and how to animate properties.

In the next chapter, you will learn how to build web applications using ASP.NET Core MVC.

14
Building Web Applications Using ASP.NET Core MVC

This chapter is about building web applications with a modern HTTP architecture on the server side using Microsoft ASP.NET Core MVC. You will learn about the startup configuration, authentication, authorization, routes, models, views, and controllers that make up ASP.NET Core MVC.

This chapter will cover the following topics:

- Understanding ASP.NET Core
- Exploring an ASP.NET Core MVC web application
- ASP.NET Core MVC controllers
- ASP.NET Core MVC models
- ASP.NET Core MVC views
- Taking ASP.NET Core MVC further

Understanding ASP.NET Core

Microsoft ASP.NET Core is part of a history of Microsoft technologies used to build web applications and services that have evolved over the years:

- **Active Server Pages (ASP)** was released in 1996, and was Microsoft's first attempt at a platform for dynamic server-side execution of web application code. ASP files are written in the VBScript language.

- **ASP.NET Web Forms** was released in 2002 with the .NET Framework, and is designed to enable non-web developers, such as those familiar with Visual Basic, to quickly create web applications by dragging and dropping visual components and writing event-driven code in Visual Basic or C#. Web Forms can only be hosted on Windows, but is still used today in products such as Microsoft SharePoint. It should be avoided for new web projects in favor of ASP.NET Core.
- **Windows Communication Foundation** (**WCF**) was released in 2006, and enables developers to build SOAP and REST services. SOAP is powerful but complex, so it should be avoided unless you need advanced features such as distributed transactions and complex messaging topologies.
- **ASP.NET MVC** was released in 2009, and is designed to cleanly separate the concerns of web developers between the *models* that represent the data, the *views* that present that data, and the *controllers* that fetch the model and pass it to a view. This separation enables improved reuse and unit testing.
- **ASP.NET Web API** was released in 2012, and enables developers to create HTTP aka REST services that are simpler and more scalable than SOAP services.
- **ASP.NET SignalR** was released in 2013, and enables real-time communication in web applications by abstracting underlying technologies and techniques, such as *Web Sockets* and *Long Polling*.
- **ASP.NET Core** was released in 2016 and combines MVC, Web API, and SignalR, running on the .NET Core. Therefore, it is cross-platform.

Good Practice
Choose ASP.NET Core to develop web applications and services because it includes three web-related technologies that are modern and cross-platform.

Classic ASP.NET versus modern ASP.NET Core

ASP.NET celebrates its 15th birthday in 2017. It's a teenager!

Until now, it has been built on top of a large assembly in the .NET Framework named `System.Web.dll`. Over the years, this assembly has accumulated a lot of features, many of which are not suitable for modern cross-platform development.

ASP.NET Core is a major redesign of ASP.NET. It removes the dependency on the `System.Web.dll` assembly and is composed of modular lightweight packages, just like the rest of .NET Core.

You can develop and run ASP.NET Core applications cross-platform on Windows, macOS, and Linux. Microsoft has even created a cross-platform, super performant web server named **Kestrel**. The entire stack is open source, and it is designed to integrate with a variety of client-side tools and frameworks, including Bower, Gulp, Grunt, AngularJS, jQuery, and Bootstrap.

Client-side web development

When building web applications, a developer needs to know more than just C# and .NET Core. On the client (that is, in the web browser), you will use a combination of the following components:

- **HTML5**: This is used for the content and structure of a web page
- **CSS3**: This is used for the styles applied to elements on the web page
- **JavaScript**: This is used for the procedural actions of the web page
- **Bower**: This is a client-side package manager for the web

This book is about C#, so we will cover some of the basics of client-side web development, but for more detail, I recommend the book *HTML5 Web Application Development By Example* by *Packt Publishing* at `https://www.packtpub.com/web-development/html5-web-application-development-example-beginners-guide`.

To make it easier to work with HTML5, CSS3, and JavaScript, both Visual Studio 2017 and Visual Studio Code have extensions such as the ones listed here:

- Mads Kristensen's extensions for Visual Studio: `https://marketplace.visualstudio.com/search?term=publisher%3A%22Mads%20Kristensen%22&target=VS&sortBy=Relevance`
- HTML Programming in VS Code: `https://code.visualstudio.com/Docs/languages/html`
- Microsoft's Visual Studio Code extensions: `https://marketplace.visualstudio.com/search?term=publisher%3A%22Microsoft%22&target=VSCode&sortBy=Relevance`

Mads Kristensen wrote one of the most popular extensions for web development with Visual Studio 2010 and later named Web Essentials. It has now been broken up into smaller extensions that can be individually installed.

Understanding HTTP

To communicate with a web server, the client makes calls over the network using a protocol known as **HTTP** (**Hypertext Transfer Protocol**). HTTP is the technical underpinning of the "Web". So, when we talk about web applications or web services, we mean they use HTTP to communicate between a client (often a web browser) and a server.

A client makes an HTTP request for a resource, such as a page identified by a **URL** (**Uniform Resource Locator**), and the server sends back an HTTP response. You can use Google Chrome and other browsers to record requests and responses.

Good Practice
Google Chrome is available on more operating systems than any other browser and it has powerful built-in developer tools, so it is a good first choice of browser. Always test your web application with Chrome and at least two other browsers, for example, **Firefox** and either **Microsoft Edge** for Windows 10 and **Safari** for macOS.

Start **Google Chrome**. To show developer tools in Chrome:

- On macOS, press *Alt* + *Cmd* + *I*
- On Windows, press *F12* or *Ctrl* + *Shift* + *I*

Click on the **Network** tab. Chrome should immediately start recording the network traffic between your browser and any web servers, as shown in the following screenshot:

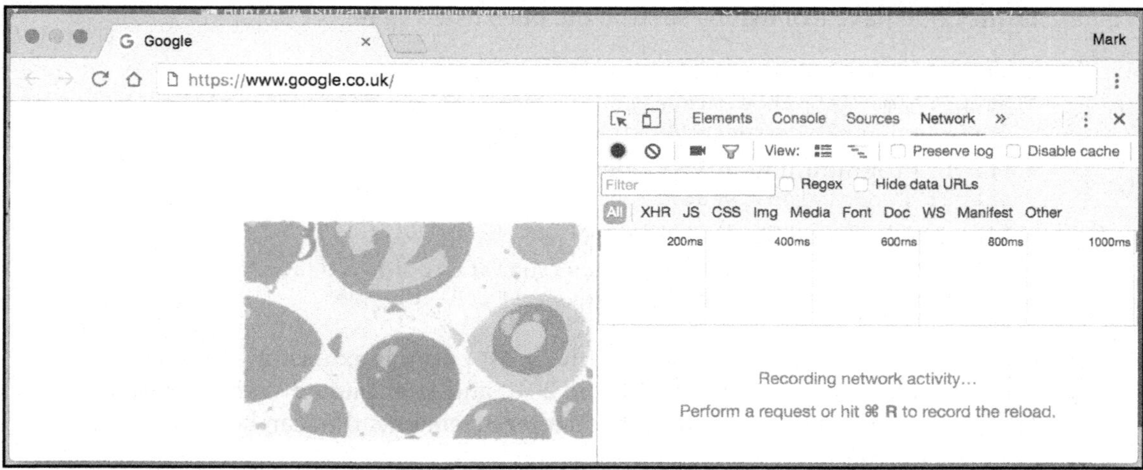

In Chrome's address box, enter `https://www.asp.net/get-started`.

In the **Developer Tools** window, in the list of recorded requests, click on the first entry, as shown in the following screenshot:

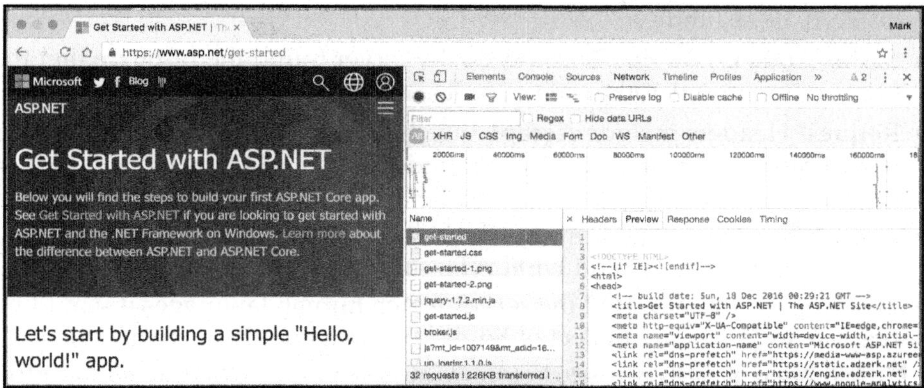

On the right-hand side, click the **Headers** tab, and you will see details about the request and the response, as shown in the following screenshot:

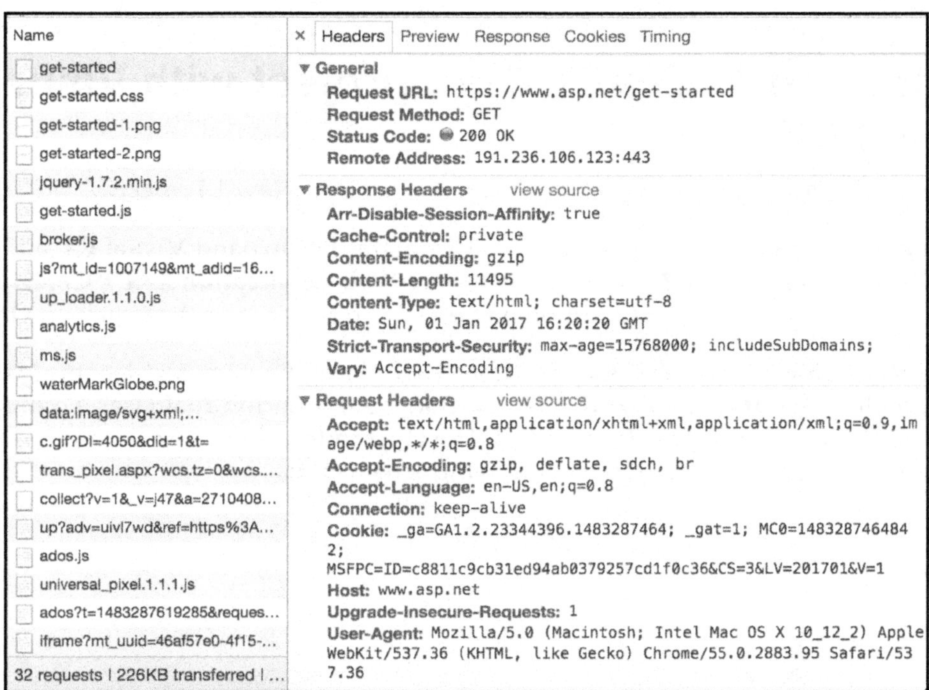

Note the following aspects:

- **Request Method** is `GET`. Other methods that HTTP defines include `POST`, `PUT`, `DELETE`, `HEAD`, and `PATCH`.
- **Status Code** is `200 OK`. This means the server found the resource that the browser requested. Other status codes include `404 Missing`.
- **Request Headers** include **Accept**, which lists what formats the browser accepts. In this case, the browser is saying it understands HTML, XHTML, XML, and others.
- **Accept-Encoding** header means the browser has told the server that it understands the GZIP and DEFLATE compression algorithms.
- The browser has also told the server which human languages it would prefer: US English and then any dialect of English (with a quality value of 0.8).
- I must have been to this site before because a Google Analytics cookie, named `_ga`, is being sent to the server so that it can track me.
- The server has sent back the response compressed using the GZIP algorithm because it knows that the client can decompress that format.

Creating an ASP.NET Core project with Visual Studio 2017

In Visual Studio 2017, press *Ctrl* + *Shift* + *N* or choose **File** | **New** | **Project...**.

In the **New Project** dialog, in the **Installed** | **Templates** list, expand **Visual C#**, and select **.NET Core**. In the center list, select **ASP.NET Core Web Application (.NET Core)**, type the name as `Ch14_WebApp`, type the solution name as `Chapter14`, and then click on **OK**.

In the **New ASP.NET Core Web Application (.NET Core)** dialog box, select the **Web Application** template. Ensure that **Authentication** is set to **Individual User Accounts** by clicking the **Change Authentication** button. The **Host in the cloud** box should be left unchecked. Click **OK**, as shown in the following screenshot:

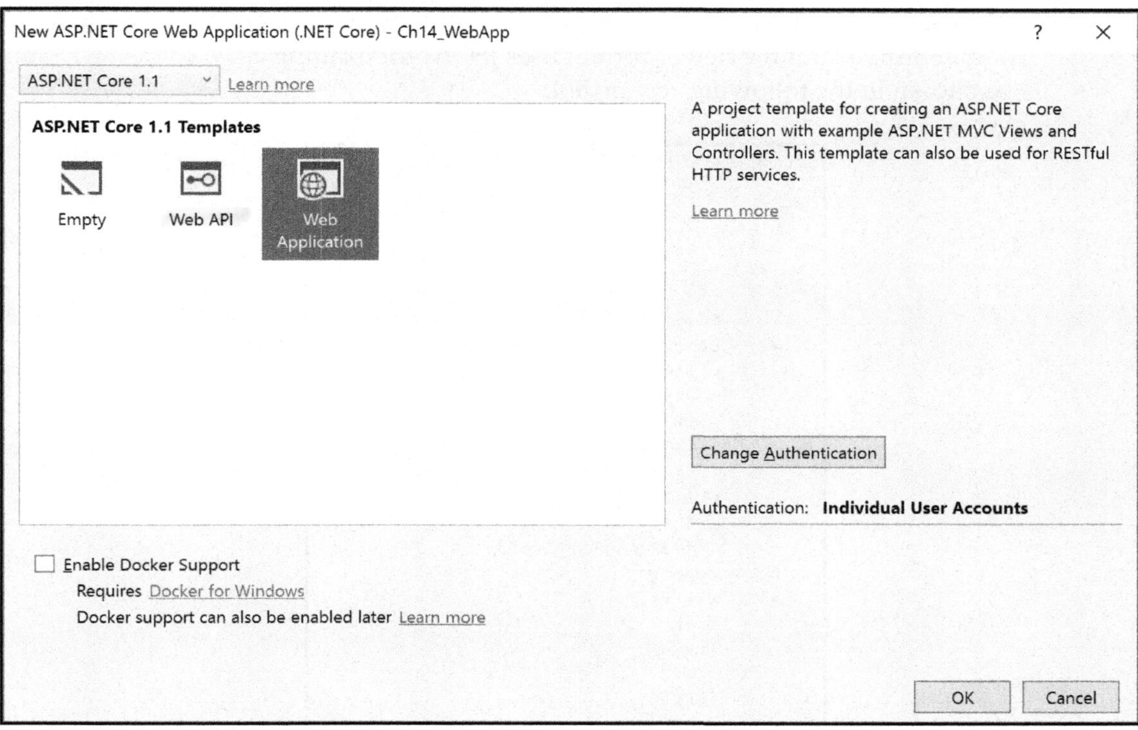

After a few seconds, your **Solution Explorer** window will look as shown in the following screenshot. Note the following points:

- `Dependencies` contain Bower packages on the client side and NuGet packages on the server side.
- The `Data` folder contains C# classes to perform initial database operations, known as migrations, to create the tables required to store users and roles for the authentication system.
- The `wwwroot` folder contains client-side files, such as CSS style sheets, images, and JavaScript libraries.
- The `Controllers`, `Models`, and `Views` folders contain ASP.NET Core classes and `.cshtml` files for execution on the server. We will look at this in more detail later.
- There are two C# classes in the root folder: `Program.cs` and `Startup.cs`.

- There are multiple configuration files. The old format used XML, for example `Web.config`, and the newer format uses JSON, for example `appsettings.json`, as shown in the following screenshot:

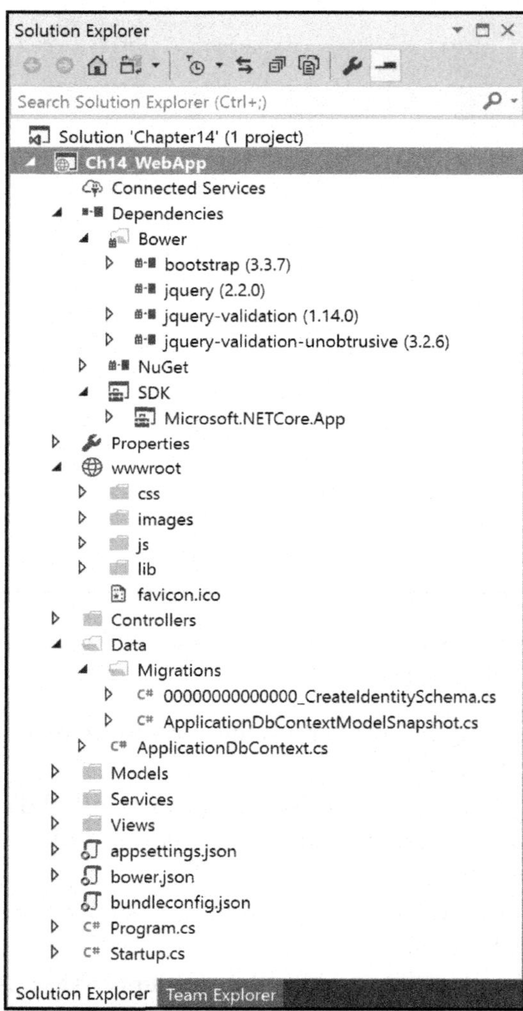

Performing database migrations

Before we test the web application, we need to ensure that the database migrations have been executed.

Open the `appsettings.json` file and note the database connection string. It should look something like this:

```
Server=(localdb)\\mssqllocaldb;Database=aspnet-Ch14_WebApp-584f323f-a60e-4933-9845-f67225753337;
Trusted_Connection=True;MultipleActiveResultSets=true
```

When the database migrations execute, it will create a database with the preceding name in Microsoft SQL Server LocalDb. You could modify the database name now to make it less GUID-y, for example, as in the following connection string:

```
Server=(localdb)\\mssqllocaldb;Database=Ch14_WebApp;
Trusted_Connection=True;MultipleActiveResultSets=true
```

Right-click on the `Ch14_WebApp` project and choose **Open Folder in File Explorer**.

Click in the address box and copy the path to the clipboard.

From the Windows Start menu, start **Developer Command Prompt for Visual Studio 2017**.

Change to the project directory and execute the database migrations by entering the following commands:

```
cd C:\Code\Chapter14\src\Ch14_WebApp
dotnet ef database update
```

You should see output, as shown in the following screenshot:

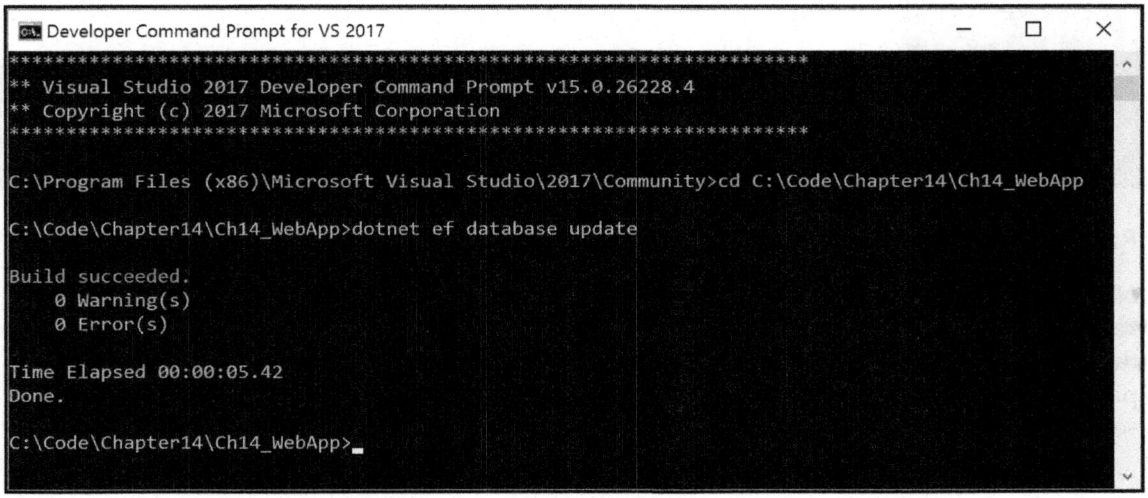

```
Developer Command Prompt for VS 2017
**********************************************************************
** Visual Studio 2017 Developer Command Prompt v15.0.26228.4
** Copyright (c) 2017 Microsoft Corporation
**********************************************************************

C:\Program Files (x86)\Microsoft Visual Studio\2017\Community>cd C:\Code\Chapter14\Ch14_WebApp

C:\Code\Chapter14\Ch14_WebApp>dotnet ef database update

Build succeeded.
    0 Warning(s)
    0 Error(s)

Time Elapsed 00:00:05.42
Done.

C:\Code\Chapter14\Ch14_WebApp>
```

In the Visual Studio 2017 toolbar, click the dropdown arrow next to **IIS Express**, choose **Web Browser**, and then **Google Chrome**, as shown in the following screenshot:

Sometimes, you must drop down the menu twice for Visual Studio to populate the browser list!

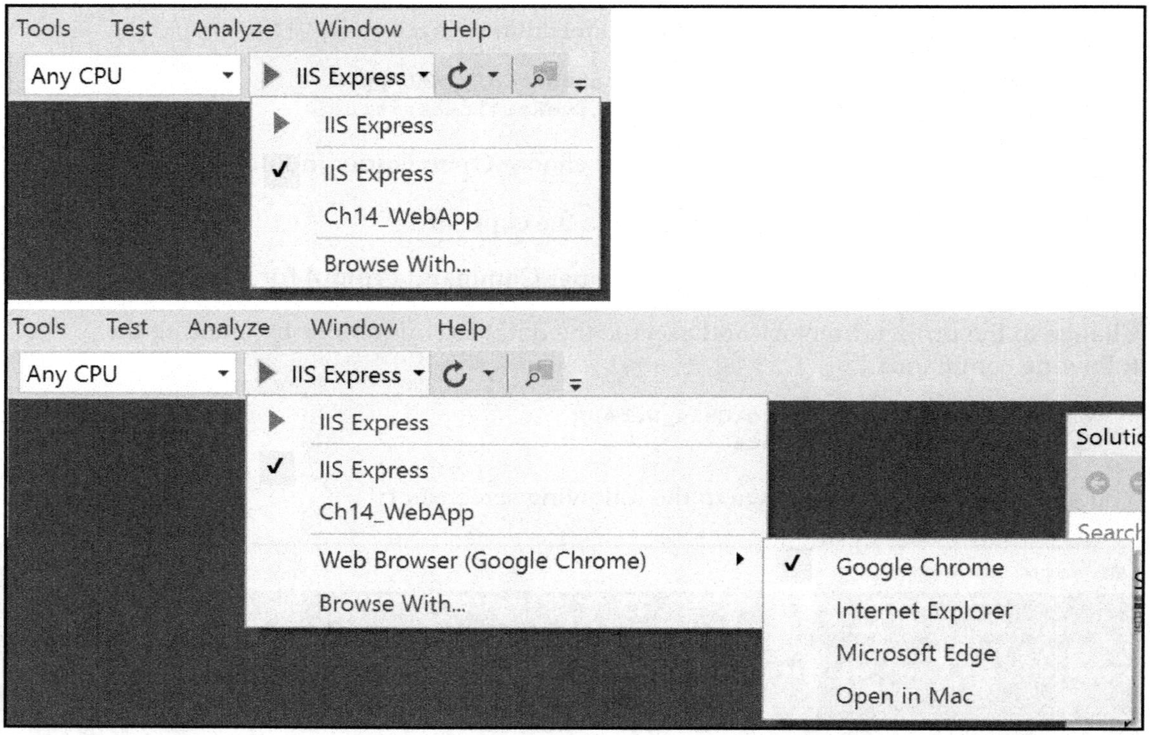

Run the application by pressing *Ctrl* + *F5*.

Note that your ASP.NET Core application is hosted in a cross-platform web server named Kestrel (here, integrated with IIS Express) using a random port number for local testing and that the sample ASP.NET Core web application project returns a site with half a dozen pages, including **Home**, **About**, **Contact**, **Register**, and **Log in**, as shown in the following screenshot:

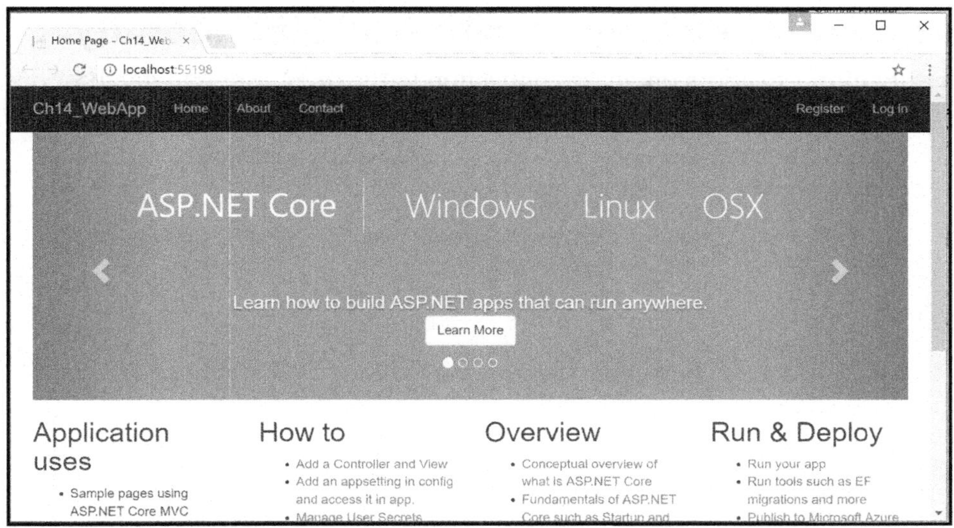

Click on the **Register** link and then complete the form to create a new account in the database that was created by the migration, as shown in the following screenshot:

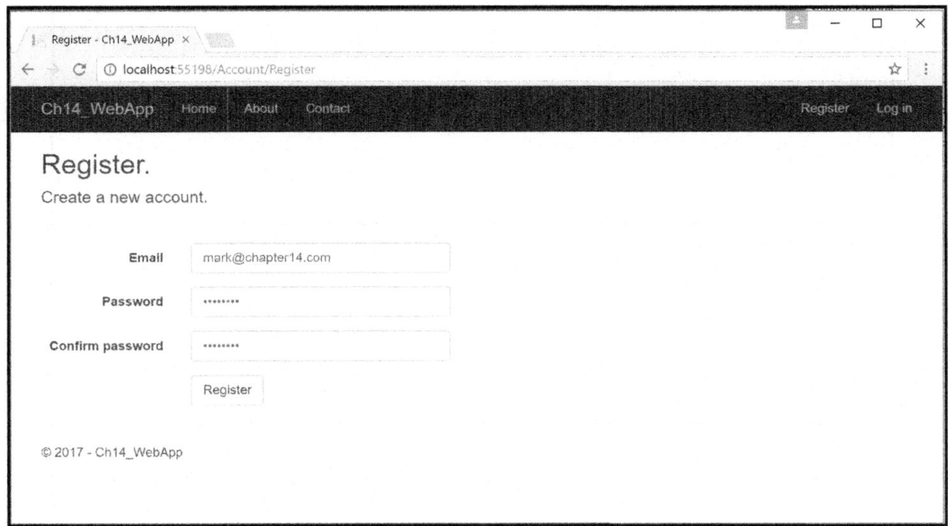

Note that if you enter a password that is not strong enough, there is built-in validation.

Close Chrome.

Reviewing authentication with ASP.NET Identity

Use **Server Explorer** to add a database connection to the `Ch14_WebApp` database, as shown in the following screenshot:

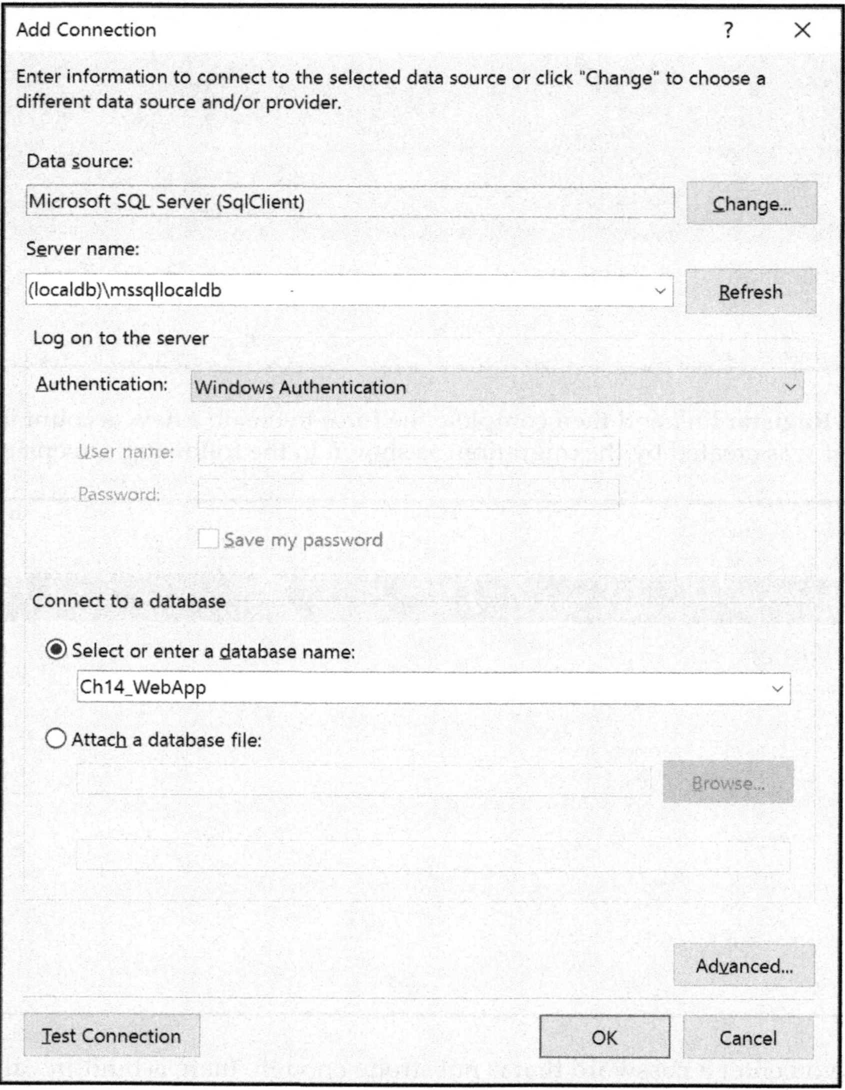

Right-click the `AspNetUsers` table, and note the row that was added to the database when you completed the register form, as shown in the following screenshot:

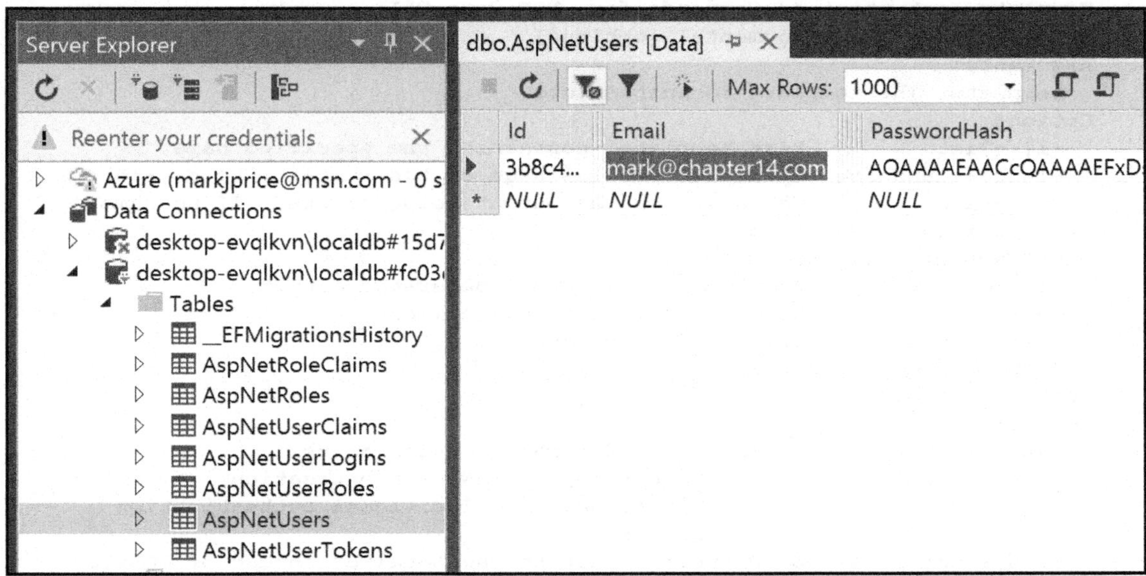

Good Practice
The ASP.NET Core web application project follows good practice by storing a hash of the password instead of the password itself. The **ASP.NET Core Identity** system can be extended to support two-factor authentication.

Creating an ASP.NET Core project with Visual Studio Code

Create a folder named `Chapter14` with a subfolder named `Ch14_WebApp`. In **Visual Studio Code**, open the `Ch14_WebApp` folder. In the **Integrated Terminal**, enter the following command to review your options when creating an ASP.NET MVC application with the CLI tool:

```
dotnet new mvc --help
```

You will see the following output:

```
bash-3.2$ dotnet new mvc --help
Template Instantiation Commands for .NET Core CLI.
Usage: dotnet new [arguments] [options]
Arguments:
  template  The template to instantiate.
Options:
  -l|--list         List templates containing the specified name.
  -lang|--language  Specifies the language of the template to create
  -n|--name         The name for the output being created. If no name
is specified, the name of th
e current directory is used.
  -o|--output       Location to place the generated output.
  -h|--help         Displays help for this command.
  -all|--show-all   Shows all templates
ASP.NET Core Web App (C#)
Author: Microsoft
Options:
  -au|--auth            The type of authentication to use
                            None           - No authentication
                            Individual     - Individual authentication
                        Default: None
  -uld|--use-local-db  Whether or not to use LocalDB instead of SQLite
                        bool - Optional
                        Default: false
  -f|--framework
                            netcoreapp1.0    - Target netcoreapp1.0
                            netcoreapp1.1    - Target netcoreapp1.1
                        Default: netcoreapp1.1
```

Options when creating a new ASP.NET Core MVC application include choosing the type of authentication to use, None or Individual, and choosing between SQL Server LocalDb and SQLite to store the users and roles.

At the Terminal prompt, enter the following command to create a new ASP.NET Core MVC web application project with individual user accounts for authentication, stored in SQLite:

```
dotnet new mvc --auth Individual
```

Note the folders and files created in the **Explorer** pane, as shown in the following screenshot, including some database migrations that must be executed to create the database for registering new users, as shown in the following screenshot:

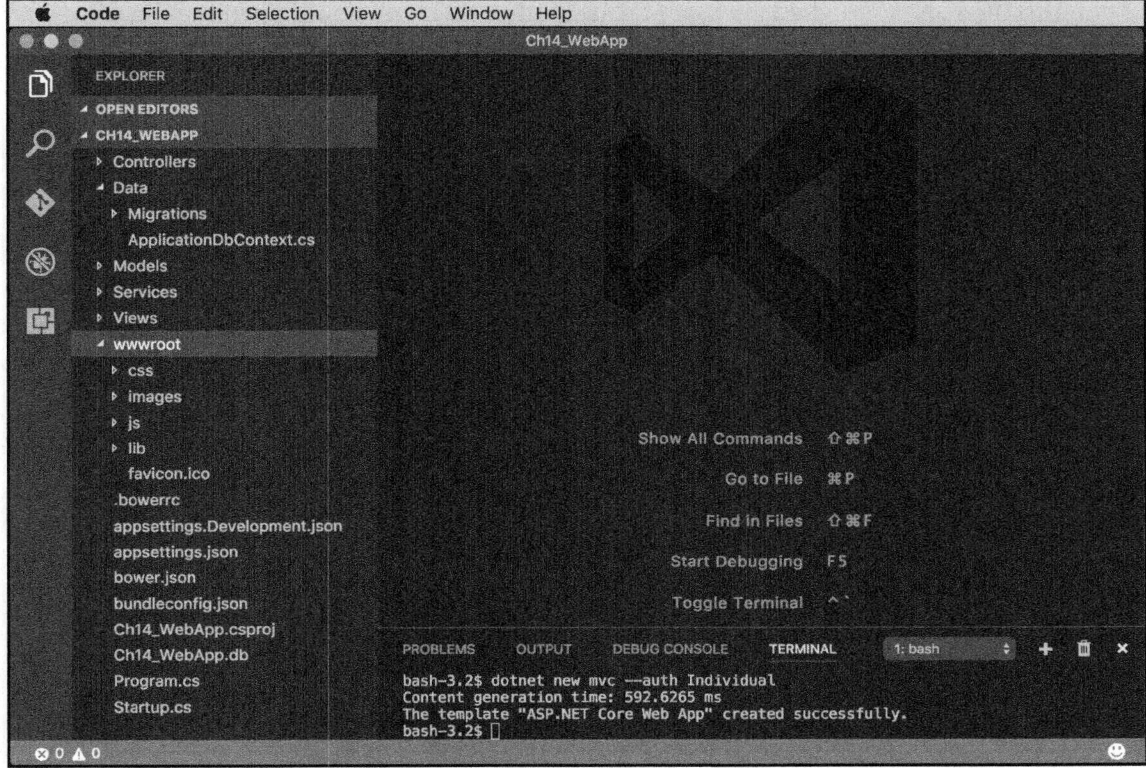

Open the `appsettings.json` file and note the database connection string. It should be something like this:

```
Data Source=.\\Ch14_WebApp.db
```

When the database migrations execute, it will create a database with the preceding name in the current folder using SQLite.

In the **Integrated Terminal**, enter the following commands to restore packages and then execute the database migrations:

```
dotnet restore
dotnet ef database update
```

In the **Explorer** pane, expand the `bin` folder and note that the database named `Ch14_WebApp.db` has been created.

If you installed an SQLite tool such as **SQLiteStudio**, then you could open the database and see the tables that the ASP.NET Identity system uses to register users and roles, as shown in the following screenshot:

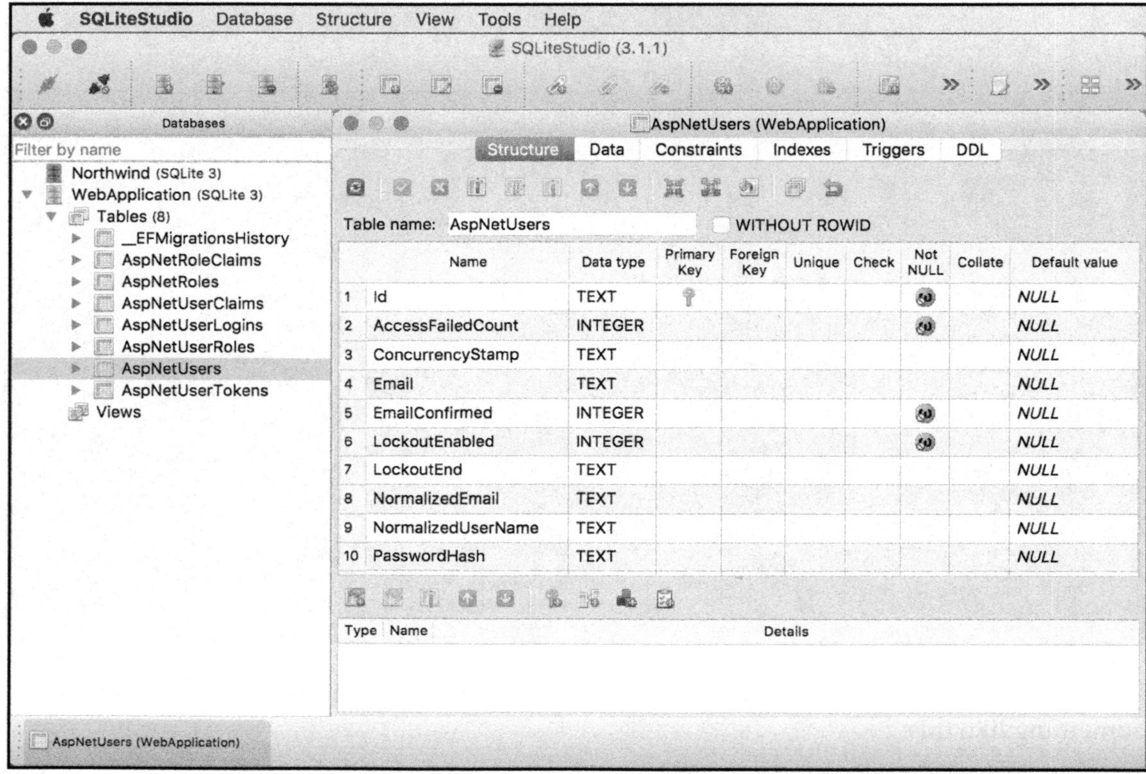

In the **Integrated Terminal**, enter the following command:

```
dotnet run
```

You will see the following output:

```
bash-3.2$ dotnet run
Hosting environment: Production
Content root path: /Users/markjprice/Code/Chapter14/Ch14_WebApp
Now listening on: http://localhost:5000
Application started. Press Ctrl+C to shut down.
```

Leave the web application running and start **Chrome**.

Navigate to `http:/localhost:5000/` and view the results, as shown in the following screenshot:

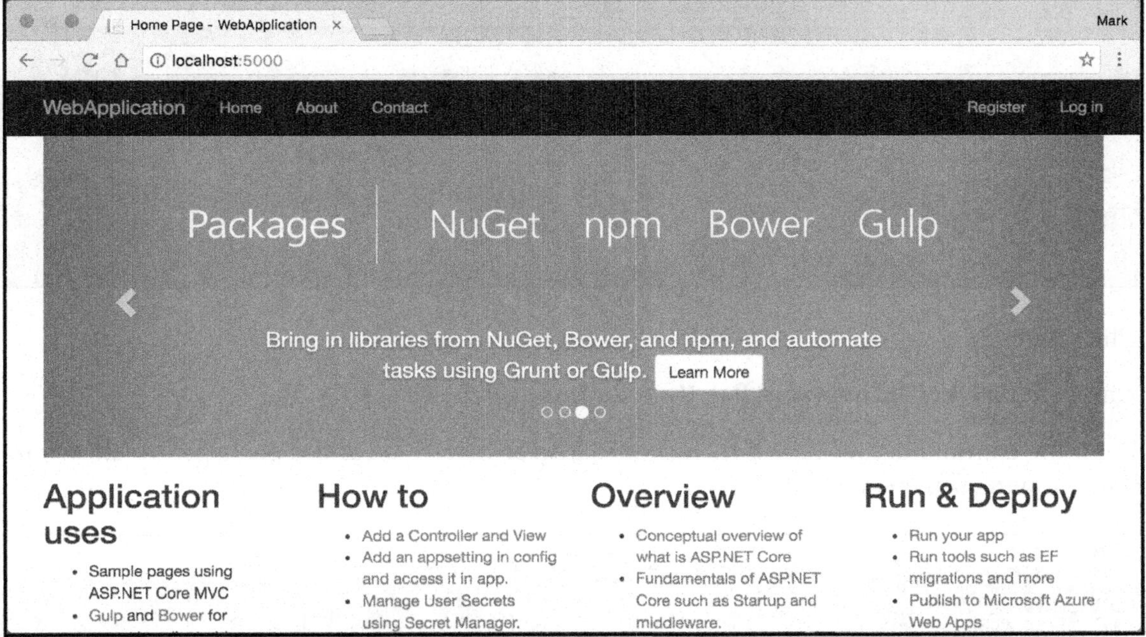

Click **Register** and complete the form to register a new user.

This ASP.NET Core web application project has the same behavior as the one created by Visual Studio 2017, except that it uses SQLite instead of SQL Server LocalDb for the ASP.NET Identity database.

Close **Chrome**, and in the **Integrated Terminal**, press *Ctrl* + *C* to stop the console application and shut down the Kestrel web server that is hosting your ASP.NET Core web application.

Managing client-side packages with Bower

In the next section, we will use Bower to manage client-side packages, for example, Bootstrap and jQuery. Bower is not installed by default.

In **Visual Studio Code**, choose **View** | **Extensions** or press *Shift* + *Cmd* + *X*.

Search for `bower` to find the most popular Bower extension, and click **Install**, as shown in the following screenshot:

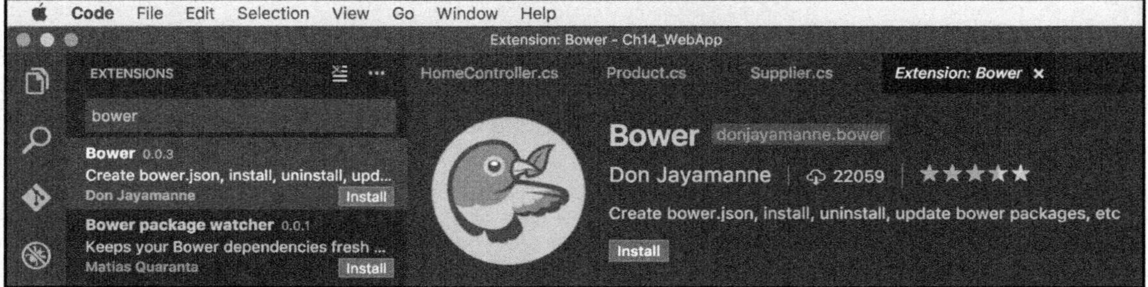

Click **Reload**.

Navigate to **View** | **Command Palette...**, or press *Shift* + *Cmd* + *P*.

Enter the command `Bower`, and then choose **Bower Install** to restore packages, as shown in the following screenshot:

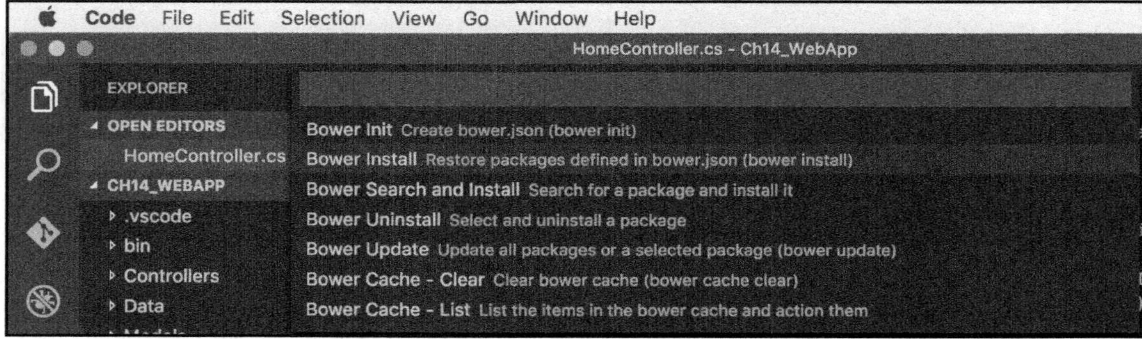

Expand `wwwroot` and note that the `lib` folder has been created with four subfolders for the packages that are specified in the `bower.json` file:

```
{
  "name": "webapplication",
  "private": true,
  "dependencies": {
    "bootstrap": "3.3.6",
    "jquery": "2.2.3",
    "jquery-validation": "1.15.0",
    "jquery-validation-unobtrusive": "3.2.6"
```

```
    }
}
```

Exploring an ASP.NET Core MVC web application

Let's walk through the parts that make up a modern ASP.NET Core MVC application.

In **Visual Studio 2017**, look at **Solution Explorer** for the `Ch14_WebApp` project. In **Visual Studio Code**, look at the **Explorer** pane. Note the following:

- `wwwroot`: This folder contains static content, such as CSS for styles, images, JavaScript, and a `favicon.ico` file.
- `Data`: This folder contains Entity Framework Core classes used by the ASP.NET Identity system to provide authentication and authorization.
- `Dependencies` (*Visual Studio 2017 only*): This folder contains a graphical representation of `Bower` and `NuGet` for modern package management. The actual files are `bower.json` and `Ch14_WebApp.csproj`. In Visual Studio 2017, you could edit the project manually by right-clicking the project and choosing **Edit** `Ch14_WebApp.csproj`.
- `Ch14_WebApp.csproj`: This file contains a list of NuGet packages, such as the Entity Framework Core, that your project requires.
- `.vscode/launch.json` (*Visual Studio Code only*) and `Properties/launchSettings.json` (*Visual Studio 2017 only*): These files configure options for starting the web application from inside your development environment.
- `Controllers`: This folder contains C# classes that have methods (known as actions) that fetch a *model* and pass it to a *view*.
- `Models`: This folder contains C# classes that represent all the data required to respond to an HTTP request.
- `Views`: This folder contains `.cshtml` files that combine HTML and C# code to enable the dynamic generation of an HTML response.
- `Services`: This folder contains C# interfaces and classes for integrating with external services, such as SMS for sending text messages.
- `appsettings.json`: This file contains settings that your web application can load at runtime, for example, the database connection string for the ASP.NET Identity system.

- `bower.json`: This file contains client-side packages that combine resources such as jQuery and Bootstrap.
- `gulpfile.js`: This file is an optional task runner that can perform actions such as bundling and minimization.
- `Program.cs`: This file is a console application that contains the `Main` entry point that performs initial configuration, compilation, and executes the web application. It can call the `UseStartup<T>()` method to specify another class that can perform additional configuration.
- `Startup.cs`: This optional file performs additional configuration of the services, for example, ASP.NET Identity for authentication, SQLite for data storage, and so on, and routes for your application.

ASP.NET Core startup

Open the `Startup.cs` file.

Note the `ConfigureServices` method that adds support for MVC along with other framework and application services such as ASP.NET Identity, as shown in the following code:

```
public void ConfigureServices(IServiceCollection services)
{
  // Add framework services.
  services.AddDbContext<ApplicationDbContext>(options =>
    options.UseSqlServer(Configuration
    .GetConnectionString("DefaultConnection")));
  services.AddIdentity<ApplicationUser, IdentityRole>()
    .AddEntityFrameworkStores<ApplicationDbContext>()
    .AddDefaultTokenProviders();

  services.AddMvc();

  // Add application services.
  services.AddTransient<IEmailSender, AuthMessageSender>();
  services.AddTransient<ISmsSender, AuthMessageSender>();
}
```

Next, we have the `Configure` method. Note the following:

- If the web application is running in the development environment, then (1) when an exception is thrown, a rich error page showing source code is displayed, and (2) browser link is enabled so that Visual Studio tools can push updates to the actively running browsers.
- Static files are enabled to allow CSS, JavaScript, and so on, to be served from the file system.
- ASP.NET Identity is enabled for authentication and authorization.
- The most important statement here is the one that calls `UseMvc` and maps a default route. This route is very flexible, because it would map to almost any incoming URL, as you will see in the next section:

```
public void Configure(IApplicationBuilder app,
  IHostingEnvironment env, ILoggerFactory loggerFactory)
{
  loggerFactory.AddConsole(Configuration.GetSection("Logging"));
  loggerFactory.AddDebug();

  if (env.IsDevelopment())
  {
    app.UseDeveloperExceptionPage();
    app.UseDatabaseErrorPage();
    app.UseBrowserLink();
  }
  else
  {
    app.UseExceptionHandler("/Home/Error");
  }

  app.UseStaticFiles();

  app.UseIdentity();

  app.UseMvc(routes =>
  {
    routes.MapRoute(
      name: "default",
      template: "{controller=Home}/{action=Index}/{id?}");
  });
}
```

Understanding the default route

The default route looks at any URL entered by the user in the address bar and matches it to extract the name of a controller, the name of an action, and an optional `id` value (the `?` symbol makes it optional). If the user hasn't entered these names, it uses defaults of `Home` for the controller and `Index` for the action (the = assignment sets a default for a named segment).

Contents in curly-brackets `{}` are called **segments**, and they are like a named parameter of a method. The value of these segments can be any string.

The responsibility of a route is to discover the name of a controller and an action.

The following table contains example URLs and how MVC would work out the names:

URL	Controller	Action	ID
`/`	Home	Index	
`/Muppet`	Muppet	Index	
`/Muppet/Kermit`	Muppet	Kermit	
`/Muppet/Kermit/Green`	Muppet	Kermit	Green
`/Products`	Products	Index	
`/Products/Detail`	Products	Detail	
`/Products/Detail/3`	Products	Detail	3

Note that if the user does not supply a name, then the defaults, **Home** and **Index**, are used as specified when the route was registered. You could change these defaults if you wanted.

ASP.NET Core MVC controllers

Now that ASP.NET Core MVC knows the name of the controller and action, it will look for a class that implements an interface named `IController`. To simplify the requirements, Microsoft supplies a class named `Controller` that your classes can inherit from.

The responsibilities of a controller are as follows:

- To extract parameters from the HTTP request
- To use the parameters to fetch the correct model and pass it to the correct view
- client as an HTTP response

To return the results from the view to the client as an HTTP responseDefining the Home controller's actions

Expand the `Controllers` folder and double-click on the file named `HomeController.cs`:

```
public class HomeController : Controller
{
  public IActionResult Index()
  {
    return View();
  }
  public IActionResult About()
  {
    ViewData["Message"] = "Your application description page.";
    return View();
  }
  public IActionResult Contact()
  {
    ViewData["Message"] = "Your contact page.";
    return View();
  }
  public IActionResult Error()
  {
    return View();
  }
}
```

If the user enters `/` or `/Home`, then it is the equivalent of `/Home/Index` because those were the defaults.

Note the following:

- None of the action methods currently use a model
- Two of the action methods use a dictionary named `ViewData` to store a `string` item named **message** that can then be read inside a view
- All of the action methods call a method named `View()` and return the results as an `IActionResult` to the client

ASP.NET Core MVC models

In ASP.NET Core MVC, the model represents the data required for a request. For example, an HTTP GET request for `http://www.example.com/products/details/3` might mean that the browser is asking for the details of product number 3.

The controller would need to use the ID value `3` to retrieve the record for that product and pass it to a view that can then turn the model into HTML for display in the browser.

In the following example, we will create an Entity Framework Core data model to directly access data in the Northwind database.

Good Practice
Use a data repository (typically implemented as a service) to manage your data instead of accessing it directly in an ASP.NET Core MVC web application.

Create Entity models for Northwind

Follow the instructions in `Chapter 8`, *Working with Databases Using the Entity Framework Core*, to create the Northwind database:

- On Windows, create it in the **(local)\mssqllocaldb** server. If you completed the earlier chapters, then you have already done this.
- On macOS, create the `Northwind.db` file in the `\bin\Debug\netcoreapp1.1\` folder by copying the `NorthwindSQLite.sql` file into that folder, and then enter the following command in **Terminal**:

```
sqlite3 Northwind.db < NorthwindSQLite.sql
```

In both **Visual Studio 2017** and **Visual Studio Code**, add three class files to the `Models` folder named `Northwind.cs`, `Category.cs`, and `Product.cs`.

`Northwind.cs` should look like this:

```
using Microsoft.EntityFrameworkCore;

namespace Packt.CS7
{
  public class Northwind : DbContext
  {
    public DbSet<Category> Categories { get; set; }
    public DbSet<Product> Products { get; set; }
```

```
        public Northwind(DbContextOptions options) : base(options)
          {}
      }
    }
```

We will set the database connection string in the ASP.NET Core startup so it does not need to be done in the `Northwind` class, but the class derived from `DbContext` must have a constructor with a `DbContextOptions` parameter.

`Category.cs` should look like this:

```
using System.ComponentModel.DataAnnotations;

namespace Packt.CS7
{
  public class Category
  {
    public int CategoryID { get; set; }
    [Required]
    [StringLength(15)]
    public string CategoryName { get; set; }
    public string Description { get; set; }
  }
}
```

`Supplier.cs` should look like this:

```
using System.ComponentModel.DataAnnotations;
using System.ComponentModel.DataAnnotations.Schema;

namespace Packt.CS7
{
  [Table("Suppliers")]
  public class Supplier
  {
    public int SupplierID { get; set; }
    [Required]
    [StringLength(15)]
    public string CompanyName { get; set; }
  }
}
```

`Product.cs` should look like this:

```
using System.ComponentModel.DataAnnotations;

namespace Packt.CS7
```

```
{
  public class Product
  {
    public int ProductID { get; set; }
    [Required]
    [StringLength(40)]
    public string ProductName { get; set; }
    public int? SupplierID { get; set; }
    public Supplier Supplier { get; set; }
    public int? CategoryID { get; set; }
    public Category Category { get; set; }
    [StringLength(20)]
    public string QuantityPerUnit { get; set; }
    public decimal? UnitPrice { get; set; }
    public short? UnitsInStock { get; set; }
    public short? UnitsOnOrder { get; set; }
    public short? ReorderLevel { get; set; }
    public bool Discontinued { get; set; }
  }
}
```

Good Practice
Create a separate class library project for your entity models. This allows easier sharing between servers and clients.

Configure Entity Framework Core as a service

Services, such as the Entity Framework Core, that are needed by MVC controllers must be registered as a service during startup.

Open the `Startup.cs` file.

Add the following statement to the `ConfigureServices` method.

For Windows with SQL Server LocalDb:

```
services.AddDbContext<Packt.CS7.Northwind>(options =>
  options.UseSqlServer(Configuration
  .GetConnectionString("NorthwindConnection")));
```

For macOS with SQLite:

```
services.AddDbContext<Packt.CS7.Northwind>(options =>
  options.UseSqlite(Configuration
  .GetConnectionString("NorthwindConnection")));
```

Open the `appsettings.json` file and add a connection string.

For Windows with SQL Server LocalDb:

```
"NorthwindConnection":
"Server=(localdb)\\mssqllocaldb;Database=Northwind;Trusted_Connect
ion=True;MultipleActiveResultSets=true"
```

For macOS with SQLite:

```
"NorthwindConnection": "Data Source=Northwind.db"
```

Create view models for requests

Imagine that when a user comes to our website, we want to show them a list of products and a count of the number of visitors we have had this month. All the data that we want to show in response to a request is the MVC model, sometimes called a **view model**, because it is a *model* that is passed to a *view*.

Add a class to the `Models` folder and name it `HomeIndexViewModel`.

Modify the class definition to make it look like this:

```
using System.Collections.Generic;

namespace Packt.CS7
{
  public class HomeIndexViewModel
  {
    public int VisitorCount;
    public ICollection<Product> Products { get; set; }
  }
}
```

Fetch the model in the controller

Open the `HomeController` class.

Import the `Packt.CS7` namespace.

Add a field to store a reference to a Northwind instance and initialize it in a constructor:

```
private Northwind db;

public HomeController(Northwind injectedContext)
{
  db = injectedContext;
}
```

Modify the contents of the Index action method to make it look like this:

```
var model = new HomeIndexViewModel
{
  VisitorCount = (new Random()).Next(1, 1001),
  Products = db.Products.ToArray()
};
return View(model); // pass model to view
```

We will simulate a visitor count using the Random class to generate a number between 1 and 1000.

ASP.NET Core MVC views

The responsibility of a view is to transform a model into HTML or other formats. There are multiple **viewengines** that can be used to do this. The default view engine for ASP.NET MVC 3 and later is called **Razor**, and it uses the @ symbol to indicate server-side code execution.

Rendering the Home controller's views

Expand the Views folder, and then expand the Home folder. Note the three files with the .cshtml file extension.

The .cshtml file extension means this is a file that mixes C# and HTML.

When the View() method is called in a controller's action method, ASP.NET Core MVC looks in the Views folder for a subfolder with the same name as the current controller, that is, **Home**. It then looks for a file with the same name as the current action, that is, Index, About, or Contact.

In the Index.cshtml file, note the block of C# code wrapped in @{ }. This will execute first and can be used to store data that needs to be passed into a shared layout file:

```
@{
  ViewData["Title"] = "Home Page";
}
```

Note the static HTML content in several <div> elements that uses Bootstrap for styling.

Good Practice
As well as defining your own styles, base your styles on a common library, such as Bootstrap, that implements responsive design. To learn more about CSS3 and responsive design, read the book *Responsive Web Design with HTML5 and CSS3 – Second Edition* by *Packt Publishing* at https://www.packtpub.com/web-development/responsive-web-design-html5-and-css3-second-edition.

Sharing layouts between views

There is a file named _ViewStart.cshtml that gets executed by the View() method. It is used to set defaults that apply to all views.

For example, it sets the Layout property of all views to a shared layout file:

```
@{
  Layout = "_Layout";
}
```

In the Shared folder, open the _Layout.cshtml file. Note that the title is being read from the ViewData dictionary that was set earlier in the Index.cshtml view.

Modify the title to have the suffix, **My First ASP.NET Core App**, as shown in the following markup:

```
<title>@ViewData["Title"] - My First ASP.NET Core App</title>
```

Note the rendering of common styles to support Bootstrap and the two sections. During *development*, the fully commented and nicely formatted versions of CSS files will be used. For *staging* and *release*, the minified versions will be used:

```
<environment names="Development">
  <link rel="stylesheet"
href="~/lib/bootstrap/dist/css/bootstrap.css" />
  <link rel="stylesheet" href="~/css/site.css" />
</environment>
<environment names="Staging,Production">
  <link rel="stylesheet" href="https://ajax.aspnetcdn.com/ajax/
           bootstrap/3.3.5/css/bootstrap.min.css"
    asp-fallback-href="~/lib/bootstrap/dist/css/bootstrap.min.css"
    asp-fallback-test-class="sr-only"
    asp-fallback-test-property="position"
    asp-fallback-test-value="absolute" />
  <link rel="stylesheet"
      href="~/css/site.min.css"
      asp-append-version="true" />
</environment>
```

~ means the `wwwroot` folder.

Note the rendering of hyperlinks to allow users to click between pages using the navigation bar at the top of every page. The `<a>` elements use "tag helper" attributes to specify the controller name and action name that will execute when the link is clicked:

```
<div class="navbar-collapse collapse">
  <ul class="nav navbar-nav">
    <li><a asp-controller="Home" asp-action="Index">Home</a></li>
    <li><a asp-controller="Home" asp-action="About">About</a></li>
    <li><a asp-controller="Home"
           asp-action="Contact">Contact</a></li>
  </ul>
</div>
```

Note the rendering of the body:

```
@RenderBody()
```

Note the rendering of script blocks at the bottom of the page so that it doesn't slow down the display of the page:

```
<environment names="Development">
  <script src="~/lib/jquery/dist/jquery.js"></script>
  <script src="~/lib/bootstrap/dist/js/bootstrap.js"></script>
  <script src="~/js/site.js" asp-append-version="true"></script>
</environment>
<environment names="Staging,Production">
  <script src="https://ajax.aspnetcdn.com/ajax/jquery/jquery-
2.1.4.min.js" asp-fallback-src="~/lib/jquery/dist/jquery.min.js"
              asp-fallback-test="window.jQuery">
  </script>
  <script
src="https://ajax.aspnetcdn.com/ajax/bootstrap/3.3.5/bootstrap.min
.js" asp-fallback-src="~/lib/bootstrap/dist/js/bootstrap.min.js"
asp-fallback-test="window.jQuery && window.jQuery.fn &&
window.jQuery.fn.modal">
  </script>
  <script src="~/js/site.min.js" asp-append-version="true">
  </script>
</environment>
```

You can add your own script blocks into an optional defined section named **scripts**:

```
@RenderSection("scripts", required: false)
```

Defining custom styles

In the `wwwroot\css` folder, open the `site.css` file.

Add a new style that will apply to an element with the `newspaper` ID like this:

```
#newspaper {
  column-count: 3;
}
```

In Visual Studio Code, you will need to add the style to `site.min.css` too. Usually you would have a build step to minify your `site.css` into a `site.min.css`, but for now, just do it manually.

Defining a typed view

To improve the IntelliSense when writing a view, you can define the type the view can expect using a `@model` directive at the top.

Back in the `Index.cshtml` view, enter the following code as the first line of the file:

```
@model Packt.CS7.HomeIndexViewModel
```

Now, whenever we enter `@Model` in this view, the IntelliSense will know the correct type and will provide IntelliSense.

To declare the type for the model, use `@model` (with lowercase `m`).

To read from the model, use `@Model` (with uppercase `M`).

In `Index.cshtml`, delete all the `<div>` elements and replace them with this markup:

```
<div class="row">
  <div class="col-md-12">
    <h1>Northwind</h1>
    <p class="lead">We have had @Model.VisitorCount
       visitors this month.
    </p>
    <h2>Products</h2>
    <div id="newspaper">
      <ul>
      @foreach (var item in @Model.Products)
      {
        <li><a asp-controller="Home"
               asp-action="ProductDetail"
               asp-route-id="@item.ProductID">
            @item.ProductName costs
            @item.UnitPrice.Value.ToString("C")
        </a></li>
      }
      </ul>
    </div>
  </div>
</div>
```

Note how easy it is to mix static HTML elements such as `<ul>` and `<li>` with C# code to output the list of product names.

Note the `<div>` element with the `id` attribute of `newspaper`. This will use the custom style that we defined earlier, so all the content in that element will display in three columns.

In **Visual Studio 2017**, press *Ctrl* + *F5*.

In **Visual Studio Code**, enter the command `dotnet run`, and then run **Chrome** and navigate to `http://localhost:5000/`.

The home page will look as shown in the following screenshot:

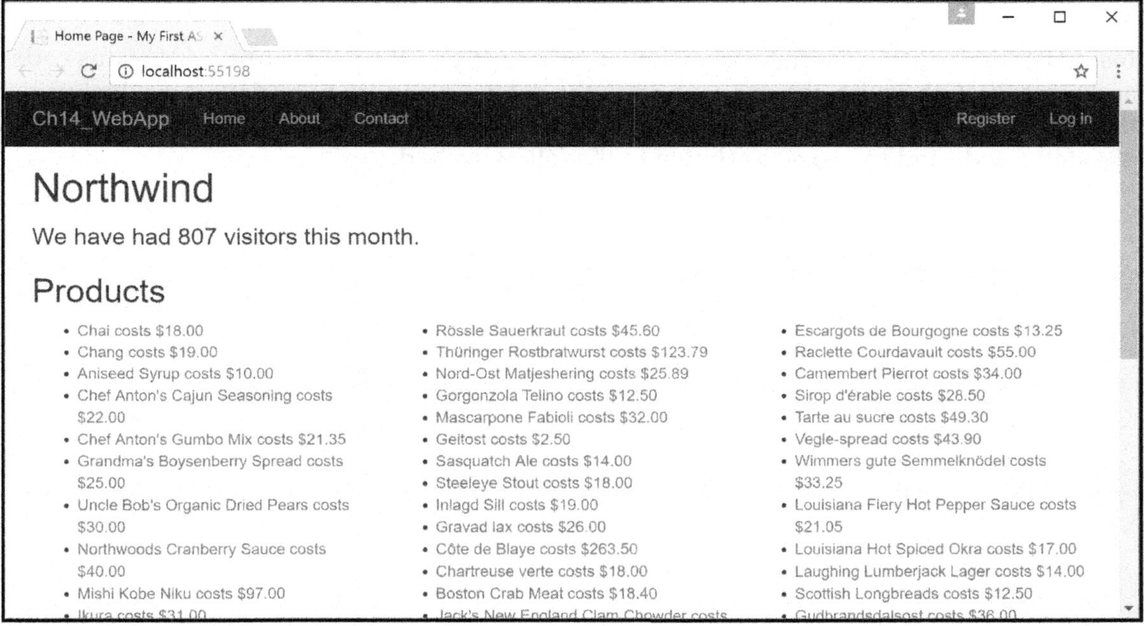

Taking ASP.NET Core MVC further

Now that you've seen the basics of how models, views, and controllers work together to provide a web application, let's look at some common scenarios, such as passing parameters and annotating models.

Passing parameters using a route value

Back in the `HomeController` class, add the following action method. It uses a class called `defaultmodelbinder` to automatically match the `id` passed in the route to the parameter named `id` in the method.

Model binders are very powerful, and the default one does a lot for you. For advanced scenarios, you can create your own by implementing the `IModelBinder` interface, but that is beyond the scope of this book.

Inside the method, we check to see whether `id` is null, and if so, it returns a 404 status code and message. Otherwise, we can connect to the database and try to retrieve a product using the `id` variable. If we find a product, we pass it to a view; otherwise, we return a different 404 status code and message, as shown in the following code:

```
public IActionResult ProductDetail(int? id)
{
  if (!id.HasValue)
  {
    return NotFound("You must pass a product ID in the route, for
      example, /Home/ProductDetail/21");
  }
  var model = db.Products.SingleOrDefault(p => p.ProductID == id);
  if (model == null)
  {
    return NotFound($"A product with the ID of {id} was not
      found.");
  }
  return View(model); // pass model to view
}
```

Now, we need to create a view for this request.

In **Visual Studio 2017**, inside the `Views` folder, right-click on **Home** and choose **Add** | **New Item...**. Choose **MVC View Page** and name it `ProductDetail.cshtml`.

In **Visual Studio Code**, inside the `Views/Home` folder, add a new file named `ProductDetail.cshtml`.

Modify the contents, as shown in the following markup:

```
@model Packt.CS7.Product
@{
  ViewData["Title"] = "Product Detail - " + Model.ProductName;
}
```

```
<h2>Product Detail</h2>
<hr />
<div>
  <dl class="dl-horizontal">
    <dt>Product ID</dt>
    <dd>@Model.ProductID</dd>
    <dt>Product Name</dt>
    <dd>@Model.ProductName</dd>
    <dt>Category ID</dt>
    <dd>@Model.CategoryID</dd>
    <dt>Unit Price</dt>
    <dd>@Model.UnitPrice.Value.ToString("C")</dd>
    <dt>Units In Stock</dt>
    <dd>@Model.UnitsInStock</dd>
  </dl>
</div>
```

Run the web application, and when the home page appears with the list of products, click one of them, for example, product 2, Chang. The result should look something like the following screenshot:

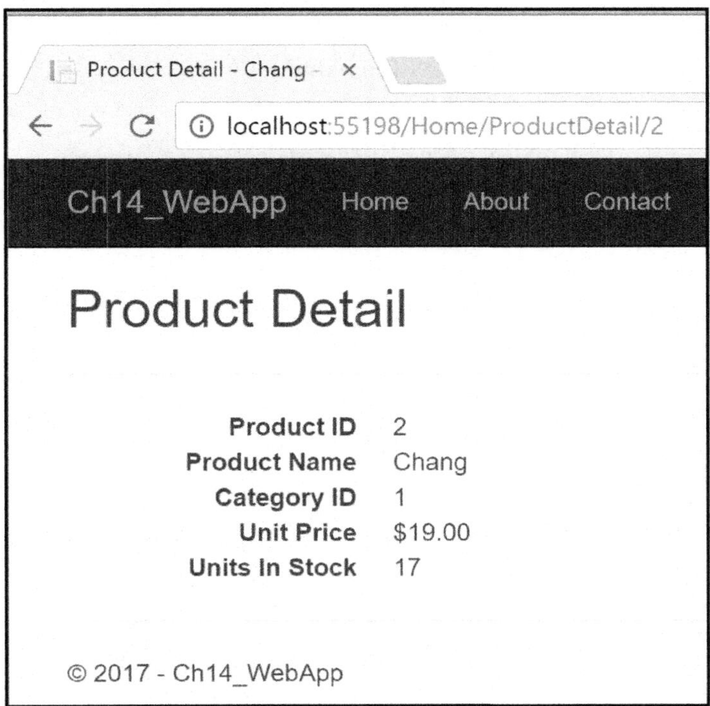

Passing parameters using a query string

In the `HomeController` class, import the `Microsoft.EntityFrameworkCore` namespace.

Add a new action method, as shown in the following code:

```
public IActionResult ProductsThatCostMoreThan(decimal? price)
{
  if (!price.HasValue)
  {
    return NotFound("You must pass a product price in the query
    string, for example, /Home/ProductsThatCostMoreThan?price=50");
  }
  var model = db.Products.Include(p => p.Category).Include(
    p => p.Supplier).Where(p => p.UnitPrice > price).ToArray();
  if (model.Count() == 0)
  {
    return NotFound($"No products cost more than {price:C}.");
  }
  ViewData["MaxPrice"] = price.Value.ToString("C");
  return View(model); // pass model to view
}
```

Inside the `Views/Home` folder, add a new file named `ProductsThatCostMoreThan.cshtml`.

Modify the contents, as shown in the following code:

```
@model IEnumerable<Packt.CS7.Product>
@{
  ViewData["Title"] =
    "Products That Cost More Than " + ViewData["MaxPrice"];
}
<h2>Products That Cost More Than @ViewData["MaxPrice"]</h2>
<table class="table">
  <tr>
    <th>
      @Html.DisplayNameFor(
        model => model.Category.CategoryName)
    </th>
    <th>
      @Html.DisplayNameFor(model => model.Supplier.CompanyName)
    </th>
    <th>
      @Html.DisplayNameFor(model => model.ProductName)
    </th>
    <th>
      @Html.DisplayNameFor(model => model.UnitPrice)
```

```
      </th>
      <th>
        @Html.DisplayNameFor(model => model.UnitsInStock)
      </th>
    </tr>
    @foreach (var item in Model)
    {
    <tr>
      <td>
        @Html.DisplayFor(modelItem => item.Category.CategoryName)
      </td>
      <td>
        @Html.DisplayFor(modelItem => item.Supplier.CompanyName)
      </td>
      <td>
        @Html.DisplayFor(modelItem => item.ProductName)
      </td>
      <td>
        @Html.DisplayFor(modelItem => item.UnitPrice)
      </td>
      <td>
        @Html.DisplayFor(modelItem => item.UnitsInStock)
      </td>
    </tr>
    }
  </table>
```

In the `Views/Home` folder, open `Index.cshtml` and add the following `div` element at the bottom of the file. This will provide a form for the user to enter a price. The user can then click on a submit button to call the action method that shows only products that cost more than the entered price:

```
<div class="row">
  <form asp-action="ProductsThatCostMoreThan" method="get">
    <input name="price" placeholder="Enter a product price" />
    <input type="submit" />
  </form>
</div>
```

Run the web application, and on the home page, scroll down and enter a price in the form, for example, `50`. Then, click **Submit Query**, as shown in the following screenshot:

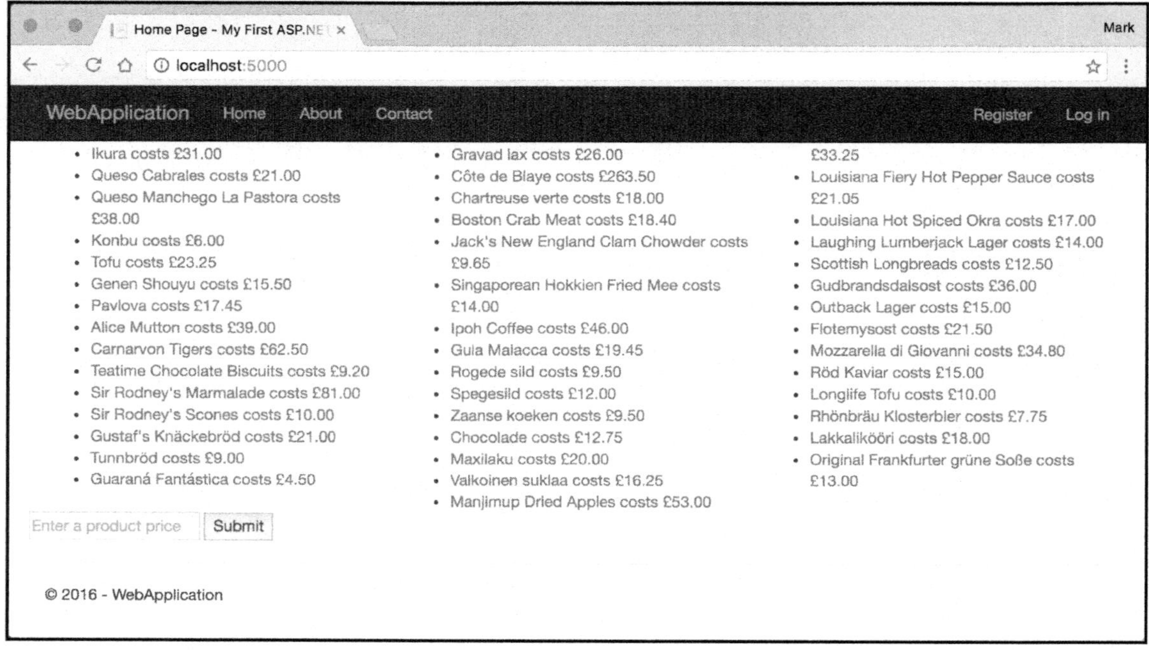

You will see a table of the products that cost more than the price that you entered, as shown in the following screenshot:

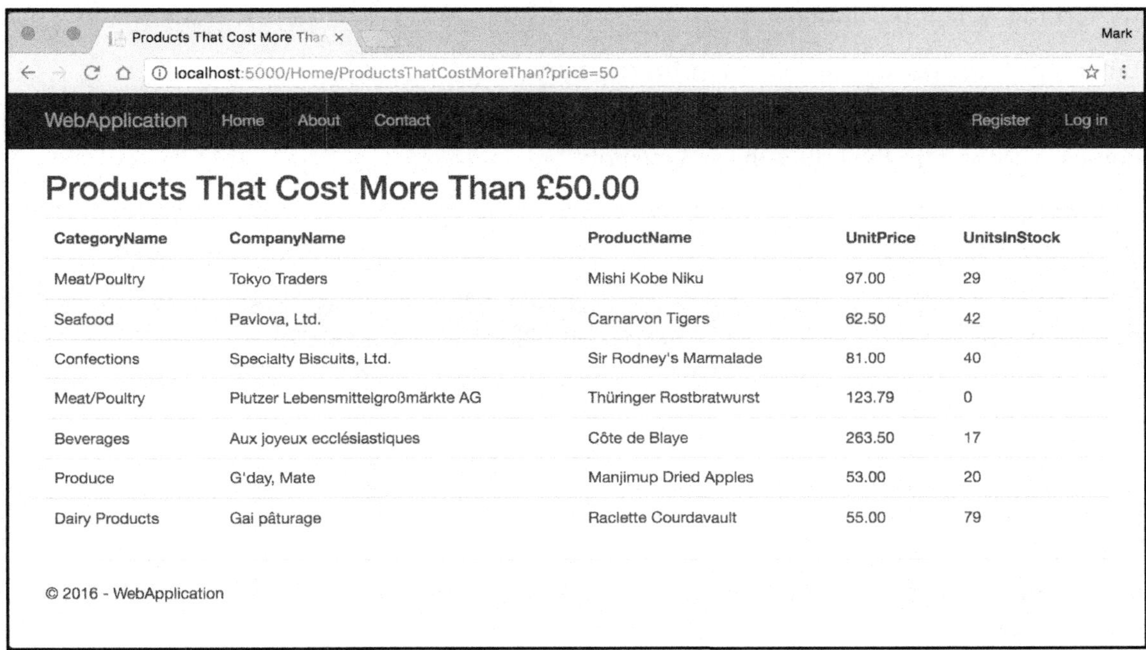

Annotating models

You might have noted that the column headings in the table used the names of the properties by default. This means that if the property is multiple words, it won't have spaces. We can use data annotations to improve this.

In the `Models` folder, open the `Product` class.

Add the `[Display]` attributes before each property that you want to have a different label, for example, **ProductName**, **UnitPrice**, **UnitsinStock**, and so on, like this code example:

```
[Display(Name = "Product Name")]
public string ProductName { get; set; }
```

Apply the `[Display]` attribute to some of the properties of the other classes, especially Category's Category Name and Supplier's Company Name.

Restart the web application.

Enter a product price and click on **Submit Query**.

Note that the column headings now reflect the display attributes and not the property names, as shown in the following screenshot:

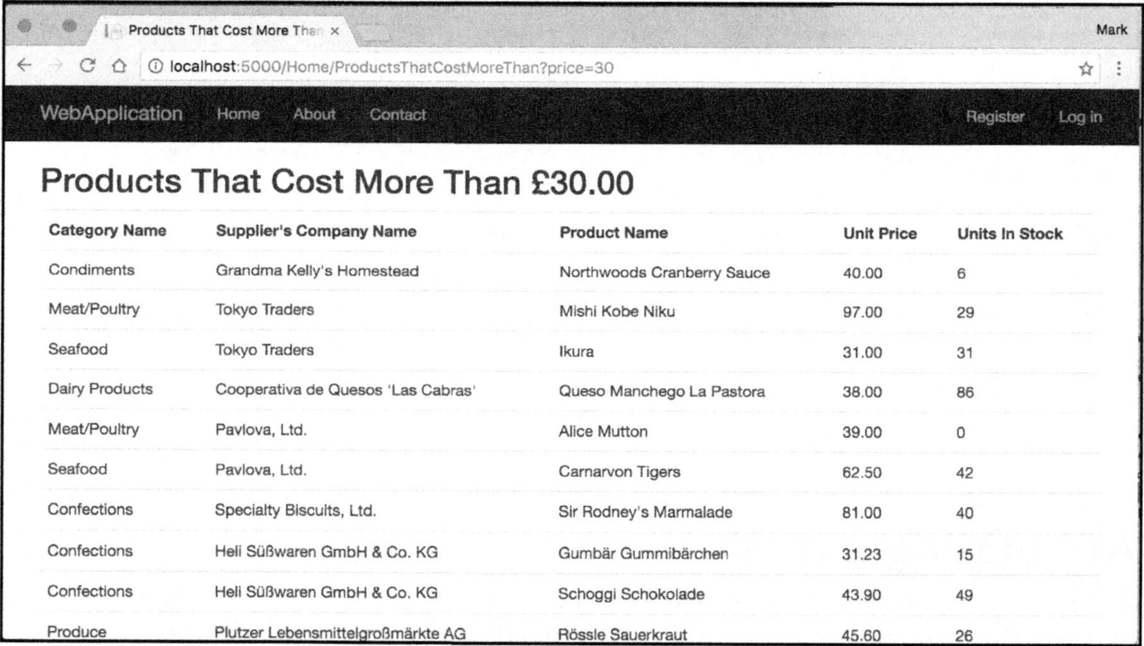

Practicing and exploring

Test your knowledge and understanding by answering some questions, get some hands-on practice, and explore this chapter's topics with deeper research.

Exercise 14.1 – test your knowledge

Answer the following questions:

1. What is the difference between a web browser and a web server?
2. What is the difference between a URI, a URL, and a URN?
3. What are the four most common HTTP methods?
4. What does it mean when a web server responds with status code 302?
5. What are the responsibilities of a route?
6. What are the responsibilities of a controller?
7. What are the responsibilities of a model?
8. What are the responsibilities of a view?

Exercise 14.2 – practice building a data-driven web application

Create an ASP.NET Core web application that connects to the Northwind sample database and enables the user to see a list of customers grouped by country. When the user clicks on a customer record, they then see a page showing the full contact details of that customer and a list of their orders.

Exercise 14.3 – explore topics

Use the following links to read more details about this chapter's topics:

- **ASP.NET Core**: `https://www.asp.net/core`
- **Introduction to ASP.NET Core**: `https://docs.microsoft.com/en-gb/aspnet/core/`
- **Overview of ASP.NET Core MVC**: `https://docs.microsoft.com/en-gb/aspnet/core/mvc/overview`
- **Working with Data in ASP.NET Core**: `https://docs.microsoft.com/en-gb/aspnet/core/data/`
- **ASP.NET Core Schedule and Roadmap**: `https://github.com/aspnet/Home/wiki/Roadmap`

Summary

In this chapter, you learned how to build an ASP.NET Core MVC web application that manages data using Entity Framework Core.

In the next chapter, you will learn how to build an ASP.NET Core Web API service that can be called from mobile apps built using Xamarin.Forms and Visual Studio for Mac.

15
Building Mobile Apps Using Xamarin.Forms and ASP.NET Core Web API

This chapter is about learning how to build C# mobile by building a cross-platform mobile app for iOS and Android. The mobile app will allow the listing and management of customers in the Northwind database.

The mobile app will call a web service built with the ASP.NET Core Web API. The server-side code will be written with **Visual Studio Code** and the client-side Xamarin.Forms mobile app will be written with **Visual Studio for Mac**.

You will need a computer with macOS to complete this chapter.

In this chapter, we will cover the following topics:

- Understanding Xamarin.Forms
- Building services using ASP.NET Core Web API and Visual Studio Code
- Building mobile apps using Xamarin.Forms and Visual Studio for Mac

Understanding Xamarin.Forms

Xamarin enables developers to build mobile apps for Apple iOS (iPhone and iPad), Google Android, and Windows Mobile using C#. It is based on a third-party open source implementation of .NET known as Mono.

How Xamarin.Forms extends Xamarin

Xamarin.Forms extends Xamarin to make cross-platform mobile development even easier by sharing most of the user experience layer, as well as the business logic layer.

Like Universal Windows Platform apps, Xamarin.Forms uses XAML to define the user interface once for all platforms using abstractions of platform-specific user interface components. Applications built with Xamarin.Forms draw the user interface using native platform widgets, so the apps look-and-feel fits naturally with the target mobile platform.

Mobile first, cloud first

Mobile apps are often supported by services in the cloud. Satya Nadella, CEO of Microsoft, famously said:

> *"To me, when we say mobile first, it's not the mobility of the device, it's actually the mobility of the individual experience. [...] The only way you are going to be able to orchestrate the mobility of these applications and data is through the cloud."*

As you have seen throughout this book, the best tool for cross-platform .NET Core development is Visual Studio Code, so we will use that to create the ASP.NET Core Web API service to support the mobile app.

To create Xamarin.Forms apps, developers can use either Visual Studio 2017 or Visual Studio for Mac (this is the new branding for Xamarin Studio). To create iOS apps, you will require a Mac and Xcode. A summary of which IDE can be used to create and compile which type of app is shown in the following table:

	iOS	Android	Windows Mobile	ASP.NET Core Web API
Visual Studio Code	✗	✗	✗	✓
Visual Studio for Mac	✓	✓	✗	✓
Visual Studio 2017	✗	✓	✓	✓

If you would like to learn more details about Xamarin, then I recommend *Xamarin Cross-platform Application Development, Second Edition* by Jonathan Peppers, and *Mastering Cross-Platform Development with Xamarin* by Can Bilgin, all by Packt Publishing.

Installing Xcode

If you have not already installed Xcode on your Mac, install it now from the App Store.

On the Apple menu, choose **App Store...**

In **App Store**, enter `xcode` in the **Search** box, and one of the first results will be **Xcode**, as shown in the following screenshot:

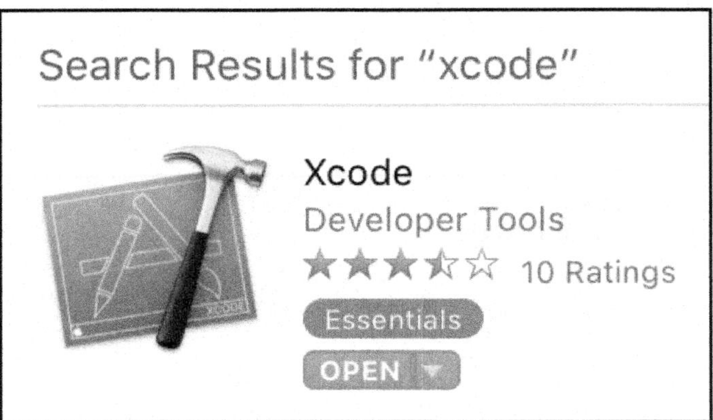

Installing Visual Studio for Mac

Go to the following link to download and install Visual Studio for Mac:

`https://developer.xamarin.com/visual-studio-mac/.`

In the **Visual Studio for Mac Preview Installer**, accept the License Terms and the Privacy Statement, click **Accept**, choose to install all components, and then click **Continue**, as shown in the following screenshot:

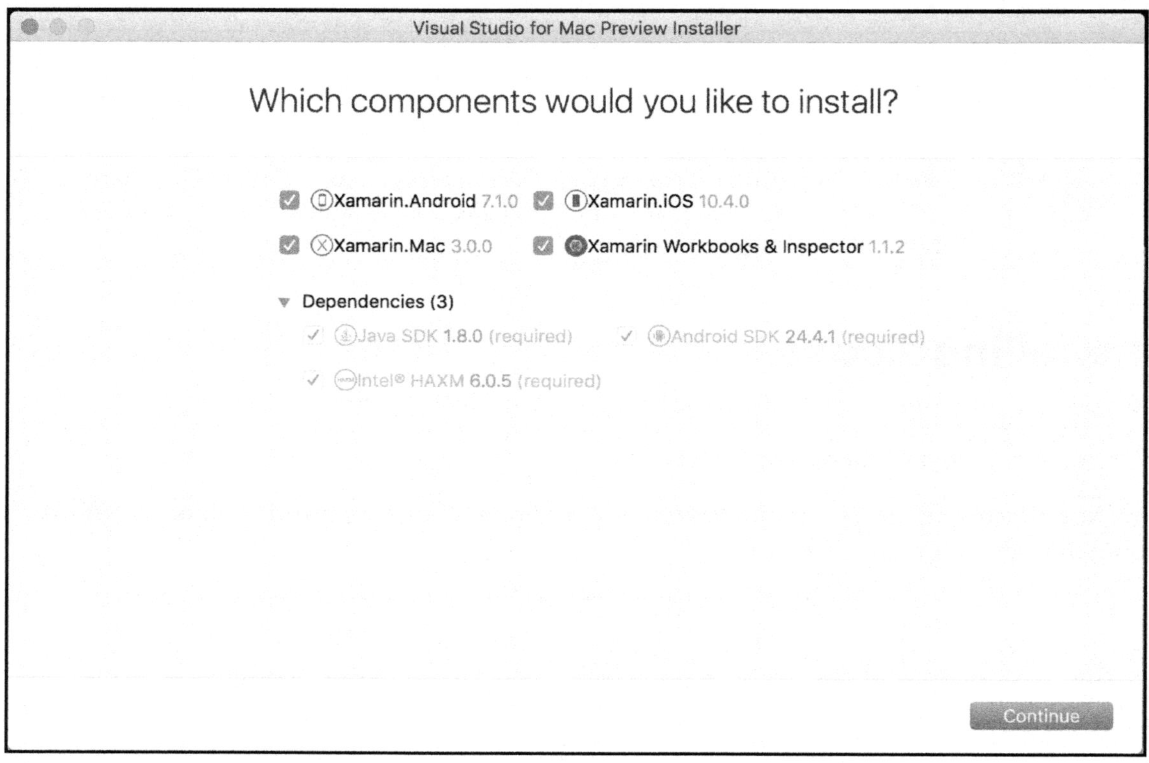

Click **Continue**, and then click **Install**.

Agree to the license terms for the components, such as the Android SDK, click **Continue**, and wait for Visual Studio for Mac to fully install, as shown in the following screenshot:

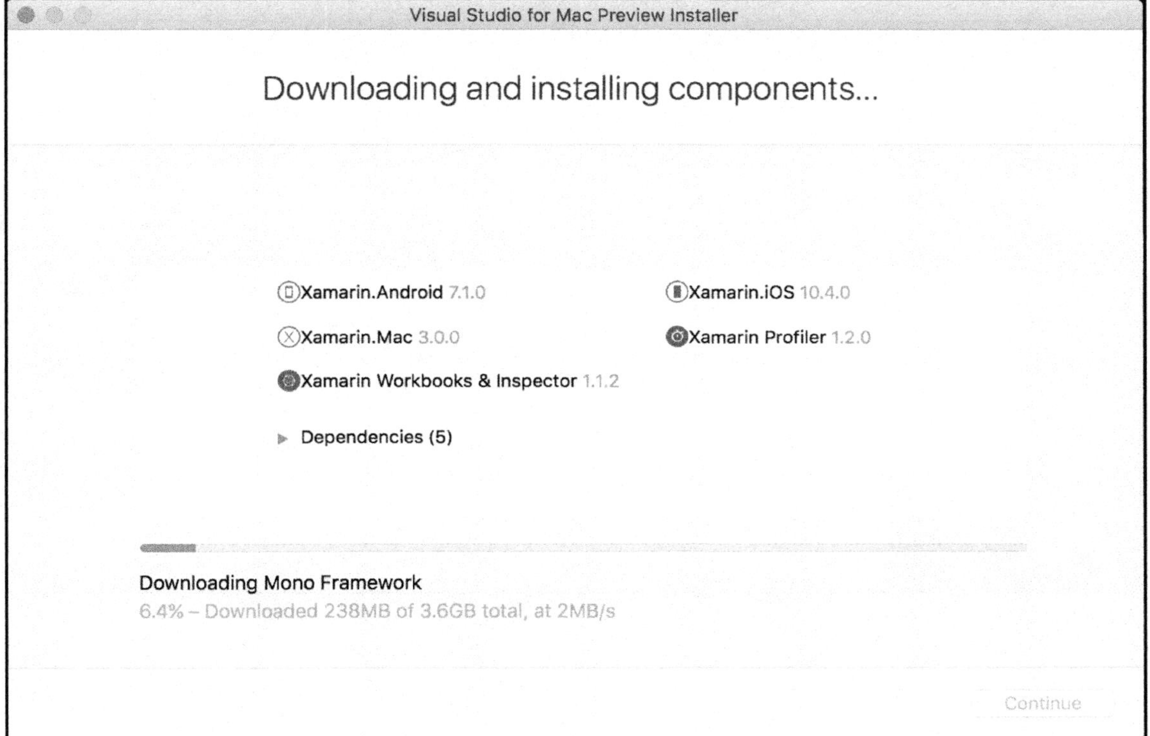

Start Visual Studio for Mac to see the **Welcome Page**, as shown in the following screenshot:

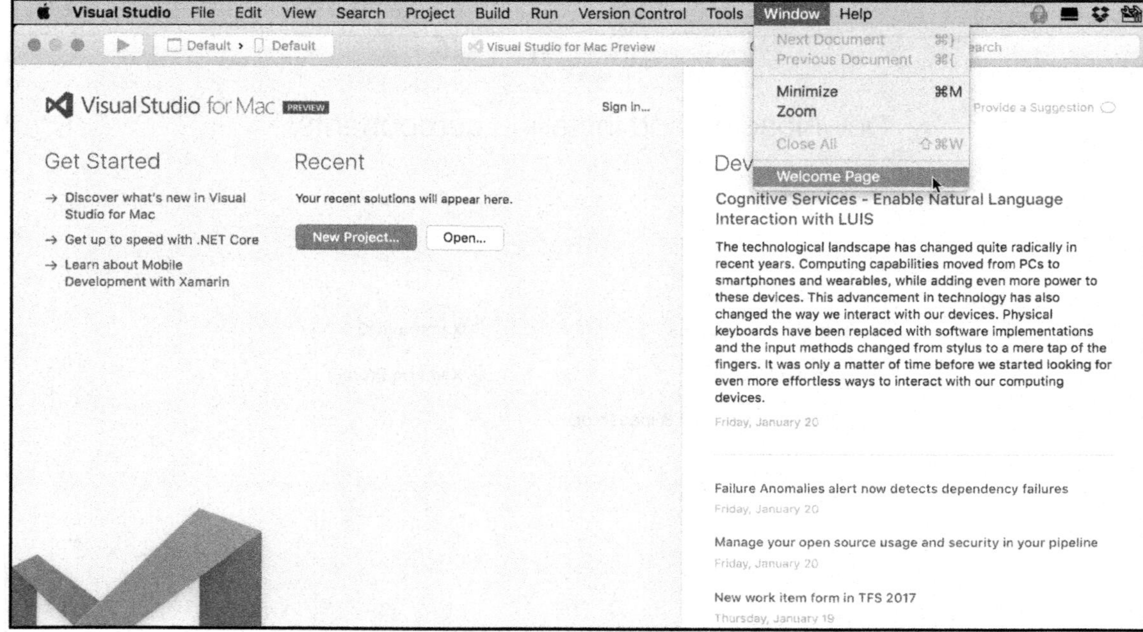

If you are prompted to update components, then click on **Restart and Install Updates**, as shown in the following screenshot:

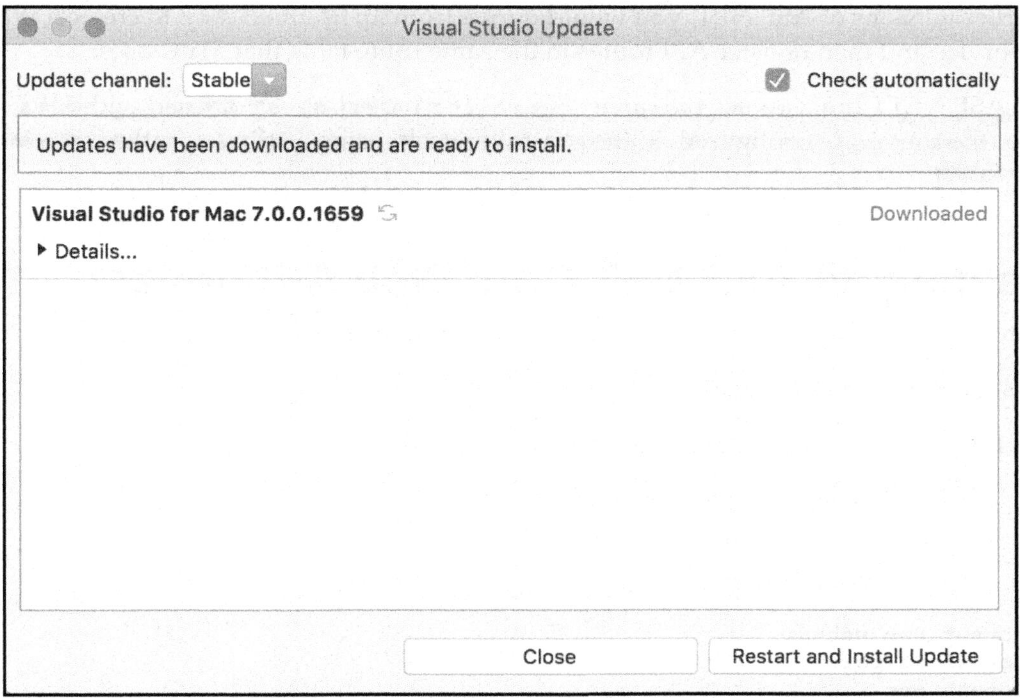

Building services using ASP.NET Core Web API and Visual Studio Code

Although HTTP was originally designed to request and respond with HTML and other resources for us to look at, it is also good to build services. Roy Fielding stated in his doctoral dissertation describing the **Representational State Transfer** (**REST**) architectural style that the HTTP standard defines:

- URLs to uniquely identify resources
- Methods to perform common tasks, such as `GET` and `DELETE`
- The ability to negotiate media formats, such as XML and JSON

To allow the easy creation of services, ASP.NET Core has combined what used to be two types of controller.

In earlier versions of ASP.NET, you would derive from `ApiController` to create a Web API service and then register API routes in the same route table that MVC uses.

With ASP.NET Core, you use the same `Controller` base class as you used with MVC, except the routes are configured on the controller itself, using attributes, rather than in the route table.

Creating an ASP.NET Core Web API project

Create a folder named `Chapter15` with a subfolder named `Ch15_WebApi`.

In Visual Studio Code, open the `Ch15_WebApi` folder.

In an Integrated Terminal, enter the following commands to:

- Create a new Web API project
- Restore dependency packages
- Start the website

```
dotnet new webapi
dotnet restore
dotnet run
```

Start Google Chrome.

Navigate to `http:/localhost:5000/api/values` and view the results, as shown in the following output:

```
["value1","value2"]
```

Close Google Chrome.

In an Integrated Terminal, press *Ctrl* + *C* to stop the console application and shut down the Kestrel web server that is hosting your ASP.NET Core web application.

Creating a web service for the Northwind database

Unlike ASP.NET Core MVC controllers, ASP.NET Core Web API controllers do not call views to return HTML responses for humans to see in browsers. Instead, they use content negotiation with the client application that made the HTTP request to return XML, JSON, or X-WWW-FORMURLENCODED data formats in the HTTP response.

The client application must then deserialize the data from the negotiated format. The most commonly used format for modern services is **JavaScript Object Notation (JSON)** because it is compact and works natively with JavaScript in a browser.

Creating the Northwind database

Create the `Northwind.db` file in the `\Ch15_WebApi\bin\Debug\netcoreapp1.1\` folder by copying the `NorthwindSQLite.sql` file into that folder and then entering the following command in **Integrated Terminal**:

```
sqlite3 Northwind.db < NorthwindSQLite.sql
```

Referencing the EF Core NuGet packages

Open the `Ch15_WebApi.csproj` file and add package references, as shown highlighted in the following code:

```
<Project Sdk="Microsoft.NET.Sdk.Web">

  <PropertyGroup>
    <TargetFramework>netcoreapp1.1</TargetFramework>
  </PropertyGroup>

  <ItemGroup>
    <Folder Include="wwwroot" />
  </ItemGroup>

  <ItemGroup>
    <PackageReference Include="Microsoft.AspNetCore"
                      Version="1.1.1" />
    <PackageReference Include="Microsoft.AspNetCore.Mvc"
                      Version="1.1.2" />
    <PackageReference Include="Microsoft.Extensions.Logging.Debug"
                      Version="1.1.1" />
    <PackageReference Include=
```

```
            "Microsoft.AspNetCore.Diagnostics.EntityFrameworkCore"
                          Version="1.1.1" />
      <PackageReference Include="Microsoft.AspNetCore.StaticFiles"
                          Version="1.1.1" />
      <PackageReference Include="Microsoft.EntityFrameworkCore.Design"
                          Version="1.1.1" />
      <PackageReference Include="Microsoft.EntityFrameworkCore.Sqlite"
                          Version="1.1.1" />
      <PackageReference
Include="Microsoft.EntityFrameworkCore.Sqlite.Design" Version="1.1.1"
PrivateAssets="All" />
      <PackageReference Include="Microsoft.EntityFrameworkCore.Tools"
Version="1.1.0" PrivateAssets="All" />
    </ItemGroup>

    <ItemGroup>
      <DotNetCliToolReference
Include="Microsoft.EntityFrameworkCore.Tools.DotNet" Version="1.0.0"
 />
      <DotNetCliToolReference
Include="Microsoft.VisualStudio.Web.CodeGeneration.Tools"
Version="1.0.0" />
    </ItemGroup>

</Project>
```

Creating the entity model and database context

Create a `Models` folder in the `Ch15_WebApi` folder.

Add two class files to the `Models` folder named `Northwind.cs` and `Customer.cs`.

`Northwind.cs` should look like this:

```
using Microsoft.EntityFrameworkCore;

namespace Packt.CS7.Models
{
  public class Northwind : DbContext
  {
    public DbSet<Customer> Customers { get; set; }

    public Northwind(DbContextOptions options) : base(options) {}
  }
}
```

`Customer.cs` should look like this:

```
using System.ComponentModel.DataAnnotations;

namespace Packt.CS7.Models
{
  public class Customer
  {
    [Key]
    [StringLength(5)]
    public string CustomerID { get; set; }

    [Required]
    [StringLength(40)]
    public string CompanyName { get; set; }

    [StringLength(30)]
    public string ContactName { get; set; }

    [StringLength(15)]
    public string City { get; set; }

    [StringLength(15)]
    public string Country { get; set; }

    [StringLength(24)]
    public string Phone { get; set; }
  }
}
```

Creating the data repository

Add two class files to the `Models` folder named `ICustomerRepository.cs` and `CustomerRepository.cs`.

`ICustomerRepository` should look like this:

```
using System.Collections.Generic;

namespace Packt.CS7.Models
{
  public interface ICustomerRepository
  {
    Customer Add(Customer c);

    IEnumerable<Customer> GetAll();
```

```
    Customer Find(string id);

    bool Remove(string id);

    Customer Update(string id, Customer c);
  }
}
```

`CustomerRepository` should look like this:

```
using System.Collections.Generic;
using System.Collections.Concurrent;
using System.Linq;

namespace Packt.CS7.Models
{
  public class CustomerRepository : ICustomerRepository
  {
    // cache the customers in a thread-safe dictionary
    // so restarting the service will reset the customers
    // in real world the repository would perform CRUD
    // on the database
    private static
    ConcurrentDictionary<string, Customer> customers;

    public CustomerRepository(Northwind db)
    {
      // load customers from database as a normal
      // Dictionary with CustomerID is the key,
      // then convert to a thread-safe
      // ConcurrentDictionary
      customers = new ConcurrentDictionary<string, Customer>(
        db.Customers.ToDictionary(c => c.CustomerID));
    }

    public Customer Add(Customer c)
    {
      // normalize CustomerID into uppercase
      c.CustomerID = c.CustomerID.ToUpper();
      // if the customer is new, add it, else
      // call Update method
      return customers.AddOrUpdate(c.CustomerID, c, Update);
    }

    public IEnumerable<Customer> GetAll()
    {
      return customers.Values;
    }
```

```
        public Customer Find(string id)
        {
          id = id.ToUpper();
          Customer c;
          customers.TryGetValue(id, out c);
          return c;
        }

        public bool Remove(string id)
        {
          id = id.ToUpper();
          Customer c;
          return customers.TryRemove(id, out c);
        }

        public Customer Update(string id, Customer c)
        {
          id = id.ToUpper();
          c.CustomerID = c.CustomerID.ToUpper();
          Customer old;
          if (customers.TryGetValue(id, out old))
          {
            if (customers.TryUpdate(id, c, old))
            {
              return c;
            }
          }
          return null;
        }
      }
    }
```

Configuring and registering the data repository

Open the `Startup.cs` file.

Import the following namespaces:

```
using Microsoft.EntityFrameworkCore;
using Packt.CS7.Models;
```

Add the following statements to the bottom of the `ConfigureServices` method that will:

- Set the Northwind database context to use SQLite and load the connection string from `appsettings.json`

- Register the `CustomerRepository` for use at runtime by ASP.NET Core

```
services.AddDbContext<Packt.CS7.Models.Northwind>(options =>
  options.UseSqlite(Configuration
  .GetConnectionString("NorthwindConnection")));

services.AddSingleton<ICustomerRepository, CustomerRepository>();
```

.Add Scoped

singleton doesn't work

Set the database connection string

Open the `appsettings.json` file and add a connection string named `NorthwindConnection`, as shown in the following code:

```
{
  "ConnectionStrings": {
    "NorthwindConnection": "Data Source=Northwind.db"
  },
  "Logging": {
    "IncludeScopes": false,
    "LogLevel": {
      "Default": "Warning"
    }
  }
}
```

Creating the Web API controller

In the **Explorer** pane, select the `Controllers` folder and add a new file named `CustomersController.cs`.

We could delete the `ValuesController.cs` file, but it is good to have a simple Web API controller in a service for testing purposes.

In the `CustomersController` class, add the following code, and note:

- The controller class registers a route that starts with `api` and includes the name of the controller, that is, `api/customers`
- The constructor uses dependency injection to instantiate the registered repository for the customers
- There are five methods to perform CRUD operations on customers—two `GETs` (all customers or one customer), `POST` (create), `PUT` (update), and `DELETE`:

```
using System.Collections.Generic;
using System.Linq;
using Microsoft.AspNetCore.Mvc;
using Packt.CS7.Models;

namespace Packt.CS7.Controllers
{
  // base address: api/customers
  [Route("api/[controller]")]
  public class CustomersController : Controller
  {
    private ICustomerRepository repo;

    // constructor injects registered repository
    public CustomersController(ICustomerRepository repo)
    {
      this.repo = repo;
    }

    // GET: api/customers
    // GET: api/customers/?country=[country]
    [HttpGet]
    public IEnumerable<Customer> GetCustomers(string country)
    {
      if (string.IsNullOrWhiteSpace(country))
      {
        return repo.GetAll();
      }
      else
      {
        return repo.GetAll()
          .Where(customer => customer.Country == country);
      }
    }

    // GET: api/customers/[id]
    [HttpGet("{id}", Name = "GetCustomer")]
    public IActionResult GetCustomer(string id)
    {
      Customer c = repo.Find(id);
      if (c == null)
      {
        return NotFound(); // 404 Resource not found
      }
      return new ObjectResult(c); // 200 OK
    }

    // POST: api/customers
```

```
// BODY: Customer (JSON, XML)
[HttpPost]
public IActionResult Create([FromBody] Customer c)
{
  if (c == null)
  {
    return BadRequest(); // 400 Bad request
  }
  repo.Add(c);
  return CreatedAtRoute("GetCustomer",
  new { id = c.CustomerID.ToLower() }, c); // 201 Created
}

// PUT: api/customers/[id]
// BODY: Customer (JSON, XML)
[HttpPut("{id}")]
public IActionResult Update(string id, [FromBody] Customer c)
{
  id = id.ToUpper();
  c.CustomerID = c.CustomerID.ToUpper();

  if (c == null || c.CustomerID != id)
  {
    return BadRequest(); // 400 Bad request
  }

  var existing = repo.Find(id);
  if (existing == null)
  {
    return NotFound(); // 404 Resource not found
  }

  repo.Update(id, c);
  return new NoContentResult(); // 204 No content
}

// DELETE: api/customers/[id]
[HttpDelete("{id}")]
public IActionResult Delete(string id)
{
  var existing = repo.Find(id);
  if (existing == null)
  {
    return NotFound(); // 404 Resource not found
  }

  repo.Remove(id);
  return new NoContentResult(); // 204 No content
```

```
        }
    }
}
```

If you have used older versions of ASP.NET Web API, then you know that in that technology, you could create C# methods that begin with any HTTP method (`GET`, `POST`, `PUT`, and so on), and the controller would automatically execute the correct one. In ASP.NET Core, this doesn't happen anymore because we are not inheriting from `ApiController`. So, you must apply an attribute such as `[HttpGet]` to explicitly map HTTP methods to C# methods. This allows us to use any name we like for the methods themselves.

Testing the web service

In an **Integrated Terminal**, start the web service by entering the following command:

```
dotnet run
```

Testing GET requests with any browser

Start Google Chrome, and in the address bar, enter the following URL:

`http://localhost:5000/api/customers`

You should see a JSON document returned containing all the 91 customers in the Northwind database, as shown in the following screenshot:

Chrome File Edit View History Bookmarks People Window Help

localhost:5000/api/customers × Mark

localhost:5000/api/customers


```
[{"customerID":"LAZYK","companyName":"Lazy K Kountry Store","city":"Walla Walla","country":"USA"},
{"customerID":"FISSA","companyName":"FISSA Fabrica Inter. Salchichas S.A.","city":"Madrid","country":"Spain"},
{"customerID":"TRAIH","companyName":"Trail's Head Gourmet Provisioners","city":"Kirkland","country":"USA"},
{"customerID":"GOURL","companyName":"Gourmet Lanchonetes","city":"Campinas","country":"Brazil"},
{"customerID":"QUICK","companyName":"QUICK-Stop","city":"Cunewalde","country":"Germany"},
{"customerID":"FRANS","companyName":"Franchi S.p.A.","city":"Torino","country":"Italy"},
{"customerID":"OCEAN","companyName":"Océano Atlántico Ltda.","city":"Buenos Aires","country":"Argentina"},
{"customerID":"VAFFE","companyName":"Vaffeljernet","city":"Århus","country":"Denmark"},
{"customerID":"LACOR","companyName":"La corne d'abondance","city":"Versailles","country":"France"},
{"customerID":"SANTG","companyName":"Santé Gourmet","city":"Stavern","country":"Norway"},
{"customerID":"THEBI","companyName":"The Big Cheese","city":"Portland","country":"USA"},
{"customerID":"GODOS","companyName":"Godos Cocina Típica","city":"Sevilla","country":"Spain"},
{"customerID":"EASTC","companyName":"Eastern Connection","city":"London","country":"UK"},
{"customerID":"BOTTM","companyName":"Bottom-Dollar Markets","city":"Tsawassen","country":"Canada"},
```

In the address bar, enter the following URL:

```
http://localhost:5000/api/customers/alfki
```

You should see a JSON document returned containing only the customer named **Alfreds Futterkiste**, as shown in the following screenshot:

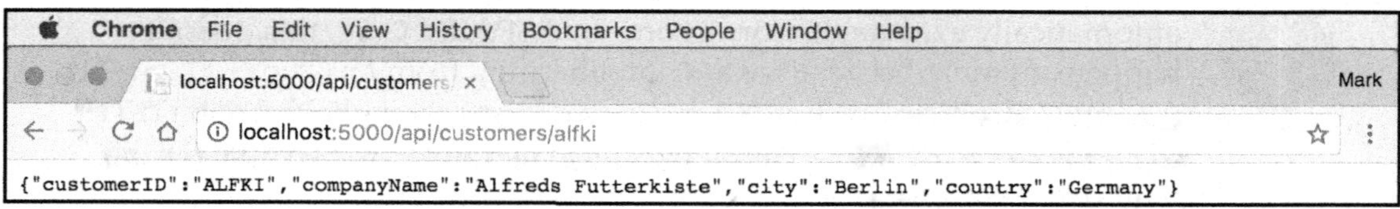

In the address bar, enter the following URL:

```
http://localhost:5000/api/customers/?country=USA
```

You should see a JSON document returned, containing the customers in the USA, as shown in the following screenshot:

Chrome File Edit View History Bookmarks People Window Help
localhost:5000/api/customers
Mark
localhost:5000/api/customers/?country=USA

[{"customerID":"LAZYK","companyName":"Lazy K Kountry Store","city":"Walla Walla","country":"USA"},
{"customerID":"TRAIH","companyName":"Trail's Head Gourmet Provisioners","city":"Kirkland","country":"USA"},
{"customerID":"THEBI","companyName":"The Big Cheese","city":"Portland","country":"USA"},
{"customerID":"SPLIR","companyName":"Split Rail Beer & Ale","city":"Lander","country":"USA"},
{"customerID":"RATTC","companyName":"Rattlesnake Canyon Grocery","city":"Albuquerque","country":"USA"},
{"customerID":"LONEP","companyName":"Lonesome Pine Restaurant","city":"Portland","country":"USA"},
{"customerID":"WHITC","companyName":"White Clover Markets","city":"Seattle","country":"USA"},
{"customerID":"HUNGC","companyName":"Hungry Coyote Import Store","city":"Elgin","country":"USA"},
{"customerID":"LETSS","companyName":"Let's Stop N Shop","city":"San Francisco","country":"USA"},
{"customerID":"OLDWO","companyName":"Old World Delicatessen","city":"Anchorage","country":"USA"},
{"customerID":"GREAL","companyName":"Great Lakes Food Market","city":"Eugene","country":"USA"},
{"customerID":"THECR","companyName":"The Cracker Box","city":"Butte","country":"USA"},
{"customerID":"SAVEA","companyName":"Save-a-lot Markets","city":"Boise","country":"USA"}]

Testing POST, PUT, DELETE, and other requests with Postman

There is a free application named **Postman** that makes it easy to test REST services like the one we just created. Postman is also available as an extension to Google Chrome, although the full application has more features.

In the real world, it would be sensible to test all the methods in our service, for example, the `POST` method, using a tool like Postman, as shown in the following screenshot, however the details of doing that are beyond the scope of this book:

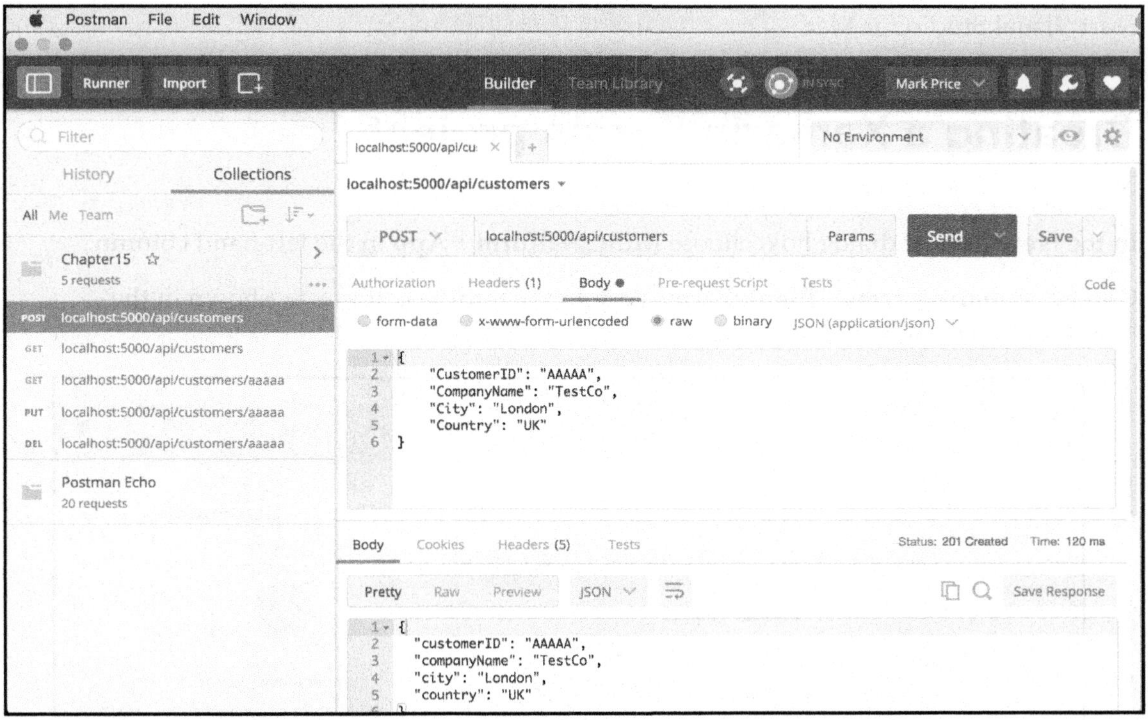

To learn more about Postman, visit the following link:
`https://www.getpostman.com/docs/`

In an **Integrated Terminal**, press *Ctrl* + *C* to stop the console application and shut down the Kestrel web server that is hosting your ASP.NET Core web application.

You are now ready to build a mobile app that calls the service.

Building mobile apps using Xamarin.Forms and Visual Studio for Mac

Start Visual Studio for Mac.

Creating a Xamarin.Forms project

Navigate to **File** | **New Solution...**

In the **New Project** dialog box, choose **Multiplatform** | **App** in the left-hand column.

Choose **Xamarin.Forms** | **Blank Forms App** in the middle column, as shown in the following screenshot:

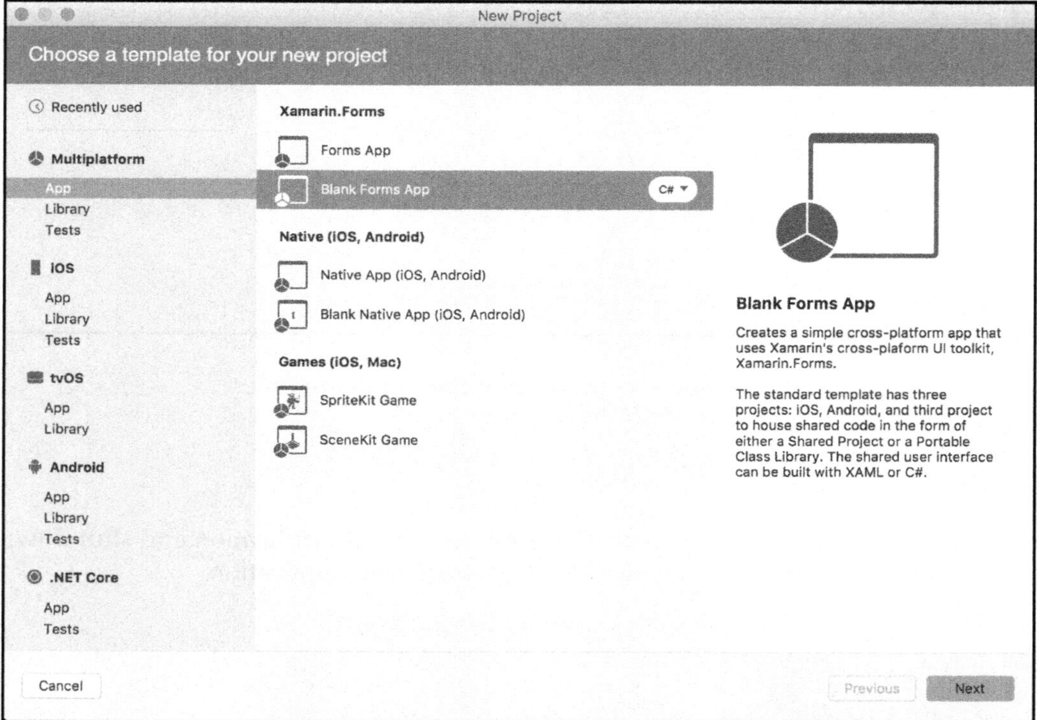

Click on **Next**.

Enter the **App Name** `Ch15_MobileApp`, and **Organization Identifier** `com.packt`, as shown in the following screenshot:

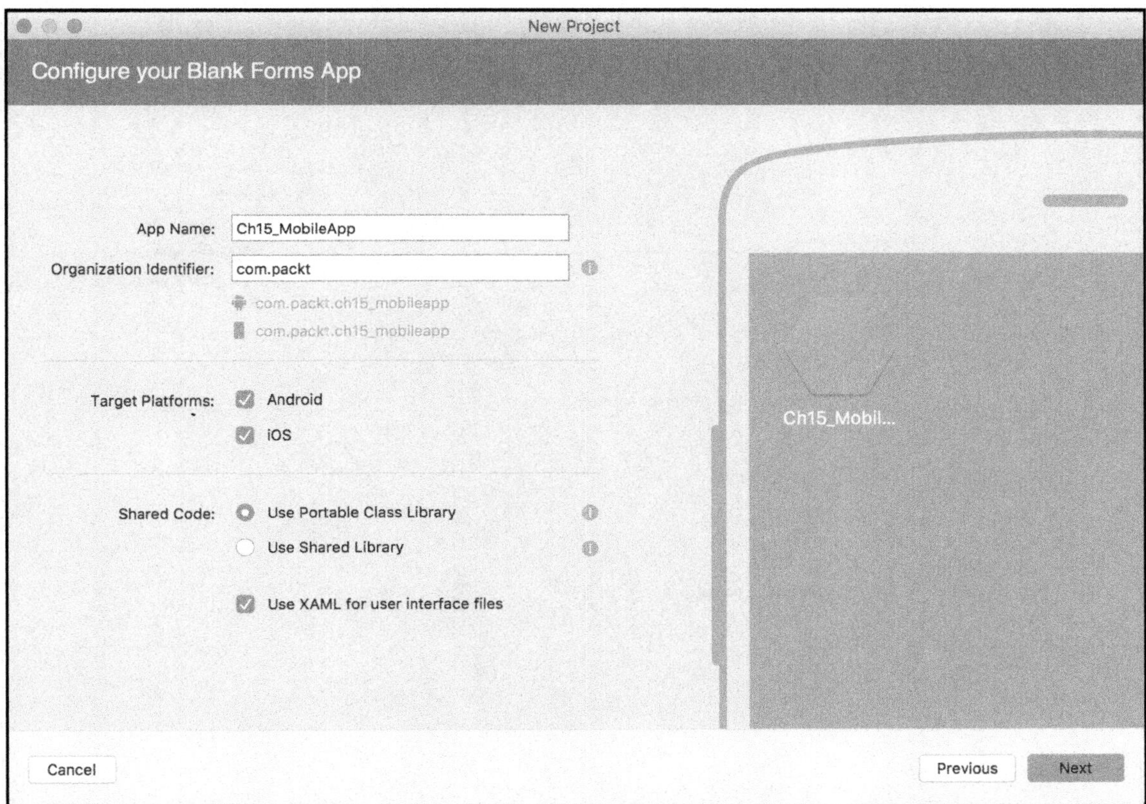

Click on **Next**.

Change the **Solution Name** to `Chapter15`, and **Location** to `/Users/[user_folder]/Code`, as shown in the following screenshot:

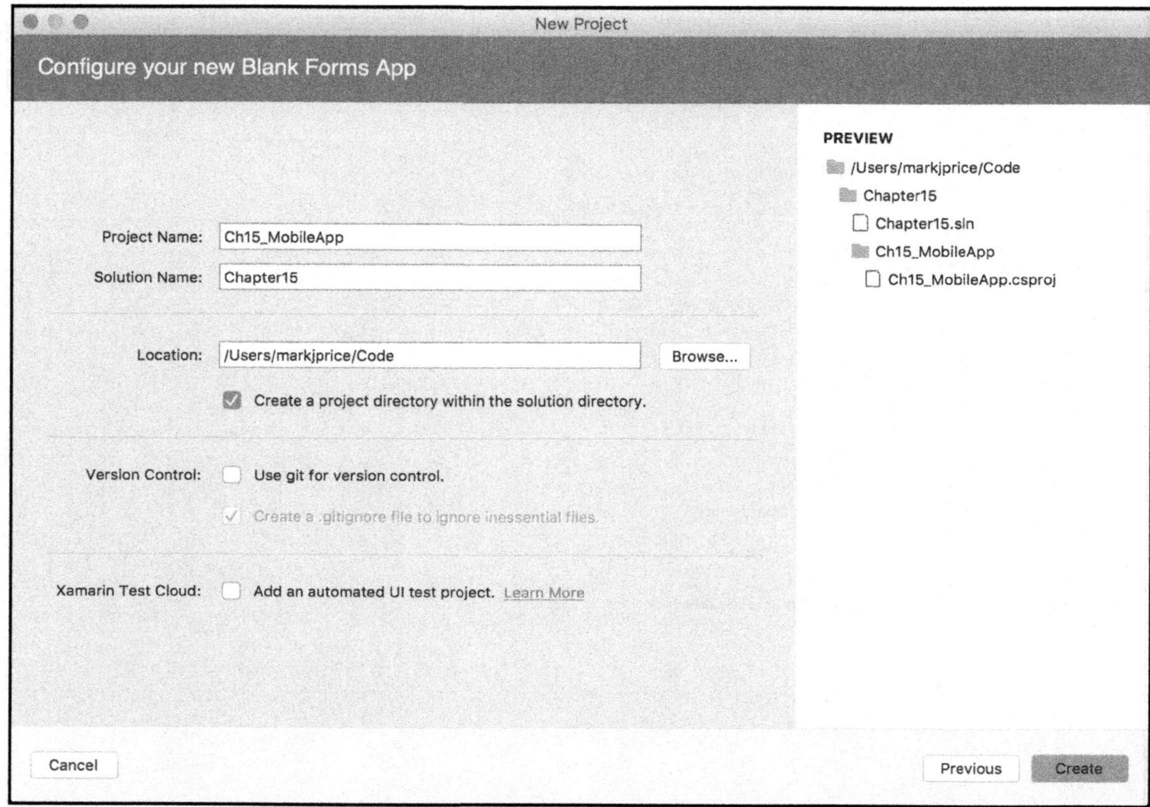

Click on **Create**.

After a few moments, the solution and project will be created, as shown in the following screenshot:

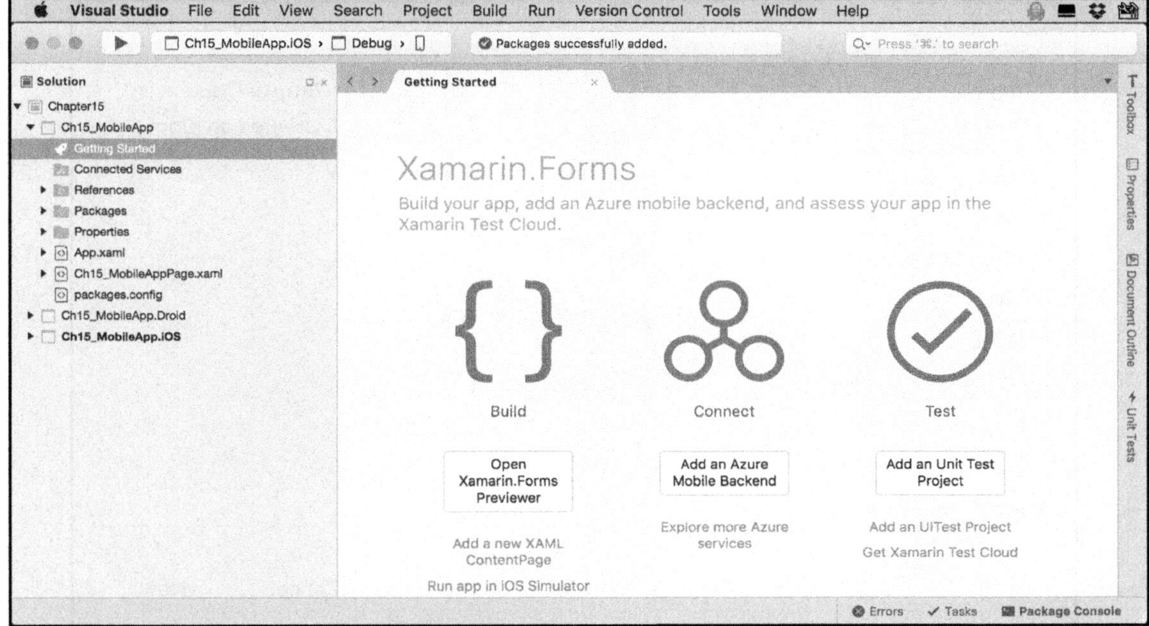

Creating a model

Right-click on the project named `Ch15_MobileApp`, choose **Add** | **New Folder**, and name it `Models`.

Right-click on the `Models` folder and choose **Add** | **New File...**

In the **New File** dialog, choose **General** | **Empty Class**, enter the name `Customer`, as shown in the following screenshot, and click on **New**:

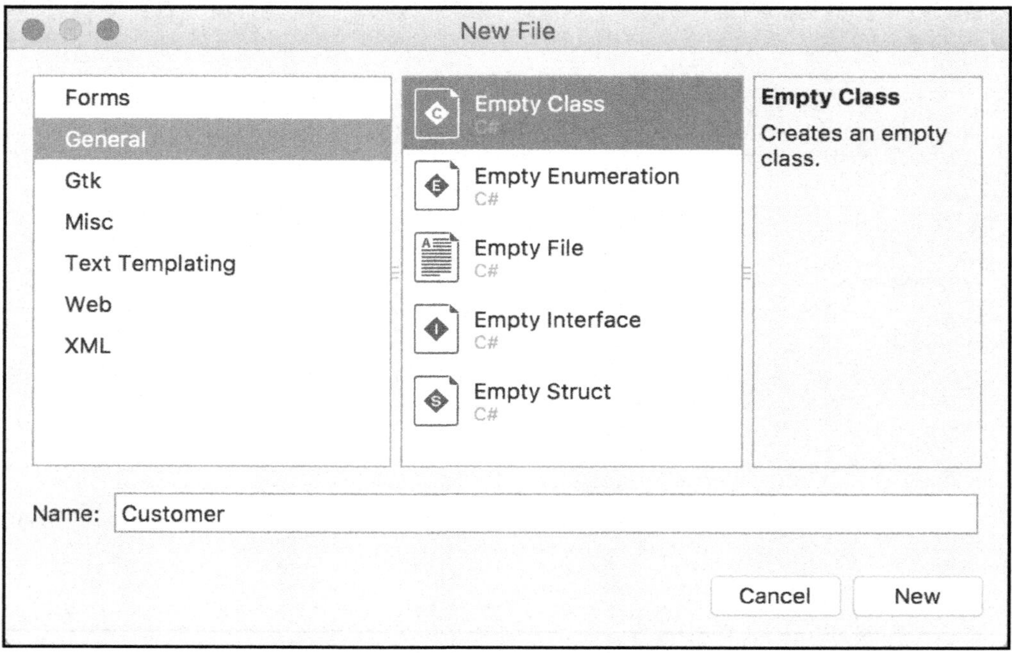

Modify the statements as shown in the following code, and note:

- The class implements `INotifyPropertyChanged` so a two-way bound user interface components such as `Editor` will update the property and vice versa. There is a `PropertyChanged` event that is raised whenever one of the properties is modified.
- After loading from the service, the customers will be cached locally in the mobile app using `ObservableCollection`. This supports notifications to any bound user interface components, such as `ListView`.
- As well as properties for storing values retrieved from the REST service, the class defines a readonly `Location` property. This will be used to bind to in a summary list of customers.
- For testing purposes, when the REST service is not available, there is a method to populate three sample customers:

```
using System.Collections.Generic;
using System.Collections.ObjectModel;
```

```
using System.ComponentModel;

namespace Ch15_MobileApp.Models
{
  public class Customer : INotifyPropertyChanged
  {
    public static IList<Customer> Customers;

    static Customer()
    {
      Customers = new ObservableCollection<Customer>();
    }

    public event PropertyChangedEventHandler PropertyChanged;

    private string customerID;
    private string companyName;
    private string contactName;
    private string city;
    private string country;
    private string phone;

    public string CustomerID
    {
      get { return customerID; }
      set
      {
        customerID = value;
        if (PropertyChanged != null) PropertyChanged(this,
          new PropertyChangedEventArgs("CustomerID"));
      }
    }

    public string CompanyName
    {
      get { return companyName; }
      set
      {
        companyName = value;
        if (PropertyChanged != null) PropertyChanged(this,
        new PropertyChangedEventArgs("CompanyName"));
      }
    }

    public string ContactName
    {
      get { return contactName; }
      set
```

```
    {
      contactName = value;
      if (PropertyChanged != null) PropertyChanged(this,
        new PropertyChangedEventArgs("ContactName"));
    }
  }
  public string City
  {
    get { return city; }
    set
    {
      city = value;
      if (PropertyChanged != null) PropertyChanged(this,
      new PropertyChangedEventArgs("City"));
    }
  }

  public string Country
  {
    get { return country; }
    set
    {
      country = value;
      if (PropertyChanged != null) PropertyChanged(this,
        new PropertyChangedEventArgs("Country"));
    }
  }

  public string Phone
  {
    get { return phone; }
    set
    {
      phone = value;
      if (PropertyChanged != null) PropertyChanged(this,
        new PropertyChangedEventArgs("Phone"));
    }
  }

  public string Location
  {
    get
    {
      return string.Format("{0}, {1}", City, Country);
    }
  }

  // for testing before calling web service
```

```
        public static void SampleData()
        {
          Customers.Clear();

          Customers.Add(new Customer
          {
            CustomerID = "ALFKI",
            CompanyName = "Alfreds Futterkiste",
            ContactName = "Maria Anders",
            City = "Berlin",
            Country = "Germany",
            Phone = "030-0074321"
          });

          Customers.Add(new Customer
          {
            CustomerID = "FRANK",
            CompanyName = "Frankenversand",
            ContactName = "Peter Franken",
            City = "München",
            Country = "Germany",
            Phone = "089-0877310"
          });

          Customers.Add(new Customer
          {
            CustomerID = "SEVES",
            CompanyName = "Seven Seas Imports",
            ContactName = "Hari Kumar",
            City = "London",
            Country = "UK",
            Phone = "(171) 555-1717"
          });
        }
      }
    }
```

Creating an interface for dialing phone numbers and implement for iOS and Android

Right-click on the `Ch15_MobileApp` folder and choose **New File...**.

Choose **General** | **Empty Interface**, name the file **IDialer**, and click on **New**, as shown in the following screenshot:

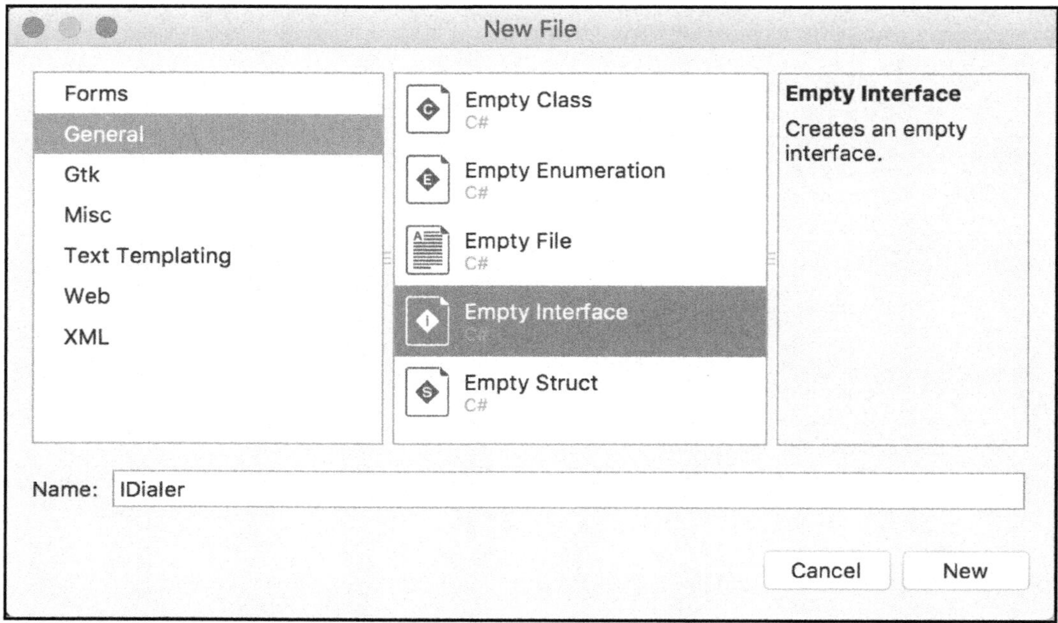

Modify the `IDialer` contents, as shown in the following code:

```
namespace Ch15_MobileApp
{
  public interface IDialer
  {
    bool Dial(string number);
  }
}
```

Right-click on the `Ch15_MobileApp.iOS` folder and choose **New File...**.

Choose **General** | **Empty Class**, name the file `PhoneDialer`, and click on **New**.

Modify its contents, as shown in the following code:

```
using Foundation;
using Ch15_MobileApp.iOS;
using UIKit;
using Xamarin.Forms;
```

```
[assembly: Dependency(typeof(PhoneDialer))]
namespace Ch15_MobileApp.iOS
{
  public class PhoneDialer : IDialer
  {
    public bool Dial(string number)
    {
      return UIApplication.SharedApplication.OpenUrl(
        new NSUrl("tel:" + number));
    }
  }
}
```

Right-click on the `Ch15_MobileApp.Droid` folder and choose **New File...**.

Choose **General** | **Empty Class**, name the file `PhoneDialer`, and click on **New**.

Modify its contents, as shown in the following code:

```
using Android.Content;
using Android.Telephony;
using Ch15_MobileApp.Droid;
using System.Linq;
using Xamarin.Forms;
using Uri = Android.Net.Uri;

[assembly: Dependency(typeof(PhoneDialer))]
namespace Ch15_MobileApp.Droid
{
  public class PhoneDialer : IDialer
  {
    public bool Dial(string number)
    {
      var context = Forms.Context;
      if (context == null)
      return false;

      var intent = new Intent(Intent.ActionCall);
      intent.SetData(Uri.Parse("tel:" + number));

      if (IsIntentAvailable(context, intent))
      {
        context.StartActivity(intent);
        return true;
      }

      return false;
   }
```

```
      public static bool IsIntentAvailable(Context context, Intent
    intent)
      {
        var packageManager = context.PackageManager;

        var list = packageManager.QueryIntentServices(intent, 0)
          .Union(packageManager.QueryIntentActivities(intent, 0));

        if (list.Any())
        return true;

        var manager = TelephonyManager.FromContext(context);
        return manager.PhoneType != PhoneType.None;
      }
    }
  }
```

In `Ch15_MobileApp.Droid`, expand **Properties**, and open `AndroidManifest.xml`.

In **Required permissions**, check the **CallPhone** permission.

Creating views for the customers list and customer details

Right-click on `Ch15_MobileAppPage.xaml`, click on **Remove**, and then click on **Remove from Project**, as shown in the following screenshot:

Right-click on the project named `Ch15_MobileApp`, choose **Add** | **New Folder**, and name it `Views`.

Right-click on the `Views` folder and choose **New File...**.

Choose **Forms** | **Forms ContentPage Xaml**, name the file `CustomersList`, and click on **New**, as shown in the following screenshot:

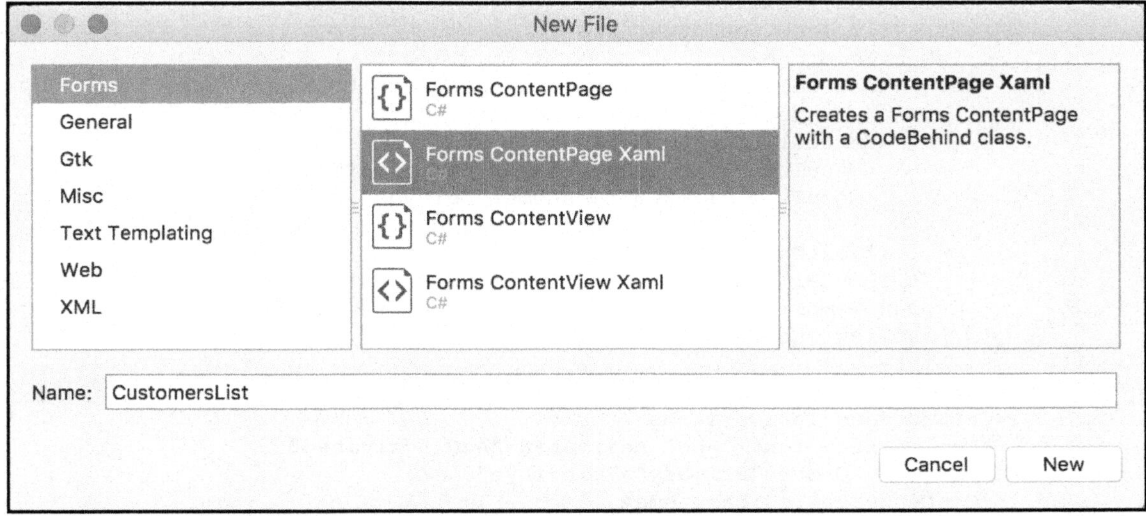

In `Ch15_MobileApp`, open `CustomersList.xaml`, and modify its contents, as shown in the following markup, and note:

- Event handlers have been written for: loading the customers when the view appears, a customer being tapped (to show detail), the list being swiped down to refresh, a customer being deleted by swiping left and then clicking a **Delete** button
- A data template defines how to display each customer: large text for the company name and smaller text for the location underneath
- An **Add** button is displayed so users can navigate to a detail view to add a new customer

```
<?xml version="1.0" encoding="UTF-8"?>
<ContentPage xmlns="http://xamarin.com/schemas/2014/forms"
  xmlns:x="http://schemas.microsoft.com/winfx/2009/xaml"
  x:Class="Ch15_MobileApp.CustomersList"
  Title="List">
  <ContentPage.Content>
    <ListView ItemsSource="{Binding .}"
      VerticalOptions="Center" HorizontalOptions="Center"
      IsPullToRefreshEnabled="True"
        ItemTapped="Customer_Tapped"
      Refreshing="Customers_Refreshing">
```

```
        <ListView.Header>
          <Label Text="Northwind Customers"
                 BackgroundColor="Silver" />
        </ListView.Header>
        <ListView.ItemTemplate>
          <DataTemplate>
              <TextCell Text="{Binding CompanyName}"
                    Detail="{Binding Location}">
              <TextCell.ContextActions>
               <MenuItem Clicked="Customer_Phoned" Text="Phone" />
               <MenuItem Clicked="Customer_Deleted"
                         Text="Delete" IsDestructive="True" />
              </TextCell.ContextActions>
            </TextCell>
          </DataTemplate>
        </ListView.ItemTemplate>
        </ListView>
        </ContentPage.Content>
      <ContentPage.ToolbarItems>
       <ToolbarItem Text="Add" Activated="Add_Activated"
                  Order="Primary" Priority="0" />
      </ContentPage.ToolbarItems>
    </ContentPage>
```

Modify the contents of `CustomersList.xaml.cs`, as shown in the following code:

```
using System.Threading.Tasks;
using Ch15_MobileApp.Models;
using Xamarin.Forms;

namespace Ch15_MobileApp
{
  public partial class CustomersList : ContentPage
  {
    public CustomersList()
    {
      InitializeComponent();
      Customer.SampleData();
      BindingContext = Customer.Customers;
    }

    async void Customer_Tapped(object sender,
    Xamarin.Forms.ItemTappedEventArgs e)
    {
      Customer c = e.Item as Customer;
      if (c == null) return;
      // navigate to the detail view and show the tapped customer
      await Navigation.PushAsync(new CustomerDetail(c));
```

```
    }

    async void Customers_Refreshing(
      object sender, System.EventArgs e)
    {
      ListView listView = sender as ListView;
      listView.IsRefreshing = true;
      // simulate a refresh
      await Task.Delay(1500);
      listView.IsRefreshing = false;
    }

    void Customer_Deleted(object sender, System.EventArgs e)
    {
      MenuItem menuItem = sender as MenuItem;
      Customer c = menuItem.BindingContext as Customer;
      Customer.Customers.Remove(c);
    }

    async void Customer_Phoned(object sender, System.EventArgs e)
    {
      MenuItem menuItem = sender as MenuItem;
      Customer c = menuItem.BindingContext as Customer;
      if (await this.DisplayAlert("Dial a Number",
        "Would you like to call " + c.Phone + "?",
        "Yes", "No"))
      {
        var dialer = DependencyService.Get<IDialer>();
        if (dialer != null)
        dialer.Dial(c.Phone);
      }
    }

    async void Add_Activated(object sender, System.EventArgs e)
    {
      await Navigation.PushAsync(new CustomerDetail());
    }
  }
}
```

Add another **Forms ContentPage Xaml** named `CustomerDetails`.

Open `CustomerDetails.xaml`, and modify its contents, as shown in the following markup:

```
<?xml version="1.0" encoding="UTF-8"?>
<ContentPage xmlns="http://xamarin.com/schemas/2014/forms"
xmlns:x="http://schemas.microsoft.com/winfx/2009/xaml"
```

```
x:Class="Ch15_MobileApp.CustomerDetail" Title="Edit Customer">
  <ContentPage.Content>
    <StackLayout VerticalOptions="Fill"
      HorizontalOptions="Fill">
      <Grid BackgroundColor="Silver">
      <Grid.ColumnDefinitions>
        <ColumnDefinition/>
        <ColumnDefinition/>
      </Grid.ColumnDefinitions>
    <Grid.RowDefinitions>
      <RowDefinition/>
      <RowDefinition/>
      <RowDefinition/>
      <RowDefinition/>
    </Grid.RowDefinitions>
      <Label Text="Customer ID"
        VerticalOptions="Center" Margin="6" />
      <Editor Text="{Binding CustomerID, Mode=TwoWay}"
              Grid.Column="1" />
      <Label Text="Company Name" Grid.Row="1"
        VerticalOptions="Center" Margin="6" />
      <Editor Text="{Binding CompanyName, Mode=TwoWay}"
        Grid.Column="1" Grid.Row="1" />
      <Label Text="Contact Name" Grid.Row="2"
        VerticalOptions="Center" Margin="6" />
      <Editor Text="{Binding ContactName, Mode=TwoWay}"
        Grid.Column="1" Grid.Row="2" />
      <Label Text="City" Grid.Row="3"
        VerticalOptions="Center" Margin="6" />
      <Editor Text="{Binding City, Mode=TwoWay}"
        Grid.Column="1" Grid.Row="3" />
      <Label Text="Country" Grid.Row="4"
        VerticalOptions="Center" Margin="6" />
      <Editor Text="{Binding Country, Mode=TwoWay}"
        Grid.Column="1" Grid.Row="4" />
      <Label Text="Phone" Grid.Row="5"
        VerticalOptions="Center" Margin="6" />
      <Editor Text="{Binding Phone, Mode=TwoWay}"
        Grid.Column="1" Grid.Row="5" />
     </Grid>
     <Button x:Name="InsertButton" Text="Insert Customer"
          Clicked="InsertButton_Clicked" />
    </StackLayout>
  </ContentPage.Content>
</ContentPage>
```

Open `CustomerDetail.xaml.cs`, and modify its contents, as shown in the following code:

```
using Ch15_MobileApp.Models;
using Xamarin.Forms;

namespace Ch15_MobileApp
{
  public partial class CustomerDetail : ContentPage
  {
    private bool newCustomer = false;

    public CustomerDetail()
    {
      InitializeComponent();
      BindingContext = new Customer();
      newCustomer = true;
      Title = "Add Customer";
    }

    public CustomerDetail(Customer customer)
    {
      InitializeComponent();
      BindingContext = customer;
      InsertButton.IsVisible = false;
    }

    async void InsertButton_Clicked(
    object sender, System.EventArgs e)
    {
      if (newCustomer)
      {
        Customer.Customers.Add((Customer)BindingContext);
      }
      await Navigation.PopAsync(animated: true);
    }
  }
}
```

Open `App.xaml.cs`.

Modify the statement that sets `MainPage` to create an instance of `CustomersList` wrapped in `NavigationPage`, as shown in the following code:

```
MainPage = new NavigationPage(new CustomersList());
```

Test the mobile app with iOS

Click on the **Start** button in the toolbar, as shown in the following screenshot, or choose **Run** | **Start Debugging**:

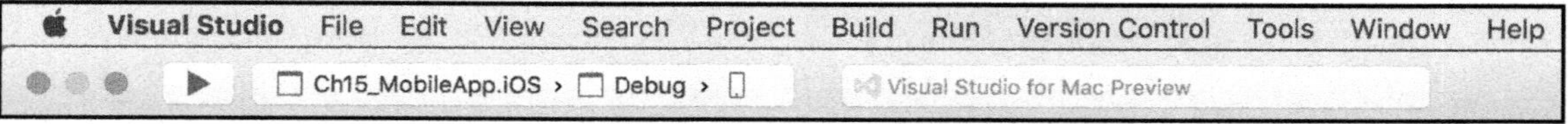

After a few moments, the **Simulator** will show your running mobile app, as shown in the following screenshot:

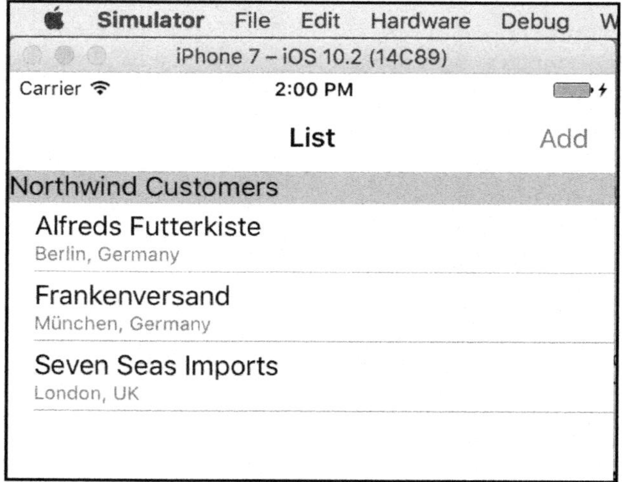

Click on a customer and modify its **Company Name**, as shown in the following screenshot:

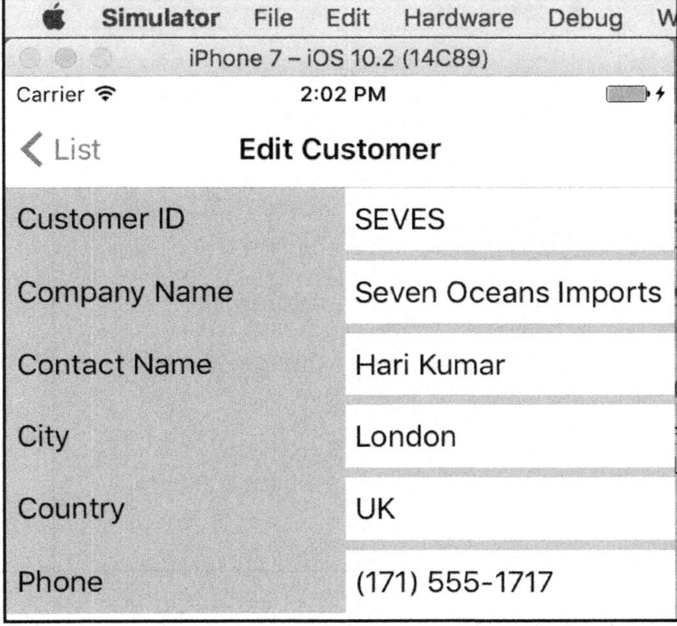

Click on **List** to return to the list of customers and note that the company name has been updated.

Click on **Add**.

Fill in the fields for a new customer, as shown in the following screenshot:

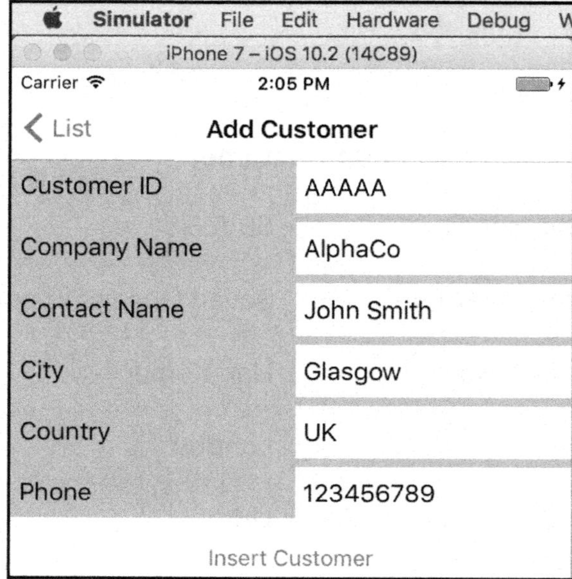

Click on **Insert Customer** and note that the new customer has been added to the list, as shown in the following screenshot:

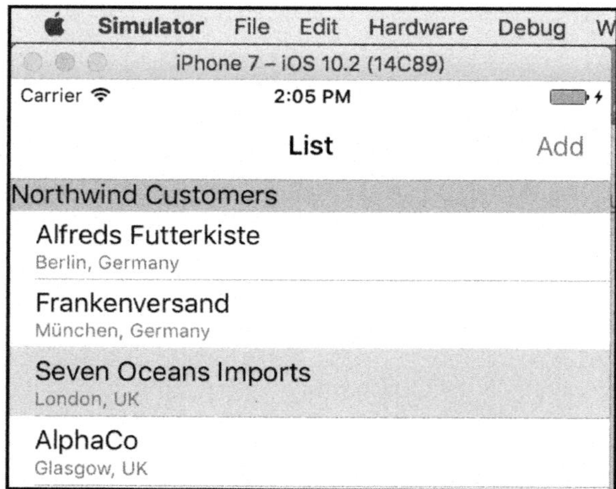

Slide one of the customers to the left to reveal two action buttons, **Phone** and **Delete**, as shown in the following screenshot:

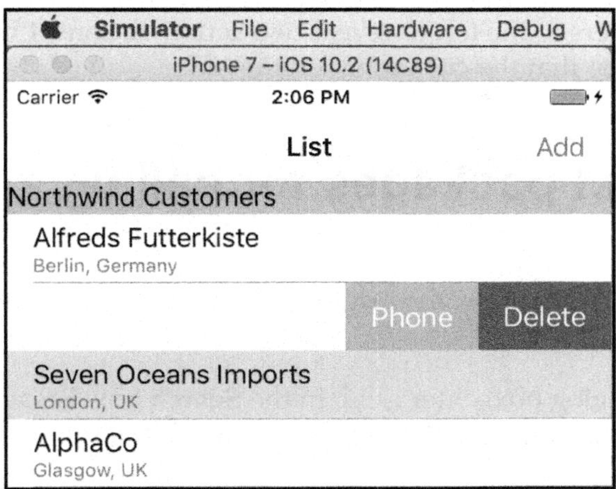

Click on **Phone** and note the prompt to the user, as shown in the following screenshot:

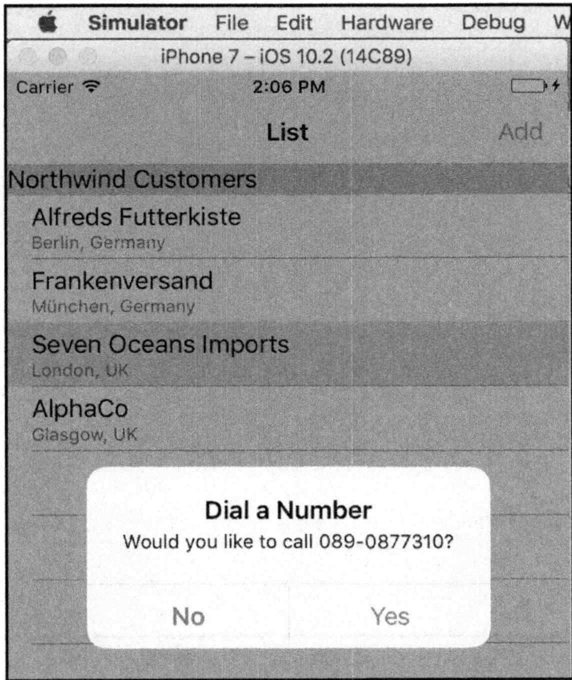

Slide one of the customers to the left to reveal two action buttons, **Phone** and **Delete**, and click on **Delete**, and note that the customer is removed.

Adding NuGet packages for calling a REST service

In the project named `Ch15_MobileApp`, right-click on the folder named `Packages` and choose **Add Packages...**.

In the **Add Packages** dialog box, enter `http` in the **Search** box. Select the package named **System.Net.Http** and click on **Add Package**, as shown in the following screenshot:

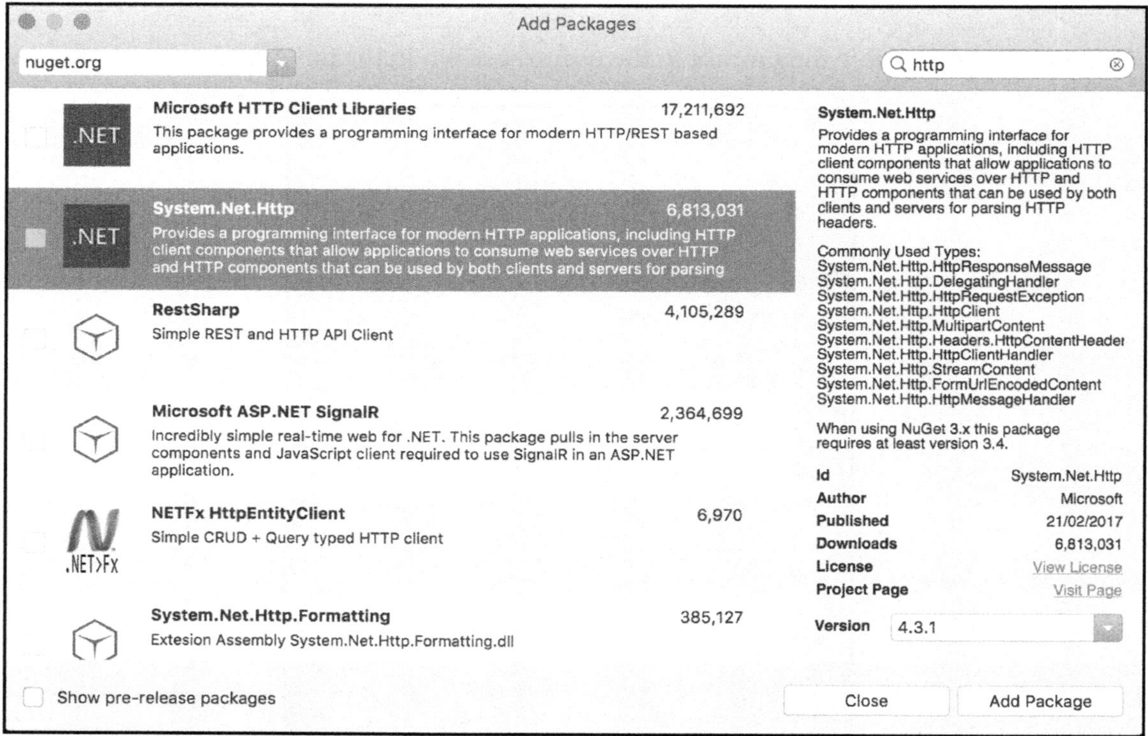

In the **License Acceptance** dialog box, click on **Accept**.

In the project named `Ch15_MobileApp`, right-click on the folder named `Packages` and choose **Add Packages...**.

In the **Add Packages** dialog box, enter `Json.NET` in the **Search** box. Select the package named **Json.NET** and click on **Add Package**.

Getting customers from the service

Open `CustomersList.xaml.cs` and import the following highlighted namespaces:

```
using System.Threading.Tasks;
using Ch15_MobileApp.Models;
using Xamarin.Forms;
using System;
using System.Linq;
using System.Collections.Generic;
using System.Net.Http;
using System.Net.Http.Headers;
using Newtonsoft.Json;
```

Modify the `CustomersList` constructor to load the list of customers using the service proxy instead of the `SampleData` method, as shown in the following code:

```
public CustomersList()
{
  InitializeComponent();

  //Customer.SampleData();

  var client = new HttpClient();
  client.BaseAddress = new Uri(
    "http://localhost:5000/api/customers");

  client.DefaultRequestHeaders.Accept.Add(
    new MediaTypeWithQualityHeaderValue("application/json"));

  HttpResponseMessage response = client.GetAsync("").Result;

  response.EnsureSuccessStatusCode();

  string content =
    response.Content.ReadAsStringAsync().Result;
  var customersFromService = JsonConvert.DeserializeObject
  <IEnumerable<Customer>>(content);

    foreach (Customer c in customersFromService
    .OrderBy(customer => customer.CompanyName))
  {
    Customer.Customers.Add(c);
```

```
        }

        BindingContext = Customer.Customers;
    }
```

In Visual Studio Code, run the `Ch15_WebApi` project.

In Visual Studio for Mac, run the `Ch15_MobileApp` project, and note that 91 customers are loaded from the web service, as shown in the following screenshot:

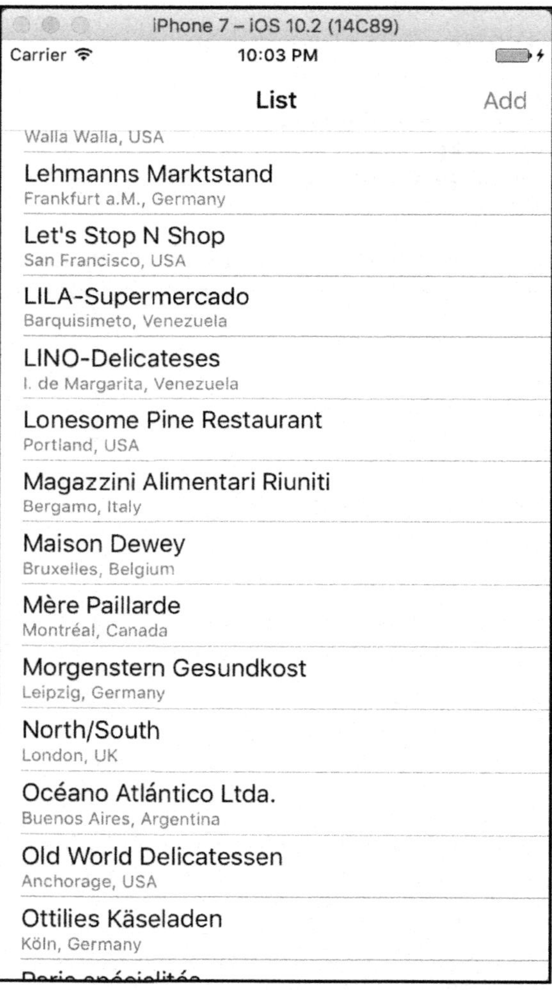

Practicing and exploring

Test your knowledge and understanding by answering some questions, get some hands-on practice, and explore this chapter's topics with deeper research.

Exercise 15.1 – test your knowledge

Answer the following questions:

1. How does ASP.NET Core distinguish a request for MVC from a request for Web API?
2. What data formats does ASP.NET Core Web API support by default?
3. What is the difference between Xamarin and Xamarin.Forms?
4. What types of cell are supported by the ListView?

Exercise 15.2 – explore topics

Use the following links to read more about this chapter's topics:

- **Building Web APIs:** `https://docs.microsoft.com/en-us/aspnet/core/mvc/web-api/`
- **Visual Studio Code for Mac developers**: `https://channel9.msdn.com/Series/Visual-Studio-Code-for-Mac-Developers`
- **Xamarin.Forms:** `https://www.xamarin.com/forms`
- **Xamarin Developer Center**: `https://developer.xamarin.com`

Summary

In this chapter, you learned how to build an ASP.NET Core Web API service that can be hosted cross-platform. You also learned how to build a mobile app using Xamarin.Forms that is cross-platform for iOS and Android (and potentially Windows Mobile) that consumes a REST/HTTP service by using the `HttpClient` and `Newtonsoft.Json` packages.

In the next chapter, you will learn how to package and deploy your .NET Core code.

16
Packaging and Deploying Your Code Cross-Platform

This chapter is about porting existing .NET Framework codebases to .NET Core, publishing your .NET Core apps and libraries, creating and distributing NuGet packages, and deploying your code cross-platform and to the cloud.

This chapter covers the following topics:

- Porting to .NET Core
- Sharing code cross-platform with .NET Standard class libraries
- Understanding NuGet packages
- Publishing your applications
- Deploying to the cloud
- Developing on and for Linux

Porting to .NET Core

If you are an existing .NET developer, then you may have existing applications written for older platforms, such as .NET Framework, that you are wondering if you should port to .NET Core.

You should consider carefully if porting is the right choice for your code. Sometimes, the best choice is not to port.

Could you port?

.NET Core has great support for the following types of applications:

- **ASP.NET Core MVC** web applications
- **ASP.NET Core Web API** web services (REST/HTTP)
- **Universal Windows Platform** (UWP) applications
- **Console** applications

.NET Core does not support the following types of applications:

- **ASP.NET Web Forms** web applications
- **Windows Forms** desktop applications
- **Windows Presentation Foundation (WPF)** desktop applications
- **Silverlight** applications

Luckily, WPF and Silverlight applications use a dialect of XAML which is like the XAML dialect used by UWP and Xamarin.Forms.

Should you port?

Even if you *could* port, *should* you? What benefits do you gain? Some common benefits include:

- **Deployment to Linux or Docker**: These OSes are lightweight and cost-effective as web application and web service platforms, especially when compared to Windows Server.
- **Removal of dependency on IIS and** `System.Web.dll`: Even if you continue to deploy to Windows Server, ASP.NET Core can be hosted on lightweight, higher performance Kestrel (or other) web servers.
- **Command-line tools** that developers and administrators use to automate their tasks are written as console applications. The ability to run a single tool cross-platform is very useful.

Differences between .NET Framework and .NET Core

There are three key differences:

- .NET Core is distributed as NuGet packages, so each application can be deployed with its own app-local copy of the version of .NET Core that it needs. .NET Framework is distributed as a system-wide shared set of assemblies (literally, in the Global Assembly Cache).
- .NET Core is split into small, layered components, so a minimal deployment can be performed. .NET Framework is a monolithic deployment.
- .NET Core removes unnecessary components. As well as removing older technologies such as Windows Forms and Web Forms, .NET Core removes non-cross-platform features such as AppDomains, .NET Remoting, and binary serialization.

Understanding the .NET Portability Analyzer

Microsoft has a useful tool that you can run against your existing applications to generate a report for porting. Watch a demonstration of the tool at the following link:

`https://channel9.msdn.com/Blogs/Seth-Juarez/A-Brief-Look-at-the-NET-Portability-Analyzer`

Sharing code cross-platform with .NET Standard class libraries

Before .NET Standard, there was **Portable Class Libraries** (**PCL**). With PCLs, you can create a library of code and explicitly specify which platforms that you want the library to support, such as Xamarin, Silverlight, Windows 8, and so on. Your library can then use the intersection of APIs that are supported by the specified platforms.

Microsoft has realized that this is unsustainable, so they have been working on .NET Standard—a single API that all future .NET platforms will support.

If you want to create a library of types that will work across .NET Framework (on Windows), .NET Core (on Windows, macOS, and Linux), and Xamarin (on iOS, Android, and Windows Mobile), you can do so most easily with .NET Standard.

The following table summarizes versions of .NET Standard, and which platforms they support. Note:

- .NET Core and Xamarin support .NET Standard 1.6
- .NET Framework 4.6.1 already supports .NET Standard 2.0, but does not support .NET Standard 1.6
- We must wait for a future release of .NET Core and Xamarin before all platforms are synchronized and support .NET Standard 2.0

Platform	**1.1**	**1.2**	**1.3**	**1.4**	**1.5**	**1.6**	**2.0**
.NET Core	→	→	→	→	→	1.0, 1.1	vNext
.NET Framework	4.5	4.5.1	4.6	→	→	→	4.6.1
Xamarin/Mono	→	→	→	→	→	4.6	vNext
UWP	→	→	→	10	→	→	vNext

Creating a .NET Standard class library

We will create a class library using .NET Standard so that it can be used cross-platform (at least in theory!).

Using Visual Studio 2017

Start Microsoft Visual Studio 2017.

In Visual Studio, press *Ctrl* + *Shift* + *N* or choose **File** | **New** | **Project...**.

In the **New Project** dialog, in the **Installed** | **Templates** list, expand **Visual C#**, and then select **.NET Standard**. In the list at the center, select **Class Library (.NET Standard)**, type the name `Ch16_SharedLibrary`, change the location to `C:\Code`, type the solution name `Chapter16`, and then click on **OK**, as shown in the following screenshot:

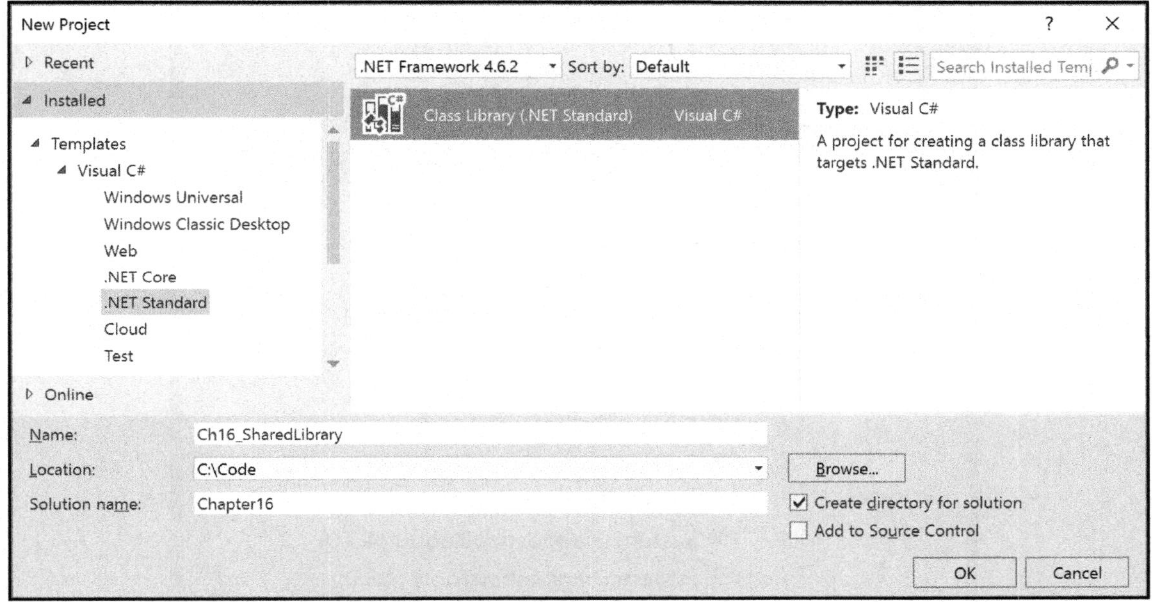

In **Solution Explorer**, expand **Dependencies**, **SDK**, and **NETStandard.Library**, and note the long list of packages that are included, as shown in the following screenshot:

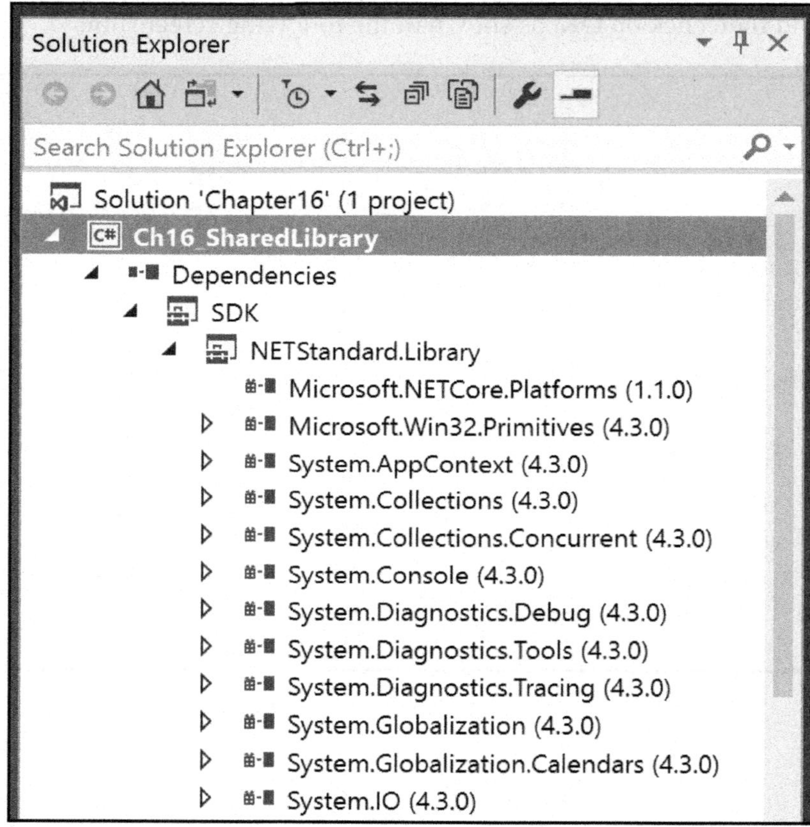

Right-click on `Ch16_SharedLibrary` and choose **Edit Ch16_SharedLibrary.csproj**.

Note a Class Library (.NET Standard) targets version 1.4 by default, as shown in the following markup:

```
<Project Sdk="Microsoft.NET.Sdk">

  <PropertyGroup>
    <TargetFramework>netstandard1.4</TargetFramework>
  </PropertyGroup>

</Project>
```

Using Visual Studio Code on macOS

In the `Code` folder in your user folder, create a subfolder named `Chapter16`, and then a sub-sub-folder named `Ch16_SharedLibrary`.

Start Visual Studio Code and open the `Code/Chapter16/Ch16_SharedLibrary` folder.

In Visual Studio Code, navigate to **View** | **Integrated Terminal**, and then enter the following command:

```
dotnet new classlib
```

Click on the `Ch16_SharedLibrary.csproj` file and then note that a class library generated by the `dotnet` CLI targets version 1.4 by default, as shown in the following markup:

```
<Project Sdk="Microsoft.NET.Sdk">

  <PropertyGroup>
    <TargetFramework>netstandard1.4</TargetFramework>
  </PropertyGroup>

</Project>
```

Understanding NuGet packages

.NET Core is split into a set of packages. Each of these packages represents a single assembly of the same name. For example, the `System.Collections` package contains the `System.Collections.dll` assembly.

The following are the benefits of packages:

- Packages can ship on their own schedule
- Packages can be tested independently of other packages
- Packages can support different OSes and CPUs
- Packages can have dependencies specific to only one library
- Apps are smaller because unreferenced packages aren't part of the distribution

The following table lists some of the more important packages:

Package	Important types
System.Runtime	Object, String, Array
System.Collections	List<T>, Dictionary<TKey, TValue>
System.Net.Http	HttpClient, HttpResponseMessage
System.IO.FileSystem	File, Directory
System.Reflection	Assembly, TypeInfo, MethodInfo

Referencing packages

Packages are referenced in the project file; for example, let us explicitly reference the `System.Collections.Specialized` package version 4.3, so that we can use the `NameValueCollection` type.

In both Visual Studio 2017 and Visual Studio Code, open `Ch16_SharedLibrary.csproj`, and add the following markup:

```
<ItemGroup>
  <PackageReference Include="System.Collections.Specialized"
                    Version="4.3" />
</ItemGroup>
```

In `Class1.cs`, import the `System.Collections.Specialized` namespace, and declare a public field of type `NameValueCollection`, as shown in the following code:

```
using System.Collections.Specialized;

namespace Ch16_SharedLibrary
{
  public class Class1
  {
    public NameValueCollection stuff;
  }
}
```

Understanding metapackages

Metapackages describe a set of packages that are used together. Metapackages are referenced just like any other NuGet package. By referencing a metapackage, you have, in effect, added a reference to each of its dependent packages.

Visual Studio 2017 nicely shows the relationship between metapackages, packages, and assemblies, as shown in the following screenshot:

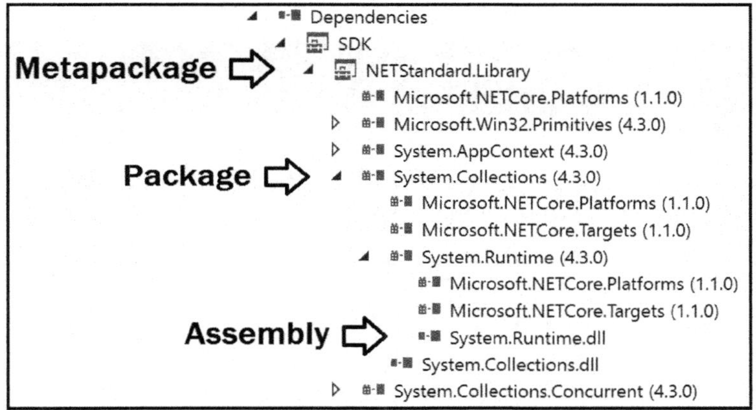

Metapackages are often just referred to as packages in Microsoft's documentation, as you are about to see.

The following list contains links to some common metapackages and packages, including an official list of their dependencies:

- `https://www.nuget.org/packages/Microsoft.NETCore.App`
- `https://www.nuget.org/packages/NETStandard.Library`
- `https://www.nuget.org/packages/Microsoft.NETCore.Runtime.CoreCLR`
- `https://www.nuget.org/packages/System.IO`
- `https://www.nuget.org/packages/System.Collections`
- `https://www.nuget.org/packages/System.Runtime`

If you were to go to the link for the `Microsoft.NETCore.App` metapackage, you would see the information shown in the following screenshot:

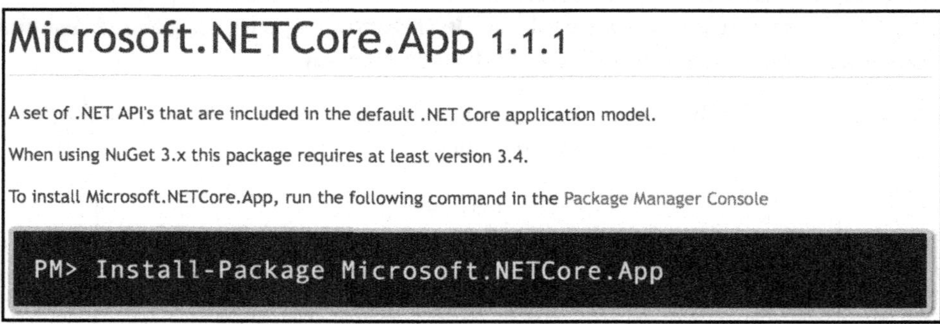

If you were to scroll down the page, you would see the list of dependencies for the metapackage, as shown in the following screenshot:

.NETCoreApp 1.1
Libuv (>= 1.9.1)
Microsoft.CodeAnalysis.CSharp (>= 1.3.0)
Microsoft.CodeAnalysis.VisualBasic (>= 1.3.0)
Microsoft.CSharp (>= 4.3.0)
Microsoft.DiaSymReader.Native (>= 1.4.1)
Microsoft.NETCore.DotNetHostPolicy (>= 1.1.0)
Microsoft.NETCore.Runtime.CoreCLR (>= 1.1.1)
Microsoft.VisualBasic (>= 10.1.0)
NETStandard.Library (>= 1.6.1)
System.Buffers (>= 4.3.0)
System.Collections.Immutable (>= 1.3.0)

Note that `Microsoft.NETCore.App` 1.1.1 has a dependency on `NETStandard.Library` 1.6.1.

Understanding Frameworks

There is a two-way relationship between frameworks and packages. Packages define the APIs, Frameworks group packages. A Framework without any packages would not define any APIs.

If you have a strong understanding of interfaces and types that implement them, you might find the following URL useful for grasping how packages and their APIs relate to frameworks such as the various .NET Standard versions: `https://gist.github.com/davidfowl/8939f305567e1755412d6dc0b8baf1b7`

.NET Core packages each support a set of frameworks. For example, the `System.IO.FileSystem` package supports the following frameworks:

- .NETStandard,Version=1.3
- .NETFramework,Version=4.6
- 6 Xamarin platforms (for example, xamarinios10)

The two most important package-based frameworks for .NET Core are these:

- `NETStandard.Library`: about 40 packages and will support all varieties of .NET with version 2.0 and later
- `Microsoft.NETCore.App`: about 60 packages that add console support and other APIs, but limits you to running on .NET Core

Remember—`Microsoft.NETCore.App` is a superset of `NETStandard.Library`.

Good Practice
Choose `NETStandard.Library` if you are creating a class library that is intended to be referenced by multiple platforms, such as .NET Framework and Xamarin, as well as .NET Core.

Fixing dependencies

To consistently restore packages and write reliable code, it's important that you fix your dependencies. Fixing dependencies means you are using the same family of packages released for a specific version of .NET Core, for example, 1.0.

To fix dependencies, every package should have a single version with no additional qualifiers. Additional qualifiers include release candidates (rc4) and wild cards (*). Wildcards are especially dangerous because it could result in the restore of incompatible packages that break your code.

The following dependencies are NOT fixed and should be avoided:

```
<PackageReference Include="System.Net.Http"
                  Version="4.1.0-*" />
```

```
<PackageReference Include="Microsoft.NETCore.App"
                  Version="1.0.0-rc4-00454-00" />
```

Good Practice
Microsoft guarantees that if you fixed your dependencies to what ships with a specific version of .NET Core, for example, 1.1, those packages will all work together. Always fix your dependencies.

Switching to a different .NET Standard

It is easy to target a different .NET Standard in a class library.

In either Visual Studio 2017 or Visual Studio Code, modify the `Ch16_SharedLibrary.csproj` file to use version 1.1, as shown highlighted in the following markup:

```
<Project Sdk="Microsoft.NET.Sdk">

  <PropertyGroup>
    <TargetFramework>netstandard1.1</TargetFramework>
  </PropertyGroup>

  <ItemGroup>
    <PackageReference Include="System.Collections.Specialized"
                      Version="4.3" />
  </ItemGroup>

</Project>
```

In Visual Studio 2017, you will note that when you save the change, you immediately get a restore error, as shown in the following screenshot:

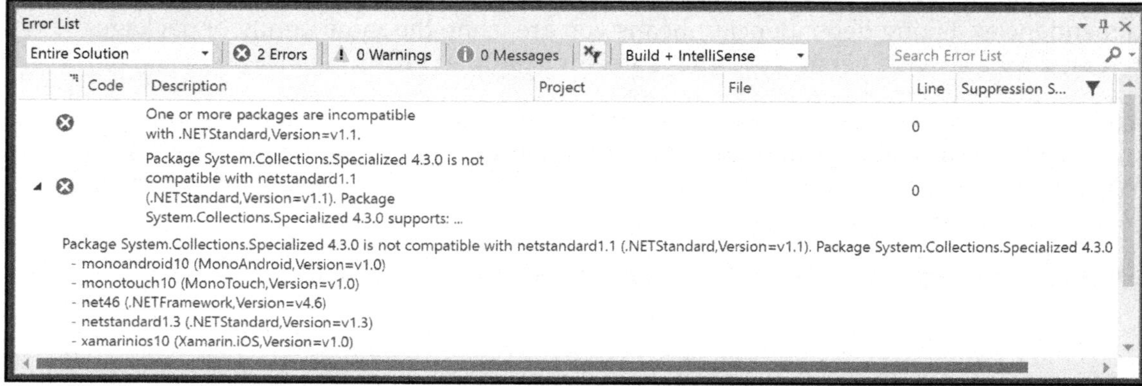

In Visual Studio Code, in the Terminal, enter the command: `dotnet restore`, and you will see a similar error message.

The error message tells us that the `System.Collections.Specialized` package that we want to use is not compatible with .NET Standard 1.1, and that the lowest version of .NET Standard that *is* compatible is version 1.3.

Modify the version to 1.3 and restore packages. This will fix the error.

Bear in mind that lower version numbers of .NET Standard are always subsets of higher version numbers.

Publishing your applications

There are two ways to publish and deploy a .NET Core application:

- Framework-dependent
- Self-contained

If you choose to deploy your application and its dependencies, but not .NET Core itself, then you rely on .NET Core already being on the target computer. This works well for web applications deployed to a server because .NET Core and lots of other web applications are likely already on the server.

Sometimes, you want to be able to give someone a USB key containing your application and know that it can execute on their computer. You want to perform a self-contained deployment. The size of the deployment files will be larger, but I will know that it will just work.

Creating a console application to publish

Add a new console application project named `Ch16_DotNetCoreEverywhere`.

Modify the code to look like this:

```
using System;

namespace Ch16_DotNetCoreEverywhere
{
```

```
        class Program
        {
          static void Main(string[] args)
          {
            Console.WriteLine("I can run everywhere!");
          }
        }
      }
```

Open `Ch16_DotNetCoreEverywhere.csproj`, and add the runtime identifiers to target four operating systems, as shown in the following markup:

```
<RuntimeIdentifiers>win10-x64;osx.10.12-x64;rhel.7-x64;ubuntu.14.04-
x64</RuntimeIdentifiers>
```

The RID value `win10-64` means Windows 10 or Windows Server 2016. The RID value `osx.10.12-x64` means macOS Sierra. You can find the full list of currently supported **Runtime IDentifier** (RID) values at the following link: https://docs.microsoft.com/en-us/dotnet/articles/core/rid-catalog

Publishing with Visual Studio 2017

In Visual Studio 2017, right-click `Ch16_DotNetCoreEverywhere`, and choose **Publish...**, and then click **Publish**, as shown in the following screenshot:

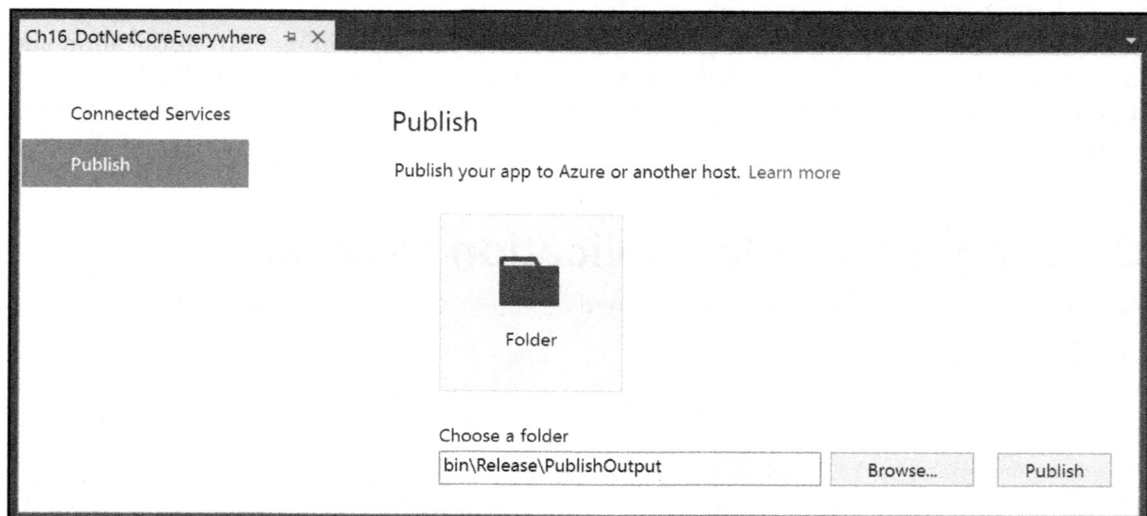

You have now published the Windows version, as shown in the following screenshot:

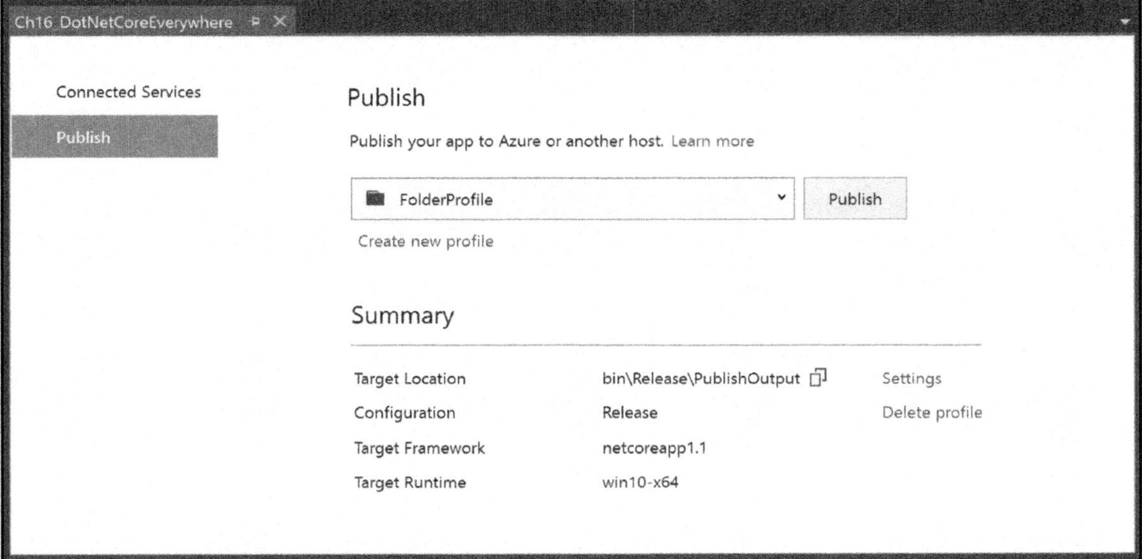

Click **Settings**, and change the **Target Runtime** to **osx.10.12-x64**, as shown in the following screenshot, and then click **Save**:

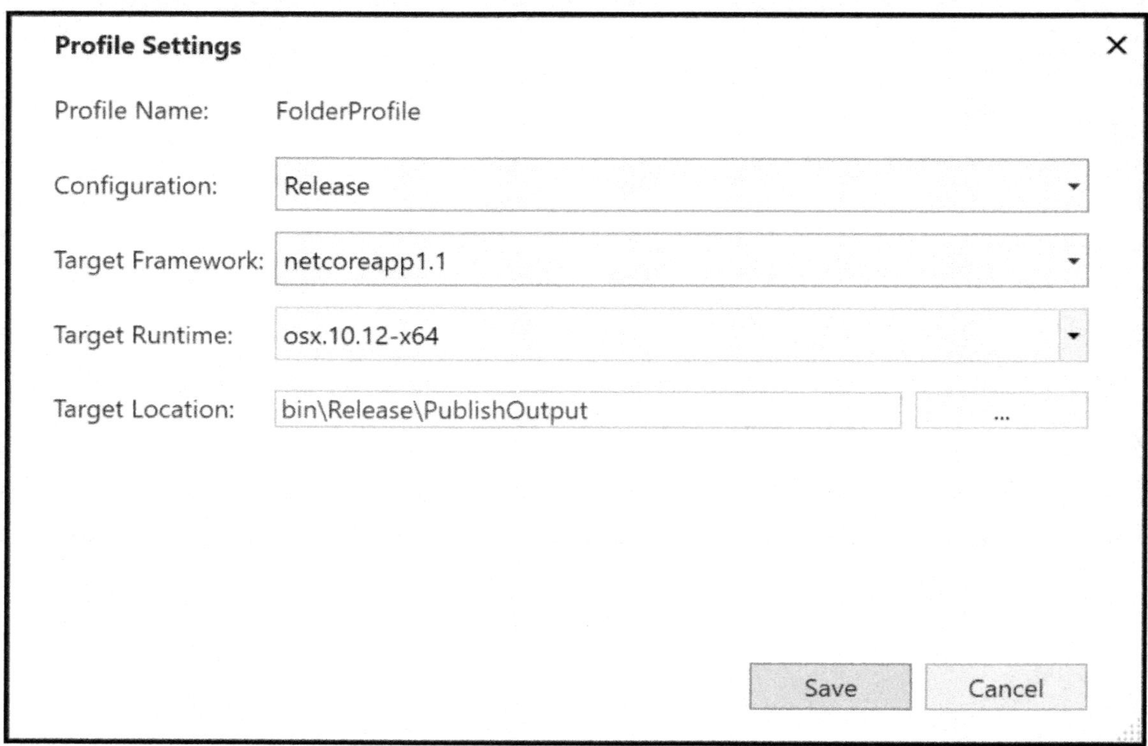

Click **Publish**.

In **Solution Explorer**, show all files, expand **bin**, **Release**, **netcoreapp1.1**, **osx.10.12-x64**, and **win10-x64**, as shown in the following screenshot, and note the application files:

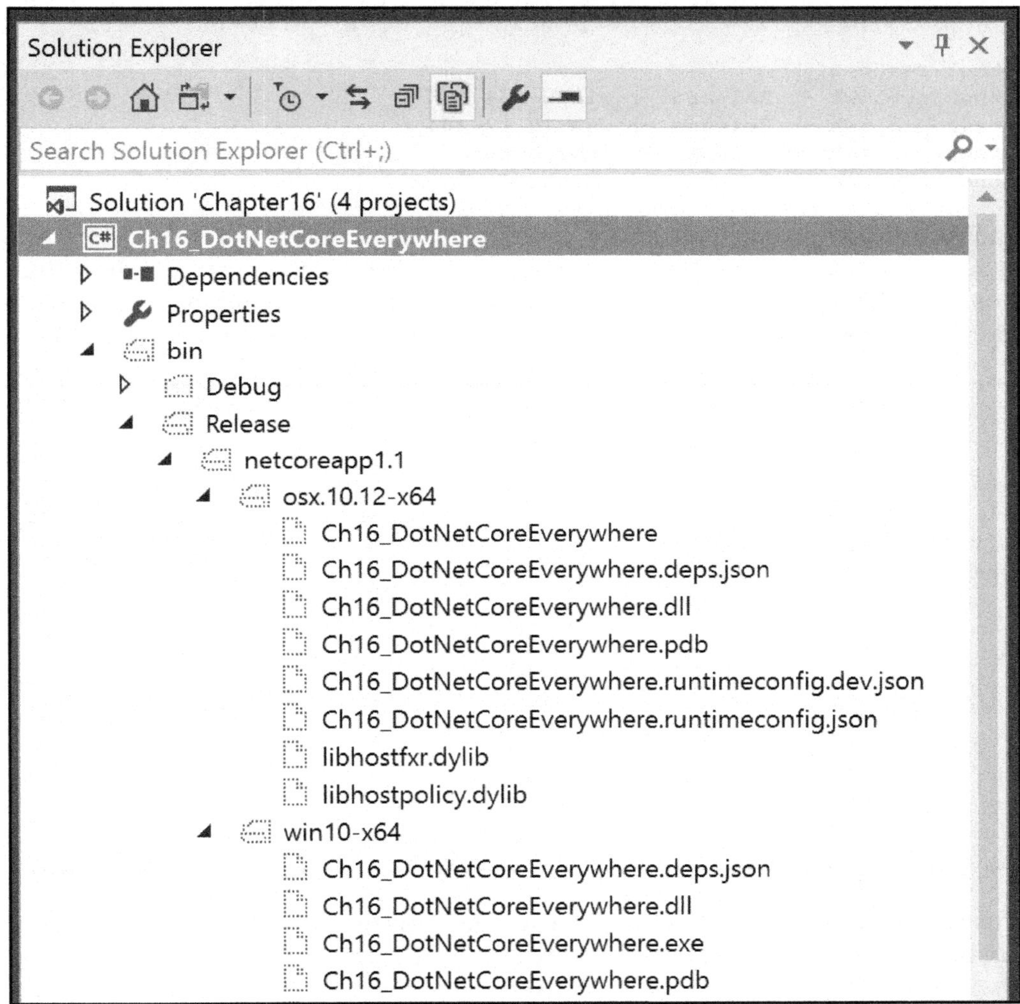

You can repeat these instructions for the other two operating systems.

Publishing with Visual Studio Code

In Visual Studio Code, in Terminal, enter the following commands to build release versions for Windows 10, macOS, Red Hat Enterprise Linux, and Ubuntu Linux:

```
dotnet restore
dotnet publish -c Release -r win10-x64
dotnet publish -c Release -r osx.10.12-x64
dotnet publish -c Release -r rhel.7-x64
dotnet publish -c Release -r ubuntu.14.04-x64
```

Open a **Finder** window, navigate to `Ch16_DotNetCoreEverywhere\bin\Release\netcoreapp1.1`, and note the output folders for the four operating systems, and the files, including a Windows executable named `Ch16_DotNetCoreEverywhere.exe`, as shown in the following screenshot:

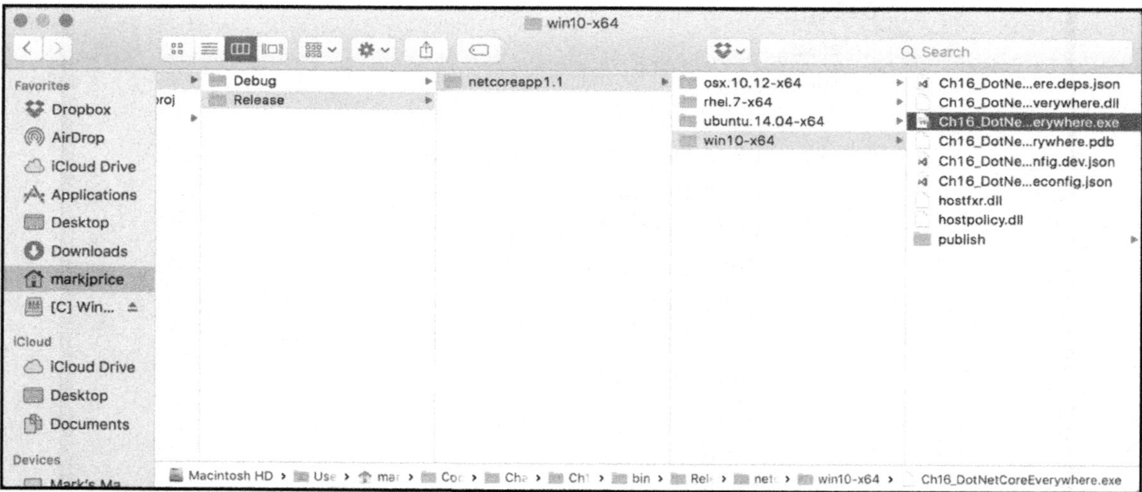

If you copy any of those folders to the appropriate operating system, the console application will run because it is a self-contained deployable .NET Core application.

Deploying to the cloud

You can deploy your .NET Core applications to the cloud using any cloud provider, for example, **Amazon Web Services** (**AWS**) or Microsoft Azure.

Creating an ASP.NET Core MVC web application to publish

In Visual Studio 2017, add a new **ASP.NET Core Web Application (.NET Core)** project named `Ch16_ImageEditorSite`. Choose the **Web Application** template and enable Docker support, as shown in the following screenshot:

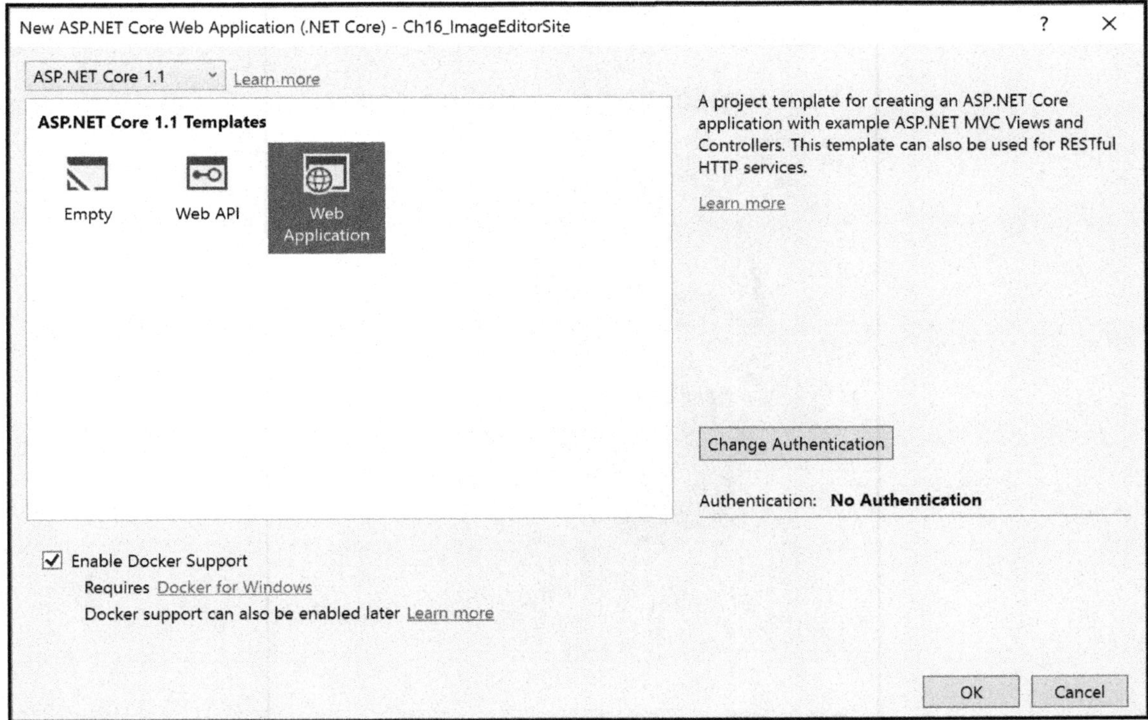

In Visual Studio Code, create a folder named `Ch16_ImageEditorSite`, and open the folder. In Terminal, enter the command: `dotnet new mvc`.

Since we are focusing on learning how to publish and deploy, rather than how to build web applications, we will use the MVC template web site as an example. The only addition I made is to add a portrait that my Mum painted of me to the About page, as shown in the following screenshot:

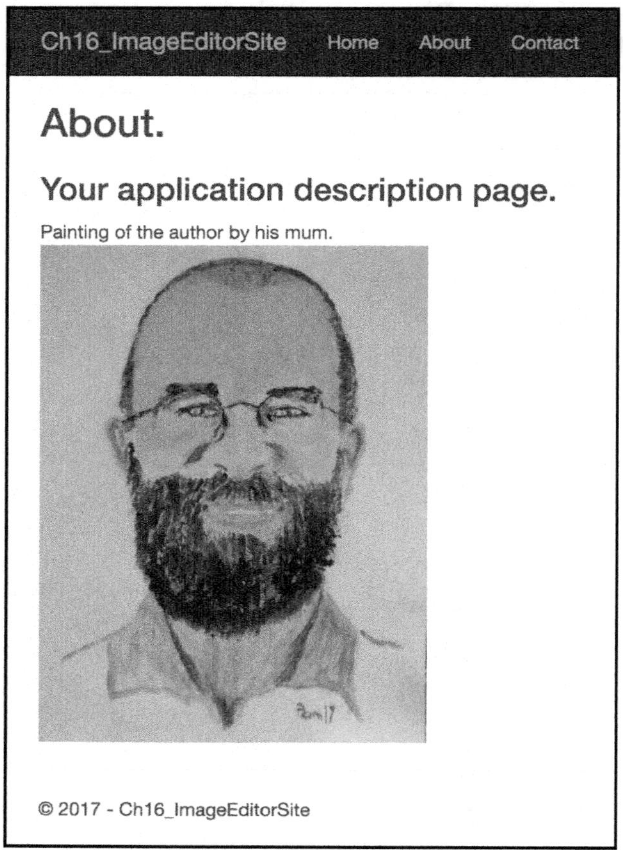

Register an Azure account

Go to `http://portal.azure.com/` and register an account to get a free trial. You will be able to continue after the end of the free trial, because we will only use the free features of Azure.

You can use any Microsoft account, for example, Hotmail, MSN, or Live account. For the first edition of this book, I registered an account named `cs6dotnetcore@outlook.com`, and I will use it for this example.

Create an Azure web app

Go to the Azure portal (`https://portal.azure.com/`) where you will see the Azure dashboard, as shown in the following screenshot:

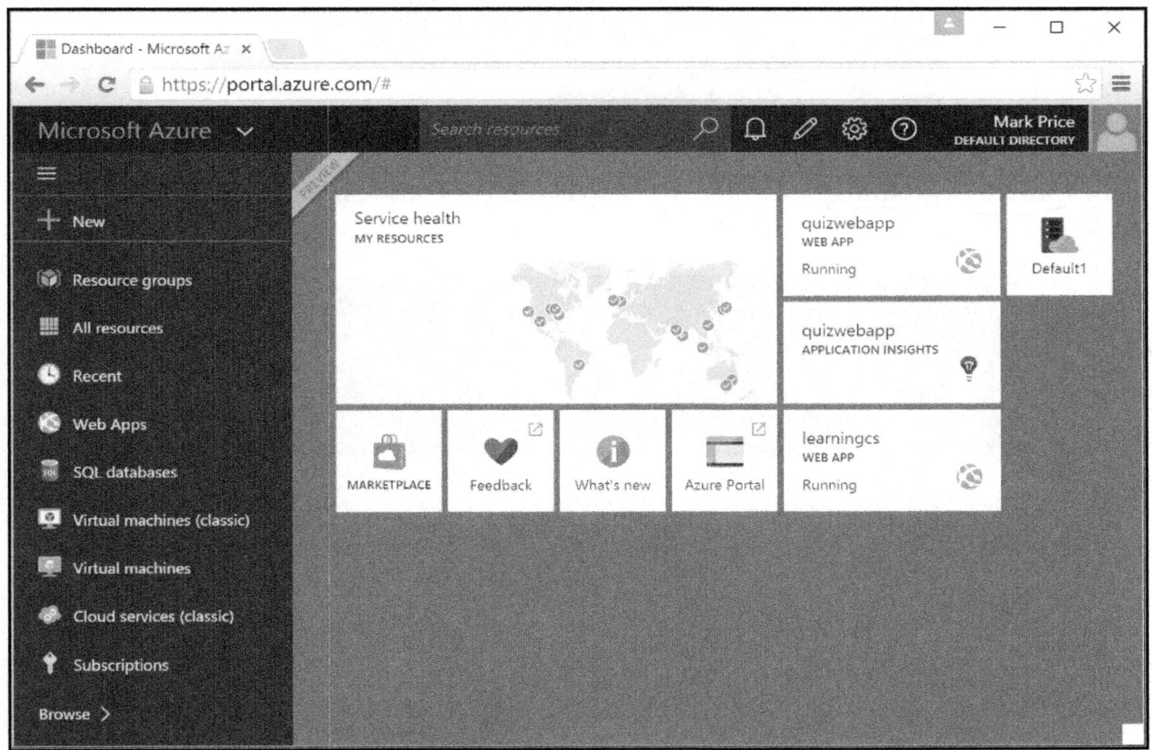

Click on **All resources** and then click on the **+ Add** button, as shown in the following screenshot:

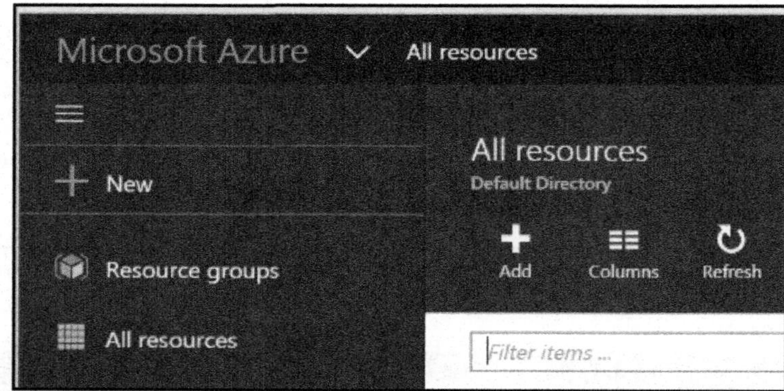

In the **Search Everything** box, enter `web app` and press *Enter*. Click on **Web App** and then click on **Create**, as shown in the following screenshot:

Search the Marketplace

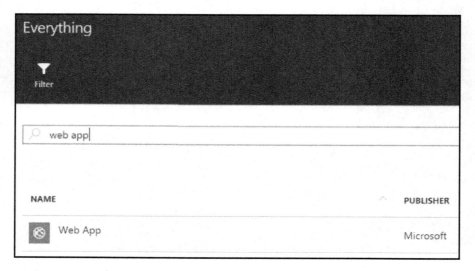

Click Create
Sign up for a new subscription

In the **Web App** blade, enter a globally unique name for your web app, as shown in the following screenshot:

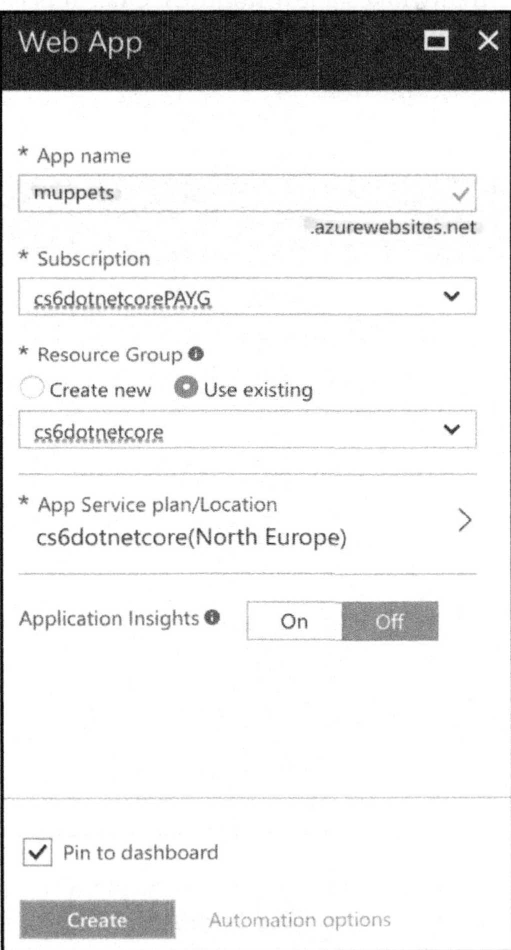

I entered `muppets`, so this name is now taken. No one else will be able to have a web app with that name. You will need to choose something different.

Leave the other options as their defaults and click on **Create**. You will be taken back to the Azure dashboard where you will see a new tile telling you that your Web App is being deployed. This process normally takes a few minutes. Once it is running, click on it, as shown in the following screenshot:

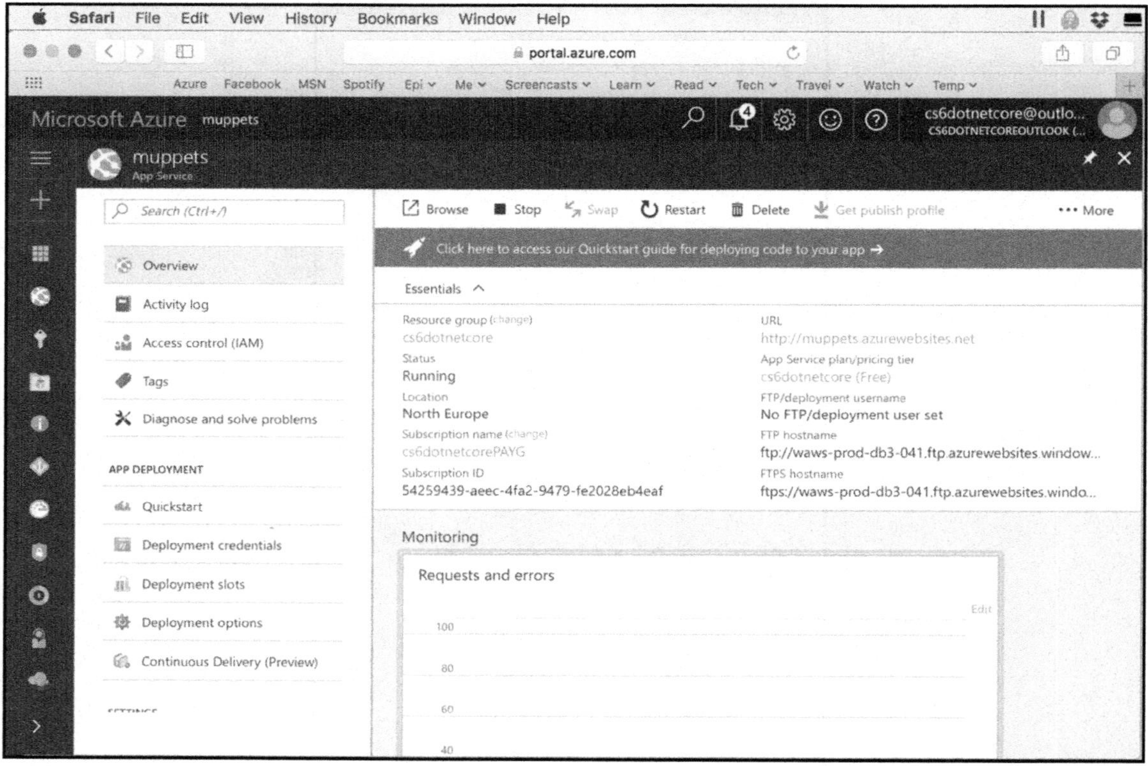

Click on the **URL** to open a browser and show the example web page. You are now ready to deploy any ASP.NET web application project (both ASP.NET 4.6 and ASP.NET Core) to your web app in Azure.

Publishing an ASP.NET web application to the web app

In the **Solution Explorer** window, right-click on the `Ch16_ImageEditorSite` project and choose **Publish...**.

Select **Azure App Service Linux (Preview)** as the publish target, as shown in the following screenshot, and click **Publish**:

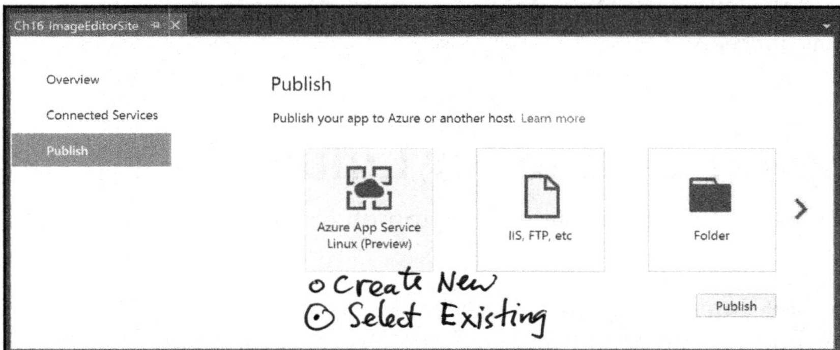

In the **Create App Service** dialog, choose the account that you previously registered, and choose the web app name that you created earlier, and click **Create**, as shown in the following screenshot:

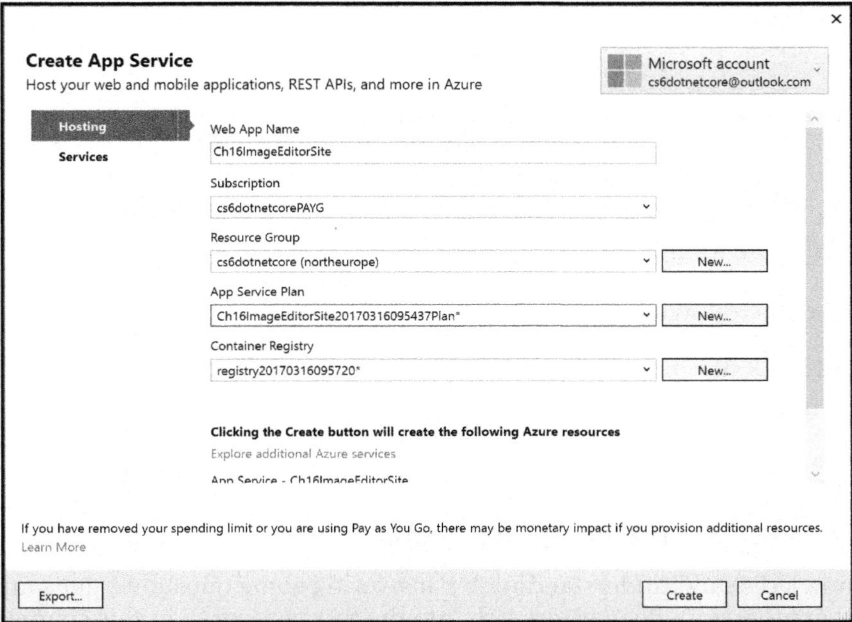

Visual Studio 2017 will download a **publishing profile** that you can use to easily deploy the web application to Azure.

Visual Studio 2017 will rebuild and deploy your application and then start a browser to show that it has succeeded.

Developing on and for Linux

The following Linux operating systems are supported as a deployment target for .NET Core:

- Red Hat Enterprise Linux 7 Server
- Ubuntu 14.04, 16.04
- Linux Mint 17
- Debian 8.2
- Fedora 23
- CentOS 7.1
- Oracle Linux 7.1
- openSUSE 13.2

If you want to choose a Linux operating systems that supports:

- Visual Studio Code for development
- SQL Server 2016 for an RDBMS
- .NET Core for a platform

Then, you have the following two choices:

- Red Hat Enterprise Linux (RHEL) 7.12
- Ubuntu 16.04

Practicing and exploring

Test your knowledge and understanding by answering some questions, get some hands-on practice, and explore with deeper research into the topics covered in this chapter.

Exercise 16.1 – test your knowledge

Answer the following questions:

1. What are some of the `dotnet` commands for working with .NET Core?
2. What are some of the operating systems that are supported by .NET Core?
3. How many web apps can you host in Microsoft Azure for free?
4. Does Microsoft Azure only support Windows as a host operating system?
5. What options does Microsoft Azure offer for data storage?

Exercise 16.2 – explore topics

Use the following links to read more about the topics covered in this chapter:

- **Porting to .NET Core from .NET Framework**: `https://docs.microsoft.com/en-us/dotnet/articles/core/porting/`
- **Packages, Metapackages and Frameworks**: `https://docs.microsoft.com/en-us/dotnet/articles/core/packages`
- **.NET Core Application Deployment**: `https://docs.microsoft.com/en-us/dotnet/articles/core/deploying/`
- **Installing ASP.NET Core 1.0 on Linux**: `https://docs.asp.net/en/latest/getting-started/installing-on-linux.html`
- **Enterprise Application Architecture with .NET Core**: `https://www.packtpub.com/application-development/enterprise-application-architecture-net-core`
- **Visual Studio Code – All the Git Features!!!**: `https://blogs.msdn.microsoft.com/user_ed/2016/02/08/visual-studio-code-all-the-git-features/`
- **Microsoft Azure: Cloud and Computing Services**: `https://azure.microsoft.com/en-us/`

Summary

In this chapter, we discussed options for porting existing .NET Framework codebases, publishing your apps and libraries, and deploying your code cross-platform and to the cloud.

Hopefully, this book and the C# 7 language and .NET Core features we've covered will inspire you to think about how you can use C# 7 and .NET Core to build well-architected and modern applications that run cross-platform on Windows, macOS, Docker, and Linux.

With C# 7 and .NET Core in your arsenal of tools and technologies, you can conquer the universe of cross-platform development and build any type of application that you need.

Answers to the Test Your Knowledge Questions

This appendix has the answers to the questions in the *Test Your Knowledge* section at the end of each chapter.

Chapter 1 – Hello, C#! Welcome, .NET Core!

1. Why can a programmer use different languages, for example C# and F#, to write applications that run on .NETCore?

- Multiple languages are supported on .NET Core because each one has a compiler that translates the source code into IL (intermediate language) code. This IL code is then compiled to native CPU instructions at runtime by the CLR.

2. What do you type at the prompt to build and execute C# source code?

- Using .NET Core CLI in a folder with a `ProjectName.csproj` file, we type `dotnet run`.

3. What is the Visual C# developer settings keyboard shortcut to save, compile, and run an application without attaching the debugger?

- Ctrl + F5.

4. What is the Visual Studio Code keyboard shortcut to view the Integrated Terminal?

- Ctrl + ` (back tick).

5. Is Visual Studio 2017 better then Visual Studio Code?

- No. Each is optimized for different tasks. Visual Studio 2017 is large, heavy-weight, and can create applications with graphical user interfaces, for example WPF, UWP, and Xamarin mobile apps, but is only available on Windows. Visual Studio Code is smaller, lighter-weight, command line and code-focused, and available cross-platform.

6. Is .NET Core better than .NET Framework?

- It depends on what you need. .NET Core is a slimmed down, cross-platform version of the more full-featured, mature .NET Framework.

7. How is .NET Native different from .NET Core?

- .NET Native is an ahead-of-time compiler that can produce native code assemblies that have better performance and reduced memory footprint, and it has its .NET assemblies statically linked, which removes its dependency on CoreCLR.

8. What is .NET Standard and why is it important?

- .NET Standard is an API that future versions of .NET Framework, .NET Core, and Xamarin will implement to provide a single, standard API that developers can learn and target.

9. What is the difference between Git and GitHub?

- Git is a source code management platform. GitHub is a popular web service that implements Git.

10. What is the name of the entry point method of a .NET console application and how should it be declared?

```
public static void Main() // minimum
public static int Main(string[] args) // recommended
```

- Its name is `Main` and the preceding code is how it is declared. An optional `string` array for command-line arguments and a return type of `int` are recommended, but they are not required.

Chapter 2 – Speaking C#

What type would you choose for the following "numbers"?

1. A person's telephone number

- `string`.

2. A person's height

- `float` or `double`.

3. A person's age

- `int` for performance or `byte` (0 to 255) for size.

4. A person's salary

- `decimal`.

5. A book's ISBN

- `string`.

6. A book's price

- `decimal`.

7. A book's shipping weight

- `float` or `double`.

8. A country's population

- `uint` (0 to about 4 billion).

9. The number of stars in the Universe

- `ulong` (0 to about 18 quadrillion) or `System.Numerics.BigInteger` (allows an arbitrarily large integer).

10. The number of employees in each of the small or medium businesses in the UK (up to about 50,000 employees per business)

- Since there are hundreds of thousands of small or medium businesses, we need to take memory size as the determining factor so choose `ushort` because it only takes 2 bytes compared to an `int`, which takes 4 bytes.

Chapter 3 – Controlling the Flow, Converting Types, and Handling Exceptions

1. Where would you look for help about a C# keyword?

- `https://docs.microsoft.com/en-us/dotnet/articles/csharp/language-reference/keywords/`

2. Where would you look for solutions to common programming problems?

- `http://stackoverflow.com`

3. What happens when you divide an `int` variable by 0?

- A `DivideByZeroException` is thrown when dividing an integer or decimal.

4. What happens when you divide a `double` variable by `0`?

- The `double` contains a special value of `Infinity`. Instances of floating-point numbers can have special values–`NaN` (not a number), `PositiveInfinity`, and `NegativeInfinity`.

5. What happens when you overflow an `int` variable, that is, set it to a value beyond its range?

- It will loop unless you wrap the statement in a `checked` block in which case an `OverflowException` will be thrown.

6. What is the difference between `x = y++;` and `x = ++y;`?

 - In `x = y++;`, `y` will be assigned to `x` and then `y` will be incremented, and in `x = ++y;`, `y` will be incremented and then the result will be assigned to `x`.

7. What is the difference between `break`, `continue`, and `return` when used inside a loop statement?

 - The `break` statement will end the whole loop and continue executing after the loop, the `continue` statement will end the current iteration of the loop and continue executing at the start of the loop block for the next iteration, and the `return` statement will end the current method call and continue executing after the method call.

8. What are the three parts of a `for` statement and which of them are required?

 - The three parts of a `for` statement are the initializer, condition, and incrementer. The condition is required to be an expression that returns `true` or `false`, but the other two are optional.

9. What is the difference between the = and == operators?

 - The = operator is the assignment operator for assigning values to variables, and the == operator is the equality check operator that returns `true` or `false`.

10. Does the following statement compile? for (; true;) ;

 - Yes. The `for` statement only requires a Boolean expression. The `initializer` and `incrementer` statements are optional. This for statement will execute the empty ; statement forever. It is an example of an infinite loop.

Exercise 3.2

1. What will happen if this code executes?

```
int max = 500;
for (byte i = 0; i < max; i++)
{
    WriteLine(i);
}
```

- The code will loop nonstop because the value of `i` can only be between `0` and `255`, so once it gets incremented beyond `255`, it goes back to `0` and therefore will always be less than `max` (`500`).
- To prevent it from looping nonstop, you can add a checked statement around the code. This would cause an exception to be thrown after `255`, like this:

```
254
255
System.OverflowException says Arithmetic operation
resulted in an overflow.
```

Chapter 4 – Using .NET Standard Types

1. What is the maximum number of characters that can be stored in a `string`?

- The maximum size of a `string` variable is 2 GB or about 1 billion characters because each `char` variable uses 2 bytes due to the internal use of Unicode (UTF-16) encoding for characters.

2. When and why should you use a `SecureString`?

- The string type leaves text data in memory for too long and it's too visible. The `SecureString` type encrypts the text and ensures that the memory is released immediately. WPF's `PasswordBox` control stores the password as a `SecureString` variable, and when starting a new process, the `Password` parameter must be a `SecureString` variable. For more discussion, visit:
- `http://stackoverflow.com/questions/141203/when-would-i-need-a-secure string-in-net`

3. When is it appropriate to use a `StringBuilder`?

- When concatenating more than about three `string` variables, you will use less memory and get improved performance using `StringBuilder` than using `string.Concat` method or the + operator.

4. When should you use a `LinkedList<T>`?

- Each item in a linked list has a reference to its previous and next siblings as well as the list itself so should be used when items need to be inserted and removed from positions in the list without actually moving the items in memory.

5. When should you use a `SortedDictionary` variable rather than a `SortedList` variable?

- The `SortedList` class uses less memory than `SortedDictionary`, `SortedDictionary` has faster insertion and removal operations for unsorted data. If the list is populated all at once from sorted data, `SortedList` is faster than `SortedDictionary`. For more discussion, visit:
- `http://stackoverflow.com/questions/935621/whats-the-difference-between-sortedlist-and-sorteddictionary`

6. What is the ISO culture code for Welsh?

```
cy-GB
```

- For a complete list of culture codes, visit: `http://timtrott.co.uk/culture-codes/`

7. What is the difference between localization, globalization, and internationalization?

- Localization affects the user interface of your application. Localization is controlled by a neutral (language only) or specific (language and region) culture. You provide multiple language versions of text and other values. For example, the label of a text box might be **First name** in English, and **Prénom** in French.
- Globalization affects the data of your application. Globalization is controlled by a specific (language and region) culture, for example, `en-GB` for British English, or `fr-CA` for Canadian French. The culture must be specific because a decimal value formatted as currency must know to use Canadian dollars instead of French Euros.
- Internationalization is the combination of localization and globalization.

8. In a regular expression, what does `$` mean?

- `$` represents the end of the input.

9. In a regular expression, how would you represent digits?

- \d+
- [0-9]+

10. Why should you not use the official standard for e-mail addresses to create a regular expression to validate a user's e-mail address?

- The effort is not worth the pain for you or your users. Validating an e-mail address using official specification doesn't check whether that address actually exists or whether the person entering the address is its owner. For more discussion, visit:

- `http://davidcel.is/posts/stop-validating-email-addresses-with-regex/`

- `http://stackoverflow.com/questions/201323/using-a-regular-expression-to-validate-an-email-address`

Chapter 5 – Debugging, Monitoring, and Testing

1. In Visual Studio 2017, what is the difference between pressing *F5, Ctrl* + *F5, Shift* + *F5,* and *Ctrl* + *Shift* + *F5?*

- *F5* saves, compiles, runs, and attaches the debugger, *Ctrl* + *F5* saves, compiles, and runs the debugger, *Shift* + *F5* stops the debugger, and *Ctrl* + *Shift* + *F5* restarts the debugger.

2. What information can you find out about a process?

- The `Process` class has many properties including: `ExitCode`, `ExitTime`, `Id`, `MachineName`, `PagedMemorySize64`, `ProcessorAffinity`, `StandardInput`, `StandardOutput`, `StartTime`, `Threads`, `TotalProcessorTime`, and so on. You can find more information about **Process Properties** at `https://msdn.microsoft.com/en-us/library/System.Diagnostics.Process_properties(v=vs.110).aspx`

3. How accurate is the `Stopwatch` class?

- The `Stopwatch` class can be accurate to within a nanosecond (a billionth of a second) but you shouldn't rely on that. You can improve accuracy by setting processor affinity as shown in the article at `http://www.codeproject.com/Articles/61964/Performance-Tests-Precise-Run-Time-Measurements-wi`

4. How do you reference another project in a `.csproj` file?

```
<ItemGroup>
<ProjectReference
Include="..\Ch05_Calculator\Ch05_Calculator.csproj" />
</ItemGroup>
```

5. When writing a unit test, what are the three As?

- Arrange, Act, Assert.

6. What dotnet command executes xUnit test?

- dotnet test

Chapter 6 – Building Your Own Types with Object-Oriented Programming

1. What are the four access modifiers and what do they do?

- `private`: This modifier makes a member only visible inside the class.
- `internal`: This modifier makes a member only visible inside the class or within the same assembly.
- `protected`: This modifier makes a member only visible inside the class or derived classes.
- `public`: This modifier makes a member visible everywhere.

2. What is the difference between the `static`, `const`, and `readonly` keywords?

- `static`: This keyword makes the member shared by all instances and accessed through the type.

- `const`: This keyword makes a field a fixed literal value that should never change.
- `readonly`: This keyword makes a field that can only be assigned at runtime using a constructor.

3. How many parameters can a method have?

- A method with 16383 parameters can be compiled, ran, and called. Any more than that and an unstated exception is thrown at runtime. IL has predefined opcodes to load up to four parameters and a special opcode to load up to 16-bits (65,536) parameters. A best practice is to limit your methods to three or four parameters. You can combine multiple parameters into a new class to encapsulate them into a single parameter. You can find more information on this at `http://stackoverflow.com/questions/12658883/what-is-the-maximum-number-of-parameters-that-a-c-sharp-method-can-be-defined-as`

4. What does a constructor do?

- A constructor allocates memory and initializes field values.

5. Why do you need to apply the `[Flags]` attribute to an `enum` type when you want to store combined values?

- If you don't apply the `[Flags]` attribute to an `enum` type when you want to store combined values, then a stored `enum` value that is a combination will return as the stored integer value instead of a comma-separated list of text values.

6. Why is the partial keyword useful?

- You can use the `partial` keyword to split the definition of a type over multiple files.

Chapter 7 – Implementing Interfaces and Inheriting Classes

1. What is a delegate?

- A delegate is a type-safe method reference. It can be used to execute any method with a matching signature.

2. What is an event?

- An event is a field that is a delegate having the `event` keyword applied. The keyword ensures that only += and -= are used; this safely combines multiple delegates without replacing any existing event handlers.

3. How is a base class and a derived class related?

- A derived class (or subclass) is a class that inherits from a base class (or superclass).

4. What is the difference between the `is` and `as` operators?

- The `is` operator returns `true` if an object can be cast to the type. The `as` operator returns a reference if an object can be cast to the type; otherwise, it returns `null`.

5. Which keyword is used to prevent a class from being derived from, or a method from being overridden?

```
sealed
```

- Find more information on the `sealed` keyword at `https://msdn.microsoft.com/en-us/library/88c54tsw.aspx`

6. Which keyword is used to prevent a class from being instantiated with the `new` keyword?

```
abstract
```

- Find more information on the `abstract` keyword at `https://msdn.microsoft.com/en-us/library/sf985hc5.aspx`

7. Which keyword is used to allow a member to be overridden?

```
virtual
```

- Find more information on the `virtual` keyword at `https://msdn.microsoft.com/en-us/library/9fkccyh4.aspx`

8. What's the difference between a destructor and a deconstructor?

- A destructor, also known as a finalizer, must be used to release resources owned by the object. A deconstructor is a new feature of C# 7 that allows a complex object to be broken down into smaller parts.

9. What are the signatures of the constructors that all exceptions should have?

- The following are the signatures of the constructors that all exceptions should have:
    - A constructor with no parameters
    - A constructor with a `string` parameter usually named `message`
    - A constructor with a `string` parameter, usually named `message`, and an `Exception` parameter usually named `innerException`

10. What is an extension method and how do you define one?

- An extension method is a compiler trick that makes a static method of a static class appear to be one of the members of a type. You define which type you want to extend by prefixing the type with `this`.

Chapter 8 – Working with Databases Using Entity Framework Core

1. Which .NET data provider would you use to work with Microsoft SQL Server 2012 Express Edition?

- .NET Core Data Provider for SQL Server.

2. When defining a `DbContext` class, what type would you use for the property that represents a table, for example, the `Products` property?

- `DbSet<T>`, where `T` is the entity type, for example, `Product`.

- For a `Products` property on another entity, for example, `Category`, that represents a one-to-many relationship between entities, use `ICollection<T>`, where `T` is the related entity type.

3. What is the EF convention for primary keys?

- The property named `ID` or `ClassNameID` is assumed to be the primary key. If the type of that property is any of the following, then the property is also marked as being an `IDENTITY` column: `tinyint`, `smallint`, `int`, `bigint`, `guid`.

4. When would you use an annotation attribute in an entity class?

- You would use an annotation attribute in an entity class when the conventions cannot work out the correct mapping between the classes and tables. For example, if a class name does not match a table name or a property name does not match a column name.

5. Why might you choose fluent API in preference to annotation attributes?

- You might choose fluent API in preference to annotation attributes when the conventions cannot work out the correct mapping between the classes and tables, and you do not want to use annotation attributes because you want to keep your entity classes clean and free from extraneous code.

Chapter 9 – Querying and Manipulating Data with LINQ

1. What are the two required parts of LINQ?

- A LINQ provider and the LINQ extension methods. You must import the `System.Linq` namespace to make the LINQ extension methods available and reference a LINQ provider assembly for the type of data that you want to work with.

2. Which LINQ extension method would you use to return a subset of properties from a type?

- The `Select` method allows projection (selection) of properties.

3. Which LINQ extension method would you use to filter a sequence?

- The `Where` method allows filtering by supplying a delegate (or lambda expression) that returns a Boolean to indicate whether the value should be included in the results.
- List five LINQ extension methods that perform aggregation.

- `Max`, `Min`, `Count`, `Average`, `Sum`, and `Aggregate`.

4. What is the difference between the Select and `SelectMany` extension methods?

- Select returns exactly what you specify to return. `SelectMany` checks that the items you have selected are themselves `IEnumerable<T>` and then breaks them down into smaller parts. For example, if the type you select is a string value (which is `IEnumerable<char>`), `SelectMany` will break each string value returned into their individual `char` values.

Chapter 10 – Working with Files, Streams, and Serialization

1. What is the difference between using the `File` class and the `FileInfo` class?

- The `File` class has static methods so it cannot be instantiated. It is best used for one-off tasks such as copying a file. The `FileInfo` class requires the instantiation of an object that represents a file. It is best used when you need to perform multiple operations on the same file.

2. What is the difference between the `ReadByte` method and the `Read` method of a stream?

- The `ReadByte` method returns a single byte each time it is called and the `Read` method fills a temporary array with bytes up to a specified length. It is generally best to use `Read` to process blocks of bytes at once.

3. When would you use the `StringReader`, `TextReader`, and `StreamReader` classes?

- `StringReader` is used for efficiently reading from a string stored in memory
- `TextReader` is an abstract class that `StringReader` and `StreamReader` both inherit from for their shared functionality
- `StreamReader` is used for reading strings from a stream that can be any type of text file, including XML and JSON

4. What does the `DeflateStream` type do?

- `DeflateStream` implements the same compression algorithm as GZIP but without a cyclical redundancy check, so although it produces smaller compressed files, it cannot perform integrity checks when decompressing.

5. How many bytes per character does the UTF-8 encoding use?

- It depends on the character. Most Western alphabet characters are stored using a single byte. Other characters may need two or more bytes.

6. What is an object graph?

- An object graph is any instance of classes in memory that reference each other, thereby forming a set of related objects. For example, a `Customer` object may have a property that references a set of `Order` instances.

7. What is the best serialization format to choose for minimizing space requirements?

- JavaScript Object Notation (JSON).

8. What is the best serialization format to choose for cross-platform compatibility?

- eXtensible Markup Language (XML), although JSON is even better these days.

Chapter 11 – Protecting Your Data

1. Of the encryption algorithms provided by .NET, which is the best choice for symmetric encryption?

- The AES algorithm is the best choice for symmetric encryption.

2. Of the encryption algorithms provided by .NET, which is the best choice for asymmetric encryption?

- The RSA algorithm is the best choice for asymmetric encryption.

3. For encryption algorithms, is it better to have a larger or smaller block size?

- For encryption algorithms, it is better to have a smaller block size.

Chapter 12 – Improving Performance and Scalability with Multitasking

1. By convention, what suffix should be applied to a method that returns a `Task` or a `Task<T>`?

- Async, for example, `OpenAsync` for a method named `Open`.

2. To use the `await` keyword inside a method, which keyword must be applied to the method declaration?

- The `async` keyword must be applied to the method declaration.

3. How do you create a child task?

- Call the `Task.Factory.StartNew` method with the `TaskCreationOptions.AttachToParent` option to create a child task.

4. Why should you avoid the `lock` keyword?

- The `lock` keyword does not allow you to specify a timeout; this can cause deadlocks. Use `Monitor.Enter` with a `TimeSpan` and `Monitor.Exit` instead.

5. When should you use the `Interlocked` class?

- If you have integers and floats that are shared between multiple threads, you should use the `Interlocked` class.

Chapter 13 – Building Universal Windows Platform Apps Using XAML

1. Which control would you choose to allow the user to easily choose their date of birth on many different types of device?

- The `DatePicker` control will allow the user to easily choose their date of birth on many different types of device.

2. Which XAML element would you use to adapt the layout of your app to handle different device families?

- The `VisualStateManager` element is used to adapt the layout of your app to handle different device families.

3. How can you set multiple properties on an XAML element as a single group?

- We can set multiple properties on an XAML element as a single group by defining a style with setters.

4. What is the difference between a control template and a data template?

- Control templates are used to define the look and feel of the external parts of a control, such as a button or list box. Data templates are used to define the look and feel of the internal content of a button or the items with a list box.

5. Can XAML bindings be two-way or just one-way?

- XAML bindings can be two-way, one-way, or one-time.

Chapter 14 – Building Web Applications Using ASP.NET Core MVC

1. What is the difference between a web browser and a web server?

- A web browser makes HTTP requests for resources and a web server sends HTTP responses back containing a mix of HTML, CSS, JavaScript, and other media formats, which the browser then displays to the end user.

2. What is the difference between a URI, a URL, and a URN?

- Uniform Resource Identifier (URI) is the more general term instead of URL or URN. A Uniform Resource Locator (URL) is a type of URI that species a location of a resource. A Uniform Resource Name (URN) is intended to serve as persistent, location-independent identifier.

3. What are the four most common HTTP methods?

- The `GET`, `POST`, `PUT`, and `DELETE` are the most common HTTP methods.

4. What does it mean when a web server responds with status code `302`?

- The web server is indicating a temporary redirect. This means that the web server found the resource but it is at a different location. A response header is used to tell the web browser about the new location. Note that status code `301` is similar but represents a permanent redirect.

5. What are the responsibilities of a route?

- At the minimum, a route must provide the name of a controller and an action. It can also provide additional parameter values defined in segments.

6. What are the responsibilities of a controller?

- A controller (and one of its actions) must examine the request and decide which model needs to be passed to which view and then return the response to the client.

7. What are the responsibilities of a model?

- A model represents all the data required for a particular request.

8. What are the responsibilities of a view?

- A view converts a model into another format, typically HTML, but it could be any media type, for example, JPEG, DOCX, JSON, XML, and so on.

Chapter 15 – Building Mobile Apps Using Xamarin.Forms and ASP.NET Core Web API

1. How does ASP.NET distinguish a request for MVC from a request for Web API?

- Multiple entries are added to the route table. By convention, Web API controllers should use attributes to register routes that look for URLs that begin with `api/`. If a URL doesn't begin with `api/` then it should match other routes registered by MVC.

2. What data formats does Web API support by default?

- x-www-formurlencoded, JSON, and XML.

3. What is the difference between Xamarin and Xamarin.Forms?

- Xamarin allows developers to build native iOS, Android, and Windows apps using existing skills, teams, and code written in C# and .NET. But the user interfaces must be developed specifically for each platform. Xamarin.Forms allows developers to build native user interfaces for iOS, Android and Windows from a single, shared C# codebase using XAML.

4. What types of cell are supported by the `ListView`?

- Data in a `ListView` is presented in cells. `TextCell` displays a string of text, optionally with a second line in smaller font with an accent color. `ImageCell` displays an image on the left with text. `SwitchCell` and `EntryCell` can be used, but this is rare. Custom cells can also be defined.

Chapter 16 – Packaging and Deploying Your Code Cross-Platform

1. What are some of the `dotnet` commands for working with .NET Core?

- `dotnet new console`, `dotnet new web`, `dotnet new mvc`, `dotnet new webapi`, `dotnet new classlib`, `dotnet restore`, `dotnet test`, `dotnet run`, `dotnet pack`, `dotnet migrate`, `dotnet publish`

2. What are some of the operating systems that are supported by .NET Core?

- Windows 7 SP1, Windows Server 2008 R2 SP1, OS X El Capitan (version 10.11) and macOS Sierra (version 10.12), Red Hat Enterprise Linux 7.2, Ubuntu 14.04 LTS, 16.04 LTS, Linux Mint 17, Debian 8.2, CentOS 7.1, Oracle Linux 7.1

3. How many web apps can you host in Microsoft Azure for free?

- 10

4. Does Microsoft Azure only support Windows as a host operating system?

- No. You can create Virtual Machines to host Linux, Docker, and other operating systems.

5. What options does Microsoft Azure offer for data storage?

- The following options are what Microsoft Azure offers for data storage:
    - Azure Storage for schema-less entities, blobs, and files
    - Azure Redis for distributed caching and general entity storage
    - Azure DocumentDb for schema-less JSON entities
    - Azure SQL Database for relational data
    - Azure Data Lake for hybrid storage and analysis

Index

B

C

D

G

H

I

J

K

L

M

N

O

P

Q

R

S

T

U

V

W

X

CPSIA information can be obtained
at www.ICGtesting.com
Printed in the USA
LVOW04s0914020917
547358LV00005B/235/P